Jutta Vesper
Diplom-Dolmetscherin aiic
Haffstraße 12
53225 Bonn

D1652225

James Helmut Zowe
53115 Bonn   VK 2508

Apelt, M.L.:
Dtsch.-Engl.Wtb.Kunstgesch.
K&V 2 33 76 20   ISBN 3-503-03003-4   WG **14600**
49,80 DM
LS 86180 vom 14.05.96   BZ

9 783503 030033   04980

German-English Dictionary: Art History – Archaeology

Deutsch-Englisches Wörterbuch für Kunstgeschichte und Archäologie

von

Mary L. Apelt

2., überarbeitete und ergänzte Auflage

ERICH SCHMIDT VERLAG

CIP-Titelaufnahme der Deutschen Bibliothek

Apelt, Mary L.:
German-English dictionary: art history – archaeology =
Deutsch-englisches Wörterbuch für Kunstgeschichte und
Archäologie / von Mary L. Apelt. – 2., überarb. u. erg. Aufl. –
Berlin : Erich Schmidt, 1990
  ISBN 3-503-03003-4

NE: HST

ISBN 3 503 03003 4, 2. Auflage
(ISBN 3 503 01619 8, Erstausgabe)
2., überarbeitete und ergänzte Auflage 1990

© Erich Schmidt Verlag GmbH & Co., Berlin 1982
Satz: Reprosatz Struve, Düsseldorf
Druck: Lengericher Handelsdruckerei, Lengerich
Printed in Germany · Nachdruck verboten
Alle Rechte vorbehalten

Preface

This dictionary will be an aid to all who are concerned with the fields of art history and archaeology. It is especially intended to be a helpful tool for the reader. For this reason, the dictionary is not limited to specialized terms from these two fields, but also includes other vocabulary often encountered when reading the professional literature, such as the various shapes, colors, materials, articles of clothing, religious objects, courtly people, titles of well-known works, dyestuffs, pigments, and mythological animals and people.

In most cases, if a direct translation of the German word exists in English, it is simply translated without explanation. However, there are some words and concepts in German which have no common equivalent in English. In such cases, a brief explanation is given in English. For a more complete explanation of such terms, the reader should refer to a German language art lexicon. The English translations do not include all possible definitions of each word; definitions are limited to those important to art history and archaeology. Further meanings can be found in a general bilingual dictionary.

The list of terms which appears here has been compiled from English and German works within the fields, professional journals, exhibition catalogues and art lexicons and dictionaries. This second, revised edition includes corrections and some 100 additional words. It is not however an exhaustive dictionary of these fields and both the author and the publisher would be grateful for any suggestions as to additions, corrections or changes.

Many people have helped me in compiling this dictionary, but I especially wish to thank my husband, Hans-Peter Apelt.

Mary L. Apelt

Vorwort

Das vorliegende Handwörterbuch möchte denjenigen eine Hilfe bieten, die im Bereich der Kunstgeschichte oder Archäologie tätig sind. Es ist vor allem als Hilfsmittel für den Leser gedacht und ist daher nicht auf Spezialausdrücke der erwähnten Fachbereiche begrenzt, sondern schließt auch Wörter ein, die des öfteren in der Fachlektüre auftauchen, wie z. B. Ausdrücke für verschiedene Formen, Farben, Materialien, Kleidungsstücke, Kultgegenstände, Hofleute, Titel bekannter Werke, Farbstoffe, Pigmente, mythologische Tiere und Personen.

In den meisten Fällen wird der deutsche Ausdruck einfach in englischer Übersetzung aufgeführt. Es gibt im Deutschen jedoch einige Wörter und Begriffe, die keine allgemeine Entsprechung im Englischen haben. In diesen Fällen wird eine kurze Erklärung im Englischen gegeben. Für eine ausführliche Erklärung dieser Begriffe sollte ein deutsches Kunstlexikon zu Rate gezogen werden. Die englische Übersetzung schließt auch nicht alle möglichen Bedeutungen eines Wortes ein; die Bedeutungen beziehen sich lediglich auf die Bereiche Kunstgeschichte und Archäologie. Darüber hinausgehende Bedeutungen sind in einem allgemeinen zweisprachigen Wörterbuch zu finden.

Die in dieses Handwörterbuch aufgenommenen Ausdrücke sind englischsprachigen und deutschen Fachbüchern und -zeitschriften entnommen, Ausstellungskatalogen, Kunstlexiken und Wörterbüchern. Die hier vorliegende, durchgesehene und um rund hundert Wörter erweiterte 2. Auflage kann jedoch kein vollständiges Wörterbuch für die genannten Bereiche sein. Die Autorin und der Verlag sind daher für jeden Hinweis bezüglich Erweiterung, Berichtigung oder Änderung dankbar.

Bei der Zusammenstellung dieses Handwörterbuchs haben mir viele geholfen, mein besonderer Dank gilt meinem Mann Hans-Peter.

Mary L. Apelt

Explanatory Notes

Words have been arranged in strict alphabetical order.

German entries:

Plural form of the noun immediately follows the noun in parantheses. Examples of plural:

Etat(s) = Etats
Brunnenhof (-höfe) = Brunnenhöfe
Gaden (–) = Gaden
Ziborium (Ziborien) = Ziborien

If there is no plural form, or if the plural is uncommon, it is not included.

Gender follows the plural form and is abbreviated *m* (masculine), *f* (feminine) and *n* (neuter). Some nouns appear only in the plural form, which is abbreviated *pl*.

Alternate spellings are listed under the German word. Common alternates are ph – f, k – c and z – c. The reader having difficulty finding a word should consider the possibility of an alternate spelling.

Names of colors are capitalized if they refer to particular pigments, but most colors can also function as adjectives.

The hyphen is used to take the place of the main word. Example:

Martersäule, Christus an der – = Christus an der Martersäule

Participles are sometimes listed instead of or in addition to the infinitive form because of adjectival use. Examples:

geschult, bemalt, signiert

German nouns derived from adjectives are declined like adjectives, for example *der Heilige, ein Heiliger*. Such words appear here with the ending required by the definite article. Example:

Heilige(n) *m, f*

Adjectives listed in connection with nouns have the ending required by the definite article. Example:

griechisches Kreuz *n*

English entries:

The comma separates translations of similar meaning. Example:

to perceive, to feel, to experience

The semicolon separates a translation and its explanation. Example:

zinken; small tools for working antler

Numbers are used for totally different translations of the same word. Example:

Becken 1. pelvis
       2. basin

Parentheses are used in two ways:

1. to include an expression which may or may not be used in actual translation. Example:

Schnitzkunst (art of) carving

2. to offer an explanation, so that confusion with other definitions of the same English word can be avoided. Example:

Grat groin (of a vault)

Italics are used in two ways:

1. for foreign words
2. to indicate the special area to which a particular translation applies. Example:

Wiegeeisen rocker, cradle *mezzotint*

Hinweise für die Benutzung des Wörterbuches

Das Wörterbuch ist alphabetisch geordnet.

Deutsche Stichwörter:

Die **Pluralform** der Nomen steht unmittelbar in Klammern hinter dem jeweiligen Nomen. Beispiele für Pluralformen:

Etat(s) = Etats
Brunnenhof (-höfe) = Brunnenhöfe
Gaden (—) = Gaden
Ziborium (Ziborien) = Ziborien

Wenn es keine Pluralform gibt oder wenn die Pluralform ungewöhnlich ist, wird sie nicht erwähnt.

Das **Genus** der Nomen steht hinter der Pluralform und ist wie folgt abgekürzt: *m* (maskulin), *f* (feminin) und *n* (neutrum). Einige Nomen erscheinen nur in der Pluralform, die mit *pl* abgekürzt ist.

Verschiedene Schreibweisen werden beim deutschen Stichwort erwähnt. Häufig erscheint die Alternative von ph – f, k – c und z – c. Bei Wörtern mit diesen Buchstaben sollte der Benutzer an die Möglichkeit verschiedener Schreibweisen denken.

Farbbezeichnungen sind mit großem Anfangsbuchstaben geschrieben, wenn sie ein bestimmtes Pigment bezeichnen. Die meisten Farbbezeichnungen werden jedoch auch als Adjektiv benutzt.

Der **Bindestrich** wird benutzt, um das Stichwort zu ersetzen, zum Beispiel:

Martersäule, Christus an der — = Christus an der Martersäule

Partizipien werden manchmal statt des Infinitivs oder zusätzlich zu einem Infinitiv aufgeführt, wenn sie als Adjektiv benutzt werden, zum Beispiel:

geschult, bemalt, signiert

Substantive, die aus Adjektiven entstanden sind, werden wie Adjektive dekliniert, zum Beispiel *der Heilige, ein Heiliger*. Diese Wörter erscheinen hier mit der Endung, die der bestimmte Artikel verlangt, also:

> Heilige(n) *m, f*

Adjektive in Verbindung mit Substantiven erscheinen mit der Endung, die der unbestimmte Artikel verlangt, also:

> griechisches Kreuz *n*

Englische Stichwörter:

Das **Komma** trennt Ausdrücke mit ähnlichem Inhalt, zum Beispiel:

> to perceive, to feel, to experience

Das **Semikolon** trennt die Übersetzung und Erklärung eines Ausdrucks, zum Beispiel:

> zinken; small tools for working antler

Die **Zahlen** numerieren völlig verschiedene Übersetzungen eines Wortes, zum Beispiel:

> Becken 1. pelvis
> 2. basin

Klammern werden benutzt

1. um Ausdrücke einzuklammern, die bei der Übersetzung vielleicht benutzt oder auch nicht benutzt werden, zum Beispiel:

   Schnitzkunst (art of) carving

2. um Erklärungen einzuklammern, die mithelfen sollen, Verwechslungen mit anderen Bedeutungen eines englischen Wortes auszuschließen, zum Beispiel:

   Grat groin (of a vault)

Kursivschrift wird benutzt

1. zur Bezeichnung von Fremdwörtern
2. zur Bezeichnung eines Spezialgebiets, für das der Ausdruck gebraucht wird, zum Beispiel:

   Wiegeweisen rocker, cradle *mezzotint*

Abakus(⸚) m	abacus
Abart(en) f	variety, deviant form
Abb. = Abbildung	illustration
Abbild(er) n	image
abbilden	to copy, to print, to portray
abbildhaft	copy-like
abbildlich	copying, depictive
Abbildung(en) f	illustration
abbinden	to set, to harden (concrete, etc.)
abblättern	to peel off
Abblättern n	peeling off (of paint)
abdecken	1. to stop out *etching, silk screen* 2. to uncover
Abdeckplatte(n) f	coping
Abdeckstein(e) m	coping stone
Abdruck(e) m	print, copy, reproduction, cast
Abendland n	Occident
abendländisch	occidental
Abendmahl n	the Last Supper, Communion
Abendmahl, das letzte —	the Last Supper
Abendmahlsdarstellung(en) f	(depiction of) the Last Supper
Abendmahlsgerät(e) n	Communion utensil
Abendmahlstisch(e) m	Communion table
abfasen	to chamfer, to bevel
abgebildet	illustrated
abgekehrt	averted
abgeschnürte Vierung f	crossing with partial walls separating it from nave and transept (compare *ausgeschiedene Vierung*)
abgestuft	1. recessed in steps, splayed 2. changing by degrees or steps
abgetreppt	recessed in steps, splayed
abgewinkelt	set or bent off at an angle, bent outward
Abgott (-götter) m	idol, image

Abguß (-güsse) *m*	casting, cast copy
Abhängling(e) *m*	pendant
abkanten	to round off (the edges), to chamfer, to bevel
Abklatsch(e) *m*	copy, impression, duplicate
abklatschen	to copy, to duplicate
Abklatschverfahren *n*	decalcomania, decal, lifting
abmalen	to paint a copy, to copy, to paint from life
abmeißeln	to chisel off, to chisel away
abmessen	to measure, to measure off
abquadern	to rusticate
Abraxen *pl*	Abraxas gems
Abri(s) *m*	abri, rock shelter
Abrollung(en) *f*	seal cylinder impression
abrunden	to round off
abschaben	to scrape off
Abschlaggerät(e) *n*	flake tool
Abschnitt(e) *m*	section, compartment
Abschrift(en) *f*	copy (of a manuscript)
Abseite(n) *f*	1. side room 2. back side 3. vertical wall under a slanting roof 4. lateral vault (or aisle) of a church
Abstieg in die Hölle, der —	the Descent into Limbo
abstrahieren	to abstract, to make abstract
abstrakt	abstract
Abstrakter Expressionismus *m*	abstract expressionism
Abstraktheit *f*	abstractness
Abstraktion(en) *f*	abstraction
Abstraktion, die Neue —	post-painterly abstraction
Abtei(en) *f*	abbey
Abteikirche(n) *f*	abbey church
Abwandlung(en) *f*	variation
abzeichnen	to copy, to draw after an original
Abziehbild(er) *n*	transfer

Abziehbilderdruck(e) *m*	decalcomania
abziehen	to pull (a proof)
Abzug (-züge) *m*	proof
Accipiesholzschnitt(e) *m*	woodcut depicting a school scene, accompanied by the text "accipies tanti doctoris dogmata sancti"
Accoudoir(s) *n*	arm rest of choir stall
Achat(e) *m*	agate
Achatglas *n*	agate glass, glass imitation of agate
Acheiropoieten *pl* *also* Acheropita	acheiropoietoi; pictures which are not man-made, miraculous pictures
achromatisch	achromatic
Achse(n) *f*	axis
Achsel(n) *f*	shoulder
achsenförmig	axial
achsial	axial
Achteck(e) *n*	octagon
achteckig	octagonal
achtkappig	eight-part (vault)
Achtort(e) *m*	equilateral octagon
Acryl *n* *also* Akryl	acrylic paint
Acrylfarbe(n) *f*	acrylic paint, acrylic color
Acrylglas *n*	acrylic glass
Actionpainting *f, n*	action painting
Adahandschriften *pl*	Ada manuscripts, Ada group
Adel *m*	nobility, aristocracy
Ader(n) *f*	vein, blood vessel
Ädikula (Ädikulä) *f*	aedicule
Adler (—) *m*	eagle
Adlerpult(e) *n*	eagle-shaped lectern
Adorant(en) *m*	orans
Adoration *f*	adoration, worship
Adresse(n) *f*	publishing information on an engraving
adsorbieren	to adsorb
Adsorption *f*	adsorption

Adyton (Adyten) *n*	adytum
Aeneolithikum *n*	Eneolithic, Copper Age
Ägäis *f*	Aegean Sea
ägäisch	Aegean
Agora *f*	agora
Agraffe(n) *f*	1. agraffe, clasp
	2. bracket connecting the keystone of an arch with the cornice
Ägypten	Egypt
Ägypter (—) *m*	Egyptian
ägyptisch	Egyptian
Ägyptologe(n) *m*	Egyptologist
Ägyptologie *f*	Egyptology
Ahnenbild(er) *n*	picture of an ancestor
Ahnenkult(e) *m*	ancestor worship
Ahorn *m*	maple
Ährenverband *m*	opus spicatum, masonry in herringbone pattern
Akademie(n) *f*	academy
Akanthus *m*	acanthus
Akanthusblatt (-blätter) *n*	acanthus leaf
Akanthusblattkranz (-kränze) *m*	acanthus vine wreath
Akanthusranke(n) *f*	acanthus vine, acanthus foliage
Akaroidharz *n*	acaroid resin, accroides, xanthorrhea
Akelei *f*	columbine
Akkulturation(en) *f*	acculturation
Akleibecher (—) *m* *also* Akleybecher	columbine-shaped goblet
Akrolith(en) *m*	acrolith
Akropolis *f*	acropolis
Akrostichon (-chen, -cha) *n*	acrostic
Akroterie(n) *f*	acroterion
Akroterion (Akroterien) *n*	acroterion
Akrylharz *n*	acrylic resin
Akrylglas *n*	plexiglas

Akt(e) *m*	nude
Aktfigur(en) *f*	nude figure
Aktstudie(n) *f*	study of a nude
Aktzeichnung(en) *f*	nude (drawing)
Alabaster *m*	alabaster
Alabastron (Alabastren) *m*	alabastron
Albarello (Albarelli) *n*	albarello
Albe(n) *f*	alb
Album (Alben) *n*	album, folio
Aldobrandinische Hochzeit, die —	the Aldobrandini Wedding (or Marriage)
Alexanderschlacht, die —	the Battle of Issus, Battle of Alexander
Algraphie(n) *f*	(planographic) print from an aluminum plate
Alhambravase(n) *f*	Alhambra vase
Alignement(s) *n*	alignment, row(s) of standing stones
Alizarin *n*	natural alizarin dye
Alizarinkrapplack *m*	alizarin crimson
Alkaliglasur(en) *f*	alkaline glaze
Alkanna *f*	alkanet, henna
Alkoholfirnis(se) *m*	spirit varnish
Alkoven (—) *m*	small side room
alla prima *n*	alla prima painting
Allegorie(n) *f*	allegory
allegorisch	allegorical
Allerheiligenbild(er) *n*	Adoration of the Trinity
Almanach(e) *m*	almanac
Almandin *m*	almandine
Altan(e) *m* also Altane(n) *f*	roofless platform, gallery, balcony
Altar (Altäre) *m*	altar
Altarapsis (-siden) *f*	(altar) apse
Altaraufbau(ten) *m*	altarpiece
Altaraufsatz (-aufsätze) *m*	altarpiece, retable
Altarbekleidung(en) *f*	antependium

Altarbild(er) *n*	altarpiece
Altarblatt (-blätter) *n*	altarpiece (painting)
Altardecke(n) *f*	altar cloth
Altarflügel (—) *m*	volet, wing panel (of an altar)
Altargemälde (—) *n*	altarpiece, altar painting
Altargerät(e) *n*	altar utensil
Altargitter (—) *n*	parclose
Altarglocke(n) *f*	altar bell
Altarleuchter (—) *m*	altar candelabra
Altarraum (-räume) *m*	chancel, sanctuary
Altarrückwand (-wände) *f*	reredos
Altarschranke(n) *f*	chancel screen, rood screen
Altarunterbau(ten) *m*	predella
Altarvorsatz (-sätze) *m*	antependium
Altarziborium (-ziborien) *n*	altar ciborium
altchristlich	early Christian
Altertum *n*	antiquity
Altertümer *pl*	antiquities, ancient relics
altertümlich	ancient
Altertumskunde *f*	the study of antiquity, archaeology
Altertumswissenschaft *f*	the study of antiquity, archaeology
Altmeister (—) *m*	old master
Altpaläolithikum *n*	lower paleolithic period
Altstadt (-städte) *f*	old (or historical) section of a city
Altsteinzeit *f*	paleolithic period
altsteinzeitlich	paleolithic
alttestamentarisch	Old Testament
Aluminium *n*	aluminum
Aluminiumblech *n*	sheet aluminum
Aluminiumdruck(e) *m*	(planographic) print from an aluminum plate
Aluminiumguß (-güsse) *m*	aluminum cast(ing)
Amarant *m*	amaranth
Amateur(e) *m*	amateur
Amazone(n) *f*	Amazon
Amazonomachie *f*	Amazonomachy

Ambo (Ambonen) *m*	ambo
Amboß (Ambosse) *m*	anvil
Amethyst(e) *m*	amethyst
Amikt(e) *m*	amice, humeral veil
Amorette(n) *f*	amoretto
Ampel(n) *f*	ampulla; lamp
Amphiprostylos (-stylen) *m*	amphiprostyle temple, amphiprostyle plan
Amphitheater (—) *n*	amphitheater
Amphora (Amphoren) *f* *also* Amphore	amphora
Ampulle(n) *f*	ampulla
Amulett(e) *n*	amulet
Anamorphose(n) *f*	anamorphosis
Anathyrose *f* *also* Anathyrosis	anathyrosis
Anatomie(n) *f*	anatomy
Anbau(ten) *m*	annex, addition
Anbetung(en) *f*	worship, adoration
Anbetung des goldenen Kalbes, die —	Worship of the Golden Calf
Anbetung der Heiligen Drei Könige, die —	Adoration of the Magi
Anbetung der Hirten, die —	Adoration of the Shepherds
Andachtsbild(er) *n*	Andachtsbild, devotional picture (or piece), piece used for private devotion
Andachtshalle(n) *f*	devotional hall
Andachtskunst *f*	devotional art
Andreaskreuz(e) *n*	St. Andrew's cross
Andruck(e) *m*	trial proof
Anfänger (—) *m*	1. beginner 2. first voissoir resting directly on the impost
Anfangsbuchstabe(n) *m*	initial
Angefälle (—) *n*	abutment
Angelseite(n) *f*	hinged side
angesetzt	attached

angewandte Kunst *f*	applied arts
angewinkelt	bent in
Angster (–) *m*	glass vessel with twisted neck(s)
Anguß *m*	1. engobe
	2. beginning of casting
Angußfarbe(n) *f*	engobe
Anhänger (–) *m*	1. friend, follower, admirer
	2. pendant (necklace)
Anker (–) *m*	1. armature butterfly, crossed sticks to support the clay
	2. metal wall brace
Ankerkreuz(e) *n*	cross ancrée
Anlage(n) *f*	structure, grounds, layout, building, plan, park
Anleger (–) *m*	register guide *printing*
Anlehnung(en) *f*	adaptation, imitation, reference
Anna Selbdritt	depiction of St. Anne, the Madonna and the Christ Child
annieten	to attach by means of rivets
anordnen	to arrange
Anordnung(en) *f*	arrangement, grouping
Anregung(en) *f*	stimulation, stimulus, impulse
anschaulich	concrete, vivid, plastic
Anschaulichkeit *f*	clearness, distinctness, vividness
Anschauung(en) *f*	view, viewing
Anschauungsrichtung(en) *f*	direction of viewing
Anschießer (–) *m*	gilder's tip
Ansicht(en) *f*	view
Ansichtsfläche(n) *f*	face, front side
Ansichtskarte(n) *f*	picture post card
Ansichtspostkarte(n) *f*	picture post card
anstreichen	to paint, to coat with paint
Anstrich(e) *m*	paint, coat of paint
Anten *pl*	antae
Antenkapitell(e) *n*	capital over the anta
Antentempel (–) *m*	Greek temple with naos, pronaos and two columns in antis
Anthemion (Anthemien) *n*	anthemion

Anthropoidsarg (-särge) *m*	anthropoid sarcophagus
anthropomorph	anthropomorphic
antik	ancient, antique
Antike *f*	Antiquity
Anti-Kunst *f*	anti-art, neo-dada
Antiphonar(ien) *n*	antiphonary
Antiquar(e) *m*	antiquary
Antiquität(en) *f*	antiquity, antique relic
antithetische Gruppe *f*	affronted figures, two mirror-image profiles facing each other
Antlitz(e) *n*	face, visage
Antoniuskreuz(e) *n*	tau cross
Anwendung(en) *f*	application, use
äolisch	Aeolic
Apodyterium (Apodyterien) *n*	dressing room in the Thermae
Apokalypse *f*	apocalypse
Apokalypsenhandschrift(en) *f*	Apocalypse manuscript, Beatus manuscript
apokalyptisch	apocalyptic
Apollontempel (—) *m*	temple of Apollo
Apophyge *f*	apophyge
Apostel (—) *m*	apostle
Apostelbalken (—) *m*	rood beam
Apostelgestalt(en) *f*	apostle figure
Apostelkrug (-krüge) *m*	pitcher or mug depicting the twelve Apostles
Apostellöffel *pl*	set of thirteen spoons depicting the Apostles and the Virgin
Apotheose(n) *f*	apotheosis
Apotropaion (Apotropaia) *n* *also* Apotropäum (Apotropäa)	apotropaic object or symbol
apotropäisch	apotropaic
Applikation(en) *f*	appliqué
Applikationsteppich(e) *m*	carpet or tapestry decorated with appliqué

applizieren	to appliqué
Aprikosengummi *m*	apricot gum
Apsidenhaus (-häuser) *n*	rectangular plan building with convex wall opposite the entrance
Apsidenkapelle(n) *f*	apsidal chapel
Apsis (Apsiden) *f*	apse
Aquädukt(e) *m*	aqueduct
Aquamanile(n) *n*	aquamanile, ewer
Aquamarin *m*	aquamarine
Aquarell(e) *n*	watercolor, aquarelle
Aquarellfarbe(n) *f*	watercolor paint
Aquarellgemälde (—) *n*	watercolor (painting)
Aquarellist(en) *m*	watercolor artist
Aquarellmalerei *f*	painting with watercolors
Aquatinta (-tinten) *f*	aquatint
Arabeske(n) *f*	arabesque
arabeskenhaft	arabesque-like
Arbeit(en) *f*	work
Archaik *f*	Archaic (period or style)
archaisch	archaic
archaisches Lächeln *n*	archaic smile
archaisieren	to archaize
archaistisch	archaistic
Archäologe(n) *m*	archaeologist
Archäologie *f*	archaeology
archäologisch	archaeological(ly)
Arche Noah *f* *also* Arche Noä	Noah's Ark
Archetyp(en) *m*	archetype
Architekt(en) *m*	architect
architektonisch	architectonic
Architektur(en) *f*	architecture
Architekturbild(er) *n*	picture of architecture, architectural vista, architectural elements in a painting
Architekturhintergrund *m*	architectural background

Architekturmalerei *f*	painting of significant architecture, architectural vista
Architekturmodell(e) *n*	architectural model
Architekturplastik(en) *f*	sculpture related to a building, architectural sculpture
Architekturzeichnung(en) *f*	architectural drawing or plan
Architrav(e) *m*	architrave, epistyle
Archivolte(n) *f*	archivolt
Arcosolium (-solien) *n*	arcosolium; arched recess in a catacomb
Areal(e) *n*	area, tract, region
Arkade(n) *f*	arcade
Arkadenreihe(n) *f*	series or row of arcades
arkadisch	Arcadian
Arkosol(ien) *n* also Arkosolium (Arkosolien)	arcosolium; arched recess in a catacomb
Arm(e) *m*	arm
Armarium (Armarien) *n*	aumbry, ambry
Armband (-bänder) *n*	bracelet
Ärmel (–) *m*	sleeve
Armenbibel *f*	Biblia Pauperum
Armhaltung(en) *f*	position of the arm
Armlehne(n) *f*	arm rest
Armpalette(n) *f*	arm palette
Armreif(e) *m*	bracelet, armband
Armschutzplatte(n) *f*	wristguard, bracer
arretinisches Gefäß(e) *n*	Arretine ware
Art(en) *f*	kind, type
Artefakt(e) *n*	artifact, artefact
art informel *f*	art informel (see *informelle Malerei*)
artes liberales *pl*	the liberal arts
Artushof (-höfe) *m*	medieval ceremonial group (and the hall in which the group met) modelled after King Arthur's Round Table

Aryballos (Aryballoi) *m*	aryballus
Asbestzement *m*	asbestos cement
Aschenurne(n) *f*	cinerary urn, urn for cremation ashes
Askos (Askoi) *m*	askos
Äskulapstab (-stäbe) *m*	Asclepius' rod
Aspergill(e) *n*	aspergill(um)
Aspersorium (-sorien) *n*	aspersorium
Asphalt *m*	1. asphalt, bitumen 2. asphaltum
Asphaltfirnis(se) *m*	asphalt-varnish (resist)
Asphaltmalerei *f*	painting technique using asphaltum as a glaze
Assemblage(n) *f*	assemblage
Assistenzfigur(en) *f*	secondary figure, figure not required by the picture subject
Ästhetik *f*	aesthetics
ästhetisch	aesthetic
Astragal(e) *m*	astragal
Astwerk *n*	branch-motif ornamentation
Asymmetrie *f*	asymmetry
asymmetrisch	asymmetrical, asymmetrically
Atelier(s) *n*	studio, atelier
Ateliermalerei *f*	painting done indoors (as opposed to plein air)
Athen	Athens
Athenäum (Athenäen) *n*	Athenaeum, Atheneum
Äther *m*	ether
ätherisch	ethereal
ätherisches Öl(e) *n*	essential oil
Atlant(en) *m*	atlas (*pl* = atlantes), telamon
Atrium (Atrien) *n*	atrium
Attikageschoß (-geschosse) *n*	attic (story)
attische Basis *f*	Attic base
Attribut(e) *n*	attribute, symbol of the depicted person
ätzen	to etch

Ätzflüssigkeit(en) f	mordant
Ätzgrund (-gründe) m	etching ground
Ätzkunst f	(art of) etching
Ätznadel(n) f	etching needle
Ätzstift(e) m	burin
Ätzung(en) f	etching
Ätzverfahren n	aquatint, etching process
Ätzwasser n	mordant, aqua fortis
Aubussonteppich(e) m	Aubusson (tapestry)
Aufbau(ten) m	structure, construction, composition, development
aufbauen	to erect, to build (on), to construct
Aufbaumerkmal(e) n	structural characteristic, structural peculiarity
Aufenthalt(e) m	stay, sojourn
Auferstehung, die —	the Resurrection
Auferstehungsengel m	Angel of the Resurrection
Auferweckung des Lazarus, die —	Lazarus Raised From the Dead
Auferweckung der Toten, die —	the Raising of the Dead
Auffassung(en) f	conception
Auffassungskraft (-kräfte) f	perception, perceptive power
Auffindung des heiligen Kreuzes, die —	the Discovery of the True Cross
Auffindung des Moses, die —	the Finding of Moses
auffrischen	to touch up
aufgemalt	painted on the surface, painted over
Aufglasurmalerei f	overglaze (painting)
aufklappbar	hinged
Auflage(n) f	1. edition 2. support, rest
Auflage, beschränkte — f	limited edition
Auflagendruck m	the printing of an edition (as opposed to pulling trial proofs)
Auflagenhöhe f	edition, number of prints pulled

Aufnäharbeit(en) *f*	appliqué
Aufnahme(n) *f*	1. photo
	2. reception, absorption
Aufnahme Marias, die —	the Assumption
aufnehmen	1. to photograph
	2. to absorb
	3. to assimilate
Aufriß (Aufrisse) *m*	elevation, front vertical view
Aufschrift(en) *f*	inscription
Aufsicht(en) *f*	view of the top, view from above
aufspannen	to mount, to stretch (a canvas)
Aufstechen (—) *n*	re-cutting of the lines on a worn copper plate after many prints have been pulled
aufstellen	to set up, to mount, to erect
Aufstellungsort(e) *m*	site, location (of a work)
Aufstrich(e) *m*	coating
Auftrag (-träge) *m*	1. commission
	2. application, coating (of paint)
Auftrag, in — geben	to commission
auftragen	to apply (paint)
Auftraggeber (—) *m*	person who commissions a work, patron, client, employer
Auftragswerk(e) *n*	commissioned piece, commissioned work
Auftritt(e) *m*	stair tread
Auge(n) *n*	1. eye
	2. oculus
	3. point of station
Augenbraue(n) *f*	eyebrow
Augendarstellung(en) *f*	depiction of eyes, eye motif, oculus
Augenpunkt(e) *m*	center of perspective, point of sight
Augenschale(n) *f*	eye kylix
Auktion(en) *f*	auction
Aula (Aulen) *f*	1. auditorium
	2. inner court
	3. aula
Aunjetitzer Kultur *f*	Únětice culture

Aureole(n) *f*	aureole
Aurignacien *n*	Aurignacian (industry)
Auripigment *n*	orpiment
Ausbau(ten) *m*	1. expansion, enlargement
	2. furnishing and detailing (of a room)
ausbauen	to enlarge, to expand (a building)
Ausblick(e) *m*	view
ausbuchten	to curve convexly, to bulge
Ausbuchtung(en) *f*	bulge, curve, convex surface
Ausdruck (-drücke) *m*	expression
Ausdrucksform(en) *f*	form of expression
Ausdruckskraft (-kräfte) *f*	power of expression
ausdrucksstark	very expressive
Ausdruckssteigerung(en) *f*	increase in expression
Ausdrucksweise(n) *f*	manner of expression
ausfachen	to nog; to fill in (the spaces between the beams on a half-timber or iron frame building)
ausfugen	to point *masonry*
Ausführung(en) *f*	execution, accomplishment
ausgehöhlt	hollowed out
ausgeschiedene Vierung *f*	crossing separated from nave and transept by four arches (see *abgeschnürte Vierung*)
ausgeschmückt	decorated
ausgemalt	painted
Ausgestaltung(en) *f*	shaping, fashioning, development
ausgewogen	(well) balanced
Ausgießung des Heiligen Geistes, die —	the Descent of the Holy Ghost, Pentecost
Ausgleichbewurf *m*	brown coat *fresco*
ausgraben	to excavate, to dig
Ausgräber (—) *m*	excavator
Ausgrabung(en) *f*	excavation
Ausgrabungsfund(e) *m*	excavated find
Ausguck(e) *m*	watch tower, observation platform

Ausguß (-güsse) *m*	spout
aushöhlen	to hollow out
Aushöhlung(en) *f*	hollow, depression, groove
auskehlen	to flute, to groove
Auskehlung(en) *f*	flute, groove
auskitten	to stop, to fill with putty
auskragen	to project, to protrude
Auskragung(en) *f*	projection (from a building), protrusion
ausladen	to project
Ausladung(en) *f*	projection (from a building)
Ausleger (–) *m*	cantilever beam
Auslöschfarben *pl*	colors which result in gray or gray-black when mixed
Auslucht(en) *f*	bay window, projection similar to a bay window
ausmalen	to paint, to decorate
Ausmalung(en) *f*	painting, decoration
Ausmaß(e) *n*	dimension, size, extent, scale
Aussage(n) *f*	statement, message, declaration
Aussagekraft (-kräfte) *f*	power of expression
Ausschmelzverfahren *n*	lost-wax process, lost pattern casting
Ausschmückung(en) *f*	decoration, ornamentation
Ausschnitt(e) *m*	1. detail (of a larger work), partial view 2. neckline
Aussehen *n*	appearance
Außenansicht(en) *f*	exterior (view)
Außenbau *m*	exterior
Aussendung der Apostel, die —	the Mission of the Apostles
Außenflügel (–) *m*	lateral or side wing, side panel
Außenkante(n) *f*	outside edge
Außenseite(n) *f*	exterior, outside
Außenwand (-wände) *f*	exterior wall, outer wall
Außenwelt *f*	external world

Außenwerk(e) *n*	outwork(s) *castle architecture*
außerkirchlich	secular
Aussparung(en) *f*	unpainted surface, reserve
ausstatten	to equip, to decorate, to furnish
Ausstattung(en) *f*	equipment, furnishings, decoration
ausstellen	to exhibit
Aussteller (−) *m*	exhibitor
Ausstellung(en) *f*	exhibition
Ausstellungshalle(n) *f*	exhibition hall
Ausstellungskatalog(e) *m*	exhibition catalog
Ausstellungsort(e) *m*	exhibition location
Ausstellungsraum (-räume) *m*	exhibition room
auswittern	to effloresce
authentifizieren	to authenticate
authentisch	authentic
Authentizität *f*	authenticity
Autodidakt(en) *m*	autodidact
Automatismus *m*	automatism, ecriture automatique
Autoschrott *m*	junk automobile parts
Autotypie(n) *f*	autotype
Avantgarde *f*	avant garde
avantgardistisch	avant garde
Aventin *m*	the Aventine Hill
Aventuringlas *n*	aventurine
Avers(e) *m*	face (of a coin), obverse
axial	axial
Axialität *f*	axiality
Axonometrie(n) *f*	axonometric projection
Azeton *n*	acetone
Azulejos *pl*	azulejos
Azurit *m*	azurite
Backe(n) *f*	cheek
Backstein(e) *m*	brick

Backsteinbau(ten) *m*	brick building, construction with bricks
Backsteingotik *f*	Brick Gothic, Backstein Gothic
Backsteinmauerwerk(e) *n*	brick masonry
Bad (Bäder) *n*	bath
Badehaus (-häuser) *n*	bath, bathhouse
Badenerkultur *f*	Baden culture, Baden-Pécel culture
Baldachin(e) *m*	baldachin, canopy
Baldachinbett(en) *n*	canopied bed
Balken (—) *m*	beam
Balkenbauart(en) *f*	trabeation, post-and-lintel construction
Balkendecke(n) *f*	trabeated ceiling, beamed ceiling
Balkengrab (-gräber) *n*	prehistorical East European grave with barrow
Balkenkopf (-köpfe) *m*	beam end
Balkenträger (—) *m*	corbel
Balkenwerk *n*	beams
Balkon(s, e) *m*	balcony
Balkonbrüstung(en) *f*	balcony railing
Ballenblume(n) *f*	ballflower
Balsam *m*	balsam
Balsamfirnis(se) *m*	balsam varnish
Baluster (—) *m*	baluster
Balustrade(n) *f*	balustrade
Bambus *m*	bamboo
Band (Bände) *m*	volume
Band (Bänder) *n*	band, ribbon, strip
Bandelwerk(e) *n*	interlacing
Banderole(n) *f*	banderole
Bandgeflecht(e) *n*	interlace, interlacing
Bandgeflecht, lombardisches *n*	Lombard band decoration
Bandkeramik(en) *f*	bandkeramik, neolithic ceramics with band ornamentation
Bandrippe(n) *f*	vault rib in the shape of a solid stone band

Bandrolle(n) f	banderole
Bandwerkmotiv(e) n	entrelac
Bank (Bänke) f	bench
Baptisterium (Baptisterien) n	baptistery
baptisteriumsartig	baptistery-like
Barbakane(n) f	barbican
barock	baroque
Barock m, n	the Baroque (period or style)
Barockkirche(n) f	baroque church
Barockkunst f	baroque art
Barockschloß (-schlösser) n	baroque palace
Barockstil m	baroque (style)
Bart (Bärte) m	beard
Bartholomäus, der heilige —	St. Bartholomew
bartlos	beardless
Bartmannskrug (-krüge) m	glazed pitcher with a bearded face under the spout
Barytgelb n	barium yellow
Barytweiß n	blanc fixe, permanent white, baryta white
Basalt m	basalt
Basaltware f	(Wedgwood's) basalt ware
Basilika (Basiliken) f	basilica
Basilisk(en) m	basilisk, cockatrice
Basis (Basen) f	base
Basrelief n	bas relief
Basselisse(s) f	low warp loom
Bast(e) m	inner bark, bast, fiber
Bastei(en) f	bastion, bulwark, projection from a fortification
Bastion(en) f	bastion, fortification
Bastseide f	raw silk
Batik f	batik
Batist m	cambric cloth
Bau(ten) m	structure, building, construction
Bauart(en) f	type of building. type of construction

Bauch (Bäuche) *m*	stomach, abdomen
Bauchamphora (-amphoren) *f*	amphora in which neck and body merge without clear borders (see *Halsamphora*)
Baudenkmal(e) *n*	architectural monument
Bauelement(e) *n*	building element, prefabricated building part
bauen	to build
Bauen *n*	building, construction
Bauentwurf (-entwürfe) *m*	building plan
Bauer(n) *m*	farmer, peasant
Bauernkunst *f*	folk art, peasant art
Baufluchtlinie(n) *f*	alignment, line formed by a row of buildings
Baugefüge (—) *n*	building structure
Baugerüst(e) *n*	scaffolding, putlog
Baugesinnung(en) *f*	building attitude, architectural concept
Bauglied(er) *n*	structural element
Baugrundverhältnis(se) *n*	building site conditions
Bauhaus *n*	Bauhaus
Bauherr(en) *m*	architect's client, person who has something built
Bauhütte(n) *f*	1. workshop where building stones were hewn 2. association of (church) builders and artisans
Bauhüttenbuch (-bücher) *n*	medieval architect's book of building plans, designs and patterns
Baukeramik(en) *f*	architectural ceramics (e. g. glazed bricks, tiles, etc.)
Baukörper (—) *m*	structure, building, main body of a building
Baukunst *f*	architecture
Bauleitung(en) *f*	head of construction, director
baulich	structural, architectural
Baumaterial(ien) *n*	building material
Baumeister (—) *m*	architect, master builder

baumeisterlich	architectural
Baumkreuz(e) *n*	crucifix with leaves, blossoms and/or fruit
Baumwolle *f*	cotton
Baumwollpapier *n*	cotton paper, paper with a high cotton content
Baunaht (-nähte) *f*	visible line between older and newer sections of a building
Bauornament(e) *n*	1. architectural ornament having structural function, e. g. lisenes, pilasters, etc. 2. ornament which is an integral part of the building (e. g. chiselled, carved, painted directly on the building elements)
Bauplan (-pläne) *m*	architectural plan, building plan
Bauplastik(en) *f*	architectural sculpture; sculpture which is related to a building
bauplastisch	in respect to the sculptural ornamentation of a building
Bauschmuck(e) *m*	decoration on a building
Baustil(e) *m*	architecture, architectural style
Baustoff(e) *m*	building material
Bausymbolik *f*	architectural symbolism, e.g. twelve columns representing the twelve Apostles
Bautastein *m*	Scandinavian Bronze Age memorial stone
Bautechnik(en) *f*	building technology
Bauteil(e) *m*	part or component of the building
Bauvorstellung(en) *f*	concept of building
Bauweise(n) *f*	manner of building, building style
bebildern	to illustrate, to decorate with pictures
Becher (—) *m*	cup, beaker, mug
Becken (—) *n*	1. pelvis 2. basin
bedeckt	covered
Bedeutung(en) *f*	meaning, significance

Bedeutungsperspektive *f*	perspective in which figures are larger or smaller according to their significance
beeinflussen	to influence
Befestigung(en) *f*	1. fastening, attaching 2. fortification
Befestigungsanlage(n) *f*	fortification, defenses
Beffroi(s) *m*	castle keep
Befund(e) *m*	result of diagnosis or examination, findings
begabt	talented
Begabung(en) *f*	talent
Begräbnis(se) *n*	burial, funeral
Begräbnisort(e) *m*	burial site
Begräbnisstätte(n) *f*	burial site
Begräbnistempel (–) *m*	funerary temple
Begriffsschrift(en) *f*	ideography, writing with ideograms
Begriffszeichen (–) *n*	ideogram
behandeln	to treat
Behandlung(en) *f*	treatment
Behang (Behänge) *m*	hanging, drapery, lambrequin
behauen	1. to hew 2. hewn
Beichtstuhl (-stühle) *m*	confessional
Beigabe(n) *f*	1. contribution, addition 2. grave objects, grave goods
beige	beige, sand-colored
Beil(e) *n*	adze
Bein(e) *n*	leg
Beinhaus (-häuser) *n*	charnel house
Beinling(e) *m*	legging
Beinschnitzerei(en) *f*	bone or ivory carving
Beinschwarz *n*	bone black
Beischlag *m*	perron
Beitel (–) *m*	gouge *woodcarving*
beitragen	to contribute
Beiwerk *n*	staffage, accessories, non-essential elements or details

Beize(n) *f*	1. stain
	2. mordant
beizen	1. to stain
	2. to bite *etching*
Bekehrung Pauli, die —	the Conversion of Paul
bekleiden	to dress, to clothe
bekleidet	dressed, clothed
Belag (Beläge) *m*	coating
Beletage(n) *f*	first upper floor, bel étage
Beleuchtung(en) *f*	lighting
Beleuchtungseffekt(e) *m*	lighting effect
belichten	to expose *photography*
Belichtung *f*	exposure
Belfried(e) *m*	belfry
Belvedere *n*	1. belvedere, gazebo
	2. popular name for palaces
Bema (Bemata) *n*	bema
bemalen	to paint
Bemalung(en) *f*	painting, painted decoration
Benzol *n*	benzol
beobachten	to observe
Beobachter (—) *m*	observer
Beobachtung(en) *f*	observation
Beobachtungsgabe *f*	observation, ability to observe, power of observation
Berapp *m*	coarse plaster
Berappung(en) *f*	scratch coat *fresco*
Bergfried(e) *m*	castle keep
Bergpredigt, die —	Sermon on the Mount
Bergkristall *m*	rock crystal
Berlinerblau *n*	Berlin blue, Prussian blue
Berlocke(n) *f*	decorative pendant, charm, trinket
Berme(n) *f*	berm
Bernstein *m*	amber
bernsteinfarben	amber-colored
Bernwardskunst *f*	art commissioned by Bishop Bernward of Hildesheim

Berufung(en) *f*	1. call
	2. the Calling of the Apostles
Berufung des hl. Petrus, die —	the Calling of St. Peter
Beryll *m*	beryl
beschädigen	to damage
beschädigt	damaged
Beschädigung(en) *f*	damage
Beschauer (—) *m*	viewer
beschlagen	to sheathe, to cover with metal
Beschlagwerk(e) *n*	strapwork
Beschneidung, die —	the Circumcision
beschränkte Auflage(n) *f*	limited edition
beschriften	to label, to inscribe
Beschriftung(en) *f*	label, inscription
Besitzerangabe(n) *f*	data on ownership
Bestattung(en) *f*	burial
Bestattungsplatz (-plätze) *m*	burial site
Bestiarium (Bestiarien) *n*	bestiary
besticken	to embroider
bestickt	embroidered
Bestoßung(en) *f*	chip, chipped off part
bethlemische Kindermord, der	the Massacre (or Slaughter) of the Innocents
Betnuß (-nüsse) *f*	small hinged sphere with religious carving inside
Beton *m*	concrete
Betonbau(ten) *m*	concrete construction, concrete building
Betonbauweise *f*	concrete construction
Betonboden (-böden) *m*	concrete floor
Beton-Fertigelement(e) *n*	precast concrete unit
Betonglasfenster (—) *n*	stained glass window set in concrete
betonieren	to reinforce with concrete, to concrete
Betonierung *f*	concrete, concreting

Betonmauer(n) *f*	concrete wall
Betonmauerstein(e) *m*	concrete building block
Betonrelief(s) *n*	relief in concrete
betrachten	to observe, to look closely (at)
Betrachter (−) *m*	viewer, observer
Betrachtungspunkt(e) *m*	viewpoint, point of station
Betrachtungsweise(n) *f*	manner of viewing, manner of looking at
Betsäule(n) *f*	roadside cross or memorial (see *Marterl*)
Bett(en) *n*	bed
Bettelordenkirche(n) *f*	churches of the Francisan, Dominican and Capucine (mendicant) orders
beweglich	flexible, moveable
Beweglichkeit(en) *f*	flexibility, mobility
bewegt	animated, lively
Bewegung(en) *f*	movement
Bewegungsfluß *m*	flow of movement
Bewegungsmotiv(e) *f*	motif of movement
Bewegungsrichtung(en) *f*	direction of movement, direction of the action
Beweinung, die −	the Lamentation
Bewurf (Bewürfe) *m*	plaster, plaster coating
Beziehung(en) *f*	relationship
Bibel(n) *f*	the Bible
Bibelhandschrift(en) *f*	Bible manuscript
Bibelillustration(en) *f*	Bible illustration
Biberschwanzdach (-dächer) *n*	roof covered with flat tiles
Bibliothek(en) *f*	library
biblisch	Biblical
Biedermeier *n*	Biedermeier (style)
Biedermeierstil *m*	Biedermeier (style)
Bienenwachs *n*	bee's-wax
Biforium (Biforien) *n*	biforium
Biga (Bigen) *f*	biga, two-horsed team

Bild

Bild(er) *n*	picture, image
Bildaufbau *m*	structure or composition of a picture
Bildauffassung(en) *f*	conception of the picture
Bildbindung *f*	cohesion of the picture
Bilddeutung(en) *f*	interpretation or meaning of a picture
Bildebene(n) *f*	picture plane, zone
bilden	1. to form, to shape 2. to constitute
bildende Kunst (Künste) *f*	fine arts, depictive art, plastic or visual arts
Bilderbogen (–, -bögen) *m*	series of pictures accompanied by a (rhymed) text
Bilderevangelium (-evangelien) *n*	illuminated evangeliar or gospel book
Bilderfeind(e) *m*	iconoclast
Bilderfreund(e) *m*	person in favor of icons during the iconoclastic controversy
Bildergeschichte(n) *f*	comic strip, picture story
Bilderkapitell(e) *n*	capital ornamented with animal or human heads
Bilderprogramm(e) *n*	pictorial program
Bilderrahmen (–) *m*	picture frame
Bilderschrift *f*	pictography
Bilderstreit *m*	the iconoclastic controversy
Bildersturm *m*	the iconoclastic controversy, iconoclasm
Bilderstürmer (–) *m*	iconoclast
bilderstürmerisch	iconoclastic
Bilderverehrung *f*	iconolatry
Bilderwand (-wände) *f*	iconostasis
Bilderzyklus (-zyklen) *m*	picture cycle, pictorial cycle
Bildfeld(er) *n*	field of the picture
Bildfläche(n) *f*	surface of the picture, picture plane
Bildfolge(n) *f*	progression (or series) of pictures
Bildformat(e) *n*	shape or size of the picture
Bildgattung(en) *f*	type of picture

Bildgefüge (–) n	structure of the picture
Bildgegenstand (-stände) m	subject, depicted object
Bildgestaltung(en) f	composition (of the picture)
Bildgießerei f	(bronze) casting
Bildgleichnis(se) n	picture parable, picture allegory
Bildhauer (–) m	sculptor
Bildhauerarbeit(en) f	sculptural work, sculpture
Bildhauerei f	sculpture
bildhauerisch	sculptural
Bildhauerkunst f	(art of) sculpture
Bildinhalt(e) m	content (of a picture)
Bildklischee(s) n	visual cliché
Bildkunst (-künste) f	depictive art, pictorial art
bildlich	visual, pictorial
Bildnerei f	sculpture
bildnerisch	pictorial, sculptural, compositional
Bildnis(se) n	portrait
Bildnisbüste(n) f	portrait bust
Bildniskopf (-köpfe) m	portrait head
Bildnismaler (–) m	portrait painter
Bildnismalerei f	portrait painting
Bildnisradierung(en) f	portrait etching
Bildnisstecher (–) m	portrait engraver
Bildnisstil(e) m	style, portrait style
Bildniszug (-züge) m	facial feature
Bildoberfläche(n) f	picture surface, picture plane
Bildpartie(n) f	part of the picture
Bildprogramm(e) n	pictorial program
Bildrand (-ränder) m	edge of the picture
Bildschnitzer (–) m	carver
Bildschnitzerei f	(art of) carving
Bildsprache(n) f	pictorial language
Bildstickerei(en) f	embroidery
Bildstock (-stöcke) m	roadside cross (see *Marterl*)
Bildteppich(e) m	tapestry, gobelin
Bildthema (-themen) n	picture theme or topic; subject

Bildtiefe(n) *f*	(spatial) depth of a picture
Bildtypus (-typen) *m*	type of picture
Bildvorstellung(en) *f*	concept of depiction, pictorial concept
Bildwerk(e) *n*	sculpture
Bildwirkerei *f*	production of loom-woven tapestry
bildwürdig	worthy of being depicted
Bildzeichen (—) *n*	symbolic picture or sign
Bimsstein *m*	pumice (stone)
Bindemittel (—) *n*	1. cement, binding agent 2. paint medium, vehicle
Binder (—) *m*	1. binder *painting* 2. header *architecture*
Bindung *f*	cohesion
Binnengarten (-gärten) *m*	inner garden
Binnenhof (-höfe) *m*	inner court, enclosed court
Binnenzeichnung(en) *f*	interior drawing, interior details (as opposed to outlines)
Bireme(n) *f*	bireme
Birkenholz *n*	birch
Birnbaumholz *n*	pear wood
birnenförmig	pear-shaped
Birnstab (-stäbe) *m*	rib or respond with pear-shaped profile
Bischof (Bischöfe) *m*	bishop
Bischofsstab (-stäbe) *m*	crosier, pastoral staff
Bischofsstuhl (-stühle) *m*	bishop's throne, cathedra
Biskuit(e) *n*	bisque, biscuit (porcelain)
Bister *m*	bistre
Bistertusche(n) *f*	bistre wash, bistre drawing ink
Bisterzeichnung(en) *f*	bistre drawing
Blacherniotissa *f*	Blacherniotissa Madonna
Blaker (—) *m*	sconce with mirror
Blankverglasung *f*	colorless glazing, colorless window(s)
Blase(n) *f*	1. blister *painting* 2. bladder (paint container)

blasen	to blow
Bläser (—) *m*	(glass) blower
blaß	pale
Blatt (Blätter) *n*	leaf, sheet, page, newspaper
Blattfries(e) *m*	vine scroll pattern
Blattgold *n*	gold leaf
Blattkapitell(e) *n*	capital decorated with leaves
Blattmaske(n) *f*	architectural ornament with a human face constructed of or surrounded by leaves
Blattmetall *n*	metal leaf
Blattornament(e) *n*	foliage ornamentation
Blattspitze(n) *f*	leaf-shaped point (on fibula, sword, arrowhead
Blattwelle(n) *f*	tongue and dart, leaf and dart
Blattwerk *n*	foliage
blau	blue
Blauen *n*	"bluing", gradual turning blue of certain colors
Blaue Reiter, der —	der Blaue Reiter, the "Blue Rider"
Blaue Vier *pl*	Blaue Vier, the "Blue Four"
bläulich	bluish
Blech *n*	sheet metal
Blechgefäß(e) *n*	tin vessel
Blei *n*	lead
bleichen	to bleach
Bleiglanzkeramik *f*	(Mayan) plumbate ware
Bleiglasfenster (-) *n*	leaded glass window, stained glass window
Bleiglasur(en) *f*	lead glaze
Bleiglätte *f*	litharge
Bleiguß (-güsse) *m*	(art of) lead casting
Bleikristall *n*	lead crystal
Bleimennige *f*	minium, red lead
Bleirute(n) *f*	lead came, lead calm; lead strip between sections of stained glass window

Bleistift(e) m	(lead) pencil
Bleistiftzeichnung(en) f	pencil drawing
Bleitafel(n) f	lead panel, lead plate
Bleiweiß n	white lead
Bleiweißpaste f	white lead in oil
Blendarkade(n) f	blind arcade
Blendbogen (−,-bögen) m	blind arch
Blende(n) f	architectural ornament applied to the wall surface, blind ornament
Blendgiebel (−) m	false front, pediment with nothing behind it
Blendmaßwerk(e) n	blind tracery
Blendtriforium (-triforien) n	blind triforium
Blick(e) m	view, glance, gaze
Blickbahn(en) f	path the eyes take when viewing an object
Blickfeld(en) n	field of vision
Blindprägung(en) f	relief printing
Blitz(e) m	lightning, thunderbolt
Blockbau(ten) m	log construction, log building
Blockbuch (-bücher) n	block book
Blockgrenze(n) f	limit (or edge) of the block
blockhaft	blocky, blocklike
Blockhaftigkeit f	blockiness
Blockhaus (-häuser) n	log house
Blockpalette(n) f	disposable palette, pad of paper palettes
Blume(n) f	flower
Blumenkranz (-kränze) m	floral wreath
Blumenstilleben (−) n	still life of flowers
Blumenstrauß (-sträuße) m	bouquet
Blumenstück(e) n	still life of flowers
Bluse(n) f	blouse
Blutemail n	ancient enamelling technique in which red enamel is poured into furrows cut into metal
Blütezeit(en) f	florescence, heyday, peak

Blutstein *m*	hematite
Boden (Böden) *m*	floor, ground
Bodenfliese(n) *f*	floor tile
Bodengrab (-gräber) *n*	relic or tomb under the altar
Bodenmosaik(en) *n*	floor mosaic
Bodenniveau *n*	ground level, floor level
Bodenplatte(n) *f*	floor section, floor slab
Bodenträger (—) *m*	floor girder
Bogen (—, Bögen) *m*	arch
Bogenansatz (-sätze) *m*	springer
Bogenfeld(er) *n*	tympanum
Bogenfeldrelief(s) *n*	tympanum relief
Bogenfibel(n) *f*	arc fibula
bogenförmig ·	arch-shaped
Bogenfries(e) *m*	arched frieze; series of blind arches
Bogengang (-gänge) *m*	arcade, arcaded walk
Bogenkonstruktion(en) *f*	construction using arches
Bogenkreis(e) *m*	archivolt
Bogenlauf (-läufe) *m*	archivolt
Bogenöffnung(en) *f*	opening of the arch, span
Bogenreihe(n) *f*	series or row of arches
Bogenstellung(en) *f*	arcade, arch over two columns (or piers)
Bogenweite(n) *f*	span
Bogenzwickel (—) *m*	spandrel
Boghazköy	Boghyzkeuy, Boghazkoy, Boghaz Keiü
Bohle(n) *f*	thick board or plank
bohren	to drill
Bohrer (—) *m*	drill
Bollwerk(e) *n*	bulwark, bastion
Bolus *m*	bole
Bolusgrund *m*	bole ground
Bootaxtkultur *f*	Boat-axe culture
Böotien	Bœotia
böotisch	Bœotian

Bootsgrab (-gräber) n	ship burial
Bordüre(n) f	edging, border
Borste(n) f	bristle
Borstenpinsel (–) m	bristle brush
Borte(n) f	border, edge, trim, braid
Böschung(en) f	escarp, slope
Bosse(n) f	1. rusticated stone 2. rough-hewn form of a sculpture
bosseln	to give (rough) shape, to rough hew
Bossenwerk(e) n	rustication
Bossiereisen (–) n	boasting chisel, point
bossieren	to give (rough) shape, to rough-in, to boast
Bossierwachs n	modelling wax
Böttgerporzellan n	Böttger porcelain; oldest German porcelain
Bottich(e) m	tub, vat
Boullearbeit(en) f	boulle-work
Boulle-Möbel pl	furniture with boulle-work, boulle
Bozzetto (Bozzetti) m	bozzetto, maquette
Brachiarium (Brachiarien) n	arm-shaped reliquary
Brakteat(en) m	bracteate, coin printed on one side
Brand (Brände) m	firing (of porcelain or ceramics)
Brandbestattung(en) f	cremation
Brandmauer(n) f	fire wall
Braue(n) f	brow, eyebrow
braun	brown
Bräunen n	the gradual darkening of an oil painting due to oxydation
Braunfarben pl	the browns, the brown color group
Braunfirnis(se) m	email brun; method of partially gilding copper
bräunlich	brownish
Brauttür(en) f	(north) church portal in front of which weddings were performed

Breccie *f*	breccia
Brechung(en) *f*	refraction
Brechungsindex (e, -indizes) *m*	refractive index
breit	broad, wide
Breite(n) *f*	breadth
Brekzie *f*	breccia
brennen	1. to burn 2. to fire (pottery, bricks)
brennende Dornbusch, der —	the Burning Bush
Brennofen (-öfen) *m*	kiln
Brenntechnik(en) *f*	firing technique
Brett(er) *n*	board, plank
Bretterboden (-böden) *m*	wood plank floor, board floor
Brettstuhl (-stühle) *m*	chair having one board as backrest with legs pegged into the seat
Breviar (Breviarien) *n* *also* Breviarium	breviary
Brevier(e) *n*	breviary
Briefmaler *pl*	late medieval painters' guild
Brillant(en) *m*	cut precious gem, esp. diamond
Brilliantgelb *n*	brilliant yellow, Naples yellow
Broderie(n) *f*	embroidery
brodieren	to embroider
Brokat(e) *m*	brocade
Bronze(n) *f*	bronze
Bronzeblech(e) *n*	bronze leaf, sheet bronze
Bronzegießerei(en) *f*	bronze foundry
Bronzeguß (-güsse) *m*	bronze, bronze casting
Bronzekrankheit *f*	bronze disease
bronzen	(of) bronze
Bronzepulver *n*	bronze powder
Bronzetafel(n) *f*	bronze plate, bronze panel
Bronzetür(en) *f*	bronze door
Bronzewerk(e) *n*	bronze
Bronzezeit *f*	Bronze Age

bronzieren	to bronze
Brosche(n) *f*	brooch
Brotvermehrung, die —	the Loaves and the Fishes
Bruch *m*	break, crack, flaw
Bruchstein(e) *m*	rubble, unworked stone
Bruchsteinmauer(n) *f*	rubble wall
Bruchstelle(n) *f*	broken place
Bruchstück(e) *n*	fragment
Brücke(n) *f*	1. bridge 2. Expressionist movement
Brünierstein(e) *m*	burnisher
Brunnen (—) *m*	fountain, spring, well
Brunnenhausszene(n) *f*	late 6th. century picture type depicting a fountain and activity around it
Brunnenhof (-höfe) *m*	courtyard with fountain
Brunnenplastik(en) *f*	fountain sculpture
Brust (Brüste) *f*	breast, chest
Brustbild(er) *n*	(half-length) portrait
Brusthöhe *f*	chest height, level of the chest
Brustkette(n) *f*	necklace, neck chain
Brustkreuz(e) *n*	pectoral cross
Bruststück(e) *n*	portrait including the entire chest
Brüstung(en) *f*	railing, balustrade, breast-high wall
Brustwehr(en) *f*	parapet, breastwork
Brutalismus *m*	Brutalism
Bucchero-Keramik(en) *f*	bucchero ware
Buch (Bücher) *n*	book
Buchdeckel (—) *m*	book cover
Buchdruck *m*	(art of) book printing
Bucheinband (-bände) *m*	binding
Buchkunst (-künste) *f*	the art(s) of book production, including bookbinding, typography, etc.
Buchmaler (—) *m*	limner, miniaturist, book illuminator
Buchmalerei *f*	book illumination
Buchrolle(n) *f*	scroll, rotulus

Buchsbaum *m*	boxwood
Buchstabe(n) *m*	letter, character
buckeln	to emboss
Buckelquader (–) *m*	rusticated ashlar, embossed stone
Buckelung(en) *f*	embossing
Bügelhenkelkrater (–, e) *m*	stirrup handle krater
Bügelkanne(n) *f*	stirrup jar, false-necked jar
Bühne(n) *f*	stage
Bühnenbild(er) *n*	stage set, scenery, backdrop
Bühnenbildner (–) *m*	stage designer
Bühnenhintergrund *m*	stage set, scenery, backdrop
Bukranion (Bukranien) *n*	bucranium, bucrane
Bund (Bünde) *m*	1. band, ring 2. girder, binder *architecture* 3. alliance, league
Bund, der Alte –	Old Testament
Bund, der Neue –	New Testament
Bündelpfeiler (–) *m*	compound pier, clustered pier
Bundeslade *f*	Ark of the Covenant
bunt	1. colored (i. e. not black and white) 2. very colorful
Buntfarbigkeit *f*	colorfulness
buntgemalt	colorfully painted, painted in color
Buntglasfenster (–) *n*	stained glass window
Buntheit *f*	1. hue 2. colorfulness
Buntkraft *f*	brilliance (of a color)
Buntscheibe(n) *f*	stained glass window
Buntstift(e) *m*	colored pencil, crayon
Buntstiftzeichnung(en) *f*	colored pencil drawing, crayon drawing
Burg(en) *f*	castle, fort
burgundisch	Burgundian
Burnus *m*	burnoose
Burse(n) *f*	1. purse 2. purse-shaped container or reliquary

busig

busig	twisted, warped (vault surface)
Büste(n) *f*	bust
Busung(en) *f*	ploughshare twist, twisted vault surface between diagonal and wall rib due to differing heights
Bütten (—) *n* *also* Büttenpapier	handmade paper with a rough edge
buttrig	buttery, short *painting*
Butzenscheibe(n) *f*	(pane of) bull's eye glass
byzantinisch	Byzantine
Byzanz *n*	Byzantium, Constantinople
Cabochon(s) *m*	cabochon
Caduceus (Caducei) *m*	caduceus
Caldarium (Caldarien) *n*	caldarium
Calefactorium (Calefactorien) *n*	heated room in a monastery
Callotfigur(en) *f*	baroque or rococo figures of dwarfs, cripples and deformed people
Camaïeu (—) *f*	1. cameo 2. camaïeu
camera obscura *f*	camera obscura
Campanile *m*	campanile
Capsa (Capsen) *f*	1. cylindrical reliquary 2. container for gospel books 3. container for Communion utensils
Capsien *n*	Capsian (culture)
Caput mortuum *n*	caput mortuum
Cardiumkeramik *f*	pottery decorated by using cardium shell
Carraramarmor *m*	Carrara marble
Cartonnier(s) *m*	artist who re-draws small original designs to full-size cartoons for weaving tapestries
Casein *n* *also* Kasein	casein

Cassone (Cassoni) *m*	cassone, wooden household chest
Cathedra (e, Cathedren) *f* *also* Kathedra	cathedra, bishop's throne
Cella(e) *f*	cella
Ceresin *n*	ceresin
Chalkographie *f*	(art of) copper engraving *obselete word*
Chalkolithikum *n*	Chalcolithic
Chalzedon *m*	chalcedony
Chemigraphie *f*	chemigraphy
Cherub(im, -inen) *m*	cherub
chiaroscuro	chiaroscuro
Chimäre(n) *f*	chimera
Chinoiserie(n) *f*	chinoiserie
Chiton(e) *m*	chiton
Chlamys (−) *f*	chlamys
Chor (Chöre) *m*	chancel, sanctuary, choir
Choranbau(ten) *m*	chancel annex
Chorempore(n) *f*	rood loft, gallery above the chancel
Chorgestühl(e) *n*	choir stalls
Chorgitter (−) *n*	cancello, chancel screen, rood screen, jubé
Chorhaupt (-häupter) *n*	apse, chevet, end of the chancel
Chorhemd(en) *n*	surplice
Chorkapelle(n) *f*	chapel in the chancel, apsidal chapel
Chörlein (−) *n*	oratory, chapel in a private home projecting like a bay window
Chorquadrat(e) *n*	chancel square
Chorraum (-räume) *m*	chancel
Chorschluß *m*	(shape of the) eastern end of the chancel
Chorschranke(n) *f*	(rood) screen, chancel screen
Chorstuhlwange(n) *f*	bench end, sidewall of choir stall
Chorturm (-türme) *m*	chancel tower
Chorumgang (-gänge) *m*	ambulatory

Chrismarium (Chrismarien) *n*	chrismatory
Chrismatorium (Chrismatorien) *n*	chrismatory
Christentum *n*	Christianity, Christendom
Christkind *n*	the Christ Child
christlich	Christian
Christophorus, der hl. —	St. Christopher
Christus *m*	Christ
Christus als Gärtner	noli me tangere
Christus in Elend *also* Christus in Rast	(sculptural) portrayal of Christ exhausted, sad, chained and/or resting
Christus-Johannes-Gruppe *f*	depiction of St. John resting his head on Christ's shoulder
Christusmonogramm(e) *n*	Christogram, chi-rho
chromatisch	chromatic
chromatische Farbqualität *f*	chromaticity
Chromatotypie(n) *f* *also* Chromatypie(n)	multi-colored print, multi-colored printing
Chromgelb *n*	chrome yellow
Chromgrün *n*	chrome green
chromieren	to (plate with) chrome
Chromolithographie(n) *f*	color lithography
Chromoxyd *n*	chromium oxide (green)
Chromrot *n*	chrome red
Chronologie(n) *f*	chronology
Chrysoberyll *m*	chrysoberyl
Chrysographie(n) *f*	chrysography; writing or painting in gold
Churriguerismus *m*	Churrigueresque (style)
Ciborium (Ciborien) *n* *also* Ziborium (Ziborien)	ciborium
Cinquecento *n*	cinquecento
Cipollin *m*	cipolin, cipollino
cire perdue *n*	cire perdue, lost wax

Cista (Cisten) *f* *also* Zista (Zisten), Ziste (Zisten)	1. prehistoric bronze bucket 2. cist; broad basket holding ceremonial utensils (ancient Greece) 3. Etruscan bronze toilet utensils; covered urn
Clairobscur *n*	chiaroscuro
Clairobscurschnitt(e) *m*	chiaroscuro woodcut
Cloisonné *n*	cloisonné
cluniazensisch	Cluny, Cluniac
Codex (Codices) *m* *also* Kodex	codex
Coelinblau *n*	cerulean blue, coelin
coemeterial	coemetrial
Coemeterium (Coemeterien) *n* *also* Zömeterium (Zömeterien)	coemeterium, catacomb
Collage(n) *f*	collage
Colophonium *n* *also* Kolophonium	rosin, colophony
Columbarium (Columbarien) *n*	columbarium
Computerkunst *f*	computer art
Confessio *f*	confessio
Copertaglasur *f*	clear, colorless lead glaze (for faience pottery)
Corten-stahl *m*	cor-ten steel
Cosmaten *pl*	Cosmati
Craquelée(s) *m, n* *also* Krakelee *n*	1. craquelure *painting* 2. crackle, crazing *porcelain*
Crayonmanier *f*	crayon manner, chalk manner
cremefarben	cream-colored
Cromlech(e, s) *m* *also* Kromlech	cromlech
Cuppa(e) *f* *also* Kuppa	bowl (of a chalice or goblet)
Custodia (Custodien) *f* *also* Kustodia	pyx or other container for storing the Host

Dach (Dächer) n	roof
dachartig	roof-like
Dachbalken (−) m	rafter, roof beam
Dachbelag (-beläge) m	roofing (material)
Dachboden (-böden) m	loft, attic
Dachdeckung(en) f	roofing (material)
Dacherker (−) m	dormer window
Dachfenster (−) n	dormer window, skylight
Dachfirst(e) m	roof ridge
Dachform(en) f	roof shape
Dachgarten (-gärten) m	roof garden
Dachgeschoß (-geschosse) n	top story, top floor
Dachgesims(e) n	roof cornice
Dachkammer(n) f	garret, attic
Dachkonstruktion(en) f	roof construction
Dachpappe f	tarpaper, roofing paper
Dachplatte(n) f	roof slab
Dachrandträger (−) m	peripheral roof girder
Dachreiter (−) m	turret, ridge-turret, flèche
Dachrinne(n) f	gutter
Dachsbeil(e) n	adze
Dachshaar(e) n	badger bristle
Dachshaarpinsel (−) m	badger brush, badger blender
Dachstroh n	thatching
Dachstuhl (-stühle) m	(roof) truss
Dachstuhl, doppeltstehender −	roof construction with queen-posts
Dachstuhl, offener −	open roof truss, roof framework visible from within the building
Dachtraufe(n) f	eaves
Dachtürmchen (−) n	louvre with lantern, turret
Dachüberstand m	verge, roof overhang, overhanging eaves
Dachuntersicht(en) f	roof undersurface
Dachziegel (−) m	roof tile
Dachzierglied(er) n	acroterion, roof ornament
Dadaismus m	Dadaism

Dadaist(en) *m*	Dadaist
dadaistisch	dadaistic
Daktyliothek(en) *f*	collection of glyptographs
Dalmatika (Dalmatiken) *f*	dalmatic
Damar *n* *also* Dammar	damar
Damarfirnis(se) *m*	damar varnish
Damarharz *n*	damar (resin)
Damast(e) *m*	damask
damaszieren	to damascene
Damaszierung(en) *f*	damascening
Dammar *n*	damar
Dämmerlicht *n*	twilight, dusk
Dammgrube(n) *f*	casting pit
Dämon(en) *m*	demon
Danielschnalle(n) *f*	bronze clasp with a depiction of Daniel and the lions
Daraufsicht *f* *also* Draufsicht	view from above, bird's eye view, view of the top
darstellen	to represent, to portray, to depict, to show
Darstellung(en) *f*	representation, portrayal, depiction
Darstellung Jesu im Tempel, die —	the Presentation in the Temple
Darstellungsmethode(n) *f*	method of depiction
Darstellungsmittel (−) *n*	medium, means of depiction
Darstellungsweise(n) *f*	manner of depicting or representing
darstellungswürdig	worthy of being depicted
datieren	to date, to establish the date of origin
Datierung(en) *f*	dating
Datierungsmittel (−) *n*	means of establishing the date of origin, means of dating
Daumen (−) *m*	thumb
Davidstern(e) *m* *also* Davidsstern	star of David, Solomon's seal

Deambulatorium (Deambulatorien) *n*	ambulatory
Decalcomanie *f*	decalcomania
Dechsel (–) *m*	adze
Decke(n) *f*	ceiling
Deckel (–) *m*	lid, cover
Deckelpokal(e) *m*	covered goblet
Deckelschale(n) *f*	covered bowl
Deckeltürmchen (–) *n*	tower-shaped lid
decken	to cover, to mask
deckend	covering, masking, opaque
Deckendekoration(en) *f*	ceiling decoration
Deckenfresko (-fresken) *n*	ceiling fresco
Deckengemälde (–) *n*	ceiling painting
Deckenmalerei(en) *f*	ceiling painting
Deckenputz *m*	ceiling plaster
Deckenträger (–) *m*	girder, ceiling beam
Deckfarbe(n) *f*	body color, opaque color, opaque paint
Deckfarbenmalerei *f*	painting with opaque colors
Deckgrün *n*	emerald green
Deckkraft *f*	hiding power, degree of opacity
Deckplatte(n) *f*	abacus
Deckweiß *n*	lithophone
Deckweiß, höhen mit –	to heighten (by underpainting with white)
Décollage(n) *f*	décollage
Dedikationsbild(er) *n*	depiction of the presentation of an artwork to the patron
Deësis (Deësen) *f*	deësis
Deformation(en) *f*	distortion, deformation
Deformierung(en) *f*	deformation
dehnbar	malleable, pliable, stretchable
dehnen	to stretch, to lengthen, to expand
Deichselkreuz(e) *n*	Y-shaped cross
Dekalkierpapier *n*	decalcomania paper, transfer paper

Dekalog *m*	Ten Commandments, Decalogue
Dekor(s) *m*	decor, ornamentation (on glass or pottery)
Dekor(e) *n*	stage scenery
Dekoration(en) *f*	decoration
Dekorationsform(en) *f*	decorational form
Dekorationsmalerei *f*	(stage) set painting, scenery painting, interior painting
dekorativ	decorative
dekorieren	to decorate, to ornament, to adorn
del.	del.
Delfter Kacheln *pl*	Delft tiles
Delfter Zeug *n*	delftware
Delphin(e) *m*	dolphin
Dendrochronologie *f*	dendrochronology, tree-ring dating
Denkbild(er) *n*	image
Denkmal (-mäler) *n*	monument
Denkmalamt (-ämter) *n*	office empowered with the care and preservation of monuments
Denkmalpflege *f*	care and preservation of monuments
Denkmalschutz *m*	protective law for the care and preservation of monuments
Depotfund(e) *m*	hoard
derb	coarse
Derbheit *f*	coarseness, roughness
Dessin(s) *n*	design, drawing
Detail(s) *n*	detail
Detailansicht(en) *f*	detail, detail view
Detailbehandlung(en) *f*	treatment of detail(s)
Detailguß (-güsse) *m*	piece mold casting
Detaillierung(en) *f*	detailing
Detailzeichnung(en) *f*	(enlarged) detail drawing
Deutschrömer (–) *m*	German painters working in Rome during the first half of the 19th. century
Deutung(en) *f*	interpretation

Devotionalbild(er) *n*	small devotional picture, small *Andachtsbild*
Devotionalien *pl*	devotional objects (such as cross, rosary, miniatures of saints, etc.)
Dextrin *n*	dextrin
Dia(s) *n*	slide
Diadem(e) *n*	diadem
diagonal	diagonal
Diagonalansicht(en) *f*	diagonal view, oblique view
Diagonale(n) *f*	diagonal (line)
Diagonalrippe(n) *f*	diagonal rib
Diakonikon *n*	diaconicon
Diamant(en) *m*	diamond
Diamantband (-bänder) *n*	nailhead (pattern)
Diamantierung(en) *f*	diamond-shaped relief band cut into a stone surface
Diamantquader (–) *m*	stone block with diamond-pointed rustication
Diamantstein(e) *m*	stone with diamond-pointed rustication
diaphan	translucent, diaphanous
Diaphanie(n) *f*	translucent picture
Diaphanradierung(en) *f*	etching drawn on a photographic plate which is then developed
Diapositiv(e) *n*	slide
Diatretglas *n*	diatreta glass
Dichroismus *m*	dichroism
Dickflüssigkeit *f*	viscosity
Dickglas *n*	dalles de vers, thick glass
Diele(n) *f*	1. board, plank, beam 2. hall, vestibule
Dielenkopf (-köpfe) *m*	mutule
Dienst(e) *m*	vaulting shaft, respond
Dienst, alter –	strong shaft bearing cross ribs
Dienst, junger –	small, weaker shaft bearing arch-forming ribs
Dienstbündel (–) *n*	clustered vaulting shafts, compound respond

Diere(n) *f*	tri-ream
diffus	diffuse
Diglyph(e) *m*	diglyph
Dimension(en) *f*	dimension
dimensional	dimensional
Dimensionierung(en) *f*	dimensions, the act of giving dimension
Dinanderie(n) *f*	dinanderie; chased copper or bronze object(s)
Diorama (Dioramen) *n*	diorama
Diorit *m*	diorite
dipteral	dipteral
Dipteros (Dipteroi) *m*	dipteral temple
Diptychon (Diptychen) *n*	diptych
Dipylon-Vase(n) *f*	Dipylon vase
Dispersionsfarbe(n) *f*	paint dispersed in synthetic resin
Divisionismus *m*	Divisionism
Docke(n) *f*	(wooden) baluster
documenta *f*	exhibition of modern art held every four years in Kassel, Germany
Doelenstück(e) *n*	Doelenstuk, Schutterstuk, marksmen's guild piece
Dogenpalast *m*	Doge's Palace
Dokument(e) *n*	document
dokumentarisch	documentary
Dolch(e) *m*	dagger
Dolmen (−) *m*	dolmen
Dom(e) *m*	cathedral, minster
Dombau *m*	cathedral architecture, cathedral building
Domikalgewölbe (−) *n*	domical vault
Dominantfarbe(n) *f*	dominant color
Domschatz (-schätze) *m*	cathedral treasure
Donator(en) *m*	donor, donor portrait
Donaukultur *f*	Danubian culture
Donauschule *f*	Danube school

Donaustil *m*	Danube School, style of the Danube School
Donnerkeil(e) *m*	thunderbolt
Doppeladler (—) *m*	double-headed eagle
Doppelantentempel (—) *m*	Greek temple with naos, pronaos, posticum and distyle in antis on both ends
Doppelausguß (-güsse) *m*	double spout
Doppelchoranlage(n) *f*	double-ended (church) plan
doppelchörig	double-ended (church)
Doppelfigur(en) *f*	addorsed figure; symmetrical figures back to back
Doppelglas *n*	double-layered glass with painting and/or foil between the layers
Doppeljoch(e) *n*	1. square Romanesque bay with two main pillars and one lateral pillar 2. Late Romanesque-Early Gothic bay with sexpartite vault
Doppelkapelle(n) *f*	palatine chapel, palatine church
Doppelkreuz(e) *n*	patriarchal cross
Doppelsäule(n) *f*	coupled columns
Doppeltafel(n) *f*	diptych
Doppelturmfassade(n) *f*	facade having two towers
Dorer *pl*	Dorians
dorisch	Doric
dorische Ordnung *f*	Doric order
Dormitorium (Dormitorien) *n*	dormitory
Dornauszieher, der —	(Street) Boy Extracting a Thorn
Dornbusch, der brennende —	the Burning Bush
Dornenkrönung, die —	Christ Crowned with Thorns
Dorsale (—) *n*	back rest of choir stall
Dose(n) *f*	box, tin, canister
Dotter (—) *n*	egg yolk
doublieren	to line, to reline, to recanvas
Doxale(s) *n*	(baroque) grill between chancel and nave

Drache(n) *m*	dragon
Drachenblut *n*	dragon's blood, red resin
Drachenkampf des hl. Georg, der −	St. George and the Dragon
Draht (Drähte) *m*	wire
Drahtemail *n*	plique-à-jour (enamel)
Drahtglas *n*	wire-reinforced glass
Drahtplastik(en) *f*	wire sculpture
Draperie(n) *f*	drapery, draping
Drapierung(en) *f*	draping, wrapping, drapery
Draufsicht *f* *also* Daraufsicht	view from above, bird's eye view, view of the top
drechseln	to turn, to shape on a lathe
Drehbank (-bänke) *f*	lathe
drehen	to turn
Dreiapsidenchor (-chöre) *m*	trichora; chancel with three apses
dreidimensional	three-dimensional
Dreidimensionalität *f*	three-dimensionality
Dreieck(e) *n*	triangle
dreieckig	triangular
Dreiecksgiebel (−) *m*	triangular gable, triangular pediment
Dreieckskomposition(en) *f*	triangular composition
Dreieinigkeit *f*	Holy Trinity
Dreifaltigkeit *f*	Holy Trinity
Dreiflügelbild(er) *n*	triptych
Dreifuß (-füße) *m*	tripod
dreijochig	three-bayed
Dreikerb *m*	triglyph
Dreikonchenanlage(n) *f* *also* Dreikonchenchor (-chöre) *m*	cloverleaf plan, trichora; church plan with an apse in the chancel and one at the end of each transept arm
Dreipaß (-pässe) *m*	trefoil
Dreipaßbogen (−, -bögen) *m*	trilobe arch, trefoil arch
dreischiffig	three-aisled
Dreischlitzplatte(n) *f*	triglyph

Dreischneuß(e) *m*	curvilinear tracery motif with three mouchettes within a circle
Dreisitz(e) *m*	sedilia
Dreisprachenstein *m*	Rosetta Stone
dreispitzig	three-pointed
Dreiviertelansicht(en) *f*	three quarter view
Dreiviertelsäule(n) *f*	column (against the wall) with a three quarter circle profile
Dreizack *m*	trident
Drillingsfenster (−) *n*	triforium
Drolerie(n) *f*	drollery
Dromos *m*	dromos
Druck(e) *m*	1. print
	2. pressure
drucken	to print
Druckerei *f*	printing shop, press
Druckerschwärze(n) *f*	black printing ink
Druckgraphik(en) *f*	prints, printed graphics
Druckkunst *f*	(art of) printing
Druckplatte(n) *f*	printing plate
Druckpresse(n) *f*	printing press
Druckschablone(n) *f*	printing stencil
Druckstock (-stöcke) *m*	printing block, printing plate
Drucktechnik(en) *f*	printing technique, printing technology
Druckverfahren (−) *n*	printing process
Druckverteilung *f*	distribution of pressure
Drudenfuß (-füße) *m*	pentacle, pentagram
Dübel (−) *m*	peg, dowel
Dübelloch (-löcher) *n*	peg hole
dübeln	to attach with a peg
Ducento *n*	dugento
duff	matt, lustreless
Dugento *n*	dugento
Duktus *m*	stroke, touch
dunkel	dark
Dunkelheit *f*	darkness

dunkeln	to darken, to become dark
dünn	thin
dünnwandig	thin-walled
Durchblick(e) *m*	view through, vista
durchbrochen	perforated, broken through
durchdringen	to penetrate
Durchdringungsraum *m*	(area of) intersection
Durchdruckverfahren *n*	soft-ground etching, vernis mou
durchfenstert	fenestrated
durchführen	to carry out, to execute (a plan)
Durchführung(en) *f*	execution (of a work)
Durchgang durch das Rote Meer, der —	Passage Through the Red Sea, Crossing the Red Sea
durchgearbeitet	detailed, worked
durchleuchten	to x-ray
durchlöchern	to perforate
Durchmesser (—) *m*	diameter
durchscheinend	translucent
durchsichtig	transparent
Durchsichtigkeit *f*	transparency
Durchschuß *m*	1. woof *weaving* 2. reglet *printing*
Durchzug durch das Rote Meer, der —	Passage through the Red Sea, Crossing the Red Sea
düster	dusky, dark, dim
Dynamik *f*	dynamism, dynamics
eben	even, level, flat, smooth
Ebenbild(er) *n*	image, likeness
Ebene(n) *f*	level, plane
Ebenholz *n*	ebony
Ebenist(en) *m*	carpenter specializing in ebony work
ecce homo	ecce homo
Ecclesia und Synagoge	Ecclesia and Synagogue, Church and Synagogue

Echinus *m*	echinus
echt	real, genuine, authentic, pure
Echtheit *f*	authenticity, purity, genuineness
Echtheitsbescheinigung(en) *f*	authentication
Eckakroterie(n) *f*	corner acroterion
Eckblatt (-blätter) *n*	spur, griffe *architecture*
Ecke(n) *f*	corner
Eckholz (-hölzer) *n*	squared timber
eckig	angular
Eckkapelle(n) *f*	corner chapel
Eckknolle(n) *f*	spur, griffe *architecture*
Eckpavillon(s) *m*	pavilion terminating the wing of a building
Eckpfeiler (—) *m*	corner pillar, angular pier
Ecksäule(n) *f*	corner column
Ecksporn (-sporen) *m*	spur, griffe *architecture*
Eckstein(e) *m*	cornerstone
Eckstütze(n) *f*	corner support
Eckzwickel (—) *m*	corner spandrel, pendentive
edel	noble, precious
Edelfrau(en) *f*	noblewoman
Edelholz (-hölzer) *n*	precious wood, rare wood
Edelmann (-männer) *m*	nobleman
Edelmetall(e) *n*	precious metal
Edelstein(e) *m*	gem, precious stone, jewel
Edelsteinreif(e) *m*	jewelled headband
Eglomisieren *n*	painting on glass (to be viewed from the unpainted side)
Ehebrecherin, Christus und die —	Christ and the Adultress, the Woman Taken in Adultery
Eiche *f*	oak
Eichenholz *n*	oak
Eidotter (—) *n*	egg yolk
Eierstab *m*	egg and dart (pattern)
eiförmig	egg-shaped
Eigenschaft(en) *f*	characteristic, peculiarity, quality

eigenständig	independent, original
Eigentümlichkeit(en) *f*	peculiarity, characteristic
Eigrund (-gründe) *m*	egg size, egg ground
einansichtig	having only one viewing point
Einarbeitung(en) *f*	bedding (of a statue)
Einband (-bände) *m*	binding, (book) cover
Einbanddeckel (—) *m*	binding, (book) cover
einbauen	to build in
Einbildungskraft (-kräfte) *f*	imaginative power
Einblattdruck(e) *m*	single-leaf print
Einblattholzschnitt(e) *m*	single-leaf woodcut
Eindruck (-drücke) *m*	impression
eindrucksvoll	impressive
einfach	simple, plain
Einfachheit *f*	simplicity
einfassen	1. to set or mount (a jewel) 2. to frame, to line
Einfassung(en) *f*	1. set(ting), mount(ing) 2. frame, framing, border
Einfriedungsmauer(n) *f*	enclosing wall
Einfluß (-flüsse) *m*	influence
Einfühlung *f*	empathy
Einfühlungsvermögen *n*	ability (or capacity) to empathize
Eingang (-gänge) *m*	entrance
Eingangsarkade(n) *f*	entrance arcade
Eingangshalle(n) *f*	entrance hall
eingefärbt	dyed
eingelegt	inlaid
eingezogener Chor *m*	chancel which is narrower than the nave
eingravieren	to engrave
Eingußkanal (-kanäle) *m*	vent for pouring molten metal into casting mold
Einheit(en) *f*	unit
Einhorn *n*	unicorn
einhüftiger Bogen *m*	quadrant arch
Einkorn *n*	einkorn; neolithic form of wheat

Einlage(n) *f*	inlay
Einlegearbeit(en) *f*	inlay, inlay work
einlegen	to inlay
einnehmen	to take up (space)
einordnen	to classify, to arrange
Einordnung(en) *f*	classification
einpunzen	to stamp, to punch in
einrahmen	to frame
Einraumkirche(n) *f*	one-roomed church
einreihen	to set in a row
einreihig	one-rowed
einritzen	to scratch in, to incise
Einsamkeit, Johannes in der —	St. John in the Wilderness
Einsatzbild(er) *n*	picture within a picture
Einsatzkapelle(n) *f*	chapel formed between interior pier buttresses
Einschlag *m*	1. woof 2. element, suggestion, touch
Einschlagen *n*	sinking in (of paint), embu
Einsicht(en) *f*	insight
Einsiedelei(en) *f*	hermitage
Einsiedler (—) *m*	hermit
einstöckig	one-storied, single-storied
Einstufung(en) *f*	categorizing, categorization, dating
Einturmfassade(n) *f*	facade having one tower
Einzelausstellung(en) *f*	one man show
Einzelbruchstück(e) *n*	single fragment
Einzelfenster (—) *n*	single window
Einzelform(en) *f*	single form, single shape, individual form
Einzelgrabkultur(en) *f*	Single-Grave culture
Einzelheit(en) *f*	detail
einzimmerig	one-roomed
Einzug in Jerusalem, der —	Entry into Jerusalem
Eisen *n*	iron

Eisenarmierung *f*	iron armature (of stained glass window)
Eisenätzung(en) *f*	(decorative) etching in iron
Eisenbau(ten) *m*	iron building, iron structure
Eisenbeton *m*	ferroconcrete, (steel) reinforced concrete
Eisenfachwerk *n*	iron framework structure
Eisenfarben *pl*	iron pigments
Eisenguß *m*	iron casting
Eisenhütte(n) *f*	foundry
Eisenocker *m*	red ochre
Eisenoxyd(e) *n*	red earth color, red iron oxide
Eisenradierung(en) *f*	iron engraving
Eisenrot *n*	Jean Cousin; dye for stained glass
Eisenträger (−) *m*	iron beam, iron girder
Eisenzeit *f*	Iron Age
eisern	(of) iron
Eisglas *n*	frosted glass
Eiszeit *f*	Ice Age
Eitempera(s) *f*	egg tempera
Eiweiß *n*	egg white
Eiweißtempera(s) *f*	tempera prepared with egg white
Eiweißvergoldung(en) *f*	glair, gilding with glair
eklektisch	eclectic
Eklektizismus *m*	eclecticism
elegant	elegant
Eleganz *f*	elegance
Elektron *n*	alloy of gold and silver, electrum
Elemi *n*	elemi
Elend, Christus in −	depiction of Christ suffering
Eleusa *f*	Eleousa Madonna
Elfenbein *n*	ivory
elfenbeinfarben	ivory-colored
Elfenbeinschnitzerei(en) *f*	ivory carving
Elfenbeinschwarz *n*	ivory black
elfenbeinweiß	ivory (colored)
Elisabethstil *m*	Elizabethan style

Ellbogen (–) *m*	elbow
Ellipse(n) *f*	ellipse
elliptisch	elliptical
elliptischer Bogen *m*	elliptical arch
Email(s) *n*	enamel
Emailarbeit(en) *f*	enamelwork
Emailchamplevé *n*	champlevé
Emailcloisonné *n*	cloisonné
Emaileinlage(n) *f*	inlaid enamel
Emaille(n) *f*	enamel
emailhaft	enamel-like
Emailfarbe(n) *f*	enamel paint
Emailfliese(n) *f*	enamel tile
emaillieren	to enamel
Emailmalerei *f*	enamel painting
Emailwaren *pl*	enamelled ware
Emblem(e) *n*	emblem, symbol, attribute
Emblematik *f*	heraldry
Emmaus, Christus in –	Christ at Emmaus, the Supper at Emmaus
Emmausjünger, die –	the Disciples at Emmaus
Emmausmahl, das –	the Supper at Emmaus
Emmer *m*	emmer
Empaquetage *f*	wrapping
Empästik *f*	antique damascene and repoussé technique
Empfängnis, die unbefleckte –	Immaculate Conception
empfinden	to perceive, to feel, to experience
Empfinden *n*	perception, feeling
Empfindsamkeit(en) *f*	sensitivity
Empirestil *m*	Empire (style)
Emplekton *n*	opus caementum masonry
Empore(n) *f*	gallery
Emulgator(en) *m*	emulsifier, emulsifying agent
Emulsion(en) *f*	emulsion
Enceinte *f*	enceinte, circumvallation

Enfilade(n) *f*	enfilade; series of rooms arranged on a continuous axis and having the doors arranged in one line
engagiert	(politically) committed
Engel (–) *m*	angel
Engelchen (–) *n*	cherub
Enghalskrug (-krüge) *m*	narrow-necked (faience) jug
Englischer Gruß *m*	the Annunciation, the Angelic Salutation
Engobe(n) *f*	engobe, slip
engobieren	to apply engobe
Enkaustik *f*	encaustic technique
entartete Kunst *f*	degenerate art
Entase(n) *f* also Entasis (Entasen) *f*	entasis
Enthauptung des hl. Johannes, die –	the Beheading of St. John
Entlastungsbogen (–, -bögen) *m*	relieving arch, discharging arch
Entlüftungskanal (-kanäle) *m*	air vent
Entrelacs *n*	entrelac
Entsendung der Apostel, die –	the Mission of the Apostles
entstanden	originated
entstehen	to originate
Entstehung *f*	origin, appearance
Entstehungsjahr(e) *n*	date of origin
Entstehungsort(e) *m*	place of origin
entwerfen	to design
Entwicklung(en) *f*	development
Entwicklungsphase(n) *f*	developmental phase, developmental stage
Entwicklungsstufe(n) *f*	developmental stage, stage of development
Entwurf (-würfe) *m*	design, plan, conception
Entwurfsplastik(en) *f*	bozzetto
Entwurfszeichnung(en) *f*	preparatory drawing, preliminary sketch

Eolith(e, en) *m*	olith
Epigone(n) *m*	epigon(e)
Epigraphik *f*	epigraphy
Epiphanie(n) *f*	epiphany, Epiphany
Epiphaniegestus *m*	gesture with raised arms
Epistelbuch (-bücher) *n*	liturgical book containing the Epistles
Epistelseite(n) *f*	south side of a church, right side of the altar
Epistolarium (Epistolarien) *n*	liturgical book containing the Epistles
Epistyl(e) *n* *also* Epistylion (Epistylien)	architrave
Epitaph(e) *n* *also* Epitaphium (Epitaphien)	epitaph
Epoche(n) *f*	epoch, era, period
Epos (Epen) *n*	epic, epic poem
Epoxydharz(e) *n*	epoxy resin
Epreuve(n) *f*	trial proof
Erbärmdebild(er) *n*	depiction of Christ suffering, Man of Sorrows
erbauen	to build, to erect
erbaut	built
Erbauung(en) *f*	construction, erection, building
Erbe *n*	heritage, inheritance
Erbe(n) *m*	heir
Erde *f*	earth, Earth
Erdfarbe(n) *f*	earth color, earth pigment
erdfarbig	earth-colored
Erdgeschoß (-geschosse) *n*	ground floor
Erechtheion *n*	Erechtheum, Erechtheion
Eremit(en) *m*	hermit
Eremitage(n) *f*	1. hermitage 2. 18th. century park pavilion 3. the Hermitage (Leningrad)
erfinden	to invent

Erfindung(en) f	invention
Erfindungsreichtum m	inventiveness
ergänzen	to complete, to restore
Ergänzfarben pl	complementary colors, contrasting colors
Ergänzung(en) f	completion, restoration, reconstruction
Ergänzungsfarben pl	complementary colors, contrasting colors
erglänzen	to shine, to glow, to sparkle
erhaben	elevated, raised, in relief
erhalten	1. to preserve, preserved 2. to acquire, acquired
Erhaltung f	preservation
Erhaltungszustand m	state of preservation, condition
erheben	to elevate, to raise, to lift
erhoben	elevated, raised
Erker (—) m	bay window, oriel
Erle f	alder wood
Erlöser (—) m	Redeemer, Saviour
Ermitage f	the Hermitage (Leningrad)
erneuern	to renew, to restore
Erneuerung(en) f	restoration
Ernteszene(n) f	harvest scene
Eröffnung(en) f	opening (day)
Eroten pl	cupids, erotes
errichten	to erect
errichtet	erected
Errichtung(en) f	erection
erschaffen	to create
Erschaffung der Welt, die —	the Creation
Erschaffung Evas, die —	the Creation of Eve
erscheinen	to appear
Erscheinung(en) f	appearance, phenomenon
Erscheinungsform(en) f	outward form, outward shape
Erweckung des Lazarus, die —	Raising Lazarus From the Dead

erweitern	to extend, to enlarge
Erweiterung(en) f	extension, enlargement
Erz(e) n	1. brass
	2. ore
erzählen	to narrate
erzählerisch	narrative
Erzählstil m	narrative style
Erzbildner (–) m	bronze sculptor
Erzbischof (-bischöfe) m	archbishop
erzbischöfliches Kreuz n	patriarchal cross
Erzengel (–) m	archangel
Erzgießer (–) m	brass founder, bronze founder
Erzherzog (-zöge) m	archduke
Erziehung der Jungfrau Maria, die –	the Education of the Virgin
Erztür(en) f	bronze door
Eschenholz n	ash (wood)
Esel (–) m	donkey
Eselsrücken (–) m	ogee arch
Eselsturm (-türme) m	spiral ramp
Esquilin m	Esquiline Hill
Essenz(en) f	essence, essential oil
Esterharz n	polyester resin
Estrade(n) f	raised platform, dais
Estrich(e) m	clay or cement flooring with no joints
Etage(n) f	floor, story
Etagere(n) f	étagère
Etat(s) m	state, trial proof
Etrusker (–) m	Etruscan
etruskisch	Etruscan
Eurydike	Eurydice
Euthynterie(n) f	euthynteria, leveling course
Eva	Eve
Evangeliar(e) n	evangeliar, gospel book
Evangeliarium (Evangeliarien) n	evangeliar, gospel book

Evangelienkonkordanz(en) f	book with parallel passages of the Gospels in parallel columns
Evangelienseite(n) f	north side of a church, left side of the altar
Evangelist(en) m	evangelist
Evangelistar(e, ien) n	liturgical book with excerpts from the Gospel
Evangelistenbogen (—, -bögen) m	evangelist table
Evangelistensymbol(e) n	Evangelist's symbol
Evangelistenzeichen (—) n	Evangelist's symbol
Evangelium (Evangelien) n	evangeliar, gospel book
Ewigkeitswert(e) m	eternal value
exakt	exact
Exaktheit f	exactness
exc.	exc.
Exedra (Exedren) f	exedra
Exlibris (—) n	bookplate, ex libris
Exonarthex (-narthizes) m	outer narthex, second narthex located in front of actual narthex
Experte(n) m	expert
Expertise(n) f	assessment, expert's opinion
Expressionismus m	Expressionism
Expressionist(en) m	Expressionist
expressionistisch	expressionist(ic)
Exvoto(s, -voten) n	ex-voto

Fabelwesen (—) n	fabulous beast, mythical beast
Fabrik(en) f	factory
Facette(n) f	facet
facettiert	facetted, having facets
Fach (Fächer) n	1. section, compartment, partition, pane 2. subject, field
Fächer (—) m	(folding) fan

fächerförmig	fan-shaped
Fächergewölbe (–) n	fan vault
Fächerpinsel (–) m	fan brush
Fächerrosette(n) f	fanlight, fan-shaped rose window
Fachwerk n	half-timber, timber framing
Fachwerkbau(ten) m	half-timber construction, half-timber building, timber framing
Fachwerkhaus (-häuser) n	half-timber house, timber frame house
Faden (Fäden) m	thread
Fadenauflage(n) f	threading, reeding *glass*
Fadeneinlage f	marvered trailing; glass threading of a different color applied to glass surface and then marvered in
Fadenglas n	threaded glass, reeded glass
Fadennetz(e) n	drawing frame
Faksimile(s) n	facsimile
Faksimiledruck(e) m	facsimile print, print after a drawing or painting
Faktur(en) f	visible sign of an artist's work process
Faldistorium (Faldistorien) n	faldistory
Falke(n) m	falcon
Fallenbild(er) n	assemblage of the remainders of an event, such as a meal (especially by Daniel Spoerri)
Fallgatter (–) n	portcullis; castle gate
fälschen	to forge
Fälscher (–) m	forger, counterfeiter
Fälschung(en) f	forgery, fake
Falte(n) f	fold, crease, wrinkle
falten	to fold, to crease
Faltenballung(en) f	concentration of folds, folds collected together
Faltenbündel (–) n	bundle of folds
Faltenschwung m	surge of folds, flow of folds

Faltenwurf *m*	drapery, arrangement of the folds
Faltstuhl (-stühle) *m*	folding chair
Falttür(en) *f*	folding door
Faltwerk *n*	1. linenfold
	2. folds
Familie(n) *f*	family
Familienbildnis(se) *n*	family portrait
Farbabstufung(en) *f*	gradation of color, nuance
Farbauftrag (-träge) *m*	application of paint
Farbbereich(e) *m*	color group
farbbestimmt	determined by color
Farbbewegung(en) *f*	movement of color(s)
Farbbindemittel (–) *n*	(paint) medium, vehicle
Farbdripping *n*	drip painting
Farbdruck(e) *m*	color print
Farbe(n) *f*	color, paint, pigment
Färbebad *n*	dye (bath)
farbecht	colorfast
Farbechtheit *f*	colorfastness
färben	to dye, to color
Farbenabstufung(en) *f*	gradation of color, nuance
Farbenfamilie(n) *f*	color group
Farbengattung(en) *f*	color group
Farbengebung(en) *f*	color, coloration
Farbenlehre(n) *f*	color theory
farbenreich	colorful
Farbenstich(e) *m*	color engraving
Farbensymbolik *f*	color symbolism
Farbenveränderung(en) *f*	change in color or tone
Farbenwahl *f*	choice of colors
Färberröte *f*	madder
Färberschablone(n) *f*	textile dyeing stencil
Farbfläche(n) *f*	colored surface, surface consisting of one color
Farbfleck(en) *m*	patch of color
Farbfolge(n) *f*	color sequence
Farbhelle *f*	brightness (of a color)

Farbhellengrad(e) *m*	degree of brightness (of a color)
Farbholzschnitt(e) *m*	color print, color woodcut
farbig	colorful, colored, in color
Farbigkeit *f*	color, colorfulness, coloration
Farbintensität *f*	color intensity, saturation
Farbkontrast(e) *m*	color contrast
Farbkörper (—) *m*	1. pigment 2. structure showing the relationship of color tones
Farbkreis *m*	color circle
farblich	in respect to color, in color
Farblicht(er) *n*	colored light
Farblithographie(n) *f*	color lithography, colored lithograph, chromolithograph(y)
farblos	colorless
Farblosigkeit *f*	colorlessness
Farbmischung(en) *f*	color mixture
Farbmischung, additive —	additive mixture (of color)
Farbmischung, subtraktive —	subtractive mixture (of color)
Farbmuster (—) *n*	color pattern
Farbnapf (-näpfe) *m*	(paint) saucer
Farbordnung(en) *f*	arrangement of colors
Farbperspektive *f*	concept of advancing and retreating colors
Farbqualität, chromatische — *f*	chromaticity
Farbraum *m*	space defined by color
Farbreichweite(n) *f*	the extent of one color's effect on the color circle
Farbrichtung(en) *f*	color
Farbschicht(en) *f*	layer of paint
Farbskala (-skalen) *f*	range of colors, color scale
Farbstich(e) *m*	color engraving
Farbstift(e) *m*	colored pencil
Farbstoff(e) *m*	dyestuff, dye, pigment, lake
Farbton (-töne) *m*	hue, tint, tone, color-tone

Farbtönung(en) *f*	nuance
Farbtonverschiebung(en) *f*	color change achieved by mixing colors where the resulting color is in a different color group
Farbtopf (-töpfe) *m*	paint pot
Färbung(en) *f*	coloration, addition of color
Farbveränderung(en) *f*	change in color
Farbwahl *f*	choice of color(s)
Farbwert(e) *m*	color value
Farbwirkung(en) *f*	effect of color
Fascie(n) *f*	fascia
Fase(n) *f*	chamfer
Faser(n) *f*	1. fiber, thread 2. (wood) grain
Faserplatte(n) *f*	wallboard, fiberboard
Faserrichtung, in −	with the grain
Faserrichtung, quer zur −	across the grain
Fassade(n) *f*	facade, front of a building
Fassadenausschnitt(e) *m*	partial view of the facade or elevation
Fassadenflucht(en) *f*	alignment or plane of the facade
Fassadengliederung(en) *f*	division of the facade, articulation of the facade
Fassadenmalerei *f*	facade painting, painting on a facade
Faßmaler (−) *m*	artist who paints or gilds wooden carvings
Fassung(en) *f*	1. setting (of a jewel), holder, frame 2. version 3. coloration, painting (on a sculpture)
Fastentuch (-tücher) *n*	Lenten veil displayed between chancel and nave
Fastenvelum (-vela) *n*	Lenten veil
Faszie(n) *f*	fascia
Faun(e) *m*	faun
Faust (Fäuste) *f*	fist

Faustkeil(e) *m*	(paleolithic) handaxe
Fauvismus *m*	Fauvism
Fayence(n) *f*	faience
Fayenceofen (-öfen) *m*	faience-tiled stove
fec..	fec.
Fechter, der borghesische —	Borghese Warrior
Feder(n) *f*	1. feather 2. pen
Federlithographie(n) *f*	lithograph done with tusche
Federmosaik(en) *n*	feather mosaic, featherwork
Federzeichnung(en) *f*	pen drawing, pen sketch
Fehlbrand (-brände) *m*	imperfect firing (of pottery)
Feigenmilch *f*	fig milk (tempera emulsion)
Feinbewurf *m*	intonaco
feingeschlämmt	well-levigated
feinkörnig	fine-grained
Feinputz *m*	intonaco
Feldspat *m*	feldspar
Feldstaffelei(en) *f*	sketching easel
Feldsteinmauerwerk *n*	rubble masonry
Fels(en) *m*	boulder, rock, cliff
Felsbild(er) *n*	rock painting, petroglyph
Felsenformation(en) *f*	rock formation
Felsentempel (—) *m*	rock-cut temple
Felsgrab (-gräber) *n*	rock-cut tomb
Felskammergrab (-gräber) *n*	rock-cut tomb
Felsmalerei(en) *f*	rock painting, petroglyph
Felsrelief(s) *n*	rock relief, relief cut into a rock face
Felsritzung(en) *f*	rock engraving, petroglyph
Felszeichnung(en) *f*	rock drawing, petroglyph
Fenster (—) *n*	window
Fensterbank (-bänke) *f*	window sill
Fensterbrett(er) *n*	window sill
Fensterbrüstung(en) *f*	section of wall under a window

Fensterfläche(n) f	window surface
Fensterform(en) f	window shape
Fensterkorb (-körbe) m	window grating
Fensterladen (-läden) m	shutter
fensterlos	windowless
Fensterpfeiler (−) m	trumeau, mullion
Fensterpfosten (−) m	mullion
Fensterraster (−) m	1. grid pattern of windows 2. window grid, window screen
Fensterreihe(n) f	row of windows
Fensterrose(n) f	rose window
Fenstersturz (-stürze) m	window lintel
Fensterwand (-wände) f	1. wall having windows 2. wall consisting of windows
Ferse(n) f	heel
Fertigbauweise f	prefabricated construction
Fertigbetonplatte(n) f	precast concrete slab
Fertigteil(e) n	prefabricated part, prefabricated element
Feston(s) n	festoon, swag
Festung(en) f	fortification, castle, stronghold
Festungsarchitektur f	fortification
Fetisch(e) m	fetish
fett	fat
Fettfarbe(n) f	1. oily paint, paint rich in oil 2. lithographic crayon
Fettfarbe(n) f	1. oily paint, paint rich in oil 2. lithographic crayon
Feuerstein(e) m	flint
feuervergoldet	fire gilded
Feuervergoldung(en) f	fire gilding, ormolu
Feuillage f	foliage, leaf ornament
Fiale(n) f	pinnacle
Fibel(n) f	clasp, fibula
Fiberglas n	fiber glass
Fichte f	fir, pine
Fichtenharz n	galipot

Figur(en) f	figure, statue
figural	figured, figural, figurative
Figurenanordnung(en) f	grouping or arrangement of the figures
Figurenbild(er) n	depiction of human(s)
Figurengruppe(n) f	group, group of figures
Figurenhöhe f	height of the figure
Figurenkapitell(e) n	figural capital
Figurenmaler (–) m	painter specializing in depictions of people
Figurenportal(e) n	portal with jamb figures or other architectural sculpture
figurenreich	ornate
Figurenschmuck(e) m	figural decoration
Figurenstaffage(n) f	staffage (figures)
Figurenwelt(en) f	vocabulary of figures
figuriertes Gewölbe n	vault with ribs forming a particular shape, e.g. stellar vault
Figurine(n) f	1. figurine 2. sketch for stage costumes or fashion
figürlich	figural, figurative
Fikellura-Vasen pl	Fikellura ware
Filigran n	filigree
Filigranarbeit(en) f	filigree
Filigranglas n	threaded glass, reeded glass
Filz m	felt
Filzstift(e) m	felt-tip pen
Finger (–) m	finger
Fingerhaltung(en) f	position of the finger(s)
Firmelung(en) f	confirmation
Firnis(se) m	varnish
First(e) m	(roof) ridge
Firstbalken (–) m	ridge beam
Firstdach (-dächer) n	ridged roof
Fisch(e) m	1. fish 2. Pisces

Fischblase(n) *f*	1. mouchette, falchion 2. vesica piscis
fischförmig	pisciform, fish-shaped
Fischgrätenmuster (−) *n*	herringbone pattern
Fischleim *m*	fish glue
Fischzug, Petri − *m*	the Miraculous Draught of Fishes
Fischzug, der wunderbare −	the Miraculous Draught of Fishes
Fixativ(e) *n*	fixative
Fixiermittel (−) *n*	fixative
Fixpunkt(e) *m*	fixed point
flach	flat, shallow
Flachbogen (−, -bögen) *m*	segmental arch
Flachdach (-dächer) *n*	flat roof, truncated roof
Flachdecke(n) *f*	flat ceiling
Flachdruck *m*	planographic printing
Fläche(n) *f*	surface, plane
Flächenaufteilung(en) *f*	division and arrangement of the surface, surface patterning or articulation
Flächenbereicherung *f*	enrichment of the surface
Flächencharakter *m*	flatness, flat characteristic(s)
flächendeckend	covering the surface
flächengliedernd	dividing or articulating the surface
flächenhaft	flat, planar, shallow
Flächenhaftigkeit *f*	flatness, emphasis on the surface plane
Flächenmalerei *f*	flat painting, painting without spatial or corporal depth
Flächenordnung(en) *f*	arrangement of the (picture) surface
Flächenstil(e) *m*	flat style, planar style
Flächenwölbung(en) *f*	curvature of the surface
flächig	flat, planar, two-dimensional
Flächigkeit *f*	flatness
Flachmeißel (−) *m*	flat chisel

Flachpinsel (−) m	flat brush
Flachrelief(s) n	low relief
Flachs m	flax
Flachstichel (−) m	flat graver, flat burin
Flachziegeldach (-dächer) n	roof covered with flat tiles
Flamboyant n	Flamboyant (style)
Flame(n) m *also* Vlame	Flemish, native of Flanders
flämisch	Flemish
Flankenbau(ten) m	flanking structure
Flasche(n) f	bottle, flask
Flaschenhals m	bottle neck
flau	dull, flat, lifeless
Flechtband (-bänder) n	interlace, interlacing
flechten	to weave, to plait
Flechtmuster (−) n	interlaced or plaited pattern
Flechtware(n) f	wicker goods, basketry
Flechtwerk(e) n	1. interlacing 2. wattle and daub 3. plait-work
Fleck(e) m	spot, patch
Fleischfarbe f	skin color
fleischig	fleshy
Fleischton (-töne) m	flesh color
Fleuron(s) m	fleuron
Fliese(n) f	tile
Fliesenboden (-böden) m	flagstone pavement, tiled floor
Flimmereffekt m	dazzle effect, moiré effect
flimmern	to flicker, to glitter
Flor(e) m	1. thin silk material, veil 2. (carpet) pile
Florentinerbraun n	Florentine brown
Florentiner Mosaik n	pietra dura
florentinisch	Florentine
Flucht(en) f	1. alignment, straight row or line; sequence of objects (e.g. buildings) in a straight line

	2. flight
	3. floor, story
Flucht nach Ägypten, die —	the Flight into Egypt
Fluchtbild(er) n	picture in perspective
Fluchtlinie(n) f	1. alignment
	2. building line
	3. *pl* parallel (converging) lines in a perspective representation
Fluchtpunkt(e) m	vanishing point
Flugblatt (-blätter) n	handbill, leaflet
Flügel (—) m	wing, panel, leaf, volet
Flügelaltar (-altäre) m	winged altarpiece, altar with polyptych
Flügelbild(er) n	(altarpiece) side wing, side panel
Flügelfenster (—) n	casement window
Flügelglas (-gläser) n	glassware with wings attached to the stem
Flügellöwe(n) m	winged lion
Flügelpferd(e) n	winged horse
Flügelretabel (—) n	winged altarpiece
Fluoreszenz f	fluorescence
Flur(e) m	corridor, hallway
Flußmittel (—) n	flux, fluxing ingredient
Flußspat m	fluorite, fluorspar
Folge(n) f	1. series
	2. result
Folie(n) f	(metal) foil
Fond(s) m	background, foundation
Fondfarbe(n) f	background color
Form(en) f	form, shape
Formalin n	Formalin
Formalinlösung(en) f	Formalin solution
Formalismus m	formalism
Format(e) n	shape, size
Formbegrenzung(en) f	limitation of shape
Formelement(e) n	formal element, element of form

Formempfinden *n*	feeling for (or sensitivity to) form or shape; perception of form
Formenbindung *f*	cohesion of the forms within a work
Formenreichtum *m*	abundance of forms or shapes
Formensprache(n) *f*	vocabulary of form or shape
Formenstrenge *f*	severity of form
Formenverschmelzung(en) *f*	blending of different forms or shapes
Formenwelt(en) *f*	vocabulary of forms or shapes
Formfülle *f*	profusion of forms or shapes
formgebend	shaping, forming, modelling
Formgeber (–) *m*	designer
Formgebung(en) *f*	design, formation, shaping
Formgeschichte(n) *f*	history of form or shape
Formkasten (-kästen) *m*	sand casting box
formlos	shapeless
Formlosigkeit *f*	shapelessness
Formmantel (-mäntel) *m*	investment *casting*
Formmodel(n) *m*	mold
Formsand *m*	foundry sand
Formschneidekunst *f*	(art of) carving figures in wood blocks for printing fabric; forerunner of woodcut
Formschneider (–) *m*	wood block carver, xylographer
Formschnitt(e) *m*	carved wooden block for printing fabric; forerunner of woodcut
Formstein(e) *m*	cut or molded building stones (or bricks) which form decoration when set in place
Formung(en) *f*	formation, shaping
Formwille *m*	the will to give form; urge to or insistence on form
Formzersetzung(en) *f*	dissolution of form
Fortifikation(en) *f*	fortification(s)
Forum (Fora, Foren) *n*	forum

Fossagrab (-gräber) *n*	rectangular (Etruscan) burial tomb
Foto(s) *n* *also* Photo	photograph
Fotograph(en) *m*	photographer
Fotomontage(n) *f*	photomontage
Foyer(s) *n*	foyer
Fragment(e) *n*	fragment
Fraktur(en) *f*	fractur, fraktur, black-letter type
Franziskus, der hl. —	St. Francis of Assissi
Frau(en) *f*	1. woman 2. wife
Frauen am Grabe, die —	the Women at the Tomb, Marys at the Tomb
Frauenseite *f*	"women's side", north side of a church
freilegen	to expose
Freilegung *f*	exposure
Freilichtmalerei *f*	plein air painting, open-air painting
Freilichtmuseum (-museen) *n*	open air museum
Freiplastik(en) *f*	free-standing sculpture
Freistatue(n) *f*	free-standing sculpture
Freitreppe(n) *f*	exterior flight of stairs
Freskant(en) *m*	fresco painter
Freskenmalerei(en) *f*	fresco painting
Freskenreste *pl*	remains of a fresco
Fresko (Fresken) *n*	fresco
Freuden, die sieben — Mariä	the Seven Joys of the Virgin
Friedensforum *n*	Forum Pacis
Friedhof (-höfe) *m*	cemetery
Fries(e) *m*	frieze, course, string course
Friesband (-bänder) *n*	frieze strip
Friessarkophag(e) *m*	frieze sarcophagus; sarcophagus in which the individual scenes are

	depicted one after another without subdivision
Frigidarium (Frigidarien) *n*	cold room in the Thermae
Frisur(en) *f*	haircut, coiffure, hairdo
Fritte(n) *f*	frit
fritten	to frit
Frittenporzellan *n*	soft paste porcelain
Fronaltar (-altäre) *m*	high altar
Fronleichnam *m*	the Body of Christ, Corpus Christi
Front(en) *f*	front, facade
Frontalblick(e) *m*	front view
Frontale (Frontalien) *n*	antependium, frontal (altar cloth)
Frontalität *f*	frontality
Frontalperspektive(n) *f*	frontal depiction, frontal perspective
Frontbetonung *f*	emphasis on the front
Frontdarstellung(en) *f*	front view, depiction of the front
Frontispiz(e) *n*	1. frontispiece *printing* 2. pediment over a projecting door, window, etc.
Froschperspektive(n) *f*	worm's-eye view
Frottage(n) *f*	frottage, rubbing
Frucht (Früchte) *f*	fruit
fruchtbar	productive, prolific
Fruchtbarkeit *f*	fertility, fruitfulness, prolificacy
Fruchtbarkeitssymbol(e) *n*	symbol of fertility
Früchtestilleben (−) *n*	still life with fruits
Fruchtgehänge *n*	swag or festoon with fruit motif
Fruchtstück(e) *n*	fruit piece, picture of fruit
frühchristlich	early Christian
frühdorisch	early Doric
Frühdruck *m*	incunabula
Frühgotik *f*	Early Gothic
Frühkultur(en) *f*	early civilization
Frühstufe(n) *f*	early stage

Frühwerk(e) n	early work
Fuchsin n	magenta dye, fuchsine
Fuge(n) f	joint
fügen	to join, to attach
Füllhorn (-hörner) n	cornucopia
Füllmauer(n) f	two parallel walls with the space between filled with stones and mortar
Fumage f	fumage
Fund(e) m	find
Fundament(e) n	foundation
Fundgegenstand (-stände) m	found object
Fundgut (-güter) n	find(s)
Fundort(e) m	place of discovery, location of the find
Fundstück(e) n	find, excavated object
Funeralwaffe(n) f	funerary weapon
Fünfpaß (-pässe) m	cinquefoil
fünfschiffig	five-aisled
Funk Art f	funk art
Funktionalismus m	functionalism
Fünte(n) f	baptismal font
Furche(n) f	groove, furrow
Furchenschmelz(e) m	ancient enamelling technique similar to champlevé
Furnier(e) n	veneer
furnieren	to veneer
Furnierholz (-hölzer) n	veneer(ing)
furniert	veneered
Fürspan(e) m	decorative clasp
Fürst(en) m	prince, sovereign
Fürstengrab (-gräber) n	royal tomb
Fürstentum (-tümer) n	principality
Fürstin(nen) f	princess
fürstlich	princely, royal
Fuß (Füße) m	1. foot 2. base, pedestal

Fußbank (-bänke) *f*	foot stool
Fußboden (-böden) *m*	floor
fußlang	1. of a length reaching to the feet
	2. as long as a foot
Fußpfette(n) *f*	wall plate *roof construction*
Fußring(e) *m*	ring-shaped vessel base
Fußschale(n) *f*	bowl with foot
Fußstellung(en) *f*	position of the feet
Fußwaschung, die —	the Washing of the Feet
Fustikholz *n*	old fustic
Fustikholz, junges —	young fustic, fustet
Futhark *n*	futhark; runic alphabet
Futtermauer(n) *f*	retaining wall
füttern	to line
Fütterung *f*	lining, padding
Futurismus *m*	Futurism

Gabe(n) *f*	offering
Gabelkreuz(e) *n*	Y-shaped cross
Gaden (—) *m*	1. one-room house
	2. clerestory
Galaktotrophusa *f*	madonna lactans; Byzantine madonna icon depicting the Virgin suckling the Child
Galerie(n) *f*	gallery
Galeriegrab (-gräber) *n*	gallery grave, allée couverte
Galerieton *m*	gallery tone
Galerist(en) *m*	art dealer, gallery owner
Galipot *m*	galipot
Gallenfarbstoff *m*	gallstone lake
Gallert(e) *n*	gelatine
Galvanoplastik *f*	galvanoplastic process, electrotypic process, electrotype
Gang (Gänge) *m*	corridor, passageway

Ganggrab (-gräber) *n*	passage grave
Ganosis (Ganosen) *f*	ganosis
Ganzfigur(en) *f*	full-figure
ganzseitig	full-page
Garbrand *m*	firing
garbrennen	to fire
Garn(e) *n*	thread, yarn
Garten (Gärten) *m*	garden
Garten, der verschlossene —	Garden Enclosed
Gartenanlage(n) *f*	garden, park
Gartenbaukunst *f*	landscaping, garden design
Gartenteppich(e) *m*	verdure
Gärtner, Christus als —	noli me tangere
Gastmahl bei Simon, das —	Supper in the House of Simon
Gastmahl des Herodes, das —	the Feast of Herod
Gastmahl des Levi, das —	Christ in the House of Levi, Supper in the House of Levi
Gattung(en) *f*	type, genre
Gaube(n) *f*	dormer window
Gaupe(n) *f*	dormer window
Gebälk *n*	entablature, beams
Gebälkfries(e) *m*	frieze decorating the entablature
Gebälkhöhe *f*	height of the entablature
Gebärde(n) *f*	gesture
Gebärdensprache(n) *f*	sign language, gesture language, vocabulary of gestures
Gebäude (—) *n*	building
Gebet(e) *n*	prayer
Gebetbuch (-bücher) *n*	prayer book
Gebetsteppich(e) *m*	prayer rug
Gebilde (—) *n*	formation, structure, product
Gebirgsbild(er) *n*	picture of mountains
Gebirgslandschaft(en) *f*	mountainous landscape
geböscht	battered, sloped

Gebote, die Zehn —	Ten Commandments, the Decalogue
Gebrauchsgegenstand (-stände) *m*	utensil, implement
Gebrauchsgraphik *f*	commercial art, advertising art, applied graphics
Gebrauchskeramik(en) *f*	household ceramics, utility ceramics
gebrochene Farbe *f*	broken color, broken tone
gebuckelt	embossed
gebundenes System *n*	system of architectural proportions based on the crossing square as module
Geburt Christi *f*	the Birth of Christ, the Nativity
gebust	twisted, warped
gedämpfte Farbe *f*	pure color changed in the direction of black, white or gray
gedrechselt	turned, shaped on a lathe
Gefach(e, Gefächer) *n*	filled space in half-timber architecture
gefälscht	faked, forged
Gefangennahme Christi, die —	the Arrest of Christ
Gefäß(e) *n*	vessel
Gefäßhals (-hälse) *m*	neck of a vessel
Gefäßwandung(en) *f*	wall or side of a vessel
gefaßt	1. set, mounted 2. painted
gefesselte Prometheus, der —	Prometheus Bound
Geflammte Ware *f*	mottled ware
Geflecht(e) *n*	plait(ing), wickerwork, wattle
Geflecht und Lehm *n*	wattle and daub
geflügelt	winged
Gefolge (—) *n*	retinue, attendants
Gefüge (—) *n*	structure, texture, framework
Gegenfarbe(n) *f*	complementary color, color on opposite side of the color wheel

Gegenlicht *n*	backlight
Gegenlicht, im —	against the light, into the light
Gegenpapst (-päpste) *m*	anti-pope
Gegenstand (-stände) *m*	object
gegenständige Gruppe *f*	affronted figures; two mirror-image profiles facing each other
gegenständlich	representational, objective
Gegenstandsfarbe(n) *f*	local color, color of the object
gegenstandslos	abstract, non-representational, non-objective
gegenstandslose Kunst *f*	abstract art, non-objective art
Gegenstandslosigkeit *f*	abstractness, non-objectivism
Gegenwart *f*	present, present day
gegenwärtig	contemporary
Gegenwartskunst *f*	contemporary art
gegliedert	arranged, divided, articulated
gegossen	cast, poured
Gehenk(e) *n*	baldric
gehöht	heightened
gehöht, weiß —	heightened (with white)
gehren	to miter
Gehrung(en) *f*	miter, miter joint
Geison(s) *n*	cornice
Geißelung Christi, die —	the Scourging of Christ, the Flagellation of Christ
Geißfuß (-füße) *m*	V-shaped gouge
Geist(er) *m*	spirit, intellect
Geist, der Heilige —	the Holy Ghost
geistlich	sacred, ecclesiastical, religious
Geistliche(n) *m*	clergyman, priest
gekleidet	clothed, dressed
gekoppelt	paired (architectural elements)
Gekreuzigte, der —	the Crucified One
gekreuzt	crossed
gekröpftes Gesims *n*	cornice or string course which continues around architectural

	elements (columns, lisenes, etc.) which are engaged with the wall
gekrümmt	bent, curved
gekuppelt	paired (architectural elements)
gekurvt	curved
Gel *n*	gel
Geländer (—) *n*	banister, railing, balustrade
Geländerstab (-stäbe) *m*	baluster
gelappt	ragged
Gelatine *f*	gelatin
gelb	yellow
Gelbglas *m*	orpiment
Gelbguß *m*	brass (alloy rich in zinc)
Gelbholz *n*	old fustic
Gelbwurz *f*	turmeric dyestuff
Geldstück(e) *n*	coin
Gelehrte(n) *m*	scholar
Gelenk(e) *n*	wrist, ankle, joint
Gemach (Gemächer) *n*	chamber, room, apartment
Gemälde (—) *n*	painting
Gemäldeausstellung(en) *f*	exhibition of paintings
Gemäldedurchleuchtung(en) *f*	examination of a painting by x-ray
Gemälderestaurierung(en) *f*	restoration of paintings
gemartert	martyred
Gemeinderaum (-räume) *m*	room or area for the congregation
Gemeinschaftsausstellung(en) *f*	joint exhibition, group exhibition
Gemme(n) *f*	glyptograph, engraved gem or seal
Gemme, erhaben geschnittene —	cameo
Gemme, vertieft geschnittene —	intaglio
genau	exact
Genauigkeit *f*	exactness
genial	genius
Genie(s) *n*	genius

Genius (Genien) *m*	genius, (Roman) tutelary spirit
Genre(s) *n*	genre
Genrebild(er) *n*	genre (painting)
Genremaler (−) *m*	genre painter
Genremalerei *f*	genre painting
Geochronologie *f*	geochronology
Geometrie *f*	geometry
geometrisch	geometric
geometrischer Stil *m*	geometric style, geometric period
Georgsaltar *m*	altar with St. George
gepflastert	paved
gepunzt	embossed, pounced
gequetschtes Relief *n*	stiacciato relief
gerade	straight
Gerade(n) *f*	straight line
Gerät(e) *n*	tool, utensil
Geräteinventar(e) *n*	industry, assemblage of tools, inventory of tools
Geräteplastik(en) *f*	sculptural ornamentation on utensils, e.g. on inkwells or hand mirrors
Gerechtigkeitsbild(er) *n*	depiction of Justice
Gericht, das Jüngste −	the Last Judgment
Gericht, das Letzte −	the Last Judgment
gerillt	grooved, fluted, ridged
gerippt	ribbed
Gerokreuz *n*	the Gero crucifix
Geröllgerät(e) *n*	pebble tool
Geröllkultur(en) *f*	Pebble Culture
gerundet	rounded
Gerüst(e) *n*	framework
Gerüstbau(ten) *m*	skeletal structure
Gesamtanlage(n) *f*	total complex, total plan
Gesamteindruck (-drücke) *m*	total impression, whole impression
Gesamtentwurf (-würfe) *m*	complete design, complete plan
Gesamthöhe *f*	total height

Gesamtlänge *f*	total length
Gesamtton *m*	total shade, total tone, overall color
Gesamtwerk *n*	complete work(s), œuvre, collected works
Gesamtwirkung(en) *f*	total effect, overall effect
Geschichte(n) *f*	history, story
Geschichtsmalerei *f*	history painting
geschickt	talented, skilled
Geschirr(e) *n*	dishes, tableware
Geschirrmalerei *f*	painting on porcelain
geschlossen	closed, complete, self-contained
Geschlossenheit *f*	completeness, self-containedness
Geschmack (Geschmäcke) *m*	taste
geschmackvoll	tasteful
Geschmeide (–) *n*	goldsmith's work, precious jewelry
geschmiedet	forged, wrought
geschnitzt	carved
Geschoß (Geschosse) *n*	story, floor
geschult	trained
geschweift	curved, arched
Geselle(n) *m*	journeyman
Gesellschaftsstück(e) *n*	work depicting the life of the aristocracy
Gesetzestafel(n) *f*	the Tables of the Law, the tablets with the Ten Commandments
Gesetzesübergabe an Petrus, die —	Delivery of the Law Scroll
Gesetzmäßigkeit(en) *f*	regularity
Gesicht(er) *n*	face
Gesichtsausdruck (-drücke) *m*	facial expression
Gesichtsmaske(n) *f*	funeral mask, facial mask
Gesichtsurne(n) *f*	prehistoric vessel with a face as decoration
Gesichtszug (-züge) *m*	facial feature
Gesims(e) *n*	cornice, string course

Gesimsung(en) *f*	cornice-work
gesintert	vitrified
Gespann(e) *n*	team (of horses)
Gesparr *n*	rafters, roof framework
Gesprenge (−) *n*	crest, Gothic altar crowning
gesprengter Giebel *m*	broken pediment, broken gable
Gestalt(en) *f*	figure
gestalten	to design, to shape, to form, to structure
Gestaltung(en) *f*	representation, structure, formation, composition, design(ing), configuration
Gestaltung, die Neue −	Neo-Plasticism, De Stijl
Geste(n) *f*	gesture
gestelzter Bogen *m*	stilted arch
Gestenmotiv(e) *n*	gesture motif
gestickt	embroidered
Gestik(en) *f*	gesturing, gestures
Gestirn(e) *n*	constellation
Gestirnsymbol(e) *n*	constellation symbol
gestrafft	tightened, tensed
gestreckt	stretched
gestrichen	painted
Gestühl(e) *n*	pews, seats, stalls
Getäfel *n*	paneling
Getreidekornabdruck(e) *m*	grain impression
getrieben	decorated with repoussé
getriebene Arbeit *f*	repoussé
gewalmtes Dach *n*	hipped roof
Gewand (Gewänder) *n*	garment, robe
Gewände (−) *n*	jamb, door post(s)
Gewändefigur(en) *f*	jamb figure, jamb statue, column figure
Gewändesäule(n) *f*	jamb (shaft)
Gewandfalte(n) *f*	fold or crease in a garment
Gewandfigur(en) *f*	draped or robed figure

Gewandfigurentypus (-typen) m	draped figure type
Gewandhaus (-häuser) n	Cloth Hall
Gewandung(en) f	garment, drapery
Gewebe (–) n	weaving, woven fabric
Geweihmotiv(e) n	antler motif
Gewichtswebstuhl (-stühle) m	warp-weighted loom
Gewölbe (–) n	vault
Gewölbe, falsches –	pseudodome, false vault, corbelled dome
Gewölbebau m	vault construction
Gewölbebogen (–, -bögen) m	formeret and/or transverse arch
Gewölbedecke(n) f	vaulted ceiling
Gewölbefach (-fächer) n	severy, cell, vault compartment
Gewölbegrat(e) m.	groin (of a vault)
Gewölbekappe(n) f	vault cell
Gewölbekonstruktion(en) f	vault construction, construction using vaults
Gewölberaum (-räume) m	room or space covered by a vault
Gewölberippe(n) f	(vault) rib
Gewölbeschub m	thrust of the vault
Gewölbeträger (–) m	vault support, column or pier supporting the vault
gewölbt	vaulted, bulged, curved
gewundene Reihung f	curved ribs of a stellar or net vault
gewundene Säule f	twisted column
Giebel (–) m	gable, pediment, tympanum
Giebelbogen (–, -bögen) m	rounded or bulged gable
Giebeldach (-dächer) n	saddleback roof
Giebelfeld n	pediment, tympanum
Giebelfenster (–) n	window in a gable
Giebelgesims(e) n	cymatium, cornice or gable moulding
Giebelschenkel (–) m	slope of the gable
Giebelschräge(n) f	slope of the gable

Giebelseite(n) *f*	(gable) front
Giebelskulptur(en) *f*	pedimental sculpture
Giebelspitze(n) *f*	peak of the gable
Giebelverzierung(en) *f*	gable ornamentation, pediment ornamentation
gießen	1. to cast
	2. to pour
Gießer (−) *m*	founder, caster, person who pours the cast
Gießform(en) *f*	mold
Gießgefäß(e) *n*	ewer, pitcher, pouring vessel
Gießgrube(n) *f*	casting pit
Gießhütte(n) *f*	foundry
Gigant(en) *m*	giant, son of Gaea
Gigantenkampf *m*	gigantomachy
Gigantomachie *f*	gigantomachy
gilben	to yellow
Gips *m*	plaster of Paris, gypsum
Gipsabguß (-güsse) *m*	plaster cast
Gipsgrund *m*	gypsum ground, gesso ground
Gipsmarmor *m*	artificial marble, scagliola
Gipsmodell(e) *n*	plaster model
Girandole(n) *f*	table candelabra with arms
Girlande(n) *f*	garland
Girlandensarkophag(e) *m*	sarcophagus decorated with relief garlands
Giseh	Giza
Gitter (−) *n*	grating, grille, screen, lattice
Gitterverzierung(en) *f*	lattice ornament
Glacis (−) *n*	glacis
Glanz *m*	brilliance, radiance, lustre, gloss
glänzen	to shine
glänzend	shining, brilliant, lustrous
Glanzstück(e) *n*	gem, masterpiece
Glas (Gläser) *n*	glass
Glasätzung(en) *f*	glass etching, etching on glass
Glasbaustein(e) *m*	glass brick

Glasblasen *n*	glass blowing
Glasbläser (−) *m*	glass blower
gläsern	(of) glass
Glasfenster (−) *n*	stained glass window, glass window
Glasfluß (-flüsse) *m*	paste, glass imitation of a jewel
Glasgemälde (−) *n*	1. stained glass window 2. painting on glass
Glasgravierung(en) *f*	glass engraving, engraving on glass
Glasgravur(en) *f*	glass engraving
Glashütte(n) *f*	glass factory
glasieren	to glaze
glasiert	glazed, enameled
Glaslüster (−) *m*	glass chandelier
Glasmacherofen (-öfen) *m*	glass maker's oven
Glasmacherpfeife(n) *f*	glass-blowing pipe
Glasmaler (−) *m*	stained glass artist
Glasmalerei(en) *f*	1. (art of) stained glass windows 2. (art of) painting on glass
Glasmasse *f*	gather, molten glass
Glasmosaikstein(e) *m*	(glass) smalto
Glaspapier *n*	sandpaper
Glaspaste(n) *f*	paste, glass imitation of a jewel
Glasperle(n) *f*	glass bead
Glaspfeife(n) *f*	glass-blowing pipe
Glasplatte(n) *f*	glass pane, glass plate
Glasporzellan *n*	vitreous porcelain
Glasradierung(en) *f*	etched drawing on glass to be viewed from the non-etched side
Glasschliff *m*	decorative cutting and polishing of glass
Glassmalte(n) *f*	glass smalto
Glasstäbe *pl*	glass rods (for the production of millefiori glass)
Glasur(en) *f*	glaze
Glasurfarbe(n) *f*	glaze color
Glasurziegel (−) *m*	glazed brick

Glasurziegelrelief(s) *n*	glazed brick relief
glatt	smooth
Glätte *f*	smoothness
glätten	to smooth, to polish, to dress
Glättung *f*	polishing
Glättungsmittel (−) *n*	polishing material
gleich	same, equal, alike
Gleichgewicht *n*	balance
gleichgroß	equal-sized, same-sized
Gleichnis(se) *n*	parable, allegory
Gleichnisgestalt(en) *f*	allegorical figure, metaphorical figure
gleichschenkelig	equilateral
gleichseitig	equilateral
gleiten	to slide
Glied(er) *n*	limb, appendage
Gliederbewegung(en) *f*	movement of the limbs
Gliedermann (-männer) *m*	lay figure, manikin
gliedern	to arrange, to divide, to distribute, to articulate
Gliederordnung(en) *f*	arrangement of the limbs (or parts)
Gliederpuppe(n) *f*	lay figure, manikin
Gliederung(en) *f*	articulation, arrangement, organization, division
Gliedmaßen *pl*	limbs, extremities
Glimmer *m*	mica
Glocke(n) *f*	bell
Glockenbecher (−) *m*	beaker, bell-beaker
Glockenbecherkultur *f*	beaker culture, bell-beaker culture
glockenförmig	campaniform, bell-shaped
Glockengehäuse (−) *n*	bellcote
Glockenguß *m*	bell casting
Glockenidol(e) *n*	terracotta figurine with bell-shaped skirt
Glockenkrater (−, e) *m*	bell krater
Glockenleiste(n) *f*	cyma recta, cyma reversa, bell-shaped profile

Glockenstuhl (-stühle) *m*	bellcote
Glockenturm (-türme) *m*	campanile, bell tower
Glorienschein *m*	aureole, glory, halo
Gloriette(n) *f*	baroque garden pavilion
Glykophilusa *f*	Madonna Glykophilusa; Byzantine Madonna pressing the Child to her cheek
Glyphe(n) *f*	glyph, glyptograph
Glypte(n) *f*	carved stone
Glyptik *f*	glyptic art, gem carving
Glyptothek *f*	collection of glyptic works and other carved sculptures
Glyzerin *n*	glycerin
Gnadenbild(er) *n*	miraculous picture or image, especially of the Virgin
Gnadenstuhl *m*	depiction of the Holy Trinity
Gobelin(s) *m*	tapestry, Gobelin
Gobelinwerkstätte(n) *f*	tapestry manufactory
Gold *n*	gold
Goldbecher (–) *m*	gold cup
Goldberyll *m*	chrysoberyl
Goldbeschlag (-beschläge) *m*	gold trim, gold fittings or hardware
Goldblech *n*	gold sheet, gold plate
Goldbrakteat(en) *m*	gold bracteate, coin printed on one side
Goldbronze *f*	ormolu
golddurchwirkt	having gold threads woven in
Goldelfenbeintechnik *f*	chryselephantine technique
Goldgewicht(e) *n*	gold weight
Goldglas *n*	glass with gold layer into which decoration is scratched
Goldgrund *m*	gold background
Goldlack *m*	gold-colored varnish
Goldleiste(n) *f*	gilt moulding, gilt edge
Goldmalerei *f*	gilt painting
Goldpurpur *m*	precipitated gold used for coloring porcelain and glass

Goldrubinglas n	ruby-red glass (made with gold chlorine)
Goldschmied(e) m	goldsmith
Goldschmiedekunst f	goldsmith's art
Goldsilberlegierung f	alloy of gold and silver; electrum
Goldstickerei(en) f	gold embroidery
Goldzeichnung(en) f	drawing with gold ink
Gönner (−) m	patron
Gönnerin(nen) f	patroness
Gorgo(nen) f	Gorgon
Gotik f	the Gothic (period or style)
gotisch	Gothic
Gott (Götter) m	god
Gott, Schöner − m	"Beau Dieu" jamb statue
Götterbild(er) n	idol, image of a god
Göttergestalt(en) f	deity, image, depiction of a god
Götterlehre f	mythology
Göttersitz(e) m	seat of the gods
Gotteshaus (-häuser) n	church, house of God
Gottesherrlichkeit f	godly splendor
Gottheit(en) f	deity
Göttin(nen) f	goddess
göttlich	godly
Gottvater m	God the Father
Götze(n) m	idol, false god
Götzenbild(er) n	idol, image
Gouache(n) f also Guasch	gouache
Gouachenmalerei f	gouache painting
Grab (Gräber) n	grave, tomb, sepulchre
Grab, das Heilige −	1. Holy Sepulchre 2. depiction of Christ's sarcophagus
Grabbeigabe(n) f	grave goods, funerary objects or furnishings
Gräberrund(e) n	grave circle
Grabgewölbe (−) n	sepulchral vault

Grabhügel (–) *m*	burial mound, tumulus
Grabinventar(e) *n*	inventory of the tomb
Grabkammer(n) *f*	burial chamber, tomb
Grabkirche(n) *f*	mortuary chapel
Grablegung(en) *f*	burial, entombment
Grabmal (-mäler) *n*	sepulchre, tomb, tombstone
Grabmonument(e) *n*	grave monument
Grabplastik(en) *f*	funerary statue, funerary sculpture
Grabplattenabdruck(e) *m*	tombstone rubbing, gravestone rubbing
Grabstätte(n) *f*	burial site, grave
Grabstein(e) *m*	gravestone, tombstone
Grabsteinrelief(s) *n*	relief on a tombstone
Grabstele(n) *f*	funerary stele
Grabstichel (–) *m*	graver, burin
Grabung(en) *f*	dig, excavation
Grabungsfund(e) *m*	excavated find
Graburne(n) *f*	funerary urn
Gradiereisen (–) *n*	toothed chisel, claw chisel
Gradierung(en) *f*	gradation
Graduale (Gradualien) *f*	Gradual (psalm)
Graf(en) *m*	count
Graffito (Graffiti) *n*	sgraffito
Gräfin(nen) *f*	countess
Gral *m*	the Holy Grail
Gralslegende *f*	legend of the Holy Grail
Granat *m*	garnet
Granatapfel (-äpfel) *m*	pomegranate
Granatapfelmuster (–) *n*	pomegranate pattern *textile*
Granierstahl(e) *m*	rocker
Granulation *f*	granulation; application of gold or silver kernels to a surface
Graphik(en) *f*	graphic arts, graphics
Graphiker (–) *m*	draftsman, graphic artist
graphisch	graphic
Graphit *m*	graphite
Graphitstift(e) *m*	lead pencil

Grat(e) *m*	1. groin 2. burr *engraving* 3. arris
Grattage *f*	grattage
grau	gray
Grauwacke *f*	graywacke
Gravettespitze(n) *f*	Gravette point
Gravettien *n*	Gravettian (industry)
Graveur(e) *m*	engraver
gravieren	to engrave
Gravierinstrument(e) *n*	graver, engraving tool
Gravierkunst *f*	(art of) engraving
graviert	engraved, enchased
Gravierung(en) *f*	engraving
Gravierzeug *n*	engraving tools
Gravur(en) *f*	engraving
Gravüre(n) *f*	1. engraving 2. intaglio printing plate or a print from it
Grazie(n) *f*	grace
Gregorsmesse(n) *f*	(depiction of) St. Gregory at Mass, the Mass of St. Gregory
Greif(e, en) *m*	griffin
Greifen (–) *m*	griffin
Greifenkessel (–) *m*	Greek bronze kettle decorated with griffin protomes
grell	glaring, harsh
Gremiale (Gremialien) *n*	gremial, bishop's lap cloth
Grenze(n) *f*	1. edge, limit 2. border
Grenzverwischung(en) *f*	softening or blurring of boundaries and edges
Grieche(n) *m*	Greek
Griechenland	Greece
Griechentum *n*	the Greeks, the Greek world, ancient Greece
griechisch	Greek
griechisches Kreuz *n*	Greek cross

Griffel (−) *m*	stylus
Grisaille(n) *f*	grisaille
Grisaillescheibe(n) *f*	grisaille window
grob	coarse
grobe Malschicht *f*	sand coat, sand finish
grobporig	coarse, large-pored
Größe(n) *f*	size, greatness, grandeur
Größenverhältnis(se) *n*	proportion
Großformat(e) *n*	large size, large scale
Großherzog (-zöge) *m*	grand duke
großräumig	spacious
Groteske(n) *f*	grotesque
Grotte(n) *f*	grotto
Grottenwerk *n*	rocaille, rockwork
Grubenschmelz *m*	champlevé
Gruft (Grüfte) *f*	sepulchre, tomb, grave
grün	green
Grund (Gründe) *m*	ground
gründen	to found
Gründer (−) *m*	founder
Grundfarbe(n) *f*	1. color of the ground or underpainting 2. main color, dominant color 3 basic color, primary color
Grundfläche(n) *f*	surface, ground
Grundform(en) *f*	basic form
grundieren	to ground (a canvas), to size, to prime
grundiert	primed, coated with ground
Grundierung(en) *f*	ground
Grundmauer(n) *f*	foundation wall
Grundriß (-risse) *m*	floor plan
Grundsteinlegung(en) *f*	ceremonial laying of the cornerstone
Grundton (-töne) *m*	dominant tone, basic tone
Grundtyp(en) *m*	basic type
Gründung(en) *f*	founding, establishment

Grundzug (-züge) *m*	basic characteristic
Grünerde *f*	green earth
Grünspan *m*	verdigris
Grünstein *m*	greenstone
Gruppe(n) *f*	group
Gruppenbild(er) *n*	group portrait
Gruppierung(en) *f*	grouping
Gruß, Englischer — *m*	the Annunciation, Angelic Salutation
Guajakholz *n*	lignum vitae
Guasch(en) *f* *also* Gouache	gouache
Guaschgrund *m*	gouache ground
Guaschmalerei *f*	gouache painting
Guilloche(n) *f*	guilloche
Gummi *n*	gum
Gummi *m*	rubber
Gummiarabikum *n*	gum arabic
Gummiarabikumlösung(en) *f*	gum arabic solution
Gummigutt *n*	gamboge
Gummiharz(e) *n*	gum resin
Gummiwalze(n) *f*	squeegee
Gummiwasser *n*	aqueous binder
Gurtbogen (—, bögen) *m*	transverse arch
Gürtel (—) *m*	belt
Gürtelschnalle(n) *f*	belt buckle
Gürtelspende, die —	Mary Lowering Her Girdle (to Thomas)
Gurtgesims(e) *n*	string course between two floors
Gurtrippe(n) *f*	longitudinal ridge-rib
Gürtung(en) *f*	belting
Guß (Güsse) *m*	cast, casting
Gußabdruck(e) *m*	cast
Gußeisen *n*	cast iron
gußeisern	(of) cast iron
Gußhohlform(en) *f*	mold

Gußkanal (-kanäle) *m*	sprue, gate
Gußmantel (-mäntel) *m*	investment
Gußmauerwerk *n*	opus caementum masonry
Gußnaht (-nähte) *f*	(casting) fin
Gußröhre(n) *f*	sprue, gate
Gußstein(e) *m*	imitation stone
Gußstück(e) *n*	cast, cast piece, casting
Gußverfahren *n*	casting
Gußwerk(e) *n*	foundry
Gutsche(n) *f*	sculpting punch
Haar(e) *n*	hair
Haarbüschel (−) *m*,*n*	tuft of hair
Haarlocke(n) *f*	lock of hair
Haarpinsel (−) *m*	hair paint brush
Haarriß (-risse) *m*	hairline crack
Haartracht(en) *f*	headdress, hairdo
Hafenbild(er) *n*	picture of a harbor, harbor scene
Hafnerkeramik *f*	hafner ware
haften	to stick, to cling, to adhere
Hagiographie *f*	hagiography
Hahnenbalken (−) *m*	purlin
Häkelarbeit *f*	crochet work
häkeln	to crochet
Haken (−) *m*	hook, peg, catch
hakenförmig	hooked, unciform, hook-shaped
Hakenkreuz(e) *n*	swastika, gammadion
halb	half
halbdeckende Farbe *f*	semi-opaque color
Halbedelstein(e) *m*	semiprecious stone
Halbfigur(en) *f*	half length figure
Halbgott (-götter) *m*	demigod
Halbkreidegrund *m*	emulsion ground
Halbkreis(e) *m*	semicircle
halbkreisartig	semicircular

Halbkugel(n) *f*	hemisphere
Halbkuppel(n) *f*	semidome
Halbmesser (−) *m*	radius
Halbprofil(e) *n*	profile showing three quarters of the face
Halbrelief(s) *n*	middle (or half) relief, mezzo-rilievo
halbrund	semicircular
Halbsäule(n) *f*	demi-column, half-column
Halbunziale(n) *f*	half-uncial
Halbzylinder (−) *m*	half cylinder
Halle(n) *f*	hall
Hallengebäude (−) *n*	hall building, building with main emphasis on the hall(s)
Hallenkirche(n) *f*	hall church
Hallstattzeit *f*	Hallstatt period
Hals (Hälse) *m*	neck
Halsamphora (-amphoren) *f*	amphora with neck and body clearly distinguished (see *Bauchamphora*)
Halsgehänge (−) *n*	necklace
Halsmuskel(n) *m*	neck muscle
Halteeisen (−) *n*	flask; steel frame for a sand mold
Haltegerüst(e) *n*	armature
halten	to hold, to support
Halterung(en) *f*	mounting, support, brace
Haltung(en) *f*	position, posture, pose, stance, attitude
Hämatit *m*	hematite, bloodstone
Hammer (Hämmer) *m*	hammer, mallet
hämmerbar	malleable
hämmern	to hammer, to planish, to work with a hammer
Hand (Hände) *f*	hand
Handbild(er) *n*	handprint
Handdruck(e) *m*	original print, hand screen; print pulled by the artist himself

Handgelenk(e) *n*	wrist
Handhabung(en) *f*	manipulation
handkoloriert	colored by hand
Handkolorierung *f*	hand coloring
Handschrift(en) *f*	1. manuscript
	2. handwriting
	3. brushwork, touch (of a painter)
Handumriß (-risse) *m*	outline of a hand
Handwalze(n) *f*	roller
Handwaschung des Pilatus, die —	Pilate Washing His Hands
Handwerker (—) *m*	craftsman, artisan
handwerklich	craftsmanlike
Handzeichnung(en) *f*	freehand drawing
Hanf *m*	hemp
Hanföl *n*	hempseed oil
Hängebrücke(n) *f*	suspension bridge
Hängekonstruktion(en) *f*	suspension construction
Hängekuppel(n) *f*	sail vault
hängen	to hang, to suspend
Hängeplastik(en) *f*	suspended sculpture
Hängeplatte(n) *f*	projecting top plate of a cornice
Hängesäule(n) *f*	king-post
Hängezwickel(n) *m*	pendentive
Hansagelb *n*	Hansa yellow
Happening(s) *n*	happening
haptisch	haptic, tactile
Hard-Edge Malerei *f*	hard-edge painting
Harmonielehre(n) *f*	theory of harmonious colors
Harnisch(e) *m*	armor
Harpunspitze(n) *f*	harpoon head, harpoon point
Harpyie(n) *f*	harpy
hart	hard, stiff, rigid
Härte *f*	hardness
Härtegrad(e) *m*	degree of hardness
Hartfaserplatte(n) *f*	hardboard, Masonite
Hartharz(e) *n*	hard resin

Hartholz *n*	hardwood
Hartmeißel (—) *m*	cold chisel
Hartporzellan(e) *n*	hard paste, hard paste porcelain
Harz(e) *n*	resin
Harzöl(e) *n*	oil distilled from resin
Harzölfirnis(se) *m*	simple-solution varnish, spirit varnish
Harzwachsfarbe(n) *f*	resin-wax paint
häßlich	ugly
Häßlichkeit *f*	ugliness
Hathorkapitell(e) *n*	Hathor (-headed) capital, Hathoric capital
Haube(n) *f*	hood, cap
Haube, welsche — *f*	tower roof similar to onion-shaped, but having two bulges
hauen	to hew
Haufebecher *pl*	nested metal cups
Haupt (Häupter) *n*	head
Hauptachse(n) *f*	main axis
Hauptansicht(en) *f*	main view
Hauptapsis *f*	main apse
Haupteingang *m*	main entrance
Hauptfigur(en) *f*	main figure
Hauptgegenstand (-stände) *m*	main object, central object
Hauptportal(e) *n*	main portal
Hauptschiffwand (-wände) *f*	nave wall
Hauptstadt (-städte) *f*	capital city
Hauptwerk(e) *n*	main work
Hauptwirkungsstätte(n) *f*	main location of (his) work or influence
Haus (Häuser) *n*	house, building
Hausenblasenleim *m*	fish glue
Hausgerät(e) *n*	domestic utensil
Hausmaler (—) *m*	free-lance porcelain painter
Haustein(e) *m*	dressed stone, evenly hewn stone block
Hausurne(n) *f*	house-shaped urn

Haut (Häute) *f*	skin
Hautelisse(s) *f*	high warp loom
Hautelisseweberei(en) *f*	high warp weaving
Hautrelief *n*	high relief, bold relief
Hedwigsgläser *pl*	Hedwig glasses
heidnisch	heathen
Heiland *m*	(Christ the) Saviour
heilig	holy, sacred
Heilige(n) *m, f*	saint
Heilige Familie, die —	1. the Nativity 2. the Holy Family (Mary, Joseph, Christ)
Heilige Grab, das —	1. the Holy Sepulchre 2. depiction of Christ's sarcophagus
Heilige Schrift *f*	the Scriptures, the Holy Bible
Heilige Sippe *f*	the Holy Family (esp. the Virgin and her relatives)
Heiligenattribut(e) *n*	attribute of a saint
Heiligenbild(er) *n*	depiction of a saint
Heiligenfigur(en) *f*	saint, saintly figure
Heiligenschein(e) *m*	halo, gloriole
Heiligtum (-tümer) *m*	shrine, sacred site, sanctuary, sacred object
Heilsgeschichte *f*	history of God's deeds; (story of) Christ's Life and Sufferings
Heilsspiegel *m*	Mirror of Salvation, speculum humanae salvationis
Heiltum (-tümer) *n*	collection of relics
Heiltumsbuch (-bücher) *n*	inventory book of a collection of relics
Heimatkunst *f*	folk art, local art
Heimatmuseum (-museen) *n*	museum of local art
Heimkehr des verlorenen Sohnes, die —	Return of the Prodigal Son
Heimsuchung Mariä, die —	the Visitation
Hekatompedon *m* *also* Hekatompedos	hecatompedon

Held(en) *m*	hero
Heldenepos (-epen) *n*	epic poem, epic
Heliographie *f*	heliography
Heliogravüre(n) *f*	photogravure
hell	light, light-colored, bright
helladisch	Helladic
hellblau	light blue
Helldunkel *n*	chiaroscuro
Hell-Dunkel-Kontrast(e) *m*	contrast between light and dark
Helldunkelmalerei *f*	chiaroscuro painting
Helldunkelschnitt(e) *m*	chiaroscuro woodcut
Hellenentum *n*	Greek culture, Greek world
hellenisch	Hellenic
Hellenismus *m*	Hellenism
hellenistisch	Hellenistic
hellfarbig	light-colored, pastel
Helligkeit *f*	brightness
Helm(e) *m*	helmet
Helm, achtseitiger	broach spire
Helmdach (-dächer) *n*	helm roof
Helmklappe(n) *f*	visor
Helmurne(n) *f*	cinerary urn with helmet lid
Hemd(en) *n*	shirt
Henkel (—) *m*	(cup or vase) handle
Henkelgefäß(e) *n*	vessel with handle(s)
Henkelkanne(n) *f*	pitcher with handle(s)
Henkelkreuz(e) *n*	ankh, ansate cross
Henna *f*	alkanet, henna
Herakles	Herakles, Hercules
Heraldik *f*	heraldry
herkömmlich	traditional
Herkunft *f*	origin
Herme(n) *f*	herm, herma
Hermenpfeiler (—) *m*	herm
Hermensäule(n) *f*	herm (column)
heroisch	heroic

Heros (Heroen) *m*	hero, demigod
Herrgottsruhbild(er) *n*	(sculptural) portrayal of Christ exhausted, sad, chained and/or resting
Herrscher (—) *m*	ruler
Herrscherbildnis(se) *n*	portrait of a ruler
hervortreten	to protrude
Hervortreten *n*	protrusion
Herz(en) *n*	heart
Herzblattwelle *f*	leaf and tongue; heart and dart
herzförmig	heart-shaped, cordate
Herz-Jesu Bild *n*	Sacred Heart depiction of Christ
Herzog (Herzöge) *m*	duke
Herzogin(nen) *f*	duchess
Herzogtum (-tümer) *n*	dukedom, duchy
Hethiter (—) *m* *also* Hettiter	Hittite
hethitisch *also* hettitisch	Hittite
Hexagon(e) *n*	hexagon
hexagonal	hexagonal
hieratisch	hieratic
Hieroglyphen *pl*	hieroglyphics
hieroglyphisch	hieroglyphic
Hieronymus, der hl. —	St. Jerome
Himmel (—) *m*	1. sky, heaven 2. canopy, baldachin
Himmelbett(en) *n*	four poster bed, canopied bed
himmelblau	sky blue
Himmelfahrt *f*	the Ascension
Himmelfahrt Mariens, die —	the Assumption of the Virgin
Himmelsthron(e) *m*	heavenly throne
himmlisch	heavenly
Hinterglasmalerei *f*	glass painting, (folk) painting on glass

Hintergrund (-gründe) *m*	background
Hintergrundlandschaft(en) *f*	background landscape
Hinterseite(n) *f*	back side
Hiob	Job
Hippokampen-Ornament *n*	hippocampus ornament
Hirnholz *n*	wood cut against the grain
Hirschhornfassung(en) *f*	(stone axe) antler sleeve
Hirt(en) *m*	shepherd
Hirte, der gute —	the Good Shepherd
Hirten, die Anbetung der —	the Adoration of the Shepherds
Hirtengott *m*	Pan
Hirtenkönige *pl*	Hyksos
Hirtenlandschaft(en) *f*	pastoral scene, pastoral landscape
Hirtenszene(n) *f*	pastoral scene
Hispanomoreske(n) *f*	Hispano-Moresque ware
Historienmalerei *f*	history painting
hl. (= heilig)	saint
hoch	high, tall
Hochaltar (-altäre) *m*	high altar
Hochburg(en) *f*	citadel
Hochdruck *m*	relief printing
hochentwickelt	highly developed
Hochgotik *f*	High Gothic
Hochhaus (-häuser) *n*	skyscraper, high-rise building
Hochkultur(en) *f*	civilization
Hochrelief(s) *n*	high relief, bold relief
Hochrenaissance *f*	High Renaissance
hochromanisch	(peak of) Romanesque
Hochschaftstuhl (-stühle) *m*	high warp loom
Hochschiffwand (-wände) *f*	nave wall (above the arches between nave and side aisle)
Hochschule für bildende Kunst *f*	art academy
Hochwand (-wände) *f*	nave wall

Hochzeit zu Kanaan, die —	the Wedding of Cana
Hockerbestattung(en) *f*	contracted inhumation; burial in crouched position
Hockerstellung *f*	crouched position
Hodegetria *f*	Hodegetria Madonna
Hof (Höfe) *m*	1. court, courtyard 2. halo
Hofarchitekt(en) *m*	royal architect, court architect
höfisch	courtly
Hofkapelle(n) *f*	royal chapel
Hofkirche(n) *f*	royal chapel, royal church
Hofmaler (—) *m*	court painter
Hofschule(n) *f*	court school (or academy)
Hofstaat *m*	court, retinue
Höhe(n) *f*	height
höhen mit Deckweiß	to heighten (by underpainting with white)
Höhenburg(en) *f*	castle protected by height
Höhepunkt *m*	peak, culmination
hohl	hollow, concave
Höhle(n) *f*	cave
Hohleisen (—) *n*	woodcutting gouge
Höhlenbewohner (—) *m*	cliff-dweller, cave dweller, cave man
Höhlenmalerei(en) *f*	cave painting
Höhlensiedlung(en) *f*	cave dwelling
Hohlfläche(n) *f*	concave surface
Hohlform(en) *f*	concave shape, hollow shape(d object)
Hohlguß (-güsse) *m*	hollow cast, hollow casting
Hohlkehle(n) *f*	concave moulding; scotia profile
Hohlleiste(n) *f*	concave or hollow moulding
Hohlmauer(n) *f*	hollow wall
Hohlmauerwerk *n*	masonry with hollow spaces within the walls
Hohlmünze(n) *f*	bracteate, hollow coin, coin printed on one side

Holzmosaik

Hohlplastik(en) *f*	hollow sculpture
Hohlraum (-räume) *m*	hollow space, cavity
Höhlung(en) *f*	hollow, depression, indent
Hohlziegel (–) *m*	1. hollow brick
	2. concave roof tile
Höhung(en) *f*	heightening (with white)
holländisch	Dutch
Hölle *f*	hell, inferno
Höllenfahrt Christi, die –	the Harrowing of Hell, the Descent to Hell, Christ in Limbo
Höllensturz der Verdammten, der, –	the Damned Cast into Hell
Holm(e) *m*	cross-beam, transom
Holographie(n) *f*	holography
Holz (Hölzer) *n*	wood
Holzbalken (–) *m*	wooden beam
Holzbalkendecke(n) *f*	wood-beamed ceiling
Holzbau(ten) *m*	wooden structure, wood construction
Holzbild(er) *n*	wooden sculpture
Holzbildhauerei *f*	(art of) wood sculpture, wood carving
Holzbildnerei *f*	(art of) wood sculpture, wood carving
Holzboden (-böden) *m*	wooden floor
Holzdecke(n) *f*	wooden ceiling
Holzfäule *f*	dry rot
Holzgalerie(n) *f*	wooden gallery
Holzhaus (-häuser) *n*	wooden house
Holzkern(e) *m*	wooden core
Holzleiste(n) *f*	wood moulding
Holzmaserung(en) *f*	grain of the wood, wood grain
Holzmesser (–) *n*	carver, woodcarving knife
Holzmöbel *pl*	wooden furniture
Holzmosaik(en) *n*	intarsia

Holznagel (-nägel) *m*	wooden peg, dowel
Holzöl *n*	tung oil
Holzpapier *n*	wood-pulp paper
Holzplastik(en) *f*	wooden sculpture
Holzrahmen (—) *m*	wooden frame
Holzsäule(n) *f*	wooden column
Holzschneidekunst *f*	xylography
Holzschnitt(e) *m*	woodcut
Holzschnitzer (—) *m*	wood carver
Holzschnitzerei *f*	(art of) wood carving
Holzskulptur(en) *f*	wooden sculpture
Holzstempel (—) *m*	wooden stamp
Holzstich(e) *m*	wood engraving
Holzstock (-stöcke) *m*	wood engraving block
Holztafel(n) *f*	wooden tablet, wooden panel
Holztafeldruck(e) *m*	block print
honiggelb	honey-colored
Horizont(e) *m*	horizon
horizontal	horizontal
Horizontale(n) *f*	horizontal line
Horizontlinie(n) *f*	horizon line
Horn (Hörner) *n*	(animal) horn
Hornblende *f*	hornblende
Horntonstein(e) *m*	Hornton stone
Hortfund(e) *m*	hoard
Hose(n) *f*	pants, trousers
Hosenkleidung *f*	legged clothing, clothing with legs
Hostie(n) *f*	Host, consecrated wafer
Hostienbüchse(n) *f*	pyx, receptacle for the Host
Hostiengefäß(e) *n*	receptacle for the Host
Hostienmühle *f*	(depiction of) the Miracle of Transubstantiation
Hostientaube(n) *f*	dove-shaped Host receptacle suspended over the altar
Hostienteller (—) *m*	paten
Hufeisenbogen (—, -bögen) *m*	horseshoe arch

hufeisenförmig	horseshoe-shaped
Hüfte(n) f	hip
Hügelaufschüttung(en) f	barrow, mound
Hügelgrab (-gräber) n	burial mound, tumulus
Hugenottenstil m	Huguenot style
Humanismus m	humanism
Humerale (Humeralien, Humeralia) f	humeral veil
Humpen (–) m	tankard, jug
Hund, laufender – m	running dog, Vitruvian scroll, wave meander
Hundszahnornament(e) n	dogtooth ornament
Hünenbett(en) n	hunebed
Hünengrab (-gräber) n	megalithic tomb
Hungertuch (-tücher) n	Lenten veil (displayed between chancel and nave)
Hüttenplastik(en) f	sculpture which is related to a building (as opposed to free-standing sculpture), architectural sculpture
Hydria (Hydrien) f	hydria (vase)
hymettischer Marmor m	marble from Mt. Hymettus
Hypäthralbasilika (-basiliken) f	hypaethral basilica
Hypäthraltempel (–) m	hypaethral temple
Hypogäum (Hypogäen) n	hypogeum
Hypokaustum (-kausten) n	hypocaust
Hypostylos (-loi) m	hypostyle hall
Hypotrachelion (-trachelien) n	hypotrachelium

Ideal(e) n	ideal
Idealansicht(en) f	ideal view, ideal viewing side
Idealgestalt(en) f	ideal figure
idealisieren	to idealize
Ideenskizze(n) f	preliminary sketch of an idea

Identifizierung(en) *f*	identification
Ideogramm(e) *n*	ideogram
Ideographie *f*	ideography
Idol(e) *n*	figurine, idol
Ikone(n) *f*	icon
Ikonodulie *f*	idolatry
Ikonographie *f*	iconography
Ikonoklasmus *m*	iconoclasm
ikonoklastisch	iconoclastic
Ikonolatrie *f*	iconolatry
Ikonologie *f*	iconology
Ikonostase (Ikonostaten) *f* *also* Ikonostasis	iconostasis
Illuminator(en) *m*	(book) illuminator, limner
illuminieren	to illuminate
Illuminieren *n*	illumination
Illuminierkunst *f*	(art of) book illumination
illuminierte Handschrift *f*	illuminated manuscript
Illusion(en) *f*	illusion
Illusionismus *m*	illusionism
illusionistisch	illusionistic
Illustration(en) *f*	illustration
Illustrator(en) *m*	illustrator
illustrieren	to illustrate
Iltishaar *n*	fitch hair
Imago (Imagines) *f*	imago, wax death mask
Immaculata *f*	the Immaculate Conception, Immaculate Mary
Impasto (Impasti) *n*	impasto
Impluvium (-vien, -via) *n*	impluvium
Impressionismus *m*	Impressionism
Impressionist(en) *m*	Impressionist
impressionistisch	impressionistic
Imprimitur(en) *f*	imprimatura, veil
inc.	inc.

indianisch	(American) Indian
Indigo *m,n*	indigo
indisch	Indian
Indischgelb *n*	Indian yellow
Individuum (Individuen) *n*	individual
Industrie(n) *f*	industry, assemblage of tools
Industriefarbe(n) *f*	industrially produced paint or dye
informelle Kunst *f* *also* informelle Malerei *f*	*art informel;* collective term for abstract movement opposed to geometric abstraction, beginning in Paris around 1945
Infrarotaufnahme(n) *f*	infrared photograph
Infrarotphotografie *f*	infrared photography
Ingenieurbau(ten) *m*	structure which especially displays technical and structural aspects, e.g. bridges, towers, dams
Inhalt(e) *m*	content(s), subject
inhaltlich	with regard to content
Initialblatt (-blätter) *n*	manuscript page having only one initial on it
Initiale(n) *f*	initial letter
Initialseite(n) *f*	manuscript page having only one initial on it
Inkarnat *n*	flesh color
Inkrustation(en) *f*	1. cladding, paneling or other wall lining 2. stone inlay
Inkunabel(n) *f*	incunabula
Innenansicht(en) *f*	inner view, view of the interior
Innenarchitekt(en) *m*	interior decorator, interior designer
Innenarchitektur *f*	1. interior decoration 2. interior architecture
Innenausstattung *f*	interior decoration or furnishings

Innendekoration(en) *f*	interior decoration
Inneneinrichtung(en) *f*	interior decoration or furnishings
Innenhof (-höfe) *m*	interior courtyard, inner courtyard
Innenraum (-räume) *m*	interior, inner chamber
Innenwand (-wände) *f*	inner wall, interior wall
Innenwelt(en) *f*	inner world
Innung(en) *f*	guild, professional association
Inschrift(en) *f*	inscription
Inschriftzeile(n) *f*	inscribed line, line of inscription
in situ	in situ
Inspiration(en) *f*	inspiration
Intaglio (Intaglien) *n*	intaglio
Intarsia (Intarsien) *f* also Intarsie(n)	intarsia, inlay
Intensität, spezifische *f*	brilliance
Intercolumnium (-columnien) *n* also Interkolumnium (-kolumnien) also Interkolumnie(n)	intercolumniation
Interieur(s) *n*	interior, depiction of an interior
Interieurmalerei *f*	painted depiction of an interior
inv.	inv.
Inventar(e) *n*	inventory
ionisch	Ionic
ionische Ordnung *f*	Ionic order
irden	earthen
Irdenware(n) *f*	earthenware
irdisch	earthly
irisieren	to be iridescent, to iridesce
irisierend	iridescent
Irrgarten (-gärten) *m*	labyrinth

Isokephalie *f*	isocephaly
isolieren	1. to insulate
	2. to isolate
Isolierglas *n*	insulating glass
Isolierschicht(en) *f*	insulating layer
Isolierung *f*	insulation
Isometrie *f*	isometric projection
Italien	Italy
italienisch	Italian
Itinerarium (Itinerarien) *n*	1. itinerary
	2. portable altar
Jacke(n) *f*	jacket
Jacquardweberei *f*	Jacquard weaving, Jacquard weave
Jade *m*	jade
jadegrün	jade green
Jadeit *m*	jadeite
Jagddarstellung(en) *f*	depiction of the hunt, hunting scene
Jagdkrug (-krüge) *m*	glazed mug or pitcher decorated with hunting scenes
Jagdmotiv(e) *n*	hunting motif
Jagdstück(e) *n*	hunting scene, still life of weapons and game
Jahreszeitendarstellung(en) *f*	depiction of the four seasons
Jahrhundert(e) *n*	century
Jahrhundertmitte *f*	mid-century
Jahrhundertwende *f*	turn of the century
Jahrtausend(e) *n*	millennium
Jahrzehnt(e) *n*	decade
Jakobus, der hl. —	St. James the Great
Jalousie(n) *f*	jalousie
Japanpapier *n*	Japanese woodcut paper
Jasper-Ware *f*	jasper ware

Jaspis(se) *m*	jasper
Jessebaum *m*	Christ's genealogy, the Tree of Jesse
Jesusknabe *m*	Jesus child, Christ child
Jett *m*	jet
Jh. (=Jahrhundert)	century
Jhdt. (=Jahrhundert)	century
Joch(e) *n*	bay
Jochbein(e) *n*	cheek bone
Jochbreite *f*	breadth of the bay
Jochweite *f*	width of the bay, distance between two columns
Johanitterkreuz(e) *n*	Maltese cross
Johannes der Evangelist	St. John the Evangelist
Johannes der Täufer	St. John the Baptist
Johannesminne *f*	sculpture depicting Christ leaning on St. John's breast
Johannespredigt *f*	St. John Preaching
Johannesschüssel(n) *f*	liturgical plate depicting St. John's head in relief
Jonas und der Wal	Jonah and the Whale
jonisch *also* ionisch	Ionic
Judaskuß, der —	the Betrayal of Christ
Judenstern(e) *m*	Star of David
Judentum *n*	Jewry, Judaism
Jugendarbeit(en) *f*	early work, work done in youth
Jugendstil *m*	modern style, art nouveau
Julisches Forum *n*	Forum of Caesar
jung	young, late, recent
Jünger (–) *m*	disciple, apostle
Jünger von Emmaus, die —	the Disciples at Emmaus
Jungfrau(en) *f*	1. virgin 2. Virgo *zodiac*

Jüngling(e) *m*	youth, boy
Jünglingsgestalt(en) *f*	figure of a youth, youthful figure
Jungpaläolithikum *n*	Upper Paleolithic
Jüngste Gericht, das −	the Last Judgment
Jungsteinzeit *f*	neolithic age or period
jungsteinzeitlich	neolithic
Jurakalk *m*	Jurassic limestone
Juwel(en) *n*	jewel
Juwelenkästchen (−) *n*	jewel box, jewel case
Kabinett(e) *n*	cabinet, small room, small room with an art collection
Kabinettmalerei *f*	1. colorless window painted with enamel and baked 2. cabinet painting, cabinet picture
Kabinettscheibe(n) *f*	stained glass window (for a profane building)
Kabinettstück(e) *n*	especially valuable work of art
Kachel(n) *f*	(ceramic) tile
Kachelofen (-öfen) *m*	ceramic-tiled stove
Kadmiumgelb *n*	cadmium yellow
Kadmiumrot *n*	cadmium red
Kaduzeus (Kaduzei) *m*	caduceus
Kaffgesims(e) *n* *also* Kappgesims	string course running under the windows
Kaiser (−) *m*	emperor
Kaiserdom(e) *m*	imperial cathedral
Kaiserfora *pl*	the Imperial forums
Kaiserkrone(n) *f*	imperial crown
Kaiserpaar(e) *n*	imperial couple
Kaiserpalast (-paläste) *m*	imperial palace
Kaiserpfalz(en) *f*	imperial palace
Kaisersaal (-säle) *m*	imperial hall
Kaisersitz(e) *m*	imperial throne, location of the imperial residence

Kaiserzeit *f*	Imperial Rome, imperial age
Kaiserzeit, die römische —	Imperial Rome
Kalander (—) *m*	calender machine
kalandern	to calender (paper)
Kalb, das goldene — *n*	the Golden Calf
Kalb(s)leder *n*	calfskin
Kaldarium (Kaldaeien) *n* *also* Caldarium	caldarium
Kalebasse(n) *f*	calabash
Kalefaktorium (-faktorien) *n*	calefactory; heated room in a monastery
Kalendarium (-darien) *n*	depictions of the (labors of the) months
Kalender (—) *m*	calendar
Kalenderbild(er) *n*	almanac picture, calendar picture
Kalk *m*	lime, limestone
Kalkmilch *f*	milk of lime
Kalkmörtel *m*	limestone mortar
Kalkputz *m*	lime stucco, mortar
Kalkschiefer, Solnhofer — *m*	Solnhofen stone
Kalkseccoverfahren *n*	limewash painting process, secco painting process employing limewater
Kalkstein *m*	limestone
Kalligraph(en) *m*	calligrapher
Kalligraphie(n) *f*	calligraphy
kalligraphisch	calligraphic
Kalotte(n) *f*	1. calotte, skull cap 2. upper half of a horizontally bisected sphere
Kaltmeißel (—) *m*	cold chisel
Kaltnadel(n) *f*	drypoint
Kaltnadelradierung(en) *f*	drypoint engraving
Kalvarienberg *m*	Mount Calvary
Kalzedon *m*	chalcedony
kalzinieren	to calcine
Kamares-Vasen *pl*	Kamares ware

Kambrik *m*	cambric cloth
Kamee(n) *f*	cameo
kameenhaft	cameo-like
Kamin(e) *m*	fireplace
Kamisol(e) *n*	camisole
Kamm (Kämme) *m*	comb
Kammer(n) *f*	chamber, small room
Kammergrab (-gräber) *n*	chamber tomb
Kammkeramik *f*	pottery with combed ornament
Kammstrich-Ornament(e) *n*	combed ornament
Kamm- und Grübchenkeramik *f*	Pit-comb ware
Kampanile *m*	campanile
Kampf (Kämpfe) *m*	battle, fight, struggle
Kämpfer (−) *m*	1. fighter, warrior 2. impost 3. dosseret, super-abacus, impost block
Kämpferhöhe *f*	height of the impost
Kämpferkapitell(e) *n*	capital with dosseret or impost block
Kampfwagen (−) *m*	war chariot
Kanalisation(en) *f*	sewer, sewage system
Kanapee(s) *n*	settee, sofa
Kandelaber (−) *m*	candelabrum, candle stand
Kanephore(n) *f*	canephora
Kanne(n) *f*	pitcher
Kannele(n) *f*	flute, groove
Kannelierung(en) *f*	fluting
Kannelüre(n) *f*	fluting
Kanon(s) *m*	canon, rule
Kanonbild(er) *n*	depiction of Christ crucified (located in a liturgical book)
Kanonbogen (−, -bögen) *m*	canon table
Kanontafel(n) *f*	canon table
Kanope(n) *f*	canopic jar

Kante(n) *f*	1. edge
	2. arris
Kantenansicht(en) *f*	profile
Kantharos (Kantharoi) *m*	cantharus
Kantholz (-hölzer) *n*	squared timber
kantig	edged, having sharp edges
kantoniert	rounded off, e. g. wall or pillar edges rounded off by adding a half or three-quarters column
Kanzel(n) *f*	pulpit
Kanzelbrüstung(en) *f*	pulpit rail
Kanzeldach (-dächer) *n*	sounding board, canopy
Kanzelhaube(n) *f*	sounding board, canopy
Kanzelhimmel (—) *m*	sounding board, canopy
Kaolin *m, n*	kaolin
Kapelle(n) *f*	chapel
Kapellenkranz (-kränze) *m*	ambulatory (wtih radial chapels)
Kapitäl(e) *n* *also* Kapitell	capital
Kapitalbuchstabe(n) *m*	capital letter
Kapitel (—) *n*	chapter
Kapitell(e) *n*	capital
Kapitellform(en) *f*	capital shape
Kapitelsaal (-säle) *m*	chapterhouse, chapter hall
Kappe(n) *f*	1. cell (of a vault)
	2. upper section resulting if two intersecting planes diagonally cut through a barrel vault
Kappgesims(e) *n* *also* Kaffgesims	string course running under the windows
Kardinalskreuz(e) *n*	patriarchal cross
Karfunkel (—) *n*	carbuncle
Karikatur(en) *f*	caricature
Karikaturist(en) *m*	caricaturist
Karikaturzeichner (—) *m*	caricaturist
Karl der Große	Charlemagne
Karmesin *n*	carmine, crimson

Karmin *n*	carmine, crimson
karminrot	carmine red, crimson red
karmosieren	to surround with small jewels
Karnation *f*	flesh tone, carnation
Karnaubawachs *n*	carnauba wax
Karneol *m*	carnelian
Karner (—) *m*	charnel house
Karnies(e) *n*	cyma recta, cyma reversa, ogee moulding, S-shaped profile
Karniesbogen (—, -bögen) *m*	ogee arch
Karolinger (—) *m*	Carolingian
karolingisch	Carolingian
Karton(s) *m*	1. cartoon, preparatory drawing 2. cardboard, heavy paper
Kartonstich(e) *m*	(copper) outline engraving
Kartusche(n) *f*	cartouche
Karyatide(n) *f*	caryatid
Kasein(e) *n*	casein
Kaseinfarbe(n) *f*	casein color
Kaseingrund *m*	casein ground
Kaseinmalerei *f*	painting with casein colors
Kasel(n) *f*	chasuble
Kasematte(n) *f*	casemate
Kassette(n) *f*	1. coffer *architecture* 2. small box
Kassettendecke(n) *f*	coffered ceiling, lacunar
Kassettierung(en) *f*	coffering
kassetiert	coffered
Kaßlerbraun *n*	Cassel earth, Cologne earth
Kastanienholz *n*	chestnut (wood)
Kastell(e) *n*	citadel, castle, stronghold
Kasten (Kästen) *m*	box
Kastenaltar (-altäre) *m*	box-shaped altar
Kastenmöbel *pl*	box-shaped medieval furniture
Kastenrahmen (—) *m*	box frame
Kastensitz(e) *m*	Romanesque box-shaped chair

Katafalk(e) *m*	catafalque
Katakombe(n) *f*	catacomb
Katalog(e) *m*	catalog
Katechu *n*	cutch, catechu
Katharinenrad *n*	St. Catherine's wheel, wheel window
Kathedra(e, -en) *f* *also* Cathedra	cathedra, bishop's throne
Kathedrale(n) *f*	cathedral
Kauterien *pl*	cauteria; equipment used in encaustic painting
Kavalierperspektive *f*	perspective from an elevated point, as if seen from horseback
Kegel (−) *m*	cone
Kegeldach (-dächer) *n*	conical roof
Kehlbalken (−) *m*	collar beam
Kehlleiste(n) *f*	concave moulding
Kehlstein(e) *m*	building stone or brick with one side or corner hollowed out
Keil(e) *m*	wedge, canvas stretcher key
keilförmig	wedge-shaped
keilförmiger Stein(e) *m*	voussoir
Keilrahmen (−) *m*	canvas stretcher
Keilschnitt *m*	chip-carving; decoration in wood by means of notching out triangular chips
Keilschrift(en) *f*	cuneiform
Keilschrifttafel(n) *f*	cuneiform tablet
Keilstein(e) *m*	voussoir
Kelch(e) *m*	1. goblet, chalice 2. calyx
kelchförmig	calyx-shaped, goblet-shaped
Kelch-Knospen-Kapitell(e) *n*	crocket capital
Kelchkrater(e, −) *m*	calyx krater
Kelchlöffel (−) *m*	chalice spoon, chalice straw
Kelchtellerchen (−) *n*	chalice paten
Kelle(n) *f*	trowel

Keller (−) m	cellar, basement
Kelt(e) m	celt, prehistoric tool
Kelten pl	Celts
Kelter, Christus in der −	depiction of Christ being tortured in a winepress
keltisch	Celtic
Kemenate(n) f	heatable room in a castle
Kenner (−) m	connoisseur, expert, specialist
Kennerschaft f	connoisseurship
Kennzeichen (−) n	characteristic
Kenotaph(e) n *also* Zenotaph	cenotaph
Kentaur(en) m *also* Zentaur	centaur
Keramik(en) f	ceramics, ceramic ware
Keramiker (−) m	ceramist
Keramikfliese(n) f	ceramic tile
Keramikfund(e) m	ceramic find
Keramikgefäß(e) n	ceramic vessel
keramisch	ceramic
keramischer Druck m	ceramic decalcomania; decoration of ceramics by means of transfers
Kerbe(n) f	notch, recess, dent, incision, chip
kerben	to notch, to indent, to chip
Kerbschnitt m	chip-carving; decoration in which triangular chips are cut away from the surface
Kerbschnittkeramik(en) f	Kerbschnitt ceramics; ceramics decorated with chip-carving
Kerbschnittverzierung(en) f	chip-carving decoration
Kerbung(en) f	notching, indentation
Kermes m	kermes dye, grain
Kern(e) m	1. core, armature 2. middle shaft of a compound pier
Kernholz n	heartwood

Kernschwarz *n*	peach black, kernel black
Kernstein(e) *m*	core
Keroplastik(en) *f* also Zeroplastik	ceroplastics, wax sculpture
Kerze(n) *f*	candle, taper
Kerzenhalter (−) *m*	candle holder
Kerzenlicht *n*	candlelight
Kerzenschein *m*	candlelight
Kerzenständer (−) *m*	candle holder, candelabrum
Kessel (−) *m*	kettle, pot, basin
Kettbaum (-bäume) *m*	warp beam
Kette(n) *f*	1. chain 2. warp *weaving*
Kettenfaden (-fäden) *m*	warp thread
Kibla *f*	qibla, kibleh
Kiefernholz *n*	pine
Kiel(e) *m*	quill
Kielbogen (−, -bögen)	ogee arch
Kielfeder(n) *f*	quill pen
Kienöl *n*	pine oil
Kienruß *m*	pine-soot black, lampblack
Kies *m*	gravel
Kieselerde *f*	silica
Kieselgel *n*	silica gel
Kieselgur *f*	diatomaceous earth
Kieselmosaik(en) *n*	pebble mosaic
Kieselstein(e) *m*	pebble, gravel
Kind(er) *n*	child
Kinderkunst *f*	children's art
Kindermord zu Bethlehem, der −	Slaughter (or Massacre) of the Innocents
Kindermord, der bethlehemische −	Slaughter (or Massacre) of the Innocents
Kinetik *f*	kinetics
kinetische Kunst *f*	kinetic art
Kinn(e) *n*	chin
Kionedonschrift *f*	(Byzantine) writing in vertical columns

Kiosk(e) *m*	kiosk
Kirche(n) *f*	church
Kirchenausstattung(en) *f*	church furnishings, church decoration
Kirchenbau(ten) *m*	church architecture, church building
Kirchenbaukunst *f*	church architecture
Kirchenburg(en) *f*	fortified church; church equipped with a defensive wall and storage vaults
Kirchenpatron(e) *m*	patron saint (of a church)
Kirchenschatz (-schätze) *m*	church treasure
Kirchentür(en) *f*	church door
kirchlich	churchly, sacred
Kirchturm (-türme) *m*	church tower
Kirschgummi *m*	cherry gum
Kissen (−) *n*	cushion, pillow
Kiste(n) *f*	box, case, chest
Kitsch *m*	kitsch
Kitt *m*	grout, mastic, putty
kitten	to spackle, to fill or stop with putty
Klammer(n) *f*	clamp, brace
Klappalette(n) *f*	folding palette
Klappaltar (-altäre) *m*	winged altarpiece
Klappaltärchen (−) *n*	folding altarpiece for a portable altar
Klassik *f*	classical period, classical style
klassisch	classical
Klassizismus *m*	classicism, Neoclassicism
Klebebild(er) *n*	collage
kleben	to glue, to stick
Klebestreifen (−) *m*	adhesive tape, pressure-sensitive tape
klebrig	sticky, tacky
Klebstoff(e) *m*	adhesive, glue
Klecks(e) *m*	spot, blot, smudge
Kleeblatt (-blätter) *n*	trefoil, cloverleaf

Kleeblattbogen (—, -bögen) *m*	trilobe arch, trefoil arch
Kleeblattchor (-chöre) *m*	cloverleaf plan; church plan with an apse in the chancel and one at the end of each transept arm
kleeblattförmig	cloverleaf, trefoil, trefled
kleeblattförmige Anlage(n) *f*	cloverleaf plan
Kleeblattkreuz(e) *n*	trefled cross
Kleid(er) *n*	garment, clothing, dress
kleiden	to clothe, to dress
Kleidung *f*	clothing, garments
Kleidungsstück(e) *n*	garment, piece of clothing
klein	small, little, short
kleinfigurig	small-figured, small scale
Kleinformat(e) *n*	small size, small scale
Kleinmeister *pl*	group of German copper engravers and woodcarvers ca. 1600, mainly producing small works
Kleinmeisterschale(n) *f*	little master cup
Kleinod(e, -ien) *n*	gem, jewel, insignia, treasure, precious object
Kleinplastik(en) *f*	small-scale sculpture
Kleister (—) *m*	paste
Kline(n) *f*	couch, furniture for reclining
Klinge(n) *f*	sword, blade
Klinker *m*	clinker, cinder block
Klischee(s) *n*	1. cliché 2. printing block
Klöppel (—) *m*	mallet
Kloster (Klöster) *n*	monastery
Klosterbibliothek(en) *f*	monastery library
Klostergewölbe (—) *n*	domical vault, cloister vault
Klosterkirche(n) *f*	monastery church
klösterlich	monastic
klugen und törichten Jungfrauen, die —	the Wise and Foolish Virgins
kluniazensisch	Cluniac

Knabe(n) *m*	youth, boy
Knabengestalt(en) *f*	youth, figure of a youth
Knagge(n) *f*	(roof) brace, console
knapp	1. concise
	2. tight
	3. scarce
Knappheit *f*	1. conciseness
	2. scarcity
Knauf (Knäufe) *m*	1. knob, knop, node (on a glass stem)
	2. column capital
Knete *f*	modelling clay
Knetton *m*	modelling clay
Knickachstempel (−) *m*	bent-axis temple
Knie (−) *n*	knee
Knielauf *m*	archaic convention used to indicate running
Kniestück(e) *n*	knee piece, three-quarter portrait
Knieverstrebung(en) *f*	(roof) brace
Knochen (−) *m*	bone
Knochenasche *f*	bone ash
Knochenschnitzerei(en) *f*	bone carving
Knollenkapitell(e) *n*	crocket capital
Knorpelwerk *n*	symmetrical baroque ornament with "gnarled" shapes
Knospe(n) *f*	(flower) bud
Knospenkapitell(e) *n*	crocket capital
Knoten (−) *m*	1. knot *fabric*
	2. burl, knot *wood*
Knotensäule(n) *f*	column or pair of columns "knotted" at mid-height
Knotenschnüre(n) *f*	quipu; Incan knotted cord
Knüpfarbeit(en) *f*	knotting, knotted work, knotted piece
knüpfen	to knot, to knit, to tie
Knüpfteppich(e) *m*	knotted carpet
Kobaltblau *n*	cobalt blue, king's blue
Kobaltgelb *n*	cobalt yellow

Kobaltviolett *n*	cobalt violet
Kodex (Kodizes) *m* *also* Codex	codex
Kohle *f*	charcoal
Kohlestift(e) *m*	charcoal crayon
Kohlezeichnung(en) *f*	charcoal drawing
Koimesis *f*	(Byzantine) depiction of the dormition of the Virgin
Kökkenmöddinger *pl*	kitchen midden
Kolkothar *m*	caput mortuum
Kollegiatkirche(n) *f*	collegiate church
Kolonialstil(e) *m*	colonial style
Kolonnade(n) *f*	colonnade
Kolonnenschrift(en) *f*	writing in vertical columns
Kolonettenkrater(e, –) *m*	column krater
Kolophonium *n* *also* Colophonium	rosin, colophony
Kolophoniumstaub *m*	powdered rosin
kolorieren	to color, to paint
Kolorierung *f*	coloring
Kolorismus *m*	colorism
Kolorist(en) *m*	colorist
Kolorit(e) *n*	color, coloring, coloration, hue, color effect
Koloß (Kolosse) *m*	colossus
kolossal	colossal, immense, enormous
Kolossalordnung *f*	colossal order, giant order
Kolossalstatue(n) *f*	colossal statue
Kolosseum *n*	Colosseum
Kolumbarium (-barien) *n*	columbarium
Kommandostab (-stäbe) *m*	(paleolithic) bâton de commandement
Kommode(n) *f*	chest of drawers, dresser
Kommunionbank (-bänke) *f*	Communion bench, Communion rail
Kommunionschüssel(n) *f*	Communion plate
kommunizierende Nebenchöre *pl*	chapels (in echelon) which have openings in the walls between them

kompensative Farben *pl*	colors which result in gray (gray-black) when mixed
Komplementäreffekt(e) *m*	effect of complementary colors
Komplementärfarbe(n) *f*	1. complementary color, color on opposite side of color wheel 2. colors which produce gray (gray-black) when mixed
Komplementärwirkung(en) *f*	effect of complementary colors
Komposition(en) *f*	composition
Kompositionsart(en) *f*	manner of composition
Kompositionslehre(n) *f*	theory of composition
Kompositionsprinzip(ien) *n*	principle of composition
Kompositkapitell(e) *n*	composite capital
Koncha(s, Konchen) *f* also Konche(n)	1. conch, apse 2. shell-shaped drinking vessel 3. baptismal font 4. chrismatory 5. shell-shaped background for sarcophagus portraits
König(e) *m*	king
königlich	royal
Königreich(e) *n*	kingdom
Königsblau *n*	king's blue
Königsgalerie(n) *f*	the Gallery of Kings (Gothic facade sculptures)
Königshalle(n) *f*	royal hall
Königshof (-höfe) *m*	royal court
Königspriester (—) *m*	royal priest
konisch	conical
konkav	concave
konkrete Kunst *f*	concrete art, abstract art
Konkurrenzentwurf (-würfe) *m*	competition design, entry
Konsekrationsmünze(n) *f*	Roman coin to commemorate the elevation of a Caesar to divine rank
Konservator(en) *m*	curator, keeper

konservieren	to conserve
Konservieren *n*	conservation
Konservierung *f*	conservation
Konsignatorium (-torien) *n*	room for confirmation, usually connected with the baptistery
Konsole(n) *f*	console, corbel, bracket
Konsoltisch(e) *m*	console table
konstantinisches Kreuz(e) *n*	cross with chi-rho
konstruieren	to build, to construct, to design
Konstruktion(en) *f*	construction, design
Konstruktivismus *m*	Constructivism
Kontamination *f*	joining parts of several works into one
Konterfei(e, s) *n*	portrait
kontinuierende Darstellung *f* *also* kontinuierliche —	continuous narration, continuous representation
Kontrapost(e) *m*	contrapposto
Kontra-Relief(s) *n*	counter relief
Kontrast(e) *m*	contrast
kontrastieren	to contrast
kontrastierend	contrasting
kontrastreich	rich in contrast
Kontur(en) *f*	contour, outline
konturieren	to give contour, to draw an outline sketch
Konturierung *f*	contouring, outlining
konturlos	without contour
Konus(se) *m*	cone
konvergent	converging, convergent
Konversationsstück(e) *n*	conversation piece
konvex	convex
Konvexbogen (—, -bögen) *m*	convex arch
konzentrisch	concentric
Kopaivabalsamöl *n*	copaiba balsam (oil)
Kopal *m*	copal

Kopalharz(e) n	copal
Kopenhagener Porzellan n	Royal Copenhagen porcelain
Kopf (Köpfe) m	head
Kopfbedeckung(en) f	headdress, head covering
Kopfbewegung(en) f	head movement
Kopfbild(er) n	portrait showing the head only
Kopfform(en) f	shape of the head
Kopfgefäß(e) n	rhyton
Kopfhaltung(en) f	position of the head
Kopfleiste(n) f	decoration on the upper page margin
Kopfputz m	headdress
Kopfreliquiar(e) n	head-shaped reliquary
Kopfschmuck m	headdress, head decoration
Kopfsteinpflaster (−) n	cobblestone paving
Kopfstütze(n) f	head rest, head support
Kopie(n) f	copy
kopieren	to copy
Kopist(en) m	copyist
koptisch	Coptic
Koralle(n) f	coral
Koran m	Koran
Koranillustration(en) f	Koran illustration
Korb (Körbe) m	basket
Korbbogen (−, -bögen) m	basket arch, anse de panier
Korbkapitell(e) n	basket capital
Kore(n) f	kore, statue of a maiden
korinthisch	Corinthian
korinthische Ordnung f	Corinthian order
körnig	grainy
Koroplastik(en) f	clay or terra cotta sculpture
Koroplastiker (−) m	coroplast, sculptor working with clay or terracotta
Körper (−) m	body
Körperachse(n) f	body axis
Körperdrehung(en) f	turning or twisting of the body

Körperfarbe(n) *f*	1. body or opaque color, opaque paint 2. color with substance or body, as opposed to light-produced color
Körperform(en) *f*	shape of the body
körperhaft	corporeal, having body
Körperhaftigkeit *f*	corporeality
Körperhaltung(en) *f*	position of the body
körperlich	corporeal, bodily
Körperlichkeit(en) *f*	corporeality
Körperlinie(n) *f*	body line
Körperverhältnis(se) *n*	body proportion
Korporale (−) *n*	corporal, altar cloth
Korridor(e) *m*	corridor
Koschenille *f*	cochineal
Kosmokrator *m*	Christ, Ruler of the World
kostbar	precious
Kostbarkeit(en) *f*	precious object
Kouros (Kouren) *m* *also* Kuros	kouros
Krabbe(n) *f*	crocket
Krage(n) *f*	console, corbel, bracket
Kragen (−) *m*	collar
Kraggesims(e) *n*	weightbearing, protruding sill or cornice
Kraggewölbe (−) *n*	pseudodome, corbelled dome, beehive dome
Kraggewölbetechnik *f*	corbelling
Kragkuppel(n) *f*	corbelled dome, beehive dome
Kragstein(e) *m*	corbel
Kragstück(e) *n*	corbel, ancon
Kragsturzbogen (−, -bögen) *m*	shouldered arch
Kragstütze(n) *f*	bracket support
Krakalee(n) *n* *also* Craquelée *m, n*	1. craquelure *painting* 2. crackle, crazing *porcelain*
Krakelüre *f*	craquelure
Kranz (Kränze) *m*	wreath, garland

Kranzgesims(e) n	cornice
Kranzleiste(n) f	dripstone, weather moulding, cornice
Krapp m	madder
krappfarben	madder-colored
Krapplack m	madder lake
Krappstoff m	alizarin
Krater(e, −) m	krater
Kratzeisen (−) n	scraping tool
kratzen	to scrape, to scratch
Kratzputz m	sgraffito
Kratzputztechnik f	sgraffito (technique)
Krayon(s) m	crayon
Krayonmanier f	crayon manner, chalk manner
Krayonstich(e) m	(engraving in) crayon manner
Krebs m	Cancer
Kredenz(en) f	sideboard, buffet
Kreide f	chalk
Kreidegrund m	gesso (ground), chalk ground
Kreidelithographie(n) f	lithograph done with lithographic crayon
Kreidemanier f	crayon manner, chalk manner
Kreidestift(e) m	chalk, chalk crayon
Kreidestrich(e) m	chalk stroke
Kreidezeichnung(en) f	chalk, chalk drawing
Kreis(e) m	circle
Kreisabschnitt(e) m	segment of a circle, foil
Kreisfenster (−) n	circular window
kreisförmig	circular
kreisrund	circular
Kreml m	kremlin, Russian fortress
Kremserweiß n	Cremnitz white, white lead
Krepidoma(s) n	crepidoma
Krepis (−) f	crepidoma
Kreta	Crete
kretisch	Cretan
Kreuz(e) n	cross

Kreuz, griechisches –	Greek cross
Kreuz, lateinisches –	Latin cross
Kreuz, päpstliches –	papal cross
Kreuzabnahme, die –	the Descent from the Cross, the Deposition of Christ
Kreuzaltar (-altäre) *m*	lay altar
Kreuzarm(e) *m*	1. arm of the cross 2. transept arm
Kreuzauffindung, die –	the Discovery of the True Cross
Kreuzaufrichtung, die –	the Raising of the Cross
Kreuzblume(n) *f*	finial
Kreuzblumenkamm (-kämme) *m*	moulding decorated with finials
Kreuzbogenfries(e) *m*	decorative frieze consisting of two overlapping rows of round arches
Kreuzdornbeere(n) *f*	buckthorn berry
Kreuzfahne(n) *f*	banner of the cross
Kreuzfahrergotik *f*	Gothic-style (buildings) in Asia Minor
Kreuzform(en) *f*	cross shape
kreuzförmig	cross-shaped, cruciform
Kreuzgang (-gänge) *m*	cloister
Kreuzgewölbe (–) *n*	groin vault
Kreuzgratgewölbe (–) *n*	groin vault
Kreuzigung, die –	the Crucifixion
Kreuzigungsgruppe(n) *f*	crucifixion group
Kreuzigungsszene(n) *f*	crucifixion scene
Kreuzkirche(n) *f*	cruciform church
Kreuzkuppelkirche(n) *f*	cruciform plan church with dome(s)
Kreuzlage(n) *f*	cross-hatching
Kreuznimbus(se) *m*	cruciform nimbus
Kreuzrippengewölbe (–) *n*	rib vault, sail vault
Kreuzschiff(e) *n*	transept
Kreuzschraffierung(en) *f*	cross-hatching
Kreuzschraffur(en) *f*	cross-hatching

Kreuztragung Christi, die —	the Bearing of the Cross
Kreuzweg, der —	the Procession to Calvary
Kreuzwegstation(en) *f*	the Stations of the Cross
Kriechblume(n) *f*	crocket
Krieger (–) *m*	warrior
Kriegsbeil(e) *n*	battleaxe
Krippe(n) *f*	crèche, crib, nativity scene
Kristall(e) *n*	crystal
Kristallglas *n*	flint glass
Kritik(en) *f*	1. criticism 2. review, critique
Kritiker (–) *m*	critic
Kromlech(e, s) *m* *also* Cromlech	cromlech
Krone(n) *f*	crown
Kronleuchter (–) *m*	chandelier
Krönung(en) *f*	coronation
Krönungsmantel (-mäntel) *m*	coronation cloak
Krönungsornat(e) *m*	coronation vestments
Krönungsschmuck *m*	coronation jewels, coronation jewelry
kröpfen	to lead (a pattern) around a building element which projects from the wall plane
Kröseleisen (–) *n*	hot iron used for cutting and smoothing stained glass before the development of diamond cutters
Krückenkreuz(e) *n*	potent cross
Krug (Krüge) *m*	jug, pitcher
krumm	crooked, curved, bent
Krümme(n) *f*	1. curvature 2. crook of bishop's crosier
krümmen	to curve, to bend, to twist, to warp
Krummstab (-stäbe) *m*	crosier, pastoral staff

Krümmung(en) *f*	curvature
Kruzifix(e) *n*	crucifix
Krypta (Krypten) *f*	crypt
kubisch	cubicular
Kubismus *m*	Cubism
Kubist(en) *m*	Cubist
Kubus (–, Kuben) *m*	cube
Kubusbau(ten) *m*	cubicular building
Küchenstück(e) *n*	painting of a kitchen scene
kufische Schrift *f*	Kufic lettering
Kugel(n) *f*	ball, globe, sphere
Kugelbau(ten) *m*	spherical building
kugelförmig	spherical
Kühlofen (-öfen) *m*	leer; glass annealing oven
Kulisse(n) *f*	stage set, scenery, backdrop
Kulissenmaler (–) *m*	set painter, scene painter
Kult(e) *m*	cult
Kultbau(ten) *m*	cult building, ceremonial building
Kultbild(er) *n*	cult image, sacred picture
kultisch	cult, cult-oriented, sacred
Kultraum (-räume) *m*	cult room, room for worship or religious ceremonies
Kultscheibe(n) *f*	(Bronze Age) cult disc, sun disc
Kultstätte(n) *f*	cult site, ceremonial site, sacred site
Kultur(en) *f*	culture, civilisation
kulturell	cultural
Kulturleistung(en) *f*	cultural achievement
kuneiform	cuneiform, wedge-shaped
Kunst (Künste) *f*	1. art 2. skill
Kunst, angewandte –	applied arts
Kunst, bildende –	fine arts, depictive art, plastic or visual arts
Kunst und Gewerbe	arts and crafts
Kunstakademie(n) *f*	art academy

Kunstauffassung(en) *f*	concept of art
Kunstauktion(en) *f*	art auction
Kunstausstellung(en) *f*	art exhibition
Kunstbetrieb(e) *m*	art trade, art world
Kunstbewegung(en) *f*	art movement
Kunstdenkmal (-mäler) *n*	art monument
Kunstdeutung *f*	art interpretation
Künstelei(en) *f*	artificiality, affectedness
Kunstentwicklung(en) *f*	artistic development, development of art
Kunsterzeugnis(se) *n*	art product, artefact
Kunsterziehung *f*	art education
Kunstfälscher (–) *m*	(art) forger, counterfeiter
Kunstfälschung(en) *f*	art forgery, fake
Kunstfertigkeit(en) *f*	artistic skill, artistic dexterity, workmanship
Kunstform(en) *f*	art form
Kunstfreund(e) *m*	art lover
Kunstgattung(en) *f*	art form, kind of art
Kunstgegenstand (-stände) *m*	art object
Kunstgeschichte *f*	art history, history of art
kunstgeschichtlich	art historical
Kunstgewerbe (–) *n*	crafts, handicrafts
Kunstgewerbemuseum (-museen) *n*	crafts museum
Kunstgewerbeschule(n) *f*	school of applied arts (or crafts)
kunstgewerblich	handicraft, in reference to crafts
Kunsthandel *m*	art trade, art market
Kunsthändler (–) *m*	art dealer
Kunsthandwerk *n*	crafts, applied arts
Kunsthandwerker (–) *m*	craftsman, artisan
Kunstharz *n*	synthetic resin
Kunstharzdispersionsfarbe(n) *f*	color dispersed in synthetic resin
Kunsthistoriker (–) *m*	art historian

Kunsthochschule(n) *f*	art academy
Kunstkammer(n) *f*	collection of cabinet pieces (both natural phenomena and art works)
Kunstkenner (–) *m*	art connoisseur
Kunstkreide *f*	artificial chalk, man-made chalk
Kunstkritik(en) *f*	art criticism
Kunstkritiker (–) *m*	art critic
Künstler (–) *m*	artist
Künstlergemeinschaft(en) *f*	artist's association
Künstlerinschrift(en) *f*	artist's signature
künstlerisch	artistic
Künstlerlexikon (-lexiken) *n*	encyclopedia (or dictionary) of artists
Künstlerlithographie(n) *f*	autolithography
Künstlermonogramm(e) *n*	artist's signature or initials
Künstlermonographie(n) *f*	monograph of an artist
Künstlersignatur(en) *f*	artist's signature
Künstlerwerkstätte(n) *f*	art workshop, atelier, studio
künstlich	artificial
Kunstliebhaber (–) *m*	art lover
Kunstmarkt *m*	art trade, art market
Kunstphilosophie *f*	philosophy of art
Kunstrichtung(en) *f*	artistic style, art movement
Kunstsachverständige(n) *f, m*	art expert
Kunstsammler (–) *m*	(art) collector
Kunstsammlung(en) *f*	art collection
Kunstschatz (-schätze) *m*	art treasure
kunstsinnig	art-minded, interested in art
Kunststein(e) *m*	1. artificial building stone made of concrete 2. imitation stone
Kunststil(e) *m*	art style
Kunststoff(e) *m*	synthetic, plastic, man-made material
Kunststoffschaum *m*	foamed plastic
Kunstversteigerung(en) *f*	art auction

kunstvoll	artistic, skillful
Kunstwerk(e) *n*	art work, work of art
Kunstzeitschrift(en) *f*	art magazine, art journal
Kunstzentrum (-zentren) *n*	art center
Kupfer *n*	copper
Kupferätzung(en) *f*	copper etching
Kupferblech *n*	copper sheet(ing)
kupferbraun	copper-colored, copper brown
Kupferdruck(e) *m*	print (from a copper plate)
Kupfergefäß(e) *n*	copper vessel
Kupfermünze(n) *f*	copper coin
Kupferplatte(n) *f*	copper plate
kupferrot	copper-colored, copper red
Kupferstecher (—) *m*	copper engraver
Kupferstechkunst *f*	(art of) copper engraving
Kupferstich(e) *m*	copper engraving
Kupferstichkabinett(e) *n*	small collection of copper engravings
Kupferzeit *f*	Copper Age, Chalcolithic
Kuppa(e) *f* *also* Cuppa	bowl (of a chalice or goblet)
Kuppel(n) *f*	dome, cupola
Kuppelbau(ten) *m*	domed building, dome construction
Kuppeldach (-dächer) *n*	dome(d) roof
Kuppelgrab (-gräber) *n*	tholos tomb, passage grave
Kuppelhaut *f*	dome covering
Kuppelmalerei *f*	dome painting
Kuppelmosaik(en) *n*	dome mosaic
Kuppelraum (-räume) *m*	room or space covered by a dome
Kuppelreliquiar(e) *n*	reliquary in the shape of a domed building
kuppelüberdeckt	covered with a dome
Kuppelzwickel (—) *m*	(dome) pendentive
Kurgan(e) *m*	kurgan grave
Kurkumagelb *n*	turmeric dyestuff

Kuros (Kuren, Kuroi) *m* *also* Kouros	kouros
kursiv	cursive
Kursivschrift *f*	italics
Kurvatur(en) *f*	curvature
Kurve(n) *f*	curve
Kurvenlineal(e) *n*	French curve, drawing curve
kurz	short
Kußtafel(n) *f*	osculatorium, peace-board, liturgical object to be kissed
Küstenlandschaft(en) *f*	costal landscape
Kustodia (Kustodien) *f* *also* Custodia	pyx or other container for storing the Host
Kustos (Kustoden) *m*	(museum) curator
Kutsche(n) *f*	coach
Kutschenlack(e) *m*	coach varnish
Kyathos (—) *m* *also* Zyathos	kiathos
kyklopisches Mauerwerk *n* *also* zyklopisches Mauerwerk	cyclopean masonry
Kylix *f*	kylix
Kyma(s) *n*	cyma
Kymation (Kymatien) *n*	cyma, profiled moulding with leaf ornamentation
Kymation, dorisches —	concave moulding, scotia profile
Kymation, ionisches —	egg and dart
Kymation, lesbisches —	tongue and dart
kypromykenisch	Cypro-Mycenean
kyrillisch	Cyrillic
Kyriotissa *f*	(Byzantine) standing Madonna pressing the Child to her breast
Labarum *n*	labarum
Labyrinth(e) *n*	labyrinth, maze
Lächeln, archaisches — *n*	archaic smile

Lack(e) *m*	1. lacquer, varnish
	2. lake (pigment)
Lackfarbstoff(e) *m*	lake (pigment)
lackieren	to varnish, to lacquer
lackiert	varnished, lacquered, painted
Lackkunst *f*	(art of making) lacquerware
Lackmus *n*	turnsole dyestuff
Lackschale(n) *f*	lacquerware bowl
Lacküberzug (-züge) *m*	lacquer or varnish coating
Lackware(n) *f*	lacquerware
Laconicum *n*	steam room in the Thermae
Lageplan (-pläne) *m*	site plan
Lagerfläche(n) *f*	supporting surface
Laibung(en) *f*	1. jamb
also Leibung	2. intrados
	3. reveal
Laibungsstatue(n) *f*	jamb statue, column figure
Laienaltar (-altäre) *m*	lay altar, rood altar
Laienmaler (−) *m*	naive painter, amateur painter
lakonisch	Laconian
Lambrequin(s) *m*	lambrequin
Lambris (−) *m*	(wall) paneling
Lamelle(n) *f*	slat, louvre
laminieren	to laminate
Lamm (Lämmer) *n*	lamb
Lampe(n) *f*	lamp
Lampenruß *m*	lampblack
Lampenschwarz *n*	lampblack
Land Art *f*	land art
Landhaus (-häuser) *n*	country house
Landschaft(en) *f*	landscape
Landschaft, heroische −	heroic landscape
Landschaft, ideale −	ideal landscape
Landschafter (−) *m*	landscape painter
Landschaftsdarstellung(en) *f*	depiction of landscape
Landschaftsgarten (-gärten) *m*	landscaped garden

Landschaftskulisse(n) *f*	landscape background, landscape setting
Landschaftsmaler (−) *m*	landscape painter
Landschaftsmalerei *f*	landscape painting
Landschaftstypus (-typen) *m*	type of landscape
lang	long
Langbau(ten) *m*	longitudinal-plan building; building with emphasis on the longitudinal axis
Langbett(en) *n*	hunebed
Länge(n) *f*	length
Langhalsvase(n) *f*	long-necked vase
Langhaus (-häuser) *n*	nave and side aisles
langobardisch	Lombardic
langobardische Kunst *f*	Lombardic art
langrechteckig	oblong
Längsachse(n) *f*	longitudinal axis
Längsbewegung(en) *f*	longitudinal movement
Langschiff(e) *n*	nave
Längsfuge(n) *f*	longitudinal joint
Längsholz *n*	wood cut along the grain
längsrechteckig	oblong
Längsschnitt(e) *m*	longitudinal section
Längsträger (−) *m*	main girder
Lanze(n) *f*	lance, spear
Lanzenspitze(n) *f*	lancehead
Lanzettbogen (−, -bögen) *m*	lancet arch
Lanzettfenster (−) *n*	lancet window
Laokoon	Laocoön
Lapislazuli *m*	lapis lazuli
lappenartig	ragged
Lärche *f*	larchwood
lasieren	to glaze, to apply a transparent coating
Laster, Tugenden und −	Virtues and Vices

Lästrygonen *pl*	Laestrigonians
Lasur(en) *f*	glaze *painting*
Lasurblau *n*	ultramarine blue
Lasurfarbe(n) *f*	transparent paint, transparent color
Lasurgrund *m*	glaze(d) ground
Lasurstein(e) *m*	lapis lazuli
Lasurstickerei(en) *f*	silk embroidery done on a gold background
Latein *n*	Latin
lateinisch	Latin
lateinisches Kreuz *n*	Latin cross
Latène-Zeit *f*	La Tène period
latènezeitlich	La Tène, of the La Tène period
Laterne(n) *f*	lantern
Latex *m*	latex
Latte(n) *f*	slat, thin board
Laub *n*	foliage, greenery
Laube(n) *f*	1. arcade 2. loggia 3. arbor
Laubengang (-gänge) *m*	covered walk, pergola, arcade
Laubfries(e) *m*	vine scroll pattern
Laubgewinde (–) *n*	garland
Laubverzierung(en) *f*	leaf work, foliage ornamentation
Laubwerk(e) *n*	leaf work, foliage
laufender Hund *m*	running dog, Vitruvian scroll, wave meander
Läufer (–) *m*	stretcher *architecture*
Laufgang (-gänge) *m*	passageway, walkway, gallery
Laurentius, der hl. –	St. Lawrence
Lavendelöl *n*	oil of lavender
lavieren	to wash *painting*
Lavieren (–) *n*	wash
lavierte Federzeichnung(en) *f*	wash drawing, pen-and-wash drawing
Lavismanier *f*	aquatint
lebendig	lively, active

Lebendigkeit *f*	liveliness
Lebensbaum *m*	Tree of Life
Lebensbrunnen *m*	fountain of life, "fons vitae"
lebensgroß	life-size
Leder *n*	leather
lederhart	leather-hard
Ledermosaik(en) *n*	decoration made of several pieces of leather, especially in bookbinding
ledern	(of) leather
Lederpolster (–) *n*	leather cushion used while engraving
Lederschnitt *m*	decorative carving in leather
Legende(n) *f*	1. legend 2. inscription
legieren	to alloy
Legierung(en) *f*	alloy
Lehm *m*	clay
Lehmputztechnik *f*	technique of wall painting done on a clay coating
Lehmverband *m*	mud bond
Lehmziegel (–) *m*	clay brick, mud brick, adobe brick
Lehmziegelbau(ten) *m*	mud brick construction, mud brick building, adobe construction
Lehmziegelmauer(n) *f*	mud brick wall, clay brick wall
Lehmziegelwand (-wände) *f*	mud brick wall, clay brick wall
Lehne(n) *f*	arm rest, back rest
Lehnstuhl (-stühle) *m*	chair with a back
Lehrgerüst(e) *n*	centering; support for holding an arch during construction
Leib(er) *m*	body
leiblich	corporeal, bodily
Leibung(en) *f* *also* Laibung	1. jamb 2. intrados 3. reveal
Leichenbrandurne(n) *f*	cinerary urn
Leichnam(e) *m*	corpse

leicht	light, light weight
Leichtbau(ten) *m*	construction with light materials
Leichtbauplatte(n) *f*	building slab of especially light material, especially pumice, foam, etc.
Leichtbauweise(n) *f*	(manner of) construction with light materials
Leichtbeton *m*	light concrete
Leichtigkeit *f*	ease, effortlessness
Leidenschaft(en) *f*	passion
leidenschaftlich	passionate
Leidensgeschichte Christi, die —	the Passion
Leidenswerkzeuge Christi, die —	Instruments of the Passion (e. g. lance, nails, switch, etc.)
Leihgabe(n) *f*	loan, loaned article
Leim(e) *m*	1. glue 2. size
Leimaufstrich(e) *m*	coat of glue size
leimen	to glue, to coat with glue or size
Leimfarbe(n) *f*	calcimine (paint), distemper
Leimfarbenmalerei(en) *f*	(painting with) calcimine paint, distemper
Leimschablone(n) *f*	glue-cutout, block-out stencil
Leimtemperafarbe(n) *f*	tempera paint (with glue binder)
Leimwasser *n*	glue solution
leinen	(of) linen
Leinen *n*	linen
Leinen, Römisches —	Roman linen canvas
Leinenband *m*	linen bookbinding
Leinöl *n*	linseed oil
Leinölfirnis mit Terpentin *m*	megilp
Leinwand *f*	1. canvas 2. screen
Leinwand, gefärbte und grundierte —	stained canvas
Leinwand, grundierte —	primed canvas

Leinwandkorn *n*	canvas texture
Leiste(n) *f*	1. moulding
	2. margin, margin decoration
Leitbild(er) *n*	ideal
Lektionar(e, ien) *n*	1. lectionary
also Lektionarium (Lektionarien)	2. lectern
Lekythos (Lekythen) *f*	lecythus
Lendentuch (-tücher) *n*	loincloth
lesbisches Kymation *n*	tongue and dart
Lesene(n) *f*	lesene, pilaster-strip
Lesepult(e) *n*	lectern
Letter(n) *f*	letter, character, type
Letterart(en) *f*	typeface
Lettner (–) *m*	1. rood screen, chancel screen, jubé
	2. lectern
Lettneraltar (-altäre) *m*	rood altar
leuchten	to shine, to gleam, to sparkle
leuchtend	luminous, radiant, glistening, brilliant
Leuchter (–) *m*	chandelier, candelabrum, candle stand
Leuchterweibchen (–) *n*	carved chandelier with female figure and antlers
Leuchtfarbe(n) *f*	luminous paint
Leuchtkraft *f*	luminosity, luminous power, radiant power
Levallois-Technik *f*	Levallois technique
Levitenstuhl (-stühle) *m*	sedilia
Lezithin *n*	lecithin
Licht(er) *n*	1. light
	2. light, area of high value
Lichtbeugung *f*	diffraction of light
Lichtbogenschweißung *f*	arc welding
Lichtbrechung(en) *f*	light refraction
Lichtdruck(e) *m*	phototypic process, phototype
lichtecht	lightfast, fast

Lichtechtheit *f*	lightfastness
Lichteffekt(e) *m*	light effect
Lichteinfall *m*	light direction, manner in which the light falls
lichtempfindlich	sensitive to light
Lichtführung *f*	direction of the light
Lichtgaden (−) *m*	clerestory
Lichtquelle(n) *f*	light source
Lichtreflex(e) *m*	light reflection
Lichtschacht (-schächte) *m*	light shaft
Lichtstrahl(en) *m*	ray of light
Lichtwirkung(en) *f*	light effect
Lichtzufuhr *f*	admission of light
lieblich	pretty, lovely
Lieblichkeit *f*	prettiness, loveliness
liegen	1. to lie, to recline 2. to be located
liegend	lying, reclining
lila	lilac, purple
Lilie(n) *f*	lily, fleur-di-lis
Limbus (Limbi) *m*	limbo, region bordering on Hell
Limosiner Email *n*	Limoges enamel
Lindenholz *n*	linden wood
Lineal(e) *n*	ruler, straightedge
Lineament(e) *n*	lineament
linear	linear
Linear-A-Schrift *f*	Linear A script
Linear-B-Schrift *f*	Linear B script
Linearbandkeramik *f*	linear Bandkeramik pottery
Linearornamentik *f*	linear ornamentation, geometric ornamentation
Linearperspektive *f*	linear perspective
Linearzeichnung(en) *f*	line drawing, outline
Linie(n) *f*	line
Linienführung *f*	draftsmanship, flow of the line
Liniengefüge (−) *n*	linear structure
Linienordnung(en) *f*	arrangement of lines

Linienstich(e) m	line engraving
Linienverlauf m	flow of the line(s)
Linienwert m	value of the line(s)
Linkswendung(en) f	turning (or twisting) to the left
Linoleumschnitt(e) m	linocut, linoleum cut
Linolplatte(n) f	linoleum plate, linoleum block
Linolschnitt(e) m	linocut, linoleum cut
linsenförmig	lenticular
Lippe(n) f	lip
Lisene(n) f	lesene, pilaster-strip
Lithofolge(n) f	series of lithographs
Lithograph(en) m	lithographer
Lithographie(n) f	lithography, lithograph
lithographieren	to lithograph
Lithographierpapier n	lithograph(ic) paper
lithographisch	lithographic
Lithokreide(n) f	lithographic crayon
Lithophanie(n) f	lithophane
Litho-Plakat(e) n	lithograph poster
Lithopone f *also* Lithophon	lithophone
Lithotusche f	tusche, lithographic ink
Liturgie(n) f	liturgy
liturgisch	liturgical
liturgische Farben pl	colors of the ecclesiastical paraments
Loch (Löcher) n	hole
Lochkamera(s) f	camera obscura
Lochstab (-stäbe) m	bâton de commandement, "baton of command"
Locke(n) f	lock, curl
locker	loose
Loculusgrab (-gräber) n	loculus
Loggia (Loggien) f	1. loggia 2. arcaded walk 3. non-protruding balcony
Lokalfarbe(n) f	local color

lokalisieren	to establish the place of origin
Lokalisierung *f*	location, placing, place of origin
lombardisches Bandgeflecht *n*	Lombard band decoration
Lorbeer *m*	laurel
Lorbeerkranz (-kränze) *m*	laurel wreath
lösen	to dissolve
Lösung(en) *f*	solution
Lösungsmittel (−) *n*	(paint) medium
Lot *n*	solder
löten	to solder
Lotos *m*	lotus
Lotosblatt (-blätter) *n*	lotus leaf
Lotosblüte(n) *f*	lotus flower
Lotosbündelsäule(n) *f*	bundled lotus column
Lotosknospe(n) *f*	lotus bud
Loutrophoros (Loutrophoroi) *m* *also* Lutrophorus	loutrophorus
Löwe(n) *m*	1. lion 2. Leo *zodiac*
Löwengrube, Daniel in der −	Daniel in the Lions' Den
Löwenkopf (-köpfe) *m*	lion's head
Löwentor *n*	Lion Gate (Mycenae)
Luftaufnahme(n) *f*	aerial photograph
Lufteinwirkung *f*	effect, action or influence of air
Luftkanal (-kanäle) *m*	vent, riser
Luftperspektive *f*	aerial perspective
Luftwirkung *f*	effect of air
Luftziegel (−) *m*	mud brick, unbaked brick
Lukarne(n) *f*	dormer window, lucarne
Lukas, der hl. −	St. Luke
Lukasbild(er) *n*	depiction of the Madonna or Christ, allegedly painted by St. Luke
Lukasbrüder *pl* *also* Lukasbrüderschaft	Nazarenes

Lukasbund *m*	Nazarenes
Lukasgilde(n) *f*	painters' guild
Lukasmadonna (-madonnen) *f*	St. Luke painting the Virgin (and Child)
Luke(n) *f*	small window
Luminarium (Luminarien) *n*	luminarium, lucernarium; light and air shaft in catacomb
Lünette(n) *f*	lunette
Lünettengemälde (–) *n*	lunette fresco, lunette painting
Lunula (e, Lunulen) *f*	1. lunette, moon-shaped Host receptacle in monstrance 2. lunula, moon-shaped Bronze Age ornament
Lüster (–) *m*	1. chandelier 2. luster
Lüsterkeramik *f*	lusterware
Lüsterschale(n) *f*	lusterware bowl
Lüsterware(n) *f*	lusterware
Lustschloß (-schlösser) *n*	pleasure palace
Luteolin *n*	luteolin dye
Lutrophorus (Lutrophoren) *m* also Loutrophoros	loutrophorus
Luzia, die hl. –	St. Lucy
Lwd. (= Leinwand)	canvas
lyraförmig	lyre-shaped
Mäander (–) *m*	fret, meander, Greek key
Mäandermuster (–) *n*	meander pattern
Macht (Mächte) *f*	power, force
Machwerk(e) *n*	inferior or clumsy work
Mädchen (–) *n*	girl, maiden
Mädchenakt(e) *m*	nude girl
Mädchenfigur(en) *f*	figure of a girl
mädchenhaft	girl-like
Madonna (Madonnen) *f*	Madonna

Madonna, das Kind anbetend	Madonna Worshiping the Child
Madonna des Sieges, die —	Santa Maria della Vittoria, Madonna of Victory
Madonna im Rosenhag	Virgin in the Rose Bower
Madonna mit dem Goldfink	Madonna of the Goldfinch
Madonna mit Kind	the Virgin and Child
Madonnenbild(er) *n*	picture of the Virgin, Madonna
madonnenhaft	madonna-like
Maestà (—) *f*	maestà, majesty
Magazin(e) *n*	store room
Magazinraum (-räume) *m*	store room
Magdalénien *n*	Magdalenian (culture)
mager	lean
magischer Realismus *m*	magic realism
Maglemosekultur *f*	Maglemosian culture
Mahagoni *n*	mahagony
Mahnbild(er) *n*	admonitory picture
Majestas Domini	Christ maestà
Majolika (Majoliken) *f*	majolica, maiolica
Majuskel(n) *f*	majuscle; capital letter
Makartbukett(e) *n*	bouquet of dried flowers, reeds, etc., as room decoration
makedonisch *also* mazedonisch	Macedonian
Makel (—) *m*	flaw, blemish, spot, stain
makellos	flawless, unblemished, perfect
Makkaroni *pl*	macaroni finger drawings
Malachit *m*	malachite
Malbedarf *m*	painting supplies
malen	to paint
Maler (—) *m*	painter
Malerbuch *n*	(Mt. Athos) painter's manual
Malerei(en) *f*	1. (art of) painting 2. painted picture, painting
Maleremail(s) *n*	Limoges enamel

Malerhandbuch (-bücher) *n*	painter's manual, painter's reference book
Malerhandbuch vom Berg Athos, das —	Mt. Athos painter's manual
malerisch	1. painterly 2. picturesque
Malerradierer (—) *m*	painter-etcher, peintre-graveur
Malerstecher (—) *m*	painter-etcher, peintre-graveur
Malerzunft (-zünfte) *f*	painters' guild
Malfarbe(n) *f*	paint, paint color
Malgrund *m*	support, surface which is painted on
Malkunst (-künste) *f*	(art of) painting
Malmesser (—) *n*	painting knife
Malpinsel (—) *m*	(painter's) brush
Malschicht(en) *f*	paint(ed) layer, layer to be painted on
Malschicht, grobe —	sand coat, sand finish
Malschlicker *m*	slip; fine-grained, runny clay
Malstock (-stöcke) *m*	mahlstick, maulstick
Maltechnik(en) *f*	painting technique
Malteserkreuz *n*	Maltese cross
Malvorgang (-gänge) *m*	process of painting, painting procedure
Malweise(n) *f*	manner of painting, painting style
Malwerk(e) *n*	painting
Mänade(n) *f*	mænad
mandelförmig	almond-shaped
Mandorla (Mandorlen) *f*	mandorla, vesica
Manganbraun *n*	manganese brown, manganese black
Manier *f*	manner, style
manieriert	mannered
Manierismus *m*	Mannerism
Manierist(en) *m*	Mannerist
Manifest(e) *n*	manifesto
Manipel(n) *f*	maniple

Mann (Männer) *m*	1. man 2. husband
Männerseite *f*	"men's side", south side of a church
männlich	male, masculine
Mansarde(n) *f*	1. mansard roof 2. room under a mansard roof
Mansardendach (-dächer) *n*	mansard roof
Manschette(n) *f*	cuff
Mantel (Mäntel) *m*	1. coat, cloak, mantle 2. investment *casting*
manueller Bilddruck(e) *m*	original print, hand screen; print pulled by the artist himself
Manuskript(e) *n*	manuscript
Mappe(n) *f*	album, portfolio
Mappenfolge(n) *f*	portfolio
Mappenwerk(e) *n*	portfolio
Märchen (—) *n*	fairy tale
märchenhaft	fabulous, magical
Marginale (Marginalien) *f*	marginal note or illustration
Maria	Mary, the Virgin
Maria auf der Mondsichel	Mary Queen of Heaven, Virgin on the Cresent, Immaculate Mary, the Immaculate Conception
Mariä Himmelfahrt	Assumption of the Virgin
Maria mit Kind	the Virgin and Child
Mariä Tempelgang	Presentation of the Virgin
marianische Symbole *pl*	symbols of the Virgin
Marien, die Drei — am Grabe	the (Three) Marys at the Tomb
Marienbild(er) *n*	(depiction of the) madonna
Marienbildtyp(en) *m*	type of madonna depiction
Marienklage, die —	Mourning of Mary
Marienkrönung, die —	Coronation of the Virgin
Marienkult *m*	veneration of the Virgin, Mariolatry
Marienleben, das —	(cycle of pictures depicting) the Life of the Virgin

Marientod, der —	Dormition (or Death) of the Virgin
marineblau	navy blue, dark blue
Marinemalerei *f*	marine painting
Marinemaler (—) *m*	marine painter
Marke(n) *f*	trademark
Marketerie *f*	marquetry
Markus, der hl. —	St. Mark
Marmor(e) *m*	marble
Marmorader(n) *f*	vein in the marble
Marmorart(en) *f*	type of marble
Marmorbildwerk(e) *n*	marble piece, marble statue
marmorieren	to marble, to decorate with a marbled pattern
Marmorierung(en) *f*	marbling
marmorn	(of) marble
Marmorplatte(n) *f*	marble slab, marble plate
Marmorsäule(n) *f*	marble column
Marmorstaub *m*	marble dust
Marmortafel(n) *f*	marble tablet
Marmortrommel(n) *f*	marble drum
Marmorverkleidung(en) *f*	marble facing, marble cladding
Marmorwerk(e) *n*	marble piece, marble work
Marsgelb *n*	Mars yellow
Marterl (—) *n*	roadside cross (usually marking a place of death, especially in the Alpine regions)
martern	to martyr
Martersäule, Christus an der —	Christ at the Pillar (or Column)
Marterwerkzeuge Christi, die —	Instruments of the Passion
Märtyrer (—) *m*	martyr
Märtyrertum *n*	martyrdom
Martyriologium (-logien) *n*	menology, register or calendar of the saints
Martyrium *n*	1. martyrdom 2. martyrium

Maschinenkunst *f*	(Tatlin's) machine art
Maserung(en) *f*	(wood) grain
Maskaron(e) *m*	mascaron
Maske(n) *f*	mask
maskenhaft	mask-like
Maß(e) *n*	measure, dimension, size, extent
Maßangabe(n) *f*	(data on) measurements
Maßeinheit(en) *f*	module, unit of measure
Massenfertigung *f*	mass production
massiv	solid
Massivbau(ten) *m*	building in which the walls are the main supporting element
Massivholz *n*	solid wood
Maßstab (-stäbe) *m*	measure, standard, scale, proportion
Maßverhältnis(se) *n*	proportion
Maßwerk(e) *n*	tracery
Mastaba(s) *f*	mastaba
Mastenbau(ten) *m*	stave construction, stave church
Mastenkirche(n) *f*	stave church
Mastix *m*	mastic
Mastixharz *n*	mastic resin
Material(ien) *n*	material
materialbedingt	determined or limited by the material
Materialbild(er) *n*	picture done with composite media, picture incorporating various materials
Materie(n) *f*	material, matter
materiell	material
Matrize(n) *f*	1. stencil 2. hollow mold, matrix
matt	dull, lustreless, mat(te)
Mattgold *n*	dull, lustreless gold
Matthäus, der hl. –	St. Matthew
Mattmalerei *f*	matte painting technique (on clay vases)
Mattoir(s) *n*	mace-head, mattoir

Mattvergoldung f	mat gilding, unburnished gilding
Mauer(n) f	wall
Mauerabdeckung(en) f	coping
Mauerabsatz (-sätze) m	offset, wall offset, water table
Maueranker (—) m	wall anchor, wall clamp
Mauerarbeit f	masonry
Mauerfläche(n) f	wall surface
Mauerflucht(en) f	plane of a wall
Mauerhut (-hüte) m	coping
Mauerkalk m	mortar
Mauerkappe(n) f	coping
Mauerkrönung(en) f	coping
mauern	to lay bricks
Mauerring(e) m	enclosing wall, circumvallation
Mauerverband (-bände) m	(masonry) bond
Mauervorsprung (-sprünge) m	protruding part of a wall
Mauerwerk n	masonry
Mauerwerk, polygonales —	polygonal masonry
Mauerwerk, zyklopisches —	cyclopean masonry
Mauerzack m	crenel
Maure(n) m	Moor
Maurer (—) m	mason, bricklayer
Maurerkelle(n) f	mason's trowel
Maureske(n) f	arabesque
maurisch	Moorish
Mausoleum (Mausoleen) n	Mausoleum, mausoleum
Mauvein n	mauve; synthetic pigment
Mäzen(e) m	patron
Mäzenatentum n	patronage
Medaille(n) f	coin, medal
Medaillon(s) n	medallion
mediceische Venus f	Medici Aphrodite, Venus de'Medici
Meduse(n) f	Medusa
meeresgrün	sea green
Meernixe(n) f	nereid, sea nymph

Meerwandel, Jesu –	Christ Walking Upon the Water
Megalith(e) m	megalith
Megalithgrab (-gräber) n	megalithic tomb
Megalith-Keramik f	pottery from neolithic period
Megalithkultur(en) f	megalithic culture
Megaron n	megaron
Mehrfarbendruck m	multicolor printing
mehrfarbig	multi-colored, polychrome
mehrschiffig	multiple-aisled
Meißel (–) m	chisel
Meißelarbeit(en) f	chiselling, chisel-work
meißeln	to chisel, to carve, to sculpture with a chisel
Meister (–) m	master
meisterhaft	masterly
meisterlich	masterly
Meisterstück(e) n	masterpiece
Meisterwerk(e) n	masterpiece
Meisterzeichen (–) n	master's mark, maker's mark, stonemason's mark
melische Aphrodite f	Venus de Milo
Memnonskoloss(e) m	statue of Memnon, colossus at Thebes
Menhir(e) m	menhir
Mennig m *also* Mennige f	minium, red lead
Menologion (-logien) n	menology, calendar or register of saints
Mensa (Mensen) f	mensa, table (slab), altar top
Mensagrab (-gräber) n	relics or tomb set into the mensa
Mensch(en) m	human being, person
Menschenbild(er) n	depiction of man
Menschengestalt(en) f	human figure
Menschenopfer (–) n	human sacrifice
Menschensohn, der –	Christ, the Son of Man
menschlich	human, humane
Merkmal(e) n	characteristic

Merkur	Mercury
Merkurstab (-stäbe) m	caduceus
merowingisch	Merovingian
Merz	Merz, a variety of Dadaism
Mesolithikum n	mesolithic period
mesolithisch	mesolithic
Meßbildverfahren n	photographic method of measuring architecture
Meßbuch (-bücher) n	missal
Meßbuchmaler (—) m	illuminator of missals
Messe(n) f	1. mass
	2. trade fair
messen	to measure
Meßgewand (-gewänder) n	chasuble
Messing n	brass
Meßkännchen (—) n	altar cruet
Meßkelch(e) m	chalice
Metall(e) n	metal
Metallbearbeitung(en) f	metalworking
Metallbeschlag (-schläge) m	metal fitting, hardware (on furniture)
Metalldruck(e) m	metal print
Metallfolie(n) f	metal foil
Metallikone(n) f	metal icon
metallisch	metallic
Metalloxyd(e) n	metallic oxide
Metallplastik(en) f	metal sculpture, cast
Metallplatte(n) f	metal plate, metal sheet
Metallrahmen (—) m	metal frame
Metallschnitt(e) m	metal cut, printing plate of soft metal
Metallurgie f	metallurgy
Metallverzierung(en) f	ornamentation of metal
Metallzusatz (-zusätze) m	addition of metal
Methode(n) f	method
Metope(n) f	metope
Mezzanin(e) n	mezzanine, entresol

Mezzotinto(s) *n*	mezzotint
Mieder (−) *n*	bodice, corset or other body-shaping undergarment
Miene(n) *f*	facial expression
Mihrab(s) *m*	mihrab, prayer niche
Mikrolith(e) *m*	microlith
Milchglas *n*	milk glass
milchigweiß	milky white
Milieumalerei *f*	naturalistic depiction of the "proletarian" milieu
Millefioriglas *n*	millefiori glass, mosaic glass
Minar(en) *n*	minaret
Minarett(e) *n*	minaret
Mineralfarbe(n) *f*	mineral pigment
Mineralgrün *n*	mineral green, malachite
Mineralmalerei *f*	mineral painting, stereochromy
Miniator(en) *m*	artist who copied the text of illuminated manuscripts
Miniatur(en) *f*	miniature
Miniaturmalerei(en) *f*	miniature painting, illumination
Minimal Art *f*	minimal art
Minium *n*	minium
Minnesänger (−) *m*	minstrel, troubador
minoisch	Minoan
Minotaurus *m*	Minotaur
Minuskel(n) *f*	minuscule; small letter
minuziös	minute, painstaking
minysche Keramik *f*	Minyan ware
Mischstil(e) *m*	composite style
Mischtechnik(en) *f*	mixed technique
Mischwesen (−) *n*	composite animal, mythical being composed of various animals
Miserikordie(n) *f*	misericord, miserere
Miserikordienbild(er) *n*	Christ with a Crown of Thorns, Man of Sorrows, mater dolorosa
Missal(e) *n* *also* Missale (−)	missal

Mithräum (Mithräen) n	mithraeum, Mithraic temple
Mitra (Mitren) f	miter, miter cap
Mitte f	middle
Mittel (−) n	means, medium, middle
Mittelachse(n) f	middle axis
Mittelalter n	Middle Ages
mittelalterlich	medieval
Mittelbild(er) n	center picture, center panel
Mittelgang (-gänge) m	center aisle
Mittelgrund m	middle distance, middle ground
Mittelmeer n	Mediterranean Sea
Mittelmeerraum m	Mediterranean region
mittelminoisch	Middle Minoan
Mittelpfeiler (−) m	central pillar
Mittelpfosten (−) m	mullion, trumeau
Mittelraum (-räume) m	central chamber, central room, central area
Mittelschiff(e) n	nave
Mittelschiffspfeiler (−) m	nave pillar, nave pier
Mittelschiffstonne(n) f	nave vault, barrel vault over the nave
Mitteltafel(n) f	center panel
Mittelton (-töne) m	middle tone, half-tone
Möbel pl	furniture
Möbelstil(e) m	furniture style
Möbelstück(e) n	piece of furniture
Mobile(s) n	mobile
Mobiliar n	furniture
Möblierung f	furniture
Mode(n) f	fashion, style
Model (−) m	1. module 2. casting mold 3. diameter of a coin 4. pattern 5. relief printing block (for fabric)
Modelbuch (-bücher) n	book of patterns
Modeldruck m	fabric or wallpaper printing with relief-cut blocks

Modell(e) *n*	model
Modellierbock (-böcke) *m*	modeling stand, turntable
modellieren	to model, to shape, to form
modellierend	modeling, shaping, forming
Modellierholz *n*	modelling tool
Modellierstuhl (-stühle) *m*	modeling stand, turntable
Modellierung(en) *f*	modeling
Modellmännchen (—) *n*	painter's wax or clay model for studying proportion and composition
modern	modern
Moderne *f*	1. modern times 2. naturalism
modernisieren	to modernize
modernistisch	modernistic
Modul(n) *m*	1. module 2. diameter of a coin or medal
Modulation(en) *f*	change in color, gradual change from one hue to another
Mohnöl *n*	poppyseed oil, poppy oil
Monasterium (Monasterien) *n*	monastery
Monatsbild(er) *n*	(depiction of) the occupations of the months
Mönch(e) *m*	monk
Mönch- und Nonnendach *n*	roofing comprised of alternate concave and convex tiles
mönchisch	monkish
Mond(e) *m*	moon
Mondlicht *n*	moonlight
Mondscheibe *f*	disc of the moon
Mondschein *m*	moonlight
Mondsichel *f*	crescent moon
Mondsichel, Maria auf der —	Mary Queen of Heaven, Virgin on the Crescent, Immaculate Mary, the Immaculate Conception
Mondstein(e) *m*	moonstone
Mondsymbol(e) *n*	symbol of the moon, lunar symbol

monochrom	monochrome
monochromatisch	monochromatic
Monochromie *f*	monochrome
Monogramm(e) *n*	monogram
Monogrammist(en) *m*	artist known only by his monogram
Monolith(en) *m*	monolith
monolithisch	monolithic
Monopteros (Monopteren) *m*	monopteral temple, monopteral building
Monotype(n) *f* *also* Monotypie	monotype
Monstranz(en) *f*	monstrance
Montage(n) *f*	montage
Monument(e) *n*	monument
monumental	monumental
Monumentalplastik(en) *f*	monumental sculpture
Moreske(n) *f*	arabesque
Morgenland *n*	Orient
Morgenland, die Drei Weisen aus dem —	the Three Magi
morgenländisch	oriental
Mörtel (—) *m*	mortar
Mörtelbau(ten) *m*	mortar construction, mortar building
Mörtelfuge(n) *f*	mortar joint
mörtellos	without mortar
Mörtelmauer(n) *f*	mortar wall
Mosaik(en) *n*	mosaic
Mosaik, Florentiner —	pietra dura
mosaikartig	mosaic-like
Mosaikboden (-böden) *m*	mosaic floor, tessellated floor
Mosaikglas *n*	millefiori glass, mosaic glass
Mosaikzyklus (-zyklen) *m*	cycle of mosaics
Mosaist(en) *m*	mosaicist
Mosaizist(en) *m*	mosaicist
Moschee(n) *f*	mosque
Moscheeampel(n) *f*	mosque lamp

Moses schlägt Wasser aus dem Felsen	Moses and the Rock of Horeb
mostrichfarben	mustard-colored
Motiv(e) *n*	motif
Moulage(n) *f*	moulage
Mound(s) *m*	(North American Indian) mound
Mousterian *n*	Mousterian (industry)
mozarabisch	Mozarabic
Ms.	MS., ms. = manuscript
Mudejarstil *m*	Mudéjar style
Muffel(n) *f*	muffle
Muffelfarbe(n) *f*	muffle color, paint melted onto a glaze in a muffle kiln
Muffelofen (-öfen) *m*	muffle kiln, muffle furnace
Muldengewölbe (−) *n*	type of cloister vault which is longer than it is wide
Multiple(s) *n*	multiple
Mumie(n) *f*	mummy
Mumienbandagen *pl*	mummy wrappings
Mumienbildnis(se) *n*	mummy portrait
Mumienporträt(s) *n*	mummy portrait
Mumiensarkophag(e) *m*	mummy sarcophagus
Mumifikation *f*	mummification
mumifiziert	mummified
Mund (Münder) *m*	mouth
Mundpartie(n) *f*	mouth, mouth section
Münster (−) *n*	cathedral, minster
Münzabdruck(e) *m*	impression of a coin
Münzbecher (−) *m*	goblet or mug decorated with coins
Münzbild(er) *n*	picture on a coin
Münze(n) *f*	coin
münzen	to stamp coins, to mint
Münzkabinett(e) *n*	small coin collection
Münzkunde *f*	numismatics
Muschel(n) *f*	seashell, scallop
Muschelgehäuse (−) *n*	seashell

Muschelgold *n*	shell gold; fine powdered gold for painting, especially on porcelain
Muschelkalk *m*	seashell limestone
Muschelmarmor *m*	shell marble
Muschelnische(n) *f*	seashell-shaped niche
Muschelornament(e) *n*	coquillage
Muschelwerk *n*	coquillage
Muse(n) *f*	Muse
Museum (Museen) *n*	museum
Musikantenbild(er) *n*	picture of a musician
Musivarbeit(en) *f*	mosaic
Musivgold *n*	mosaic gold
musivische Glasmalerei *f*	stained glass painting
Muskel(n) *m*	muscle
Muskelmann (-männer) *m*	écorché
Muskelpartie(n) *f*	muscle, muscle section, muscle part
Muster (—) *n*	pattern, design, model
Musterbild(er) *n*	ideal, paragon
Musterbuch (-bücher) *n*	pattern book; collection of designs, patterns, ornaments, etc.
Musterzeichnung(en) *f*	cartoon
Muttergottes *f*	mother of God
Muttergottesikone(n) *f*	icon of the Madonna (or Virgin)
Muttergottesleuchter (—) *m*	chandelier with Madonna and antlers
Mutterkirche, die —	the Mother Church, mater ecclesia
Mutulus (Mutuli) *m*	mutule
Mütze(n) *f*	cap
Mykene	Mycenæa
mykenisch	Mycenæan
Myrrhe *f*	myrrh
Mythendarstellung(en) *f*	depiction of myth(s)
Mythologie(n) *f*	mythology
mythologisch	mythological
Mythos (Mythen) *m*	myth

Nabelscheibe(n) *f*	bull's eye glass
Nabis *pl*	Nabis
nach der Schrift	proof after letter, after all letters, avec la lettre
nachahmen	to imitate, to copy
Nachahmer (−) *m*	imitator
Nachahmung(en) *f*	imitation, copy(ing)
nachbilden	to copy, to imitate
Nachbildkontrast *m*	phenomenon of negative afterimage
Nachbildung(en) *f*	copy, imitation
nach Chr. (= nach Christus)	A. D.
nachchristlich	A. D.
nachdunkeln	to darken
Nachdunkeln *n*	gradual darkening (of oil colors)
nachfärben	to color or dye again
Nachfolger (−) *m*	successor
Nachimpressionismus *m*	Post-Impressionism
Nachimpressionist(en) *m*	Post-Impressionist
Nachkriegszeit *f*	post-war period
Nachmalerische Abstraktion *f*	Post-Painterly Abstraction
Nachstecher (−) *m*	engraver whose main work is producing engravings after paintings
Nachstich(e) *m*	engraving after a painting
Nachtstück(e) *n*	nocturne, night piece
nachwirken	to continue to have an effect, to continue to influence
Nachwirkung(en) *f*	continuing influence or effect
Nacken (−) *m*	nape of the neck, back of the neck
nackt	nude, bare
Nadel(n) *f*	needle, pin
Nadelholz *n*	soft wood
Nadelstichel (−) *m*	etching needle
Nagel (Nägel) *m*	nail
Nagelkopf *m*	nailhead (pattern)

nageln	to nail
nähen	to sew
nahestehen	to be closely related (to)
Naht (Nähte) *f*	seam, seam line
naiv	naive
Najade(n) *f*	naiad
Namenszug (-züge) *m*	1. signature
	2. monogram
Naos (—) *m*	naos
Napf (Näpfe) *m*	bowl, basin, cup, (paint) saucer
Narthex (Narthizes) *m*	narthex
Narziß	Narcissus
Nase(n) *f*	1. nose
	2. cusp *tracery*
Nasenschmuck *m*	nose ornament, nose ring
Nasenstein(e) *m*	brick with a cusp cut into it
naß in naß	wet-into-wet
Natur *f*	nature
Naturalismus *m*	naturalism
Naturalist(en) *m*	naturalist
Naturbeobachtung(en) *f*	observation or study of nature
Naturdarstellung(en) *f*	depiction of nature
Naturfarbe(n) *f*	natural color
Naturform(en) *f*	natural form, natural shape
naturgetreu	faithful (reproduction), true to nature
natürlich	natural
Naturlicht *n*	natural light
Naturnachahmung(en) *f*	imitation of nature
Naturnähe *f*	closeness to nature
Naturpapier *n*	naturally colored drawing paper
Naturstein(e) *m*	natural stone
Naturtreue *f*	faithfulness to nature
Naturvolk (-völker) *n*	primitive people
naturvölkische Kunst *f*	primitive art
Naturwiedergabe *f*	depiction of nature, reproduction or rendering of nature

Naturwirklichkeit(en) *f*	reality (in nature)
Nautiluspokal(e) *m*	nautilus shell mounted as a goblet
naxischer Marmor *m*	marble from Naxos
Nazarener *pl*	Nazarenes
n. Chr. (= nach Christus)	A. D.
Neapelgelb *n*	Naples yellow
Nebenaltar (-altäre) *m*	side altar
Nebenapsis (-apsiden) *f*	side apse, apsidole
Nebenchor (-chöre) *m*	side chancel, chancel at the end of the side aisle
Nebenchöre, kommunizierende —	chapels (in echelon) which have openings in the walls between them
Nebenkapelle(n) *f*	subsidiary chapel
Nebenkuppel(n) *f*	lateral dome
Nebenmotiv(e) *n*	secondary motif
Nebenraum (-räume) *m*	side room
Nebenrippe(n) *f*	lierne
Nebenstütze(n) *f*	lateral support, auxiliary support
Nebenszene(n) *f*	secondary scene, scene on a side panel
Negativtechnik *f*	negative painting
Neidkopf (-köpfe) *m*	carved animal or demon head attached to a building to repel evil spirits
Nekropole(n) *f*	necropolis
Nelkenöl *n*	oil of cloves
Neo-Dada	Neo-Dada
Neoimpressionismus *m*	neoimpressionism, pointillism
Neoklassizismus *m*	neoclassicism
Neolithikum *n*	neolithic period
neolithisch	neolithic
Neo-Plastizismus *m*	Neo-Plasticism, De Stijl
Nephrit *m*	nephrite
Nereide(n) *f*	nereid
Netz(e) *n*	net
netzartig	net-like, reticular

Netzätzung(en) *f*	autotype
Netzgewölbe (—) *n*	net vault, reticulated vault
Netzglas *n*	glass with threading applied in a net pattern
Netzmittel (—) *n*	wetting agent
Netzrahmen (—) *m*	drawing frame
Netzverband *m*	opus reticulatum
Neubau(ten) *m*	new construction, new building
Neuer Realismus *m*	New Realism, nouveau réalisme
Neuerwerbung(en) *f*	new acquisition
Neugotik *f*	Gothic Revival
Neuklassizismus *m*	neoclassicism
neutestamentarisch	New Testament
Neuzeit *f*	modern times, era from the Renaissance onward
Nickel *n*	nickle
Niederländer (—) *m*	Netherlander, Dutch
niederländisch	Netherlandish
Niederlassung(en) *f*	settlement
Niellierarbeit *f*	niello work
niellieren	to decorate with niello
Niello(s, Niellen, Nielli) *n*	niello
Niet(en) *m* *also* Niete(n) *f*	rivet
nieten	to rivet
Nikopoia *f*	Nikopeia, Byzantine Madonna icon with the Virgin as the Bringer of Victory (enthroned with the Child on her lap)
Niltal *n*	Nile Valley
Nimbus(se, Nimben) *m*	halo, nimbus
Niobiden *pl*	Niobe's children
Niobidengruppe *f*	group with Niobe's fourteen children
Nische(n) *f*	niche
nischenartig	niche-like
Nischensarkophag(e) *m*	sarcophagus in which the scenes are depicted separately, divided by

	columns or pilasters (see: *Friessarkophag*)
Nodus (Nodi) *m*	knop
Nomadenvolk (-völker) *n*	nomads, nomadic people
nonfigurative Kunst *f*	non-objective art, abstract art
Nonnenchor (-chöre) *m*	nuns' gallery
Nonnenkloster (-klöster) *n*	cloister, convent
Non-Objektivismus *m*	Non-Objectivism, Constructivism
Notenkopfware *f*	Bandkeramik with pitted decoration resembling musical notation
Nothelfer (−) *m*	intercessor, the Fourteen Auxiliary Saints
Notname(n) *m*	invented name (for an artist known only by his work)
Novecento *n*	novecento
Nuance(n) *f*	nuance
nuancenreich	rich in nuance, finely nuanced
nuanciert	nuanced
Numismatik *f*	numismatics
Nuppe(n) *f*	knop, decorative knob on glassware or ceramics
Nuppenbecher (−) *m*	straight-sided glass decorated with glass knops
Nurage(n) *f* also Nuraghe	nuraghe
Nußbaum *m*	walnut
Nußöl *n*	(wal)nut oil
Nute(n) *f*	groove
Nymphäum (Nymphäen) *n*	nymphaeum
Nymphenburger Porzellan *n*	Nymphenburg porcelain

Obelisk(en) *m*	obelisk
Oberarm(e) *m*	upper arm
Oberbau(ten) *m*	superstructure
Oberfläche(n) *f*	surface, upper surface

Oberflächen- bearbeitung(en) *f*	working or processing of the surface
Oberflächenstruktur(en) *f*	surface structure
Obergaden (—) *m*	clerestory
Obergeschoß (-geschosse) *n*	upper floor
Obergewand (-gewänder) *n*	over garment
Oberkörper (—) *m*	upper part of the body, torso
Oberlicht *n*	light from above
Oberschenkel (—) *m*	thigh
Objekt(e) *n*	object
objet trouvé *n*	objet trouvé, found object
Obsidian *m*	obsidian
Obsidianklinge(n) *f*	obsidian blade, obsidian knife
Ochsenauge(n) *n*	1. bull's eye glass 2. elliptical roof opening, Œil-de-Bœuf window
Ochsenschädel (—) *m*	bucranium, ox skull
ocker	ochre
Ocker *m,n*	ochre
Odaliske(n) *f*	odalisque
Odeion(s) *n* *also* Odeon	odeum
Odeum (Odeen) *n*	odeum
Œuvre *n* *also* Oeuvre	oeuvre; an artist's entire output
Oeuvrekatalog(e) *m*	oeuvre catalogue
Oeuvreverzeichnis(se) *n*	oeuvre catalogue, catalogue raisonné
Ofen (Öfen) *m*	furnace, oven, kiln
Ofenruß *m*	chimney soot, lampblack
Offenbarung(en) *f*	revelation, manifestation, Revelation, Apocalypse
Offizin(en) *f*	printing shop, press
Öffnung(en) *f*	opening, hole, gap
Offsetdruck(e) *m*	offset print, offset printing
Ohr(en) *n*	ear
Ohrenhenkel (—) *m*	ear-shaped handle

Ohrensessel (—) n	wing chair
Ohrgehänge (—) n	earring, ear pendant
Ohrmuschelstil m	baroque architectural decoration style featuring "gnarled" forms
Ohrring(e) m	earring
Oinochoe(n) f	oenochoe
Oktateuch m	octateuch
Oktogon(e) n	octagon, octagonal building
Okzident m	Occident
Öl(e) n	oil
Öl, ätherisches —	essential oil
Ölberg, der —	Mount of Olives
Ölberggruppe f	Mount of Olives group
Ölbergstunde, die —	Christ on the Mount of Olives, the Agony in the Garden
Ölbild(er) n	oil painting
Ölfarbe(n) f	oil paint
Ölgemälde (—) n	oil painting
Ölgrundleinwand f	canvas prepared with an oil ground
Olifant(e) m	oliphant
olivgrün	olive green
Öllasur(en) f	oil glaze
Ölmalerei f	(art of) oil painting, painting in oils
Ölskizze(n) f	oil sketch
Öltempera(s) f	oil tempera
Ölvergoldung f	mordant gilding
Olymp m	Mt. Olympus
Omphalos m	indent on the bottom of a bowl
Omphalosschale(n) f	bowl with *Omphalos*
Onyx m	onyx
opak	opaque
Opal(e) m	opal
Opaleszenz f	opalescence
Opalglas n	opaline
opalisierend	opalescent
Op-Art f	op art, optical illusion art

Operment *n*	orpiment
Opfer (−) *n*	sacrifice
Opfer, das − Abels	Abel's Sacrifice
Opfer, das − Abrahams	Abraham's Sacrifice of Isaac
Opferaltar (-altäre) *m*	sacrificial altar
Opferbeil(e) *n*	ceremonial axe, sacrificial axe
Opferdiener (−) *m*	attendant at a sacrifice
Opfergabe(n) *f*	sacrificial offering
opfern	to sacrifice
Opferstätte(n) *f*	sacrificial site
Opferstein(e) *m*	sacrificial slab, sacrificial stone
Opfertier(e) *n*	sacrificial animal
Opferung Isaaks, die −	the Sacrifice of Isaac
Opferzeremonie(n) *f*	sacrificial ceremony
Opisthodomos (Opisthodomoi) *m*	opisthodomos
Oppidum (Oppida) *n*	oppidum, Celtic settlement or town
optisch	optical, optically
optische Mischung *f*	additive mixture of colors within the eye
optische Täuschung(en) *f*	optical illusion
Opus (Opera) *n*	work, work of art
Orakel (−) *n*	oracle
orange	orange
orangenfarben	orange, orange-colored
Orangerie(n) *f*	orangery
Orans *m* also Orant	orant, orans
Orantenstellung(en) *f*	orant position (arms crossed over breast)
Oratorium(Oratorien) *n*	oratory, small chapel
Ordensburg(en) *f*	castle of a particular order (e.g. of the Teutonic Order)
Ordnung(en) *f*	order, arrangement
Ordnung, dorische −	Doric order
Ordnung, ionische −	Ionic order

Ordnung, korinthische −	Corinthian order
Ordnung, toskanische −	Tuscan order
Orgel(n) *f*	organ
Orgelbauer (−) *m*	organ builder
Orgelprospekt(e) *m*	organ case, decorative side of organ pipework
orientalisieren	to Orientalize
orientalisierender Stil *m*	Orientalizing style
Orientierung(en) *f*	orientation, placement, position
original	original
Original(e) *n*	original
Originaldruck(e) *m*	original print
Originalgemälde (−) *n*	original painting
Originalgröße *f*	original size, actual size
Originalität(en) *f*	originality
originell	original, novel
Ornament(e) *n*	ornament
ornamental	ornamental
Ornamentgeschichte *f*	history of ornamentation
ornamentieren	to ornament
Ornamentierung *f*	ornamentation
Ornamentik *f*	ornamentation
Ornamentstich(e) *m*	copper engraving of an ornamental pattern
Ornat(e) *n*	robe, vestment
Orphismus *m*	Orphism, Orphic Cubism
Ort(e) *m*	place, location, site, town
orthogonal	orthographic, orthogonal
Orthostaten *pl*	arthostats
Orthostatenrelief(s) *n*	orthostat decorated in relief, relief on an orthostat
örtlich	local
Ortrippe(n) *f*	transverse rib
Osculatorium (Osculatorien) *n*	osculatorium, peace-board, liturgical object to be kissed
Öse(n) *f*	ring, loop, eye
Ossarium (Ossarien) *n* *also* Ossuarium	ossuary

Ostchor (-chöre) *m*	east sanctuary, east choir
Ostensorium (Ostensorien) *n*	ostensoir, monstrance
Ostgiebel (—) *m*	east pediment
Ostkirche *f*	Eastern Orthodox Church
Ostrakon (Ostraka) *n*	ostracon
oströmisch	east Roman
Ostung(en) *f*	orientation toward the east
ottonisch	Ottonian
Oval(e) *n*	oval
oval	oval
Oxydation *f*	oxydation
Paar(e) *n*	pair, couple
Pacificale *n*	osculatorium, peace-board, liturgical object to be kissed
Page(n) *m*	page, boy attendant
Pagode(n) *f*	pagoda
Palaiologenzeitalter *n*	Palaeologian period, Palaelogian epoch
Palais (—) *n*	palace
Paläographie *f*	paleography; study of antique writings and writing materials
Paläolithiker (—) *m*	paleolithic man
Paläolithikum *n*	Paleolithic Age
paläolithisch	paleolithic
Palas(se) *m*	main living quarters in medieval castle
Palast (Paläste) *m*	palace
Palastanlage(n) *f*	palace building(s) and grounds, palace complex
palastartig	palatial
Palästra (Palästren) *f*	palestra
Palaststil *m*	Palace Style
Palatin *m*	Palatine Hill
Palette(n) *f*	palette

Palettemesser (–) n	palette knife
Palimpsest(e) m,n	palimpsest
Palisade(n) f	palisade
Palisanderholz n	palisander, rosewood
Palladianismus m	Palladianism, Palladian
Palladium (Palladien) n	Palladium
Pallium (Pallien) n	pallium, pall
Palmensäule(n) f	palmiform column
Palmesel (–) m	lifesize wooden donkey bearing a Christ figure, used in Palm Sunday processions
Palmette(n) f	palmette
Palmgewölbe (–) n	fan vault
Palmtuch (-tücher) n	Lenten veil (displayed between chancel and nave)
Palstab (-stäbe) m	palstave, Bronze Age axe
panathenäische Preisamphora (-amphoren) f *also* Preisamphore(n)	Pan-Athenaic amphora
Paneel(e) n	panel, paneling, sunken panel
paneelieren	to panel
Panorama (Panoramen) n	panorama
Pantheon(s) n	Pantheon
Pantograph(en) m	pantograph
Pantographie(n) f	drawing made by using a pantograph
pantographisch	pantographic, by using a pantograph
Pantokrator m	Pantocrator, Christ Omnipotent
Papier n	paper
Papierklebebild(er) n	papiers collés, paper collage
Papiermaché n	papier mâché
Papiermasse f	papier mâché
Papierschablone(n) f	paper stencil
Pappe f	pasteboard, cardboard
Pappel f	poplar, poplar wood
Pappmaché n	papier mâché
Papst (Päpste) m	pope

Papstbildnis(se) *n*	papal portrait
päpstliches Kreuz *n*	papal cross
Papyrus (Papyri) *m*	papyrus
Papyrusblatt (-blätter) *n*	papyrus leaf
Papyrusbündelsäule(n) *f*	bundled papyrus column
Papyrushandschrift(en) *f*	papyrus manuscript
Papyrusrolle(n) *f*	papyrus scroll, papyrus manuscript
Paradies(e) *n*	1. paradise
	2. atrium (of basilica), paradisus
Paradiesflüsse, die vier –	the four rivers of Paradise (Pison, Gihon, Tigris, Euphrates)
Paradiesgärtlein (–) *n*	Paradise Garden, depiction of the Virgin and Child in a garden
Paradigma (Paradigmen) *n*	paradigm
parallel	parallel
Parallelchor (-chöre) *m*	chancel to right or left of main chancel
Parallelperspektive(n) *f*	parallel perspective
Parament(e) *n*	(ecclesiastical) parament
Paravent(s) *m,n*	decorative folding screen
Parergon (Parerga) *n*	parergon
parischer Marmor *m*	Parian marble
Pariserblau *n*	Paris blue, Prussian blue
Parkett(e) *n*	1. wood strip used in parquetage
	2. parquet, parquet floor
Parkettboden (-böden) *m*	parquet floor
Parkettieren *n*	parquetage, cradling
Parterre *n*	ground level, ground floor
Parterrewohnung(en) *f*	ground floor apartment
Partie(n) *f*	part, section, area
Paß (Pässe) *m*	foil
Passepartout(s) *n*	passe-partout
Passion *f*	the Passion
Passionale (–) *n*	passional
Passionsgeschichte *f*	Passion of Christ
Passionssarkophag(e) *m*	sarcophagus with depictions of the Passion

Passionssäule(n) *f*	1. depiction of the Flagellation of Christ
	2. column depicting the Passion and Instruments of the Passion, topped by a rooster
Passionstafel(n) *f*	passion panel
Passionswerkzeuge *pl*	Instruments of the Passion, Symbols of the Passion
Passionszyklus (-zyklen) *m*	passion cycle, depictions of events from the Passion in chronological order
Paste(n) *f*	paste, paste gem
Pastell(e) *n*	pastel, pastel painting
Pastellbild(er) *n*	pastel, pastel painting
Pastellfarbe(n) *f*	pastel, crayon
Pastellmaler (—) *m*	pastelist, pastel artist
Pastellmalerei(en) *f*	pastel, pastel painting
Pastellstift(e) *m*	pastel crayon
Pastellzeichnung(en) *f*	drawing in pastel crayons
Pasticcio (s, Pasticci) *n*	pastiche, pasticcio
Pastophorium (Pastophorien) *n*	pastophory
Pastorale(s) *n* also Pastorale(n) *f*	pastoral scenes
pastos	thick, opaque, relief-like
pastose Malweise *f*	pastose painting technique
Patene(n) *f*	paten
Patina *f*	patina
Patriarchenkreuz(e) *n*	patriarchal cross
Patrize(n) *f*	1. stamp (in relief)
	2. concave (open) mold, patrix
Patron(e) *m*	1. patron saint
	2. founder of a church
	3. patron
Patrone(n) *f*	model, pattern, stencil
Pauschmalglas (-gläser) *n*	gold glass, double-walled glass with gold decoration between
Pause(n) *f*	tracing

pausen	to trace
Pauspapier *n*	tracing paper
Pauspulver *n*	pounce powder
Pausrad (-räder) *n*	perforating wheel, tracing wheel
Pavillon(s) *m*	pavilion
Paviment(e) *n*	pavement, floor
Paxtafel(n) *f*	peace-board, osculatorium, liturgical object to be kissed
Pech *n*	pitch
Pechnase(n) *f*	machicolation
Pedum (Peda) *n*	crosier
Pektorale(s, Pektoralien) *n*	pectoral, pectoral cross
Pelz(e) *m*	fur
Pendentif(e) *n*	pendentive
Pendentifkuppel(n) *f*	dome resting on pendentives
Pentagramm(e) *n*	pentacle
Pentateuch *m*	pentateuch, Torah
pentelisch	Pendelikon
Pentimenti *pl*	pentimenti
Peplos (Peplen) *m*	peplos, peplus
Perforation(en) *f*	perforation
perforieren	to perforate
pergamenische Kunst *f*	Pergamene art, art of the Pergamene School
Pergament(e) *n*	parchment, vellum
Pergamenteinband (-bände) *m*	parchment book binding
pergamenten	(of) parchment
Pergamentleim(e) *m*	parchment glue
Pergamentpapier *n*	1. parchment paper, vellum paper 2. waxed paper
Pergamentrolle(n) *f*	parchment scroll
Pergamon-Altar *m*	Pergamum Altar
Pergola (Pergolen) *f*	pergola
Perikopenbuch (-bücher) *n*	lectionary, pericope book
Peripteros (Peripteren) *m*	peripteral temple
Peristyl(e) *n*	peristyle

Perle(n) *f*	pearl, bead
Perlenschnur *f*	1. bead moulding, bead and reel pattern
	2. string of pearls or beads
Perlmutt *n* *also* Perlmutter *f*	mother-of-pearl
Perlstab (-stäbe) *m*	bead moulding, bead and reel
Perlstäbchen (−) *n*	bead moulding, bead and reel
Permanentfarbstoff(e) *m*	lightfast pigment
Permanentgrün *n*	permanent green
Perpendikularstil *m*	Perpendicular Style
Perserschutt *m*	the Persian dump (on the Acropolis)
persisch	Persian
Person(en) *f*	person
Personifikation(en) *f*	personification
personifizieren	to personify
Persönlichkeitsstil(e) *m*	personal style
Perspektive(n) *f*	perspective
Perspektive, umgekehrte −	inverted perspective
perspektivisch	perspective
Perücke(n) *f*	wig
Pestblatt (-blätter) *n*	woodcut prayer against the plague
Pestkreuz(e) *n*	crucifix depicting ugly realism of the crucified body
Pestsäule(n) *f*	column erected in memory of the plague
Petersbau *m*	the construction of St. Peter's
Petersdom *m*	St. Peter's Cathedral
Petri Verleugnung	Denial of Peter
Petrus, der hl. −	St. Peter
Petrus, der sinkende −	the Navicella, St. Peter Sinking
Petrusgrab *n*	St. Peter's grave
Petschaft(e) *n*	stamp seal, signet
Pettenkofersches Verfahren *n*	Pettenkofer process
Pfahl (Pfähle) *m*	stake, pile

Pfahlbau(ten) m	lake-dwelling, building on stilts or piles
Pfalz(en) f	palace, imperial residence
Pfalzkapelle(n) f	palatine church, palatine chapel
Pfau(en) m	peacock
Pfeifenton m	kaolin, China clay
Pfeilbogen (−, -bögen) m	bow, hunting bow
Pfeiler (−) m	pier, pillar
Pfeilerabstand (-abstände) m	distance between pillars
Pfeilerbasilika (-basiliken) f	basilica with nave walls resting on pillars
Pfeilerbogen (−, -bögen) m	pier arch
Pfeilerfigur(en) f	pillar figure, pillar statue
pfeilergestützt	supported by pillars
Pfeilerweite(n) f	intercolumniation
Pfeilhöhe(n) f	rise (of an arch)
Pfeilspitze(n) f	arrowhead
Pferd(e) n	horse
Pfette(n) f	purlin
Pfingsten n, f	Pentecost
Pfingstwunder n	miracle of Pentecost
Pflanze(n) f	plant
Pflanzenfarbstoff(e) m	vegetable dye, vegetable color
Pflanzenöl(e) n	vegetable oil
Pflanzenornament(e) n	ornament with plant motif
Pflanzensäule(n) f	(Egyptian) column in plant form
Pflaster (−) n	pavement, paved floor
pflastern	to pave, to cobble
Pflasterstein(e) m	paving stone
Pforte(n) f	door in an outside wall, gate
Pfosten (−) m	post, stud, stake
Phantasie(n) f	imagination, fantasy
Phantasiebild(er) n	vision
Pharao(nen) m	Pharaoh
Phiale(n) f	phiale
Philosophensarkophag(e) m	philosopher sarcophagus

Phlyakenvase(n) *f*	phylakikoi, Phlyax vase
Phönix *m*	Phoenix
phönizisch	Phœnician
Photo(s) *n* also Foto(s)	photograph
Photochemigraphie(n) *f*	engraving produced photographically
Photograph(en) *m*	photographer.
Photographie *f*	photography
photographieren	to photograph
Photogravüre(n) *f*	photogravure
Photomontage(n) *f*	photomontage; collage of photos
phrygisch	Phrygian
Physiognomie(n) *f*	physiognomy
Physiologus (Physiologen) *m*	Physiologus (bestiary)
Piedestal(s) *n*	pedestal
Pietà(s) *f*	pietà
Pigment(e) *n*	pigment
Piktographie *f*	pictography
Pilaster (—) *m*	pilaster
Pilgerfahrt(en) *f*	pilgrimage
Pilgerkirche(n) *f*	pilgrimage church
Pilgerstraße(n) *f*	pilgrimage road
Pinakothek(en) *f*	Pinacotheca, picture gallery
Pinie(n) *f*	pine
Pinienzapfen (—) *m*	pine cone, pine cone motif
Pinsel (—) *m*	paintbrush
Pinsel und Tusche	brush and ink
Pinselei *f*	daubing, dabbling
Pinselführung(en) *f*	brushwork, handling of the brush, touch
pinseln	to paint
Pinselstiel(e) *m*	brush handle
Pinselstrich(e) *m*	brush stroke, touch
Pinselzeichnung(en) *f*	brush drawing
Pinselzug (-züge) *m*	brush stroke

Pinte(n) *f*	stoneware mug or tankard
pinx.	pinx.
Piscina (Piscinien) *f*	piscina, sacrarium
Pithos (Pithoi) *m*	pithos
Plafond(s) *m*	flat ceiling, plafond
Plafondmalerei *f*	plafond painting, painting on a flat ceiling
Plakat(e) *n*	poster
Plakatfarbe(n) *f*	poster color, poster paint
plakativ	poster-like; particularly effective visually
Plakatkunst *f*	poster art
Plakatmontage(n) *f*	poster montage
Plakatstil *m*	poster style, poster-like style
Plakette(n) *f*	plaque(tte)
plan	flat, even, level, smooth
Plan (Pläne) *m*	plan, design
Planet(en) *m*	planet
Planetendarstellung(en) *f*	depiction of the planets
planieren	to smooth, to planish
Planierhammer (—) *m*	planishing hammer
Plastik *n*	plastic
Plastik(en) *f*	sculpture, plastic art
Plastilin *n*	modelling clay
plastisch	sculptural, three-dimensional, plastic
Plastizität *f*	plasticity; sculptured volume
Platereskenstil *m*	Plateresque style
Platin *n*	platinum
Platte(n) *f*	slab, plate
Plattenfibel(n) *f*	two-piece fibula, two-disc fibula
Plattenfuge(n) *f*	joint between two slabs or plates
plattieren	to plate (with metal)
Plattner (—) *m*	artist who makes and decorates armor
Plattnerkunst *f*	the art of decorating armor

Platytera *f*	(Byzantine) Madonna in supplication with Child appearing before her
Platz (Plätze) *m*	1. place, space, room 2. (city) square, public square 3. seat
Pleinair-Malerei *f*	plein air painting
Plenarium (Plenarien) *n*	liturgical book containing the readings for Mass or a survey of Mass segments
Plexiglas *n*	plexiglas
Plinthe(n) *f*	plinth
plissiert	pleated
Plumbate-Keramik *f*	(Mayan) plumbate ware
Podest(e) *n*	podium, base
Podium (Podien) *n*	podium, dais
Podiumstempel (—) *m*	temple built on a high podium accessible by an exterior stairway
Pointillismus *m*	Pointillism
Pointillist(en) *m*	Pointillist
Pokal(e) *m*	goblet, cup
polieren	to polish
Polierstahl (-stähle) *m*	burnisher
poliert	polished
Polimentleim *m*	rabbitskin glue
Polimentvergoldung(en) *f*	gilding with gold leaf
politisch engagierte Kunst *f*	politically committed art
Pollenanalyse *f*	pollen analysis, palynology
Polsterquader (—) *m*	stone block with rounded edges
Polsterung(en) *f*	cushion, cushioning, upholstery
polychrom	polychrome
Polychromie *f*	polychromy
Polyesterharz *n*	polyester resin
Polygon(e) *n*	polygon
polygonal	polygonal
polygonales Mauerwerk *n*	polygonal masonry

Polymer(e) *n*	polymer color
Polypenvase *f*	the Octopus Vase
Polyptychon (-chen, -cha) *n*	polyptych
Polyurethan *n*	polyurethane
pompeianisch *also* pompejanisch	Pompeian
Ponderation(en) *f*	equilibrium; balanced distribution of masses *sculpture*
Pontifikale (Pontefikalien) *n*	pontifical book, pontifical vestments
Pop-Art *f*	Pop Art
Porostein(e) *m*	poros stone
Porphyr *m*	porphyry
Portal(e) *n*	portal
Portalgewände (—) *n*	portal jamb
Portalpfeiler (—) *m*	trumeau, portal trumeau
Portalplastik(en) *f*	portal sculpture
Portatile (Portatilien) *n*	portable altar
Portikus *m*	portico
Portlandvase *f*	Portland vase
Portlandzement *m*	Portland cement
Porträt(s) *n* *also* Portrait(s)	portrait
Porträtbüste(n) *f*	portrait bust
porträthaft	portrait-like
porträtieren	to paint a portrait
Porträtist(en) *m*	portraitist
Porträtstudie(n) *f*	portrait study
Porträttafel(n) *f*	portrait panel
Porzellan(e) *n*	porcelain, china
porzellanen	(of) porcelain
Porzellanerde *f*	China clay
Porzellangefäß(e) *n*	porcelain vessel
Porzellanglasur(en) *f*	glaze or enamel on porcelain
Porzellanmalerei *f*	painting on porcelain
Porzellanplastik(en) *f*	porcelain sculpture
Pose(n) *f*	pose

posieren	to pose
Position(en) *f*	position, location
Postament(e) *n*	base, pedestal
Pottasche *f*	potash
Pozzograb (-gräber) *n*	rectangular or round tomb for accommodation of cinerary urns (Etruscan)
Prachtamphora (-amphoren) *f*	ceremonial amphora
Prachtarchitektur(en) *f*	display architecture, architecture meant to impress the viewer
Prachthandschrift(en) *f*	ceremonial manuscript, display manuscript
prachtvoll	splendid
Prägedruck *m*	relief printing with a deeply etched plate
prägen	to stamp, to shape, to coin
Prägestempel (–) *m*	goffer, gauffer; stamp for impressing leather, metal, cardboard, etc.
Prähistorie *f*	prehistory, prehistoric times
präkolumbianisch	pre-Columbian
Präraffaeliten *pl*	Pre-Raphaelites
Predella (Predellen) *f*	predella
Prellstein(e) *m*	spur stone
Presbyterium (Presbyterien) *n*	presbytery, presbytery room
Preußischblau *n*	Prussian blue
Priesche(n) *f*	gallery
Priester (–) *m*	priest
Priesterin(nen) *f*	priestess
Priesterschaft(en) *f*	priesthood
Primamalerei *f*	alla prima, direct painting
Primärfarbe(n) *f*	primary color, basic color
primitive Kunst *f*	1. art produced by a primitive people 2. prehistorical art 3. naive art

Prisma (Prismen) *n*	prism
Privatbesitz, im —	(in) private ownership
Privathaus (-häuser) *n*	private residence
Privatsammlung(en) *f*	private collection
Probeabzug (-züge) *m*	trial proof
Probedruck(e) *m*	trial proof
Probeplastik(en) *f*	bozzetto, maquette, test sculpture
Profanbau(ten) *m*	secular architecture, secular building
Profil(e) *n*	profile
Profil, verlorenes — *n*	profil perdu; profile of an averted head actually showing less than a full profile
Profilansicht(en) *f*	side view, profile
Programm(e) *n*	program, plan
Proletkult *m*	Proletcult
Pronaos (Pronaoi) *m*	pronaos
Prophet(en) *m*	prophet
Prophetenschnalle(n) *f*	bronze clasp with a depiction of Daniel and the lions
Prophezeiung, die — Simeons	Simon's Prophecy (concerning Jesus)
Proportion(en) *f*	proportion
Proportionierung(en) *f*	proportion(s), proportioning
Proportionslehre(n) *f*	theory of proportion
Propyläen *pl*	propylaeum
Proskynese(n) *f* also Proskynesis (Proskynesen)	(depiction of) adoration in a position of genuflection
Prospekt(e) *m*	1. painted stage backdrop 2. decorative side of an organ; organ case 3. realistic view of a town or landscape; veduta
prostyl	prostyle
Prostylos (Prostyloi) *m*	prostyle temple
Proszenium (Proszenien) *n*	proscenium
Prothesis *f*	prothesis

protogeometrisch	protogeometric
protokorinthische Vase(n) *f*	proto-Corinthian vase
Protome(n) *f*	protome; bust or half-figure
Protorenaissance *f*	Proto-Renaissance
Prototyp(en) *m*	prototype
Provenienz(en) *f*	provenance, origin
Prozeß (Prozesse) *m*	process, procedure
Prozessionsstraße(n) *f*	processional street, Via Sacra
Prozeßkunst *f*	process art
Prunkgewand (-gewänder) *n*	parade dress, ceremonial dress
Prunkmöbel *pl*	ornamental furniture
Prunkschüssel(n) *f*	ornamental bowl, ceremonial bowl
Prunkstück(e) *n*	ornamental piece, display piece, showpiece, splendid piece
Prunkwaffe(n) *f*	richly decorated weapon, ceremonial weapon
Psalter (—) *m*	Psalter
Pseudobasilika (-basiliken) *f*	hall church with raised nave but no nave windows
Pseudodipteros (-dipteroi) *m*	pseudo-dipteral temple
Pseudoperipteros (-peripteren) *m*	pseudo-peripteral temple
Psykter(e) *m*	psykter
Puffärmel (—) *m*	puffed sleeve
Pult(e) *n*	lectern
Pultdach (-dächer) *n*	lean-to roof
Punkte (Punkte) *m*	point, dot
punktieren	1. to point *sculpture* 2. to dot, to stipple *engraving*
Punktiergerät(e) *n*	pointing machine
Punktiermanier *f*	dotted manner, manière criblée
Punktiermaschine(n) *f*	pointing machine
Punktierrad (-räder) *n*	perforating wheel, tracing wheel
Punktierstich(e) *m*	dotted manner engraving
Punktstich(e) *m*	dotted manner engraving

Punzarbeit *f*	embossing
Punze(n) *f*	punch, stamp
punzen	to punch, to emboss
Punzenmanier *f*	dotted manner, manière criblée
Punzenmuster (–) *n*	embossed design, embossing pattern
Purismus *m*	purism
Purist(en) *m*	purist
Purpur *m*	Tyrian purple, murex purple
Purpurin *n*	purpurin
purpurn	bluish-red
Putte(n) *f*	putto
Putto (Putti, Putten) *m*	putto
Putz *m*	plaster, plaster coat
Putzarbeit *f*	plaster work
Putzmosaikverfahren (–) *n*	mosaic technique in which visible plaster is part of the picure
Putzschicht(en) *f*	layer of plaster
Puzzolanerde *f*	Puzzolana, Pozzuoli red
Pylon(en) *m* also Pylone(n) *f*	pylon
Pyramide(n) *f*	pyramid
Pyramidendach (-dächer) *n*	tetrahedron roof
pyramidenförmig	pyramidal
Pyramidenkomposition(en) *f*	pyramidal composition
Pyxis (Pyxiden) *f*	pyx
Qibla *f*	qibla, kibleh
Quader (–) *m*	ashlar, square hewn stone
Quadermauerwerk *n*	rustication, masonry made of ashlars
Quaderraum (-räume) *m*	room or area covered by a flat ceiling
Quadrat(e) *n*	square
quadratisch	square

quadratischer Schematismus *m*	system of architectural proportions based on the crossing square as module
Quadratmeter (−) *n*	square meter
Quadratnetz(e) *n*	squaring-off grid, graticulation grid
Quadratur(en) *f*	ad quadratum; architectural form based on the square
Quadraturmalerei(en) *f*	illusionistic room painting which makes the room seem larger or deeper
Quadrierung(en) *f*	1. squaring, squaring off, graticulation 2. plaster wall painted in imitation of rustication
Quadriga (Quadrigen) *f*	quadriga
Quarz *m*	quartz
Quast(e) *m* *also* Quaste(n) *f*	tassel, tuft, knot
Quattrocento *n*	quattrocento
Quelle(n) *f*	1. source 2. spring, fountain
Quellenwerk(e) *n*	source, source book, documentary source
quer	diagonal, oblique, slanting, crosswise
Querapsis (-apsiden) *f*	transept apse
Querbau(ten) *m*	any (external) structure perpendicular to the nave
Quere *f*	diagonal, transverse or oblique line
Quergurt(e) *m*	transverse arch
Querhaus (-häuser) *n*	transept (and any structure parallel to it)
Querhausarm (-arme) *m*	transept arm
Querschiff(e) *n*	transept
Querschiffkonche(n) *f*	transept conch, transept apse
Querschnitt(e) *m*	cross section
Querschnittform *f*	shape or profile of the cross section
Quersprosse(n) *f*	cross bar
Querzetin *n*	quercitron

Quipu(s) *n*	quipu; Indian knotted cord
Quirin *m*	Quirinal Hill
Rad (Räder) *n*	wheel
Radfenster (−) *n*	wheel window, rose window
Radialsymmetrie *f*	radial symmetry
radieren	to etch
Radierkunst *f*	(art of) etching
Radiernadel(n) *f*	etching needle
Radierung(en) *f*	etching
Radiographie(n) *f*	radiography; picture produced by x-rays
Radiokarbondatierung(en) *f*	radiocarbon dating
Radiokarbonmethode *f*	radiocarbon dating
Radius (Radien) *m*	radius
raffiniert	refined
rahmen	to frame
Rahmen (−) *m*	frame
Rahmennetz(e) *n*	drawing frame
Rahmenwerk(e) *n*	framework
Rahmung(en) *f*	frame, framing
Rakel(n) *f*	squeegee
Rakeltiefdruck(e) *m*	intaglio printing technique where excess ink is removed from the plate with a squeegee
Rampe(n) *f*	ramp
Rand (Ränder) *m*	edge, cant, border
Randleiste(n) *f*	side margin (and decoration)
Randornament(e) *n*	ornamentation on the edge or margin
Randschrift(en) *f*	margin inscription, legend (of coins)
Randzeichnung(en) *f*	marginal drawing
Ranke(n) *f*	vine, vine foliage
Rankenfries(e) *m*	vine scroll pattern

Rankenwerk *n*	vine scroll decoration
Raphia *f*	raffia
Rapport *m*	rythmic reappearance of the same design
Rapport, unendlicher —	regularly repeating (textile) pattern
Rapportmuster (—) *n*	repeating pattern
Raspel(n) *f*	rasp
Raster (—) *m*	grid, screen
Rasterschema (-schemen) *n*	grid design, grid pattern
Rathaus (-häuser) *n*	town hall, city hall
Raub der Europa, der —	the Rape of Europa
Raub der Sabinerinnen, der —	the Rape of the Sabine Women
Räuchergefäß(e) *n*	incense container, censer
Rauchfaß (-fässer) *n*	censer, thurible
Rauhputz *m*	brown coat, arriccio
Raum (Räume) *m*	space, room, area
Raumausstattung(en) *f*	furnishing(s), interior decoration
Raumbegrenzung *f*	limitation of space
raumbestimmend	space determining, space defining
Raumbeziehung(en) *f*	spatial relationship
Raumbild(er) *n*	depiction of space, pictorial space
raumbildend	space defining, space shaping
Raumdynamik *f*	spatial dynamics
Raumentfaltung *f*	development of space
Raumfolge(n) *f*	(floor) plan, arrangement of rooms
Raumgefüge *n*	structure of the space
Raumgliederung(en) *f*	organization of space, arrangement of space
raumgrenzend	space limiting, space delineating
Raumharmonie *f*	spatial harmony
Raumillusion *f*	illusion of space
Raumkunst *f*	(art of) interior decorating
räumlich	spatial, spatially
Räumlichkeit(en) *f*	spaciousness, spatiality, room
raumlos	spaceless

Raumordnung *f*	arrangement of space, arrangement of rooms
raumplastisch	three-dimensional, architectural
Raumstatik *f*	statics, spatial statics
Raumstruktur(en) *f*	structure of space
Raumteiler (—) *m*	room divider
Raumtiefe(n) *f*	depth, spatial depth
Raumverschwendung *f*	waste of space
Raumverzerrung(en) *f*	spatial distortion
Raumwirkung *f*	spatial effect, three-dimensional effect
Rauschgelb *n*	orpiment
Rauschrot *n*	realgar
Raute(n) *f*	rhombus, lozenge
Rautendach (-dächer) *n*	helm roof
Rautenfries *m*	rhomboid pattern
Rayonismus *m*	Rayonnism
Ready-made(s) *n*	ready-made
Realgar *m*	realgar
Realismus *m*	realism, Realism
Realist(en) *m*	Realist
realistisch	realistic
Rebenschwarz *n*	vine black
Rechteck(e) *n*	rectangle
rechteckig	rectangular
Rechteckplatte(n) *f*	rectangular section or plate
Rechtecktempel (—) *m*	rectangular temple
Rechtswendung(en) *f*	turning (or twisting) to the right
rechtwinklig	rectangular, right-angled
Rednertribüne(n) *f*	speaker's stage, Rostra
Refektorium (Refektorien) *n*	refectory
regelmäßig	regular, regularly
Regenbogen (—, -bögen) *m*	rainbow
Regenbogenfarbe(n) *f*	diffraction color, prismatic color
regenerieren	to renew the gloss of dull varnish

Regentenstück(e) *n*	regent-piece, (Dutch) painting depicting a regent
Reglette(n) *f*	reglet
Regula(e) *f*	regula, regulus
Reiber (−) *m*	brayer
Reiberdruck(e) *m*	hand method of printing wood blocks or lithographs by rubbing
Reich(e) *n*	realm, empire
Reichsapfel *m*	orb, imperial orb
Reichsinsignien *pl*	imperial insignia; a collection of imperial emblems, now in Vienna
Reichskleinod(ien) *n*	imperial insignia
Reichszepter *n*	imperial scepter
reif	mature
Reif(e) *m*	ring, band, headband
Reifestil *m*	mature style
Reihe(n) *f*	row series
Reihenhaus (-häuser) *n*	row house
Reihung(en) *f*	1. arrangement in a row, alignment 2. rhythm, rhythmic reappearance of the same design or unit
Reihung, gewundene −	curved ribs of a stellar or net vault
rein	pure
reinbunte Farbe(n) *f*	pure color
Reinheit *f*	purity
Reinigungsbrunnen (−) *m*	(Islamic) fountain for ablution
Reisealtärchen (−) *n*	portable altar
Reiseziborium (-ziborien) *n*	portable ciborium
Reißbrett(er) *n*	drawing board
Reiswerkkirche(n) *f*	stave church
Reiter (−) *m*	rider, horseman
Reiter, der Blaue −	der Blaue Reiter
Reiterfigur(en) *f*	mounted figure
Reiterstandbild(er) *n*	equestrian statue
Reiterstatue(n) *f*	equestrian statue

Reittier(e) *n*	steed
Reklamekunst *f*	advertising art
rekonstruieren	to reconstruct
Rekonstruktion(en) *f*	reconstruction
Rekonstruktionszeichnung(en) *f*	reconstruction drawing
rektifiziertes Terpentinöl *n*	rectified turpentine
Relief(s, e) *n*	relief
Relief, gequetschtes — *n*	stiacciato relief
Relief, versenktes —	sunk relief, hollow relief
reliefartig	relief-like
Reliefdarstellung(en) *f*	depiction on relief(s)
Reliefdekor *m*	relief decoration, relief ornamentation
Reliefdruck *m*	relief printing
Relieffries(e) *m*	frieze in relief, relief ornament
reliefiert	decorated with relief, in relief
Reliefintarsia (-intarsien) *f*	combination of woodcarving and intarsia
reliefmäßig	relief-like
Reliefschmuck *m*	relief ornamentation
Reliefstele(n) *f*	stele decorated in relief
reliefverziert	decorated in relief
Reliefware(n) *f*	reliefware, pottery or ceramics decorated with reliefs
Reliquiar(e) *n*	reliquary
Reliquie(n) *f*	relic
Reliquienbehälter (—) *m*	reliquary, receptacle for relics
Reliquienschrank (-schränke) *m*	reliquary
Reliquienschrein(e) *m*	reliquary
Remarquedruck(e) *m*	remarque proof
Remter (—) *m*	refectory
Ren(e) *n*	reindeer
Renaissance *f*	Renaissance
Rentiergeweih(e) *n*	reindeer antler
Rentierzeit *f*	Magdalenian period, Magdalenian culture

Rentoilieren n	transfer (to a new support) *conservation*
Replik(en) f *also* Replika (Repliken)	replica
Repoussoir(s) n	repoussoir
Reproduktion(en) f	reproduction
Reproduktionsholzschnitt(e) m	woodcut reproduction of a painting
Reproduktionsstich(e) m	engraved reproduction of a painting
Reproduktionsverfahren (−) n	reproduction process, duplication process
reproduzieren	to reproduce
Residenz(en) f	residence
Restaurator(en) m	conservator
restaurieren	to conserve, to restore
Restaurierung(en) f	restoration
Retabel (−) n	altarpiece, retable, reredos
Retrospektive(n) f	retrospective
Retusche(n) f	retouched spot, touched up spot
retuschieren	to retouch
Revers(e) m	reverse, back of a coin
Rezipient(en) m	metal base for enamelwork
rhodisch	Rhodian
Rhombendach (-dächer) n	rhomboid roof
Rhomboid(e) n	rhomboid
Rhombus (Rhomben) m	rhombus
Rhyton (Rhyta) n	rhyton
Richtung(en) f	1. direction 2. style, movement
Richtungsbau(ten) m	axial building, longitudinal-plan building, building having a longitudinal axis
richtungsbetont	having emphasis on direction or movement (especially a building plan)
Riefe(n) f	flute, groove
Riefelung(en) f	parallel grooves, incised hatching

Riegel (–) *m*	1. transom
	2. diagonal beam in half-timber construction
Riesen *m*	pinnacle crowned with a finial
riesenhaft	gigantic
riesig	gigantic, huge
Riet(e) *n*	reed, weaving reed
Rille(n) *f*	groove, furrow, flute, channel
Ring(e) *m*	ring
Ringglas (-gläser) *n*	ring-shaped bottle with a hole through the middle
Ringgraben (-gräben) *m*	moat, fosse
Ringhenkel (–) *m*	ring-shaped handle
Ringkrug (-krüge) *m*	ring-shaped flask with a hole through the middle
Ringmauer(n) *f*	circumvallation
Ringtonne(n) *f*	annular barrel vault; curved (circular or semi-circular) barrel vault
Rinne(n) *f*	trough, gutter
Rinnleiste(n) *f*	drip moulding, cymatium
Rippe(n) *f*	rib
Rippengewölbe (–) *n*	rib vault
Rippenkuppel(n) *f*	ribbed dome
Rippenwölbung(en) *f*	ribbed vault(ing)
Rippenwerk *n*	ribs (of a vault)
Risalit(e) *m*	protruding facade bay
Riß (Risse) *m*	1. crack, split, break, flaw
	2. sketch, plan, design
Ritter (–) *m*	knight
Ritterburg(en) *f*	knight's castle
Rittersaal (-säle) *m*	knight's hall, baronial hall
Ritterspiel(e) *n*	tournament, joust
Rittertum *n*	knighthood
Ritual(e, Ritualien) *n*	ritual, ritual book
rituell	ritual, ritually
Ritus (Riten) *m*	rite
Ritzbild(er) *n*	incised picture, scratched picture

Ritzdekor(s) *m*	incised decoration
ritzen	to incise, to scratch
Ritzgriffel (−) *m*	stylus, needle
Ritzzeichnung(en) *f*	incised drawing
Rizinusöl *n*	castor oil
Rocaille(s) *f, n*	rocaille, rockwork
Rock (Röcke) *m*	gown, skirt, frock
roh	rough, raw, unfinished
Rohbau(ten) *m*	framework, skeleton, unfinished building
Rohmarmor *m*	unworked marble
Rohrfeder(n) *f*	reed pen, bamboo cane pen
Rohseide *f*	raw silk
Rokoko *n*	rococo
Roland(e) *m*	Roland column
Rolandsäule(n) *f*	Roland column
Rolle(n) *f*	1. scroll 2. role
Rollenbild(er) *n*	roll painting, continuous cylindrical canvas which is rolled when viewed
Rollenfries(e) *m*	billet moulding, roll moulding
Rollenporträt(s) *n*	portrait of an actor in his theatrical role
Rollsiegel (−) *n*	seal cylinder
Rollwerk *n*	scrollwork
Rom	Rome
Romanik *f*	Romanesque style, Romanesque period
romanisch	Romanesque
Romanismus *m*	Romanism
Romanist(en) *m*	Romanist
Romantik *f*	Romanticism, Romantic movement
Romantiker (−) *m*	Romantic
romantisch	romantic
Römer (−) *m*	1. Roman 2. roemer; glass with broad green stem

Römertum n	ancient Rome, the Romans, the Roman world
Römerzeit f	Roman times
römisch	Roman
röntgen	to x-ray
Röntgenstil m	x-ray style
rosa	pink, rose
Rose(n) f	1. rose 2. rose window
Rosenfenster (−) n	rose window, wheel window
Rosenhag, Madonna im −	Virgin in the Rose Bower
Rosenholz n	rosewood
Rosenkranz (-kränze) m	1. rosary 2. rose garland, rose wreath
Rosenkranzbild(er) n	(depiction of) Virgin of the Rose-Crown, Madonna of the Rosary
Rosenkranzfest, das −	Festival of the Rose-Garlands
Rosette(n) f	rosette
Rosette-Stein m	Rosetta Stone
Rosmarinöl n	oil of rosemary
Roß (Rösser) n	horse
Rost m	rust
rostfarben	rust-colored
rostfreier Stahl m	stainless steel
Rostra (Rostren) f	rostrum
rot	red
Roteisenstein m	hematite
Rötel m	ruddle, red chalk, sanguine
Rötelstift(e) m	red chalk crayon, red chalk pencil
Rötelzeichnung(en) f	red chalk drawing, sanguine drawing
rotfigurig	red-figured
rötlich	reddish
Rotmarderpinsel (−) m	red sable brush
Rotunde(n) f	rotunda
Roulette(n) f	roulette *engraving*
Rubensstecher (−) m	engraver specializing in the reproduction of Rubens' paintings

Rubin(e) *m*	ruby
Rubinätzung(en) *f*	ruby etching (on glass)
Rubinglas *n*	ruby glass
Rubrik(en) *f*	rubric
rubrizieren	to rubricate
Rubrizieren *n*	rubrication
Rückansicht(en) *f*	back view
Rücken (−) *m*	1. back
	2. extrados
Rückenakt(e) *m*	nude showing the back view
Rückenblatt (-blätter) *n*	back of an altarpiece
Rückenlehne(n) *f*	back rest, chair back
Rückenpfeiler (−) *m*	back pillar
Rückkehr des verlorenen Sohnes, die −	the Return of the Prodigal Son
Rücklaken (−) *n*	narrow woven wall hanging or covering for backs of choir stalls
Rückseite(n) *f*	back side
Rückwand (-wände) *f*	back panel, backing
Rudiment(e) *n*	fragment, remains (pl.)
Ruhe auf der Flucht, die −	Rest on the Flight to Egypt, Repose on the Flight to Egypt
Ruine(n) *f*	ruin
Ruinenmalerei(en) *f*	painting of ruins
Ruinenstätte(n) *f*	site of ruins
Rumpf (Rümpfe) *m*	torso, trunk
rund	round
Rundansicht(en) *f*	panoramic view
Rundbau(ten) *m*	circular-plan building
Rundbild(er) *n*	panorama
Rundblick(e) *m*	panoramic view
Rundbogen (−, -bögen) *m*	round arch, semicircular arch, Roman arch
Rundbogenblende(n) *f*	blind round arch (frieze)
Rundbogenfenster (−) *n*	window shaped like a round arch
Rundbogenfries(e) *m*	blind arcade, round arch frieze
rundbogig	having a round arch

Runddienst(e) m	respond with round profile
Rundfenster (—) n	round window
Rundform(en) f	circular shape, circular form
rundhohl	concave
Rundpfeiler (—) m	circular pier, circular pillar
Rundpinsel (—) m	round brush
Rundplastik(en) f	three-dimensional sculpture, sculpture in the round
rundplastisch	three-dimensional
Rundstab (-stäbe) m	astragal
Rundtempel (—) m	tholos, round temple
Rundturm (-türme) m	circular tower
Rundung(en) f	rounding
Rune(n) f	rune
Runenschrift(en) f	runic writing
Runenstein(e) m	rune stone
Runzel(n) f	wrinkle in the skin
Rupfen m	burlap, sack cloth
Ruß m	lampblack, soot
Rußschwarz n	soot black
Rüstbalken (—) m	putlog, scaffold beam
Rustika f	rustication
Rustika-Quader (—) m	rusticated block, rusticated ashlar
Rüstloch (-löcher) n	putlog hole, scaffolding hole
Rüststange(n) f	putlog
Rüstung(en) f	armor
Rute(n) f	came, calm, strip
Saal (Säle) m	hall
saalartig	hall-like
Saalkirche(n) f	one-aisled church
Säbel (—) m	saber
Sabiner pl	Sabines
Sabinerin(nen) f	Sabine woman
sachlich	objective, objectively

Sachlichkeit *f*	objectivity
Sachlichkeit, die Neue —	Neue Sachlichkeit, New Objectivity
Safflor *m*	safflor, safflower pigment
Safran *m*	saffron
safrangelb	saffron, saffron yellow
Sage(n) *f*	fable, myth, saga
Sägedach (-däcker) *n*	sawtooth (factory) roof
sagenhaft	mythical, fabulous, fantastic
Sägezahnfries(e) *m*	zigzag band, zigzag ornament
sakral	sacred
Sakralarchitektur *f*	sacred architecture
Sakralbau(ten) *m*	sacred structure, sacred building
Sakralbaukunst *f*	church architecture, architecture of sacred buildings
Sakramentar(e) *n* *also* Sakramentarium (Sakramentarien)	sacramentary, liturgical book
Sakramenthäuschen (—) *n*	tabernacle, sacrament house
Sakristei(en) *f*	sacristy, vestry
Salbe(n) *f*	ointment, oil, salve
Salbgefäß(e) *n*	unguentarium, ointment jar, ointment vessel
Salier (—) *m*	Salian
salische Epoche *f*	Salian period
Salvatorbild(er) *n*	Christ in Majesty
Salzfaß (-fässer) *n*	salt cellar
Samariter, der gute —	the Good Samaritan
Samariterin, Jesus und die —	Christ and the Woman of Samaria
sammeln	to collect
Sammler (—) *m*	collector
Sammlung(en) *f*	collection
Samt *m*	velvet
Sand *m*	sand
Sandarak *m*	sandarac
Sandelholz *n*	sandalwood
sandfarben	sand-colored

Sandformverfahren n	sand casting
Sandguß m	sand casting
Sandstein m	sandstone
sanft	soft, mellow
Sänfte(n) f	sedan chair
Sanktuarium (Sanktuarien) n	1. sanctuary 2. place where relics are kept
Saphir(e) m	sapphire
Sardonyx m	sardonyx
Sarg (Särge) m	coffin
Sarkophag(e) m	sarcophagus
Sarkophagdeckel (−) m	sarcophagus lid
Sarkophagplastik(en) f	sarcophagus sculpture
Satin m	satin
Satinage f	calendering (of paper)
Satiniermaschine(n) f	calender, calender machine
satt	deep, dark, rich, intense, saturated
Satteldach (-dächer) n	saddleback roof
sattgrün	deep, rich green
Sättigung f	saturation, color saturation
Sättigungsgrad m	degree of saturation (of a color)
Satyr(n) m	satyr
Satzspiegel (−) m	printed portion of a page
Säulchen (−) n	colonnette, small column
Säule(n) f	column
Säulenarkadensarkophag(e) m	same as *Säulensarkophag*, but the columns are joined by arches
Säulenbasilika (-basiliken) f	basilica whose nave walls are supported only by columns
Säuleneingang (-gänge) m	columned entrance
Säulenfassade(n) f	columned facade
Säulenfigur(en) f	column figure, column statue
Säulenfuß (-füße) m	column base, plinth, base
Säulengang (-gänge) m	colonnade, columned walk
säulengestützt	supported by columns, hypostyle
säulengetragen	supported by columns, hypostyle
säulenhaft	columnar, column-like

Säulenhalle(n) *f*	columned hall, hypostyle hall
Säulenkapitell(e) *n*	column capital
Säulenknauf (-knäufe) *m*	column capital
Säulenkranz (-kränze) *m*	wreath of columns, circle of columns
Säulenordnung(en) *f*	order, column order
Säulenpfeilerbasilika (-basiliken) *f*	basilica with both columns and pillars as supports
Säulenportal(e) *n*	columned portal
Säulenreihe(n) *f*	row of columns
Säulensaal (-säle) *m*	columned hall, hypostyle hall
Säulensarkophag(e) *m*	sarcophagus, the front of which is divided by columns or pilasters
Säulenschaft (-schäfte) *m*	column shaft
Säulenschwellung(en) *f*	entasis
Säulenstatue(n) *f*	column figure, statue in front of or connected to a column
Säulenstellung(en) *f*	position of the column(s)
Säulentrommel(n) *f*	column drum, drum
Säulenvorhalle(n) *f*	columned front hall
Säulenvorlage(n) *f*	column placed in front of a wall
Saum (Säume) *m*	seam, hem
Säure(n) *f*	acid, mordant
Säurebad *n*	mordant bath, acid bath
Sauveterrien *n*	Sauveterrian culture
sc.	sculp.
Scagliola *f*	scagliola
Schabblatt (-blätter) *n*	scratchboard, scraperboard
Schabeisen (−) *n*	burnisher, scraper
schaben	to scrape
Schaber (−) *m*	scraper
Schabkunst *f*	mezzotint
Schabkunstblatt (-blätter) *n*	mezzotint engraving
Schabkünstler (−) *m*	mezzotint artist
Schablone(n) *f*	stencil, pattern, template
Schablonendruck *m*	silk screen
Schabmanier *f*	mezzotint

Schabtechnik *f*	drawing technique employing scratchboard
Schachbrettfries(e) *m*	billet pattern or moulding, checkerboard pattern
Schachbrettmuster (−) *n*	checkerboard pattern
Schachbrettsystem(e) *n*	grid system, grid plan
Schächer am Kreuz, der −	the Thief on the Cross
Schächerkreuz(e) *n*	Y-shaped cross
Schacht (Schächte) *m*	shaft
Schachtgrab (-gräber) *n*	shaft grave
Schachtgräberring(e) *m*	shaft grave circle
Schachtkammergrab (-gräber) *n*	shaft and chamber tomb
Schädel (−) *m*	skull
Schäferszene(n) *f*	pastoral scene
schaffen	to create
Schaffen *n*	work, œuvre
Schaffensdrang *m*	urge or desire to create
Schaffenskraft (-kräfte) *f*	creative power, creative energy
Schaffensperiode(n) *f*	creative period
Schaffensprozeß *m*	creative process
Schaffung *f*	creation
Schaft (Schäfte) *m*	shaft
Schaftring(e) *m*	shaft-ring, annulet
Schale(n) *f*	1. bowl 2. shell
Schalenboden (-böden) *m*	inner bottom of a bowl
Schalenbrunnen (−) *m*	fountain with a series of basins
Schaleninnenbild(er) *n*	picture on the inside surface of a bowl
Schalenkonstruktion(en) *f*	concrete shell construction, shell construction
Schalldeckel (−) *m*	sounding board
Schalung(en) *f*	1. shell *architecture* 2. outer boards of a wooden house 3. foundation for roofing material 4. formwork (for concrete), shuttering

Schamotte *f*	fireclay
Schamotteziegel (−) *m*	fire brick
Schanze(n) *f*	bulwark
Schanzwerk *n*	fortifications, bulwark
Scharffeuerfarbe(n) *f*	heat-resistant underglaze pigment
scharlachrot	scarlet
Scharnier(e) *n*	hinge
Scharnierdeckel (−) *m*	hinged cover, hinged lid
Schärpe(n) *f*	baldric, sash
Scharriereisen (−) *n*	mason's tool for incising hatching
Scharrierung(en) *f*	incised hatching (on the face of a building stone)
Scharte(n) *f*	embrasure
Schartenbacke(n) *f*	merlon
Schatten (−) *m*	shadow, shade
Schattenbild(er) *n*	silhouette
Schattenfarbe *f*	umber
Schattenkontrast(e) *m*	contrast of shadows
Schattenmalerei *f*	(manner of) painting which includes or emphasizes shadows or shading
Schattenriß (-risse) *m*	silhouette
Schattenverteilung(en) *f*	distribution of light and shade
schattieren	to shade, to tint
Schattierung(en) *f*	shade, nuance, tint, shading
schattig	shady, shadowy
Schatulle(n) *f*	jewelry box
Schatz (Schätze) *m*	treasure
Schatzhaus (-häuser) *n*	treasury, treasure house
Schatzkammer(n) *f*	treasury, treasure chamber
Schaubühne(n) *f*	stage
Schaukasten (-kästen) *m*	display case
Schaumgummi *m*	foam rubber
Schautreppe(n) *f*	observers' steps, steps from which an activity can be observed
Scheibe(n) *f*	1. pane of glass 2. disc

Scheibenfibel(n) *f*	disc fibula
Scheibenkreuz(e) *n*	crucifix with disc-shaped backing
Scheibenriß (-risse) *m*	design for a stained glass window
Scheidbogen (—, -bögen) *m*	arch separating the nave and the side aisle
Scheide(n) *f*	scabbard, sheath
Scheidewasser *n*	aqua fortis
Scheidmauer(n) *f*	wall (above the arch) separating the nave and the side aisle
Schein(e) *m*	illusion, appearance, shine, gleam, aura
Scheinarchitektur *f*	illusionistic architectural decoration painted on a wall
Scheinarkade(n) *f*	blind arcade
Scheinärmel (—) *m*	false sleeve, the illusion of sleeves
Scheinbild(er) *n*	illusion
scheinen	1. to seem, to appear 2. to shine
Scheintür(en) *f*	dummy door, false door
Scheitel (—) *m*	1. crown, highest point 2. part in the hair
Scheitelhöhe *f*	crown, apex (of a vault)
Scheitelkapelle(n) *f*	chapel at the vertex of the Gothic church sanctuary; Lady Chapel
Scheitelpunkt(e) *m*	crown (of an arch)
Scheitelrippe(n) *f*	transverse ridge rib
scheitrechter Sturz *m* *also* scheitrechter Sturzbogen	flat arch
Schellack(e) *m*	shellac
Schellackpolitur *f*	French polish
Schema(ta) *n*	scheme, diagram, system, plan
Schematismus, quadratischer — *m*	use of the crossing square as module for the entire floor plan
Schemel (—) *m*	stool, footstool
Schenkel (—) *m*	upper leg, thigh
Scherbe(n) *f*	fragment, sherd, shard, potsherd

Scherben (−) m	baked ceramic material; layer under the glaze
Schere(n) f	scissors
Scherenschnitt(e) m	cut-out silhouette portrait
Scherenstuhl (-stühle) m	folding chair
Schicht(en) f	level, layer, stratum, horizon
Schichtenmalerei f	painting in layers (as opposed to alla prima)
Schichtmauerwerk n	layered masonry; masonry with alternating layers of different bonds and/or building materials
Schichtung(en) f	layering, arrangement in layers
schichtweise	in layers, layered
Schicksal(e) n	fate
Schiebetür(en) f	sliding door
schief	slanting, lop-sided, crooked, skew
Schiefer m	slate, schist
Schieferdach (-dächer) n	slate roof
Schieferplatte(n) f	slate slab, slate plate
Schießscharte(n) f	embrasure, meutrière, opening in fortress wall for shooting
Schiff(e) n	1. ship 2. aisle or section of a church
Schiffchen (−) n	1. weaving shuttle 2. small boat or ship 3. incense boat
Schiffsbestattung(en) f	boat burial
Schiffskanzel(n) f	ship-shaped pulpit
Schild(e) m	shield
Schildbogen (−, -bögen) m	formeret, wall rib, lateral transverse arch
schildern	to portray, to depict
Schilderung(en) f	portrayal, depiction
Schildhalter (−) m	supporter *heraldry*
Schildpatt n	tortoise shell
Schildrippe(n) f	wall rib, rib at intersection of vault and wall
Schildwand (-wände) f	wall section under the formeret

Schilf(e) *n*	reeds
Schilfrohrfeder(n) *f*	reed pen
Schiller *m*	iridescence
Schillerfarbe(n) *f*	shot color, iridescent color
Schillerglanz *m*	luster, iridescence
schillern	to opalesce, to change color(s)
schillernd	iridescent
Schimäre(n) *f*	chimera
Schindel(n) *f*	shingle
Schindeldach (-dächer) *n*	shingle roof
Schindelstil *m*	Shingle Style
Schirm(e) *m*	1. umbrella 2. screen
Schirmgewölbe (—) *n*	umbrella dome, parachute dome
Schlachtenbild(er) *n*	battle-piece, battle scene
Schlachtstück(e) *n*	battle-piece, battle scene
Schläfe(n) *f*	temple
Schlaglicht(er) *n*	intense ray of light, intense light distinctly setting off the objects it strikes
Schlagschatten (—) *m*	cast shadow
schlämmen	to levigate
Schlämmkreide *f*	precipitated chalk, whiting
Schlange(n) *f*	snake, serpent
Schlangenkult(e) *m*	snake cult
Schlegel (—) *m*	mallet, sculptor's mallet
Schleier (—) *m*	veil
Schleife(n) *f*	bow, loop
schleifen	to grind, to polish, to whet
Schleifer (—) *m*	polisher, grinder, gem cutter
Schleifkanne(n) *f*	heavy covered pewter pitcher with beak-shaped spout
Schleifrillen *pl*	ridges on medieval church portals, allegedly the result of whetting swords there before battle
Schleifstein(e) *m*	whetstone
Schlemmkreide *f*	chalk priming (for painting on wooden sculpture)

Schleppe(n) f	train of cloth
schlicht	simple, unadorned
Schlicker m	slip, engobe
Schliff(e) m	polish, grinding, finish
Schlingornamentik f	looped decoration, loops
Schloß (Schlösser) n	palace
Schloßanlage(n) f	palace and grounds, palace complex
Schloßgraben (-gräben) m	moat, fosse
Schloßkapelle(n) f	palace chapel
Schloßkirche(n) f	palace church
Schloßtor(e) n	palace gate, portal
Schloßtyp(en) m	type of palace
Schlüpfpforte(n) f	postern
Schlüsselübergabe an Petrus, die —	Delivery of the Keys to St. Peter
Schlußfirnis(se) m	final varnish
Schlußlasur(en) f	final glaze
Schlußstein(e) m	1. (vault) boss 2. (arch) keystone
schmächtig	slender, slim, slight
schmal	narrow
Schmalt m	enamel
Schmalte(n) f	1. smalto 2. smalt, cobalt enamel
Schmelz m	enamel
Schmelzarbeit(en) f	enamel, enameling
Schmelzfarbe(n) f	enamel paint, enamel color
Schmelzfarbenmalerei(en) f	enamel painting
Schmelzglas n	enamel
Schmelzglasur(en) f	enamel glaze
Schmelzmalerei f	enameling, enamel painting
Schmerzen, die sieben — Mariä	the Seven Sorrows of the Virgin
Schmerzensmann m	Man of Sorrows, Christ with a Crown of Thorns
Schmerzensmutter f	mater dolorosa, Mother of Sorrows

Schmiedeeisen *n*	wrought iron
schmiedeeisern	(of) wrought iron
Schmiedekunst *f*	(art of) metalworking
schmieden	to forge, to work metal
Schmiege(n) *f*	chamfer, bevel
Schminkpalette(n) *f*	(cosmetic) palette, stone palette
Schmirgelpapier *n*	sandpaper
Schmuck *m*	1. decoration 2. jewelry
Schmuckbedürfnis *n*	the need for decoration or ornamentation
schmücken	to decorate, to adorn, to trim
schmückend	decorative
Schmuckform(en) *f*	decorative form, type of decoration
Schmuckgegenstand (-stände) *m*	decorative object
Schmuckkasten (-kästen) *m*	jewelry box
Schmuckleiste(n) *f*	decorative moulding
schmucklos	undecorated, unadorned
Schmucklosigkeit *f*	plainness
Schmuckschrift(en) *f*	calligraphy
Schmuckstück(e) *n*	ornament, piece of jewelry
Schnabel (−) *m*	1. beak 2. spout
schnabelförmig	beaked, beak-shaped
Schnabelkanne(n) *f*	beaked jug, long-spouted pitcher
Schnabeltasse(n) *f*	beaked cup
Schnalle(n) *f*	buckle, clasp
Schnecke(n) *f*	1. snail 2. snail-shaped decoration (e. g. volute or spiral staircase)
schneckenförmig	snail-shaped
Schneckengehäuse (−) *n*	snail shell
Schneckenlöckchen (−) *n*	snail-shaped curl
Schneidemesser (−) *n*	carver, wood-carving knife
schneiden	to cut
Schneidenadel(n) *f*	drypoint needle

Schneuß(e) *m*	mouchette, falchion
Schnitt(e) *m*	cut, section
Schnitt, der goldene –	golden section
Schnittebene(n) *f*	cross-section, intersecting plane
Schnittervase *f*	the Harvester Vase (Hagia Triada)
Schnittfläche(n) *f*	plane of intersection
Schnittlinie(n) *f*	line of intersection
Schnittpunkt(e) *m*	point of intersection
Schnittzeichnung(en) *f*	sectional drawing
Schnitzaltar (-altäre) *m*	carved altarpiece
Schnitzbank (-bänke) *f*	woodcarver's workbench, banker
Schnitzbild(er) *n*	carving, carved statue
Schnitzeisen (–) *n*	woodcarving chisel
schnitzen	to carve
Schnitzer (–) *m*	carver
Schnitzerei(en) *f*	carving
Schnitzkunst *f*	(art of) carving
Schnitzmesser (–) *n*	woodcarving knife
Schnitzwerk(e) *n*	carving
Schnörkel (–) *m*	scroll, volute, ornamental flourish
Schnupftabakdose(n) *f*	snuff box
Schnuramphore(n) *f*	globular amphora (corded ware)
Schnurkeramik *f*	corded ware
schön	beautiful, pretty, lovely
Schöndruck *m*	printing on only one side of the paper
Schöne Madonna (Madonnen) *f*	"Beautiful Madonna", Soft Style depiction of the Madonna
Schöner Gott *m*	Beau Dieu jamb statue
Schönheit(en) *f*	beauty
Schönheitsideal(e) *n*	ideal of beauty
schöpfen	to create
Schöpfer (–) *m*	creator
schöpferisch	creative
Schöpferkraft (-kräfte) *f*	creative power, creativity
Schöpfung(en) *f*	creation
Schöpfungsgeschichte *f*	story of Creation

Schöpfungskraft (-kräfte) *f*	creative power, creativity
Schöpfungstage, die sieben —	the Seven Days of the Creation
Schornstein(e) *m*	chimney
Schoß (Schöße) *m*	lap, womb
Schraffen *pl*	lines of a hatching pattern
schraffieren	to hatch
Schraffierung(en) *f*	hatching
Schraffur(en) *f*	hatching
schräg	diagonal, oblique, slanting, slanted, tilted
Schrägansicht(en) *f*	diagonal view, oblique view
Schräge(n) *f*	incline, slope, oblique line
Schräggeison(s) *n*	raking geison
Schrägkante(n) *f*	chamfer
Schrägkreuz(e) *n*	St. Andrew's cross
Schräglinie(n) *f*	diagonal, diagonal line
Schrank (Schränke) *m*	cupboard, closet, cabinet
Schraube(n) *f*	screw
schraubenförmig	spiral
Schreiber (—) *m*	1. pen 2. scribe, writer
Schreiberfigur(en) *f*	seated scribe (statue)
Schreiberwerkstätte(n) *f*	scriptorium
Schreibfeder(n) *f*	writing quill
Schreibpinsel (—) *m*	lettering brush
Schreibstube(n) *f*	scriptorium
Schreibtisch(e) *m*	desk
Schrein(e) *m*	1. shrine 2. center panel of an altarpiece
Schreinalter (-altäre) *m*	winged altarpiece
Schreiner (—) *m*	joiner, cabinet maker
Schreinfigur(en) *f*	carved figure for the middle section of an altarpiece
Schrift(en) *f*	writing, script, book hand
Schrift, die Heilige —	the Scriptures
Schrift, nach der —	proof after letter, after all letters, avec la lettre

Schrift, vor der —	proof before letter, before all letters, avant la lettre
Schriftband (-bänder) *n*	banderole
Schriftbild(er) *n*	object poem
Schriftdekor *m*	letter decoration, letters, writing
Schriftgelehrten, Christus unter den —	Christ Among the Doctors, the Dispute in the Temple
Schriftquelle(n) *f*	written source, document
Schriftrolle(n) *f*	scroll
Schrifttyp(en) *m*	typeface
Schriftzeichen (—) *n*	written letter, character, type
Schrittstellung *f*	stance
Schrotblatt (-blätter) *n*	print produced by *Schrotschnitt* technique
Schroteisen (—) *n*	chisel
schroten	to chisel
Schrotmeißel (—) *m*	chisel
Schrotschnitt(e) *m*	printing technique similar to woodcut using a metal plate
Schub *m*	thrust
Schubkraft (-kräfte) *f*	thrust
Schublade(n) *f*	drawer
Schularbeit(en) *f*	school work, piece done completely by workshop member(s)
Schule(n) *f*	school
schulen	to train
Schüler (—) *m*	pupil, student
Schulter(n) *f*	1. shoulder 2. section of vase below the neck
Schulterbogen (—, -bögen) *m*	shouldered arch
Schuppenmuster (—) *n*	scalloped pattern, fish scale pattern
Schurz(e) *m*	loincloth
Schuß *m*	woof, weft
Schüssel(n) *f*	bowl, dish
Schußfaden (-fäden) *m*	weft thread

Schütze(n) *m*	1. Sagittarius 2. weaving shuttle
Schutzengel (–) *m*	guardian angel, especially Raphael with Tobias
Schützenstück(e) *n*	Doelenstuk, Schutterstuk, marksmen's guild piece
Schutzgottheit(en) *f*	protective deity
Schutzmantelmadonna *f*	Madonna of Mercy, mater misericordiae
Schutzpatron(e) *m*	patron saint
Schwalbenschwanzfuge(n) *f*	dovetail joint
schwarz	black
schwarze Kunst *f*	mezzotint
Schwärze *f*	1. blackness, darkness 2. printer's ink
schwärzen	to blacken, to darken
schwarzfigurig	black-figured
Schwarzholz *n*	ebony
Schwarzkreidezeichnung(en) *f*	black chalk drawing
Schwarzkunst *f*	mezzotint
schwärzlich	blackish, dark
Schwarzlot *n*	black enamel (used for painting interior details of a stained glass window)
schwarzweiß	black and white
schwefelgelb	sulfur yellow
Schwefelsilber *n*	niello
Schweifwerk *n*	baroque scrollwork
Schweinfurtergrün *n*	emerald green
schweißen	to weld
Schweißtuch (-tücher) *n*	vernicle, sudarium, cloth with an image of Christ's face, St. Veronica's veil
Schweißtuch der hl. Veronika, das—	the veil of St. Veronica, vernicle
Schwelle(n) *f*	threshold
schwer	1. heavy 2. difficult

Schwert(er) *n*	sword
Schwertgriff(e) *m*	sword grip, sword handle
Schwertlilie(n) *f*	iris, fleur-di-lis
Schwibbogen (—, -bögen) *m*	strainer arch
Schwundriß (-risse) *m*	crack caused by shrinkage
Schwundsprung (-sprünge) *m*	crack caused by shrinkage
sculp.	sculp.
Seccomalerei *f*	secco painting
Secento *n*	seicento
Sechseck(e) *n*	hexagon
sechseckig	hexagonal
Seebild(er) *n*	sea piece, seascape
Seegemälde (—) *n*	sea piece, seascape
Seele(n) *f*	soul
Seelenwägung, die —	the Weighing of the Souls
Seestück(e) *n*	sea piece, seascape
Segelgewölbe (—) *n*	sail vault
Segensgestus *m*	gesture of blessing
Segmentbogen (—, -bögen) *m*	segmental arch
Segmentgiebel (—) *m*	gable in shape of a segmental arch
Sehachse(n) *f*	line of vision
Seherfahrung(en) *f*	visual experience
Sehne(n) *f*	tendon, sinew
Sehpyramide *f*	cone of vision
Seicento *n*	seicento
Seide(n) *f*	silk
seiden	(of) silk, silken
Seidenstickerei(en) *f*	silk embroidery
Seidenstoff(e) *m*	silk cloth, silk
Seidenweberei *f*	silk weaving
Seifenlauge *f*	lye
Seite(n) *f*	1. side 2. page

Seitenansicht(en) *f*	side view
seitenfüllend	page-filling, filling the entire page
Seitenlänge(n) *f*	lateral length, length of a side
Seitenschiff(e) *n*	lateral aisle, side aisle
Seitenschub *m*	lateral thrust
seitlich	lateral, laterally
Sekkomalerei *f*	secco painting
Sekundärfarbe(n) *f*	secondary color
Seladon *n*	celadon, celadon ware
seladongrün	celadon green
Seladonporzellan *n*	celadon porcelain; green-glazed Chinese ware
Selbdritt, Anna —	(depiction of) St. Anne, the Virgin and the Christ Child
Selbstbildnis(se) *n*	self portrait
selbständig	independent, free-lance
seldschukisch	Seljuk
Semantik *f*	semantics
Semeiotik *f* *also* Semiotik *f*	semiotics
Sendgerichtshalle(n) *f*	hall in which church trials of laymen were held
senkrecht	vertical, perpendicular
Senkrechte(n) *f*	vertical line
Sense(n) *f*	sickle, scythe
Sepia *f*	sepia
Sepiazeichnung(en) *f*	pen or brush drawing with sepia
Sepulcrum (Sepulcra) *n*	sepulchrum, altar cavity for relics
Seraph(im) *m*	seraph
Serie(n) *f*	series
Serienfertigung(en) *f*	series production
Serife(n) *f*	serif
serifenlos	sans-serif
Serigraphie(n) *f*	serigraph, silk screen
Serpentin *m*	serpentine
Sessel (—) *m*	arm chair, easy chair
Setzstufe(n) *f*	stair riser

Sezession(en) *f*	secession
Sezessionstil *m*	art nouveau in Austria, Vienna Sezession
Sfumato *n*	sfumato
Sgraffito(s, Sgraffiti) *n*	sgraffito
Sheddach (-dächer) *n*	sawtooth (factory) roof
Sibylle(n) *f*	sibyl
Sichel(n) *f*	1. crescent 2. scythe
sichelförmig	crescent-shaped
sichtbar	visible
Sichtbarkeit *f*	visibility
Sichtbeton *m*	exposed concrete
Siebdruck(e) *m*	silk screen
sieben freien Künste, die —	the seven liberal arts
Sieben Freuden Mariä, die —	the Seven Joys of the Virgin
Sieben Schmerzen Mariä, die —	the Seven Sorrows of the Virgin
Sieben Weltwunder, die —	Seven Wonders of the World
Siebrahmen (—) *m*	silk screen printing frame
Siedlung(en) *f*	settlement, housing complex, housing development
Sieg(e) *m*	victory
Siegel (—) *n*	seal
Siegelabdruck(e) *m*	seal impression
Siegelabrollung(en) *f*	seal(ing) cylinder impression
Siegelkunde *f*	sigillography, study of seals
Siegellack *m*	sealing wax
Siegelring(e) *m*	seal ring
Siegelschneidekunst *f*	(art of making) seals
Siegelwachs *n*	sealing wax
Siegelzylinder (—) *m*	seal(ing) cylinder
Sieger (—) *m*	victor
Siegesgöttin(nen) *f*	goddess of victory
Siegessäule(n) *f*	victory column
Siegesstele(n) *f*	victory stele

siegreich	victorious
siena	red-brown
sienesisch	Sienese
Sigillum (Sigilla) *n*	1. lid of a relic sepulchre 2. seal
Signatur(en) *f*	signature
signiert	signed
Signierung(en) *f*	signature, signing
Signum (Signa) *n*	sign, mark, initials
Sikkativ(e) *n*	siccative, drier
Silbenschrift(en) *f*	syllabary; writing system in which each symbol represents a syllable
Silbenzeichen (–) *n*	symbol for a syllable, character
Silber *n*	silver
Silberblech *n*	thin sheet of silver
Silbergerät(e) *n*	silver utensil, silverware
silbergrau	silver gray
Silberlot *n*	silver stain *stained glass*
silbern	(of) silver
Silberplattierung *f*	silver plating
Silberschale(n) *f*	silver bowl
Silberschmelz *m*	cloisonné done on silver
Silberschmied(e) *m*	silversmith
Silberschmiedekunst *f*	(art of) silversmithing
Silbersmalte(n) *f*	silver smalto
Silberstift(e) *m*	silver point
silbrig	silvery
Silen	Silenus
Silene *pl*	sileni
Silhouette(n) *f*	silhouette
Silikagel *n*	silica gel
Silikatfarbe(n) *f*	paint with ethyl silicate as a vehicle
Silikatmalerei *f*	mineral painting, stereochromy
Sima (Simen) *f*	sima, cymatium
Sims(e) *n*	cornice, sill
Simson	Samson

Simultanität *f*	1. simultaneity
	2. simultaneous representation
Simultankontrast *m*	simultaneous contrast
Simultanwirkung *f*	simultaneous contrast, effect of simultaneous contrast
Singerie(n) *f*	singerie; depiction of a monkey aping a human occupation
sinkende Petrus, der —	the Navicella, St. Peter Sinking
Sinn(e) *m*	sense
Sinnbild(er) *n*	symbol
sinnbildlich	symbolic
sinnlich	sensuous
Sinnzeichen (—) *n*	symbol
Sinopia (Sinopien) *f*	sinopia, sinopia underdrawing
sintern	to vitrify, to fuse
Sinterung *f*	vitrification
Sintflut *f*	flood, Deluge
Sippe, die heilige —	the Holy Family (especially the Virgin and her relatives)
Sippenbild(er) *n*	depiction of St. Anne and the Virgin with various other members of the Holy Family
Sirene(n) *f*	Siren
Sitte(n) *f*	custom, tradition
Sittenbild(er) *n*	genre painting
Situla (Situlen) *f*	situla; bucket-shaped metal vessel
Sitz(e) *m*	seat, chair
Sitzbild(er) *n*	statue of a seated figure
sitzen	to sit
sitzend	sitting
Sitzkissen (—) *n*	chair cushion
Sitzkoloss(e) *m*	seated colossus
Sitzstufe(n) *f*	steps for sitting on (e. g. in a Greek theater)
Sixtinische Kapelle *f*	Sistine Chapel
Skarabäus (Skarabäen) *m*	scarab
Skelett(e) *n*	skeleton

Skelettbau(ten) *m*	skeleton building, skeleton construction
Skelettbauweise(n) *f*	skeleton construction
Skene(n) *f*	scene, theater stage
Skenographie *f*	scenography
Skizze(n) *f*	sketch
Skizzenbuch (-bücher) *n*	sketchbook
skizzenhaft	sketchy
skizzieren	to sketch
Skorpion(e) *m*	1. scorpion 2. Scorpio
Skriptorium (Skriptorien) *n*	scriptorium
skulptieren	to sculpt
Skulptur(en) *f*	sculpture
Skulpturnische(n) *f*	niche for the accommodation of sculpture
Skurz *m*	scorzo, iscorzo
Skyphos (Skyphoi) *m*	skyphos
Skythen *pl*	Scyths, Scythians
Smalte(n) *f*	1. smalto 2. smalt, cobalt enamel
Smaragd(e) *m*	emerald
Sockel (—) *m*	socle, pedestal, base
Sockelgeschoß (-geschosse) *n*	basement level, foundation
sockellos	having no socle or base
Sockelzone(n) *f*	socle area
Soffitte(n) *f*	soffitte
Sohlbank (-bänke) *f*	window sill, window ledge
Solitär(e) *m*	solitaire, single set gem
Söller (—) *m*	roofless balcony borne on supports from the ground
Solnhofer Kalkschiefer *m*	Solnhofen stone
Solnhofer Schiefer *m*	Solnhofen stone
Solutréen *n*	Solutrean (industry)
Sondergotik *f*	German late Gothic architecture style

Sonne(n) *f*	sun
Sonnenblende(n) *f*	sun blind, sun break, brise-soleil
Sonnengott (-götter) *m*	sun god
Sonnenlicht *n*	sunlight
Sonnenscheibe(n) *f*	(disc of the) sun
Sonnenspektrum *n*	solar spectrum
Sonnenstrahl(en) *m*	ray of sunlight, sunbeam
Sonnensymbol *n*	sun symbol
Sonnenwagen (–) *m*	sun chariot
Sonnenwagen von Trundholm *m*	Trundholm sun chariot
Sonnenzeichen (–) *n*	symbol or sign of the sun
Sonntagsmaler (–) *m*	Sunday painter, naive painter, amateur painter
Sopraporte(n) *f*	sopraporta, overdoor, dessus de porte
Sozialistischer Realismus *m*	Socialist Realism
Spachtel (–) *m* *also* Spachtel(n) *f*	spatula
spachteln	to work with a spatula, to apply paint with a spatula or knife
Spandrille(n) *f*	spandrel
Spange(n) *f*	clip, fibula, band
Spannbalken (–) *m*	tie-beam
Spannbeton *m*	prestressed concrete
spannen	to stretch, to strain
Spannrahmen (–) *m*	stretching frame
Spannung(en) *f*	tension
Spannweite(n) *f*	span
Spannzange(n) *f*	stretching pliers
Sparren (–) *m*	rafter
Sparrenwerk(e) *n*	rafters, framework
Spatel(s) *m*	spatula
Spätgotik *f*	Late Gothic, Perpendicular
späthellenistisch	late Hellenistic
spätmykenisch	late Mycenaean

Spätzeit *f*	Late Period
Speckstein *m*	soapstone, steatite
Speer(e) *m*	spear, lance, javelin
Speerschleuder(n) *f*	spear thrower
Speerspitze(n) *f*	spearhead
Speerträger (—) *m*	spear bearer, lance bearer
Spektralfarbe(n) *f*	spectral color
Sperrholz *n*	plywood
spezifische Intensität *f*	brilliance
Sphingen *pl*	*plural form of Sphinx*
Sphinx(e, Sphingen) *m*	(Egyptian) sphinx
Sphinx(en) *f*	(Greek) sphinx
Sphragistik *f*	sphragistics; the study of seals
Spiegel (—) *m*	mirror
Spiegelbild(er) *n*	reflection
Spiegelgalerie(n) *f*	hall of mirrors
Spiegelgewölbe (—) *n*	type of cloister vault with flat top
Spiegelkabinett(e) *n*	small, mirrored room for the display of porcelain and small works of art
Spiegelmalerei *f*	painting on glass, glass painting
Spiegelsaal (-säle) *m*	hall of mirrors
Spiegelung(en) *f*	reflection
Spielbein *n*	free leg
Spielkarte(n) *f*	playing card
Spielteppich(e) *m*	game carpet; carpet with figures and spaces for playing a game
Spindel(n) *f*	center post of spiral stair
Spindeltreppe(n) *f*	spiral stair, vyse
Spinell(e) *m*	spinel
Spirale(n) *f*	spiral, spiral-shaped ornament
Spiralsäule(n) *f*	1. column decorated with spirals 2. spiral-shaped column, Salomonica
Spiritus *m*	alcohol
Spiritusfirnis(se) *m*	spirit varnish
spitz	pointed, sharp

Spitzbogen (–, -bögen) *m*	pointed arch
spitzbogig	shaped like a pointed or lancet arch, having a pointed arch
Spitze(n) *f*	1. peak, point 2. lace
Spitzeisen (–) *n*	point *sculpture*
Spitzenbild(er) *n*	lace-like silhouette
Spitzenkunst *f*	(art of making) lace
Spitzgiebel (–) *m*	peaked gable
Spitzhammer (-hämmer) *m*	pointed sculptor's hammer
Spitzmeißel (–) *m*	point, pointed chisel
Spitzmütze(n) *f*	pointed cap
Spitzzahnfries(e) *m*	dog-tooth ornament
Spitzzahnornament(e) *n*	dog-tooth ornament
Splintholz *n*	sapwood
Spolium (Spolien) *n*	part of a work which was originally in another work; bootied piece
Sprengwedel (–) *m*	aspergill, aspergillum
Sprengwerk *n*	construction in which two diagonal braces help support a beam over a wide opening
sprenkeln	to spatter, to sprinkle
Sprieße(n) *f*	brace, supporting beam
Sprießholz *n*	brace, supporting beam
springen	to crack
Spritzbewurf *m*	scratch coat *fresco*
Spritzmalerei *f*	spray painting
Spritzpistole(n) *f*	spray gun, airbrush
spröde	brittle
Sprödigkeit *f*	brittleness
Sprossenstuhl (-stühle) *m*	chair form in which the back legs and back rest are one piece (or one line)
Spruchband (-bänder) *n*	banderole
Sprung (Sprünge) *m*	crack, flaw
Staat(en) *m*	state
Staatsbibliothek(en) *f*	state library, national library
Stab (Stäbe) *m*	staff, stick, rod, bar, stave

Stabbogen (−, -bögen) *m*	tied arch
stabil	stabile, stable
Stabile(s) *n*	stabile
Stabkirche(n) *f*	stave church
Stabwerk(e) *n*	mullions, bar tracery
Stadion (Stadien) *n*	stadium
Stadium (Stadien) *n*	stage, level
Stadt (Städte) *f*	city
Stadtansicht(en) *f*	cityscape, veduta
Stadtbaukunst *f*	city planning
Stadtbaumeister (−) *m*	city architect, city planner, building commissioner
Städtebau *m*	city planning
Stadtlandschaft(en) *f*	cityscape
Stadtmauer(n) *f*	city wall
Stadtplanung *f*	city planning
Stadttor(e) *n*	city gate
Stadttorsarkophag(e) *m*	city-gate sarcophagus
Stadtvedute(n) *f*	veduta
Staffage(n) *f*	staffage; incidental people or animals in a painting
Staffel(n) *f*	1. predella 2. echelon
Staffelchor (-chöre) *m*	(chancel with) chapels in echelon
Staffelei(en) *f*	easel
Staffeleibild(er) *n*	easel painting, picture painted on an easel
Staffelgiebel (−) *m*	corbie gable, stepped gable
Staffelhalle(n) *f*	hall church with raised nave but no nave windows
Staffierer (−) *m*	artist who paints or gilds sculpture
Staffiermaler (−) *m*	artist who paints or gilds sculpture
Staffiermalerei *f*	the painting or gilding of (wooden) sculpture
Stahl *m*	steel
Stahlbau(ten) *m*	steel construction, steel building
Stahlbauelement(e) *n*	steel structural element

Stahlbeton *m*	ferroconcrete, (steel) reinforced concrete
Stahlbetonkonstruktion(en) *f*	reinforced concrete construction, ferroconcrete construction
stahlblau	steel blue
Stahlfeder(n) *f*	steel drawing pen
stahlgrau	steel gray
Stahlskelettbau(ten) *m*	steel frame building
Stahlstich(e) *m*	steel engraving
Stahlstütze(n) *f*	steel support
Stahlträger (−) *m*	steel girder
Stalaktiten-Gewölbe (−) *n*	vault with stalactite work
Stallen *pl*	choir stalls
Stamm (Stämme) *m*	1. stem, trunk 2. tribe
Stammbaum (-bäume) *m*	genealogical table, family tree
Stammbaum Christi, der −	Tree of Jesse
stammen	to originate, to come (from)
Stamnos *m*	stamnos
Standarte(n) *f*	standard, flag
Standbein *n*	engaged leg
Standbild(er) *n*	statue
Ständer (−) *m*	upright beam
Ständerbau(ten) *m*	wood frame construction
Standeskultur(en) *f*	class society, society based on rank
Standöl *n*	stand oil
Stangenglas (-gläser) *n*	cylindrical glass
Stanze(n) *f*	1. stanza 2. stamp, punch
stanzen	to punch, to stamp
Stärke *f*	1. strength 2. thickness 3. starch, glue
Stärkegummi *m*	dextrin
Stärkekleister (−) *m*	starch paste
starr	rigid, stiff
Starrheit *f*	rigidity, rigidness

Statik *f*	statics
statisch	static
Stätte(n) *f*	site, location
statuarisch	statuesque, statue-like
Statue(n) *f*	statue
statuenhaft	statuesque
Statuette(n) *f*	statuette
staufische Kunst *f*	Staufen art; art of the Hohenstaufen empire
Staurothek(en) *f*	cruciform reliquary (containing relics of the cross)
Steatit *m*	steatite
Stecheisen (−) *n*	punch
stechen	to engrave
Stecher (−) *m*	engraver
Steg(e) *m*	fillet, listel
stehen	1. to stand 2. to be located
steif	stiff
steigender Bogen (−, Bögen) *m*	quadrant arch
Steigung *f*	stair riser
Steildach (-dächer) *n*	slanted roof, pitched roof
Stein(e) *m*	stone
Steinart(en) *f*	type of stone
Steinbalken (−) *m*	lintel, stone beam
Steinbau(ten) *m*	stone construction, stone building
Steinbearbeitungstechnik(en) *f*	technique of working or processing stone
Steinbildhauer (−) *m*	stone sculptor
Steinblock (-blöcke) *m*	block of stone
Steinbock *m*	Capricorn
Steinbuntdruck(e) *m*	color lithograph
Steindruck(e) *m*	lithography, lithograph
Steindrucker (−) *m*	lithographer
Steindruckerei(en) *f*	lithographic press
Steindruckfarbe(n) *f*	lithographic ink

steinern	(of) stone
Steinfragment(e) *n*	stone fragment
Steingebälk *n*	stone entablature
Steingerät(e) *n*	stone tool
Steinguß *m*	the casting of imitation stone
Steingut *n*	(white) earthware, pottery
Steininschrift(en) *f*	petroglyph, inscription in stone
Steinkammergrab (-gräber) *n*	megalithic tomb
Steinkistengrab (-gräber) *n*	cist grave
Steinkopf (-köpfe) *m*	stone head
Steinkreide *f*	native chalk
Steinmalerei(en) *f*	stone mosaic
Steinmeißel (–) *m*	stone chisel
Steinmetz(e) *m*	stone mason
Steinmetzkunst *f*	(art of) stone masonry
Steinmetzzeichen (–) *n*	stone mason's mark, maker's mark
Steinperle(n) *f*	stone bead
Steinplastik(en) *f*	stone sculpture
Steinplatte(n) *f*	stone slab, stone plate
Steinsarg (-särge) *m*	stone coffin, sarcophagus
Steinschneidekunst *f*	(art of) gem cutting, glyptics
Steinschneider (–) *m*	lapidary, cameo cutter
Steinskulptur(en) *f*	stone sculpture
Steintonne(n) *f*	stone barrel vault
Steinumfriedung(en) *f*	stone enclosure
Steinwerkzeug(e) *n*	stone tool
Steinzeichner (–) *m*	lithographer
Steinzeichnung(en) *f*	lithograph
Steinzeit *f*	Stone Age
Steinzeug *n*	(salt-glazed) stoneware
Stele(n) *f*	stele
Stellung(en) *f*	position
Stellungsmotiv(e) *n*	position motif
Stellwand (-wände) *f*	partition, partition wall
Stempel (–) *m*	stamp, punch

Stempelkeramik *f*	ceramic ware with impressed decoration
stempeln	to stamp, to impress
Stempelschneider (−) *m*	carver of stamps or seals
Stempelsiegel (−) *n*	stamp seal
Stengelkohle(n) *f*	charcoal, charcoal crayon
sterblich	mortal
Stereobat(en) *m*	stereobate
Stereochromie *f*	stereochromy, mineral painting
Stereometrie(n) *f*	stereometry
stereometrisch	stereometric
Stern(e) *m*	star
Sternbild(er) *n*	1. constellation 2. sign of the zodiac
sternförmig	stellate, star-shaped
Sterngewölbe (−) *n*	stellar vault
Sternkranzsarkophag(e) *m*	sarcophagus decorated with stars and wreaths, especially in the spandrels between the figures
Stich(e) *m*	engraving
Stichbalken (−) *m*	hammer beam
Stichbandkeramik *f*	stroke-ornamented ware
Stichblatt (-blätter) *n*	protective metal plate between sword blade and grip
Stichbogen (−, -bögen) *m*	segmental arch
Stichel (−) *m*	graver, burin
Stichhöhe(n) *f*	rise (of an arch)
Stichkappe(n) *f*	curved undersurface above a lunette
Stichverfahren (−) *n*	engraving process, engraving procedure
Stickerei(en) *f*	embroidery
Stiege(n) *f*	stairway; steep and narrow stair
Stiegenhaus (-häuser) *n*	stairway, staircase
Stier(e) *m*	1. bull 2. Taurus
Stier, der farnesische −	Farnese bull
Stierkapitell(e) *n*	(double) bull capital, capital with bull protome(s)

Stieropfer (—) n	sacrifice of a bull
Stift(e) n	foundation, cloister, convent, chapter
Stift(e) m	1. pencil, crayon, chalk, style, stylus 2. peg, pin
stiften	to donate, to endow
Stifter (—) m	donor, founder
Stifterbildnis(se) n	donor portrait
Stifterfigur(en) f	figure or statue of the donor
Stifterwappen (—) n	donor's coat-of-arms
Stifthalter (—) m	portcrayon
Stiftmosaik(en) n	pegged mosaic, cone mosaic
Stiftskirche(n) f	collegiate church
Stiftung(en) f	endowment, charity, foundation
Stigma (Stigmen) n	stigma
Stigmatisation f	stigmatization
Stil(e) m	style
Stilanalyse(n) f	analysis of style
Stilbezeichnung(en) f	designation or name of a style
Stilbruch (-brüche) m	breach in style
Stilform(en) f	style
stilgeschichtlich	regarding the history of a style
Stilisierung(en) f	stylization
stilistisch	stylistic
Stilleben (—) n	still life
Stillebenmalerei f	still life painting
Stilmerkmal(e) n	characteristic of a style
Stilrichtung(en) f	style
Stilstufe(n) f	stage in the development of a style
Stilus (Stili) m	stylus, style
Stilwandel (—) m	change in style
Stilwandlung(en) f	change in style
Stilwille m	style, urge to create style
Stimmung(en) f	mood, atmosphere
Stimmungslandschaft(en) f	mood landscape, landscape intended to evoke a mood

Stipes *m*	stipes; part of altar which supports the mensa
Stipesgrab (-gräber) *n*	relics or tomb inside the stipes
Stirn(en) *f*	1. forehead 2. front side of an arch
Stirnmauer(n) *f*	front wall
Stirnreif(e) *m*	headband
Stirnseite(n) *f*	front, front side
Stirnziegel (–) *m*	acroterion, antefixa
Stoa *f*	stoa
Stockbrunnen (–) *m*	fountain consisting of a pier or column and a basin
Stockhammer (-hämmer) *m*	bushhammer *sculpture*
Stockwerk(e) *n*	story, floor
Stoff(e) *m*	material, cloth
Stoffbahn(en) *f*	train of cloth or material
Stoffdruck *m*	textile printing
Stoffragment(e) *n*	fragment of fabric
Stoichedon *n*	arrangement of letters on Greek inscriptions in rows under each other with no spaces between words
Stola (Stolen) *f*	stola
Stollen (–) *m*	1. post, support 2. tunnel
Stollenkrypta (-krypten) *f*	crypt consisting of individual chambers
Stollenschrank (-schränke) *m*	tallboy, medieval chest on legs with sliding drawers
Stöpsel (–) *m*	stopper
Storchschnabel (–) *m*	pantograph
Stößel (–) *n*	muller
Stoßzahn (-zähne) *m*	tusk
straff	tight
Straffheit *f*	tightness
Strahl(en) *m*	beam, ray
strahlen	to shine, to radiate
strahlend	shining, radiant

Strahlengewölbe (−) *n*	fan vault
Strahlenkranz (-kränze) *m*	halo, nimbus, glory
Strahlenkranzmadonna *f*	depiction of the Virgin with radiating lines surrounding her
Strahlenkrone(n) *f*	halo, nimbus, glory
Strahlenperspektive(n) *f*	angular perspective, oblique perspective
Strahlensymmetrie *f*	radial symmetry
Strahlkraft *f*	radiance, radiant power
Strandszene(n) *f*	beach scene
Straße(n) *f*	street
Straßenbild(er) *n*	street scene
Straßenszene(n) *f*	street scene
Stratigraphie *f*	stratigraphy
Straußenei(er) *n*	ostrich egg
Strebe(n) *f*	buttress, strut
Strebebogen (−, -bögen) *m*	flying buttress (arch), quadrant arch
Strebepfeiler (−) *m*	pier buttress
Strebewerk(e) *n*	buttressing
Streckung(en) *f*	stretching, elongation
Streifen (−) *m*	band, strip, stripe
Streifenornamentik *f*	striped decoration, stripes
Streitaxt (-äxte) *f*	battleaxe
Streitwagen (−) *m*	battle chariot, war chariot
streng	severe, strict
Strenge *f*	severity, strictness
strenger Stil *m*	Severe Style
Streumuster (−) *n*	pattern of irregularly strewn flowers and/or leaves
Strich(e) *m*	stroke, line
Strichätzung(en) *f*	autotype, etching of a drawing for relief printing
Strichelung(en) *f*	striations, grooves
Strichplatte(n) *f*	key block, key plate *multicolor printing*

Strichzeichnung(en) *f*	line drawing
strigiliert	decorated with S-shaped striations, strigal patterned
Strohdach (-dächer) *n*	thatched roof
strohfarben	straw-colored
Strömung(en) *f*	current, trend
Strontiumgelb *n*	strontium yellow
Struktur(en) *f*	structure
Strukturelement(e) *n*	structural element
strukturell	structural, structurally
Stuck *m*	plaster, stucco
Stück(e) *n*	piece
Stuckmarmor *m*	scagliola
Stuckrelief(s) *n*	stucco relief
Stuckschicht(en) *f*	stucco coating, stucco layer
Studie(n) *f*	study
Studio(s) *n*	studio, atelier, artist's workshop
Stufe(n) *f*	step, stage
stufenförmig	step-shaped, stepped
Stufengiebel (−) *m*	corbie gable, stepped gable
Stufenhallenkirche(n) *f*	hall church with raised nave but no nave windows
Stufenportal(e) *n*	portal recessed in several steps, portal with splayed jambs
Stufenpyramide(n) *f*	step-pyramid
Stufentempel (−) *m*	ziggurat
Stufenunterbau(ten) *m*	crepidoma, stair foundation
Stuhl (Stühle) *m*	chair
Stukkateur(e) *m*	plasterer, stucco worker
Stukkatur(en) *f*	stucco, stucco work
Stukkierung(en) *f*	stucco, stucco work
stumpf	dull, lustreless
Stundenbuch (-bücher) *n*	Book of Hours
Stundenglas (-gläser) *n*	hour glass
Stupa(s) *m*	stupa
Sturz(e) *m*	lintel, transom
Sturz, scheitrechter −	flat arch

Sturzbecher (–) *m*	funnel-shaped glass or tumbler with no base
Sturzbogen (–, -bögen) *m*	flat arch
Stützbalken (–) *m*	supporting beam, strut
Stütze(n) *f*	support
Stützelement(e) *n*	supporting element
stützen	to support, to prop
Stützenträger (–) *m*	support girder
Stützenwechsel (–) *m*	alternating system of supports; rhythmic alternation of pillars and columns
Stutzkuppel(n) *f*	sail vault
Stützmauer(n) *f*	supporting wall, retaining wall
Stylobat(en) *m*	stylobate
Styropor *n*	styrofoam
Substanzfarbe(n) *f*	color having substance; colors, dyes, pigments, paints etc. as opposed to colored light
Substruktion(en) *f*	substructure, foundation
Sudatorium (Sudatorien) *n*	steam room in the Thermae
Sujet(s) *n*	subject, picture theme
Sukzessivkontrast *m*	phenomenon of negative afterimage
sumerische Kunst *f*	Sumerian art
Sündenfall, der –	the Fall of Man
Sündflut *f*	flood, Deluge
Suppedaneum (Suppedanea) *n*	1. suppedaneum; foot rest on the cross 2. top step to altar
Supraporte(n) *f*	sopraporta, overdoor, dessus de porte
Suprematismus *m*	Suprematism
Suprematist(en) *m*	Suprematist
surreal	surreal, surrealistic
Surrealismus *m*	Surrealism
Surrealist(en) *m*	Surrealist
Symbol(e) *n*	symbol
Symbolfarbe(n) *f*	symbolic color, color having symbolic meaning

Symbolfigur(en) *f*	symbolic figure
Symbolform(en) *f*	symbolic form, symbolic shape
symbolhaft	symbolic
Symbolik *f*	symbolism
Symbolinhalt(e) *m*	symbolic meaning
symbolisch	symbolic
symbolisieren	to symbolize
Symbolismus *m*	Symbolism
Symbolist(en) *m*	Symbolist
Symbolkeramik *f*	Symbolkeramik; Los Millares pottery ware
Symbolsprache(n) *f*	symbolism, vocabulary of symbols
Symbolwert(e) *m*	symbolic value
Symmetrie *f*	symmetry
Symmetrieachse *f*	axis of symmetry, central axis
Symmetrieebene *f*	plane of symmetry
symmetrisch	symmetric, symmetrical, symmetrically
Synagoge(n) *f*	synagogue
Synchronismus *m*	synchronism
System(e) *n*	system, plan
systematisch	systematic, systematically
Szene(n) *f*	scene
Szenenfolge(n) *f*	series of scenes, order of the scenes
Szenographie *f*	scenography
Szepter (—) *n*	scepter
szythisch	Scythian

Tabernakel (—) *m, n*	tabernacle
Tablinum (Tablina) *n*	tablinum
Tabu(s) *n*	taboo
Tachismus *m*	Tachisme
Taenia (Taenien) *f*	tenia
Tafel(n) *f*	panel, tablet, plate
Tafelbild(er) *n*	panel painting

Tafelmalerei *f*	panel painting
Täfelung(en) *f*	paneling
Täfelwerk *n*	paneling
Tageslicht *n*	daylight
Tagewerk *n*	giornata; fresco work done in one day
Taille(n) *f*	waist
Taillierung(en) *f*	tailoring
Talent(e) *n*	talent, talented person
talentiert	talented
talentvoll	talented
Talisman(e) *m*	talisman
Talmud *m*	Talmud
Tambour(e) *m*	tambour
Tambourkuppel(n) *f*	dome resting on a tambour
Tambourzone(n) *f*	tambour area
Tanagrafigur(en) *f*	Tanagra statuette, Tanagra figurine
Tannenholz *n*	fir wood
Tänzer (—) *m*	dancer
Tapete(n) *f*	wallpaper
Tapetendruck *m*	the printing of wallpaper
Tapisserie(n) *f*	tapestry
Tasche(n) *f*	bag, sack, pocket
Tasse(n) *f*	cup
tasten	to touch, to feel
Tasterzirkel (—) *m*	calliper
Tastsinn *m*	sense of touch
tatauieren	to tattoo
tätowieren	to tattoo
Tätowierung(en) *f*	tattoo, tattooing
Tau(e) *n*	cable, cable moulding
Tau, gedrehtes —	cable moulding
Taube(n) *f*	dove
Taufbecken (—) *n*	baptismal font
Taufe, die — Christi	Baptism of Christ
Täufer, Johannes der —	John the Baptist
Taufkapelle(n) *f*	baptistry, baptismal chapel

Taufkirche(n) *f*	baptistry
Taufstein(e) *m*	baptismal font
Taukreuz(e) *n*	tau cross
tauschieren	to Damascene
tauschiert	Damascened
Tauschierung(en) *f*	Damascening
Täuschung(en) *f*	illusion
Täuschung, optische —	optical illusion
Tausendblumen-teppich(e) *m*	mille-fleur-tapisserie
Teakholz *n*	teak
Technik(en) *f*	1. technique 2. technology
Teer *m*	tar
Teerfarbe(n) *f*	coal-tar color, coal-tar dye
Teerfarblack(e) *m*	coal-tar lake
Teerfarbstoff(e) *m*	coal-tar color, synthetic organic pigment
Teigdruck *m*	woodcut process in which paper is covered with a pasty mass before printing
Teigfarbe(n) *f*	pastel, pastel paint
Teil(e) *m, n*	part, portion, section
Teilansicht(en) *f*	partial view, portion, detail
Teilbestattung(en) *f*	inhumation of part of the body
Teint *m*	color of the skin
Tektonik *f*	tectonics
tektonisch	tectonic
Teller (—) *m*	plate, dish
Tempel (—) *m*	temple
Tempelbau(ten) *m*	temple, temple building, temple construction
Tempelgang Mariä, der —	Presentation of the Virgin
Tempelkammer(n) *f*	temple chamber
Tempelruine(n) *f*	temple ruins
Tempera(s) *f*	tempera
Temperafarbe(n) *f*	tempera, tempera paint
Temperamalerei *f*	tempera painting

Teneberleuchter (–) *m*	Tenebrae candelabrum; candelabrum used during Passion week
Tenebrosmalerei *f*	tenebrism, tenebrist painting
Tepidarium (Tepidarien) *n*	tepidarium
Teppich(e) *m*	carpet, tapestry
Teppichfolge(n) *f*	series of tapestries
Terpentin *n*	turpentine
Terpentin, Venezianer –	Venice turpentine
Terpentinöl *n*	oil of turpentine
Terpentingeist *m*	spirit of turpentine, oil of turpentine
Terraindarstellung(en) *f*	depiction of terrain, landscape
Terrakotta *f*	terracotta
Terra Sigillata *f*	terra sigillata
Terrasse(n) *f*	terrace
terrassiert	terraced
Terrazzo *m*	terrazzo
Terrine(n) *f*	tureen
Tessellatum *n*	mosaic technique using pre-cut tesserae (as opposed to *Vermiculatum*)
Testament, das Alte –	Old Testament
Testament, das Neue –	New Testament
Tetrachromie(n) *f*	four-color print
Tetramorph(en) *m*	tetramorph; four-headed, winged cherub
Teufel (–) *m*	devil
Textbild(er) *n*	1. picture with text incorporated 2. text as picture
textil	textile
Textilien *pl*	textiles
Textur(en) *f*	texture
Thaumatologie *f*	thaumatology
Theater (–) *n*	theater
Theaterdekoration(en) *f*	stage set, scenery
Thema (Themen) *n*	theme, subject, topic
Themenkreis(e) *m*	themes, thematic subjects, available thematic subjects

Theophaniebild(er) *n*	theophany, theophany picture
Thermen *pl*	thermae
Thermolumineszenz *f*	thermoluminescence (dating)
Thixotropie *f*	thixotrophy
Tholos (Tholoi) *m*	tholos; columned circular structure
Thomaswunder, das —	the Incredulity of Thomas
Thron(e) *m*	throne
thronend	enthroned
Thronhimmel (—) *m*	canopy, baldachin over a throne
Thronsaal (-säle) *m*	throne room
Thuja *f*	thuja wood, arbor vitae
Thyrsus (Thyrsi) *m*	thyrsus; staff symbolic of Bacchus
Thyrsusstab (-stäbe) *m*	thyrsus, thyrsus staff
Tiara (Tiaren) *f*	tiara
tief	deep
Tiefdruck *m*	intaglio printing, gravure printing
Tiefe(n) *f*	depth
Tiefenbau *m*	deep structure, internal structure
Tiefengestein *n*	plutonic rock
Tiefenwirkung(en) *f*	effect of depth
Tiefschaftstuhl (-stühle) *m*	low warp loom
Tiefschnittschmelz *m*	bassetaille
Tiekholz *n*	teak
Tier(e) *n*	animal
Tierfarbstoff(e) *m*	animal dye
Tiergefäß(e) *n*	animal-shaped vessel, rhyton
Tiergestalt(en) *f*	animal figure
Tierkreis *m*	zodiac
Tierkreisbild(er) *n*	sign of the zodiac
Tierkreiszeichen (—) *n*	sign of the zodiac
Tierornament(e) *n*	zoomorphic ornament
Tierornamentik *f*	Germanic animal ornament, animal interlace, zoomorphic ornament
Tierra di Siena gebrannt	burnt sienna
Tierra di Siena natur	raw sienna
Tierstaffage(n) *f*	staffage animal(s)
Tierstil *m*	animal style

Tierstück(e) *n*	animal depiction
Tiersymbolik *f*	animal symbolism
Tinte(n) *f*	ink
Tintenfaß (-fässer) *n*	inkwell
Tisch(e) *m*	table
Tischbein(e) *n*	table leg
Tischler (—) *m*	carpenter
Tischstaffelei(en) *f*	table easel
Titanomachie *f*	Titanomachy
Titanweiß *n*	titanium white
Titelblatt (-blätter) *n*	title page, frontispiece
Titeleinfassung(en) *f*	framework or border of title page
Titelheilige(n) *m, f*	titular saint
Titelkupfer (—) *n*	copper-engraved frontispiece
Titulus (Tituli) *m*	medieval picture caption, often in verse
tizianrot	golden red
TL-Datierung *f*	thermoluminescence dating
Tod *m*	death
Tod, der — Mariä *also* Tod, der — Mariens	Dormition of the Virgin, Death of the Virgin
Toga (Togen) *f*	toga
Togge(n) *f*	baluster
Ton (Töne) *m*	1. clay 2. tone, shade
Tonbozzetto (-bozzetti) *m*	clay bozzetto
Tondo(s, Tondi) *n*	tondo
Tonerde *f*	clay
tönern	(of) clay
Tongefäß(e) *n*	clay vessel, clay container
Tonholzschnitt(e) *m*	chiaroscuro woodcut
Tonhülle(n) *f*	clay cover
Tonletter(n) *f*	clay printing letter, clay type
Tonmalerei *f*	painting technique emphasizing color value and avoiding strong color contrasts
Tonmetope(n) *f*	clay metope

Tonnengewölbe (−) n	barrel vault, wagon vault, tunnel vault
tonnengewölbt	covered with a barrel vault
Tonpapier n	tinted paper, colored paper
Tonpatrize(n) f	clay stamp
Tonplastik(en) f	clay sculpture
Tonplatte(n) f	woodcut block for making a color print
Tonscherbe(n) f	clay shard, clay fragment
Tonschlicker m	slip
Tonstich(e) m	wood engraving
Tonstiftmosaik(en) n	clay pegged mosaic, clay cone mosaic
Tontafel(n) f	clay tablet
Tontafelhülle(n) f	clay tablet cover
Tönung(en) f	tint, shading
Tonware(n) f	earthenware, clay pottery
Tonwert(e) m	tone value
Tonziegel (−) m	clay brick
Topas m	topaz
Topf (Töpfe) m	pot, vessel, jar
Töpfer (−) m	potter
Töpferei(en) f	pottery, potter's workshop
Töpfererde f	potter's clay
Töpfergeschirr n	pottery, earthenware
Töpferkunst f	(art of making) pottery
Töpferscheibe(n) f	potter's wheel
Töpferton m	potter's clay
Töpferware(n) f	pottery, earthenware, crockery
Töpferzeug n	pottery, earthenware, crockery
Topographie(n) f	topography, topographical landscape
Tor(e) n	gate
Toreutik f	toreutics; (art of) metal working, especially embossing
Torhalle(n) f	gate hall, porch
Torhaus (-häuser) n	gate, gate house

Torinschrift(en) *f*	gate inscription
Torkret *m*	spray concrete
Torques (—) *m*	torc, torque; Celtic neck ring
Torso (Torsen) *m*	torso
Torturm (-türme) *m*	gate tower
Torus (Tori) *m*	torus
toskanische Ordnung *f*	Tuscan order
Totem (—) *n*	totem, totem pole
Totempfahl (-pfähle) *m*	totem pole
Totenbahre(n) *f*	funeral bier
Totenbuch, das —	the Book of the Dead
Totenmaske(n) *f*	death mask
Totenschild(e) *m*	hatchment, memorial shield
Totentanz (-tänze) *m*	Dance of Death, danse macabre
Totentempel (—) *m*	mortuary temple
Tracht(en) *f*	traditional costume
Trachyt *m*	trachyte
Tradition(en) *f*	tradition
traditionell	traditional, traditionally
Tragaltar (-altäre) *m*	portable altar
Tragantschleim *m*	gum tragacanth
tragen	to carry, to bear, to support, to wear
Träger (—) *m*	girder, beam
Tragfigur(en) *f*	processional statue, statue to be carried in a procession
Traghimmel (—) *m*	portable canopy, portable baldachin
Tragik *f*	tragedy
Tragkonstruktion(en) *f*	weight-bearing structure
Tragkraft *f*	weight-bearing capacity
Tragsessel (—) *m*	sedan chair
Tragstahl-Skelett(e) *n*	supporting steel construction, steel skeleton
Tragstein(e) *m*	corbel, console
Tragwand (-wände) *f*	supporting wall, load-bearing wall
Trajanssäule *f*	Column of Trajan

Trakt(e) *m*	wing of a building
Transept(e) *n*	transept
Transfiguration, die —	the Transfiguration
transluzid	translucid
transparent	transparent
Transparentbild(er) *n*	transparent picture
Transparentpapier *n*	tracing paper, transparent paper
Trapez(e) *n*	trapezoid
Trapezkapitell, byzantinisches *n*	Byzantine trapezoidal capital
Traufe(n) *f*	eaves
Traufleiste(n) *f*	drain, gutter, trough
Traufrinne(n) *f*	gutter, drain
Travée(n) *f*	bay
Travée, rhythmische —	rhythmically divided bay
Travertin *m*	travertine
Trecento *n*	trecento
Treibarbeit(en) *f*	repoussé
Treibholz *n*	driftwood
Treibpech *n*	pad used in doing repoussé work
Tremolierstich(e) *m*	assayer's test, purity test for silver
Trennwand (-wände) *f*	partition, partition wall
Trepanation(en) *f*	trepanation, trepanning, trephining
Treppe(n) *f*	stairway, steps, stairs
Treppenabsatz (-sätze) *m*	landing
Treppenanfänger (—) *m*	newel post
Treppengiebel (—) *m*	corbie gable, stepped gable
Treppenhaus (-häuser) *n*	staircase
Treppenpfosten (—) *m*	newel, newel post
Treppenpodest(e) *n*	landing
Treppenspindel(n) *f*	center post of a spiral stair
Treppenturm (-türme) *m*	stair turret, stair tower
Tretscheibe(n) *f*	potter's kickwheel
Triangulatur(en) *f*	use of triangles as modules or to determine architectural shape
Tribüne(n) *f*	tribune

Trichorum (Trichoren) *n*	cloverleaf plan church; church with an apse in the chancel and one at the end of each transept arm
Trichterbecher (—) *m*	funnel beaker
Trichterbecherkultur *f*	TRB culture
trichterförmig	funnel-shaped
Trident(e) *m*	trident
Triere(n) *f*	trireme; Greek warship
Trifolium (-folien) *n*	trefoil, cloverleaf
Triforium (Triforien) *n*	triforium
Triglyph(e) *m* *also* Triglyphe(n) *f*	triglyph
Triklinium (Triklinien) *n*	triclinium
Trikonchos *m*	cloverleaf plan church; church with an apse in the chancel and one at the end of each transept arm
Trinität *f*	Trinity
Trinkgefäß(e) *n*	drinking vessel
Triptychon (Triptychen) *n*	triptych
Triton(en) *m*	Triton
Trittwebstuhl (-stühle) *m*	treadle-operated loom
Triumphbalken (—) *m*	rood beam, rood
Triumphbogen (—, -bögen) *m*	1. triumphal arch 2. rood
Triumphkreuz(e) *n*	Christus triumphens, crucifix depicted on the rood
Triumphkreuzgruppe(n) *f*	rood crucifixion group
Triumphsäule(n) *f*	triumphal column
Triumphwagen (—) *m*	chariot
Triumphzug (-züge) *m*	triumphal procession
Trochilus *m*	scotia, concave moulding in an Attic base
trocken	dry
Trockenmauerwerk(e) *n*	dry joint masonry, masonry construction using no mortar
Trockenmittel (—) *n*	drier, siccative
Trockenstoff(e) *m*	drier, siccative
Troer (—) *m*	Trojan

Troia *also* Troja	Troy
Trommel(n) *f*	drum, tambour
Trompe(n) *f*	squinch
Trompe l'oeil *m*	trompe l'oeil
Trompenkuppel(n) *f*	dome resting on squinches
Tropaion (Tropaia) *n*	trophy, trophy monument
Tropfen (–) *m*	1. guttae 2. drop
Tropfenauflage *f*	prunts; molten drops of glass fused onto a glass surface
Tropfenplatte(n) *f*	mutule
Tropfleiste(n) *f*	drip; part of cornice preventing water from running down the wall
Tropfsteingewölbe (–) *n*	vault with stalactite work
Trophäe(n) *f*	trophy, trophy motif
trüb	cloudy, muddy, dim
trüben	to cloud
Truhe(n) *f*	chest, trunk
Trumeau(s) *m*	1. trumeau 2. narrow mirror between two windows
Trümmer *pl*	ruins
Trutzwaffe(n) *f*	hand weapon
Tube(n) *f*	tube
Tuch (Tücher) *n*	cloth, piece of cloth
Tuchhalle(n) *f*	Cloth Hall
Tudorblatt (-blätter) *n*	tudor flower
Tudorbogen (–, -bögen) *m*	Tudor arch
Tudorstil *m*	Tudor style
Tuffstein *m*	tufa, tuff
Tugenden und Laster	Virtues and Vices
Tula-Arbeit(en) *f*	tula work; niello work done in Tula, Russia
Tülle(n) *f*	spout
Tulpenkanzel(n) *f*	tulip-shaped pulpit

Tumba (Tumben) *f*	sacrophagus-like tomb with a relief of the deceased on the top
Tummler (–) *m*	round bottomed glass which rights itself when tipped
Tumulusgrab (-gräber) *n*	tumulus, tumulus grave
Tünche(n) *f*	whitewash
Tungöl *n*	tung oil
Tunika (Tuniken) *f*	tunic
Tüpfel (–) *m*	spot, dot
tüpfeln	to stipple
Tür(en) *f*	door
Türangel(n) *f*	door hinge
Türeinfassung(en) *f*	door frame, architrave
Türfeld(er) *n*	door panel, tympanum, surface of the door
Türgesims(e) *n*	cornice or moulding of a door
Türgriff(e) *m*	door handle, door knob
Türkis *m*	turquoise
Türkischrot *n*	Turkey red
türkisfarben	turquoise, turquoise-colored
Türklopfer (–) *m*	door knocker
Turm (Türme) *m*	tower
Turmalin *m*	tourmaline
Turmbau zu Babel, der –	the Tower of Babel
Türmchen (–) *n*	turret
Turmform(en) *f*	tower shape, shape of a tower and/or its roof
Turmgruppe(n) *f*	group of towers
Turmhelm(e) *m*	spire
Turmmonstranz(en) *f*	tower monstrance
Turmspitze(n) *f*	spire
Türöffnung(en) *f*	doorway, door opening
Türpfeiler (–) *m*	trumeau
Türpfosten (–) *m*	door jamb
Türrahmen (–) *m*	door frame, architrave
Türrelief(s) *n*	door relief
Türschwelle(n) *f*	threshold, door sill

Türsturz(e) m	door lintel
Türzarge(n) f	door frame, architrave
Tuschätzung(en) f	aquatint
Tusche(n) f	1. drawing ink
	2. lithographic tusche
Tusche, Pinsel und —	brush and ink
tuschen	to draw with ink
Tuschfarbe(n) f	drawing ink
Tuschfeder(n) f	drawing pen
Tuschmalerei f	painting with black ink
Tuschmanier f	aquatint
Tuschpinsel (—) m	ink drawing brush
Tuschzeichnung(en) f	ink drawing, pen and ink drawing
Tympanon (Tympana) n	tympanum
Typographie(n) f	typography
Typologie(n) f	1. theory that all New Testament events were predicted in the Old Testament
	2. typology; the study of symbols and types
typologischer Bilderkreis(e) m	typological Biblical illustrations

Überbau(ten) m	superstructure
Überbleibsel (—) n	rest, remains, remnant
überdacht	roofed, covered with a roof
Überdachung(en) f	roof, roof cover, roofing
übereck	diagonally, across
übereckstehend	cater-cornered, diagonally situated
übereinandergestellt	placed on top of one another, stacked
Übereinstimmung(en) f	agreement, correspondence
Überfangglas n	flashed glass, cased glass
Überfangverfahren n	glass flashing process; technique of fusing colorless glass with colored glass

Überflutung, optische — f	simultaneous contrast
Übergang (-gänge) m	transition
Übergangsphase(n) f	transitional phase, transitional stage
Übergangsstil(e) m	transitional style
Überglasurdekor m	overglaze decoration
Überkragungsgewölbe (—) n	corbelling, false vault
Überkragungskuppel(n) f	corbelling, false vault
überkuppelt	domed, covered with a dome
überlebensgroß	over life-size
überliefern	to hand down (through the years), to preserve, to transmit
Überlieferung(en) f	history, tradition, provenance
Überlieferungsgeschichte(n) f	provenance
übermalen	to overpaint
Übermalung(en) f	overpainting
Übernahme f	acceptance, adoption
übernehmen	to accept, to adopt, to take
Überrest(e) m	remain(s), remainder, ruin(s)
überschneiden	to overlap
Überschneidung(en) f	overlapping
überschnitten	overlapped
überspannen	to span
Überstrich(e) m	coating, top coat
überwölbt	covered by a vault
Überzug (-züge) m	coating
Uffizien f	Uffizi
Ultramarin n	ultramarine blue
Ultraviolett n	ultraviolet light
umbauen	to rebuild, to renovate, to convert
Umbra f	umber
Umdruck m	transfer lithography
Umdruckpapier n	transfer paper
Umfassungsbau(ten) m	enclosing structure, exterior contours of a building
Umfassungsmauer(n) f	enclosure wall, circumvallation

Umfriedung(en) *f*	enclosure
Umgang (-gänge) *m*	ambulatory
Umgebung *f*	vicinity, environment
umgekehrte Perspektive *f*	inverted perspective
Umgreifung *f*	architectural system in which one wall rib spans two of the arches separating the nave from the side aisle
Ummauerung(en) *f*	circumvallation
umrahmt	framed
Umrahmung(en) *f*	framing, frame
Umriß (Umrisse) *m*	outline, contour
umrissen	outlined, contoured
Umrißlinie(n) *f*	contour line, outline
Umrißstich(e) *m*	outline engraving
Umrißzeichnung(en) *f*	sketch, contour drawing
umspannen	to transfer to a new support *conservation*
Umwelt *f*	environment
unbefleckte Empfängnis, die —	Immaculate Conception
unbehauen	unhewn, unworked
unbekleidet	unclothed, undressed
unbemalt	unpainted
unbunt	1. not colorful 2. non-colored; gray, white or black
undurchsichtig	opaque, non-transparent
Undurchsichtigkeit *f*	opacity
ungefaßt	1. unset, unmounted *jewelry* 2. unpainted *sculpture*
ungegenständlich	non-objective, abstract
ungläubige Thomas, der —	Doubting Thomas
Unikum(s, Unika) *n*	only copy
unregelmäßig	irregular
unschätzbar	priceless, inestimable
unsigniert	unsigned
unsterblich	immortal

Unterarm(e) *m*	lower arm
Unterbau(ten) *m*	base, foundation, substructure
Unterdach (-dächer) *n*	roof substructure
Unterfläche(n) *f*	lower surface, bottom, soffit
Untergeschoß (-geschosse) *n*	lower floor, ground floor
Untergewand (-gewänder) *n*	under garment
Unterglasurmalerei *f*	underglaze, underglaze painting
Unterkörper (−) *m*	lower part of the body
Unterlage(n) *f*	undersurface, base
unterlebensgroß	under life-size
Unterleib(er) *m*	abdomen
Untermalung(en) *f*	underpainting
Untermalungsschicht(en) *f*	underpainting layer
Unterputz *m*	underlayer of plaster
Untersatz (-sätze) *m*	base, stand
Unterschenkel (−) *m*	lower leg, section between foot and knee
Unterschneidung(en) *f*	chamfered or recessed underside
Untertuschung(en) *f*	underpainting, sketchy underpainting
unversehrt	undamaged
Unzialbuchstabe(n) *m*	uncial letter
Unziale(n) *f*	uncial, uncial book hand
Unzialschrift(en) *f*	uncial, uncial book hand
üppig	sumptuous
Urbild(er) *n*	original picture, prototype
Urfirnisware *f*	Urfirnis; ware of Early Helladic Greece
Urform(en) *f*	original shape, prototype shape
Urgeschichte *f*	protohistory
Urheber (−) *m*	author, creator, inventor
Urkunde(n) *f*	document
urkundlich	documentary, in documents, by means of documents
Urne(n) *f*	urn
Urnenfeld(er) *n*	urnfield
Urnenfelderkultur(en) *f*	urnfield culture

Ursprung (Ursprünge) *m*	origin
ursprünglich	original, originally |//

Valeur(s) *f*	value, color value
Valeurmalerei *f*	painting technique emphasizing color value and avoiding strong color contrasts
Vanitasstilleben (—) *n*	vanitas still life; still life with symbols of the transcience of earthly pleasures
variieren	to vary
Vase(n) *f*	vase
Vasenbild(er) *n*	vase scene, picture on a vase
Vasenfragment(e) *n*	potsherd, shard, fragment
Vasenkunst *f*	(art of making) vases
Vasenmalerei *f*	vase painting, pottery painting
v. Chr. = vor Christus	B. C.
Vedute(n) *f*	veduta
Vedutenmalerei *f*	veduta painting
Velin *n*	vellum, vellum paper
Velinpapier *n*	vellum paper
Velourpapier *n*	pastel paper with a velour finish
Velum (Vela) *n*	liturgical parament: 1. priest's shoulder garment 2. cloth to cover the Communion vessels
Venedig	Venice
venezianisches Glas *n*	Venetian glass
Venizianischrot *n*	Venetian red
Veranda (Veranden) *f*	porch
Verband (Verbände) *m*	bond, masonry bond
Verbildlichung(en) *f*	depiction, illustration
Verbindung(en) *f*	link, relationship, connection
Verbindungsbau(ten) *m*	connecting structure or building
verblassen	to fade
verbleichen	to fade, to bleach out

verblenden	to cover common building material with a layer of more valuable material
verchromen	to chrome, to plate with chrome
verchromt	chrome plated
verdübeln	to attach by means of a peg, to peg
verdünnen	to thin
Verdünnungsmittel (−) *n*	thinner, paint thinner
Verdüre(n) *f*	verdure tapestry
Verfahren (−) *n*	method, procedure, process
verfälschen	to forge, to falsify
Verfälschung(en) *f*	forgery, falsification
verfeinern	to refine, to improve
Verflächigung(en) *f*	flattening
verformbar	shapeable, moldable
Vergitterung(en) *f*	grillework
verglasen	to glaze, to provide with windows
Verglasung(en) *f*	glass, glazing
vergolden	to gild
Vergolderkissen (−) *n*	gilder's cushion
vergoldet	gilded, gilt
Vergoldung(en) *f*	gilding
vergöttlichen	to deify
vergrößern	to enlarge
Vergrößerung(en) *f*	enlargement
Verhältnis(se) *n*	relationship, situation
verhauen	to make an error in sculpting, to stun
Verismus *m*	Verism
verjüngen, sich −	to taper
Verjüngung(en) *f*	taper, tapering
Verklärung Christi, die −	the Transfiguration
verkleiden	to panel, to face, to clad
Verkleidung(en) *f*	facing, cladding, sheathing, revetment
verkörpern	to embody
Verkörperung(en) *f*	embodiment

Verkröpfung(en) *f*	the continuation of a cornice or string course around architectural elements which are engaged with the wall, e. g. around columns, lisenes, etc.
Verkündigung(en) *f*	1. the Annunciation 2. announcement
Verkündigung der Hirten, die — *also* Verkündigung an die Hirten, die —	the Annunciation to the Shepherds
Verkündigungsengel *m*	angel of the Annunciation
Verkürzung(en) *f*	foreshortening
verlängern	to extend, to lengthen
Verlängerung(en) *f*	extension, lengthening
Verleugnung Petri, die —	the Denial of Peter
Verlobung der hl. Katharina, die —	the Mystic Marriage of St. Catherine
Verlorene Form *f*	lost-wax process
verlorene Sohn, der —	the Prodigal Son
verlorenes Profil *n*	profil perdu; picture of an averted head showing only the cheek profile
vermeil	vermeil red
Vermeil *n*	vermeil
Vermiculatum *n*	mosaic technique using stones cut to fit (as opposed to *Tessellatum*)
vernickeln	to nickel plate
vernickelt	nickel plated
Vernis mou (—) *n*	vernis mou
Vernissage(n) *f*	vernissage, exhibition opening, varnishing day
Veronikabild(er) *n*	St. Veronica and Her Veil
Veronikatuch *n*	the veil of St. Veronica; sudarium
Verputz(e) *m*	plaster, plaster coating
verputzen	1. to plaster 2. to restore badly
verputzt	plastered

Verrat des Judas, der —	the Betrayal of Christ
Versal(ien) *m*	large capital initial letter
Versammlungshalle(n) *f*	meeting hall
verschiedenfarben	variously colored
Verschlossener Garten *m*	Garden Enclosed
verschönen	to beautify, to embellish, to adorn
verschönern	to decorate, to embellish, to make more beautiful
Verschönerung(en) *f*	embellishment, improvement
verschränken	to interlace, to interlock
Verschränkung(en) *f*	interlacing
verschwimmen	to become blurred or hazy, to merge or melt into one another
verschwommen	indistinct, blurred, hazy
Verschwommenheit *f*	blurriness, haziness
versehrt	damaged
versenktes Relief *n*	sunk relief, hollow relief
versilbern	to silverplate
versinnbildlichen	to symbolize
Versinnbildlichung(en) *f*	symbolization
Verspottung Christi, die —	Mocking of Christ
versteckt	hidden
Versteigerung(en) *f*	auction
verstreben	to brace
Verstrebung(en) *f*	strut, brace
Versuchsplastik(en) *f*	bozzetto, maquette, test sculpture
Versuchung, die —	the Temptation
vertieft	recessed, sunk
Vertiefung(en) *f*	recess, sunken area
vertikal	vertical
Vertikale(n) *f*	vertical, vertical line
Vertikalschnitt(e) *m*	vertical section
Vertreibung aus dem Paradies, die —	Expulsion from the Garden of Eden
Vertreibung der Wechsler, die —	Cleansing of the Temple
vervielfältigen	to duplicate

Vervielfältigung(en) *f*	duplication
Vervielfältigungsverfahren (—) *n*	duplication process
Verwahrfund(e) *m*	discovery of cached objects, hoard
Verwandschaft(en) *f*	relationship
Verweilraum (-räume) *m*	central plan room, centrally positioned room
Verwendung(en) *f*	use, application
Verwitterung(en) *f*	1. decomposition, weathering 2. efflorescence
Verzeichnis(se) *n*	list, register, catalogue
Verzeichnung(en) *f*	mistake (in drawing)
verzerren	to distort
Verzerrung(en) *f*	distortion
verzieren	to decorate, to adorn
verziert	decorated
Vesperbild(er) *n*	Vesperbild, pietà
Vestalin(nen) *f*	vestal virgin
Vestibül(e) *n* also Vestibulum (Vestibula)	vestibule
Vesuv *m*	Mt. Vesuvius
Vieleck *n*	polygon
vieleckig	polygonal
Vielfarbenholzschnitt(e) *m*	polychrome woodcut, multicolor woodcut
vielfarbig	polychrome, multicolor
vielgeschossig	many-floored, many-storied
Vielpaß (-pässe) *m*	multi-foil, multi-foil window
vielschichtig	multi-leveled, multi-layered
Vierblatt (-blätter) *n*	pointed quatrefoil
viereckig	quadrangular
Vierfarbendruck(e) *m*	four-color print, four-color printing process
Vierflügelanlage(n) *f*	building plan with four wings
Viergespann(e) *n*	quadriga
Vierkantpfeiler (—) *m*	four-cornered pillar
Vierpaß (-pässe) *m*	quatrefoil

Vierpaß-Säule(n) *f*	composite column with a quatrefoil cross section
Viertelstab (-stäbe) *m*	quarter round, quadrant moulding, moulding with quarter-circle profile
Vierung(en) *f*	1. division into four sections 2. crossing
Vierungskuppel(n) *f*	dome at the crossing, central dome
Vierungspfeiler (−) *m*	pillar or pier at the crossing
Vierungsquadrat(e) *n*	square delineating the crossing, crossing square
Vierungsturm (-türme) *m*	crossing tower
Vierzehnheiligen *pl*	the Fourteen Auxiliary Saints, the Fourteen Holy Helpers
Vignette(n) *f*	vignette
Viktoriagrün *n*	Victoria green
Villa (Villen) *f*	villa
Vinyl-Farbe(n) *f*	acrylic paint, acrylic color
violett	violet purple
Visierung(en) *f*	work drawing, plan, design
Visitatio *f*	the Visitation
Vitensammlung(en) *f*	collection of artists' biographies
Vitrine(n) *f*	display case
vlämisch *also* flämisch	Flemish
Vließ, das goldene −	the Golden Fleece
Vogel (Vögel) *m*	bird
Vogelperspektive *f*	aerial view, bird's-eye view
Vogelsonnenbarke(n) *f*	bird, boat and sun disc
Völkerwanderung(en) *f*	1. Migration Period, Barbarian Invasions 2. the migration of an entire people
Volkskunst *f*	folk art, peasant art
vollenden	to finish, to perfect, to complete
Vollkommenheitsideal(e) *n*	ideal of perfection, model of perfection
Vollkuppel(n) *f*	hemispherical dome on a cylindrical base

Vollplastik(en) *f*	three-dimensional sculpture, sculpture in the round
vollplastisch	three-dimensional
vollrund	three-dimensional
Volumen (−) *n*	1. volume, bulk 2. early book form in which each page was rolled separately
Volute(n) *f*	volute
Volutenkrater (−) *m*	volute krater
vor der Schrift	proof before letter, before all letters, avant la lettre
vorarchaisch	prearchaic
Vorarlberger Schema *n*	the Vorarlberg plan *architecture*
Vorbild(er) *n*	model, prototype
vorbildlich	model, exemplary
vorchristlich	pre-Christian, before Christ
Vorderansicht(en) *f*	front view
Vordergiebel (−) *m*	front gable, front pediment
Vordergrund *m*	foreground
Vorderseite(n) *f*	front, face, obverse
Vorderteil(e) *n, m*	front section, front end
Vordringen *n*	protrusion, projection
Vorentwurf (-entwürfe) *m*	rough draft
vorfabrizieren	to prefabricate
vorfabriziert	prefabricated
Vorform(en) *f*	prototype, model
Vorgänger (−) *m*	predecessor, forerunner
vorgefertigt	prefabricated
vorgehängte Wand *f*	curtain wall
vorgelagert	built or situated in front of
Vorgeschichte *f*	prehistoric times, prehistory
vorgeschichtlich	prehistoric
Vorhalle(n) *f*	narthex, antechamber, antechurch, porch
Vorhangbogen (−, -bögen) *m*	curtain arch
Vorhof (-höfe) *m*	outer court, vestibule

Vorhölle *f*	limbo
vorkaiserlich	pre-Imperial, pre-Caesar
vorkarolingisch	pre-Carolingian
vorkragen	to protrude from the plane of the building
Vorlage(n) *f*	1. prototype, model, original, origin, source 2. vertical building element placed in front of the wall, e. g. a respond
Vorlagebuch (-bücher) *n*	pattern book, design book
Vorlagensammlung(en) *f*	craftsman's pattern book, book of designs
vorlagern	to build or situate in front of
Vorratsgefäß(e) *n*	storage jar, storage vessel
Vorratsraum (-räume) *m*	storeroom
vorromanisch	pre-Romanesque
Vorsatzpapier *n*	fly-leaf paper, paper glued to the inside of the bookbinding
vorspringen	to protrude, to project
Vorsprung (-sprünge) *m*	projection, protrusion
Vorstellung(en) *f*	mental conception, imagination
Vortragekreuz(e) *n*	processional cross (on a long staff)
Vorzeichnung(en) *f*	preliminary sketch, preliminary drawing
Votivaxt (-äxte) *f*	ceremonial axe
Votivbild(er) *n*	votive image
Votivkapelle(n) *f*	votive chapel, chapel built in fulfillment of a vow
Votivkunst *f*	votive art, religious folk art

Waage(n) *f*	1. scale, balance 2. Libra
waagerecht	horizontal, horizontally
Waagerechte(n) *f*	horizontal, horizontal line
Wachs(e) *n*	wax
Wachsabdruck(e) *m*	impression in wax

Wachsausschmelzverfahren *n*	lost-wax process
Wachsbild(er) *n*	wax sculpture, ceroplastic work
Wachsbildnerei *f*	ceroplastics, wax modelling, wax-work
Wachsbossierer (—) *m*	wax modeller
Wachsentwurf (-entwürfe) *m*	wax model, preliminary study in wax
Wachsfarbenmalerei *f*	encaustic painting
Wachsfigur(en) *f*	wax figure, wax statue
Wachskreide(n) *f*	wax crayon
Wachsmalerei *f*	encaustic painting
Wachsmalstift(e) *m*	wax crayon
Wachsmaske(n) *f*	wax mask
Wachsschablone(n) *f*	wax stencil, batik stencil
Wachstafel(n) *f*	wax tablet
Wachsüberzug (-züge) *m*	wax coating
Wachtturm (-türme) *m*	watchtower, bartizan
Wade(n) *f*	calf, lower leg
Waffe(n) *f*	weapon
Wagen (—) *m*	carriage, car, chariot, coach
Wagenfahrer (—) *m*	charioteer, coachman
Wagenlenker (—) *m*	charioteer, coachman
Wagenrennen (—) *n*	chariot race
wahrnehmen	to perceive
Wahrnehmung(en) *f*	perception
Waid *m*	woad dyestuff
Wal, Jonas und der —	Jonah and the Whale
Waldglas *n*	forest glass, verre de fougère
Waldlandschaft(en) *f*	forest landscape
Wall (Wälle) *m*	rampart
Wallanlage(n) *f*	system of ramparts, rampart complex
Wallfahrt(en) *f*	pilgrimage
Wallfahrtskirche(n) *f*	pilgrimage church
Wallgraben (-gräben) *m*	moat
Wallschild(e) *m*	ravelin

Walm(e) *m*	hip, roof hip
Walmdach (-dächer) *n*	hipped roof
Walmkappe(n) *f*	shaped brick for the transition from the roof ridge to the rib
Walnußkernöl *n*	walnut oil
Walnußöl *n*	walnut oil
Walroßzahn (-zähne) *m*	walrus tusk
Walze(n) *f*	roller
Walzeisen *n*	sheet iron
Walzholz (-hölzer) *n*	warp beam
Wams (Wämser) *n*	doublet, jerkin
Wand (Wände) *f*	wall, side
Wand, spanische —	decorative folding screen
Wandaufbau *m*	structure of the wall(s)
Wandbehang (-behänge) *m*	tapestry, wall tapestry, hanging
Wandbewurf (-bewürfe) *m*	plaster
Wandbild(er) *n*	mural, wall painting
Wandbilderzyklus (-zyklen) *m*	mural cycle
Wandelaltar (-altäre) *m*	winged altarpiece which shows different scenes when closed or opened
Wandelgang (-gänge) *m*	roof-covered promenade, peripatos
Wandelhalle(n) *f*	roof-covered promenade, peripatos
Wandfläche(n) *f*	wall surface, wall space, wall plane
Wandfliese(n) *f*	wall tile
Wandflucht *f*	wall plane, wall surface
Wandform(en) *f*	wall shape
Wandgemälde (—) *n*	mural, wall painting, fresco
wandgliedernd	articulating the wall, dividing the wall
Wandgliederung(en) *f*	wall articulation, division of the wall
Wandgrab (-gräber) *n*	tomb with relief decoration either in or in front of a wall
Wandleuchter (—) *m*	sconce
Wandmalerei *f*	mural, wall painting, fresco painting

Wandmosaik(en) *n*	wall mosaic
Wandnischengrabmal (-mäler) *n*	wall niche tomb
Wandpfeiler (–) *m*	engaged pier, engaged pillar, wall pier
Wandpfeilerhalle(n) *f*	hall church with two-storied side aisles and having a transept narrower than the nave
Wandpfeilerkirche(n) *f*	pier church
Wandputz *m*	plaster, wall plaster
Wandsäule(n) *f*	engaged column
Wandtäfelung(en) *f*	wainscot(ing), wall paneling
Wandung(en) *f*	wall, side
Wandverkleidung(en) *f*	wall paneling, wall sheathing
Wandvertiefung(en) *f*	niche, recess in the wall
Wandvorlage(n) *f*	vertical building element placed in front of the wall
Wandzone(n) *f*	wall register
Wange(n) *f*	1. cheek 2. side wall (of a stairway or choir stall), stair string 3. vault cell 4. base section resulting if two intersecting planes diagonally cut through a barrel vault
Wappen (–) *n*	coat-of-arms, insignia
Wappenkunde *f*	heraldry
Wappenkunst *f*	heraldry
Wappenlilie(n) *f*	fleur-de-lys
Wappenscheibe(n) *f*	window with a coat-of-arms (painted) on it
Wappenschild(er) *m*	escutcheon
Wappentier(e) *n*	heraldic animal
Warp(e) *m*	warp
Wartturm (-türme) *m*	watchtower, bartizan
Wasserburg(en) *f*	castle protected by water
Wasserfarbe(n) *f*	watercolor
Wasserfarbenmalerei *f*	watercolor, watercolor painting

wasserfest	waterproof
Wasserglas *n*	water glass, liquid silicate
Wasserkanne(n) *f*	ewer, water pitcher
Wasserkrug (-krüge) *m*	ewer, water jug
Wasserlaub *n*	tongue and dart
wasserlöslich	water soluble
Wassermann *m*	Aquarius
Wassernase(n) *f*	drip; part of cornice preventing water from running down the wall
Wasserschlag *m*	weathering, off-set
Wasserspeier (—) *m*	gargoyle
Wasserstrich(e) *m*	1. coating of a water medium 2. water-tempera brush line
wasserunlöslich	insoluble in water
Wasserversorgungsanlage(n) *f*	water supply system
Wasserzeichen (—) *n*	watermark
Wau *m*	weld, gaude yellow
Webeblatt *n*	weaving reed
weben	to weave
Weber (—) *m*	weaver
Weberei(en) *f*	weaving, weaving mill
Weberschiffchen (—) *n*	weaving shuttle
Webstuhl (-stühle) *m*	loom
Webverfahren (—) *n*	weaving process, weaving method
Wechselrahmen (—) *m*	passe-partout
Wechselwirkung(en) *f*	reciprocal influence, reciprocal effect
Wedel (—) *m*	brush, fan, frond
Wedgwoodware *f*	Wedgwood ware
Weft(e) *n*	weft, woof
Wegraum (-räume) *m*	room plan emphasizing direction or motion from entrance to main feature
Wehklage, die —	the Lamentation
Wehrbau(ten) *m*	defense architecture, defensive structure

Wehrgang (-gänge) *m*	defense passage along top of castle wall
Wehrgehenk(e) *n*	baldric
Wehrkirche(n) *f*	fortified church, rampart church
Wehrmauer(n) *f*	enceinte, parapet, defensive wall
weiblich	female, feminine
weich	soft
Weiche *f*	softness
Weicher Stil *m*	Weicher Styl, Soft Style
Weichgrundätzung(en) *f*	soft ground etching, vernis mou
Weichharz(e) *n*	soft resin
Weichheit *f*	softness
Weichholz *n*	softwood
Weichporzellan(e) *n*	soft paste, soft paste porcelain
Weihbecken (–) *n*	aspersorium
Weihbild(er) *n*	votive image, sacred image
Weihbrunnen (–) *m*	aspersorium
Weihe(n) *f*	consecration, dedication, initiation
Weihe Jesu im Tempel, die –	the Presentation in the Temple
Weihenbild(er) *n*	votive image, votive statue
Weihgeschenk(e) *n*	ex-voto, votive offering
Weihnachtsbild(er) *n*	Nativity scene
Weihnachtskrippe(n) *f*	crèche, Nativity scene
Weihrauch *m*	incense, frankincense
Weihrauchbehälter (–) *m*	incense container, censer
Weihrauchschiffchen (–) *n*	censer, incense boat
Weihwasserbecken (–) *n*	stoup, aspersorium
Weihwasserkessel (–) *m*	aspersorium, receptacle for holy water
Weihwedel (–) *m*	aspergill(um)
Weinranke(n) *f*	grapevine, vine ornament
Weisen, die Drei – aus dem Morgenland	the Three Magi
weiß	white
weißen	to paint white, to whitewash
Weißgrundmalerei *f*	white-ground, white-ground painting

Weißhöhung(en) f	heightening (with white)
Weißlinienschnitt(e) m	white-line woodcut
Weißschnitt(e) m	white-line woodcut
Weite(n) f	width
Weiterentwicklung(en) f	further development
weiträumig	spacious
Weiträumigkeit f	spaciousness
Welfenschatz m	Guelph treasure
Wellblech n	corrugated iron
Welle(n) f	wave
Wellenband (-bänder) n	running dog, Vitruvian scroll, wave meander
Wellendekor m	wave decoration, waves
Weller m	wall filling used in half-timber architecture
welsche Haube(n) f	tower roof similar to onion-shaped, but having two bulges
Welt(en) f	world
Weltausstellung(en) f	world's fair, international exhibition
Weltgericht n	Last Judgment
weltlich	wordly, secular
Weltrund n	globe
Weltwunder, die sieben —	the Seven Wonders of the World
Wendelring(e) m	late Nordic Bronze Age twisted neck ring
Wendelstein(e) m	spiral staircase tower on an exterior wall
Wendeltreppe(n) f	spiral stair, vyse
Wenzelbibel f	King Wenceslaus' Bible
Werbegraphik(en) f	advertising art, advertising graphics
Werft(e) m	warp
Werk(e) n	work, piece, œuvre
Werkkunstschule(n) f	school of applied arts
Werkmittel (—) n	medium
Werkstatt (-stätten) f	workshop, atelier
Werkstattarbeit(en) f	workshop production, shop-work

Werkstätte(n) *f*	workshop, atelier
Werkstattstaffelei(en) *f*	studio easel
Werkstein(e) *m*	ashlar, evenly hewn stone block
Werkverfahren (−) *n*	technique, work procedure
Werkverzeichnis(se) *n*	œuvre catalogue, catalogue raisonné
Werkzeichnung(en) *f*	working drawing, cartoon, building plan
Werkzeug(e) *n*	tool
Wert(e) *m*	value, worth
wertlos	worthless
wertvoll	valuable
Wesen (−) *n*	being, essence, nature, character, characteristic
Wesensbestimmung(en) *f*	attribute, identification
Weserrenaissance *f*	German renaissance style in the Weser region
Westbau *m*	western side of Romanesque church
Westfries(e) *m*	western frieze
Westgiebel (−) *m*	west pediment
westgotische Kunst *f*	Visigoth art
weströmisch	west Roman
Westteil(e) *m*	western section
Westwerk(e) *n*	westwork
Wettbewerb(e) *m*	competition
Wetzstein(e) *m*	whetstone
Widder (−) *m*	1. ram 2. Aries
Widerdruck *m*	printing on both sides of the paper
Widerlager (−) *n*	abutment
widerspiegeln	to reflect, to mirror
Wiederaufbau *m*	reconstruction
wiederaufbauen	to rebuild, to reconstruct
Wiederentdeckung(en) *f*	rediscovery
Wiederfindung Jesu im Tempel, die −	Jesus Found in the Temple
Wiedergabe(n) *f*	reproduction, depiction, rendering
wiedergeben	to reproduce, to depict, to render

wiederherstellen	to restore to original condition
Wiederherstellung(en) *f*	restoration
Wiederkreuz(e) *n*	cross-crosslet
Wiederkunft Christi, die —	the Second Coming
Wiegeeisen (—) *n*	rocker, cradle *mezzotint*
Wiegendruck(e) *m*	incunabula
Wien	Vienna
Wiener Werkstätten *pl*	"Vienese Workshops" established during the Sezession
Wikinger (—) *m*	Viking
Wimperg(e) *m*	triangular gable over Gothic portals and windows
windbewegter Akanthus *m*	wind-blown acanthus; depiction of movement of acanthus leaves
Windeisen (—) *n*	metal support to protect stained glass window from wind
Winkel (—) *m*	angle
winkelig	angular
winzig	tiny
Wirbelknochen (—) *m*	bead and reel moulding
Wirbelrosette(n) *f*	whorl rosette, twirled rosette
wirken	1. to have an effect, to work 2. to weave (with a needle as opposed to a shuttle)
Wirker (—) *m*	weaver, carpet weaver
Wirklichkeit(en) *f*	reality
Wirklichkeitsdarstellung(en) *f*	depiction of reality
wirklichkeitsfremd	unrealistic, not faithful to reality
Wirklichkeitstreue *f*	fidelity, faithfulness to reality
Wirklichkeitswiedergabe(n) *f*	reproduction or depiction of reality
Wirkmeister (—) *m*	master weaver
Wirkstuhl (-stühle) *m*	loom, tapestry loom
Wirkteppich(e) *m*	tapestry or carpet made on a loom with the aid of a needle instead of shuttle
Wirkung(en) *f*	effect

Wirkungskreis(e) *m*	sphere of influence
Wirtel (−) *m*	shaft-ring, annulet
Wischer (−) *m*	tortillon, stump, stomp
Wismutmalerei *f*	painting on a chalk ground which has been coated with bismuth
Wismuthnitrat *n*	bismuth white
Wissenschaft(en) *f*	science
Wissenschaftler (−) *m*	scientist, scholar, academician
Witterungseinfluß (-flüsse) *m*	effect of weather
wohlgestaltet	nicely shaped, well-shaped
Wohnarchitektur *f*	residential architecture
Wohnbau(ten) *m*	residential architecture, residential building
Wohnhaus (-häuser) *n*	residence, apartment house
Wohnturm (-türme) *m*	residential tower, high-rise apartment building
Wohnung(en) *f*	apartment, flat
Wölbedach (-dächer) *n*	vaulted roof
wölben	to vault, to cover with a vault
Wölbung(en) *f*	vault, vaulting, curvature
Wölbungsart(en) *f*	type of vault
Wölbungstechnik(en) *f*	technique of building a vault, vault building technology
Wolke(n) *f*	cloud
Wolkenkratzer (−) *m*	skyscraper
Wolle *f*	wool
Wollrock (-röcke) *m*	woolen cloak, woolen garment
wuchtig	heavy, ponderous
Wulst (Wülste) *m*	1. echinus 2. swelling, bulge 3. torus profile
Wunder (−) *n*	miracle
Wundertaten Christi, die −	Christ's Miracles
Wundmal(e) *n*	stigma
Wundmale Christi, die −	the Stigmata
Würdenträger (−) *m*	dignitary

Würfel (–) m	1. cube, tessera 2. die
Würfelband (-bänder) n	billet, billet moulding
Würfelfries(e) m	billet, billet moulding
Würfelhocker (–) m	Egyptian block statue
Würfelkapitell(e) n	cushion capital
Wurstkrug (-krüge) m	ring-shaped flask with a hole through the middle
Wurzel Jesse, die –	Tree of Jesse
Xylograph(en) m	xylographer; artist who cuts the block for a woodcut
Xylographie f	xylography, (art of) wood cutting
Xylol n	xylene, xylol
Zackenbogen (–, -bögen) m	round arch with chevron decorative bands
Zackenfries(e) m	zigzag, zigzag ornament
zackig	toothed, zigzag
Zähflüssigkeit f	viscosity
Zahlensymbol(e) n	numerical symbol
Zahneisen (–) n	cold chisel
Zahnschnitt(e) m	dentil, dentil pattern
Zahnschnittfries(e) m	dentil, dentil pattern
Zahnstock (-stöcke) m	carved wood or bone tool for making stamped decoration on (prehistoric) pottery
Zaponlack(e) m	cellulose lacquer
Zarge(n) f	border, edge, frame
zart	delicate
Zartheit f	delicacy
zartblau	delicate blue
Zebraholz n	zebra wood, zebrano
Zeder f	cedar
Zedernholz n	cedar wood

Zedernholzöl *n*	oil of cedar
Zehe(n) *f*	toe
Zeichen (—) *n*	sign, symbol
Zeichenblock (-blöcke) *m*	tablet of drawing paper
Zeichenbrett(er) *n*	drawing board
Zeichenfeder(n) *f*	drawing pen
Zeichengrund *m*	drawing surface
Zeichenkamera(s) *f*	camera obscura
Zeichenkohle(n) *f*	charcoal, charcoal crayon
Zeichenkunst *f*	(art of) drawing
Zeichenmaschine(n) *f*	drafting machine
Zeichenmittel (—) *n*	drawing material, drawing medium
Zeichenpapier *n*	drawing paper, drafting paper
Zeichenschule(n) *f*	drawing school, art school
Zeichenstift(e) *m*	pencil, drawing pencil
Zeichentisch(e) *m*	drawing table
zeichnen	to draw
Zeichner (—) *m*	draftsman, graphic artist
zeichnerisch	graphic
Zeichnung(en) *f*	drawing
Zeigefinger (—) *m*	index finger
Zeile(n) *f*	line, row
Zeilenbau *m*	construction of row houses
Zeit(en) *f*	time, period, age
Zeitalter (—) *n*	age, era
Zeitbestimmung *f*	dating, establishment of the date of origin
Zeitgenosse(n) *m*	contemporary
zeitgenössisch	contemporary
Zeitrechnung, vor der —	B. C.
Zeitstil(e) *m*	style of a period, style of the time
Zelle(n) *f*	cell, cloison
Zelleneinlage(n) *f*	Germanic decoration of metal with glass or semi-precious stones set in cells
Zellengewölbe (—) *n*	net vault
Zellenschmelz *m*	cloisonné

Zellentechnik *f*	technique of setting garnets in gold cells
Zellenverglasung *f*	Germanic decoration of metal with glass or semi-precious stones set in cells
Zeltdach (-dächer) *n*	tetrahedron roof
Zement *m, n*	cement
Zenotaph(e) *n* *also* Kenotaph	cenotaph
Zentaur(en) *m* *also* Kentaur	centaur
Zentralbau(ten) *m*	central-plan building
Zentralperspektive(n) *f*	central perspective
zentrieren	to center, to place in the center
Zentrum (Zentren) *n*	center
zentrumsbetont	emphasizing the center, central-plan
Zepter (−) *n*	scepter
zerbrechlich	fragile, brittle
Zerbrechlichkeit *f*	fragility, brittleness
Zeremonialbeil(e) *n*	ceremonial axe
Zerographie *f*	cerography
Zeroplastik(en) *f* *also* Keroplastik	ceroplastics, wax sculpture
Zerrbild(er) *n*	caricature
zerstören	to destroy
zerstört	destroyed
Zettel (−) *m*	1. piece of paper 2. warp threads, system of warp threads
Zettelbaum (-bäume) *m*	warp beam
Zeug *n*	1. material, fabric 2. utensils, implements
Zeugdruck *m*	textile printing (with wood blocks)
Zeusadler (−) *m*	Zeus' eagle
Ziborium (Ziborien) *n*	ciborium
Zickzackband (-bänder) *n*	zigzag pattern, chevron
zickzackförmig	zigzag
Ziegel (−) *m*	brick

Ziegelbau(ten) *m*	brick building, brick construction
Ziegelmauer(n) *f*	brick wall
Ziegelmauerwerk *n*	brick masonry
Ziegelstein(e) *m*	brick
Ziegelwürfelkapitell(e) *n*	cushion capital made of bricks
Zierat(e) *m*	decoration
Zierbuchstabe(n) *m*	decorative initial, decorative letter
Zierde(n) *f*	ornament, decoration
zieren	to decorate, to ornament
Zierform(en) *f*	decorative form, ornamental form
Ziergefäß(e) *n*	decorative vessel
Ziergiebel (−) *m*	ornamental gable, ornamental pediment
Zierglied(er) *n*	ornament
Zierleiste(n) *f*	decorative book margin, decorative moulding
Ziernagel (-nägel) *m*	decorative nail, upholsterer's nail
Zierwerk(e) *n*	decoration, ornamentation
Zikkurat(en) *f* *also* Zikkurrat	ziggurat, zikkurrat
Zimier(e) *n*	helmet decoration, crest
Zimmer (−) *n*	room
Zimmerei(en) *f*	carpentry, carpenter's workshop
Zimmerflucht(en) *f*	row of adjacent, connected rooms; rooms arranged along one axis
Zimmermann (-leute) *m*	carpenter
zimmern	to make out of wood, to build
Zimmerwerkstatt (-stätten) *f*	carpentry shop
Zingel (−) *m*	castle wall, circumvallation
Zingulum (Zingula) *n*	cord, cincture (worn over the alb)
Zink *m, n*	zinc
Zinkätzung(en) *f*	etching on a zinc plate
Zinkdruck(e) *m*	zincography
Zinken *pl*	zinken; small tools for working antler
Zinkflachdruck(e) *m*	lithography using a zinc plate

Zinkgelb n	zinc yellow
Zinkographie(n) f	zincography
Zinkweiß n	zinc white
Zinn n	1. tin
	2. pewter
Zinne(n) f	crenellation, battlement
Zinngefäß(e) n	tin vessel, pewter vessel
Zinnglasur(en) f	tin enamel; opaque fayence glaze
Zinnober m	cinnabar, sinopia
zinnoberrot	vermilion
Zinsgroschen, der —	the Tribute Money
Zirbelholz n	cedar
Zirkel (−) m	1. compass
	2. circle
ziselieren	to chisel, to chase
Ziselierung(en) f	chiseling, (en)chasing
Zista (Zisten) f	1. prehistoric bronze bucket
also Ziste	2. cist; basket holding ceremonial utensils (ancient Greece)
also Cista	3. Etruscan bronze toilet utensils; covered urn
Zisterzienser-Baukunst f	Cistercian architecture
Zitadelle(n) f	citadel
Zivilisation(en) f	civilization
Zodiakus m	zodiac
Zömeterium (Zömeterien) n	coemeterium, catacomb
also Coemeterium	
Zone(n) f	zone, register, area
Zonenbecher (−) m	beaker with decoration arranged in zones
Zopf (Zöpfe) m	braid
Zopfmaler (−) m	painter of the *Zopfstil* (late Baroque period)
Zopfstil m	German art style between 1760 − 1780
Zottenrock (-röcke) m	Sumerian robe
Zug (Züge) m	1. trait, characteristic, facial feature

	2. ceremonial procession
	3. movement
Zug der hl. drei Könige, der —	Journey of the Magi
Zugbrücke(n) *f*	draw bridge
zugeordnet	arranged toward
Zunft (Zünfte) *f*	guild, craftsmen's guild
zurückführen	to go back (to), to attribute (to), to stem (from)
zurückspringen	to recede
zurückspringend	recessed, receding
zuschreiben	to attribute (to), to ascribe (to)
Zuschreibung(en) *f*	attribution, ascription
Zustand (Zustände) *m*	1. condition
	2. state *printing*
Zustandsdruck(e) *m*	trial proof, state
Zweck(e) *m*	aim, end, object, purpose
Zwecke(n) *f*	tack
zweckfrei	not intended for a special use or purpose
zweckmäßig	functional, suitable for the purpose
zweidimensional	two-dimensional
Zweifarbendruck *m*	two-color printing, two-color print
zweigeschossig	two-floored, two-storied
Zweischneuß(e) *m*	circular tracery form with two mouchettes
Zweistromland *n*	Mesopotamia
Zweitguß *m*	second casting
Zweiturmfassade(n) *f*	facade having two towers
Zwerchgiebel (—) *m*	dormer window
Zwerchhaus (-häuser) *n*	dormer window
Zwergarkade(n) *f*	arched frieze, connected series of arches as decoration
Zwerggalerie(n) *f*	dwarf gallery
Zwickel (—) *m*	spandrel
Zwiebeldach (-dächer) *n*	onion-shaped roof, onion-shaped tower, bulbous dome

Zwiebelhaube(n) *f*	onion-shaped roof, onion-shaped tower, bulbous dome
Zwiebelmuster (–) *n*	blue onion pattern
Zwiebelturm (-türme) *m*	tower with onion-shaped roof
Zwilling(e) *m*	1. twin
	2. Gemini
Zwillingsfenster (–) *n*	biforium
Zwinger (–) *m*	pathway or open area between outer and inner defense walls
Zwischenfarbe(n) *f*	intermediate color
Zwischenfirnis(se) *m*	intermediate varnish, isolating varnish
Zwischengoldglas (-gläser) *n*	gold glass; double-walled glass with gold decoration between walls
Zwischenmauer(n) *f*	partition wall
Zwischenraum (-räume) *m*	gap, space between
Zwischenrippe(n) *f*	tierceron
Zwischenstütze(n) *f*	intermediate support
Zwischenwand (-wände) *f*	partition wall, non-supporting inner wall
Zyanin *n*	cyanine blue
Zyathos (–) *m*	kiathos
also Kyathos	
Zygoma (Zygomata) *n*	arch or vault over one bay
Zyklopenmauer(n) *f*	cyclopean wall, cyclopean masonry
zyklopisch	cyclopean
also kyklopisch	
zyklopisches Mauerwerk *n*	cyclopean masonry
Zyklus (Zyklen) *m*	cycle
Zylinder (–) *m*	cylinder
zylindrisch	cylindrical

Wir empfehlen:

English-German Dictionary: Art History - Archaeology

Englisch-Deutsches Wörterbuch für Kunstgeschichte und Archäologie
von Mary L. Apelt
253 Seiten, Taschenlexikonformat, kartoniert, DM 49,–
ISBN 3 503 02259 7

In Fortführung des hier in 2., überarbeiteter und ergänzter Auflage vorgelegten ‚German-English Dictionary: Art History — Archaeology' hat die Autorin eine korrespondierende englisch-deutsche Fassung veröffentlicht, so daß dieses wichtige Fachlexikon nun als abgerundete Arbeitshilfe zur Verfügung steht. Mehr als 8 000 englische Begriffe werden in diesem Band mit ihren jeweiligen deutschen Entsprechungen und, wo nötig, mit Bedeutungserklärungen in lexikalischer Form nachgewiesen. Dabei sind nicht nur Fachausdrücke erfaßt, sondern auch im fachsprachlichen Umkreis häufig gebrauchte Begriffe.

Reading Knowledge in German for Art Historians and Archaeologists

Ein englisch-deutscher Lesekurs für Kunstgeschichte und Archäologie
von Mary L. und Hans-Peter Apelt
2., durchgesehene Auflage, 152 Seiten, DIN A 5, kartoniert, DM 29,80
ISBN 3 503 02228 7

Die Autoren haben aus ihrer großen Erfahrung im Deutschunterricht für Ausländer mit diesem Lehrbuch einen sprachlichen Einführungskurs für englischsprachige Studenten vorgelegt, der das Studium der deutschen Kunstgeschichte und Archäologie ermöglicht. Aber auch für andere geistesgeschichtliche Fächer hat sich dieser Lesekurs sehr bewährt. Die Lesefähigkeit deutscher wissenschaftlicher Texte wird in systematisch aufgebauten Lektionen und Übungen erarbeitet. Der erforderliche Wortschatz wird in gezielter Anordnung vermittelt.

Einführung in die deutsche Sprache der Wissenschaften

Ein Lehrbuch für Ausländer
von Günter Schade
10., überarbeitete Auflage, 310 Seiten, DIN A 5, kartoniert, DM 38,60
ISBN 3 503 02278 3

Dieses weit verbreitete Lehrbuch ist in erster Linie für die Unterrichtung der Ausländer bestimmt, die an deutschsprachigen Universitäten studieren oder wissenschaftlich arbeiten wollen. Es erfaßt die Wissenschaftssprache aller Fachrichtungen. Die einzelnen sprachlichen Phänomene werden im syntaktischen Zusammenhang aufgezeigt, um die deutsche Sprachstruktur durchsichtig zu machen.

ERICH SCHMIDT VERLAG

Jutta Vesper
Diplom-Dolmetscherin aiic
Haffstraße 12
53225 Bonn

James Helmut Zowe
53115 Bonn   VK 25088

Apelt,M.L.:
Engl.-Dtsch.Wtb.Kunstgesch.
K&V **3 08 53 60** ISBN 3-503-02259-7 WG **14500**
49,00 DM
LS 86180 vom 14.05.96   BZ

9 783503 022595   04900

English-German Dictionary:
Art History — Archaeology

English-Deutsches Wörterbuch für Kunstgeschichte und Archäologie

von

Mary L. Apelt

ERICH SCHMIDT VERLAG

CIP-Kurztitelaufnahme der Deutschen Bibliothek

Apelt, Mary L.:
English-German dictionary: art history — archaeology
= Englisch-deutsches Wörterbuch für Kunstgeschichte
und Archäologie / von Mary L. Apelt. — Berlin :
Erich Schmidt, 1987
ISBN 3-503-02259-7

NE: HST

ISBN 3 503 02259 7

© Erich Schmidt Verlag GmbH, Berlin 1987
Satz: Reprosatz Struve, Düsseldorf
Druck: Lengericher Handelsdruckerei, Lengerich
Printed in Germany · Nachdruck verboten
Alle Rechte vorbehalten

Preface

This dictionary will be an aid to all who are concerned with the fields of art history and archaeology. It is especially intended to be a helpful tool for the reader. For this reason, the dictionary is not limited to specialized terms from these two fields, but also includes other vocabulary often encountered when reading the professional literature, such as the various shapes, colors, materials, articles of clothing, religious objects, courtly people, titles of well-known works, dyestuffs, pigments, and mythological animals and people.

In most cases, if a direct translation of the English word exists in German, it is simply translated without explanation. However, there are some words and concepts in English which have no common equivalent in German. In such cases, a brief explanation is given in German. For a more complete explanation of such terms, the reader should refer to an English language art lexicon. The English translations do not include all possible definitions of each word; definitions are limited to those important to art history and archaeology. Further meanings can be found in a general bilingual dictionary.

The list of terms which appears here has been compiled from English and German works within the fields, professional journals, exhibition catalogues and art lexicons and dictionaries. Since this dictionary is mainly intended to be a reader's aid, it is not an exhaustive lexicon for the mentioned fields — a work which would necessarily consist of several volumes. However, both the author and the publisher would be grateful for any suggestions as to additions, corrections or changes.

Mary L. Apelt

Vorwort

Das vorliegende Handwörterbuch möchte denjenigen eine Hilfe bieten, die im Bereich der Kunstgeschichte oder Archäologie tätig sind. Es ist vor allem als Hilfsmittel für den Leser gedacht und ist daher nicht auf Spezialausdrücke der erwähnten Fachbereiche begrenzt, sondern schließt auch Wörter ein, die des öfteren in der Fachlektüre auftauchen, wie zum Beispiel Ausdrücke für verschiedene Formen, Farben, Materialien, Kleidungsstücke, Kultgegenstände, Hofleute, Titel bekannter Werke, Farbstoffe, Pigmente, mythologische Tiere und Personen.

In den meisten Fällen wird der englische Ausdruck einfach in deutscher Übersetzung aufgeführt. Es gibt im Englischen jedoch einige Wörter und Begriffe, die keine allgemeine Entsprechung im Deutschen haben. In diesen Fällen wird eine kurze Erklärung im Deutschen gegeben. Für eine ausführliche Erklärung dieser Begriffe sollte ein englisches Kunstlexikon zu Rate gezogen werden. Die deutsche Übersetzung schließt auch nicht alle möglichen Bedeutungen eines Wortes ein; die Bedeutungen beziehen sich lediglich auf die Bereiche Kunstgeschichte und Archäologie. Darüber hinausgehende Bedeutungen sind in einem allgemeinen zweisprachigen Wörterbuch zu finden.

Die in dieses Handwörterbuch aufgenommenen Ausdrücke sind englischsprachigen und deutschen Fachbüchern und -zeitschriften entnommen, Ausstellungskatalogen, Kunstlexiken und Wörterbüchern. Da dieses Handwörterbuch vor allem als Hilfe für den Leser gedacht ist, kann es kein vollständiges Wörterbuch für die genannten Bereiche sein — ein solches Werk müßte mehrere Bände umfassen. Die Autorin und der Verlag sind jedoch für jeden Hinweis bezüglich Erweiterung, Berichtigung oder Änderung dankbar.

Mary L. Apelt

Explanatory Notes

Words and multi-word expressions have been arranged in strict alphabetical order, not under a main word heading.

>Example:
>
>red earth color
>Redeemer
>red-figured
>red iron oxide

English entries:

>The **hyphen** is used to take the place of the main word. Example:
>
>| | | |
>|---|---|---|
>| acanthus | | |
>| wind-blown — | = | wind-blown acanthus |
>| Denial of Peter, the — | = | the Denial of Peter |
>
>**Past participles** are sometimes listed instead of or in addition to the infinitive form because of frequent adjectival use. Example:
>
>colored, contoured, enameled
>
>**Adverbs** are not usually listed separately. They may be found under the related adjective.
>
>Example:
>
>| | | |
>|---|---|---|
>| natural | = | natürlich |
>| naturally (not listed) | = | natürlich |
>
>**Italics** are used to indicate the grammatical function of a word.
>
>Example:
>
>| | |
>|---|---|
>| abstract *v.* | (verb) |
>| abstract *adj.* | (adjective) |

German entries:

Nouns are immediately followed by gender. Examples:

Abri *m*	= masculine
Abtei *f*	= feminine
Blatt *n*	= neutral
Möbel *pl*	= only in plural

The **comma** separates translations of similar meaning.

Example:

absorbieren, aufnehmen

Numbers are used for totally different translations of the same word.

Example:

brush   1. Pinsel *m*
           2. Bürste *f*

Hinweise für die Benutzung des Wörterbuches

Das Wörterbuch ist alphabetisch geordnet; Wörter, Wortzusammensetzungen und -zusammenstellungen erscheinen immer in der Reihenfolge des Alphabets und sind auch im Einzelfall nicht unter einem Stich- oder Grundwort zusammengefaßt, zum Beispiel:

    red earth color
    Redeemer
    red-figured
    red iron oxide

Englische Stichwörter:

    Der **Bindestrich** wird benutzt, um das Stichwort zu ersetzen, zum Beispiel

acanthus	
wind-blown —	= wind-blown acanthus
Denial of Peter, the —	= the Denial of Peter

    Statt der Infinitivform der Verben erscheint des öfteren direkt das **Partizip Perfekt**, wenn dieses primär als Adjektiv benutzt wird, zum Beispiel

        colored, contoured, enameled

Adverbien sind im allgemeinen nicht besonders aufgeführt, ihre Bedeutung ist aus dem entsprechenden Adjektiv zu erschließen, zum Beispiel

natural	= natürlich
naturally (nicht aufgeführt)	= natürlich

Kursivschrift wird benutzt, um auf die grammatische Funktion eines Wortes hinzuweisen, zum Beispiel

abstract *v.*	(Verb)
abstract *adj.*	(Adjektiv)

Deutsche Stichwörter:

Der Hinweis auf das **Genus der Nomen** steht direkt hinter dem Nomen. Nomen, die nur im Plural vorkommen, sind mit *pl* bezeichnet, zum Beispiel

    Abri *m*   = maskulin
    Abtei *f*   = feminin
    Blatt *n*   = neutrum
    Möbel *pl* = nur als Plural

Das **Komma** trennt Ausdrücke mit ähnlichem Inhalt, zum Beispiel

    absorbieren, aufnehmen

Zahlen werden benutzt, um auf unterschiedliche Bedeutungen eines Wortes hinzuweisen, zum Beispiel

    brush   1. Pinsel *m*
            2. Bürste *f*

abacus	Abakus *m*, Deckplatte *f*
abbey	Abtei *f*
abbey church	Abteikirche *f*
abbozzo	Entwurfszeichnung *f*
abdomen	Bauch *m*, Unterleib *m*
Abel's Sacrifice	das Opfer Abels
ablution fountain	Reinigungsbrunnen *m*
Abraham's Sacrifice of Issac	das Opfer Abrahams
Abraxas gems	Abraxen *pl*
abri	Abri *m*
absorb	absorbieren, aufnehmen
absorption	Absorption *f*, Aufnahme *f*
abstract *v.*	abstrahieren
abstract *adj.*	abstrakt, gegenstandslos, ungegenständlich
abstract art	gegenstandslose Kunst *f*, konkrete Kunst *f*
abstract expressionism	Abstrakter Expressionismus *m*
abstraction	Abstraktion *f*
abstractness	Abstraktheit *f*, Gegenstandslosigkeit *f*
abutment	Angefälle *n*, Widerlager *n*
academician	Akademiker *m*, Wissenschaftler *m*
academy	Akademie *f*
acanthus	Akanthus *m*
wind-blown —	windbewegter Akanthus *m*
acanthus foliage	Akanthusranke *f*
acanthus leaf	Akanthusblatt *n*
acanthus vine	Akanthusranke *f*
acanthus vine wreath	Akanthusblattkranz *m*
acaroid resin	Akaroidharz *n*
accept	annehmen, übernehmen
acceptance	Annahme *f*, Übernahme *f*
accessories	Beiwerk *n*, Zubehör *n*

accomplishment	Leistung *f*, Ausführung *f*, Vollendung *f*
accroides	Akaroidharz *n*
acculturation	Akkulturation *f*
acetone	Azeton *n*
acheiropoietoi	Acheiropoieten *pl*, Acheropita *pl*
achromatic	achromatisch
acid	Säure *f*
acid bath	Säurebad *n*
acquire	erhalten, erwerben
acquisition	Erwerbung *f*
acrolith	Akrolith *m*
acropolis	Akropolis *f*
acrostic	Akrostichon *n*
acroterion	Akroterie *f*, Akroterion *n*, Stirnziegel *m*, Dachzierglied *n*
corner –	Eckakroterie *f*
acrylic	Acryl-, Akryl-
acrylic color	Acrylfarbe *f*, Vinyl-Farbe *f*
acrylic glass	Acrylglas *n*
acrylic paint	Acryl *n*, Akryl *n*, Acrylfarbe *f*, Vinyl-Farbe *f*
acrylic resin	Akrylharz *n*
action painting	Actionpainting *f, n*
active	aktiv, tätig, wirkend
actual size	Originalgröße *f*
A. D.	nach Christus, nach Chr., n. Chr.
Ada group	Adahandschriften *pl*
adaptation	Bearbeitung *f*, Anlehnung *f*
addition	Anbau *m*, Beigabe *f*, Erweiterung *f*
additive mixture	additive Farbmischung *f*
addorsed figure	Doppelfigur *f*
adhere	haften
adhesive	Klebstoff *m*
adhesive tape	Klebestreifen *m*

admirer	Anhänger m, Verehrer m
admonitory picture	Mahnbild n
adobe	Lehmziegel m, Lehmziegelbau m
adopt	übernehmen
adoption	Übernahme f
adoration	Adoration f, Anbetung f
Adoration of the Magi, the —	die Anbetung der Heiligen Drei Könige
Adoration of the Shepherds, the —	die Anbetung der Hirten
Adoration of the Trinity	Allerheiligenbild n
adorn	dekorieren, zieren, schmücken, verschönen, verzieren
ad quadratum	Quadratur f
adsorb	adsorbieren
adsorption	Adsorption f
advancing and retreating colors	Farbperspektive f
advertising art	Gebrauchsgraphik f, Reklamekunst f, Werbegraphik f
advertising graphics	Werbegraphik f
adytum	Adyton n
adze	Dechsel m, Beil n, Dachsbeil n
aedicule	Ädikula f
Aegean	ägäisch
Aegean Sea	Ägäis f
Aeolic	äolisch
aerial perspective	Luftperspektive f
aerial photograph	Luftaufnahme f
aerial view	Vogelperspektive f
aesthetic	ästhetisch
aesthetics	Ästhetik f
affected	affektiert, unnatürlich, gekünstelt
affectedness	Affektiertheit f, Künstelei f
affronted figures	antithetische Gruppe, gegenständige Gruppe f
after all letters	nach der Schrift

agate	Achat *m*
agate glass	Achatglas *n*
age	1. Zeitalter *n*, Zeit *f*
	2. Alter *n*
Agony in the Garden	Ölbergstunde *f*
agora	Agora *f*
agraffe	Agraffe *f*
agreement	Übereinstimmung *f*
aim	Zweck *m*, Ziel *n*, Absicht *f*
airbrush	Spritzpistole *f*
air vent	Entlüftungskanal *m*
aisle	1. Schiff *n*, Seitenschiff *n*
	2. Flur *m*, Gang *m*
alabaster	Alabaster *m*
alabastron	Alabastron *m*
alb	Albe *f*
albarello	Albarello *n*
album	Album *n*, Mappe *f*
alcohol	Spiritus *m*, Alkohol *m*
alcove	Bettnische *f*, Alkoven *m*, Nische *f*
alder wood	Erle *f*
Aldobrandini Wedding (or Marriage)	Aldobrandinische Hochzeit *f*
Alhambra vase	Alhambravase *f*
alignment	1. Alignement *m*
	2. Baufluchtlinie *f*, Fassadenflucht *f*, Flucht *f*, Fluchtlinie *f*, Reihung *f*
alike	gleich
alizarin	Krappstoff *m*
alizarin crimson	Alizarinkrapplack *m*
alizarin dye	Alizarin *n*
alkaline glaze	Alkaliglasur *f*
alkanet	Alkanna *f*, Henna *f*
alla prima	Primamalerei *f*
alla prima painting	alla prima *n*, Primamalerei *f*
allée couverte	Galeriegrab *n*

allegorical	allegorisch
allegorical figure	Gleichnisgestalt *f*
allegory	Allegorie *f*, Gleichnis *n*
alliance	Bund *m*
alloy *v.*	legieren
alloy *n.*	Legierung *f*
almanac	Almanach *m*
almanac picture	Kalenderbild *n*
almandine	Almandin *m*
almond-shaped	mandelförmig
altar	Altar *m*
portable —	Tragaltar *m*
altar apse	Altarapsis *f*
altar bell	Altarglocke *f*
altar ciborium	Altarziborium *n*
altar cloth	Altardecke *f*, Korporale *n*
altar crowning	Gesprenge *n*
altar cruet	Meßkännchen *n*
altar painting	Altargemälde *n*, Altarblatt *n*
altarpiece	1. Altaraufsatz *m*, Altaraufbau *m*, Retabel *n*
	2. Altarbild *n*, Altargemälde *n*, Altarblatt *n*
side wing of —	Flügelbild *n*
winged —	Flügelaltar *m*, Klappaltar *m*
altar top	Mensa *f*
altar utensil	Altargerät *n*
aluminum	Aluminium *n*
sheet —	Aluminiumblech *n*
aluminum casting	Aluminiumguß *m*
amaranth	Amarant *m*
amateur	Amateur *m*
amateur painter	Laienmaler *m*
Amazon	Amazone *f*
Amazonomachy	Amazonomachie *f*
amber	Bernstein *m*
amber-colored	bernsteinfarben

ambo	Ambo *m*
ambry	Armarium *n*
ambulatory	Chorumgang *m*, Deambulatorium *n*, Umgang *m*
American Indian *adj.*	indianisch
American Indian *n.*	Indianer
amethyst	Amethyst *m*
amice	Amikt *m*
amoretto	Amorette *f*
amphiprostyle temple	Amphiprostylos *m*
amphitheater	Amphitheater *n*
amphora	Amphora *f*, Amphore *f*
globular —	Schnuramphore *f*
ampulla	Ampel *f*, Ampulle *f*
amulet	Amulett *n*
analysis	Analyse *f*
anamorphosis	Anamorphose *f*
anathyrosis	Anathyrose *f*, Anathyrosis *f*
anatomy	Anatomie *f*
ancestor	Ahne *m, f*
ancestor worship	Ahnenkult *m*
ancient	altertümlich, antik
ancient Greece	Griechentum *n*
ancient relics	Altertümer *pl*
ancient Rome	Römertum *n*
ancon	Kragstück *n*
Andachtsbild	Andachtsbild *n*, Devotionalbild *n*
angel	Engel *m*
Angelic Salutation	Englischer Gruß *m*
Angel of the Annunciation	Verkündigungsengel *m*
Angel of the Resurrection	Auferstehungsengel *m*
angle	Winkel *m*
angular	winklig, eckig
angular perspective	Strahlenperspektive *f*
angular pier	Eckpfeiler *m*

animal	Tier *n*
mythological composite –	Mischwesen *n*, Fabelwesen *n*
animal dye	Tierfarbstoff *m*
animal figure	Tiergestalt *f*
animal interlace	Tierornamentik *f*
animal-shaped	tierförmig
animal-shaped vessel	Tiergefäß *n*
animal style	Tierstil *m*
animal symbolism	Tiersymbolik *f*
animated	bewegt, lebhaft
ankh	Henkelkreuz *n*
ankle	Fußknöchel *m*
anneal	kühlen
annealing oven	Kühlofen *m*
annex	Anbau *m*
annular barrel vault	Ringtonne *f*
annulet	Schaftring *m*, Wirtel *m*
Annunciation	Englischer Gruß *m*, Verkündigung *f*
Annunciation to the Shepherds	Verkündigung der Hirten *f*, Verkündigung an die Hirten *f*
ansate cross	Henkelkreuz *n*
anse de panier	Korbbogen *m*
antae	Anten *pl*
antecedent	Vorbild *n*, Vorgänger *m*, Vorlage *f*
antechamber	Vorhalle *f*
antechurch	Vorhalle *f*
antediluvian	vorsintflutlich
antefixa	Stirnziegel *m*
antependium	Altarbekleidung *f*, Alarvorsatz *m*, Frontale *n*
Anthemion	Anthemion *n*
anthropoid sarcophagus	Anthropoidsarg *m*
anthropomorphic	anthropomorph
anti-art	Anti-Kunst *f*

antiphonary	Antiphonar *n*
anti-pope	Gegenpapst *m*
antiquary	Antiquar *m*
antique *adj.*	antik, altertümlich
antique *n.*	Antiquität *f*
antiquity	1. Altertum *n*, Antike *f*
	2. Antiquität *f*
study of —	Altertumswissenschaft *f*, Altertumskunde *f*
antis, in —	zwischen den Anten
antler motif	Geweihmotiv *n*
antler sleeve	Hirschhornfassung *f*
anvil	Amboß *m*
apartment	Wohnung *f*
apartment house	Wohnhaus *n*
ape	Affe *m*
apex	Scheitelhöhe *f*, Scheitel *m*
apocalypse	Apokalypse *f*, Offenbarung *f*
Apocalypse manuscript	Apokalypsenhandschrift *f*
apocalyptic	apokalyptisch
Apollo, temple of —	Apollontempel *m*
apophyge	Apophyge *f*
apostle	Apostel *m*
apostle figure	Apostelgestalt *f*
Apostles, the Mission of the —	die Aussendung der Apostel, die Entsendung der Apostel
apotheosis	Apotheose *f*
apotropaic	apotropäisch
apotropaic object	Apotropaion *n*, Apotropäum *n*
appear	1. erscheinen, entstehen
	2. scheinen
appearance	1. Entstehung *f*, Erscheinung *f*
	2. Aussehen *n*, Schein *m*
appendage	Glied *n*
application	1. Anwendung *f*, Verwendung *f*
	2. Auftrag *m*
applied arts	angewandte Kunst *f*, Kunsthandwerk *n*

arch

applied graphics	Gebrauchsgraphik *f*
appliqué *n.*	Applikation *f*, Aufnäharbeit *f*
appliqué *v.*	applizieren
apply	1. anwenden, verwenden, gebrauchen 2. auftragen
apricot gum	Aprikosengummi *m*
apse	Apsis *f*, Altarapsis *f*, Chorhaupt *n*, Koncha *f*, Konche *f*
main —	Hauptapsis *f*
apse echelon	Staffelchor *m*; abgetreppt angeordnete Nebenchöre
apsidal chapel	Apsidenkapelle *f*, Chorkapelle *f*
apsidole	Nebenapsis *f*
aqua fortis	Ätzwasser *n*
aquamanile	Aquamanile *n*
aquamarine	Aquamarin *m*
aquarelle	Aquarell *n*
Aquarius	Wassermann *m*
aquatint	Aquatinta *f*, Ätzverfahren *n*, Lavismanier *f*, Tuschätzung *f*, Tuschmanier *f*
aqueduct	Aquädukt *m*
aqueous binder	Gummiwasser *n*
arabesque	Arabeske *f*, Maureske *f*, Moreske *f*
arabesque-like	arabeskenhaft
arbor	Laube *f*
arbor vitae	Thuja *f*
arcade	Arkade *f*, Bogengang *m*, Laube *f*, Laubengang *m*
arcaded walk	Bogengang *m*, Loggia *f*
Arcadian	arkadisch
arc fibula	Bogenfibel *f*
arch	Bogen *m*
basket —	Korbbogen *m*
blind —	Blendbogen *m*
blind round —	Rundbogenblende *f*

archaeological

convex —	Konvexbogen *m*
curtain —	Vorhangbogen *m*
discharging —	Entlastungsbogen *m*
elliptical —	elliptischer Bogen *m*
flat —	scheitrechter Sturz *m*, scheitrechter Sturzbogen *m*
horseshoe —	Hufeisenbogen *m*
lancet —	Lanzettbogen *m*
lateral transverse —	Schildbogen *m*
ogee —	Eselsrücken *m*, Karniesbogen *m*, Kielbogen *m*
pier —	Pfeilerbogen *m*
pointed —	Spitzbogen *m*
quadrant —	einhüftiger Bogen *m*, steigender Bogen *m*, Strebebogen *m*
relieving —	Entlastungsbogen *m*
Roman —	Rundbogen *m*
round —	Rundbogen *m*
segmental —	Flachbogen *m*, Segmentbogen *m*, Stichbogen *m*
semicircular —	Rundbogen *m*
shouldered —	Kragsturzbogen *m*, Schulterbogen *m*
stilted —	gestelzter Bogen *m*
strainer —	Schwibbogen *m*
tied —	Stabbogen *m*
transverse —	Gurtbogen *m*, Gewölbebogen *m*, Quergurt *m*
trefoil —	Kleeblattbogen *m*, Dreipaßbogen *m*
trilobe —	Kleeblattbogen *m*, Dreipaßbogen *m*
Tudor —	Tudorbogen *m*
archaeological	archäologisch
archaeologist	Archäologe *m*
archaeology	Archäologie *f*, Altertumskunde *f*, Altertumswissenschaft *f*
archaic	archaisch

Archaic	Archaik *f*
archaic smile	archaisches Lächeln *n*
archaistic	archaistisch
archaize	archaisieren
archangel	Erzengel *m*
archbishop	Erzbischof *m*
archduke	Erzherzog *m*
arched	gewölbt
arched frieze	Bogenfries *m*, Zwergarkade *f*
archetype	Archetyp *m*, Original *n*, Vorbild *n*
architect	Architekt *m*, Baumeister *m*
architectonic	architektonisch
architect's client	Bauherr *m*
architectural	baulich, baumeisterlich, raumplastisch, Architektur-, Bau-
architectural background	Architekturhintergrund *m*
architectural ceramics	Baukeramik *f*
architectural concept	Baukonzept *n*, Baugesinnung *f*
architectural drawing	Architekturzeichnung *f*
architectural model	Architekturmodell *n*
architectural monument	Baudenkmal *n*
architectural ornament	Bauornament *n*
architectural plan	Bauplan *m*, Bauzeichnung *f*, Bauentwurf *m*
architectural sculpture	Architekturplastik *f*, Bauplastik *f*
architectural style	Baustil *m*
architectural symbolism	Bausymbolik *f*
architecture	Architektur *f*, Baukunst *f*, Baustil *m*
architrave	Architrav *m*, Epistyl *n*, Epistylion *n*, Türeinfassung *f*, Türrahmen *m*, Türzarge *f*
archivolt	Archivolte *f*, Bogenkreis *m*, Bogenlauf *m*
arch-shaped	bogenförmig
arcosolium	Arcosolium *n*, Arkosol *n*, Arkosolium *n*

arc welding	Lichtbogenschweißung *f*
area	1. Fläche *f*, Raum *m*
	2. Zone *f*, Bereich *m*, Gebiet *n*, Partie *f*
Aries	Widder *m*
aristocracy	Aristokratie *f*, Adel *m*
Ark, Noah's —	Arche Noah *f*
Ark of the Covenant	Bundeslade *f*
arm	Arm *m*
armature	Kern *m*, Haltegerüst *n*
armature butterfly	Anker *m*
armband	Armreif *m*, Armband *n*
arm chair	Sessel *m*
armor	Harnisch *m*, Rüstung *f*
armor decoration	Plattnerkunst *f*
arm palette	Armpalette *f*
arm rest	Armlehne *f*, Lehne *f*
choir stall —	Accoudoir *n*
arrange	anordnen, ordnen, einordnen, gliedern
arrangement	Anordnung *f*, Gliederung *f*, Ordnung *f*, Einrichtung *f*, Verteilung *f*
arrangement in a row	Reihung *f*
arrangement in layers	Schichtung *f*
arrangement of rooms	Raumfolge *f*
arrangement of space	Raumgliederung *f*, Raumordnung *f*
Arrest of Christ	Gefangennahme Christi *f*
Arretine ware	arretinisches Gefäß *n*
arriccio	Rauhputz *m*
arris	Grat *m*, Kante *f*
arrowhead	Pfeilspitze *f*
art	Kunst *f*
depictive —	Bildkunst *f*
history of —	Kunstgeschichte *f*
philosophy of —	Kunstphilosophie *f*

art academy	Kunstakademie *f*, Kunsthochschule *f*, Hochschule für bildende Kunst *f*
art auction	Kunstauktion *f*, Kunstversteigerung *f*
art center	Kunstzentrum *n*
art connoisseur	Kunstkenner *m*
art critic	Kunstkritiker *m*
art criticism	Kunstkritik *f*
art dealer	Kunsthändler *m*, Galerist *m*
art deco	Art Déco *f*
art education	Kunsterziehung *f*
artefact	Artefakt *n*, Kunsterzeugnis *n*
art exhibition	Kunstausstellung *f*
art expert	Kunstsachverständige *f*, *m*
art forgery	Kunstfälschung *f*
art form	Kunstform *f*, Kunstgattung *f*
art historian	Kunsthistoriker *m*
art historical	kunstgeschichtlich, kunsthistorisch
art history	Kunstgeschichte *f*
articulate	gliedern
articulation	Gliederung *f*
artifact	Artefakt *n*, Kunsterzeugnis *n*
artificial	künstlich, Kunst-
artificial chalk	Kunstkreide *f*
artificiality	Künstlichkeit *f*, Künstelei *f*
artificial marble	Gipsmarmor *m*
artificial material	Kunststoff *m*
art informel	art informel *f*, informelle Kunst *f*, informelle Malerei *f*
art interpretation	Kunstdeutung *f*
artisan	Handwerker *m*, Kunsthandwerker *m*
artist	Künstler *m*
artistic	künstlerisch, kunstvoll
artistic skill	Kunstfertigkeit *f*
artistic style	Kunstrichtung *f*, Kunststil *m*

artists' association	Künstlergemeinschaft *f*
artist's initials	Künstlermonogramm *n*
artist's signature	Künstlerinschrift *f*, Künstlermonogramm *n*, Künstlersignatur *f*
artist's workshop	Studio *n*, Werkstätte *f*, Atelier *n*, Künstlerwerkstätte *f*
art journal	Kunstzeitschrift *f*
art lover	Kunstfreund *m*, Kunstliebhaber *m*
art magazine	Kunstzeitschrift *f*
art market	Kunsthandel *m*, Kunstmarkt *m*
art movement	Kunstbewegung *f*, Kunstrichtung *f*
art nouveau	Jugendstil *m*
art object	Kunstgegenstand *m*
arts and crafts	Kunst und Gewerbe
arts, applied —	angewandte Kunst *f*
arts, the liberal —	artes liberales *pl*, die sieben freien Künste *pl*
art school	Kunstschule *f*
art style	Kunststil *m*
art trade	Kunsthandel *m*, Kunstmarkt *m*, Kunstbetrieb *m*
art treasure	Kunstschatz *m*
art work	Kunstwerk *n*
aryballos	Aryballos *m*
asbestos	Asbest *m*
asbestos cement	Asbestzement *m*
Ascension	Himmelfahrt *f*
Asclepius' rod	Äskulapstab *m*
ascribe to	zuschreiben
ascription	Zuschreibung *f*
ash	Asche *f*
ashlar	Quader *m*, Werkstein *m*
rusticated —	Buckelquader *m*, Rustika-Quader *m*
ash wood	Eschenholz *n*
askos	Askos *m*

aspergill(um)	Aspergill *n*, Sprengwedel *m*, Weihwedel *m*
aspersorium	Aspersorium *n*, Weihbecken *n*, Weihbrunnen *m*, Weihwasserbecken *n*, Weihwasserkessel *m*
asphalt	Asphalt *m*
asphaltum	Asphalt *m*
asphalt-varnish	Asphaltfirnis *m*
assayer's test	Tremolierstich *m*
assemblage	Assemblage *f*
assemblage of tools	Geräteinventar *n*, Industrie *f*
assessment	Expertise *f*, Einschätzung *f*
Assumption of the Virgin	Himmelfahrt Mariens *f*, Mariä Himmelfahrt *f*, Aufnahme Marias *f*
astragal	Astragal *m*, Rundstab *m*
astylar	säulenlos
asymmetrical	asymmetrisch
asymmetry	Asymmetrie *f*
atelier	Atelier *n*, Künstlerwerkstätte *f*, Studio *n*, Werkstatt *f*, Werkstätte *f*
Athenaeum	Athenäum *n*
Atheneum	Athenäum *n*
Athens	Athen
atlas	Atlant *m*
atmosphere	Stimmung *f*, Atmosphäre *f*
atrium	1. Atrium *n* 2. Paradies *n*
attach	befestigen, ansetzen, fügen, anfügen
attaching	Befestigung *f*
attendants	Gefolge *n*, Begleitung *f*, Dienerschaft *f*
attic	Attikageschoß *n*, Dachboden *m*, Dachkammer *f*
Attic base	attische Basis *f*

attribute	Attribut *n*, Eigenschaft *f*, Merkmal *n*, Emblem *n*, Wesensbestimmung *f*
attribute to	zurückführen, zuschreiben
attribution	Zuschreibung *f*
Aubusson	Aubussonteppich *m*
auction	Auktion *f*, Versteigerung *f*
auditorium	Aula *f*
aula	Aula *f*
aumbry	Armarium *n*
aureole	Aureole *f*, Glorienschein *m*
Aurignacian	Aurignacien *n*
authentic	authentisch, echt
authenticate	authentifizieren
authentication	Echtheitsbescheinigung *f*
authenticity	Authentizität *f*, Echtheit *f*
author	Autor *m*, Urheber *m*, Verfasser *m*
autodidact	Autodidakt *m*
autolithography	Künstlerlithographie *f*
automatism	Automatismus *m*
autotype	Autotypie *f*, Netzätzung *f*, Strichätzung *f*
avant garde *adj.*	avantgardistisch
avant garde *n.*	Avantgarde *f*
avant la lettre	vor der Schrift
avec la lettre	nach der Schrift
Aventine Hill	Aventin *m*
aventurine	Aventuringlas *n*
averted	abgekehrt, abgewendet
axial	axial, achsenförmig, achsial
axial building	Richtungsbau *m*
axiality	Axialität *f*
axis	Achse *f*
central —	Symmetrieachse *f*, Zentralachse *f*
axis of symmetry	Symmetrieachse *f*
axonometric projection	Axonometrie *f*

azulejos	Azulejos *pl*
azurite	Azurit *m*
back	Rücken *m*
backdrop	Bühnenbild *n*, Bühnenhintergrund *m*, Kulisse *f*
background	Hintergrund *m*, Fond *m*
background color	Hintergrundfarbe *f*, Fondfarbe *f*
background landscape	Hintergrundlandschaft *f*
backing	Rückwand *f*
backlight	Gegenlicht *n*
back panel	Rückwand *f*
back pillar	Rückenpfeiler *m*
back rest	Rückenlehne *f*, Lehne *f*
choir stall —	Dorsale *n*
back side	Rückseite *f*, Hinterseite *f*, Abseite *f*
Backstein Gothic	Backsteingotik *f*
back view	Rückansicht *f*
Baden culture	Badenerkultur *f*
Baden-Pecél culture	Badenerkultur *f*
badger blender	Dachshaarpinsel *m*
badger bristle	Dachshaar *n*
badger brush	Dachshaarpinsel *m*
bag	Tasche *f*
balance	1. Gleichgewicht *n* 2. Waage *f*
balanced	ausgewogen, abgewogen
balcony	Balkon *m*, Altan *m*, Altane *f*
balcony railing	Balkonbrüstung *f*
baldachin	Baldachin *m*, Himmel *m*
portable —	Traghimmel *m*
baldric	Schärpe *f*, Wehrgehenk *n*, Gehenk *n*
ballflower	Ballenblume *f*
balsam	Balsam *m*

balsam varnish	Balsamfirnis *m*
baluster	Baluster *m*, Geländerstab *m*, Togge *f*, Docke *f*
balustrade	Balustrade *f*, Brüstung *f*, Geländer *n*
bamboo	Bambus *m*
bamboo cane pen	Rohrfeder *f*
band	1. Band *n*, Schnur *f*, Bund *m* 2. Reif *m*, Spange *f* 3. Streifen *m*
banderole	Banderole *f*, Bandrolle *f*, Schriftband *n*, Spruchband *n*
bandkeramik	Bandkeramik *f*
banister	Geländer *n*
banker	Schnitzbank *f*
banner	Banner *n*, Fahne *f*
baptismal chapel	Taufkapelle *f*
baptismal font	Taufbecken *n*, Taufstein *m*, Fünte *f*, Koncha *f*, Konche *f*
Baptism of Christ	Taufe Christi *f*
baptistery	Baptisterium *n*
baptistry	Taufkapelle *f*, Taufkirche *f*
bar	Stab *m*
Barbarian Invasions	Völkerwanderung *f*
Barbarian style	Stilbezeichnung für Verzierungen und Schmuck der Völkerwanderung
barbican	Barbakane *f*
bare	nackt, kahl
bargeboard	Dielenköpfe verdeckendes Brett zur Giebelverzierung
barium yellow	Barytgelb *n*
baroque	barock, Barock-
Baroque	Barock *m*, *n*
baroque art	Barockkunst *f*
baroque church	Barockkirche *f*
baroque palace	Barockschloß *n*
baroque style	Barockstil *m*

barrel vault	Tonnengewölbe *n*
barrow	Hügelaufschüttung *f*
bartizan	Wachtturm *m*, Wartturm *m*
bar tracery	Stabwerk *n*
baryta white	Barytweiß *n*
basalt	Basalt *m*
basalt ware	Basaltware *f*
base	Basis *f*, Sockel *m*, Fuß *m*, Säulenfuß *m*, Unterbau *m*, Unterlage *f*, Untersatz *m*, Postament *n*
basement	Keller *m*, Fundament *n*, Souterrain *n*
basement level	Sockelgeschoß *n*, Kellergeschoß *n*
basic	Grund-
basic color	Grundfarbe *f*, Primärfarbe *f*
basic form	Grundform *f*
basilica	Basilika *f*
basilisk	Basilisk *m*
basin	Becken *n*, Schale *f*, Schüssel *f*, Kessel *m*
basket	Korb *m*
basket arch	Korbbogen *m*
basket capital	Korbkapitell *n*
basketry	Flechtware *f*
bas-relief	Basrelief *n*
bassetaille	Tiefschnittschmelz *m*
bast	Bast *m*
bastion	Bastei *f*, Bastion *f*, Bollwerk *n*, Schanze *f*
bath	Bad *n*, Badehaus *n*
bathhouse	Badehaus *n*
batik	Batik *f*
batik stencil	Wachsschablone *f*
bâton de commandement	Kommandostab *m*, Lochstab *m*
batter	Böschung *f*, geböschte Mauer *f*
battle	Kampf *m*, Schlacht *f*

battleaxe	Streitaxt *f*, Kriegsbeil *n*
battle chariot	Streitwagen *m*, Kampfwagen *m*
battlement	Zinne *f*
Battle of Alexander	Alexanderschlacht *f*
Battle of Issus	Alexanderschlacht *f*
battle-piece	Schlachtenbild *n*, Schlachtstück *n*
battle scene	Schlachtenbild *n*, Schlachtstück *n*
Bauhaus	Bauhaus *n*
bay	Joch *n*, Travée *f*
bay window	Erker *m*, Auslucht *f*
B. C.	vor Christus, v. Chr., vor der Zeitrechnung
beach scene	Strandszene *f*
bead	Perle *f*
bead and reel	Perlstab *m*, Perlstäbchen *n*, Perlenschnur *f*
bead moulding	Perlstab *m*, Perlstäbchen *n*, Perlenschnur *f*
beak	Schnabel *m*
beaked	schnabelförmig, Schnabel-
beaked cup	Schnabeltasse *f*
beaked jug	Schnabelkanne *f*
beaker	Becher *m*
Beaker culture	Glockenbecherkultur *f*
beak-shaped	schnabelförmig
beam	1. Balken *m*, Diele *f*, Träger *m* 2. Strahl *m*
cantilever –	Ausleger *m*
ceiling –	Deckenträger *m*
collar –	Kehlbalken *m*
hammer –	Stichbalken *m*
I- –	Doppel-T-Träger *m*
ridge –	Firstbalken *m*
rood –	Apostelbalken *m*, Triumphbalken *m*
roof –	Dachbalken *m*
supporting –	Stützbalken *m*, Sprieße *f*, Sprießholz *n*

upright —	Ständer *m*
warp —	Kettbaum *m*, Zettelbaum *m*
wooden —	Holzbalken *m*
beamed ceiling	Balkendecke *f*
beam end	Balkenkopf *m*, Dielenkopf *m*
beams	Balkenwerk *n*, Gebälk *n*
bear	tragen
beard	Bart *m*
beardless	bartlos
Bearing of the Cross	Kreuztragung Christi *f*
beast, mythical —	Fabelwesen *n*
Beatus manuscript	Apokalypsenhandschrift *f*
Beau Dieu jamb statue	Schöner Gott *m*
beautiful	schön
beautify	verschönen, verschönern, schön machen
beauty	Schönheit *f*
bed	1. Bett *n*
	2. Unterbau *m*, Lagerung *f*, Bettung *f*, Untermauerung *f*
bedding	Einarbeitung *f*, Unterlage *f*
beehive dome	Kraggewölbe *n*, Kragkuppel *f*
beeswax	Bienenwachs *n*
before all letters	vor der Schrift
beginner	Anfänger *m*
Beheading of St. John	Enthauptung des hl. Johannes *f*
beige	beige
bel étage	Beletage *f*
belfry	Belfried *m*, Glockenturm *m*
bell	Glocke *f*
bell-beaker	Glockenbecher *m*
bell-beaker culture	Glockenbecherkultur *f*
bell casting	Glockenguß *m*
bellcote	Glockengehäuse *n*, Glockenstuhl *m*
bell krater	Glockenkrater *m*
bell-shaped	glockenförmig
bell-shaped profile	Glockenleiste *f*

33

bell tower	Glockenturm *m*
belt	Gürtel *m*
belt buckle	Gürtelschnalle *f*
belt course	Fries *m*
belting	Gürtung *f*
belvedere	Belvedere *n*
bema	Bema *n*
bench	Bank *f*
bench end	Chorstuhlwange *f*
bend	krümmen, biegen
bent-axis temple	Knickachstempel *m*
benzol	Benzol *n*
Berlin blue	Berlinerblau *n*
berm	Berme *f*
beryl	Beryll *m*
bestiary	Bestiarium *n*
Betrayal of Christ	Verrat des Judas *m*, Judaskuß *m*
bevel *v.*	abfasen, abkanten
bevel *n.*	Schmiege *f*
Bible	Bibel *f*
Bible illustration	Bibelillustration *f*
Bible manuscript	Bibelhandschrift *f*
Biblia Pauperum	Armenbibel *f*
Biblical	biblisch
Biedermeier	Biedermeier *n*, Biedermeierstil *m*
bier	Bahre *f*
biforium	Biforium *n*, Zwillingsfenster *n*
biga	Biga *f*
billet	Würfelband *n*, Würfelfries *m*
billet moulding	Würfelband *n*, Würfelfries *m*, Schachbrettfries *m*, Rollenfries *m*
binder	1. Bund *m* 2. Binder *m*
binding	Bucheinband *m*, Einband *m*, Einbanddeckel *m*
binding medium	Bindemittel *n*

birch	Birkenholz n
bird	Vogel m
bird, boat and sun disc	Vogelsonnenbarke f
bird's eye view	Vogelperspektive f, Draufsicht f, Daraufsicht f
bireme	Bireme f
Birth of Christ	Geburt Christi f
biscuit	Biskuit n
bishop	Bischof m
bishop's throne	Bischofsstuhl m, Cathedra f, Kathedra f
bismuth white	Wismuthnitrat n
bisque	Biskuit n
bistre	Bister m
bistre drawing	Bisterzeichnung f
bistre drawing ink	Bistertusche f
bistre wash	Bistertusche f
bite	beizen
bitumen	Asphalt m
Blacherniotissa Madonna	Blacherniotissa f
black	schwarz, Schwarz-
black and white	schwarzweiß
black chalk drawing	Schwarzkreidezeichnung f
blacken	schwärzen
black enamel	Schwarzlot n
black-figured	schwarzfigurig
black ink painting	Tuschmalerei f
black-letter type	Fraktur f
blackness	Schwärze f
black printing ink	Druckerschwärze f
bladder	Blase f
blade	Klinge f
blanc fixe	Barytweiß n
Blaue Reiter, der —	der Blaue Reiter
bleach	bleichen
bleach out	verbleichen
blemish	Fehler m, Makel m

blind arcade	Blendarkade *f*, Rundbogenfries *m*, Scheinarkade *f*
blind arch	Blendbogen *m*
blind ornament	Blende *f*
blind round arch	Rundbogenblende *f*
blind story	Triforium *m*
blind tracery	Blendmaßwerk *n*
blind triforium	Blendtriforium *n*
blister	Blase *f*
block	Block *m*
block book	Blockbuch *n*
blockiness	Blockhaftigkeit *f*
blocklike	blockhaft
block-out stencil	Leimschablone *f*
block print	Holztafeldruck *m*
blocky	blockhaft
bloodstone	Hämatit *m*
blood vessel	Ader *f*, Blutgefäß *n*
blot	Klecks *m*, Fleck *m*
blouse	Bluse *f*
blow	blasen
blower, glass —	Bläser *m*, Glasbläser *m*
blue	blau
Blue Four, the —	Blaue Vier *pl*
blue onion pattern	Zwiebelmuster *n*
Blue Rider, the —	der Blaue Reiter *m*
bluing	Blauen *n*
bluish	bläulich
blurred	verschwommen
blurriness	Verschwommenheit *f*
board	Brett *n*, Diele *f*
board floor	Bretterboden *m*
boast	bossieren
boasting chisel	Bossiereisen *n*
Boat-axe culture	Bootaxtkultur *f*
boat burial	Schiffsbestattung *f*, Bootsgrab *n*

bodice	Mieder *n*
bodily	körperlich, leiblich
body	Körper *m*, Leib *m*
position of the —	Körperhaltung *f*
shape of the —	Körperform *f*
body axis	Körperachse *f*
body color	Deckfarbe *f*, Körperfarbe *f*
body line	Körperlinie *f*
Body of Christ	Fronleichnam *m*
body proportion	Körperverhältnis *n*
Boeotia	Böotien
Boeotian	böotisch
Boghaz Keiü, Boghaz-keuy, Boghazkoy	Boghasköy
bold relief	Hochrelief *n*, Hautrelief *n*
bole	Bolus *m*
bole ground	Bolusgrund *m*
bond	Verband *m*, Mauerverband *m*
bone	Knochen *m*
bone ash	Knochenasche *f*
bone black	Beinschwarz *n*
bone carving	Knochenschnitzerei *f*, Beinschnitzerei *f*
bone sculpture	Knochenschnitzerei *f*, Beinschnitzerei *f*
book	Buch *n*
book cover	Buchdeckel *m*, Einband *m*, Einbanddeckel *m*
book hand	Schrift *f*, Schriftart *f*
book illumination	Buchmalerei *f*, Illuminierkunst *f*
book illuminator	Buchmaler *m*
book of Epistles	Epistelbuch *n*
Book of Hours	Stundenbuch *n*
Book of the Dead	Totenbuch *n*
bookplate	Exlibris *n*
book printing	Buchdruck *m*

border	1. Bordüre *f*, Rand *m*, Einfassung *f*, Zarge *f*, Borte *f*
	2. Grenze *f*
Borghese Warrior	borghesischer Fechter *m*
boss	Schlußstein *m*
Böttger porcelain	Böttgerporzellan *n*
bottle	Flasche *f*
bottle neck	Flaschenhals *m*
bottom	Boden *m*, Unterfläche *f*, Grund *m*
boulder	Fels *m*
boulle	Boulle-Möbel *pl*
boulle-work	Boullearbeit *f*
bouquet	Blumenstrauß *m*
bow	1. Pfeilbogen *m*
	2. Schleife *f*
bowl	Schüssel *f*, Schale *f*, Napf *m*
inner bottom of —	Schalenboden *m*
bowl with foot	Fußschale *f*
bowl with cover	Deckelschale *f*
Bow porcelain	Porzellan aus Stratford-le-Bow
box	Dose *f*, Büchse *f*, Schachtel *f*, Kasten *m*, Kästchen *n*, Kiste *f*
box frame	Kastenrahmen *m*
box-shaped altar	Kastenaltar *m*
boxwood	Buchsbaum *m*
boy	Jüngling *m*, Junge *m*, Knabe *m*
Boy Extracting a Thorn	Dornauszieher *m*
bozzetto	Bozzetto *m*, Entwurfsplastik *f*, Probeplastik *f*, Versuchsplastik *f*
brace *v.*	verstreben
brace *n.*	Verstrebung *f*, Strebebalken *m*, Strebeband *n*, Halterung *f*, Klammer *f*, Sprieße *f*, Sprießholz *n*
roof —	Knagge *f*, Knieverstrebung *f*
wall —	Anker *m*
bracelet	Armband *n*, Armreif *m*

bracer	Armschutzplatte f
bracket	Krage f, Konsole f
bracket support	Kragstütze f
bracteate	Brakteat m, Hohlmünze f
braid	Zopf m, Borte f
branch-motif ornamentation	Astwerk n
brass	Messing n, Erz n
brass founder	Erzgießer m
brayer	Reiber m
breach in style	Stilbruch m
breadth	Breite f
break	Bruch m, Riß m
breast	Brust f
breast-high wall	Brüstung f
breastwork	Brustwehr f
breccia	Breccie f, Brekzie f
breviary	Breviar n, Breviarium n, Brevier n
brick	Ziegel m, Ziegelstein m, Backstein m
fire –	Schamotteziegel m
mud –	Lehmziegel m, Luftziegel m
unbaked –	Luftziegel m
brick building	Backsteinbau m, Ziegelbau m
brick construction	Ziegelbau m
brick cushion capital	Ziegelwürfelkapitell n
Brick Gothic	Backsteingotik f
bricklayer	Maurer m
brick masonry	Backsteinmauerwerk n, Ziegelmauerwerk n
brick wall	Ziegelmauer f
bridge	Brücke f
bright	hell
brightness	1. Helligkeit f 2. Farbhelle f
degree of –	Farbhellengrad m

brilliance	1. Glanz *m*, Leuchtkraft *f*, Buntkraft *f*
	2. spezifische Intensität *f*
brilliant	glänzend, strahlend, leuchtend
brilliant yellow	Brilliantgelb *n*
brise-soleil	Sonnenblende *f*
bristle	Borste *f*
bristle brush	Borstenpinsel *m*
brittle	spröde, zerbrechlich
brittleness	Sprödigkeit *f*, Zerbrechlichkeit *f*
broach spire	achtseitiger Helm *m*
broad	breit
brocade	Brokat *m*
broken color	gebrochene Farbe *f*
broken gable	gesprengter Giebel *m*
broken pediment	gesprengter Giebel *m*
broken place	Bruchstelle *f*
broken tone	gebrochene Farbe *f*
bronze *adj.*	bronzen, Bronze-
bronze *n*	Bronze *f*, Bronzeguß *m*, Bronzewerk *n*
Bronze Age	Bronzezeit *f*
bronze casting	Bronzeguß *m*, Bildgießerei *f*
bronze disease	Bronzekrankheit *f*
bronze door	Bronzetür *f*, Erztür *f*
bronze founder	Erzgießer *m*, Bronzegießer *m*
bronze foundry	Bronzegießerei *f*
bronze leaf	Bronzeblech *n*
bronze panel	Bronzetafel *f*
bronze powder	Bronzepulver *n*
bronze sculptor	Erzbildner *m*
brooch	Brosche *f*
brow	Braue *f*
brown	braun
brown coat	Rauhputz *m*, Ausgleichbewurf *m*
brown color group	Braunfarben *pl*
brownish	bräunlich

brush	1. Pinsel *m*, Malpinsel *m*
	2. Wedel *m*
	3. Bürste *f*
brush and ink	Pinsel und Tusche
brush drawing	Pinselzeichnung *f*
brush handle	Pinselstiel *m*
brush handling	Pinselführung *f*
brush stroke	Pinselstrich *m*, Pinselzug *m*
brushwork	Pinselführung *f*, Handschrift *f*
Brutalism	Brutalismus *m*
bucchero ware	Bucchero-Keramik *f*
buckle	Schnalle *f*
buckthorn berry	Kreuzdornbeere *f*
bucrane	Bukranion *n*, Ochsenschädel *m*
bucranium	Bukranion *n*, Ochsenschädel *m*
bud	Knospe *f*, Blütenknospe *f*
bud capital	Knospenkapitell *n*
buffet	Kredenz *f*
Buhl	Boullearbeit *f*
build	bauen, erbauen, konstruieren
builder	Baumeister *m*
build in	einbauen
building	1. Gebäude *n*, Bau *m*, Haus *n*, Baukörper *m*, Anlage *f*
	2. Bauen *n*, Erbauung *f*
manner of –	Bauweise *f*
building element	Bauelement *n*, Bauteil *m*
building line	Fluchtlinie *f*
building material	Baustoff *m*, Baumaterial *n*
building plan	Bauentwurf *m*, Bauplan *m*, Werkzeichnung *f*
building plans, book of –	Bauhüttenbuch *n*
building site conditions	Baugrundverhältnis *n*
building style	Baustil *m*, Bauweise *f*
building technology	Bautechnik *f*
bulbous dome	Zwiebelhaube *f*, Zwiebeldach *n*
bulge *v.*	ausbuchten

bulge *n.*	Ausbuchtung *f*, Wulst *m*, Echinus *m*
bulged	gewölbt
bulged gable	Giebelbogen *m*
bulk	Masse *f*, Volumen *n*, Umfang *m*
bull	Stier *m*
bull capital	Stierkapitell *n*
bull sacrifice	Stieropfer *n*
bull's eye glass	Butzenscheibe *f*, Nabelscheibe *f*, Ochsenauge *n*
bulwark	Bollwerk *n*, Bastei *f*, Schanze *f*, Schanzwerk *n*
bundle	Bündel *n*
bundled lotus column	Lotosbündelsäule *f*
bundled papyrus column	Papyrusbündelsäule *f*
Burgundian	burgundisch
burial	Begräbnis *n*, Bestattung *f*, Grablegung *f*
burial chamber	Grabkammer *f*
burial mound	Grabhügel *m*, Hügelgrab *n*
burial site	Grabstätte *f*, Begräbnisort *m*, Begräbnisstätte *f*, Bestattungsplatz *m*
burin	Ätzstift *m*, Grabstichel *m*, Stichel *m*
burl	Knoten *m*
burlap	Rupfen *m*
burn	brennen
Burning Bush, the —	der brennende Dornbusch
burnisher	Brünierstein *m*, Polierstahl *m*, Schabeisen *n*
burnoose	Burnus *m*
burnt sienna	Tierra di Siena gebrannt
burr	Grat *m*
bushhammer	Stockhammer *m*
bust	Büste *f*
portrait —	Bildnisbüste *f*
buttery	buttrig

calligraphy

buttress	Strebe *f*
flying —	Strebebogen *m*
pier —	Strebepfeiler *m*
buttressing	Strebewerk *n*
Byzantine	byzantinisch
Byzantium	Byzanz *n*

cabinet	Kabinett *n*, Schrank *m*
cabinet maker	Schreiner *m*, Tischler *m*
cabinet painting	Kabinettmalerei *f*
cable	Tau *n*
cable moulding	Tau *n*, gedrehtes Tau *n*
cabochon	Cabochon *m*
cache	Hort *m*, Depot *n*
cadmium red	Kadmiumrot *n*
cadmium yellow	Kadmiumgelb *n*
caduceus	Caduceus *m*, Kaduzeus *m*, Merkurstab *m*
calabash	Kalebasse *f*
calcimine paint	Leimfarbe *f*
calcine	kalzinieren
caldarium	Caldarium *n*, Kaldarium *n*
calefactory	Kalefaktorium *n*
calendar	Kalender *m*
calendar picture	Kalenderbild *n*
calender *v.*	kalandern
calender *n.*	Satiniermaschine *f*, Kalander *m*
calendering	Satinage *f*
calf	1. Kalb *n* 2. Wade *f*
calfskin	Kalbleder *n*, Kalbsleder *n*
calligrapher	Kalligraph *m*
calligraphic	kalligraphisch
calligraphic decoration	Schriftdekor *m*
calligraphy	Kalligraphie *f*, Schmuckschrift *f*

Calling of the Apostles, the —	die Berufung
Calling of St. Peter, the —	die Berufung des hl. Petrus
calliper	Tasterzirkel *m*
calm	Rute *f*
lead —	Bleirute *f*
calotte	Kalotte *f*
calyx	Kelch *m*
calyx krater	Kelchkrater *m*
calyx-shaped	kelchförmig
camaïeu	Camaïeu *f*
cambric cloth	Batist *m*, Kambrik *m*
came	Rute *f*
lead —	Bleirute *f*
cameo	Kamee *f*, Camaïeu *f*, erhaben geschnittene Gemme *f*
cameo cutter	Steinschneider *m*
cameo-like	kameenhaft
camera obscura	camera obscura *f*, Lochkamera *f*, Zeichenkamera *f*
camisole	Kamisol *n*
campaniform	glockenförmig
campanile	Campanile *m*, Kampanile *m*, Glockenturm *m*
cancel	(durch eine Querlinie nach der Auflage) entwerten
cancello	Chorgitter *n*
Cancer	Krebs *m*
candelabrum	Kandelaber *m*, Kerzenständer *m*, Leuchter *m*
candle	Kerze *f*
candle holder	Kerzenhalter *m*, Kerzenständer *m*, Kandelaber *m*, Leuchter *m*
candlelight	Kerzenlicht *n*, Kerzenschein *m*
canephora	Kanephore *f*
canister	Dose *f*, Kanister *m*
canon	Kanon *m*

canon table	Kanonbogen *m*, Kanontafel *f*
canopic jar	Kanope *f*
canopied bed	Baldachinbett *n*, Himmelbett *n*
canopy	Baldachin *m*, Himmel *m*, Kanzeldach *n*, Kanzelhaube *f*, Kanzelhimmel *m*, Thronhimmel *m*
portable —	Traghimmel *m*
cant	1. Rand *m*, Kante *f* 2. Schmiege *f*
cantharus	Kantharos *m*
cantilever beam	Ausleger *m*
canvas	Leinwand *f*, Lwd.
primed —	grundierte Leinwand *f*
canvas stretcher	Keilrahmen *m*
canvas stretcher key	Keil *m*
canvas texture	Leinwandkorn *n*
cap	Mütze *f*, Haube *f*
capital	Kapitell *n*, Kapitäl *n*
basket —	Korbkapitell *n*
brick cushion —	Ziegelwürfelkapitell *n*
bud —	Knospenkapitell *n*
bull —	Stierkapitell *n*
composite —	Kompositkapitell *n*
crocket —	Kelch-Knospen-Kapitell *n*, Knollenkapitell *n*, Knospenkapitell *n*
cushion —	Würfelkapitell *n*
figural —	Figurenkapitell *n*
papyrus —	Papyruskapitell *n*
trapezoidal —	Trapezkapitell *n*
capital city	Hauptstadt *f*
capital letter	Kapitalbuchstabe *m*, Majuskel *f*
capital shape	Kapitellform *f*
Capricorn	Steinbock *m*
Capsian culture	Capsien *n*
caput mortuum	Caput mortuum *n*, Kolkothar *m*
carbon 14 dating	Radiocarbondatierung *f*

carbuncle	Karfunkel *n*
cardboard	Karton *m*, Pappe *f*
caricature	Karikatur *f*, Zerrbild *n*
caricaturist	Karikaturist *m*, Karikaturzeichner *m*
carmine	Karmin *n*, Karmesin *n*
carmine red	karminrot
carnation	Karnation *f*
carnauba wax	Karnaubawachs *n*
carnelian	Karneol *m*
Carolingian *adj.*	karolingisch
Carolingian *n*	Karolinger *m*
carpenter	Tischler *m*, Zimmermann *m*, Schreiner *m*
carpentry	Zimmerei *f*
carpentry shop	Zimmerwerkstatt *f*, Zimmerei *f*
carpet	Teppich *m*
knotted –	Knüpfteppich *m*
Oriental –	Orientteppich *m*
carpet pile	Flor *m*
Carrara marble	Carraramarmor *m*
carriage	Wagen *m*, Kutsche *f*
carry	tragen
Carrying of the Cross	Kreuztragung Christi *f*
carry out	durchführen
cart	Wagen *m*, Fuhrwerk *n*
cartoon	Karton *m*, Musterzeichnung *f*, Werkzeichnung *f*
cartouche	Kartusche *f*
carve	schnitzen, meißeln
carved	geschnitzt, Schnitz-
carved altarpiece	Schnitzaltar *m*
carved statue	Schnitzbild *n*
carved stone	Glypte *f*
carver	1. Bildschnitzer *m*, Schnitzer *m* 2. Holzmesser *n*, Schneidemesser *n*

carving	Schnitzbild n, Schnitzwerk n, Schnitzerei f
art of —	Bildschnitzerei f, Schnitzkunst f
wood —	Holzbildhauerei f, Holzbildnerei f, Holzschnitzerei f
caryatid	Karyatide f
case	Kiste f
cased glass	Überfangglas n
casein	Casein n, Kasein n
casein color	Kaseinfarbe f
casein ground	Kaseingrund m
casemate	Kasematte f
casement window	Flügelfenster n
casket	1. Sarg m 2. Kasten m, Kästchen n
Cassel earth	Kaßlerbraun n
cassone	Cassone m
cast v.	gießen
cast n.	Guß m, Abdruck m, Gußabdruck m, Gußstück n, Metallplastik f
cast copy	Abguß m
caster	Gießer m
casting	1. Abguß m, Guß m, Gußstück n 2. Gußverfahren n, Bildgießerei f
piece mold —	Detailguß m
second —	Zweitguß m
casting fin	Gußnaht f
casting mold	Model m
casting pit	Gießgrube f, Dammgrube f
cast iron adj.	gußeisern
cast iron n.	Gußeisen n
castle	Burg f, Festung f, Kastell n
castle keep	Bergfried m, Beffroi m
castle wall	Zingel m, Enceinte f, Mauer f
castor oil	Rizinusöl n
cast piece	Gußstück n

cast shadow	Schlagschatten *m*
catacomb	Katakombe *f*, Coemeterium *n*, Zömeterium *n*
catafalque	Katafalk *m*
catalog	Katalog *m*, Verzeichnis *n*
catch	Haken *m*
catechu	Katechu *n*
categorization	Einstufung *f*
categorize	einstufen
category	Kategorie *f*
cater-cornered	übereckstehend
cathedra	Cathedra *f*, Kathedra *f*, Bischofsstuhl *m*
cathedral	Dom *m*, Kathedrale *f*, Münster *n*
cathedral treasure	Domschatz *m*
cauteria	Kauterien *pl*
cave	Höhle *f*
cave dweller	Höhlenbewohner *m*
cave dwelling	Höhlensiedlung *f*
cave man	Höhlenbewohner *m*
cave painting	Höhlenmalerei *f*, Felsmalerei *f*
cavetto	Hohlleiste *f*
cavity	Hohlraum *m*
cedar	Zeder *f*, Zedernholz *n*, Zirbelholz *n*
ceiling	Decke *f*, Zimmerdecke *f*, Plafond *m*
ceiling beam	Deckenträger *m*
ceiling decoration	Deckendekoration *f*
ceiling fresco	Deckenfresko *n*
ceiling painting	Deckengemälde *n*, Deckenmalerei *f*
ceiling plaster	Deckenputz *m*
celadon	Seladon *n*
celadon green	seladongrün
celadon porcelain	Seladonporzellan *n*
celadon ware	Seladon *n*

cell	Zelle *f*, Gewölbefach *n*, Wange *f*
cella	Cella *f*
cellar	Keller *m*
cellulose laquer	Zaponlack *m*
celt	Kelt *m*
Celtic	keltisch
Celts	Kelten *pl*
cement	1. Zement *m, n* 2. Bindemittel *n*
cemetery	Friedhof *m*
cenotaph	Kenotaph *n*, Zenotaph *n*
censer	Räuchergefäß *n*, Rauchfaß *n*, Weihrauchbehälter *m*, Weihrauchschiffchen *n*
centaur	Kentaur *m*, Zentaur *m*
center *v.*	zentrieren
center *n.*	Mittelpunkt *m*, Zentrum *n*
center aisle	Mittelgang *m*, Mittelschiff *n*
centering	Lehrgerüst *n*, Bogengerüst *n*, Gewölbegerüst *n*
center of perspective	Augenpunkt *m*
center panel	Mittelbild *n*, Mitteltafel *f*
central axis	Zentralachse *f*, Symmetrieachse *f*
central dome	Vierungskuppel *f*
central figure	Hauptfigur *f*
central object	Hauptgegenstand *m*
central perspective	Zentralperspektive *f*
central pillar	Mittelpfeiler *m*
central-plan building	Zentralbau *m*
century	Jahrhundert *n*, Jh., Jhdt.
ceramic	keramisch, Keramik-
ceramic decalcomania	keramischer Druck *m*
ceramic material, fired –	Scherben *m*
ceramics	Keramik *f*
ceramic tile	Kachel *f*, Keramikfliese *f*
ceramic-tiled stove	Kachelofen *m*
ceramic vessel	Keramikgefäß *n*

ceramic ware	Keramik *f*
ceramist	Keramiker *m*
ceremonial amphora	Prachtamphora *f*
ceremonial axe	Opferbeil *n*, Votivaxt *f*, Zeremonialbeil *n*
ceremonial bowl	Prunkschüssel *f*
ceremonial building	Kultbau *m*
ceremonial dress	Prunkgewand *n*
ceremonial procession	Zug *m*, Prozession *f*
ceremonial room	Kultraum *m*
ceremonial site	Kultstätte *f*
ceremonial weapon	Prunkwaffe *f*
ceremony	Zeremonie *f*
ceresin	Ceresin *n*
cerography	Zerographie *f*
ceroplastics	Keroplastik *f*, Zeroplastik *f*, Wachsbildnerei *f*
cerulean blue	Coelinblau *n*
chain	Kette *f*
chair	Stuhl *m*
folding —	Klappstuhl *m*, Faltstuhl *m*
chair back	Rückenlehne *f*
chair cushion	Sitzkissen *n*
chalcedony	Chalzedon *m*, Kalzedon *m*
Chalcolithic	Chalkolithikum *m*, Kupferzeit *f*
chalice	Kelch *m*, Meßkelch *m*
chalice paten	Kelchtellerchen *n*
chalice spoon	Kelchlöffel *m*
chalice straw	Kelchlöffel *m*
chalk	1. Kreide *f*, Kreidestift *m* 2. Kreidezeichnung *f*
precipitated —	Schlammkreide *f*
chalk crayon	Kreidestift *m*
chalk drawing	Kreidezeichnung *f*
chalk ground	Kreidegrund *m*
chalk manner	Kreidemanier *f*, Crayonmanier *f*, Krayonmanier *f*

chalk priming	Schlemmkreide *f*
chalk stroke	Kreidestrich *m*
chamber	Kammer *f*, Gemach *n*, Stube *f*
chamber tomb	Kammergrab *n*
chamfer *v.*	abfasen, abkanten
chamfer *n.*	Fase *f*, Schmiege *f*, Schrägkante *f*
champlevé	Emailchamplevé *n*, Grubenschmelz *m*
chancel	Chor *m*, Chorraum *m*, Altarraum *m*
chancel annex	Choranbau *m*
chancel screen	Altarschranke *f*, Chorgitter *n*, Chorschranke *f*, Lettner *m*
chancel square	Chorquadrat *n*
chancel tower	Chorturm *m*
chandelier	Kronleuchter *m*, Leuchter *m*, Lüster *m*
channel	Rille *f*, Kannele *f*, Auskehlung *f*
chapel	Kapelle *f*, Chorkapelle *f*
subsidiary —	Nebenkapelle *f*
chapels in echelon	Staffelchor *m*, kommunizierende Nebenchöre *pl*
chapter	1. Kapitel *n* 2. Stift *n*
chapter hall	Kapitelsaal *m*
chapter house	Kapitelsaal *m*
character	1. Schriftzeichen *n*, Silbenzeichen *n*, Buchstabe *m*, Letter *f* 2. Wesen *n*, Charakter *m*
characteristic *adj.*	charakteristisch, wesentlich
characteristic *n.*	Eigenschaft *f*, Eigentümlichkeit *f*, Kennzeichen *n*, Merkmal *n*, Zug *m*
charcoal	Kohle *f*, Stengelkohle *f*, Zeichenkohle *f*
charcoal crayon	Kohlestift *m*, Stengelkohle *f*, Zeichenkohle *f*

charcoal drawing

charcoal drawing	Kohlezeichnung *f*
chariot	Wagen *m*, Streitwagen *m*, Triumphwagen *m*, Kampfwagen *m*
charioteer	Wagenfahrer *m*, Wagenlenker *m*
chariot race	Wagenrennen *n*
Charlemagne	Karl der Große
charm	1. Berlocke *f* 2. Reiz *m*
charnel house	Beinhaus *n*, Karner *m*
chase	zisilieren
chasing	Ziselierung *f*
chassis	Untergestell *n*
chasuble	Kasel *f*, Meßgewand *n*
checkerboard pattern	Schachbrettfries *m*, Schachbrettmuster *n*
cheek	Backe *f*, Wange *f*
cheekbone	Backenknochen *m*, Jochbein *n*
chemigraphy	Chemigraphie *f*
cherry gum	Kirschgummi *m*
cherub	Cherub *m*, Engelchen *n*
chest	1. Brust *f* 2. Kiste *f*, Truhe *f*, Kästchen *n* Kasten *m*
chestnut	Kastanienholz *n*
chest of drawers	Kommode *f*
chevet	Chorhaupt *n*
chevet en echelon	Staffelchor *m*; abgetreppt angeordnete Nebenchöre
chevron	Zickzackband *n*
chiaroscuro *adj.*	chiaroscuro, Helldunkel-, Clairobscur-
chiaroscuro *n.*	Clairobscur *n*, Helldunkel *n*
chiaroscuro painting	Helldunkelmalerei *f*, Clairobscurmalerei *f*
chiaroscuro woodcut	Helldunkelschnitt *m*, Clairobscurschnitt *m*, Tonholzschnitt *m*
chignon	Dutt *m*, Haarknoten *m*
child	Kind *n*

children's art	Kinderkunst *f*
chimera	Chimäre *f*, Schimäre *f*
chimney	Schornstein *m*
chimney soot	Ofenruß *m*
chin	Kinn *n*
china	Porzellan *n*
China clay	Pfeifenton *m*, Porzellanerde *f*, Kaolin *m, n*
chinoiserie	Chinoiserie *f*
chip *v.*	kerben
chip *n.*	1. Bestoßung *f*, Splitter *m* 2. Kerbe *f*
chip-carving	Kerbschnitt *m*, Keilschnitt *m*
chi-rho monogram	Christusmonogramm *n*
chisel *v.*	zisilieren, meißeln, schroten
chisel *n.*	Meißel *m*, Schroteisen *n*, Schrotmeißel *m*
chiseling	Ziselierung *f*, Meißelarbeit *f*
chisel off	abmeißeln
chisel work	Meißelarbeit *f*
chiton	Chiton *m*
chlamys	Chlamys *f*
choir	Chor *m*
choir stall	Chorgestühl *n*, Stallen *pl*
choir stall sidewall	Chorstuhlwange *f*
chrism	Chrisam *n, m*, Chrisma *n*
chrismatory	Chrismarium *n*, Chrismatorium *n*, Koncha *f*, Konche *f*
Christ	Christus
Christ Among the Doctors	Christus unter den Schriftgelehrten
Christ and the Adultress	Christus und die Ehebrecherin
Christ and the Woman of Samaria	Jesus und die Samariterin
Christ at Emmaus	Christus in Emmaus
Christ at the Column	Christus an der Martersäule
Christ at the Pillar	Christus an der Martersäule
Christ Child	Christkind *n*, Jesusknabe *m*

Christ Crowned with Thorns	die Dornenkrönung
Christendom	Christentum *n*
Christian	christlich
Christianity	Christentum *n*
Christ in Limbo	die Höllenfahrt Christi
Christ in Majesty	Salvatorbild *n*
Christ in the House of Levi	das Gastmahl des Levi
Christ maestà	Majestas Domini
Christogram	Christusmonogramm *n*
Christ Omnipotent	Pantokrator *m*
Christ on the Mount of Olives	die Ölbergstunde
Christ, Ruler of the World	Kosmokrator *m*
Christ's genealogy	Jessebaum *m*, der Stammbaum Christi
Christ's Life and Sufferings	Heilsgeschichte *f*
Christ's Miracles	die Wundertaten Christi
Christ Suffering	Christus in Elend, Christus in Rast
Christ the Saviour	Heiland *m*
Christ, the Son of Man	der Menschensohn
Christus triumphens	Triumphkreuz *n*
Christ Walking Upon the Water	Jesu Meerwandel
Christ with a Crown of Thorns	die Dornenkrönung, Miserikordienbild *n*, Schmerzensmann *m*
chromatic	chromatisch
cromaticity	chromatische Farbqualität *f*
chrome *v.*	chromieren, verchromen
chrome *n.*	Chrom *n*
chrome green	Chromgrün *n*
chrome plated	verchromt
chrome red	Chromrot *n*
chrome yellow	Chromgelb *n*

chromium oxide	Chromoxyd n
chromolithograph(y)	Farblithographie f
chronology	Chronologie f
chryselephantine technique	Goldelfenbeintechnik f
chrysoberyl	Chrysoberyll m, Goldberyll m
chrysography	Chrysographie f
church	Kirche f, Gotteshaus n
fortified –	Kirchenburg f, Wehrkirche f
hall –	Hallenkirche f
one-roomed –	Einraumkirche f
pier –	Wandpfeilerkirche f
pilgrimage –	Pilgerkirche f, Wallfahrtskirche f
Church and Synagoge	Ecclesia und Synagoge
church architecture	Kirchenbau m, Kirchenbaukunst f, Sakralbaukunst f
church furnishings	Kirchenausstattung f
churchly	kirchlich
church tower	Kirchturm m
church treasure	Kirchenschatz m
Churrigueresque	Churriguerismus m
ciborium	Ciborium n, Ziborium n
cincture	Zingulum n
cinder block	Klinker m
cinerarium	Aschenurne f
cinerary urn	Aschenurne f, Leichenbrandurne f
cinnabar	Zinnober m
cinquecento	Cinquecento n
cinquefoil	Fünfpaß m
cipolin	Cipollin m
cipollino	Cipollin m
circle	Kreis m, Zirkel m
circular	kreisförmig, kreisrund, Kreis-, Rund-
circular pier	Rundpfeiler m
circular-plan building	Rundbau m
circular shape	Rundform f

circular window	Kreisfenster *n*
Circumcision, the —	die Beschneidung
circumvallation	Enceinte *f*, Mauerring *m*, Ringmauer *f*, Umfassungsmauer *f*, Ummauerung *f*, Zingel *m*
circus	Zirkus *m*
cire perdue	cire perdue *n*
cist	Cista *f*, Zista *f*, Ziste *f*
Cistercian architecture	Zisterzienser-Baukunst *f*
cist grave	Steinkistengrab *n*
citadel	Zitadelle *f*, Hochburg *f*, Kastell *n*
city	Stadt *f*
city architect	Stadtbaumeister *m*
city gate	Stadttor *n*
city-gate sarcophagus	Stadttorsarkophag *m*
city hall	Rathaus *n*
city planner	Stadtbaumeister *m*, Stadtplaner *m*
city planning	Stadtplanung *f*, Stadtbaukunst *f*, Städtebau *m*
cityscape	Stadtansicht *f*, Stadtlandschaft *f*
city wall	Stadtmauer *f*
civilization	Zivilisation *f*, Hochkultur *f*, Kultur *f*
clad	verkleiden, verblenden
cladding	Verkleidung *f*, Inkrustation *f*
clamp	Klammer *f*
clapboard	Hausverschalung aus Brettern mit keilförmigem Profil
clasp	Schnalle *f*, Agraffe *f*, Fibel *f*, Fürspan *m*
classical	klassisch
classical period	Klassik *f*
classical style	Klassik *f*
classicism	Klassizismus *m*
classification	Einordnung *f*, Klassifikation *f*
classify	einordnen, klassifizieren
claw chisel	Gradiereisen *n*

clay *adj.*	tönern, Ton-, Lehm-
clay *n.*	Ton *m*, Lehm *m*, Tonerde *f*
modelling —	Knete *f*, Knetton *m*
clay bozzetto	Tonbozzetto *m*
clay brick	Lehmziegel *m*, Tonziegel *m*
clay brick wall	Lehmziegelmauer *f*, Lehmziegelwand *f*
clay cone mosaic	Tonstiftmosaik *n*
clay container	Tongefäß *n*
clay cover	Tonhülle *f*
clay fragment	Tonscherbe *f*
clay metope	Tonmetope *f*
clay pegged mosaic	Tonstiftmosaik *n*
clay pottery	Tonware *f*
clay printing letter	Tonletter *f*
clay sculpture	Koroplastik *f*, Tonplastik *f*
clay shard	Tonscherbe *f*
clay stamp	Tonpatrize *f*
clay tablet	Tontafel *f*
clay tablet cover	Tontafelhülle *f*
clay type	Tonletter *f*
clay vessel	Tongefäß *n*
Cleansing of the Temple	die Vertreibung der Wechsler
clear	klar
clerestory	Gaden *m*, Lichtgaden *m*, Obergaden *m*
clergyman	Geistliche *m*
cliché	Klischee *n*
client	Auftraggeber *m*
cliff	Fels *m*
cliff-dweller	Höhlenbewohner *m*
cling	haften
clinker	Klinker *m*
clip	Spange *f*
cloak	Mantel *m*
cloison	Zelle *f*

cloisonné	Cloisonné n, Zellenschmelz m, Emailcloisonné n
cloisonné on silver	Silberschmelz m
cloister	1. Kreuzgang m 2. Nonnenkloster n, Stift n
cloister vault	Klostergewölbe n
close	Einfriedung, besonders um Kirchen u. ä.
closet	Schrank m
cloth	Stoff m, Tuch n
clothe	kleiden, bekleiden
Cloth Hall	Gewandhaus n, Tuchhalle f
clothing	Kleidung f
cloud v.	trüben
cloud n.	Wolke f
cloudy	trüb
cloverleaf	Kleeblatt n, Trifolium n
cloverleaf plan	kleeblattförmige Anlage f, Dreikonchenanlage f
cloverleaf plan church	Kleeblattchor m, Dreikonchenchor m, Trichorum n
cloverleaf-shaped	kleeblattförmig, Kleeblatt-
clumsy	ungewandt, plump, ungeschickt
Cluniac	cluniazensisch, kluniazensisch
clustered pier	Bündelpfeiler m
clustered vaulting shafts	Dienstbündel n
coach	Kutsche f, Wagen m
coachman	Wagenlenker m, Wagenfahrer m, Kutscher m
coach varnish	Kutschenlack m
coal-tar color	Teerfarbe f, Teerfarbstoff m
coal-tar dye	**Teerfarbe f**
coal-tar lake	Teerfarblack m
coarse	grob, derb
coarseness	Grobheit f, Derbheit f
coarse plaster	Berapp m
coarse-pored	grobporig

coastal landscape	Küstenlandschaft *f*
coat	Mantel *m*
coated with ground	grundiert
coating	Aufstrich *m*, Belag *m*, Überstrich *m*, Überzug *m*, Auftrag *m*
coat-of-arms	Wappen *n*
cobalt blue	Kobaltblau *n*
cobalt enamel	Schmalte *f*, Smalte *f*
cobalt violet	Kobaltviolett *n*
cobalt yellow	Kobaltgelb *n*
cobblestone paving	Kopfsteinpflaster *n*
cochineal	Koschenille *f*
cockatrice	Basilisk *m*
codex	Codex *m*, Kodex *m*
coelin	Coelinblau *n*
coemeterium	Coemeterium *n*, Zömeterium *n*
coemetrial	coemetrial
coffer	Kassette *f*
coffered	kassettiert, Kassetten-
coffered ceiling	Kassettendecke *f*
coffering	Kassettierung *f*
coffin	Sarg *m*
cohesion	Bindung *f*
coiffure	Frisur *f*
coil technique	frühe Töpfertechnik, bei der Tonwülste spiralig aufeinandergelegt werden
coin *v*.	prägen, münzen
coin *n*.	Münze *f*, Medaille *f*, Geldstück *n*
coin collection	Münzkabinett *n*, Münzsammlung *f*
coin impression	Münzabdruck *m*
cold chisel	Hartmeißel *m*, Kaltmeißel *m*, Zahneisen *n*
collage	Collage *f*, Klebebild *n*
paper —	Papierklebebild *n*
photo —	Photomontage *f*

collar	Kragen *m*
collar beam	Kehlbalken *m*
collect	sammeln
collection	Sammlung *f*
private —	Privatsammlung *f*
collector	Sammler *m*, Kunstsammler *m*
collector's mark	Sammlersiegel *n*, Sammlerzeichen *n*
collegiate church	Kollegiatkirche *f*, Stiftskirche *f*
Cologne earth	Kaßlerbraun *n*
colonial style	Kolonialstil *m*
colonnade	Kolonnade *f*, Säulengang *m*
colonnette	Säulchen *n*
colophony	Colophonium *n*, Kolophonium *n*
color *v.*	färben, kolorieren
color *n.*	1. Farbe *f*, Kolorit *n* 2. Farbengebung *f*, Farbgebung *f*, Farbigkeit *f*
advancing —	optisch in den Vordergrund tretende Farbe
background —	Fondfarbe *f*, Hintergrundfarbe *f*
body —	Deckfarbe *f*, Körperfarbe *f*
broken —	gebrochene Farbe *f*
complementary —	Komplementärfarbe *f*, Gegenfarbe *f*, Ergänzfarben *pl*, Ergänzungsfarben *pl*
contrasting —	Ergänzungsfarbe *f*
diffraction —	Regenbogenfarbe *f*
dominant —	Grundfarbe *f*, Hauptfarbe *f*
fugitive —	unbeständige Farbe *f*, unechte Farbe *f*
in —	farbig, bunt
local —	Lokalfarbe *f*
opaque —	Deckfarbe *f*, Körperfarbe *f*
overall —	Gesamtton *m*
patch of —	Farbfleck *m*
primary —	Primärfarbe *f*, Grundfarbe *f*

prismatic —	Regenbogenfarbe *f*
pure —	Spektralfarbe *f*, reinbunte Farbe *f*
receding —	optisch in den Hintergrund tretende Farbe
secondary —	Sekundärfarbe *f*
semi-opaque —	halbdeckende Farbe *f*
shot —	Schillerfarbe *f*
symbolic —	Symbolfarbe *f*
coloration	Farbengebung *f*, Farbigkeit *f*, Färbung *f*, Kolorit *n*, Fassung *f*
color change	Modulation *f*
color circle	Farbkreis *m*
color contrast	Farbkontrast *m*
colored	bunt, farbig, gefärbt, koloriert, Farb-, Bunt-
colored light	Farblicht *n*
colored paper	Tonpapier *n*
colored pencil	Buntstift *m*, Farbstift *m*
colored pencil drawing	Buntstiftzeichnung *f*
color engraving	Farbenstich *m*, Farbstich *m*
colorfast	farbecht
colorfastness	Farbechtheit *f*
colorful	bunt, buntfarbig, vielfarbig, farbenreich, farbig
colorfulness	Buntfarbigkeit *f*, Buntheit *f*, Farbigkeit *f*
color group	Farbenfamilie *f*, Farbbereich *m*, Farbengattung *f*
coloring	Farbe *f*, Färbung *f*, Kolorierung *f*, Kolorit *n*
colorism	Kolorismus *m*
colorist	Kolorist *m*
colorless	farblos
colorless glazing	Blankverglasung *f*
colorlessness	Farblosigkeit *f*
color lithograph	Steinbuntdruck *m*, Farblithographie *f*, Chromolithographie *f*

color mixture	Farbmischung *f*
color pattern	Farbmuster *n*
color print	Farbdruck *m*, Farbholzschnitt *m*
color range	Farbskala *f*
color saturation	Sättigung *f*
color scale	Farbskala *f*
color symbolism	Farbensymbolik *f*
color theory	Farbenlehre *f*
color-tone	Farbton *m*
color value	Farbwert *m*, Valeur *f*
color woodcut	Farbholzschnitt *m*
colossal	kolossal, Kolossal-
colossal order	Kolossalordnung *f*
colossal statue	Kolossalstatue *f*
Colosseum	Kolosseum *n*
colossus	Koloß *m*
columbarium	Columbarium *n*, Kolumbarium *n*
columbine	Akelei *f*
columbine-shaped goblet	Akeleibecher *m*, Akeleybecher *m*
column	Säule *f*
engaged —	Wandsäule *f*
palmiform —	Palmensäule *f*
position of —	Säulenstellung *f*
rostral —	Gedenksäule für einen Seesieg
triumphal —	Siegessäule *f*
twisted —	gewundene Säule *f*
column base	Säulenfuß *m*
column capital	Säulenkapitell *n*, Säulenknauf *m*, Knauf *m*
column drum	Säulentrommel *f*
columned	mit Säulen versehen, Säulen-
columned facade	Säulenfassade *f*
column figure	Säulenfigur *f*, Säulenstatue *f*, Gewändefigur *f*, Laibungsstatue *f*
column krater	Kolonettenkrater *m*
column-like	säulenhaft

Column of Trajan	Trajansäule *f*
column order	Säulenordnung *f*
columns, coupled —	Doppelsäule *f*
columns, supported by —	säulengestützt, säulengetragen
column shaft	Säulenschaft *m*
column statue	Säulenfigur *f*, Säulenstatue *f*
comb	Kamm *m*
combed ornament	Kammstrich-Ornament *n*
combed ornament pottery	Kammkeramik *f*
comic strip	Bildergeschichte *f*, Comics *pl*, Comic strip *m*
commercial art	Gebrauchsgraphik *f*
commission *v.*	in Auftrag geben
commission *n.*	Auftrag *m*
commissioned work	Auftragswerk *n*
committed	engagiert
Communion	Abendmahl *n*
Communion bench	Kommunionbank *f*
Communion plate	Kommunionschüssel *f*
Communion rail	Kommunionbank *f*
Communion table	Abendmahlstisch *m*
Communion utensil	Abendmahlsgerät *n*
compartment	Fach *n*
compass	Zirkel *m*
competition	Wettbewerb *m*
competition design	Konkurrenzentwurf *m*
complementary color	Komplementärfarbe *f*, Gegenfarbe *f*, Ergänzfarben *pl*, Ergänzungsfarben *pl*
complete	ergänzen, vervollständigen, beendigen, vollenden
complete works	Gesamtwerk *n*, Oeuvre *n*
completion	Ergänzung *f*, Vervollständigung *f*, Beendigung *f*
composite animal	Mischwesen *n*
composite capital	Kompositkapitell *n*
composite style	Mischstil *m*

composition	Komposition *f*, Anordnung *f*, Aufbau *m*, Gestaltung *f*
principle of —	Kompositionsprinzip *n*
theory of —	Kompositionslehre *f*
compound pier	Bündelpfeiler *m*
compound respond	Dienstbündel *n*
computer art	Computerkunst *f*
concave	konkav, hohl, rundhohl, Hohl-
concave mold	Patrize *f*
concave moulding	Hohlkehle *f*, Hohlleiste *f*, Kehlleiste *f*, dorisches Kymation *n*
concave roof tile	Hohlziegel *m*
concave surface	Hohlfläche *f*
concentric	konzentrisch
concept	Vorstellung *f*, Begriff *m*, Konzeption *f*
pictorial —	Bildvorstellung *f*
conception	Entwurf *m*, Plan *m*, Auffassung *f*, Konzipierung *f*, Vorstellung *f*
conch	Koncha *f*, Konche *f*
concise	knapp
conciseness	Knappheit *f*
concrete *adj.*	1. konkret, anschaulich 2. Beton-
concrete *v.*	betonieren
concrete *n.*	Beton *m*
exposed —	Sichtbeton *m*
prestressed —	Spannbeton *m*
reinforced —	Eisenbeton *m*, Stahlbeton *m*
spray —	Torkret *m*
concrete art	konkrete Kunst *f*
concrete building block	Betonmauerstein *m*
concrete construction	Betonbau *m*, Betonbauweise *f*
concrete floor	Betonboden *m*
concrete shell construction	Schalenkonstruktion *f*
concrete slab, precast —	Fertigbetonplatte *f*
concrete unit, precast —	Beton-Fertigelement *n*

contemporary

concrete wall	Betonmauer *f*
concreting	Betonierung *f*
condition	Erhaltungszustand *m*, Zustand *m*
cone	Konus *m*, Kegel *m*
cone mosaic	Stiftmosaik *n*
cone of vision	Sehpyramide *f*
confessio	Confessio *f*
confessional	Beichtstuhl *m*
configuration	Gestaltung *f*
confirmation	Firmelung *f*, Konfirmation *f*
conical	konisch, Kegel-
conical roof	Kegeldach *n*
connection	Verbindung *f*
connoisseur	Kenner *m*
connoisseurship	Kennerschaft *f*
consecration	Weihe *f*, Weihung *f*, Einweihung *f*
conservation	Konservierung *f*, Konservieren *n*, Restaurierung *f*
conservator	Restaurator *m*
conserve	konservieren, restaurieren
console	Konsole *f*, Knagge *f*, Krage *f*, Tragstein *m*, Kragstein *m*
console table	Konsoltisch *m*
Constantinople	Konstantinopel, Byzanz
constellation	Sternbild *n*, Gestirn *n*
constellation symbol	Gestirnsymbol *n*
constitute	bilden
construct	bauen, errichten, aufbauen, konstruieren
construction	Bau *m*, Bauen *n*, Erbauung *f*, Konstruktion *f*, Aufbau *m*, Gebäude *n*
prefabricated —	Fertigbauweise *f*
type of —	Bauart *f*
Constructivism	Konstruktivismus *m*, Non-Objektivismus *m*
contemporary *adj.*	gegenwärtig, zeitgenössisch

contemporary n.	Zeitgenosse m
contemporary art	Gegenwartskunst f
content(s)	Inhalt m
continuous narration	kontinuierende Darstellung f, kontinuierliche Darstellung f
contour	Umriß m, Kontur f
contour drawing	Umrißzeichnung f
contoured	umrissen
contouring	Konturierung f
contour line	Umrißlinie f
contracted inhumation	Hockerbestattung f
contrapposto	Kontrapost m
contrast v.	kontrastieren
contrast n.	Kontrast m
simultaneous —	Simultankontrast m, Simultanwirkung f
contrasting	kontrastierend
contrasting colors	Ergänzfarben pl, Ergänzungsfarben pl
contribute	beitragen
contribution	1. Beitrag m 2. Beigabe f
convent	Nonnenkloster n, Stift n
convergent	konvergent
converging	konvergent
conversation piece	Konversationsstück n
Conversion of Paul, the —	die Bekehrung Pauli
convert	umbauen, umwandeln
convex	konvex, Konvex-
convex arch	Konvexbogen m
copaiba balsam	Kopaivabalsamöl n
copal	Kopal m, Kopalharz m
coping	Abdeckplatte f, Mauerabdeckung f, Mauerkappe f, Mauerhut m, Mauerkrönung f
coping stone	Abdeckstein m
copper adj.	kupfern, Kupfer-

copper n.	Kupfer n
Copper age	Kupferzeit f, Aeneolithikum n
copper brown	kupferbraun
copper coin	Kupfermünze f
copper-colored	kupferbraun, kupferrot
copper engraver	Kupferstecher m
copper engraving	1. Kupferstechkunst f 2. Kupferstich m
copper etching	Kupferätzung f
copper plate	Kupferplatte f
copper red	kupferrot
copper sheet	Kupferblech n
copper vessel	Kupfergefäß n
Coptic	koptisch
copy v.	abbilden, abmalen, abzeichnen, kopieren, nachahmen, nachbilden, abklatschen
copy n.	Kopie f, Abdruck m, Abschrift f, Abklatsch m, Nachahmung f, Nachbildung f
copyist	Kopist m
copy-like	abbildhaft
coquillage	Muschelornament n, Muschelwerk n
coral	Koralle f
corbel	Konsole f, Krage f, Kragstein m, Kragstück n, Balkenträger m, Tragstein m
corbelled dome	Kragkuppel f, Kraggewölbe n, falsches Gewölbe n
corbelling	Kraggewölbetechnik f, Überkragungsgewölbe n, Überkragungskuppel f
corbel table	auf Kragsteinen ruhender Fries
corbie gable	Staffelgiebel m, Stufengiebel m, Treppengiebel m
cord	1. Strick m, Schnur f 2. Zingulum m

cordate	herzförmig
corded ware	Schnurkeramik *f*
core	Kern *m*, Kernstein *m*
Corinthian	korinthisch
Corinthian order	korinthische Ordnung *f*
corner	Ecke *f*
corner acroterion	Eckakroterie *f*
corner column	Ecksäule *f*
corner pillar	Eckpfeiler *m*
corner spandrel	Eckzwickel *m*
cornerstone	Eckstein *m*, Grundstein *m*
cornerstone laying	Grundsteinlegung *f*
corner support	Eckstütze *f*
cornice	Gesims *n*, Geison *n*, Kranzgesims *n*, Kranzleiste *f*, Sims *n*
cornice moulding	Giebelgesims *n*
cornice-work	Gesimsung *f*
cornucopia	Füllhorn *n*
coronation	Krönung *f*
coronation cloak	Krönungsmantel *m*
coronation jewelry	Krönungsschmuck *m*
coronation jewels	Krönungsschmuck *m*
Coronation of the Virgin	die Marienkrönung
coronation vestments	Krönungsornat *m*
coroplast	Koroplastiker *m*
corporal	Korporale *n*
corporeal	körperhaft, körperlich, leiblich
corporeality	Körperhaftigkeit *f*, Körperlichkeit *f*
corpse	Leiche *f*, Leichnam *m*
Corpus Christi	Fronleichnam *m*
correspondence	Übereinstimmung *f*, Entsprechung *f*
corridor	Gang *m*, Flur *m*, Korridor *m*
corrugated iron	Wellblech *n*
corset	Mieder *n*
cor-ten steel	Corten-stahl *m*

Cosmatis, the —	Cosmaten *pl*
cosmetic palette	Schminkpalette *f*
costume	Kostüm *n*, Tracht *f*
traditional —	Tracht *f*
cotton	Baumwolle *f*
cotton paper	Baumwollpapier *n*
couch	Couch *f*, Kline *f*
coulisse	Gleitbahn *f*, Gleitschiene *f*
count	Graf *m*
counterfeiter	Fälscher *m*, Kunstfälscher *m*
counter relief	Kontra-Relief *n*
countess	Gräfin *f*
country house	Landhaus *n*
couple	Paar *n*
coupled columns	Doppelsäule *f*
course	Fries *m*
belt —	Gesims *n*, Fries *m*
court	Hof *m*, Hofstaat *m*
court academy	Hofschule *f*
court architect	Hofarchitekt *m*
courtly	höfisch
court painter	Hofmaler *m*
court school	Hofschule *f*
courtyard	Hof *m*
cove	Hohlleiste *f*, Kehlleiste *f*
Covenant, Ark of the —	Bundeslade *f*
cover *v.*	decken, bedecken
cover *n.*	Deckel *m*
covered	bedeckt, Deckel-
covered bowl	Deckelschale *f*
covered goblet	Deckelpokal *m*
covered walk	Laubengang *m*
coving	Hohlleiste *f*, Kehlleiste *f*
crack *v.*	springen, reißen
crack *n.*	Riß *m*, Sprung *m*
crackle	Krakalee *f*, Craqueleé *m, n*

cradle	1. Wiege *f* 2. Wiegeeisen *n*
cradling	Parkettieren *n*
crafts	Kunstgewerbe *n*, Kunsthandwerk *n*
craftsman	Handwerker *m*, Kunsthandwerker *m*
craftsmanlike	handwerklich
craftsmen's guild	Zunft *f*
crafts museum	Kunstgewerbemuseum *n*
craquelure	1. Krakalee *f*, Craqueleé *m*, *n* 2. Krakelüre *f*
crater	s. krater
crayon	Buntstift *m*, Krayon *m*, Pastellfarbe *f*, Stift *m*
crayon drawing	Bunstiftzeichnung *f*
crayon lithograph	Kreidelithographie *f*
crayon manner	Crayonmanier *f*, Krayonmanier *f*, Kreidemanier *f*
crazing	Krakalee *f*, Craqueleé *m*, *n*
cream-colored	cremefarben, kremfarben
crease *v.*	falten
crease *n.*	Falte *f*
create	schaffen, schöpfen, erschaffen
creation	Schöpfung *f*, Schaffung *f*, Erschaffung *f*
Creation, the story of —	Schöpfungsgeschichte *f*
Creation, the —	die Erschaffung der Welt
Creation of Eve, the —	die Erschaffung Evas
creative	schöpferisch
creative period	Schaffensperiode *f*
creative power	Schaffenskraft *f*, Schöpferkraft *f*, Schöpfungskraft *f*
creative process	Schaffensprozeß *m*
creativity	Schöpferkraft *f*, Schöpfungskraft *f*
creator	Schöpfer *m*, Urheber *m*
crèche	Krippe *f*, Weihnachtskrippe *f*

cremation	Brandbestattung *f*, Verbrennung *f*, Leichenverbrennung *f*
Cremnitz white	Kremserweiß *n*
crenel	Mauerzack *m*, Schießscharte *f*
crenellation	Zinne *f*
crepidoma	Krepidoma *n*, Krepis *f*, Stufenunterbau *m*
crescent	Sichel *f*
crescent moon	Mondsichel *f*
crescent-shaped	sichelförmig, Sichel-
crest	1. Gesprenge *n* 2. Zimier *n*
Cretan	kretisch
Crete	Kreta
crib	Krippe *f*
crimson	Karmin *n*, Karmesin *n*
crimson red	karminrot
critic	Kritiker *m*
criticism	Kritik *f*
critique	Kritik *f*
crochet	häkeln
crochet work	Häkelarbeit *f*
crockery	Töpferware *f*, Töpferzeug *n*
crocket	Krabbe *f*, Kriechblume *f*
crocket capital	Kelch-Knospen-Kapitell *n*, Knollenkapitell *n*, Knospenkapitell *n*
cromlech	Cromlech *m*, Kromlech *m*
crooked	krumm, schief
crosier	Bischofsstab *m*, Krummstab *m*, Pedum *n*
cross	Kreuz *n*, Kruzifix *n*
banner of the —	Kreuzfahne *f*
Greek —	griechisches Kreuz *n*
Latin —	lateinisches Kreuz *n*
Maltese —	Malteserkreuz *n*, Johannitterkreuz *n*

papal —	päbstliches Kreuz *n*
patriarchal —	erzbischöfliches Kreuz *n*, Kardinalskreuz *n*, Patriarchenkreuz *n*, Doppelkreuz *n*
pectoral —	Brustkreuz *n*, Pektorale *n*
potent —	Krückenkreuz *n*
roadside —	Bildstock *m*, Marterl *n*, Betsäule *f*
St. Andrew's —	Schrägkreuz *n*, Andreaskreuz *n*
tau —	Antoniuskreuz *n*, Taukreuz *n*
trefled —	Kleeblattkreuz *n*
Y-shaped —	Deichselkreuz *n*, Gabelkreuz *n*, Schächerkreuz *n*
cross ancrée	Ankerkreuz *n*
cross bar	Quersprosse *f*
cross-beam	Holm *m*
cross-crosslet	Wiederkreuz *n*
crossed	gekreuzt
cross-hatching	Kreuzlage *f*, Kreuzschraffierung *f*, Kreuzschraffur *f*
crossing	Vierung *f*
crossing pillar	Vierungspfeiler *m*
crossing square	Vierungsquadrat *n*
Crossing the Red Sea	der Durchgang durch das Rote Meer, der Durchzug durch das Rote Meer
crossing tower	Vierungsturm *m*
cross section	Querschnitt *m*
cross section profile	Querschnittform *f*
cross shape	Kreuzform *f*
cross-shaped	kreuzförmig
crosswise	quer
crouched position	Hockerstellung *f*
crouched position burial	Hockerbestattung *f*
crown	1. Krone *f* 2. Scheitel *m*, Scheitelpunkt *m*, Scheitelhöhe *f*
Crown Derby	feines Porzellan aus Derby, England

crowning, altar —	Gesprenge *n*
crown jewels	Kronjuwelen *pl*
Crucified One, the —	der Gekreuzigte
crucifix	Kruzifix *n*
Crucifixion	Kreuzigung *f*
crucifixion group	Kreuzigungsgruppe *f*
crucifixion scene	Kreuzigungsszene *f*
cruciform	kreuzförmig
cruciform church	Kreuzkirche *f*
cruciform nimbus	Kreuznimbus *m*
cruciform reliquary	Staurothek *f*
cruet	Meßkännchen *n*
crypt	Krypta *f*
crystal	Kristall *n*
lead —	Bleikristall *n*
cube	Kubus *m*, Würfel *m*
cubicular	kubisch, Kubus-
cubicular building	Kubusbau *m*
cubiform	kubisch
Cubism	Kubismus *m*
Cubist	Kubist *m*
cuff	Manschette *f*
culmination	Höhepunkt *m*
cult *adj.*	kultisch, Kult-
cult *n.*	Kult *m*
cult building	Kultbau *m*
cult disc	Kultscheibe *f*
cult image	Kultbild *n*
cult object	Kultgegenstand *m*
cult site	Kultstätte *f*
cultural	kulturell, Kultur-
cultural achievement	Kulturleistung *f*
culture	Kultur *f*
cuneiform *adj.*	kuneiform
cuneiform *n.*	Keilschrift *f*
cuneiform tablet	Keilschrifttafel *f*

cup	Tasse *f*, Becher *m*, Pokal *m*
cupboard	Schrank *m*, Geschirrschrank *m*
cupids	Eroten *pl*
cupola	Kuppel *f*
curator	Kustos *m*, Konservator *m*
curl	Locke *f*, Haarlocke *f*
current *adj.*	aktuell, gegenwärtig
current *n.*	Strömung *f*
cursive	kursiv
curtain	1. Vorhang *m* 2. Burgmauer *f*
curtain arch	Vorhangbogen *m*
curtain wall	vorgehängte Wand *f*, nicht tragende (Außen-)Wand
curvature	Krümme *f*, Krümmung *f*, Kurvatur *f*, Wölbung *f*
curve *v.*	krümmen
curve *n.*	Kurve *f*, Ausbuchtung *f*
curved	gekurvt, gekrümmt, krumm, geschweift, gewölbt
cushion	Polsterung *f*, Kissen *n*
cushion capital	Würfelkapitell *n*
cushioning	Polsterung *f*
cusp	Nase *f*
custom	Sitte *f*
cut *v.*	schneiden
cut *n.*	Schnitt *m*
cutch	Katechu *n*
cyanine blue	Zyanin *n*
cycle	Zyklus *m*
picture –	Bilderzyklus *m*
cyclopean	zyklopisch, kyklopisch
cyclopean masonry	zyklopisches Mauerwerk *n*, Zyklopenmauer *f*
cyclopean wall	Zyklopenmauer *f*
cylinder	Zylinder *m*
cylinder impression	Siegelabrollung *f*

cylindrical	zylindrisch
cylix	Kylix *f*
cyma	Kyma *n*, Kymation *n*
cyma recta	Glockenleiste *f*, Karnies *n*
cyma reversa	Glockenleiste *f*, Karnies *n*
cymatium	Sima *f*, Giebelgesims *n*, Rinnleiste *f*
Cypro-Mycenean	kypromykenisch
Cyrillic	kyrillisch
dabbling	Pinselei *f*
Dadaism	Dadaismus *m*
Dadaist	Dadaist *m*
dadaistic	dadaistisch
dado	Würfel *m*
dagger	Dolch *m*
daguerreotype	Daguerreotypie *f*
dais	Podium *n*, erhöhte Plattform *f*, Estrade *f*
dalmatic	Dalmatika *f*
damage *v.*	beschädigen
damage *n*	Beschädigung *f*
damaged	beschädigt, versehrt
damar	Damar *n*, Dammar *n*
damar resin	Damarharz *n*
damar varnish	Damarfirnis *m*
Damascene	damaszieren, tauschieren
Damascening	Damaszierung *f*, Tauschierung *f*
damask	Damast *m*
Damned Cast into Hell, the —	der Höllensturz der Verdammten
Dance of Death	Totentanz *m*
dancer	Tänzer *m*
Daniel in the Lions' Den	Daniel in der Löwengrube
danse macabre	Totentanz *m*
Danube school	Donauschule *f*, Donaustil *m*

Danubian culture	Donaukultur *f*
dark	dunkel, dunkel-, düster, satt, schwarz, schwärzlich
dark blue	dunkelblau, marineblau
darken	dunkeln, nachdunkeln, schwärzen
darkness	Dunkelheit *f*, Schwärze *f*
data	Angabe *f*, Daten *pl*
ownership –	Besitzerangabe *f*
date *v.*	datieren
date *n*	Datum *n*
dating	Datierung *f*, Zeitbestimmung *f*, Einstufung *f*
carbon 14 –	Radiocarbondatierung *f*
means of –	Datierungsmittel *n*
radiocarbon –	Radiocarbondatierung *f*
thermoluminescence –	TL-Datierung *f*
tree-ring –	Dendrochronologie *f*
daubing	Pinselei *f*
daylight	Tageslicht *n*
dazzle effect	Flimmereffekt *m*
death	Tod *m*
death mask	Totenmaske *f*
Death of the Virgin	der Marientod, der Tod Mariä, der Tod Mariens
decade	Jahrzehnt *n*
decadent art	1. dekadente Kunst *f* 2. entartete Kunst *f*
decal	Abklatschverfahren *n*
decalcomania	Abklatschverfahren *n*, Abziehbilderdruck *m*, Decalcomanie *f*
decalcomania papier	Dekalkierpapier *n*
Decalogue	Dekalog *m*, die Zehn Gebote
decastyle	zehnsäulig
declaration	Aussage *f*
décollage	Décollage *f*
decomposition	Verwitterung *f*
decor	Dekor *m*

decorate	dekorieren, schmücken, verschönern, verzieren, ausmalen, ausstatten, zieren
Decorated Style	dekorierter Stil *m*; Baustil der englischen Hochgotik
decoration	Dekoration *f*, Schmuck *m*, Zierat *m*, Zierde *f*, Zierwerk *n*, Ausmalung *f*, Ausschmückung *f*, Ausstattung *f*
decorational form	Dekorationsform *f*
decorative	dekorativ, schmückend, Zier-, Schmuck-
decorative art	dekorative Kunst *f*
decorative form	Schmuckform *f*, Zierform *f*
decorative letter	Zierbuchstabe *m*
decorative moulding	Schmuckleiste *f*
decorative object	Schmuckgegenstand *m*
decorative vessel	Ziergefäß *n*
decorator	Dekorateur *m*, Dekorationsmaler *m*, Innenarchitekt *m*
dedicate	weihen, einweihen, widmen
dedication	Weihe *f*, Einweihung *f*, Widmung *f*
deep	1. satt, intensiv 2. tief
deep structure	Tiefenstruktur *f*, Tiefenbau *m*
deësis	Deësis *f*
defense architecture	Wehrbau *m*, Wehrarchitektur *f*
defensive structure	Wehrbau *m*, Befestigungsanlage *f*
defensive wall	Wehrmauer *f*
deformation	Deformation *f*, Deformierung *f*
degenerate art	entartete Kunst *f*
degree	Grad *m*, Stufe *f*
degree of brightness	Farbhellengrad *m*
degree of opacity	Deckkraft *f*
degree of saturation	Sättigungsgrad *m*
deify	vergöttlichen
deity	Göttergestalt *f*, Gottheit *f*

del.	del.
Delft tiles	Delfter Kacheln *pl*
delftware	Delfter Zeug *n*
delicacy	Zartheit *f*, Feinheit *f*, Zierlichkeit *f*
delicate	zart, fein
Delivery of the Keys to St. Peter	die Schlüsselübergabe an Petrus
Delivery of the Law Scroll	die Gesetzesübergabe an Petrus
Deluge	Sintflut *f*, Sündflut *f*
demi-column	Halbsäule *f*
demigod	Halbgott *m*, Heros *m*
demon	Dämon *m*
dendrochronology	Dendrochonologie *f*
Denial of Peter, the —	Petri Verleugnung, die Verleugnung Petri
dent	Kerbe *f*, Einschnitt *m*, Beule *f*
dentil	Zahnschnitt *m*
dentil pattern	Zahnschnittfries *m*
depict	darstellen, wiedergeben, schildern
depicted object	Bildgegenstand *m*
depiction	Darstellung *f*, Schilderung *f*, Wiedergabe *f*, Verbildlichung *f*
manner of —	Darstellungsweise *f*
means of —	Darstellungsmittel *n*
method of —	Darstellungsmethode *f*
depiction of man	Menschenbild *n*
depiction of nature	Naturdarstellung *f*, Naturwiedergabe *f*
depiction of reality	Wirklichkeitsdarstellung *f*
depiction of space	Raumbild *n*
depictive	bildlich, abbildlich
depictive art	bildende Kunst *f*, Bildkunst *f*
Deposition of Christ, the —	die Kreuzabnahme
depression	Höhlung *f*, Aushöhlung *f*, Vertiefung *f*

depth	Tiefe *f*, Raumtiefe *f*
Derby porcelain	Porzellan aus Derby, England
Descent from the Cross, the —	die Kreuzabnahme
Descent into Limbo, the —	der Abstieg in die Hölle
Descent of the Holy Ghost, the —	die Ausgießung des Heiligen Geistes
Descent to Hell, the —	die Höllenfahrt Christi
design *v.*	entwerfen, gestalten, konstruieren, planen
design *n.*	Entwurf *m*, Dessin *n*, Konstruktion *f*, Muster *n*, Plan *m*, Riß *m*. Visierung *f*, Gestaltung *f*, Formgebung *f*
interior —	Innenarchitektur *f*
design book	Vorlagebuch *n*, Vorlagesammlung *f*
designer	Formgeber *m*, Gestalter *m*
interior —	Dekorateur *m*, Innenarchitekt *m*
stage —	Bühnenbildner *m*
desk	Schreibtisch *m*
dessus de porte	Sopraporte *f*, Supraporte *f*
De Stihl	Neoplastizismus *m*, die Neue Gestaltung *f*
destroy	zerstören
detail	1. Detail *n*, Einzelheit *f* 2. Detailansicht *f*, Teilansicht *f*, Ausschnitt *m*
treatment of —	Detailbehandlung *f*
detail drawing	Detailzeichnung *f*
detailed	durchgearbeitet, detailliert
detailing	Detaillierung *f*
detail view	Detailansicht *f*
development	Entwicklung *f*, Aufbau *m*, Ausbau *m*, Ausgestaltung *f*, Entfaltung *f*
developmental phase	Entwicklungsphase *f*

developmental stage	Entwicklungsstufe *f*
deviant form	Abart *f*
deviate	abweichen
devil	Teufel *m*, Satan *m*
devotional art	Andachtskunst *f*
devotional hall	Andachtshalle *f*
devotional objects	Devotionalien *pl*
devotional picture	Andachtsbild *n*, Devotionalbild *n*
dexterity	Kunstfertigkeit *f*
dextrin	Dextrin *n*, Stärkegummi *n*
diaconicon	Diakonikon *n*
diadem	Diadem *n*
diagonal	diagonal, schräg, quer, übereck, Diagonal-, Schräg-
diagonal line	Quere *f*, Schräglinie *f*, Diagonale *f*
diagonal rib	Diagonalrippe *f*
diagonal view	Diagonalansicht *f*, Schrägansicht *f*
diagram	Diagramm *n*, Schema *n*
diameter	Durchmesser *m*
diamond	Diamant *m*
diaper	wiederholtes, rautenförmiges Muster
diaphanous	diaphan
diastyle	mit weit auseinanderstehenden Säulen versehen
diatomaceous earth	Kieselgur *f*
diatreta glass	Diatretglas *n*
dice	Würfel *pl*
dichroism	Dichroismus *m*
die	1. Prägestempel *m* 2. Würfel *m*
diffraction	Lichtbeugung *f*
diffraction color	Regenbogenfarbe *f*
diffuse	diffus
dig *v.*	ausgraben, graben
dig *n.*	Ausgrabung *f*, Grabung *f*
diglyph	Diglyph *m*

dignitary	Würdenträger *m*
dim	düster, trüb
dimension	Dimension *f*, Ausmaß *n*, Maß *n*
dimensional	dimensional
dinanderie	Dinanderie *f*
diorama	Diorama *n*
diorite	Diorit *m*
dipteral	dipteral
dipteral temple	Dipteros *m*
diptych	Diptychon *n*, Doppeltafel *f*
Dipylon vase	Dipylon-Vase *f*
direction	Richtung *f*
direct painting	Primamalerei *f*
disc	Scheibe *f*
disc fibula	Scheibenfibel *f*
discharging arch	Entlastungsbogen *m*
disciple	Jünger *m*
Disciples at Emmaus, the —	die Emmausjünger, die Jünger von Emmaus
Discovery of the True Cross, the —	die Kreuzauffindung, die Auffindung des heiligen Kreuzes
dish	Teller *m*, Schüssel *f*, Platte *f*
dishes	Geschirr *n*
disk	Scheibe *f*
display case	Schaukasten *m*, Vitrine *f*
Dispute in the Temple, the —	Christus unter den Schriftgelehrten
dissolve	lösen
distemper	Leimfarbe *f*, Leimfarbenmalerei *f*
distinct	deutlich, klar
distinctness	Deutlichkeit *f*, Klarheit *f*, Anschaulichkeit *f*
distort	verzerren
distortion	Verzerrung *f*
distribute	verteilen, gliedern
distribution	Verteilung *f*
divide	teilen, trennen, unterteilen, gliedern

division

division	Teilung *f*, Trennung *f*, Unterteilung *f*, Gliederung *f*
Divisionism	Divisionismus *m*
document	Urkunde *f*, Dokument *n*, Schriftquelle *f*
documentary	urkundlich, dokumentarisch
documentary source	Quellenwerk *n*, Schriftquelle *f*
dodecastyle	zwölfsäulig
Doelenstuk	Doelenstück *n*, Schützenstück *n*
Doge's Palace	Dogenpalast *m*
dog-tooth ornament	Spitzzahnfries *m*, Spitzzahnornament *n*, Hundzahnornament *n*
dolmen	Dolmen *m*
dolphin	Delphin *m*
dome	Kuppel *f*
beehive –	falsches Gewölbe *n*, Kraggewölbe *n*, Kragkuppel *f*
bulbous –	Zwiebelhaube *f*
corbelled –	falsches Gewölbe *n*, Kraggewölbe *n*, Kragkuppel *f*
parachute –	Schirmgewölbe *n*
ribbed –	Rippenkuppel *f*
umbrella –	Schirmgewölbe *n*
dome construction	Kuppelbau *m*
domed	überkuppelt, Kuppel-
domed building	Kuppelbau *m*
domed roof	Kuppeldach *n*
dome mosaic	Kuppelmosaik *n*
dome painting	Kuppelmalerei *f*
domestic utensil	Hausgerät *n*
domical vault	Domikalgewölbe *n*, Klostergewölbe *n*
dominant color	Dominantfarbe *f*, Hauptfarbe *f*
donate	stiften
donjon	Bergfried *m*
donkey	Esel *m*

doublet

donor	Stifter *m*, Donator *m*
donor figure	Stifterfigur *f*
donor portrait	Stifterbildnis *n*, Donator *m*
donor's coat-of-arms	Stifterwappen *n*
door	Tür *f*
bronze —	Bronzetür *f*, Erztür *f*
door cornice	Türgesims *n*
door frame	Türrahmen *m*, Türeinfassung *f*, Türzarge *f*
door handle	Türgriff *m*
door hinge	Türangel *f*
door jamb	Türpfosten *m*
door knob	Türgriff *m*
door knocker	Türklopfer *m*
door lintel	Türsturz *m*
door moulding	Türgesims *n*
door panel	Türfeld *n*
door post	Gewände *n*
door sill	Türschwelle *f*
doorway	Türöffnung *f*, Tür *f*
Dorians	Dorer *pl*
Doric	dorisch
Doric order	dorische Ordnung *f*
dormer window	Dachfenster *n*, Dacherker *m*, Gaube *f*, Gaupe *f*, Lukarne *f*, Zwerchgiebel *m*, Zwerchhaus *n*
Dormition of the Virgin	der Marientod, der Tod Mariä, der Tod Mariens
dormitory	Dormitorium *n*
dosseret	Kämpfer *m*
dot *v.*	punktieren
dot *n*	Punkt *m*, Tüpfel *m*
dotted manner	Punktiermanier *f*, Punzenmanier *f*
dotted manner engraving	Punktierstich *m*, Punktstich *m*
double-ended church	Doppelchoranlage *f*
double-headed eagle	Doppeladler *m*
doublet	Wams *n*

Doubting Thomas	der ungläubige Thomas
dove	Taube *f*
dovetail joint	Schwalbenschwanzfuge *f*
dowel	Dübel *n*, Holznagel *m*
drafting machine	Zeichenmaschine *f*
drafting paper	Zeichenpapier *n*
draftsman	Zeichner *m*, Graphiker *m*
draftsmanship	Linienführung *f*
dragon	Drache *m*
Dragon, St. George and the —	der Drachenkampf des hl. Georg
dragon's blood	Drachenblut *n*
drain	Traufleiste *f*, Traufrinne *f*, Abfluß *m*, Kanalisation *f*
drape	Vorhang *m*
drapery	Draperie *f*, Behang *m*, Faltenwurf *m*, Gewandung *f*
draping	Draperie *f*, Drapierung *f*
draw	zeichnen
draw bridge	Zugbrücke *f*
drawer	Schublade *f*, Schubfach *n*
drawing	1. Zeichnung *f* 2. Zeichenkunst *f*
pen —	Federzeichnung *f*
pencil —	Bleistiftzeichnung *f*
drawing board	Reißbrett *n*, Zeichenbrett *n*
drawing curve	Kurvenlineal *n*
drawing frame	Fadennetz *n*, Netzrahmen *m*, Rahmennetz *n*
drawing ink	Tusche *f*, Tuschfarbe *f*
drawing material	Zeichenbedarf *m*, Zeichenmittel *n*
drawing medium	Zeichenmittel *n*
drawing paper	Zeichenpapier *n*
drawing pen	Tuschfeder *f*, Zeichenfeder *f*
drawing pencil	Zeichenstift *m*
drawing school	Zeichenschule *f*
drawing surface	Zeichengrund *m*

drawing table	Zeichentisch *m*
dress *v.*	1. bekleiden, kleiden
	2. glätten, behauen
dress *n.*	**Kleid** *n*
dressed stone	**Haustein** *m*
dresser	**Kommode** *n*, **Schrank** *m*
drier	Sikkativ *n*, Trockenmittel *n*, Trockenstoff *m*
driftwood	Treibholz *n*
drill *v.*	bohren
drill *n.*	Bohrer *m*
drinking vessel	Trinkgefäß *n*
drip	Tropfleiste *f*, Wassernase *f*
drip moulding	Rinnleiste *f*
drip painting	Farbdripping *n*
dripstone	Kranzleiste *f*
drollery	Drolerie *f*
dromos	Dromos *m*
drop	Tropfen *m*
drum	Trommel *f*, Säulentrommel *f*
dry	trocken, Trocken-
dry joint masonry	Trockenmauerwerk *n*
drypoint	Kaltnadel *f*, Schneidenadel *f*
drypoint engraving	Kaltnadelradierung *f*
dry rot	Holzfäule *f*
duchess	Herzogin *f*
duchy	Herzogtum *n*
dugento	Ducento *n*, Dugento *n*
duke	Herzog *m*
dukedom	Herzogtum *n*
dull	matt, stumpf, flau
dummy door	Scheintür *f*
duplicate *v.*	vervielfältigen, abklatschen, kopieren
duplicate *n.*	Duplikat *n*, Kopie *f*, Abklatsch *m*
duplication	Vervielfältigung *f*, Duplikation *f*

duplication process	Vervielfältigungsverfahren *n*, Reproduktionsverfahren *n*
dusky	düster
Dutch	holländisch, niederländisch
dwarf gallery	Zwerggalerie *f*
dye *v.*	färben, einfärben
dye *n.*	Farbstoff *m*
dye bath	Färbebad *n*
dyestuff	Farbstoff *m*
dynamics	Dynamik *f*
dynamism	Dynamik *f*

eagle	Adler *m*
ear	Ohr *n*
early	früh, Früh-
early Christian	frühchristlich, altchristlich
early civilization	Frühkultur *f*
early Doric	frühdorisch
Early Gothic	Frühgotik *f*
early stage	Frühstufe *f*
early work	Frühwerk *n*, Jugendarbeit *f*
ear pendant	Ohrgehänge *n*
earring	Ohrring *m*, Ohrgehänge *n*
earth	Erde *f*
Earth	Erde *f*
earth color	Erdfarbe *f*
earth-colored	erdfarbig, erdfarben
earthen	irden
earthenware	Irdenware *f*, Tonware *f*, Töpfergeschirr *n*, Töpferware *f*, Töpferzeug *n*
earthly	irdisch
earth pigment	Erdfarbe *f*
ease	Leichtigkeit *f*
easel	Staffelei *f*
sketching —	Feldstaffelei *f*

studio —	Werkstattstaffelei f
table —	Tischstaffelei f
easel painting	Staffeleibild n
Eastern Orthodox Church	Ostkirche f
east pediment	Ostgiebel m
east Roman	oströmisch
east sanctuary	Ostchor m
easy chair	Sessel m
eaves	Traufe f
ebauche	Entwurfszeichnung f
ebony	Ebenholz n, Schwarzholz n
ecce homo	ecce homo
Ecclesia and Synagogue	Ecclesia und Synagoge
ecclesiastical	geistlich, kirchlich
echelon	Staffel f
echinus	Echinus m, Wulst m
echoppe	Radiernadel für feinste Linien
eclectic	eklektisch
eclecticism	Eklektizismus m
écorché	Muskelmann m
ecriture automatique	Automatismus m
ectypum	Ektypon n
edge	Rand m, Kante f, Grenze f, Zarge f, Borte f
edging	Bordüre f, Einfassung f
edition	1. Auflage f 2. Auflagenhöhe f
limited —	beschränkte Auflage f
Education of the Virgin, the —	die Erziehung der Jungfrau Maria
effect	Wirkung f
effect of air	Lufteinwirkung f, Luftwirkung f
effect of weather	Witterungseinfluß m
effloresce	auswittern
efflorescence	Verwitterung f
effortlessness	Leichtigkeit f
egg and dart	Eierstab m, ionisches Kymation n

egg ground	Eigrund *m*
egg-shaped	eiförmig
eggshell porcelain	Eierschalenporzellan *n*
egg size	Eigrund *m*
egg tempera	Eitempera *f*
egg white	Eiweiß *n*
egg yolk	Dotter *n*, Eidotter *n*
Egypt	Ägypten
Egyptian *adj.*	ägyptisch
Egyptian *n,*	Ägypter *m*
Egyptologist	Ägyptologe *m*
Egyptology	Ägyptologie *f*
einkorn	Einkorn *n*
elbow	Ellbogen *m*
electrotype	Galvanoplastik *f*
electrotypic process	Galvanoplastik *f*
electrum	Elektron *n*, Goldsilberlegierung *f*
elegance	Eleganz *f*
elegant	elegant
element	Element *n*
elemi	Elemi *n*
Eleousa Madonna	Eleusa *f*
elevate	erheben
elevation	Aufriß *m*
Elizabethan style	Elisabethstil *m*
ellipse	Ellipse *f*
elliptical	elliptisch
elliptical arch	elliptischer Bogen *m*
elongate	strecken, verlängern
elongation	Streckung *f*
email brun	Braunfirnis *m*
embellish	verschönen, verschönern, schmücken
embellishment	Verschönerung *f*
emblem	Emblem *n*, Sinnbild *n*, Symbol *n*
embodiment	Verkörperung *f*

enamel paint

embody	verkörpern
emboss	buckeln, punzen
embossed design	Punzenmuster *n*
embossed stone	Buckelquader *m*
embossing	Buckelung *f*, Punzarbeit *f*
embrasure	Scharte *f*, Schießscharte *f*
embroider	besticken, brodieren
embroidery	Broderie *f*, Stickerei *f*, Bildstickerei *f*
embu	Einschlagen *n*
emerald	Smaragd *m*
emerald green	Deckgrün *n*, Schweinfurtergrün *n*
Emmaus, Christ at —	Christus in Emmaus
Emmaus, the Disciples at —	die Emmausjünger
Emmaus, the Supper at —	das Emmausmahl
emmer	Emmer *m*
empathy	Einfühlung *f*
empathize, ability to —	Einfühlungsvermögen *n*
emporer	Kaiser *m*
empire	Reich *n*
Empire style	Empirestil *m*
emulsifier	Emulgator *m*
emulsifying agent	Emulgator *m*
emulsion	Emulsion *f*
emulsion ground	Halbkreidegrund *m*
enamel *v.*	emaillieren
enamel *n.*	Emaille *f*, Email *n*, Schmalt *m*, Schmelz *m*, Schmelzarbeit *f*, Schmelzglas *n*
enamel color	Schmelzfarbe *f*
enameled	emailliert, glasiert
enameled ware	Emailware *f*
enamel glaze	Schmelzglasur *f*
enameling	Schmelzarbeit *f*, Schmelzmalerei *f*
enamel-like	emailhaft
enamel paint	Emailfarbe *f*, Schmelzfarbe *f*

enamel painting	Emailmalerei *f*, Schmelzfarbenmalerei *f*, Schmelzmalerei *f*
enamel tile	Emailfliese *f*
enamelwork	Emailarbeit *f*
encaustic painting	Enkaustik *f*, Wachsfarbenmalerei *f*, Wachsmalerei *f*
encaustic technique	Enkaustik *f*
enchase	gravieren, ziselieren
enchasing	Gravierung *f*, Ziselierung *f*
enciente	Enciente *f*, Wehrmauer *f*
enclosed court	Binnenhof *m*
enclosing structure	Umfassungsbau *m*
enclosing wall	Mauerring *m*, Umfassungsmauer *f*, Einfriedungsmauer *f*
enclosure	Umfriedung *f*
endow	stiften
endowment	Stiftung *f*
Eneolithic	Aeneolithikum *m*
enfilade	Enfilade *f*
engaged column	Wandsäule *f*
engaged leg	Standbein *n*
engaged pier	Wandpfeiler *m*
engaged pillar	Wandpfeiler *m*
engobe	Engobe *f*, Anguß *m*, Angußfarbe *f*
engrave	gravieren, stechen, eingravieren
engraver	Stecher *m*, Graveur *m*
portrait —	Bildnisstecher *m*
engraving	1. Gravierkunst *f* 2. Gravierung *f*, Stich *m*, Gravur *f*, Gravüre *f*
engraving after a painting	Nachstich *m*
engraving cushion	Lederpolster *n*
engraving on glass	Glasgravierung *f*
engraving tool	Gravierinstrument *n*
enlarge	vergrößern, erweitern, ausbauen
enlargement	Vergrößerung *f*, Erweiterung *f*, Ausbau *m*

enormous	kolossal, riesig, gewaltig
entablature	Gebälk *n*
entasis	Entase *f*, Entasis *f*, Säulenschwellung *f*
enthroned	thronend
entombment	Grablegung *f*, Begräbnis *n*, Beerdigung *f*
entrance	Eingang *m*
main –	Haupteingang *m*
entrance hall	**Eingangshalle** *f*
entrelac	**Entrelacs** *n*, **Bandwerkmotiv** *n*
entresol	**Mezzanin** *n*
Entry into Jerusalem	der Einzug in Jerusalem
environment	Umgebung *f*, Umwelt *f*
eolith	Eolith *m*
epic	Epos *n*, Heldenepos *n*
epic poem	Epos *n*, Heldenepos *n*
epigon	Epigone *f*
epigraphy	Epigraphik *f*
epiphany	Epiphanie *f*
Epiphany	Epiphanie *f*
Epistle book	Epistolarium *n*
epistyle	Architrav *n*
epitaph	Epitaph *n*, Epitaphium *n*
epoch	Epoche *f*
epoxy resin	Epoxydharz *n*
equal	gleich
equal-sized	gleichgroß
equestrian statue	Reiterstandbild *n*, Reiterstatue *f*
equilateral	**gleichseitig, gleichschenkelig**
equilateral octagon	**Achtort** *m*
equilibrium	Ponderation *f*, Gleichgewicht *n*
equip	ausstatten
equipment	Ausstattung *f*
era	Epoche *f*, Zeitalter *n*
Erechtheion	Erechtheion *n*
Erechtheum	Erechtheion *n*

erect	errichten, aufbauen, bauen, erbauen, aufstellen
erection	Errichtung *f*, Erbauung *f*, Bau *m*
erotes	Eroten *pl*
escarp	Böschung *f*
escutcheon	Wappenschild *m*
Esquiline Hill	Esquilin *m*
essence	1. Essenz *f* 2. Wesen *n*
essential oil	ätherisches Öl *n*, Essenz *f*
establish	gründen
establishment	Gründung *f*
étagerè	Etagere *f*
etch	ätzen, radieren
etching	1. Ätzung *f*, Radierung *f* 2. Radierkunst *f*
soft-ground –	Weichgrundätzung *f*, Durchdruckverfahren *n*
etching ground	Ätzgrund *m*
etching needle	Ätznadel *f*, Nadelstichel *m*, Radiernadel *f*
etching on glass	Glasätzung *f*
etching process	Ätzverfahren *n*
eternal value	Ewigkeitswert *m*
ether	Äther *m*
ethereal	ätherisch
Etruscan *adj.*	etruskisch
Etruscan *n*	Etrusker *m*
Eurydice	Eurydike
euthynteria	Euthynterie *f*
evangeliar	Evangeliar *n*, Evangeliarium *n*, Evangelium *n*
evangelist	Evangelist *m*
evangelist's symbol	Evangelistensymbol *n*, Evangelistenzeichen *n*
evangelist table	Evangelistenbogen *m*
Eve	Eva
even	eben, plan, gerade, glatt, flach

ewer	Aquamanile *f*, Gießgefäß *n*, Wasserkanne *f*, Wasserkrug *m*
exact	exakt, genau
exactness	Exaktheit *f*, Genauigkeit *f*
exc.	exc.
excavate	ausgraben
excavated find	Ausgrabungsfund *m*, Grabungsfund *m*, Fund *m*
excavation	Ausgrabung *f*, Grabung *f*
excavator	Ausgräber *m*
execute	durchführen, ausführen
execution	Ausführung *f*, Durchführung *f*
exedra	Exedra *f*
exemplary	vorbildlich
exhibit	ausstellen
exhibition	Ausstellung *f*
exhibition catalog	Ausstellungskatalog *m*
exhibition hall	Ausstellungshalle *f*
exhibition opening	Vernissage *f*, Ausstellungseröffnung *f*
exhibition room	Ausstellungsraum *m*
exhibitor	Aussteller *m*
ex libris	Exlibris *n*
exonarthex	Exonarthex *m*
expand	erweitern, ausbauen
expansion	Erweiterung *f*, Ausbau *m*
expert	Experte *m*, Kenner *m*
expert's opinion	Expertise *f*
expose	1. belichten 2. freilegen
exposed concrete	Sichtbeton *m*
exposure	1. Belichtung *f* 2. Freilegung *f*
express	ausdrücken
expression	Ausdruck *m*
manner of —	Ausdrucksweise *f*
power of —	Ausdruckskraft *f*, Aussagekraft *f*

Expressionism	Expressionismus *m*
Expressionist	Expressionist *m*
expressionist	expressionistisch
Expulsion from the Garden of Eden	die Vertreibung aus dem Paradies
extend	verlängern, erweitern
extension	Verlängerung *f*, Erweiterung *f*, Vergrößerung *f*, Anbau *m*
extent	Ausmaß *n*, Maß *n*
exterior	1. Außenseite *f*, Äußere *n* 2. Außenansicht *f* 3. Außenbau *m*
exterior stairs	Freitreppe *f*
exterior wall	Außenwand *f*
extrados	Rücken *m*
extremities	Gliedmaßen *pl*, Glieder *pl*
ex-voto	Exvoto *n*, Weihgeschenk *n*
eye	1. Auge *n* 2. Öse *f*
eyebrow	Augenbraue *f*, Braue *f*
eye kylix	Augenschale *f*
fable	Fabel *f*, Sage *f*, Legende *f*
fabric	Stoff *m*, Zeug *n*
fabulous	märchenhaft, sagenhaft, legendenhaft
fabulous beast	Fabelwesen *n*
facade	Fassade *f*, Front *f*, Vorderseite *f*
face *v.*	verkleiden
face *n.*	1. Gesicht *n*, Antlitz *n* 2. Vorderseite *f*, Ansichtsfläche *f* 3. Avers *m*
facet	Facette *f*
facetted	facettiert
facial expression	Gesichtsausdruck *m*, Miene *f*
facial feature	Gesichtszug *m*, Bildniszug *m*, Zug *m*

facing	Verkleidung *f*, Verblendung *f*
facsimile	Faksimile *n*
facsimile print	Faksimiledruck *m*
factory	Fabrik *f*
fade	verblassen, verbleichen
faience	Fayence *f*
faience-tiled stove	Fayenceofen *m*
fairy tale	Märchen *n*
faithful to nature	naturgetreu
fake *v.*	fälschen, verfälschen
fake *n.*	Fälschung *f*, Kunstfälschung *f*
falchion	Fischblase *f*, Schneuß *m*
falcon	Falke *m*
faldistory	Faldistorium *n*
Fall of Man, the —	der Sündenfall
false door	Scheintür *f*
false front	Blendgiebel *m*
false god	Götze *m*
false-necked jar	Bügelkanne *f*
false sleeve	Scheinärmel *m*
false vault	falsches Gewölbe *n*, Überkragungsgewölbe *n*, Überkragungskuppel *f*
falsification	Verfälschung *f*
falsify	verfälschen
family	Familie *f*
family portrait	Familienbildnis *n*
family tree	Stammbaum *m*
fan	Fächer *m*, Wedel *m*
fan brush	Fächerpinsel *m*
fanlight	Fächerrosette *f*
fan-shaped	fächerförmig
fantasy	Phantasie *f*
fan vault	Fächergewölbe *n*, Palmgewölbe *n*, Strahlengewölbe *n*
farmer	Bauer *m*
Farnese bull	der farnesische Stier

fascia	Fascie *f*, Faszie *f*
fashion *v.*	gestalten, bilden, formen
fashion *n.*	Mode *f*
fasten	befestigen
fastening	Befestigung *f*
fat	fett, dick
fate	Schicksal *n*
faun	Faun *m*
Fauvism	Fauvismus *m*
Feast of Herod, the —	das Gastmahl des Herodes
feather	Feder *f*
feather mosaic	Federmosaik *n*
featherwork	Federmosaik *n*
fec.	fec.
feel	empfinden, fühlen, tasten
feeling	Empfinden *n*, Empfindung *f*, Gefühl *n*
Feet, the Washing of the —	die Fußwaschung
feldspar	Feldspat *m*
felt	Filz *m*
felt-tip pen	Filzstift *m*
female	weiblich
feminine	weiblich
fenestrated	gefenstert, mit Fenstern versehen
fenestration	Anordnung der Fenster
ferroconcrete	Eisenbeton *m*, Stahlbeton *m*
ferroconcrete construction	Stahlbetonkonstruktion *f*
fertility	Fruchtbarkeit *f*
fertility symbol	Fruchtbarkeitssymbol *n*
Festival of the Rose-Garlands	das Rosenkranzfest
festoon	Feston *n*
fetish	Fetisch *m*
fiber	Faser *f*, Fiber *f*, Bast *m*
fiberboard	Faserplatte *f*
fiber glass	Fiberglas *n*
fibula	Fibel *f*, Spange *f*

fidelity	Wirklichkeitstreue *f*, Treue *f*
field	1. Fach *n*
	2. Feld *n*, Bildfeld *n*, Fläche *f*, Grund *m*
field of vision	Blickfeld *n*
fight	Kampf *m*
fighter	Kämpfer *m*
fig milk	Feigenmilch *f*
figural	figural, figürlich, Figuren-
figural capital	Figurenkapitell *n*
figural decoration	Figurenschmuck *m*
figurative	figural, figürlich
figure	Figur *f*, Gestalt *f*, Form *f*, Statue *f*
main −	Hauptfigur *f*
figured	figural
figurine	**Figurine *f*, Figürchen *n*, Statuette *f*, Idol *n***
Fikellura ware	Fikellura-Vasen *pl*
filigree	**Filigran *n*, Filigranarbeit *f***
fill	**füllen**
fillet	Steg *m*
fin	Gußnaht *f*
final glaze	Schlußglasur *f*
final varnish	Schlußfirnis *m*
find	Fund *m*, Fundgut *n*, Fundstück *n*, Ausgrabungsfund *m*
location of the −	Fundort *m*
Finding of Moses, the −	die Auffindung des Moses
findings	Befund *m*, Ergebnis *n*
fine arts	bildende Kunst *f*
fine-grained	feinkörnig
finger	Finger *m*
finial	Kreuzblume *f*
finish *v.*	vollenden, beendigen, vervollkommnen
finish *n.*	Schliff *m*, Putz *m*, Politur *f*

fir	Fichte *f*, Tannenholz *n*
fire	brennen, garbrennen
fire brick	Schamotteziegel *m*
fireclay	Schamotte *f*
fire gilded	feuervergoldet
fire gilding	Feuervergoldung *f*
fireplace	Kamin *m*, Feuerstelle *f*
fire wall	Brandmauer *f*
firing	Garbrand *m*, Brand *m*
firing technique	Brenntechnik *f*
fish	Fisch *m*
fish glue	Fischleim *m*, Hausenblasenleim *m*
fish scale pattern	Schuppenmuster *m*
fish-shaped	fischförmig
fist	Faust *f*
fitch hair	Iltishaar *n*
fittings	Ausrüstung *f*, Ausstattung *f*
five-aisled	fünfschiffig
fixative	Fixativ *n*, Fixiermittel *n*
fixed point	Fixpunkt *m*
flag	Fahne *f*, Flagge *f*, Standarte *f*
Flagellation of Christ, the —	die Geißelung Christi
flagstone	Steinplatte *f*, Fliese *f*
flagstone pavement	Steinplattenboden *m*, Fliesenboden *m*
flake tool	Abschlaggerät *n*
Flamboyant	Flamboyant *n*
flashed glass	Überfangglas *n*
flashed pottery	Töpferware, deren Oberfläche beim Brennen verfärbt wurde
flask	1. Flasche *f* 2. Halteeisen *n*
flat *adj.*	1. flach, eben, plan, flächenhaft, flächig, Flach- 2. flau, stumpf, matt
flat *n.*	Wohnung *f*

flat arch	scheitrechter Sturz *m*, scheitrechter Sturzbogen *m*, Sturzbogen *m*
flat brush	Flachpinsel *m*
flat burin	Flachstichel *m*
flat chisel	Flachmeißel *m*
flat graver	Flachstichel *m*
flatness	1. Flächenhaftigkeit *f*, Flächigkeit *f* 2. Flauheit *f*, Stumpfheit *f*, Mattheit *f*
flat painting	Flächenmalerei *f*
flat roof	Flachdach *n*
flat style	Flächenstil *m*
flaw	Fehler *m*, Makel *m*, Sprung *m*, Riß *m*, Bruch *m*
flawed	fehlerhaft
flawless	fehlerfrei, makellos, perfekt
flax	Flachs *m*
flèche	Dachreiter *m*
Flemish	flämisch, vlämisch
flesh color	Fleischton *m*, Inkarnat *n*, Karnation *f*
fleshy	fleischig
fleur-de-lis	Wappenlilie *f*, Lilie *f*, Schwertlilie *f*
fleuron	Fleuron *m*
flexibility	Beweglichkeit *f*
flexible	beweglich
flicker	flimmern
flight	Flucht *f*
Flight into Egypt, the —	die Flucht nach Ägypten
flint	Feuerstein *m*
flint glass	Kristallglas *n*
Flood, the —	Sintflut *f*, Sündflut *f*
floor	1. Boden *m*, Fußboden *m* 2. Geschoß *n*, Stockwerk *n*, Etage *f*, Flucht *f*

floor girder	Bodenträger *m*
flooring	Fußboden *m*, Paviment *n*
floor mosaic	Bodenmosaik *n*
floor plan	Grundriß *m*
floor tile	Bodenfliese *f*
floral wreath	Blumenkranz *m*
Florentine	florentinisch
Florentine brown	Florentinerbraun *n*
florescence	Blütezeit *f*
flow	Fluß *m*
flower	Blume *f*
flowers, still life of —	Blumenstilleben *n*, Blumenstück *n*
flow of line	Linienverlauf *m*
flow of movement	Bewegungsfluß *m*
fluorescence	Fluoreszenz *f*
fluorite	Flußspat *m*
fluorspar	Flußspat *m*
flute *v.*	auskehlen
flute *n.*	Kannele *f*, Auskehlung *f*, Riefe *f*, Rille *f*
fluted	gerillt
fluting	Kannelierung *f*, Kannelüre *f*, Auskehlung *f*
flux	Flußmittel *n*
flying buttress	Strebebogen *m*, Strebewerk *n*
fly-leaf paper	Vorsatzpapier *n*
foamed plastic	Kunststoffschaum *m*
foam rubber	Schaumgummi *m*
foil	1. Folie *f* 2. Kreisabschnitt *m*, Paß *m*
fold *v.*	falten
fold *n.*	Falte *f*
folding altarpiece	Klappaltärchen *n*
folding chair	Faltstuhl *m*, Klappstuhl *m*, Scherenstuhl *m*
folding door	Falttür *f*
folding palette	Klappalette *f*

folding room screen	spanische Wand *f*, Paravent *m, n*
folds	Faltwerk *n*
foliage	Blattwerk *n*, Feuillage *f*, Laub *n*, Laubwerk *n*
foliage ornamentation	Blattornament *n*, Laubverzierung *f*
folio	1. Album *n* 2. Folio *n*
folk art	Volkskunst *f*, Bauernkunst *f*, Heimatkunst *f*
follower	Anhänger *m*
fons vitae	Lebensbrunnen *m*
font	Taufbecken *n*, Fünte *f*
foot	Fuß *m*
footstool	Fußbank *f*, Schemel *m*
foreground	Vordergrund *m*
forehead	Stirn *f*
forerunner	Vorgänger *m*
foreshortening	Verkürzung *f*
forest glass	Waldglas *n*
forest landscape	Waldlandschaft *f*
forge	1. fälschen, verfälschen 2. schmieden
forger	Fälscher *m*, Kunstfälscher *m*
forgery	Fälschung *f*, Verfälschung *f*
form *v.*	bilden, gestalten, modellieren, formen
form *n.*	Form *f*, Gestalt *f*
history of —	Formgeschichte *f*
formal	formal, förmlich, Form-
formal element	Formelement *n*
Formalin	Formalin *n*
Formalin solution	Formalinlösung *f*
formalism	Formalismus *m*
formation	1. Formgebung *f*, Formung *f*, Gestaltung *f* 2. Gebilde *n*, Formation *f*, Form *f*
formative	formbildend

formeret	Gewölbebogen *m*, Schildbogen *m*
forming	formgebend
formless	formlos
formwork	Schalung *f*
fort	Burg *f*, Feste *f*, Festung *f*
fortification	Festung *f*, Fortifikation *f*, Festungsarchitektur *f*, Schanzwerk *n*, Bastion *f*, Befestigung *f*, Befestigungsanlage *f*
fortified church	Wehrkirche *f*, Kirchenburg *f*
forum	Forum *n*
Forum of Caesar	Julisches Forum *n*
Forum Pacis	Friedensforum *n*
fosse	Ringgraben *m*, Schloßgraben *m*
found *v.*	1. gründen, stiften 2. gießen
found *adj.*	gefunden, Fund-
foundation	1. Unterbau *m*, Grundmauer *f*, Substruktion *f* 2. Stift *n*, Stiftung *f* 3. Fond *m*
foundation wall	Grundmauer *f*
founder	1. Gießer *m* 2. Stifter *m*, Patron *m*, Gründer *m*
founding	1. Gründung *f* 2. Gußverfahren *n*
found object	Fundgegenstand *m*, objet trouvé *n*
foundry	Gießhütte *f*, Eisenhütte *f*, Gießerei *f*
bronze —	Bronzegießerei *f*
foundry sand	Formsand *m*
fountain	Brunnen *m*, Quelle *f*
fountain of life	Lebensbrunnen *m*
fountain sculpture	Brunnenplastik *f*
four-color print	Tetrachromie *f*, Vierfarbendruck *m*
four-cornered pillar	Vierkantpfeiler *m*
four-poster bed	Himmelbett *f*

four rivers of Paradise	die vier Paradiesflüsse
four seasons, depiction of —	Jahreszeitendarstellung *f*
Fourteen Auxiliary Saints	Vierzehnheiligen *pl*, Nothelfer *pl*
Fourteen Holy Helpers	Vierzehnheiligen *pl*, Nothelfer *pl*
foyer	Foyer *n*
fractur	Fraktur *f*
fragile	zerbrechlich
fragility	Zerbrechlichkeit *f*
fragment	Fragment *n*, Bruchstück *n*, Scherbe *f*
fabric —	Stoffragment *n*
vase —	Vasenfragment *n*, Scherbe *f*
fraktur	Fraktur *f*
frame *v.*	einfassen, einrahmen, rahmen
frame *n.*	Einfassung *f*, Fassung *f*, Rahmen *m*, Rahmung *f*, Umrahmung *f*, Zarge *f*
framework	Gerüst *n*, Rahmenwerk *n*, Gefüge *n*, Rohbau *m*, Sparrenwerk *n*
framing	Einfassung *f*, Rahmung *f*, Umrahmung *f*
frankincense	Weihrauch *m*
freehand drawing	Handzeichnung *f*
free-lance	selbständig
free leg	Spielbein *n*
free-standing sculpture	Freiplastik *f*, Freistatue *f*
French curve	Kurvenlineal *n*
French polish	Schellackpolitur *f*
fresco	Fresko *n*, Wandgemälde *n*
fresco painter	Freskant *m*
fresco painting	Freskenmalerei *f*, Freskomalerei *f*, Wandmalerei *f*
fresco remains	Freskenreste *pl*
fresco secco	fresco secco *n*
fret	Mäander *m*
friable	bröcklig

friend	Freund *m*, Anhänger *m*
frieze	Fries *m*
arched —	Bogenfries *m*, Zwergarkade *f*
frieze sarcophagus	Friessarkophag *m*
frieze strip	Friesband *n*
frit *v.*	fritten
frit *n.*	Fritte *f*
frock	Rock *m*, Mönchskutte *f*, Kittel *m*, Kleid *n*
frond	Wedel *m*
front	Stirnseite *f*, Vorderseite *f*, Schauseite *f*, Ansichtsfläche *f*, Fassade *f*, Front *f*, Avers *m*
frontal *adj.*	frontal
frontal *n.*	Frontale *n*
frontal perspective	Frontalperspektive *f*
frontality	Frontalität *f*
front end	Vorderteil *n, m*
front gable	Vordergiebel *m*
frontispiece	Frontispiz *n*, Titelblatt *n*
front pediment	Vordergiebel *m*
front section	Vorderteil *n, m*
front view	Frontalblick *m*, Frontdarstellung *f*, Vorderansicht *f*
front wall	Vordermauer *f*, Stirnmauer *f*
frosted glass	Eisglas *n*
frottage	Frottage *f*
fruit	Frucht *f*, Obst *n*
fruitfulness	Fruchtbarkeit *f*
fruit piece	Fruchtstück *n*, Früchtestilleben *n*
fuchsine	Fuchsin *n*
fugitive color	unbeständige Farbe *f*, unechte Farbe *f*
full-figure	Ganzfigur *f*
full-page	ganzseitig
fumage	Fumage *f*
functional	funktionell, zweckmäßig

functionalism	Funktionalismus *m*
funeral	Begräbnis *n*, Bestattung *f*
funeral bier	Totenbahre *f*
funeral mask	Totenmaske *f*
funerary objects	Grabbeigabe *f*
funerary statue	Grabplastik *f*
funerary stele	Grabstele *f*
funerary temple	Begräbnistempel *m*
funerary urn	Graburne *f*
funerary weapon	Funeralwaffe *f*
funk art	Funk Art *f*
funnel beaker	Trichterbecher *m*
funnel-shaped	trichterförmig, Trichter-
fur	Pelz *m*
furnace	Ofen *m*
furnish	ausstatten, möbelieren, einrichten
furnishings	Ausstattung *f*, Einrichtung *f*, Inneneinrichtung *f*, Raumausstattung *f*
furniture	Möbel *pl*, Möblierung *f*, Mobiliar *n*, Möbelstück *n*
furniture style	Möbelstil *m*
furrow	Furche *f*, Rille *f*
fuse	sintern
fustet	junges Fustikholz *n*
fustic, old —	Fustikholz *n*, Gelbholz *n*
fustic, young —	junges Fustikholz *n*
futhark	Futhark *n*
Futurism	Futurismus *m*
gable	Giebel *m*
broken —	gesprengter Giebel *m*
corbie —	Stufengiebel *m*, Treppengiebel *m*, Staffelgiebel *m*
stepped —	Stufengiebel *m*, Treppengiebel *m*, Staffelgiebel *m*

gable moulding	Giebelgesims *n*
galipot	Fichtenharz *n*, Galipot *m*
gallery	Galerie *f*, Altan *m*, Altane *f*, Empore *f*, Laufgang *m*, Priesche *f*
dwarf —	Zwerggalerie *f*
nuns' —	Nonnenchor *m*
gallery grave	Galeriegrab *n*
Gallery of Kings	Königsgalerie *f*
gallery owner	Galerist *m*
gallery tone	Galerieton *m*
gallstone lake	Gallenfarbstoff *m*
galvanoplastic process	Galvanoplastik *f*
gamboge	Gummigutt *n*
gammadion	Hakenkreuz *n*
ganosis	Ganosis *f*
gap	Öffnung *f*, Lücke *f*, Zwischenraum *m*
garden	Garten *m*, Gartenanlage *f*
garden design	Gartenbaukunst *f*
Garden Enclosed	der verschlossene Garten, Verschlossener Garten *m*
gargoyle	Wasserspeier *m*
garland	Girlande *f*, Kranz *m*, Laubgewinde *n*
garment	Kleid *n*, Kleidungsstück *n*, Gewand *n*, Gewandung *f*, Kleidung *f*
garnet	Granat *m*
garret	Dachkammer *f*
gate	1. Tor *n*, Torhaus *n* 2. Gußkanal *m*, Gußröhre *f*
gate hall	Torhalle *f*
gate house	Torhaus *n*
gate tower	Torturm *m*
gather	Glasmasse *f*
gaude yellow	Wau *m*
gauffer	Prägestempel *m*

gaze	Blick *m*
gazebo	Belvedere *n*
gel	Gel *n*
gelatine	Gelatine *f*, Gallert *n*, Gallerte *f*
gem	1. Edelstein *m* 2. Kleinod *n*, Prachtstück *n*, Glanzstück *n*
gem carving	Glyptik *f*
gem cutter	1. Steinschneider *m* 2. Schleifer *m*
gem cutting	Steinschneidekunst *f*
Gemini	Zwilling *m*
genealogical table	Stammbaum *m*
genius *adj.*	genial
genius *n.*	1. Genie *n* 2. Genius *m*
genre	Genre *n*, Gattung *f*
genre painter	Genremaler *m*
genre painting	Genrebild *n*, Genremalerei *f*, Sittenbild *n*
genuine	echt, authentisch
geochronology	Geochronologie *f*
geometric	geometrisch
geometric ornamentation	Linearornamentik *f*
geometric style	geometrischer Stil *m*
geometry	Geometrie *f*
Germanic art	germanische Kunst *f*
Gero crucifix	Gerokreuz *n*
gesso ground	Kreidegrund *m*, Gipsgrund *m*
gesture	Gebärde *f*, Geste *f*, Gestik *f*
gesture motif	Gestenmotiv *n*
gestures	Gestik *f*
vocabulary of –	Gebärdensprache *f*
gesturing	Gestik *f*
giant	Gigant *m*, Riese *m*
giant order	Kolossalordnung *f*
gigantic	riesenhaft, riesig

gigantomachy	Gigantenkampf *m*, Gigantomachie *f*
gild	vergolden
gilded	vergoldet
gilder's cushion	Vergolderkissen *n*
gilder's tip	Anschießer *m*
gilding	Vergoldung *f*
matte —	Mattvergoldung *f*
gilding with glair	Eiweißvergoldung *f*
gilding with gold leaf	Polimentvergoldung *f*
gild painting	Goldmalerei *f*
gilt	vergoldet
gilt moulding	Goldleiste *f*
gilt painting	Goldmalerei *f*
gingerbread style	spätviktorianischer, mit Verzierungen überladener Baustil
giornata	Tagewerk *n*
girder	Träger *m*, Bund *m*
floor —	Bodenträger *m*
main —	Längsträger *m*
peripheral roof —	Dachrandträger *m*
support —	Stützenträger *m*
girl	Mädchen *n*
girl-like	mädchenhaft
Giza	Giseh
glacis	Glacis *n*
glair	Eiweißvergoldung *f*
glance	Blick *m*
glaring	grell
glass *adj.*	gläsern, Glas-
glass *n.*	1. Glas *n* 2. Verglasung *f*
flashed —	Überfangglas *n*
frosted —	Eisglas *n*
gold —	Zwischengoldglas *n*, Pauschmalglas *n*
millefiori —	Millefioriglas *n*

molten —	Glasmasse *f*
mosaic —	Millefioriglas *n*
reeded —	Filigranglas *n*, Fadenglas *n*
stained —	Buntglas *n*, Glasmalerei *f*
threaded —	Filigranglas *n*, Fadenglas *n*
wire-reinforced —	Drahtglas *n*
glass annealing oven	Kühlofen *m*
glass bead	**Glasperle** *f*
glass blower	Glasbläser *m*
glass blowing	Glasblasen *n*
glass-blowing pipe	Glasmacherpfeife *f*, Glaspfeife *f*
glass brick	Glasbaustein *m*
glass engraving	Glasgravierung *f*, Glasgravur *f*
glass etching	Glasätzung *f*
glass factory	Glashütte *f*
glass flashing process	Überfangverfahren *n*
glass maker's oven	Glasmacherofen *m*
glass painting	Hinterglasmalerei *f*, Spiegelmalerei *f*
glass pane	Glasplatte *f*, Glasscheibe *f*
glass rods	Glasstäbe *pl*
glass smalto	Glassmalte *f*
glass window	**Glasfenster** *n*
glaze *v.*	1. verglasen 2. lasieren, glasieren
glaze *n.*	Glasur *f*, Lasur *f*
lead —	Bleiglasur *f*
glazed	glasiert, Glasur-
glazed brick	Glasurziegel *m*
glazed brick relief	Glasurziegelrelief *n*
glaze ground	Lasurgrund *m*
glazing	Verglasung *f*
gleam *v.*	leuchten, glänzen, schimmern, scheinen
gleam *n.*	Schein *m*, Glanz *m*
glisten	leuchten, strahlen

glitter	flimmern, glitzern, schimmern
globe	Weltrund *n*, Kugel *f*, Globus *m*
globular amphora	Schnuramphore *f*
gloriole	s. glory
glory	Glorienschein *m*, Heiligenschein *m*, Hof *m*, Strahlenkrone *f*, Strahlenkranz *m*, Nimbus *m*, Aureole *f*
gloss	Glanz *m*, Firnis *m*
glow	erglänzen, glühen, strahlen, glänzen
glue *v.*	kleben, leimen
glue *n.*	Klebstoff *m*, Leim *m*, Stärke *f*
glue-cutout	Leimschablone *f*
glue solution	Leimwasser *n*
glycerin	Glyzerin *n*
glyph	Glyphe *f*
glyptics	Glyptik *f*, Steinschneidekunst *f*, Gemmoglyptik *f*
glyptograph	1. Gemme *f* 2. Glyphe *f*
glyptology	Gemmenkunde *f*
Gobelin	Gobelin *m*, Bildteppich *m*
goblet	Kelch *m*, Pokal *m*
god	Gott *m*
goddess	Göttin *f*
goddess of victory	Siegesgöttin *f*
godly	göttlich
godly splendor	Gottesherrlichkeit *f*
God the Father	Gottvater *m*
goffer	Prägestempel *m*
gold *adj.*	golden, Gold-
gold *n.*	Gold *n*
golden	golden, Gold-
Golden Calf, the —	das goldene Kalb
Golden Fleece, the —	das goldene Vließ
golden red	tizianrot
golden section	der goldene Schnitt

gold glass	Pauschmalglas *n*, Zwischengoldglas *n*
gold ground	Goldgrund *m*
gold ink drawing	Goldzeichnung *f*
gold leaf	Blattgold *n*
gold plate	Goldblech *n*
gold sheet	Goldblech *n*
goldsmith	Goldschmied *m*
goldsmith's art	Goldschmiedekunst *f*
gold varnish	Goldlack *m*
gold weight	Goldgewicht *n*
Good Samaritan, the —	der gute Samariter
Good Shepherd, the —	der gute Hirt
Gorgo(n)	Gorgo *f*
gospel book	Evangeliar *n*, Evangeliarium *n*, Evangelium *n*
Gothic *adj.*	gotisch
Gothic *n.*	Gotik *f*
Gothic Revival	Neugotik *f*
gouache	Gouache *f*, Guasch *f*
gouache ground	Guaschgrund *m*
gouache painting	Gouachenmalerei *f*, Guaschmalerei *f*
gouge	Beitel *m*
V-shaped —	Geißfuß *m*
woodcutting —	Hohleisen *n*
gown	Rock *m*, Damenkleid *n*
grace	Grazie *f*
gradation	Gradierung *f*, Abstufung *f*
Gradual	Graduale *f*
grain	1. Maserung *f*, Faser *f* 2. Kermes *m*
across the —	quer zur Faserrichtung
with the —	in Faserrichtung
wood —	Holzmaserung *f*
grain impression	Getreidekornabdruck *m*
grainy	körnig
grand duke	Großherzog *m*

grandeur	Größe *f*
granulation	Granulation *f*
grapevine	Weinranke *f*
graphic	graphisch, zeichnerisch
graphic artist	Graphiker *m*, Zeichner *m*
graphic arts	Graphik *f*
graphics	Graphik *f*
advertising —	Gebrauchsgraphik *f*, Reklamekunst *f*, Werbekunst *f*
graphite	Graphit *m*
graticulation	Quadrierung *f*
graticulation grid	Quadratnetz *n*
grating	Gitter *n*
grattage	Grattage *f*
grave	Grab *n*, Grabstätte *f*, Gruft *f*
gallery —	Galeriegrab *n*
passage —	Ganggrab *n*
shaft —	Schachtgrab *n*
stipes —	Stipesgrab *n*
grave circle	Gräberrund *n*
grave goods	Grabbeigabe *f*, Beigabe *f*
gravel	Kies *m*, Kieselstein *m*
grave monument	Grabmonument *n*
grave objects	Grabbeigabe *f*, Beigabe *f*
graver	Grabstichel *m*, Gravierinstrument *n*, Stichel *m*
gravestone	Grabstein *m*, Grabplatte *f*
gravestone rubbing	Grabplattenabdruck *m*
Gravette point	Gravettespitze *f*
Gravettian	Gravettian *n*
gravure printing	Tiefdruck *m*
gray	grau
graywacke	Grauwacke *f*
great	groß, Groß-
greatness	Größe *f*
Greece	Griechenland
Greek *adj.*	griechisch

ground

Greek *n.*	Grieche *m*
Greek cross	griechisches Kreuz *n*
Greek culture	Griechentum *n*, Hellenentum *n*
Greek key	Mäander *m*
green	grün
green earth	Grünerde *f*
greenery	Laub *n*
greenstone	Grünstein *m*
gremial	Gremiale *n*
grid	Raster *m*
grid pattern	Rasterschema *n*
grid system	Schachbrettsystem *n*
griffe	Eckknolle *f*, Ecksporn *m*, Eckblatt *n*
griffin	Greif *m*, Greifen *m*
grille	Gitter *n*
grillework	Vergitterung *f*
grind	schleifen
grinder	Schleifer *m*
grinding	Schliff *m*
grisaille	Grisaille *f*
grisaille window	Grisaillescheibe *f*
groin	Grat *m*, Gewölbegrat *m*
groin vault	Kreuzgewölbe *n*, Kreuzgratgewölbe *n*
groove *v.*	auskehlen, aushöhlen
groove *n.*	Auskehlung *f*, Aushöhlung *f*, Furche *f*, Kannele *f*, Nute *f*, Riefe *f*, Rille *f*
grotesque *adj.*	grotesk
grotesque *n.*	Groteske *f*
grotto	Grotte *f*
ground *v.*	grundieren
ground *n.*	1. Boden *m*, Erde *f*, Grund *m*, Grundfläche *f* 2. Grundierung *f*
bole —	Bolusgrund *m*

ground floor	Erdgeschoß *n*, Parterre *n*
ground floor apartment	Parterrewohnung *f*
ground level	Bodenniveau *n*, Parterre *n*
grounds	Anlage *f*, Park *m*, Gartenanlage *f*
group	Gruppe *f*
group exhibition	Gemeinschaftsausstellung *f*
grouping	Gruppierung *f*, Anordnung *f*
group portrait	Gruppenbild *n*
grout	Kitt *m*
guardian angel	Schutzengel *m*
Guelph treasure	Welfenschatz *m*
guild	Innung *f*, Zunft *f*
guilloche	Guilloche *f*
gum	Gummi *n*
gum arabic	Gummiarabikum *n*
gum arabic solution	Gummiarabikumlösung *f*
gum resin	Gummiharz *n*
gum tragacanth	Tragantschleim *m*
guttae	Tropfen *m*
gutter	Rinne *f*, Dachrinne *f*, Traufleiste *f*, Traufrinne *f*
gypsum	Gips *m*
gypsum ground	Gipsgrund *m*
hafner ware	Hafnerkeramik *f*
hagiography	Hagiographie *f*
hair	Haar *n*
haircut	Frisur *f*
hairdo	Frisur *f*
hairline crack	Haarriß *m*
hair paint brush	Haarpinsel *m*
half	halb, Halb-
half-column	Halbsäule *f*
half cylinder	Halbzylinder *m*
half-figure	Protome *f*, Halbfigur *f*
half-length figure	Halbfigur *f*

half-length portrait	Brustbild *n*
half-timber	Fachwerk *n*
half-timber construction	Fachwerkbau *m*
half-timber house	Fachwerkhaus *n*
half-tone	Mittelton *m*
half-uncial	Halbunziale *f*
hall	1. Halle *f*, Saal *m* 2. Diele *f*, Flur *m*, Korridor *m*, Gang *m*
hypostyle —	Hypostylos *m*, Säulenhalle *f*; Halle mit säulengetragenem Dach
hall church	Hallenkirche *f*
hallmark	Feingehaltsstempel *m*
hall of mirrors	Spiegelgalerie *f*, Spiegelsaal *m*
Hallstatt period	Hallstattzeit *f*
halo	Glorienschein *m*, Aureole *f*, Heiligenschein *m*, Hof *m*, Nimbus *m*, Strahlenkranz *m*, Strahlenkrone *f*
hammer *v.*	hämmern
hammer *n.*	Hammer *m*
hammer beam	Stichbalken *m*
hand	Hand *f*
handaxe	Faustkeil *m*
handbill	Flugblatt *n*
hand colored	handkoloriert
hand coloring	Handkolorierung *f*
handicrafts	Kunstgewerbe *n*
handle	Henkel *m*
handprint	Handbild *n*
hand screen	Handdruck *m*, manueller Druck *m*
hand weapon	Handwaffe *f*, Trutzwaffe *f*
handwriting	Handschrift *f*
hang	hängen
hanging	Behang *m*, Wandbehang *m*
Hansa yellow	Hansagelb *n*
happening	Happening *n*

haptic

haptic	haptisch
harbor scene	Hafenbild *n*
hard	hart, Hart-
hardboard	Hartfaserplatte *f*
hard-edge painting	Hard-Edge Malerei *f*
harden	1. härten
	2. abbinden
hardness	Härte *f*
degree of —	Härtegrad *m*
hard paste	Hartporzellan *n*
hard paste porcelain	Hartporzellan *n*
hard resin	Hartharz *n*
hardwood	Hartholz *n*
harmonious colors, theory of —	Harmonielehre *f*
harpoon point	Harpunspitze *f*
harpy	Harpyie *f*
Harrowing of Hell, the —	die Höllenfahrt Christi
harsh	grell
Harvester Vase	Schnittervase *f*
harvest scene	Ernteszene *f*
hatch	schraffieren
hatching	Schraffur *f*, Schraffierung *f*
hatching lines	Schraffen *pl*
hatchment	Totenschild *m*
Hathoric capital	Hathorkapitell *n*
haunch	Bogenschenkel *m*; Bogenteil zwischen Kämpfer und Scheitel
haziness	Verschwommenheit *f*
hazy	verschwommen
head	Kopf *m*, Haupt *n*
position of the —	Kopfhaltung *f*
shape of the —	Kopfform *f*
headband	Reif *m*, Stirnreif *m*
head covering	Kopfbedeckung *f*
head decoration	Kopfschmuck *m*

headdress	Haartracht *f*, Kopfbedeckung *f*, Kopfputz *m*, Kopfschmuck *m*
header	Binder *m*
head rest	Kopfstütze *f*
head support	Kopfstütze *f*
heart	Herz *n*
heart and dart	Herzblattwelle *f*
heart-shaped	herzförmig, Herz-
heartwood	Kernholz *n*
heathen	heidnisch
heaven	Himmel *m*
heavenly	himmlisch
heavenly throne	Himmelsthron *m*
heavy	schwer, wuchtig
hecatompedon	Hekatompedon *n*, Hekatompedos *m*
Hedwig glasses	Hedwigsgläser *pl*
heel	Ferse *f*
height	Höhe *f*
heightened	gehöht, weiß gehöht
heightening	Höhung *f*, Weißhöhung *f*
heighten with white	mit Deckweiß höhen
heir	Erbe *m*
heliography	Heliographie *f*
helix	1. Spirale *f*, Schnecke *f* 2. Volute eines ionischen bzw. korinthischen Kapitells
hell	Hölle *f*
Helladic	helladisch
Hellenic	hellenisch
Hellenism	Hellenismus *m*
Hellenistic	hellenistisch
helmet	Helm *m*
helmet decoration	Helmschmuck *m*, Zimier *n*
helm roof	Helmdach *n*, Rautendach *n*
hem	Saum *m*
hematite	Hämatit *m*, Blutstein *m*, Roteisenstein *m*

hemisphere	Hemisphäre f, Halbkugel f
hemp	Hanf m
hempseed oil	Hanföl n
henna	Henna f, Alkanna f
henostyle	einsäulig
Herkales	Herakles
heraldic animal	Wappentier n
heraldry	Heraldik f, Wappenkunde f, Wappenkunst f, Emblematik f
Hercules	Herakles
heritage	Erbe n
herm	Herme f, Hermenpfeiler m
herma	Herme f
herm column	Hermensäule f
hermit	Einsiedler m, Eremit m
hermitage	Einsiedelei f, Eremitage f
Hermitage, the —	Eremitage f, Ermitage f
hero	Held m, Heros m
heroic	heroisch
heroic landscape	heroische Landschaft f
herringbone pattern	Fischgrätenmuster n
hew	behauen, hauen
hexagon	Hexagon n, Sechseck n
hexagonal	hexagonal, sechseckig
heyday	Blütezeit f
hidden	versteckt, verhüllt
hiding power	Deckkraft f
hieratic	hieratisch
hieroglyphic	hieroglyphisch
hieroglyphics	Hieroglyphen pl
high	hoch, Hoch-
high altar	Hochaltar m, Fronaltar m
High Gothic	Hochgotik f
highlight *painting*	Licht n
high relief	Hochrelief n, Hautrelief n
High Renaissance	Hochrenaissance f

high-rise apartment building	Wohnturm *m*
high-rise building	Hochhaus *n*
high warp loom	Hochschaftsstuhl *m*, Hautelisse *f*
high warp weaving	Hautelisseweberei *f*
hinge	Scharnier *n*, Angel *f*
hinged	aufklappbar, Klapp-
hip	1. Hüfte *f* 2. Walm *m*
hipped roof	Walmdach *n*, gewalmtes Dach *n*
hippocampus ornament	Hippokampen-Ornament *n*
Hispano-Moresque ware	Hispanomoreske *f*
history	Geschichte *f*, Überlieferung *f*
history of art	Kunstgeschichte *f*
history of ornamentation	Ornamentgeschichte *f*
history painting	Geschichtsmalerei *f*, Historienmalerei *f*
Hittite *adj.*	hethitisch, hettitisch
Hittite *n.*	Hethiter *m*, Hettiter *m*
hoard	Hort *m*, Hortfund *m*, Depotfund *m*, Verwahrfund *m*
Hodegetria Madonna	Hodegetria *f*
hold	halten
holder	Fassung *f*, Halter *m*, Griff *m*
hole	Loch *n*, Öffnung *f*
hollow *adj.*	hohl, Hohl-
hollow *n.*	Aushöhlung *f*, Höhlung *f*, Vertiefung *f*
hollow brick	Hohlziegel *m*
hollow cast	Hohlguß *m*
hollow coin	Hohlmünze *f*
hollow mold	Matrize *f*
hollow moulding	Hohlleiste *f*
hollow out	aushöhlen
hollow relief	versenktes Relief *n*
hollow sculpture	Hohlplastik *f*
hollow space	Hohlraum *m*

hollow wall	Hohlmauer *f*
holography	Holographie *f*
holy	heilig
Holy Bible	Bibel *f*, Heilige Schrift *f*
Holy Family	die Heilige Familie, die Heilige Sippe
Holy Ghost	der Heilige Geist
Holy Grail	Gral *m*
Holy Sepulchre	das Heilige Grab
Holy Trinity	Dreieinigkeit *f*, Dreifaltigkeit *f*
depiction of the —	Gnadenstuhl *m*
honey-colored	honiggelb
hood	Haube *f*
hook	Haken *m*
hook-shaped	hakenförmig, Haken-
horizon	1. Horizont *m* 2. Schicht *f*
horizon line	Horizontlinie *f*
horizontal	horizontal, waagerecht
horizontal line	Horizontale *f*, Waagerechte *f*
horn	Horn *n*
hornblende	Hornblende *f*
horn of plenty	Füllhorn *n*
Hornton stone	Horntonstein *m*
horse	Pferd *n*, Roß *n*
horseman	Reiter *m*
horseshoe arch	Hufeisenbogen *m*
horseshoe-shaped	hufeisenförmig
Host	Hostie *f*
hour glass	Stundenglas *n*
house	Haus *n*
household ceramics	Gebrauchskeramik *f*
house of God	Gotteshaus *n*
house-shaped urn	Hausurne *f*
housing complex	Siedlung *f*
housing development	Siedlung *f*

hue	Buntheit *f*, Farbton *m*, Kolorit *n*
Hugenot style	Hugenottenstil *m*
human	menschlich, Menschen-
human being	Mensch *m*
humane	menschlich, human
human figure	Menschengestalt *f*
humanism	Humanismus *m*
human sacrifice	Menschenopfer *n*
humeral veil	Humerale *f*, Amikt *m*
hunebed	Hünenbett *n*, Langbett *n*
hunting bow	Pfeilbogen *m*
hunting motif	Jagdmotiv *n*
hunting scene	Jagddarstellung *f*, Jagdstück *n*
husband	Mann *m*, Ehemann *m*
hydria	Hydria *f*
Hyksos	Hirtenkönige *pl*
hypaethral basilica	Hypäthralbasilika *f*
hypaethral temple	Hypäthraltempel *m*
hyperbolic	hyperbolisch
hypocaust	Hypokaustum *n*
hypogeum	Hypogäum *n*
hypostyle	säulengetragen
hypostyle hall	Säulenhalle *f*, Hypostylos *m*
hypotrachelium	Hypotrachelion *n*
I-beam	Doppel-T-Träger *m*
Ice Age	Eiszeit *f*
icon	Ikone *f*
iconoclasm	Bildersturm *m*, Ikonoklasmus *m*
iconoclast	Bilderfeind *m*, Bilderstürmer *m*
iconoclastic	bilderstürmerisch, ikonoklastisch
iconoclastic controversy	Bilderstreit *m*, Bildersturm *m*
iconography	Ikonographie *f*
iconolatry	Bilderverehrung *f*, Ikonolatrie *f*

iconology	Ikonologie *f*
iconostasis	Ikonostase *f*, Ikonostasis *f*, Bilderwand *f*
ideal *adj.*	ideal, vorbildlich, Ideal-
ideal *n.*	Ideal *n*, Leitbild *n*, Musterbild *n*, Vorbild *n*, Vollkommenheitsideal *n*
ideal figure	Idealgestalt *f*
idealize	idealisieren
ideal landscape	ideale Landschaft *f*
ideal of beauty	Schönheitsideal *n*
ideal viewing side	Idealansicht *f*
identification	1. Identifizierung *f* 2. Wesensbestimmung *f*
ideogram	Ideogramm *n*, Begriffszeichen *n*
ideography	Ideographie *f*, Begriffsschrift *f*
idol	Götze *f*, Götzenbild *n*, Idol *n*, Abgott *m*, Götterbild *n*
idolatry	Ikonodulie *f*
illuminate	illuminieren
illuminated evangeliar	Bilderevangelium *n*
illuminated manuscript	illuminierte Handschrift *f*
illumination	Buchmalerei *f*, Illuminieren *n*, Miniaturmalerei *f*
illuminator	Illuminator *m*, Buchmaler *m*, Miniaturmaler *m*
illusion	Illusion *f*, Schein *m*, Scheinbild *n*, Täuschung *f*
illusionism	Illusionismus *m*
illusionistic	illusionistisch
illusion of space	Raumillusion *f*
illustrate	bebildern, illustrieren
illustration	Abbildung *f*, Abb., Illustration *f*, Verbildlichung *f*
illustrator	Illustrator *m*
image	1. Abbild *n*, Bild *n*, Ebenbild *n*, Denkbild *n* 2. Götzenbild *n*, Abgott *m*

imagination	Phantasie *f*, Einbildung *f*, Vorstellung *f*
imaginative power	Einbildungskraft *f*, Vorstellungskraft *f*
imagine	sich vorstellen, sich einbilden, sich denken
imago	Imago *f*
imitate	nachahmen, nachbilden, kopieren, imitieren
imitation	Anlehnung *f*, Nachahmung *f*, Nachbildung *f*
imitation of nature	Naturnachahmung *f*
imitation stone	Gußstein *m*, Kunststein *m*
imitator	Nachahmer *m*
Immaculate Conception	die unbefleckte Empfängnis, Immaculata *f*, Maria auf der Mondsichel
Immaculate Mary	Immaculata *f*
immense	immens, unermeßlich, kolossal
immortal	unsterblich
impasto	Impasto *n*
imperial	kaiserlich, Kaiser-, Reichs-
imperial age	Kaiserzeit *f*
imperial cathedral	Kaiserdom *m*
imperial crown	Kaiserkrone *f*
Imperial forums, the —	Kaiserfora *pl*
imperial hall	Kaisersaal *m*
imperial insignia	Reichskleinod *n*, Reichsinsignien *pl*
imperial orb	Reichsapfel *m*
imperial palace	Kaiserpalast *m*, Kaiserpfalz *f*
imperial residence	Kaisersitz *m*, Pfalz *f*
Imperial Rome	Kaiserzeit *f*, die römische Kaiserzeit
imperial scepter	Reichszepter *n*
imperial throne	Kaisersitz *m*
implement	Gerät *n*, Werkzeug *n*, Gebrauchsgegenstand *m*
impluvium	Impluvium *n*

impost	Kämpfer *m*
impost block	Kämpfer *m*
impost height	Kämpferhöhe *f*
impress	1. beeindrucken
	2. stempeln, prägen
impression	1. Eindruck *m*
	2. Abklatsch *m*
overall —	Gesamteindruck *m*
Impressionism	Impressionismus *m*
Impressionist	Impressionist *m*
impressionistic	impressionistisch
impressive	eindrucksvoll
imprimatura	Imprimitur *f*
improve	verbessern, vervollkommnen, verfeinern, verschönern
improvement	Verbesserung *f*, Verschönerung *f*, Verfeinerung *f*, Vervollkommnung *f*
impulse	Anregung *f*, Impuls *m*, Anstoß *m*
in antis	zwischen den Anten
inc.	inc.
incense	Weihrauch *m*
incense boat	Schiffchen *n*, Weihrauchschiffchen *n*
incense container	Räuchergefäß *n*, Rauchfaß *n*, Weihrauchbehälter *m*
incise	einritzen, ritzen, einscheiden
incised decoration	Ritzdekor *m*
incised drawing	Ritzzeichnung *f*
incised hatching	Riefelung *f*, Scharrierung *f*
incised picture	Ritzbild *n*
incision	Kerbe *f*, Einschnitt *m*
incline	Schräge *f*
in color	farbig
Incredulity of Thomas, the —	das Thomaswunder
incunabula	Inkunabel *f*, Frühdruck *m*, Wiegendruck *m*

indent *v.*	kerben, einkerben
indent *n.*	Kerbe *f*
indentation	Kerbung *f*, Einkerbung *f*
independent	eigenständig, selbständig
index finger	Zeigefinger *m*
Indian *adj.*	indisch
Indian *n.*	Inder *m*
American — *adj.*	indianisch
American — *n.*	Indianer *m*
Indian yellow	Indischgelb *n*
indigo	Indigo *m, n*
indistinct	undeutlich, unklar, verschwommen, verworren
individual	Individuum *n*
indoor painting	Ateliermalerei *f*
industry	Industrie *f*, Geräteinventar *n*
inestimable	unschätzbar
inferno	Hölle *f*
influence *v.*	beeinflussen
influence *n.*	Einfluß *m*
infrared	infrarot
infrared photograph	Infrarotaufnahme *f*
infrared photography	Infrarotphotographie *f*
inheritance	Erbe *n*
inhumation	Bestattung *f*, Beerdigung *f*
contracted —	Hockerbestattung *f*
partial —	Teilbestattung *f*
initial	Anfangsbuchstabe *m*, Initiale *f*, Versal *m*, Signum *n*
decorative —	Zierbuchstabe *m*
ink	Tinte *f*, Tusche *f*
black printing —	Druckerschwärze *f*
lithographic —	Lithotusche *f*, Steindruckfarbe *f*
ink drawing	Tuschzeichnung *f*
ink drawing brush	Tuschpinsel *m*
inkwell	Tintenfaß *n*
inlaid	eingelegt

inlaid enamel	Emaileinlage *f*
inlay *v.*	einlegen
inlay *n.*	Einlegearbeit *f*, Einlage *f*, Intarsia *f*, Intarsie *f*
stone —	Inkrustation *f*
inlay work	Einlegearbeit *f*
inner chamber	Innenraum *m*
inner court	Innenhof *m*, Binnenhof *m*, Aula *f*
inner garden	Binnengarten *m*
inner view	Innenansicht *f*
inner wall	Innenwand *f*
Innocents, the Massacre of the —	der bethlehemische Kindermord, der Kindermord zu Bethlehem
in relief	erhaben, reliefiert
inscribe	beschriften
inscribed line	Inschriftzeile *f*
inscription	Inschrift *f*, Aufschrift *f*, Beschriftung *f*, Legende *f*
insight	Einsicht *f*
insignia	1. Kleinod *n*, Insignien *pl* 2. Wappen *n*
in situ	in situ
insoluble	wasserunlöslich
inspiration	Inspiration *f*
Instruments of the Passion	die Leidenswerkzeuge Christi, die Marterwerkzeuge Christi, die Passionswerkzeuge
insulate	isolieren
insulating glass	Isolierglas *n*
insulating layer	Isolierschicht *f*
insulation	Isolierung *f*
intaglio	Intaglio *n;* vertieft geschnittene Gemme
intaglio printing	Tiefdruck *m*
intarsia	Intarsia *f*, Intarsie *f*, Holzmosaik *n*
intellect	Geist *m*
intense	intensiv, stark, satt

intensity, color −	Farbintensität *f*
intercessor	Nothelfer *m*
intercolumniation	Intercolumnium *n*, Interkolumnium *n*, Interkolumnie *f*, Pfeilerweite *f*
interior	Innenraum *m*, Interieur *n*, Innenseite *f*
interior decorating	Innenarchitektur *f*, Raumkunst *f*
interior decoration	Inneneinrichtung *f*, Innenausstattung *f*, Raumausstattung *f*, Innendekoration *f*
interior decorator	Innenarchitekt *m*, Dekorateur *m*
interior wall	Innenwand *f*
interlace *v.*	verschränken, flechten
interlace *n.*	Bandgeflecht *n*, Flechtband *n*
animal −	Tierornamentik *f*
interlace pattern	Flechtmuster *n*
interlacing	Bandelwerk *n*, Bandgeflecht *n*, Flechtband *n*, Flechtwerk *n*, Verschränkung *f*
intermediate color	Zwischenfarbe *f*
intermediate support	Zwischenstütze *f*
intermediate varnish	Zwischenfirnis *m*
internal structure	Tiefenstruktur *f*, Tiefenbau *m*
international exhibition	Weltausstellung *f*, Messe *f*
interpretation	Deutung *f*, Auslegung *f*, Interpretation *f*
intersecting plane	Schnittebene *f*
intersection	Durchdringungsraum *m*, Schnittpunkt *m*
line of −	Schnittlinie *f*
plane of −	Schnittfläche *f*
point of −	Schnittpunkt *m*
intonaco	Feinbewurf *m*, Feinputz *m*
intrados	Laibung *f*, Leibung *f*
inv.	inv.
invent	erfinden
invention	Erfindung *f*

inventiveness	Erfindungsreichtum *m*
inventor	Erfinder *m*, Urheber *m*
inventory	Inventar *n*, Verzeichnis *n*
tomb —	Grabinventar *n*
inventory of tools	Geräteinventar *n*
inverted perspective	umgekehrte Perspektive *f*
investment	Gußmantel *m*, Formmantel *m*, Mantel *m*
Ionic	ionisch, jonisch
Ionic order	ionische Ordnung *f*
iridesce	irisieren, schillern
iridescence	Schiller *m*, Schillerglanz *m*
iridescent	schillernd, irisierend
iridescent color	Schillerfarbe *f*
iris	Schwertlilie *f*
iron *adj.*	eisern, Eisen-
iron *n.*	Eisen *n*
Iron Age	Eisenzeit *f*
iron armature	Eisenarmierung *f*
iron beam	Eisenträger *m*
iron building	Eisenbau *m*
iron casting	Eisenguß *m*
iron engraving	Eisenradierung *f*
iron framework structure	Eisenfachwerk *n*
iron girder	Eisenträger *m*
iron pigments	Eisenfarben *pl*
iron structure	Eisenbau *m*
irregular	unregelmäßig
iscorzo	Skurz *m*
isocephaly	Isokephalie *f*
isolate	isolieren
isolating varnish	Zwischenfirnis *m*
isometric projection	Isometrie *f*
Italian *adj.*	italienisch
Italian *n.*	Italiener *m*
itinerary	Itinerarium *n*
ivory	Elfenbein *n*

ivory black	Elfenbeinschwarz n
ivory carving	Elfenbeinschnitzerei f
ivory-colored	elfenbeinfarben, elfenbeinweiß

jacket	Jacke f
Jacquard weaving	Jacquardweberei f
jade	Jade m
jade green	jadegrün
jadeite	Jadeit m
jalousie	Jalousie f
jamb	Gewände n, Laibung f, Leibung f
jamb shaft	Gewändesäule f
jamb statue	Gewändefigur f, Laibungsstatue f
jar	Krug m, Kanne f, Topf m
stirrup —	Bügelkanne f
storage —	Vorratsgefäß n
jasper	Jaspis m
jasper ware	Jasper-Ware f
javelin	Speer m
Jean Cousin	Eisenrot n
jerkin	Wams n
Jesse, Tree of —	Jessebaum m, der Stammbaum Christi
Jesus child	Jesusknabe m, Christkind n
Jesus Found in the Temple	die Wiederfindung Jesu im Tempel
jet	Jett m
jewel	Edelstein m, Juwel n, Kleinod n
jewel box	Schmuckkasten m, Juwelenkästchen n, Schatulle f
jewelery	Schmuck m
piece of —	Schmuckstück n
Jewry	Judentum n
Job	Hiob
John the Baptist	Johannes der Täufer
join	fügen
joiner	Schreiner m

joint	1. Fuge *f*
	2. Gelenk *n*
dovetail —	Schwalbenschwanzfuge *f*
miter —	Gehrung *f*
mortar —	Mörtelfuge *f*
joint exhibition	Gemeinschaftsausstellung *f*
jointless	fugenlos, nahtlos
Jonah and the Whale	Jonas und der Wal
journeyman	Geselle *m*
Journey of the Magi	der Zug der hl. drei Könige
joust	Ritterspiel *n*, Turnier *n*
jubé	Chorgitter *n*, Lettner *m*
Judaism	Judentum *n*
jug	Humpen *m*, Krug *m*, Kanne *f*
junk (automobile) parts	Autoschrott *m*
Jurassic limestone	Jurakalk *m*
Justice, depiction of —	Gerechtigkeitsbild *n*

Kamares ware	Kamares-Vasen *pl*
kaolin	Kaolin *m, n*, Pfeifenton *m*, Porzellanerde *f*
keep	Bergfried *m*
keeper	Konservator *m*
Kerbschnitt ceramics	Kerbschnittkeramik *f*
kermes dye	Kermes *m*
kernel black	Kernschwarz *n*
kettle	Kessel *m*
key	Schlüssel *m*
canvas stretcher —	Keil *m*
key block	Strichplatte *f*
key plate	Strichplatte *f*
keystone	Schlußstein *m*
kiathos	Kyathos *m*, Zyathos *m*
kibleh	Kibla *f*, Quibla *f*
kickwheel	Tretscheibe *f*
kiln	Brennofen *m*, Ofen *m*

muffle –	Muffelofen *m*
tunnel –	Tunnelofen *m*
kind	Art *f*, Gattung *f*
kinetic art	kinetische Kunst *f*
kinetics	Kinetik *f*
king	König *m*
kingdom	Königreich *n*
king-post	Hängesäule *f*
king's blue	Kobaltblau *n*, Königsblau *n*
King Wenceslaus' Bible	Wenzelbibel *f*
kiosk	Kiosk *m*
kitchen midden	Kökkenmöddinger *pl*
kitchen scene	Küchenstück *n*
kitsch	Kitsch *m*
knee	Knie *n*
kneel	knien
knee piece	Kniestück *n*
knight	Ritter *m*
knighthood	Rittertum *n*
knight's castle	Ritterburg *f*
knight's hall	Rittersaal *m*
knit	stricken, knüpfen
knob	Knauf *m*
knop	Knauf *m*, Nodus *m*, Nuppe *f*
knot *v.*	knoten, knüpfen
knot *n.*	Knoten *m*
knotted carpet	Knüpfteppich *m*
knotted column	Knotensäule *f*
knotted work	Knüpfarbeit *f*
knotting	Knüpfarbeit *f*
Koran	Koran *m*
Koran illustration	Koranillustration *f*
kore	Kore *f*
kouros	Kouros *n*, Kuros *m*
krater	Krater *m*
bell –	Glockenkrater *m*

calyx —	Kelchkrater m
column —	Kolonettenkrater m
stirrup handle —	Bügelhenkelkrater m
volute —	Volutenkrater m
kremlin	Kreml m
Kufic lettering	kufische Schrift f
kurgan grave	Kurgan m
kylix	Kylix f
eye —	Augenschale f
labarum	Labarum n
label v.	beschriften
label n.	Beschriftung f
labors of the months	Kalendarium n, Monatsbild n
labyrinth	Labyrinth n, Irrgarten m
lace	Spitze f
lacemaking	Spitzenkunst f
Laconian	lakonisch
lacquer v.	lackieren
lacquer n.	Lack m
lacquer coating	Lacküberzug m
lacquerware	Lackware f, Lackkunst f
lacquerware bowl	Lackschale f
lacunar	Kassettendecke f
Lady Chapel	Scheitelkapelle f
Laestrigonians	Lästrygonen pl
lake	Lack m, Lackfarbstoff m, Farbstoff m
lake-dwelling	Pfahlbau m
lamb	Lamm n
lambrequin	Lambrequin m, Behang m
Lamentation, the —	die Wehklage, die Beweinung
laminate	laminieren
lamp	Lampe f, Ampel f
lampblack	Lampenruß m, Lampenschwarz n, Ofenruß m, Kienruß m, Ruß m

lance	Lanze *f*, Speer *m*
lance bearer	Speerträger *m*
lancehead	Lanzenspitze *f*
lancet arch	Lanzettbogen *m*
lancet window	Lanzettfenster *n*
land art	Land Art *f*
landing	Treppenpodest *n*, Treppenabsatz *m*
landscape	Landschaft *f*
heroic —	heroische Landschaft *f*
mood —	Stimmungslandschaft *f*
type of —	Landschaftstypus *m*
landscape background	Landschaftskulisse *f*, Landschaftshintergrund *m*
landscape painter	Landschafter *m*, Landschaftsmaler *m*
landscape painting	Landschaftsmalerei *f*
landscaping	Gartenbaukunst *f*
lantern	Laterne *f*
Laocoön	Laokoon
lap	Schoß *m*
lapidary	1. Steinschneider *m* 2. Steinkenner *m*
lapis lazuli	Lapislazuli *m*, Lasurstein *m*
larchwood	Lärche *f*
large	groß, Groß-
large-pored	grobporig
large scale	Großformat *n*
Last Judgment	das Jüngste Gericht, das Letzte Gericht, das Weltgericht
Last Supper	Abendmahl *n*, das letzte Abendmahl
late	jung, spät, Jung-, Spät-
Late Gothik	Spätgotik *f*
late Hellenistic	späthellenistisch
late Mycenean	spätmykenisch
La Tène	latènezeitlich

La Tène period	Latène-Zeit *f*
Late Period	Spätzeit *f*
lateral	seitlich, Seiten-
lateral aisle	Seitenschiff *n*
lateral dome	Nebenkuppel *f*
lateral support	Nebenstütze *f*
lateral thrust	Seitenschub *m*
lateral transverse arch	Schildbogen *m*
late work	Spätwerk *n*
latex	Latex *m*
lathe	Drehbank *f*
Latin *adj.*	lateinisch
Latin *n.*	Latein *n*
Latin cross	lateinisches Kreuz *n*
lattice	Gitter *n*
lattice ornament	Gitterverzierung *f*
laurel	Lorbeer *m*
laurel wreath	Lorbeerkranz *m*
lay altar	Laienaltar *m*, Kreuzaltar *m*
layer	Schicht *f*
layered	schichtweise, geschichtet, Schicht-
layered masonry	Schichtmauerwerk *n*
layering	Schichtung *f*
lay figure	Gliedermann *m*, Gliederpuppe *f*
lay-in	Untermalung *f*
layout	1. Anlage *f*, Plan *m* 2. Entwurfsskizze *f* 3. Layout *n*
Lazarus Raised From the Dead	die Auferweckung des Lazarus
lead	Blei *n*
white –	Bleiweiß *n*
lead calm	Bleirute *f*
lead came	Bleirute *f*
lead casting	Bleiguß *m*
lead crystal	Bleikristall *n*
leaded glass window	Bleiglasfenster *n*

lead glaze	Bleiglasur *f*
lead panel	Bleitafel *f*
lead pencil	Bleistift *m*, Graphitstift *m*
lead plate	Bleitafel *f*
leaf	1. Blatt *n* 2. Flügel *m*, Altarflügel *m*
bronze —	Bronzeblech *n*
gold —	Blattgold *n*
metal —	Blattmetall *n*
leaf and dart	Blattwelle *f*, Herzblattwelle *f*
leaflet	Flugblatt *n*
leaf ornament	Feuillage *f*, Laubverzierung *f*
leaf work	Laubverzierung *f*, Laubwerk *n*
league	Bund *m*
lean	mager
lean-to roof	Pultdach *n*
leather *adj.*	ledern, Leder-
leather *n.*	Leder *n*
leather-hard	lederhart
lecithin	Lezithin *n*
lectern	Lektionar *n*, Lektionarium *n*, Lesepult *n*, Pult *n*, Lettner *m*
lectionary	Lektionar *n*, Lektionarium *n*, Perikopenbuch *n*
lecythus	Lekythos *f*
leer	Kühlofen *m*
leg	Bein *n*
engaged —	Standbein *n*
free —	Spielbein *n*
legend	1. Legende *f* 2. Randschrift *f*, Inschrift *f*
legging	Beinling *m*
length	Länge *f*
total —	Gesamtlänge *f*
lengthen	verlängern, ausdehnen
lengthening	Verlängerung *f*

Lenten veil	Fastenvelum *n*, Hungertuch *n*, Palmtuch *n*, Fastentuch *n*
lenticular	linsenförmig
Leo	Löwe *m*
lesene	Lesene *f*, Lisene *f*
letter	Buchstabe *m*, Letter *f*
lettering brush	Schreibpinsel *m*
Levallois technique	Levallois-Technik *f*
level *adj.*	eben, plan, gerade
level *n.*	Ebene *f*, Schicht *f*
leveling course	Euthynterie *f*
levigate	schlämmen
liberal arts	artes liberales *pl*, die sieben freien Künste
Libra	Waage *f*
library	Bibliothek *f*
lid	Deckel *m*
hinged —	Scharnierdeckel *m*
tower-shaped —	Deckeltürmchen *n*
lie	liegen
lierne	Nebenrippe *f*
lifeless	leblos, flau
Life of the Virgin, the —	das Marienleben
life-size	lebensgroß
over —	überlebensgroß
under —	unterlebensgroß
lift	heben, erheben
lifting	Abklatschverfahren *n*
light *adj.*	1. hell, hell- 2. leicht, Leicht-
light *n.*	Licht *n*
admission of —	Lichtzufuhr *f*
against the —	im Gegenlicht
ray of —	Lichtstrahl *m*
light-colored	hell, hellfarbig, hell-
light concrete	Leichtbeton *m*
light diffraction	Lichtbeugung *f*

light effect	Lichteffekt *m*, Lichtwirkung *f*
lightfast	lichtecht
lightfastness	Lichtechtheit *f*
lightfast pigment	Permanentfarbstoff *m*
lighting	Beleuchtung *f*
lighting effect	Beleuchtungseffekt *m*
lightning	Blitz *m*
light reflection	Lichtreflex *m*
light refraction	Lichtbrechung *f*
light sensitive	lichtempfindlich
light shaft	Lichtschacht *m*
light source	Lichtquelle *f*
light-weight	leicht
lignum vitae	Guajakholz *n*
likeness	1. Ähnlichkeit *f* 2. Ebenbild *n*, Abbild *n*
lilac	lila
lily	Lilie *f*
limb	Glied *n*
limbo	Limbus *m*, Vorhölle *f*
limbs	Gliedmaßen *pl*, Glieder *pl*
arrangement of the —	Gliederanordnung *f*
movement of the —	Gliederbewegung *f*
lime	Kalk *m*
limestone	Kalk *m*
limestone mortar	Kalkmörtel *n*
lime stucco	Kalkputz *m*
limewash painting process	Kalkseccoverfahren *n*
limit	Grenze *f*
limitation of space	Raumbegrenzung *f*
limited edition	begrenzte Auflage *f*
limner	Buchmaler *m*, Illuminator *m*
Limoges enamel	Limosiner Email *n*, Maleremail *n*
linden wood	Lindenholz *n*
line *v.*	1. einfassen 2. füttern 3. linieren 4. doublieren

line *n.*	1. Linie *f*, Strich *m*
	2. Zeile *f*
	3. Reihe *f*
flow of the —	Linienführung *f*, Linienverlauf *m*
value of the —	Linienwert *m*
lineament	Lineament *m*
line and wash	lavierte Federzeichnung *f*
linear	linear
Linear A script	Linear-A-Schrift *f*
Linear B script	Linear-B-Schrift *f*
linear Bandkeramik pottery	Linearbandkeramik *f*
linear ornamentation	Linearornamentik *f*
linear perspective	Linearperspektive *f*
linen *adj.*	leinen, Leinen-
linen *n.*	Leinen *n*
linen bookbinding	Leinenband *m*
linenfold	Faltwerk *n*
lining	1. Fütterung *f*
	2. Doublieren *n*
link	Verbindung *f*, Glied *n*, Bindeglied *n*
linocut	Linoleumschnitt *m*, Linolschnitt *m*
linoleum cut	Linoleumschnitt *m*, Linolschnitt *m*
linoleum plate	Linolplatte *f*
linseed oil	Leinöl *n*
lintel	Steinbalken *m*, Sturz *m*
lion	Löwe *m*
Lion Gate	Löwentor *n*
lip	Lippe *f*
liquid silicate	Wasserglas *n*
list	Verzeichnis *n*, Liste *f*
listel	Steg *m*
litharge	Bleiglätte *f*
lithograph *v.*	lithographieren

lithograph n.	Lithographie f, Steindruck m, Steinzeichnung f
lithographer	Lithograph m, Steindrucker m, Steinzeichner m
lithographic	lithographisch, Litho-
lithographic crayon	Fettfarbe f, Lithokreide f
lithographic ink	Lithotusche f, Steindruckfarbe f
lithographic press	Steindruckerei f
lithographic tusche	Tusche f
lithograph paper	Lithographierpapier n
lithography	Lithographie f, Steindruck m
lithophane	Lithophanie f
lithophone	Deckweiß n, Lithophone f
little	klein, Klein-
little master cup	Kleinmeisterschale f
liturgical	liturgisch
liturgical book	Sakramentar n, Sakramentarium n
liturgy	Liturgie f
liveliness	Lebendigkeit f
lively	bewegt, lebendig
loan	Leihgabe f
Loaves and the Fishes, the —	die Brotvermehrung
local	lokal, örtlich, Lokal-
local art	Heimatkunst f
local color	Lokalfarbe f, Gegenstandsfarbe f
localization	Lokalisierung f, Bestimmung f
location	1. Lokalisierung f 2. Ort m, Position f, Stätte f, Standort m, Aufstellungsort m
lock	1. Locke f, Haarlocke f 2. Schloß n
loculus	Lokulusgrab n
loft	Dachboden m, Boden m
rood —	Chorempore f
log building	Blockbau m

loggia	Loggia f, Laube f
log house	Blockhaus n
loincloth	Lendentuch n, Schurz m
Lombard band decoration	lombardisches Bandgeflecht n
Lombardic	langobardisch
long	lang, Lang-
longitudinal axis	Längsachse f
longitudinal joint	Längsfuge f
longitudinal movement	Längsbewegung f
longitudinal-plan building	Langbau m, Richtungsbau m
longitudinal ridge-rib	Gurtrippe f
longitudinal section	Längsschnitt m
long-necked vase	Langhalsvase f
loom	Webstuhl m, Wirkstuhl m
high warp –	Hautelisse f, Hochschaftstuhl m
low warp –	Basselisse f, Tiefschaftstuhl m
treadle-operated –	Trittwebstuhl m
warp-weighted –	Gewichtswebstuhl m
loop	Öse f, Schlinge f, Schleife f
looped decoration	Schlingornamentik f
loose	locker, los
lop-sided	schief
lost pattern casting	Ausschmelzverfahren n
lost wax	cire perdue n
lost-wax process	Ausschmelzverfahren n, Verlorene Form f, Wachsausschmelzverfahren n
lotus	Lotos m
lotus bud	Lotosknospe f
lotus flower	Lotosblüte f
lotus leaf	Lotosblatt n
loutrophorus	Loutrophoros m, Lutrophorus m
louvre	Lamelle f
loveliness	Lieblichkeit f
lovely	lieblich, schön
low	niedrig, tief, Tief-
lower arm	Unterarm m

lower floor	Untergeschoß *n*
lower paleolithic period	Altpaläolithikum *n*
low relief	Flachrelief *n*
low warp loom	Basselisse *f*, Tiefschaftstuhl *m*
lozenge	Raute *f*, Rhombus *m*
lucarne	Lukarne *f*
lucenarium	Luminarium *n*
luminarium	Luminarium *n*
luminosity	Leuchtkraft *f*
luminous	leuchtend, Leucht-
luminous paint	Leuchtfarbe *f*
luminous power	Leuchtkraft *f*
lunar disc	Mondscheibe *f*
lunar symbol	Mondsymbol *n*
lunette	Lünette *f*, Lunula *f*
lunette painting	Lünettengemälde *n*
lunula	Lunula *f*
luster	1. Lüster *m*
	2. Schillerglanz *m*, Glanz *m*
lusterware	Lüsterkeramik *f*, Lüsterware *f*
lusterware bowl	Lüsterschale *f*
lustre	Schillerglanz *m*, Glanz *m*
lustreless	duff, matt, stumpf
lustrous	glänzend
luteolin dye	Luteolin *n*
lye	Seifenlauge *f*
lyre-shaped	lyraförmig
macaroni finger drawing	Makkaroni *pl*
Macedonian	makedonisch, mazedonisch
mace-head	Mattoir *n*
machicolation	Pechnase *f*
machine art	Maschinenkunst *f*
madder	Krapp *m*, Färberröte *f*
madder-colored	krappfarben
madder lake	Krapplack *m*

Madonna	Madonna *f*, Madonnenbild *n*, Marienbild *n*, Muttergottesbild *n*
Madonna Glykophilusa	Glykophilusa *f*
Madonna Lactans	Galaktotrophusa *f*
madonna-like	madonnenhaft
Madonna of Mercy	Schutzmantelmadonna *f*
Madonna of the Goldfinch	Madonna mit dem Goldfink
Madonna of the Rosary	Rosenkranzbild *n*
Madonna of Victory	die Madonna des Sieges
Madonna Worshiping the Child	Madonna, das Kind anbetend
maenad	Mänade *f*
maestà	Maestà *f*
Magdalenian period	Magdalénien *n*, Rentierzeit *f*
magenta	Fuchsin *n*
magical	märchenhaft, zauberhaft
magic realism	Magischer Realismus *m*
magilp	Leinölfirnis mit Terpentin
Maglemosian culture	Maglemosekultur *f*
mahagony	Mahagoni *n*
mahlstick	Malstock *m*
maiden	Mädchen *n*, Jungfrau *f*
main apse	Hauptapsis *f*
main axis	Hauptachse *f*
main color	Grundfarbe *f*
main entrance	Haupteingang *m*
main figure	Hauptfigur *f*
main girder	Längsträger *m*
main view	Hauptansicht *f*
main work	Hauptwerk *n*
maiolica	Majolika *f*
majesty	Maestà *f*
majolica	Majolika *f*
majuscle	Majuskel *f*
maker's mark	Meisterzeichen *n*, Steinmetzzeichen *n*

malachite	Malachit *m*, Mineralgrün *n*
male	männlich
malleable	dehnbar, hämmerbar
mallet	Klöppel *m*, Schlegel *m*, Hammer *m*
Maltese cross	Malteserkreuz *n*, Johanitterkreuz *n*
man	Mann *m*, Mensch *m*
mandorla	Mandorla *f*
manganese black	Manganbraun *n*
manganese brown	Manganbraun *n*
manière criblée	Punktiermanier *f*, Punzenmanier *f*
manifestation	Offenbarung *f*
manifesto	Manifest *n*
manikin	Gliedermann *m*, Gliederpuppe *f*
maniple	Manipel *f*
manipulation	Handhabung *f*, Behandlung *f*
man-made chalk	Kunstkreide *f*
man-made material	Kunststoff *m*
manner	Manier *f*, Weise *f*, Art *f*
mannered	manieriert
Mannerism	Manierismus *m*
Mannerist	Manierist *m*
Man of Sorrows	Erbärmdebild *n*, Miserikordienbild *n*, Schmerzensmann *m*
mansard	Mansarde *f*
mansard roof	Mansarde *f*, Mansardendach *n*
mantle	1. Mantel *m* 2. Kamineinfassung *f*, Kaminsims *n*
manuscript	Manuskript *n*, Ms., Handschrift *f*
maple	Ahorn *m*
maquette	Bozzetto *m*, Probeplastik *f*, Versuchsplastik *f*
marble *adj.*	marmorn, Marmor-
marble *v.*	marmorieren
marble *n.*	Marmor *m*
marble cladding	Marmorverkleidung *f*

marble dust	Marmorstaub *m*
marble piece	Marmorbildwerk *n*
marble slab	Marmorplatte *f*
marble statue	Marmorbildwerk *n*, Marmorstatue *f*
marble tablet	Marmortafel *f*
marble type	Marmorart *f*
marble vein	Marmorader *f*
marble work	Marmorwerk *n*
marbling	Marmorierung *f*
margin	Leiste *f*, Randleiste *f*
decorative —	Zierleiste *f*
margin inscription	Randschrift *f*
margin ornamentation	Randornament *n*
marginal illustration	Marginale *f*
marginal note	Marginale *f*
marine painter	Marinemaler *m*
marine painting	Marinemalerei *f*
Mariolatry	Marienkult *m*
mark	Signum *n*
marksmen's guild piece	Doelenstück *n*, Schützenstück *n*
marquetry	Marketerie *f*
Mars yellow	Marsgelb *n*
martyr *v.*	martern
martyr *n.*	Märtyrer *m*
martyrdom	Märtyrertum *n*, Martyrium *n*
martyrium	Martyrium *n*
marvered trailing	Fadeneinlage *f*
Mary Lowering Her Girdle	die Gürtelspende
Mary Queen of Heaven	Maria auf der Mondsichel
Marys at the Tomb	die Frauen am Grabe, die Drei Marien am Grabe
mascaron	Maskaron *m*
masculine	männlich
mask *v.*	1. decken 2. maskieren
mask *n.*	Maske *f*

mask-like	maskenhaft
mason	Maurer *m*
Masonite	Hartfaserplatte *f*
masonry	Mauerarbeit *f*, Mauerwerk *n*
cyclopean —	Zyklopenmauer *f*, zyklopisches Mauerwerk *n*
dry joint —	Trockenmauerwerk *n*
rubble —	Feldsteinmauerwerk *n*
masonry bond	Mauerverband *m*, Verband *m*
mason's trowel	Maurerkelle *f*
mass	1. Messe *f* 2. Masse *f*, Menge *f*
Massacre of the Innocents	der Kindermord zu Bethlehem, der bethlehemische Kindermord
Mass of St. Gregory	Gregorsmesse *f*
mass production	Massenfertigung *f*
mastaba	Mastaba *f*
master	Meister *m*
masterly	meisterhaft, meisterlich
masterpiece	Meisterstück *n*, Meisterwerk *n*, Glanzstück *n*
master's mark	Meisterzeichen *n*
mastery	Meisterschaft *f*, Beherrschung *f*
mastic	Mastix *m*, Kitt *m*
mastic resin	Mastixharz *n*
mat	*s.* matte
mater dolorosa	Miserikordienbild *n*, Schmerzensmutter *f*
mater ecclesia	die Mutterkirche
mater misericordiae	Schutzmantelmadonna *f*
material *adj.*	materiell
material *n.*	Material *n*, Materie *f*, Stoff *m*, Zeug *n*
matrix	Matrize *f*
matte	matt, duff, glanzlos, Matt-
matte gilding	Mattvergoldung *f*
matte painting	Mattmalerei *f*

matter	Materie f
mattoir	Mattoir n
mature	reif
mature style	Reifestil m
maulstick	Malstock m
mausoleum	Mausoleum n
mauve	Mauvein n
maze	Labyrinth n
meander	Mäander m
meander pattern	Mäandermuster n
meaning	Bedeutung f
means	Mittel n
measure v.	abmessen, messen
measure n.	Maß n, Maßstab m
unit of —	Maßeinheit f
measurement	Messung f, Maßangabe f, Maß n
medal	Medaille f
medallion	Medallion n
Medici Aphrodite	mediceische Venus f
medieval	mittelalterlich
Mediterranean region	Mittelmeerraum m
Mediterranean Sea	Mittelmeer n
medium	1. Mittel n, Darstellungsmittel n, Werkmittel n 2. Farbbindemittel n, Lösungsmittel n
Medusa	Meduse f
meeting hall	Versammlungshalle f
megalith	Megalith m
megalithic	megalithisch, Megalith-
megalithic culture	Megalithkultur f
megalithic tomb	Megalithgrab n, Hunengrab n, Steinkammergrab n
megaron	Megaron n
megilp	Leinölfirnis mit Terpentin
mehrab	Mihrab m
mellow	sanft, mild

Memnon statue	Memnonskoloß *m*
mendicant orders	Bettelorden *pl*
menhir	Menhir *m*
menology	Martyriologium *n*, Menologion *n*
menorah	Menora *f*
mensa	Mensa *f*
mental conception	Vorstellung *f*
Mercury	Merkur
merlon	Schartenbacke *f*
mermaid	Wassernixe *f*
Merovingian	merowingisch
Merz	Merz
mesolithic	mesolithisch
mesolithic period	Mesolithikum *n*
Mesopotamia	Zweistromland *n*, Mesopotamien *n*
message	Aussage *f*
metal *adj.*	metallen, Metall-
metal *n.*	Metall *n*
metal cut	Metallschnitt *m*
metal fitting	Metallbeschlag *m*
metal foil	Folie *f*, Metallfolie *f*
metal leaf	Blattmetall *n*
metallic	metallisch
metallic oxide	Metalloxyd *n*
metallurgy	Metallurgie *f*
metal plate	Metallplatte *f*
metal print	Metalldruck *m*
metalworking	Metallbearbeitung *f*, Toreutik *f*, Schmiedekunst *f*
metaphorical figure	Gleichnisgestalt *f*
method	Methode *f*, Verfahren *n*
metope	Metope *f*
meutrière	Scharte *f*, Schießscharte *f*
mezzanine	Mezzanin *n*
mezzo-rilievo	Halbrelief *n*
mezzotint	Mezzotinto *n*, Schabkunst *f*, Schabmanier *f*, Schwarzkunst *f*, schwarze Kunst *f*

mezzotint artist	Schabkünstler *m*
mezzotint engraving	Schabkunstblatt *n*
mica	Glimmer *m*
microlith	Mikrolith *m*
mid-century	Jahrhundertmitte *f*
middle	Mitte *f*
Middle Ages	Mittelalter *n*
middle axis	Mittelachse *f*
middle distance	Mittelgrund *m*
middle ground	Mittelgrund *m*
Middle Minoan	mittelminoisch
middle relief	Halbrelief *n*
middle shaft	Kern *m*
middle tone	Mittelton *m*
Migration Period	Völkerwanderung *f*
mihrab	Mihrab *m*
milk glass	Milchglas *n*
milk of lime	Kalkmilch *f*
milky white	milchigweiß
millefiori glass	Millefioriglas *n*, Mosaikglas *n*
mille-fleur-tapisserie	Tausendblumenteppich *m*
millennium	Jahrtausend *n*
minaret	Minar *n*, Minarett *n*
mineral green	Mineralgrün *n*, Malachit *m*
mineral painting	Mineralmalerei *f*, Silikatmalerei *f*, Stereochromie *f*
mineral pigment	Mineralfarbe *f*
miniature	Miniatur *f*
miniature painting	Miniaturmalerei *f*
miniaturist	Buchmaler *m*, Miniaturmaler *m*
minimal art	Minimal Art *f*
minium	Bleimennige *f*, Mennig *m*, Mennige *f*, Minium *n*
Minoan	minoisch
Minotaur	Minotaurus *m*
minster	Münster *n*, Dom *m*
minstrel	Minnesänger *m*

mint	münzen
minuscule	Minuskel *f*
minute	minutiös
Minyan ware	minysche Keramik *f*
miracle	Wunder *n*, Wundertat *f*
Miracle of Pentecost	Pfingstwunder *n*
Miracle of Transubstantiation, the −	Hostienmühle *f*
Miraculous Draught of Fishes, the −	Petri Fischzug, der wunderbare Fischzug
mirror *v*.	wiederspiegeln
mirror *n*.	Spiegel *m*
Mirror of Human Salvation	Heilsspiegel *m*
mirrors, hall of −	Spiegelgalerie *f*, Spiegelsaal *m*
miserere	Miserikordie *f*
misericord	Miserikordie *f*
missal	Meßbuch *n*, Missal *n*, Missale *n*
missal illuminator	Meßbuchmaler *m*
Mission of the Apostles, the −	die Aussendung der Apostel, die Entsendung der Apostel
miter *v*.	gehren
miter *n*.	1. Gehrung *f* 2. Mitra *f*
miter cap	Mitra *f*
miter joint	Gehrung *f*
mithraeum	Mithräum *n*
Mithraic temple	Mithräum *n*
mixed technique	Mischtechnik *f*
moat	Ringgraben *m*, Schloßgraben *m*, Wallgraben *m*
mobile	Mobile *n*
mobility	Beweglichkeit *f*
Mocking of Christ	die Verspottung Christi
model *v*.	modellieren
model *n*.	1. Modell *n*, Muster *n*, Vorbild *n*, Vorlage *f* 2. Patrone *f*

modelling

modelling *adj.*	modellierend, formgebend, Modellier-
modelling *n.*	Modellierung *f*, Formgebung *f*
modelling clay	Knete *f*, Knetton *m*, Plastilin *n*
modelling stand	Modellierbock *m*, Modellierstuhl *m*
modelling tool	Modellierholz *n*
modelling wax	Bossierwachs *n*
modern	modern
modernistic	modernistisch
modernize	modernisieren
modern style	Jugendstil *m*
modern times	Moderne *f*, Neuzeit *f*
modillion	Konsole *f*, Krage *f*
module	Model *m*, Modul *m*, Maßeinheit *f*
moiré effect	Flimmereffekt *m*
mold	Formmodel *n*, Gießform *f*, Gußhohlform *f*
moldable	verformbar
molding	*s.* moulding
molten glass	Glasmasse *f*
monastery	Kloster *n*, Monasterium *n*
monastery church	Klosterkirche *f*
monastery library	Klosterbibliothek *f*
monastic	klösterlich
monk	Mönch *m*
monkey	Affe *m*
monkish	mönchisch
monochromatic	monochromatisch
monochrome *adj.*	monochrom
monochrome *n.*	Monochromie *f*
monogram	Monogramm *n*
monograph	Monographie *f*
monolith	Monolith *m*
monolithic	monolithisch
monopteral	Monopteros *m*
monotype	Monotype *f*, Monotypie *f*

monster	Ungeheuer *n*, Monstrum *n*
monstrance	Monstranz *f*, Ostensorium *n*
montage	Montage *f*
monument	Denkmal *n*, Monument *n*
monumental	monumental
monumental sculpture	Monumentalplastik *f*
mood	Stimmung *f*
mood landscape	Stimmungslandschaft *f*
moon	Mond *m*
moonlight	Mondlicht *n*, Mondschein *m*
moonstone	Mondstein *m*
moon symbol	Mondsymbol *n*
Moor	Maure *m*
Moorish	maurisch
mordant	Ätzflüssigkeit *f*, Ätzwasser *n*, Beize *f*, Säure *f*
mordant bath	Säurebad *n*
mordant gilding	Ölvergoldung *f*
mortal	sterblich
mortar	Mörtel *m*, Kalkputz *m*, Mauerkalk *m*
without —	mörtellos
mortar construction	Mörtelbau *m*
mortar joint	Mörtelfuge *f*
mortar wall	Mörtelmauer *f*
mortuary temple	Totentempel *m*
mosaic	Mosaik *n*, Musivarbeit *f*
cone —	Stiftmosaik *n*
pebble —	Kieselmosaik *n*
pegged —	Stiftmosaik *n*, Tonstiftmosaik *n*
mosaic floor	Mosaikboden *m*
mosaic glass	Mosaikglas *n*, Millefioriglas *n*
mosaic gold	Musivgold *n*
mosaicist	Mosaist *m*, Mosaizist *m*
mosaic-like	mosaikartig
Moses and the Rock of Horeb	Moses schlägt Wasser aus dem Felsen

mosque	Moschee *f*
mosque lamp	Moscheeampel *f*
Mother Church, the —	die Mutterkirche
mother of God	Muttergottes *f*
mother-of-pearl	Perlmutt *n*, Perlmutter *f*
Mother of Sorrows	Schmerzensmutter *f*
motif	Motiv *n*
motive	Motiv *n*
mottled ware	Geflammte Ware *f*
motto	Devise *f*, Motto *n*
mouchette	Fischblase *f*, Schneuß *m*
moulage	Moulage *f*
moulding	Leiste *f*
bead —	Perlenschnur *f*, Perlstab *m*, Perlstäbchen *n*
billet —	Würfelband *n*, Würfelfries *m*, Rollenfries *m*, Schachbrettfries *m*
cable —	Tau *n*, gedrehtes Tau *n*
concave —	Hohlkehle *f*, Hohlleiste *f*, Kehlleiste *f*, dorisches Kymation *n*
decorative —	Zierleiste *f*
drip —	Rinnleiste *f*
hollow —	Hohlleiste *f*
ogee —	Karnies *n*
quadrant —	Viertelstab *m*
roll —	Rollenfries *m*
wood —	Holzleiste *f*
mound	Hügelaufschüttung *f*, Mound *m*
mount	aufspannen, aufstellen, einfassen, fassen
Mount Calvary	Kalvarienberg *m*
mounted figure	Reiterfigur *f*
mounting	Einfassung *f*, Halterung *f*
Mount of Olives	der Ölberg
Christ on the —	die Ölbergstunde
Mount of Olives group	Ölberggruppe *f*

multiple

Mourning of Mary	die Marienklage
Mousterian	Mousterian *n*
mouth	Mund *m*
moveable	beweglich
movement	Bewegung *f*
direction of –	Bewegungsrichtung *f*
flow of –	Bewegungsfluß *m*
Mozarabic	mozarabisch
MS., ms.	Ms.
Mt. Athos painter's manual	das Malerhandbuch vom Berg Athos
Mt. Olympus	Olymp *m*
Mt. Vesuvius	Vesuv *m*
mud bond	Lehmverband *m*
mud brick	Lehmziegel *m*, Luftziegel *m*
mud brick building	Lehmziegelbau *m*
mud brick wall	Lehmziegelmauer *f*, Lehmziegelwand *f*
muddy	trüb, unklar
Mudéjar style	Mudejarstil *m*
muffle	Muffel *f*
muffle color	Muffelfarbe *f*
muffle furnace	Muffelofen *m*
muffle kiln	Muffelofen *m*
mug	Becher *m*, Krug *m*
muller	Stößel *n*
mullion	Fensterpfeiler *m*, Fensterpfosten *m*, Mittelpfosten *m*, Stabwerk *n*
multi-color(ed)	mehrfarbig, vielfarbig
multi-color print	Chromatotypie *f*, Mehrfarbendruck *m*, Chromatypie *f*
multi-color printing	Chromatotypie *f*, Mehrfarbendruck *m*
multi-color woodcut	Vielfarbenholzschnitt *m*
multi-foil	Vielpaß *m*
multi-leveled	vielschichtig
multiple	Multiple *n*

multiple-aisled	mehrschiffig
mummification	Mumifikation *f*
mummify	mumifizieren
mummy	Mumie *f*
mummy portrait	Mumienbildnis *n*, Mumienporträt *n*
mummy sarcophagus	Mumiensarkophag *m*
mummy wrappings	Mumienbandagen *pl*
mural	Wandbild *n*, Wandgemälde *n*, Wandmalerei *f*
mural cycle	Wandbilderzyklus *m*
murex purple	Purpur *m*
muscle	Muskel *m*
Muse	Muse *f*
museology	Museumskunde *f*
museum	Museum *n*
open air —	Freilichtmuseum *n*
museum curator	Kustos *m*
mustard-colored	mostrichfarben
mutule	Mutulus *m*, Dielenkopf *m*, Tropfenplatte *f*
Mycenaea	Mykene
Mycenaean	mykenisch
myrrh	Myrrhe *f*
Mystic Marriage of St. Catherine, the —	die Verlobung der hl. Katherina
myth	Mythos *m*, Mythus *m*, Mythe *f*, Sage *f*
mythical	mythisch, sagenhaft
mythical beast	Fabelwesen *n*
mythological	mythologisch
mythology	Mythologie *f*, Götterlehre *f*
Nabis	Nabis *pl*
naiad	Najade *f*
nail *v.*	nageln

nail *n.*	Nagel *m*
nailhead pattern	Diamantband *n*, Nagelkopf *m*
naive	naiv
naive art	naive Kunst *f*, primitive Kunst *f*
naive painter	naiver Maler *m*, Laienmaler *m*, Sonntagsmaler *m*
naos	Naos *m*
nape of the neck	Nacken *m*
Naples yellow	Neapelgelb *n*, Brilliantgelb *n*
Narcissus	Narziß
narrate	erzählen
narration, continuous —	kontinuierende Darstellung *f*, kontinuierliche Darstellung *f*
narrative	erzählerisch
narrative style	Erzählstil *m*
narrow	schmal, eng
narrow-necked jug	Enghalskrug *m*
narthex	Narthex *m*, Vorhalle *f*
national library	Staatsbibliothek *f*
native chalk	Steinkreide *f*
Nativity, the —	Geburt Christi *f*, die Heilige Familie
Nativity scene	Krippe *f*, Weihnachtsbild *n*, Weihnachtskrippe *f*
natural	natürlich, Natur-
natural alizarin dye	Alizarin *n*
natural color	Naturfarbe *f*
naturalism	Naturalismus *m*, Moderne *f*
naturalist	Naturalist *m*
natural light	Naturlicht *n*
natural shape	Naturform *f*
natural stone	Naturstein *m*
nature	1. Natur *f* 2. Wesen *n*
true to —	naturgetreu
nave	Mittelschiff *n*, Hauptschiff *n*, Langschiff *n*

nave pillar	Mittelschiffspfeiler *m*
nave wall	Hauptschiffwand *f*, Hochwand *f*
Navicella, the —	der sinkende Petrus
navy blue	marineblau
Nazarenes	Nazarener *pl*, Lukasbrüder *pl*, Lukasbrüderschaft *f*, Lukasbund *m*
neck	Hals *m*
neck chain	Halskette *f*, Kette *f*, Brustkette *f*
necklace	Kette *f*, Halskette *f*, Brustkette *f*, Halsgehänge *n*
neckline	Ausschnitt *m*
necropolis	Nekropole *f*
needle	1. Nadel *f* 2. Ritzgriffel *m*
negative afterimage	Nachbildkontrast *m*, Sukzessivkontrast *m*
negative painting	Negativtechnik *f*
neoclassicism	Neoklassizismus *m*, Neuklassizismus *m*, Klassizismus *m*
Neo-Dada	Neo-Dada, Anti-Kunst *f*
neoimpressionism	Neoimpressionismus *m*
neolithic	jungsteinzeitlich, neolithisch
neolithic age	Jungsteinzeit *f*, Neolithikum *n*
Neo-Plasticism	Neo-Plastizismus *m*, die Neue Gestaltung
nephrite	Nephrit *m*
nereid	Nereide *f*, Meernixe *f*
net	Netz *n*
net-like	netzartig
Netherlander	Niederländer *m*
Netherlandish	niederländisch
net vault	Netzgewölbe *n*, Zellengewölbe *n*
Neue Sachlichkeit	die Neue Sachlichkeit
new acquisition	Neuerwerbung *f*
newel	Treppenpfosten *m*, Treppenanfänger *m*
New Objectivity	die Neue Sachlichkeit

New Realism	Neuer Realismus *m*
newspaper	Zeitung *f*, Blatt *n*
New Testament *adj.*	neutestamentarisch
New Testament *n.*	das Neue Testament, der Neue Bund
niche	Nische *f*, Wandvertiefung *f*
niche-like	nischenartig
nickel	Nickel *n*
nickel plate	vernickeln
niello	Niello *n*, Schwefelsilber *n*
niello work	Niellierarbeit *f*
night piece	Nachtstück *n*
Nikopeia	Nikopoia *f*
Nile Valley	Niltal *n*
nimbus	Nimbus *m*, Hof *m*, Heiligenschein *m*, Strahlenkranz *m*, Strahlenkrone *f*
cruciform —	Kreuznimbus *m*
Noah's Ark	Arche Noah *f*
nobility	Adel *m*
noble	edel, Edel-
nobleman	Edelmann *m*
noblewoman	Edelfrau *f*
nocturne	Nachtstück *n*
node	Knauf *m*
nog	ausfachen
noli me tangere	Christus als Gärtner
nomadic people	Nomadenvolk *n*
nomads	Nomadenvolk *n*, Nomaden *pl*
non-objective	gegenstandslos, ungegenständlich
non-objective art	gegenstandslose Kunst *f*, non-figurative Kunst *f*
non-objectivism	Gegenstandslosigkeit *f*
Non-Objectivism	Non-Objektivismus *m*
non-representational	gegenstandslos
nose	Nase *f*
nose ornament	Nasenschmuck *m*

notch v.	kerben
notch n.	Kerbe f
notching	Kerbung f
nouveau réalisme	Neuer Realismus m
novecento	Novecento n
novel	originell, neuartig, ungewöhnlich
nuance	Nuance f, Farbabstufung f, Farbenabstufung f, Farbtönung f, Schattierung f
nuanced	nuanciert
nude adj.	nackt
nude n.	Akt m
nude back	Rückenakt m
nude drawing	Aktzeichnung f
nude figure	Aktfigur f
nude girl	Mädchenakt m
nude study	Aktstudie f
numerical symbol	Zahlensymbol n
numismatics	Numismatik f, Münzkunde f
nun	Nonne f
nuns' gallery	Nonnenchor m
nuraghe	Nurage f, Nuraghe f
nut oil	Nußöl n
nymphaeum	Nymphäum n
Nymphenburg porcelain	Nymphenburger Porzellan n
oak	Eiche f, Eichenholz n
obelisk	Obelisk m
object	Gegenstand m, Objekt n
objective	gegenständlich, sachlich
objectivity	Sachlichkeit f
object poem	Schriftbild n
objet trouvé	objet trouvé n
oblique	quer, schräg, Schräg-
oblique line	Quere f, Schräge f
oblique perspective	Strahlenperspektive f

oblique view	Diagonalansicht *f*, Schrägansicht *f*
oblong	langrechteckig, längsrechteckig
observation	Beobachtung *f*, Betrachtung *f*
observe	beobachten, betrachten
observer	Beobachter *m*, Betrachter *m*
obsidian	Obsidian *m*
obsidian blade	Obsidianklinge *f*
obsidian knife	Obsidianklinge *f*
obverse	Avers *m*, Vorderseite *f*
Occident	Abendland *n*, Okzident *m*
occidental	abendländisch, okzidental, okzidentalisch
occupations of the months	Monatsbild *n*, Kalendarium *n*
ochre *adj.*	ocker
ochre *n.*	Ocker *m, n*
octagon	Achteck *n*, Oktogon *n*
octagonal	achteckig
octateuch	Oktateuch *m*
Octopus Vase, the —	Polypenvase *f*
oculus	Auge *n*
odalisque	Odaliske *f*
odeum	Odeion *n*, Odeon *n*, Odeum *n*
Œil-de-Bœuf window	Ochsenauge *n*
oenochoe	Oinochoe *f*
œuvre	Gesamtwerk *n*, Œuvre *n*, Oeuvre *n*, Schaffen *n*, Werk *n*
œuvre catalogue	Œuvrekatalog *m*, Oeuvreverzeichnis *n*, Werkverzeichnis *n*
offering	Gabe *f*, Opfergabe *f*
offset	Mauerabsatz *m*, Wasserschlag *m*
offset printing	Offsetdruck *m*
ogee arch	Eselsrücken *m*, Karniesbogen *m*, Kielbogen *m*
ogee moulding	Karnies *n*
oil	Öl *n*
essential —	ätherisches Öl *n*, Essenz *f*
oil glaze	Öllasur *f*

oil of cedar	Zedernholzöl n
oil of cloves	Nelkenöl n
oil of lavender	Lavendelöl n
oil of rosemary	Rosmarinöl n
oil of turpentine	Terpentinöl n, Terpentingeist m
oil paint	Ölfarbe f
oil painting	Ölgemälde n, Ölbild n, Ölmalerei f
oil sketch	Ölskizze f
oil tempera	Öltempera f
oily paint	Fettfarbe f
oinochoe	Oinochoe f
ointment	Salbe f
ointment jar	Salbgefäß n
old fustic	Fustikholz n, Gelbholz n
old master	Altmeister m
Old Testament *adj.*	alttestamentarisch
Old Testament *n.*	das Alte Testament, der Alte Bund
oliphant	Olifant m
olive green	olivgrün
one-aisled church	Saalkirche f
one man show	Einzelausstellung f
one-roomed	einzimmerig
one-roomed church	Einraumkirche f
one-rowed	einreihig
one-storied	einstöckig
onion-shaped roof	Zwiebeldach n
onion-shaped tower	Zwiebelturm m, Zwiebelhaube f
only copy	Unikum n
onyx	Onyx m
op art	Op-Art f
opacity	Undurchsichtigkeit f
degree of —	Deckkraft f
opal	Opal m
opalesce	opaliszieren, opalisieren, schillern
opalescence	Opaleszenz f
opalescent	opalisierend

opaline	Opalglas *n*
opaque	opak, deckend, undurchsichtig, pastos
opaque color	Deckfarbe *f*
opaque paint	Deckfarbe *f*
open-air museum	Freilichtmuseum *n*
open-air painting	Pleinairmalerei *f*, Freilichtmalerei *f*
opening	1. Eröffnung *f* 2. Öffnung *f*
open roof truss	offener Dachstuhl *m*
opisthodomos	Opisthodomos *m*
oppidum	Oppidum *n*
optical	optisch
optical illusion	optische Täuschung *f*
optical illusion art	Op-Art *f*
opus caementum masonry	Emplekton *n*, Gußmauerwerk *n*
opus reticulatum	Netzverband *m*
opus spicatum	Ährenverband *m*
oracle	Orakel *n*
oracle bones	mit Schriftzeichen versehene Tierknochen und Schildkrötenpanzer zur Orakelbefragung
orange	orange, orangenfarben
orangery	Orangerie *f*
orans	Adorant *m*
orant	Orans *m*, Orant *m*
orant position	Orantenstellung *f*
oratory	Oratorium *n*, Chörlein *n*
orb	Reichsapfel *m*
order	Ordnung *f*, Säulenordnung *f*
Corinthian –	korinthische Ordnung *f*
Doric –	dorische Ordnung *f*
Ionic –	ionische Ordnung *f*
Tuscan –	toskanische Ordnung *f*
ore	Erz *n*
organ	Orgel *f*

organ builder	Orgelbauer *m*
organ case	Orgelprospekt *m*, Prospekt *m*
organization	Organisierung *f*, Organisation *f*, Ordnung *f*
oriel	Erker *m*
Orient	Morgenland *n*, Orient *m*
oriental	morgenländisch, orientalisch
Oriental carpet	Orientteppich *m*
Orientalize	orientalisieren
Orientalizing style	orientalisierender Stil *m*
orientation	Orientierung *f*, Richtung *f*
origin	Ursprung *m*, Herkunft *f*, Entstehung *f*, Provenienz *f*, Anfang *m*
date of –	Entstehungsdatum *n*, Entstehungsjahr *n*
place of –	Entstehungsort *m*
original *adj.*	1. eigenständig, originell 2. original, ursprünglich
original *n.*	1. Original *n* 2. Vorlage *f*, Urbild *n*
originality	Originalität *f*
original painting	Originalgemälde *n*
original print	Handdruck *m*, manueller Bilddruck *m*, Originaldruck *m*
original size	Originalgröße *f*
originate	entstehen, stammen
ormolu	Feuervergoldung *f*, Goldbronze *f*
ornament *v.*	ornamentieren, dekorieren, schmücken
ornament *n.*	Ornament *n*, Schmuck *m*, Verzierung *f*, Schmuckstück *n*, Zierat *m*
ornamental	ornamental, dekorativ
ornamental flourish	Schnörkel *m*
ornamental form	Zierform *f*
ornamental piece	Prunkstück *n*

ornamentation	Ornamentierung *f*, Ornamentik *f*, Zierwerk *n*, Ausschmückung *f*, Dekor *m*
history of —	Ornamentgeschichte *f*
ornate	figurenreich
Orphic Cubism	Orphismus *m*
Orphism	Orphismus *m*
orphrey	Goldborte *f*
orpiment	Auripigment *n*, Operment *n*, Gelbglas *m*, Rauschgelb *n*
orthogonal	orthogonal
orthographic	1. orthographisch 2. orthogonal
orthostats	Orthostaten *pl*
orthostyle	mit geradlinig angeordneten Säulen versehen
osculatorium	Osculatorium *n*, Kußtafel *f*, Pacificale *n*, Paxtafel *f*
ossuary	Ossarium *n*, Ossuarium *n*
ostensoir	Ostensorium *n*
ostracon	Ostrakon *n*
ostrich egg	Straußenei *n*
Ottonian	ottonisch
outer garment	Obergewand *n*
outer narthex	Exonarthex *m*
outer side	Außenseite *f*
outer wall	Außenwand *f*
outline	Umriß *m*, Umrißlinie *f*, Kontur *f*
outline engraving	Umrißstich *m*, Kartonstich *m*
outside edge	Außenkante *f*
outworks	Außenwerk *n*
oval *adj.*	oval, Oval-
oval *n.*	Oval *n*
oven	Ofen *m*
overall color	Gesamtton *m*
overall effect	Gesamtwirkung *f*
overdoor	Sopraporte *f*, Supraporte *f*

over garment	Obergewand *n*
overglaze decoration	Überglasurdekor *m*
overglaze painting	Aufglasurmalerei *f*
overhanging eaves	Dachüberstand *m*
overhead light	Oberlicht *n*
overlap	überschneiden
overlapping	Überschneidung *f*
over life-size	überlebensgroß
overpaint	übermalen
overpainting	Übermalung *f*
owner	Besitzer *m*
ownership	Besitz *m*
private —	im Privatbesitz
ownership information	Besitzerangabe *f*
ox skull	Ochsenschädel *m*
oxydation	Oxydation *f*
darkening due to —	Bräunen *n*

pad	Kissen *n*, Polster *n*
padding	Polsterung *f*, Fütterung *f*
page	1. Seite *f*, Blatt *n*
	2. Page *m*
pagoda	Pagode *f*
painstaking	minuziös, sorgfältig
paint *v.*	malen, bemalen, ausmalen, anmalen, streichen, anstreichen, pinseln
paint *n.*	Farbe *f*, Ölfarbe *f*, Malfarbe *f*
paintbox	Malkasten *m*
paintbrush	Pinsel *m*, Malpinsel *m*
painted	bemalt, gemalt, ausgemalt, gefaßt, gestrichen, lackiert
painter	Maler *m*
painter-etcher	Malerradierer *m*, Malerstecher *m*
painterly	malerisch
painter's brush	Malpinsel *m*, Pinsel *m*

painters' guild	Lukasgilde *f*, Malerzunft *f*
painter's manual	Malerbuch *n*, Malerhandbuch *n*
painting	1. Gemälde *n*, Malerei *f*, Malwerk *n*
	2. Malkunst *f*, Malerei *f*
	3. Bemalung *f*, Anstrich *m*, Ausmalung *f*
	4. Fassung *f*
black ink –	Tuschmalerei *f*
genre –	Genrebild *n*, Sittenbild *n*
painting knife	Malmesser *n*
painting on glass	Glasgemälde *n*, Glasmalerei *f*, Hinterglasmalerei *f*, Spiegelmalerei *f*, Eglomisieren *n*
painting on porcelain	Porzellanmalerei *f*, Geschirrmalerei *f*
painting process	Malvorgang *m*
painting supplies	Malbedarf *m*
painting technique	Maltechnik *f*
paint layer	Malschicht *f*
paint medium	Bindemittel *n*, Farbbindemittel *n*, Lösungsmittel *n*
paint pot	Farbtopf *m*
paint saucer	Napf *m*, Farbnapf *m*
paint thinner	Verdünnungsmittel *n*
paint vehicle	Farbbindemittel *n*
pair	Paar *n*
paired	gekoppelt, gekuppelt
palace	Palast *m*, Pfalz *f*, Schloß *n*, Palais *n*
palace and grounds	Schloßanlage *f*, Palastanlage *f*
palace chapel	Schloßkapelle *f*
palace church	Schloßkirche *f*
palace gate	Schloßtor *n*
Palace Style	Palaststil *m*
Palaeologian period	Palaiologenzeitalter *n*
palatial	palastartig, schloßartig
palatine chapel	Pfalzkapelle *f*, Doppelkapelle *f*

Palatine Hill	Palatin *m*
pale	blaß, bleich
paleography	Paläographie *f*
paleolithic	altsteinzeitlich, paläolithisch
Paleolithic Age	Paläolithikum *n*, Altsteinzeit *f*
paleolithic man	Paläolithiker *m*
paleolithic period, lower –	Altpaläolithikum *n*
paleolithic period, upper –	Jungpaläolithikum *n*
palestra	Palästra *f*
palette	Palette *f*
arm –	Armpalette *f*
cosmetic –	Schminkpalette *f*
disposable –	Blockpalette *f*
folding –	Klappalette *f*
palette knife	Palettemesser *n*
palimpsest	Palimpsest *m, n*
palisade	Palisade *f*
palisander	Palisanderholz *n*
pall	Pallium *n*
Palladianism	Palladianismus *m*
Palladium	Palladium *n*
pallium	Pallium *n*
palmette	Palmette *f*
palmiform column	Palmensäule *f*
palstave	Palstab *m*
palynology	Pollenanalyse *f*
Pan	Pan, Hirtengott *m*
Pan-Athenaic amphora	panathenäische Preisamphora *f*
pane	1. Scheibe *f*, Fensterscheibe *f* 2. Fach *n*
panel *v.*	paneelieren, verkleiden, täfeln
panel *n.*	1. Paneel *n* 2. Flügel *m* 3. Tafel *f*
back –	Rückwand *f*
paneling	Paneel *n*, Täfelung *f*, Täfelwerk *n*, Getäfel *n*, Inkrustation *f*, Lambris *m*

panel painting	Tafelbild *n*, Tafelmalerei *f*
panel wall	nicht tragende (Außen-)Wand
panorama	Panorama *n*, Rundbild *n*
panoramic view	Rundansicht *f*, Rundblick *m*
Pantheon	Pantheon *n*
Pantocrator	Pantokrator *m*
pantograph	Pantograph *m*, Storchschnabel *m*
pantographic	pantographisch
pants	Hose *f*
papal cross	päpstliches Kreuz *n*
paper	Papier *n*
paper collage	Papierklebebild *n*
paper stencil	Papierschablone *f*
papier mâché	Papiermasse *f*, Papiermaché *n*, Pappmaché *n*
papiers collés	Papierklebebild *n*
papyrus	Papyrus *m*
papyrus capital	Papyruskapitell *n*
papyrus leaf	Papyrusblatt *n*
papyrus manuscript	Papyrushandschrift *f*, Papyrusrolle *f*
papyrus scroll	Papyrusrolle *f*
parable	Gleichnis *n*
parachute dome	Schirmgewölbe *n*
paradigm	Paradigma *n*
paradise	Paradies *n*
Paradise Garden	Paradiesgärtlein *n*
paradisus	Paradies *n*
paragon	Musterbild *n*, Vorbild *n*
parallel	parallel, Parallel-
parallel perspective	Parallelperspektive *f*
parament	Parament *n*
parapet	Brustwehr *f*, Wehrmauer *f*
parchment *adj.*	pergamenten, Pergament-
parchment *n.*	Pergament *n*
parchment binding	Pergamenteinband *m*
parchment glue	Pergamentleim *m*

parchment paper	Pergamentpapier *n*
parchment scroll	Pergamentrolle *f*
parclose	Altargitter *n*
parergon	Parergon *n*
Parian marble	parischer Marmor *m*
Paris blue	Pariserblau *n*
park	Park *m*, Anlage *f*, Gartenanlage *f*
parquet	Parkett *n*
parquetage	Parkettieren *n*
parquet floor	Parkettboden *m*
part	Partie *f*, Teil *m, n*
partial view	Ausschnitt *m*, Teilansicht *f*
partition	Fach *n*
partition wall	Stellwand *f*, Trennwand *f*, Zwischenmauer *f*, Zwischenwand *f*
parvis	offener Vorhof einer Kirche
passage grave	Ganggrab *n*, Kuppelgrab *n*
Passage Through the Red Sea	Durchgang durch das Rote Meer, Durchzug durch das Rote Meer
passageway	Gang *m*, Laufgang *m*, Korridor *m*
passe-partout	Passepartout *n*, Wechselrahmen *m*
passion	Leidenschaft *f*
Passion, the —	die Leidensgeschichte Christi, die Passion
Passion, Instruments of the —	die Leidenswerkzeuge Christi, die Marterwerkzeuge Christi, die Passionswerkzeuge
passional	Passionale *n*
passionate	leidenschaftlich
passion cycle	Passionszyklus *m*
Passion of Christ	Passionsgeschichte *f*
passion panel	Passionstafel *f*
paste	1. Kleister *m*, Leim *m* 2. Glasfluß *m*, Glaspaste *f*, Paste *f*
pasteboard	Pappe *f*
paste gem	Paste *f*
pastel *adj.*	hellfarbig

pastel n.	1. Pastell n, Pastellbild n, Pastellmalerei f
	2. Pastellfarbe f, Teigfarbe f
pastel artist	Pastellmaler m
pastel crayon	Pastellstift m
pastel drawing	Pastellzeichnung f
pastelist	Pastellmaler m
pastel paint	Teigfarbe f, Pastelfarbe f
pastel painting	Pastell n, Pastellbild n, Pastellmalerei f
pasticcio	Pasticcio n
pastiche	Pasticcio n
pastophory	Pastophorium n
pastoral scene	Hirtenlandschaft f, Hirtenszene f, Schäferszene f, Pastorale n, f
pastoral staff	Bischofsstab m, Krummstab m
pastose painting	pastose Malweise f
patch	Fleck m
patch of color	Farbfleck m
paten	Hostienteller m, Patene f
patina	Patina f
patio	Patio m; offener Lichthof
patriarchal cross	Doppelkreuz n, Erzbischöfliches Kreuz n, Kardinalskreuz n, Patriarchenkreuz n
patrix	Patrize f
patron	Patron m, Auftraggeber m, Gönner m, Mäzen m
patronage	Mäzenatentum n
patroness	Gönnerin f
patron saint	Kirchenpatron m, Patron m, Schutzpatron m
pattern	Muster n, Model m, Modell n, Vorlage f, Patrone f, Schablone f
bead and reel –	Perlenschnur f
checkerboard –	Schachbrettmuster n, Schachbrettfries m

pattern book

diaper —	wiederholtes, rautenförmiges Muster
fish scale —	Schuppenmuster *n*
interlace —	Flechtmuster *n*
meander —	Mäandermuster *n*
nailhead —	Nagelkopf *m*, Diamantband *n*
repeating —	Rapportmuster *n*
rhomboid —	Rautenfries *m*
vine scroll —	Blattfries *m*, Laubfries *m*, Rankenfries *m*
zigzag —	Zackenfries *m*, Zickzackband *n*
pattern book	Modelbuch *n*, Musterbuch *n*, Vorlagebuch *n*, Bauhüttenbuch *n*
pave	pflastern
pavement	Paviment *n*, Pflaster *n*
pavilion	Pavillon *m*
paving stone	Pflasterstein *m*
peace-board	Kußtafel *f*, Osculatorium *n*, Paxtafel *f*, Pacificale *n*
peach black	Kernschwarz *n*
peacock	Pfau *m*
peak	Höhepunkt *m*, Gipfel *m*, Spitze *f*
pearl	Perle *f*
pear-shaped	birnenförmig
pear wood	Birnbaumholz *n*
peasant	Bauer *m*
peasant art	Bauernkunst *f*, Volkskunst *f*
pebble	Kieselstein *m*
Pebble Culture	Geröllkultur *f*
pebble mosaic	Kieselmosaik *n*
pebble tool	Geröllgerät *n*
pectoral	Pektorale *n*
pectoral cross	Pektorale *n*, Brustkeuz *n*
peculiarity	Eigenschaft *f*, Eigentümlichkeit *f*
pedestal	Sockel *m*, Fuß *m*, Piedestal *n*, Postament *n*
pediment	Giebel *m*, Giebelfeld *n*

blind —	Blendgiebel *m*
broken —	gesprengter Giebel *m*
ornamental —	Ziergiebel *m*
triangular —	Dreiecksgiebel *m*
pediment ornamentation	Giebelverzierung *f*
peel off	abblättern
peg *v.*	verdübeln, dübeln
peg *n.*	Dübel *m*, Haken *m*, Stift *m*
pegged mosaic	Stiftmosaik *n*, Tonstiftmosaik *n*
peg hole	Dübelloch *n*
peintre-graveur	Malerradierer *m*, Malerstecher *m*
pelican	Pelikan *m*
pelvis	Becken *n*
pen	Schreiber *m*, Feder *f*
drawing —	Zeichenfeder *f*
quill —	Schreibfeder *f*, Kielfeder *f*
reed —	Rohrfeder *f*, Schilfrohrfeder *f*
pen and ink drawing	Tuschzeichnung *f*
pen-and-wash drawing	lavierte Federzeichnung *f*
pencil	Bleistift *m*, Stift *m*, Zeichenstift *m*, Graphitstift *m*
colored —	Farbstift *m*
pencil drawing	Bleistiftzeichnung *f*
pendant	Abhängling *m*, Berlocke *f*, Anhänger *m*
Pendelikon	pentelisch
pendentive	Hängezwickel *m*, Kuppelzwickel *m*, Eckzwickel *m*, Pendentif *n*
penetrate	durchdringen
pentacle	Drudenfuß *m*, Pentagramm *n*
pentagram	Drudenfuß *m*, Pentagramm *n*
pentastyle	fünfsäulig
pentateuch	Pentateuch *m*
Pentecost	Pfingsten *n, f*, die Ausgießung des Heiligen Geist
miracle of —	Pfingstwunder *n*

pentimenti	Pentimenti *pl*
peplos	Peplos *m*
peplus	Peplos *m*
perceive	empfinden, wahrnehmen
perception	Empfinden *n*, Wahrnehmung *f*, Auffassungskraft *f*
perfect *adj.*	vollendet, vollkommen, makellos, perfekt
perfect *v.*	vollenden, vervollkommnen
perfection	Vollkommenheit *f*
perforate	durchlöchern, perforieren
perforating wheel	Punktierrad *n*, Pausrad *n*
perforation	Perforation *f*
Pergamene art	pergamenische Kunst *f*
Pergamum Altar	Pergamon-Altar *m*
pergola	Laubengang *m*, Pergola *f*
pericope book	Perikopenbuch *n*
period	Epoche *f*, Zeit *f*, Periode *f*
peripatos	Wandelgang *m*, Wandelhalle *f*
peripheral roof girder	Dachrandträger *m*
peripteral temple	Peripteros *m*
peristalith	Kreis von aufrecht stehenden, ein Hügelgrab umschließenden Steinen
peristyle	Peristyl *n*
permanent green	Permanentgrün *n*
permanent white	Barytweiß *n*
perpendicular	senkrecht
Perpendicular	Spätgotik *f*
Perpendicular Style	Perpendikularstil *m*
perron	Beischlag *m*
Persian	persisch
Persian dump	Perserschutt *m*
person	Mensch *m*, Person *f*
personal style	Persönlichkeitsstil *m*
personification	Personifizierung *f*, Personifikation *f*, Verkörperung *f*

personify	personifizieren, verkörpern
perspective *adj.*	perspektivisch
perspective *n.*	Perspektive *f*
aerial −	Luftperspektive *f*
angular −	Strahlenperspektive *f*
center of −	Augenpunkt *m*
inverted −	umgekehrte Perspektive *f*
linear −	Linearperspektive *f*
oblique −	Strahlenperspektive *f*
parallel −	Parallelperspektive *f*
petroglyph	Felsbild *n*, Felsmalerei *f*, Felsritzung *f*, Felszeichnung *f*, Steininschrift *f*
Pettenkofer process	Pettenkofersches Verfahren *n*
pews	Gestühl *n*
pewter	Zinn *n*
pewter vessel	Zinngefäß *n*
Pharaoh	Pharao *m*
phenomenon	Phänomen *n*, Erscheinung *f*
phiale	Phiale *f*
philosopher sarcophagus	Philosophensarkophag *m*
philosophy	Philosophie *f*
philosophy of art	Kunstphilosophie *f*
Phoenician	phönizisch
Phoenix	Phönix *m*
photo	Aufnahme *f*, Foto *n*, Photo *n*
photo collage	Fotomontage *f*
photograph *v.*	photographieren, aufnehmen
photograph *n.*	Photo *n*, Foto *n*
photographer	Fotograph *m*, Photograph *m*
photography	Photographie *f*
photogravure	Photogravüre *f*, Heliogravüre *f*
photomontage	Photomontage *f*
phototype	Lichtdruck *m*
phototypic process	Lichtdruck *m*
Phrygian	phrygisch
phylacteries	Phylakterien *pl*, Gebetsriemen *pl*

phylakikoi	Phylakenvase *f*
physiognomy	Physiognomie *f*
Physiologus	Physiologus *m*
pictography	Piktographie *f*, Bilderschrift *f*
pictorial	bildlich, bildnerisch
pictorial art	Bildkunst *f*
pictorial concept	Bildvorstellung *f*
pictorial language	Bildsprache *f*
pictorial program	Bilderprogramm *n*, Bildprogramm *n*
picture	Bild *n*
picture allegory	Bildgleichnis *n*
picture composition	Bildaufbau *m*, Bildgestaltung *f*
picture content	Bildinhalt *m*
picture cycle	Bilderzyklus *m*
picture depth	Bildtiefe *f*
picture field	Bildfeld *n*
picture frame	Bilderrahmen *m*
picture parable	Bildgleichnis *n*
picture plane	Bildebene *f*, Bildfläche *f*, Bildoberfläche *f*
picture post card	Ansichtskarte *f*
picturesque	malerisch
picture structure	Bildaufbau *m*, Bildgefüge *n*
picture theme	Bildthema *n*, Bildinhalt *m*, Sujet *n*
picture type	Bildgattung *f*, Bildtypus *m*
picture within a picture	Einsatzbild *n*
piece	Stück *n*, Werk *n*
piece mold casting	Detailguß *m*
piece of clothing	Kleidungsstück *n*
piece of furniture	Möbelstück *n*
piece of jewelry	Schmuckstück *n*
pier	Pfeiler *m*
angular —	Eckpfeiler *m*
clustered —	Bündelpfeiler *m*
compound —	Bündelpfeiler *m*

crossing –	Vierungspfeiler *m*
engaged –	Wandpfeiler *m*
wall –	Wandpfeiler *m*
pier arch	Pfeilerbogen *m*
pier buttress	Strebepfeiler *m*
pier church	Wandpfeilerkirche *f*
pietà	Pietà *f*, Vesperbild *n*
pietra dura	Florentiner Mosaik *n*
pigment	Pigment *n*, Farbe *f*, Farbkörper *m*, Farbstoff *m*
pilaster	Pilaster *m*
pilaster-strip	Lesene *f*, Lisene *f*
Pilate Washing His Hands	die Handwaschung des Pilatus
pile	Pfahl *m*
carpet –	Flor *m*
pilgrim	Pilger *m*
pilgrimage church	Pilgerkirche *f*, Wallfahrtskirche *f*
pilgrimage road	Pilgerstraße *f*
pillar	Pfeiler *m*
corner –	Eckpfeiler *m*
crossing –	Vierungspfeiler *m*
engaged –	Wandpfeiler *m*
pillar figure	Pfeilerfigur *f*
pillars, distance between –	Pfeilerabstand *m*
pillars, supported by –	pfeilergestützt
pin	Nadel *f*, Pinne *f*, Stift *m*
Pinacotheca	Pinakothek *f*
pine	Fichte *f*, Kiefernholz *n*, Pinie *f*
pine cone	Pinienzapfen *m*
pine cone motif	Pinienzapfen *m*
pine oil	Kienöl *n*
pine-soot black	Kienruß *m*
pink	rosa, rosarot, blaßrot
pinnacle	Fiale *f*
pinnacle with finial	Riesen *m*
pinx.	pinx.
Pisces	Fisch *m*

pisciform	fischförmig
piscina	Piscina *f*
pitch	1. Pech *n*
	2. Neigung *f*, Schräge *f*, Gefälle *n*
pitched roof	Steildach *n*
pitcher	Kanne *f*, Gießgefäß *n*, Krug *m*
Pit-comb ware	Kamm- und Grübchenkeramik *f*
pithos	Pithos *m*
pix	s. pyx
place *v.*	1. lokalisieren
	2. stellen, legen, hängen
place *n.*	Ort *m*, Platz *m*, Stelle *f*
placement	Orientierung *f*
place of discovery	Fundort *m*
place of origin	Lokalisierung *f*, Entstehungsort *m*
placing	Lokalisierung *f*
plafond	Plafond *m*
plafond painting	Plafondmalerei *f*
plain	einfach, schlicht, schmucklos
plainness	Schmucklosigkeit *f*, Einfachheit *f*
plait *v.*	flechten
plait *n.*	Geflecht *n*, Zopf *m*
plaited pattern	Flechtmuster *n*
plaiting	Geflecht *n*
plait-work	Flechtwerk *n*
plan *v.*	planen, entwerfen
plan *n.*	Plan *m*, Programm *n*, Entwurf *m*, Grundriß *m*, Riß *m*, Schema *n*, System *n*, Visierung *f*, Zeichnung *f*
planar	flächenhaft, flächig
planar style	Flächenstil *m*
plane	Fläche *f*, Ebene *f*
plane of intersection	Schnittfläche *f*
plane of symmetry	Symmetrieebene *f*
planet	Planet *m*
planish	planieren, hämmern

planishing hammer	Planierhammer *m*
plank	Brett *n*, Diele *f*, Bohle *f*
planographic printing	Flachdruck *m*
plant	Pflanze *f*
plaque	Plakette *f*
plaquette	Plakette *f*
plaster *v.*	verputzen
plaster *n.*	1. Putz *m*, Stuck *m*, Verputz *m* Bewurf *m*, Wandbewurf *m*, Wandputz *m* 2. Gips *m*
plaster cast	Gipsabguß *m*
plaster coat	Putz *m*, Verputz *m*, Bewurf *m*
plastered	verputzt
plasterer	Stukkateur *m*
plaster layer	Putzschicht *f*
plaster model	Gipsmodell *n*
plaster of Paris	Gips *m*
plaster work	Putzarbeit *f*
plastic *adj.*	1. plastisch, anschaulich 2. Kunstoff-
plastic *n.*	Kunststoff *m*, Plastik *n*
plastic arts	bildende Kunst *f*
plasticity	Plastizität *f*
plate *v.*	plattieren
plate *n.*	1. Platte *f* 2. Teller *m* 3. Tafel *f*, Illustration *f*, Abbildung *f*
plate mark	Prägung des Druckplattenrandes
Plateresque style	Platereskenstil *m*
plate with chrome	verchromen
plate with gold	vergolden
plate with nickel	vernickeln
plate with silver	versilbern
platform	Plattform *f*
platinum	Platin *n*
playing card	Spielkarte *f*

pleasure palace	Lustschloß *n*
pleated	plissiert
plein air painting	Pleinair-Malerei *f*, Freilichtmalerei *f*
plexiglas	Plexiglas *n*, Akrylglas *n*
pliable	biegsam, dehnbar
plinth	Plinthe *f*, Säulenfuß *m*
plique-à-jour	Drahtemail *n*
ploughshare twist	Busung *f*
plumbate ware	Plumbate-Keramik *f*, Bleiglanzkeramik *f*
plutonic rock	Tiefengestein *n*
plywood	Sperrholz *n*
pochade	flüchtige Skizze *f*
pocket	Tasche *f*
podium	Podium *n*, Podest *n*
point *v.*	1. punktieren 2. ausfugen
point *n.*	1. Punkt *m* 2. Spitze *f* 3. Bossiereisen *n*, Spitzeisen *n*, Spitzmeißel *m*
vanishing —	Fluchtpunkt *m*
pointed	spitz, Spitz-
pointed arch	Spitzbogen *m*
pointed chisel	Spitzmeißel *m*
pointed quatrefoil	Vierblatt *n*
Pointillism	Pointillismus *m*, Neoimpressionismus *m*
Pointillist	Pointillist *m*
pointing machine	Punktiergerät *n*, Punktiermaschine *f*
point of intersection	Schnittpunkt *m*
point of sight	Augenpunkt *m*
point of station	Auge *n*, Augenpunkt *m*, Betrachtungspunkt *m*
polish *v.*	polieren, glätten, schleifen
polish *n.*	Schliff *m*, Politur *f*, Glanz *m*

polisher	Schleifer *m*
polishing	Glättung *f*
polishing material	Glättungsmittel *n*
politically committed	engagiert
politically committed art	politisch engagierte Kunst *f*
pollen analysis	Pollenanalyse *f*
polychrome	mehrfarbig, polychrom, vielfarbig
polychrome woodcut	Vielfarbenholzschnitt *m*
polychromy	Polychromie *f*
polyester resin	Polyesterharz *n*, Esterharz *n*
polygon	Polygon *n*, Vieleck *n*
polygonal	polygonal, vieleckig
polygonal masonry	polygonales Mauerwerk *n*
polymer color	Polymer *n*
polyptych	Polyptychon *n*
polyptych altar	Flügelaltar *m*
polyurethane	Polyurethan *n*
pomegranate	Granatapfel *m*
pomegranate pattern	Granatapfelmuster *n*
Pompeian	pompeianisch, pompejanisch
ponderous	wuchtig, schwer
pontifical book	Pontifikale *n*
pontifical vestments	Pontifikale *n*
Pop Art	Pop-Art *f*
pope	Papst *m*
poplar wood	Pappel *f*
poppy oil	Mohnöl *n*
poppyseed oil	Mohnöl *n*
porcelain *adj.*	porzellanen, Porzellan-
porcelain *n.*	Porzellan *n*
painting on –	Porzellanmalerei *f*
porcelain sculpture	Porzellanplastik *f*
porcelain vessel	Porzellangefäß *n*
porch	Veranda *f*, Vorhalle *f*
poros stone	Porostein *m*
porphyry	Porphyr *m*

portable altar	Tragaltar *m*, Itinerarium *n*, Portatile *n*, Reisealtärchen *n*
portable baldachin	Traghimmel *m*, Reiseziborium *n*
portal	Portal *n*
portal sculpture	Portalplastik *f*
portcrayon	Stifthalter *m*
portcullis	Fallgatter *n*
portfolio	Mappe *f*, Mappenfolge *f*, Mappenwerk *n*
portico	Portikus *m*
portion	1. Teil *m, n* 2. Teilansicht *f*
Portland cement	Portlandzement *m*
Portland vase	Portlandvase *f*
portrait	Porträt *n*, Portrait *n*, Bildnis *n*, Brustbild *n*, Konterfei *n*
donor —	Stifterbildnis *n*
family —	Familienbildnis *n*
portrait bust	Bildnisbüste *f*, Porträtbüste *f*
portrait engraver	Bildnisstecher *m*
portrait etching	Bildnisradierung *f*
portraitist	Porträtist *m*
portrait painter	Bildnismaler *m*
portrait painting	Bildnismalerei *f*
portrait study	Porträtstudie *f*
portrait style	Bildnisstil *m*
portray	darstellen, abbilden, schildern, porträtieren
portrayal	Darstellung *f*, Schilderung *f*
pose *v.*	posieren
pose *n.*	Pose *f*
position	Position *f*, Stellung *f*, Haltung *f*, Orientierung *f*
post	Pfosten *m*, Pfahl *m*, Stollen *m*
post-and-lintel construction	Balkenbauart *f*
poster	Plakat *n*
poster art	Plakatkunst *f*

poster color	Plakatfarbe *f*
poster montage	Plakatmontage *f*
postern	Schlüpfpforte *f*
poster paint	Plakatfarbe *f*
poster style	Plakatstil *m*
Post-Impressionism	Nachimpressionismus *m*
Post-Impressionist	Nachimpressionist *m*
Post-Painterly Abstraction	die Neue Abstraktion *f*, Nachmalerische Abstraktion *f*
posture	Haltung *f*
post-war period	Nachkriegszeit *f*
pot	Kessel *m*, Topf *m*
potash	Pottasche *f*
potent cross	Krückenkreuz *n*
potsherd	Vasenfragment *n*
potter	Töpfer *m*
potter's clay	Töpfererde *f*, Töpferton *m*
potter's kickwheel	Tretscheibe *f*
potter's wheel	Töpferscheibe *f*
potter's workshop	Töpferei *f*
pottery	Töpferei *f*, Töpfergeschirr *n*, Töpferware *f*, Töpferzeug *n*
clay —	Tonware *f*
pottery making	Töpferkunst *f*
pounce	punzen
pounce powder	Pauspulver *n*
pour	gießen
pouring vessel	Gießgefäß *n*
powdered rosin	Kolophoniumstaub *m*
power	Macht *f*, Kraft *f*
power of expression	Ausdruckskraft *f*, Aussagekraft *f*
power of observation	Beobachtungsgabe *f*
Pozzuoli red	Puzzolanerde *f*
prayer	Gebet *n*
prayer book	Gebetbuch *n*
prayer niche	Mihrab *m*, Gebetsnische *f*
prayer rug	Gebetsteppich *m*

prayer wheel	Gebetsmühle *f*
prearchaic	vorarchaisch
pre-Caesar	vorkaiserlich
pre-Carolingian	vorkarolingisch
precast concrete unit	Beton-Fertigelement *n*
pre-Christian	vorchristlich
precious	edel, kostbar, Edel-
precious metal	Edelmetall *n*
precious object	Kleinod *n*, Kostbarkeit *f*
precious stone	Edelstein *m*
precious wood	Edelholz *n*
precipitated chalk	Schlämmkreide *f*
precipitated gold	Goldpurpur *m*
pre-Columbian	präkolumbianisch
predecessor	Vorgänger *m*
predella	Predella *f*, Altarunterbau *m*, Staffel *f*
prefabricate	vorfabrizieren, vorfertigen
prefabricated building part	Bauelement *n*, Fertigteil *n*
prefabricated construction	Fertigbauweise *f*
prefabricated element	Fertigteil *n*
prehistoric	vorgeschichtlich, prähistorisch
prehistory	Prähistorie *f*, Vorgeschichte *f*
pre-Imperial	vorkaiserlich
preliminary drawing	Vorzeichnung *f*, Entwurfszeichnung *f*, Ideenskizze *f*, Karton *m*
Pre-Raphaelites	Präraffaeliten *pl*
pre-Romanesque	vorromanisch
presbytery	Presbyterium *n*
present	Gegenwart *f*
Presentation in the Temple, the —	die Darstellung Jesu im Tempel, die Weihe Jesu im Tempel
Presentation of the Virgin	Mariä Tempelgang, der Tempelgang Mariä
preservation	Erhaltung *f*
preserve	1. erhalten, bewahren, konservieren 2. überliefern

press	Druckerei *f*, Druckerpresse *f*, Offizin *f*
pressure	Druck *m*
distribution of —	Druckverteilung *f*
pressure-sensitive tape	Klebestreifen *m*
prestressed concrete	Spannbeton *m*
prettiness	Lieblichkeit *f*
pretty	lieblich, schön
priceless	unschätzbar
priest	Priester *m*, Geistliche *m*
priestess	Priesterin *f*
priesthood	Priesterschaft *f*
primary color	Primärfarbe *f*, Grundfarbe *f*
prime	grundieren
primed canvas	grundierte Leinwand *f*
priming	Grundierung *f*
primitive art	primitive Kunst *f*, naturvölkische Kunst *f*
primitive people	Naturvolk *n*
prince	Fürst *m*, Prinz *m*
princely	fürstlich, prinzlich
princess	Fürstin *f*, Prinzessin *f*
principality	Fürstentum *n*
principle	Prinzip *n*
print *v.*	drucken
print *n.*	Druck *m*, Abdruck *m*
printed graphics	Druckgrafik *f*
printer	Drucker *m*
printer's ink	Schwärze *f*, Druckerschwärze *f*
printing	Druckkunst *f*, Buchdruck *m*
printing block	1. Klischee *n*, Druckstock *m* 2. Model *m*
printing ink	Schwärze *f*, Druckerschwärze *f*
printing plate	Druckplatte *f*, Druckstock *m*
printing press	Druckerei *f*, Druckpresse *f*
printing process	Druckverfahren *n*
printing shop	Druckerei *f*, Druckerpresse *f*, Offizin *f*

printing stencil | Druckschablone *f*
printing technique | Drucktechnik *f*
prints pulled, number of — | Auflagenhöhe *f*
prism | Prisma *n*
prismatic color | Regenbogenfarbe *f*
private collection | Privatsammlung *f*
private ownership | im Privatbesitz
private residence | Privathaus *n*
procedure | Verfahren *n*, Prozeß *m*
process | Verfahren *n*, Prozeß *m*
process art | Prozeßkunst *f*
procession | Prozession *f*, Zug *m*
processional cross | Vortragekreuz *n*
processional statue | Tragfigur *f*
processional street | Prozessionsstraße *f*
Procession to Calvary | der Kreuzweg
Prodigal Son, the — | der verlorene Sohn
productive | fruchtbar
profile | Profil *n*, Profilansicht *f*, Kantenansicht *f*
  bell-shaped — | Glockenleiste *f*
  cross sectional — | Querschnittform *f*
  scotia — | Hohlkehle *f*, dorisches Kymation *n*
  S-shaped — | Karnies *n*
profil perdu | verlorenes Profil *n*
program | Programm *n*
project *v.* | ausladen, vorspringen
project *n.* | Projekt *n*
projection | Ausladung *f*, Auskragung *f*, Vorsprung *m*
Proletcult | Proletkult *m*
prolific | fruchtbar
prolificacy | Fruchtbarkeit *f*
promenade | Promenade *f*, Wandelanlage *f*
Prometheus Bound | der gefesselte Prometheus
pronaos | Pronaos *m*

proof	Abzug *m*
proof after letter	nach der Schrift
proof before letter	vor der Schrift
prop	stützen
prophet	Prophet *m*
proportion	Proportion *f*, Größenverhältnis *n*, Maßstab *m*, Maßverhältnis *n*
theory of —	Proportionslehre *f*
proportioning	Proportionierung *f*
propylaeum	Propyläen *pl*
proscenium	Proszenium *n*
prostyle	prostyl
prostyle temple	Prostylos *m*
protective deity	Schutzgottheit *f*
prothesis	Prothesis *f*
proto-Corinthian vase	protokorinthische Vase *f*
protogeometric	protogeometrisch
protohistory	Urgeschichte *f*
protome	Protome *f*
Proto-Renaissance	Protorenaissance *f*
prototype	Prototyp *m*, Urbild *n*, Vorbild *n*, Vorform *f*, Vorlage *f*
prototype shape	Urform *f*
protrude	hervortreten, auskragen, vorspringen
protrusion	Auskragung *f*, Vorsprung *m*, Hervortreten *n*
provenance	Provenienz *f*, Überlieferung *f*, Überlieferungsgeschichte *f*
prunts	Tropfenauflage *f*
Prussian blue	Berlinerblau *n*, Pariserblau *n*, Preußischblau *n*
Psalter	Psalter *m*
pseudo-dipteral temple	Pseudodipteros *m*
pseudodome	falsches Gewölbe *n*, Kraggewölbe *n*
pseudo-peripteral temple	Pseudoperipteros *m*
psykter	Psykter *m*

public square	Platz *m*
pull *printing*	abziehen
pulpit	Kanzel *f*
pulpit rail	Kanzelbrüstung *f*
pumice	Bimsstein *m*
punch *v.*	punzen, stanzen
punch *n.*	Punze *f*, Stecheisen *n*, Stanze *f*, Stempel *m*
punch in	einpunzen
pupil	Schüler *m*
pure	echt, rein
pure color	reinbunte Farbe *f*
purism	Purismus *m*
purist	Purist *m*
purity	Reinheit *f*
purlin	Hahnenbalken *m*, Pfette *f*
purple	lila
purpose	Zweck *m*
purpurin	Purpurin *n*
purse	Burse *f*, Geldbeutel *m*, Tasche *f*
putlog	Baugerüst *n*, Rüstbalken *m*, Rüststange *f*
putlog hole	Rüstloch *n*
putto	Putte *f*, Putto *m*
putty	Kitt *m*
Puzzolana	Puzzolanerde *f*
pylon	Pylon *m*, Pylone *f*
pyramid	Pyramide *f*
pyramidal	**pyramidenförmig, Pyramiden-**
pyramidal composition	Pyramidenkomposition *f*
pyx	Pyxis *f*, Hostienbüchse *f*, Hostiengefäß *n*, Custodia *f*, Kustodia *f*
pyxis	s. pyx
qibla	Qibla *f*, Kibla *f*
quadrangle	von Gebäuden umschlossener, rechteckiger Hof

quadrangular	viereckig
quadrant arch	einhüftiger Bogen *m*, steigender Bogen *m*, Strebebogen *m*
quadrant moulding	Viertelstab *m*
quadriga	Quadriga *f*, Viergespann *n*
quality	1. Qualität *f* 2. Eigenschaft *f*
quarter round	Viertelstab *m*
quartz	Quarz *m*
quartefoil	Vierpaß *m*
quattrocento	Quattrocento *n*
queen-post roof construction	doppeltstehender Dachstuhl *m*
quercitron	Querzetin *n*
quill	Kiel *m*
quill pen	Kielfeder *f*, Schreibfeder *f*
quipu	Quipu *n*, Knotenschnüre *f*
Quirinal Hill	Quirin *m*
quoin	1. Eckstein *m* 2. mit Ecksteinen versehene Gebäudeecke
rabbet	Fuge *f*
rabbitskin glue	Polimentleim *m*
radial symmetry	Radialsymmetrie *f*, Strahlensymmetrie *f*
radiance	Glanz *m*, Strahlkraft *f*
radiant	leuchtend, glänzend, strahlend
radiant power	Leuchtkraft *f*, Strahlkraft *f*
radiate	strahlen
radiocarbon dating	Radiokarbondatierung *f*, Radiokarbonmethode *f*
radiography	Radiographie *f*
radius	Radius *m*, Halbmesser *m*
raffia	Raphia *f*
rafter	Dachbalken *m*, Sparren *m*
rafters	Gesparr *n*, Sparrenwerk *n*

ragged	lappenartig, gelappt
railing	Brüstung *f*, Geländer *n*
rainbow	Regenbogen *m*
raise	1. heben, erheben
	2. errichten, aufrichten
Raising Lazarus From the Dead	die Erweckung des Lazarus
Raising of the Cross, the —	die Kreuzaufrichtung
Raising of the Dead, the —	die Auferweckung der Toten
raking geison	Schräggeison *n*
ram	Widder *m*
ramp	Rampe *f*
rampart	Wall *m*, Wallanlage *f*
rampart church	Wehrkirche *f*
rampart complex	Wallanlage *f*
range of colors	Farbskala *f*
Rape of Europa, the —	der Raub der Europa
Rape of the Sabine Women, the —	der Raub der Sabinerinnen
rare	selten, rar
rare wood	Edelholz *n*
rasp	Raspel *f*
ravelin	Wallschild *m*
raw	roh, unbearbeitet
raw sienna	Tierra di Siena natur
raw silk	Rohseide *f*, Bastseide *f*
ray	Strahl *m*
ray of light	Lichtstrahl *m*
Rayonnism	Rayonismus *m*
ready-made	Ready-made *n*
real	echt, wahr
realgar	Rauschrot *n*, Realgar *m*
realism	Realismus *m*
Realism	Realismus *m*
Realist	Realist *m*
realistic	realistisch
reality	Wirklichkeit *f*

depiction of —	Wirklichkeitsdarstellung *f*
faithfulness to —	Wirklichkeitstreue *f*
realm	Reich *n*
rebate	Fuge *f*
rebite	nachätzen, nachbeizen
rebuild	umbauen, wiederaufbauen
recanvas	doublieren
recede	zurücktreten, zurückspringen
recent	jung, neu
reception	Aufnahme *f*, Empfang *m*
recess	Vertiefung *f*, Nische *f*, Kerbe *f*
reciprocal effect	Wechselwirkung *f*
recline	liegen
reconstruct	rekonstruieren
reconstruction	Rekonstruktion *f*, Ergänzung *f*, Wiederaufbau *m*
reconstruction drawing	Rekonstruktionszeichnung *f*
rectangle	Rechteck *n*
rectangular	rechteckig, rechtwinklig, Rechteck-
rectangular temple	Rechtecktempel *m*
rectified turpentine	rektifiziertes Terpentinöl *n*
red	rot
red-brown	siena
red chalk	Rötel *m*
red chalk crayon	Rötelstift *m*
red chalk drawing	Rötelzeichnung *f*
red chalk pencil	Rötelstift *m*
reddish	rötlich
red earth color	Eisenoxyd *n*
Redeemer	Erlöser *m*
red-figured	rotfigurig
red iron oxide	Eisenoxyd *n*
rediscover	wiederentdecken
rediscovery	Wiederentdeckung *f*
red lead	Bleimennige *f*, Mennig *m*, Mennige *f*
red ochre	Eisenocker *m*

red resin	Drachenblut *n*
red sable brush	Rotmarderpinsel *m*
redye	nachfärben
reed	Riet *n*, Schilf *n*
reeded glass	Fadenglas *n*, Filigranglas *n*
reeding	Fadenauflage *f*
reed pen	Rohrfeder *f*, Schilfrohrfeder *f*
refectory	Refektorium *n*, Remter *m*
reference	Anlehnung *f*
refine	verfeinern
reflect	wiederspiegeln
reflection	Spiegelbild *n*, Spiegelung *f*
refraction	Brechung *f*, Lichtbrechung *f*
refractive index	Brechungsindex *m*
regenerate	regenerieren
regent-piece	Regentenstück *n*
region	Region *f*, Gebiet *n*, Gegend *f*, Areal *n*
register	1. Verzeichnis *n* 2. Zone *f*
register guide	Anleger *m*
reglet	Reglette *f*, Durchschuß *m*
regula	Regula *f*
regular	regelmäßig, gleichmäßig
regularity	Regelmäßigkeit *f*, Gesetzmäßigkeit *f*
regulus	Regula *f*
reindeer	Ren *n*, Rentier *n*
reindeer antler	Rentiergeweih *n*
reinforce	verstärken
reinforced concrete	Eisenbeton *m*, Stahlbeton *m*
relationship	Verhältnis *n*, Beziehung *f*, Verbindung *f*, Verwandschaft *f*
relic	Reliquie *f*
relic collection	Heiltum *n*
relief	Relief *n*
counter —	Kontra-Relief *n*

decorated in —	reliefverziert, reliefiert
in —	reliefiert, erhaben, Relief-
stiacciato —	gequetschtes Relief *n*
relief decoration	Reliefdekor *m*
relief-like	reliefartig, reliefmäßig
reliefware	Reliefware *f*
relieving arch	Entlastungsbogen *m*
religion	Religion *f*
religious	geistlich, religiös
reline	doublieren
relining	Doublieren *n*
reliquary	Reliquiar *n*, Reliquienbehälter *m*, Reliquienschrank *m*, Reliquienschrein *m*
arm-shaped —	Brachiarium *n*
head-shaped —	Kopfreliquiar *n*
remains	Überrest *m*, Rest *m*, Überbleibsel *n*, Rudiment *n*
remarque proof	Remarquedruck *m*
remnant	Überbleibsel *n*, Rest *m*, Überrest *m*
Renaissance	Renaissance *f*
render	wiedergeben, darstellen
rendering	Wiedergabe *f*, Darstellung *f*
renew	erneuern
renovate	umbauen, erneuern, renovieren, wiederherstellen
repeating pattern	Rapportmuster *n*
replica	Replik *f*, Replika *f*
Repose on the Flight to Egypt	die Ruhe auf der Flucht
repoussé	getriebene Arbeit *f*, Treibarbeit *f*
repoussoir	Repoussoir *n*
represent	darstellen
representation	Darstellung *f*, Schilderung *f*
representational	gegenständlich
reproduce	reproduzieren, wiedergeben

reproduction	Reproduktion *f*, Abdruck *m*, Wiedergabe *f*
reproduction process	Reproduktionsverfahren *n*
reredos	Altarrückwand *f*, Retabel *n*
reserve	Aussparung *f*
residence	1. Residenz *f* 2. Wohnhaus *n*
residential architecture	Wohnarchitektur *f*
residential building	Wohnbau *m*, Wohnhaus *n*, Wohnblock *m*
residential tower	Wohnturm *m*
resin	Harz *n*
resin-wax paint	Harzwachsfarbe *f*
resist	Reservage *f*
resist dyeing	Reservedruck *m*
respond	Dienst *m*
clustered —	Dienstbündel *n*
round-profiled —	Runddienst *m*
rest	Auflage *f*
Rest on the Flight to Egypt	die Ruhe auf der Flucht
restoration	Restaurierung *f*, Wiederherstellung *f*, Ergänzung *f*, Erneuerung *f*
restoration of paintings	Gemälderestaurierung *f*
restore	restaurieren, wiederherstellen, ergänzen, erneuern
result	Folge *f*, Ergebnis *n*
results	Befund *m*, Ergebnisse *pl*
Resurrection, the —	die Auferstehung
retable	Retabel *n*, Altaraufsatz *m*
retaining wall	Futtermauer *f*, Stützmauer *f*
reticular	netzartig, Netz-
reticulated vault	Netzgewölbe *n*
retinue	Gefolge *n*, Hofstaat *m*
retouch	retuschieren
retouched spot	Retusche *f*
retrospective	Retrospektive *f*

Return of the Prodigal Son, the —	die Heimkehr des verlorenen Sohnes, die Rückkehr des verlorenen Sohnes
reveal	Leibung *f*, Laibung *f*
revelation	Offenbarung *f*
Revelation, the —	die Offenbarung
reverse	Revers *m*
revetment	Verkleidung *f*
review	Kritik *f*, Besprechung *f*
Rhodian	rhodisch
rhomboid	Rhomboid *n*
rhomboid pattern	Rautenfries *m*
rhomboid roof	Rhombendach *n*
rhombus	Rhombus *m*, Raute *f*
rhythm	Reihung *f*, Rhythmus *m*
rhyton	Rhyton *n*, Kopfgefäß *n*, Tiergefäß *n*
rib	Rippe *f*, Gewölberippe *f*
ribbed dome	Rippenkuppel *f*
ribbed vaulting	Rippenwölbung *f*
ribbon	Band *n*
ribs	Rippenwerk *n*
rib vault	Rippengewölbe *n*, Kreuzrippengewölbe *n*
rich	satt, reich
rich in contrast	kontrastreich
rider	Reiter *m*
ridge	First *m*
ridge beam	Firstbalken *m*
ridged roof	Firstdach *n*
ridge-turret	Dachreiter *m*
right-angled	rechtwinklig, rechteckig
rigid	hart, starr
rigidity	Starrheit *f*
ring	Ring *m*, Reif *m*, Bund *m*, Öse *f*
rise	Stichhöhe *f*, Pfeilhöhe *f*
riser	1. Luftkanal *m* 2. Setzstufe *f*, Steigung *f*

rite	Ritus *m*
ritual *adj.*	rituell
ritual *n.*	Ritual *n*
ritual book	Ritual *n*
Rivers of Paradise	die vier Paradiesflüsse
rivet *v.*	nieten, annieten
rivet *n.*	Niet *m*, Niete *f*
roadside cross	Betsäule *f*, Bildstock *m*, Marterl *n*
robe	Gewand *n*, Ornat *n*
rocaille	Rocaille *f, n*, Grottenwerk *n*
rock	Fels *m*
rock crystal	Bergkristall *m*
rock-cut temple	Felsentempel *m*
rock-cut tomb	Felsgrab *n*, Felskammergrab *n*
rock drawing	Felszeichnung *f*
rock engraving	Felsritzung *f*
rocker	Granierstahl *m*, Wiegeeisen *n*
rock formation	Felsenformation *f*
rock painting	Felsbild *n*, Felsmalerei *f*
rock relief	Felsrelief *n*
rock shelter	Abri *m*
rockwork	Rocaille *f, n*, Grottenwerk *n*
rococo	Rokoko *n*
rod	Stab *m*
roemer	Römer *m*
Roland column	Roland *m*, Rolandsäule *f*
role	Rolle *f*
roller	Handwalze *f*, Walze *f*
roll moulding	Rollenfries *m*
roll painting	Rollenbild *n*
Roman *adj.*	römisch
Roman *n.*	Römer *m*
Roman arch	Rundbogen *m*
Romanesque	romanisch
Romanesque period	Romanik *f*
Romanesque style	Romanik *f*

Romanism	Romanismus *m*
Romanist	Romanist *m*
Roman linen canvas	Römisches Leinen *n*
Romantic	Romantiker *m*
romantic	romantisch
Romanticism	Romantik *f*
Romantic style	Romantik *f*
Roman times	Römerzeit *f*
Roman world	Römertum *n*
Rome	Rom
ancient –	Römertum *n*
rood	Triumphbalken *m*, Triumphbogen *m*
rood altar	Laienaltar *m*, Lettneraltar *m*
rood beam	Apostelbalken *m*, Triumphbalken *m*
rood crucifixion group	Triumphkreuzgruppe *f*
rood loft	Chorempore *f*
rood screen	Altarschranke *f*, Chorgitter *n*, Chorschranke *f*, Lettner *m*
roof	Dach *n*
conical –	Kegeldach *n*
flat –	Flachdach *n*
helm –	Rautendach *n*
hipped –	gewalmtes Dach *n*, Walmdach *n*
mansard –	Mansarde *f*, Mansardendach *n*
pitched –	Steildach *n*
rhomboid –	Rhombendach *n*
ridged –	Firstdach *n*
saddleback –	Giebeldach *n*, Satteldach *n*
sawtooth –	Sägedach *n*, Sheddach *n*
shingle –	Schindeldach *n*
tetrahedron –	Zeltdach *n*
thatched –	Strohdach *n*
truncated –	Flachdach *n*
roof beam	Dachbalken *m*
roof brace	Knagge *f*, Knieverstrebung *f*

roof construction	Dachkonstruktion *f*
roof cornice	Dachgesims *n*
roofed	überdacht
roof garden	Dachgarten *m*
roof girder	Dachträger *m*
peripheral —	Dachrandträger *m*
roof hip	Walm *m*
roofing	Überdachung *f*
roofing material	Dachdeckung *f*, Dachbelag *m*
roofing paper	Dachpappe *f*
roof-like	dachartig
roof overhang	Dachüberstand *m*
roof ridge	Dachfirst *m*
roof shape	Dachform *f*
roof substructure	Unterdach *n*
roof tile	Dachziegel *m*
roof truss	Dachstuhl *m*
open —	offener Dachstuhl *m*
roof undersurface	Dachuntersicht *f*
room	1. Zimmer *n*, Raum *m*, Räumlichkeit *f*, Gemach *n* 2. Platz *m*, Raum *m*, Räumlichkeit *f*
room divider	Raumteiler *m*
rosary	Rosenkranz *m*
rose *adj.*	rosa, Rosen-
rose *n.*	Rose *f*
rose garland	Rosenkranz *m*
Rose-Garlands, Festival of the —	das Rosenkranzfest
Rosetta Stone	Dreisprachenstein *m*, Rosette-Stein *m*
rosette	Rosette *f*
whorl —	Wirbelrosette *f*
rose window	Fensterrose *f*, Radfenster *n*, Rose *f*, Rosenfenster *n*
rose wood	Rosenholz *n*, Palisanderholz *n*

rose wreath	Rosenkranz *m*
rosin	Colophonium *n*, Kolophonium *n*
Rostra	Rednertribüne *f*
rostral column	Gedenksäule für einen Seesieg
rostrum	Rostra *f*
rotulus	Buchrolle *f*
rotunda	Rotunde *f*
rough	rauh, roh, derb, grob
rough draft	Vorentwurf *m*
rough hew	bosseln
roughness	Derbheit *f*, Rauheit *f*, Grobheit *f*, Roheit *f*
rough sketch	flüchtige Skizze *f*
roulette	Roulette *f*
round	rund, Rund-
round arch	Rundbogen *m*
blind —	Rundbogenblende *f*
round arch frieze	Rundbogenfries *m*
round brush	Rundpinsel *m*
rounding	Rundung *f*
round off	abrunden, abkanten
round temple	Rundtempel *m*
round window	Rundfenster *n*
row	Reihe *f*, Zeile *f*
row house	Reihenhaus *n*
royal	königlich, fürstlich, Hof-, Königs-, Fürsten-
royal architect	Hofarchitekt *m*
royal chapel	Hofkapelle *f*, Hofkirche *f*
Royal Copenhagen porcelain	Kopenhagener Porzellan *n*
royal court	Königshof *m*
royal tomb	Königsgrab *n*, Fürstengrab *n*
rubber	Gummi *m*
rubbing	Frottage *f*
rubble	Bruchstein *m*
rubble masonry	Feldsteinmauerwerk *n*

rubble wall	Bruchsteinmauer *f*
rubric	Rubrik *f*
rubricate	rubrizieren
rubrication	Rubrizieren *n*
ruby	Rubin *m*
ruby etching	Rubinätzung *f*
ruby glass	Rubinglas *n*
ruby-red glass	Goldrubinglas *n*
ruddle	Rötel *m*
rug	Teppich *m*
ruin	Ruine *f*
ruins	Trümmer *pl*, Ruinen *pl*
site of —	Ruinenstätte *f*
rule	Regel *f*, Kanon *m*
ruler	1. Herrscher *m*
	2. Lineal *n*
rune	Rune *f*
rune stone	Runenstein *m*
runic alphabet	Futhark *n*
runic writing	Runenschrift *f*
running dog	laufender Hund *m*, Wellenband *n*
rust	Rost *m*
rust-colored	rostfarben
rusticate	abquadern
rusticated ashlar	Buckelquader *m*, Rustika-Quader *m*
rusticated block	Rustika-Quader *m*
rusticated stone	Bosse *f*
rustication	Bossenwerk *n*, Quadermauerwerk *n*, Rustika *f*
saber	Säbel *m*
Sabines	Sabiner *pl*
Sabine woman	Sabinerin *f*
sack	Tasche *f*
sack cloth	Rupfen *m*

sacramentary	Sakramentar *n*, Sakramentarium *n*
sacrament house	Sakramenthäuschen *n*
sacrarium	Piscina *f*
sacred	heilig, sakral, kultisch, kirchlich, geistlich
sacred architecture	Sakralarchitektur *f*, Sakralbaukunst *f*
sacred building	Sakralbau *m*, Kultbau *m*
Sacred Heart depiction	Herz-Jesu-Bild *n*
sacred object	Heiligtum *n*
sacred picture	Kultbild *n*, Weihbild *n*
sacred site	Kultstätte *f*, Heiligtum *n*
sacrifice *v.*	opfern
sacrifice *n.*	Opfer *n*
Sacrifice of Isaac, the —	die Opferung Isaaks
sacrificial altar	Opferaltar *m*
sacrificial animal	Opfertier *n*
sacrificial axe	Opferbeil *n*
sacrificial ceremony	Opferzeremonie *f*
sacrificial offering	Opfergabe *f*
sacrificial servant	Opferdiener *m*
sacrificial site	Opferstätte *f*
sacrificial slab	Opferstein *m*
sacrificial stone	Opferstein *m*
sacristy	Sakristei *f*
saddleback roof	Giebeldach *n*, Satteldach *n*
safflor	Safflor *m*
safflower pigment	Safflor *m*
saffron *adj.*	safrangelb
saffron *n.*	Safran *m*
saffron yellow	safrangelb
saga	Sage *f*
Sagittarius	Schütze *f*
sail vault	Segelgewölbe *n*, Hängekuppel *f*, Kreuzrippengewölbe *n*, Stutzkuppel *f*
saint	Heilige *m*, *f*, hl.

titular —	Titelheilige *m, f*
saint's attribute	Heiligenattribut *n*
Salian	Salier *m*
Salian period	salische Epoche *f*
Salomonica	Spiralsäule *f*
salt cellar	Salzfaß *n*
salve	Salbe *f*
Samaritan, the Good —	der gute Samariter
same	gleich
same-sized	gleichgroß
Samson	Simson, Samson
sanctuary	Sanktuarium *n*, Altarraum *m*, Chor *n*, Heiligtum *n*
sand	Sand *m*
sandalwood	Sandelholz *n*
sandarac	Sandarak *m*
sand casting	Sandformverfahren *n*, Sandguß *m*
sand casting box	Formkasten *m*
sand coat	grobe Malschicht *f*
sand-colored	sandfarben, beige
sand finish	grobe Malschicht *f*
sandpaper	Glaspapier *n*, Schmirgelpapier *n*
sandstone	Sandstein *m*
sanguine	Rötel *m*
sanguine drawing	Rötelzeichnung *f*
sans-serif	serifenlos
Santa Maria della Vittoria	die Madonna des Sieges
sapphire	Saphir *m*
sapwood	Splintholz *n*
sarcophagus	Sarkophag *m*, Steinsarg *m*
sarcophagus lid	Sarkophagdeckel *m*
sarcophagus sculpture	Sarkophagplastik *f*
sardonyx	Sardonyx *m*
sash	Schärpe *f*
satin	Satin *m*
saturated	satt

saturation	Farbintensität *f*, Sättigung *f*
color −	Sättigung *f*
degree of −	Sättigungsgrad *m*
satyr	Satyr *m*
saucer	Farbnapf *m*, Napf *m*
Sauveterrian culture	Sauveterrien *n*
Saviour	Erlöser *m*, Heiland *m*
saw	Säge *f*
sawtooth roof	Sägedach *n*, Sheddach *n*
scabbard	Scheide *f*
scaffold beam	Rüstbalken *m*
scaffolding	Baugerüst *n*
scaffolding hole	Rüstloch *n*
scagliola	Scagliola *f*, Gipsmarmor *m*, Stuckmarmor *m*
scale	1. Maßstab *m*, Ausmaß *n*, Größenordnung *f* 2. Waage *f*
scallop	Muschel *f*
scalloped pattern	Muschelwerk *n*, Schuppenmuster *n*
scarab	Skarabäus *m*
scarce	knapp, selten, rar
scarcity	Knappheit *f*
scarlet	scharlachrot
scene	1. Szene *f* 2. Skene *f*
scene painter	Kulissenmaler *m*
scenery	Bühnenbild *n*, Bühnenhintergrund *m*, Kulisse *f*, Theaterdekoration *f*
scenery painting	Dekorationsmalerei *f*, Kulissenmalerei *f*
scenography	Skenographie *f*, Szenographie *f*
scepter	Szepter *n*, Zepter *n*
scheme	Schema *n*
schist	Schiefer *m*
scholar	Gelehrte *m*, Wissenschaftler *m*

school

school	Schule *f*
school of applied arts	Kunstgewerbeschule *f*, Werkkunstschule *f*
school of crafts	Kunstgewerbeschule *f*
school work	Schularbeit *f*
Schutterstuk	Doelenstück *f*, Schützenstück *n*
science	Wissenschaft *f*
scientist	Wissenschaftler *m*
scissors	Schere *f*
scone	Wandleuchter *m*
Scorpio	Skorpion *m*
scorpion	Skorpion *m*
scorzo	Skurz *m*
scotia	Trochilus *m*
scotia profile	Hohlkehle *f*, dorisches Kymation *n*
Scourging of Christ, the —	die Geißelung Christi
scrape	kratzen, schaben
scrape off	abschaben
scraper	Schabeisen *n*, Schaber *m*
scraperboard	Schabblatt *n*
scraping tool	Kratzeisen *n*
scratch	kratzen, ritzen
scratchboard	Schabblatt *n*
scratch coat	Spritzbewurf *m*, Berappung *f*
scratched picture	Ritzbild *n*
scratch in	einritzen
screen	1. Gitter *n*, Schranke *f*, Schirm *m*, spanische Wand *f*, Paravent *m, n* 2. Leinwand *f* 3. Raster *m*
screw	Schraube *f*
scribe	Schreiber *m*
scrimshaw	feine Schnitzerei aus Elfenbein, Muscheln, Walfischknochen usw.
script	Schrift *f*
scriptorium	Schreiberwerkstätte *f*, Schreibstube *f*, Skriptorium *n*

Scriptures, the —	die Heilige Schrift
scroll	1. Buchrolle *f*, Schriftrolle *f*, Rolle *f*
	2. Schnörkel *m*
scrollwork	Rollwerk *n*
sculp.	sc., sculp.
sculpt	skulptieren
sculpting punch	Gutsche *f*
sculptor	Bildhauer *m*
sculptor's mallet	Schlegel *m*
sculptural	bildhauerisch, bildnerisch, plastisch
sculpture	1. Plastik *f*, Bildwerk *n*, Skulptur *f*
	2. Bildhauerkunst *f*, Bildhauerei *f*, Bildnerei *f*, Bildhauerarbeit *f*
clay —	Tonplastik *f*
free-standing —	Freiplastik *f*
stone —	Steinplastik *f*, Steinskulptur *f*
sculpture in the round	Rundplastik *f*, Vollplastik *f*
scumble	verwischen
scythe	Sense *f*, Sichel *f*
Scythian	szythisch, skythisch
Scythians	Szythen *pl*, Skythen *pl*
Scyths	Szythen *pl*, Skythen *pl*
sea green	meeresgrün
seal	Siegel *n*, Sigillum *n*
seal cylinder	Rollsiegel *n*, Siegelzylinder *m*
seal cylinder impression	Abrollung *f*
seal impression	Siegelabdruck *m*
sealing wax	Siegellack *m*, Siegelwachs *n*
seal ring	Siegelring *m*
seals, art of making —	Siegelschneidekunst *f*
seals, study of —	Siegelkunde *f*, Sphragistik *f*
seam	Naht *f*, Saum *m*
seam line	Naht *f*
sea nymph	Meernixe *f*
sea piece	Seebild *n*, Seegemälde *n*, Seestück *n*

seascape	Seebild *n*, Seegemälde *n*, Seestück *n*
seashell	1. Muschel *f*, Muschelgehäuse *n* 2. Muschelornament *n*, Muschelwerk *n*
seashell limestone	Muschelkalk *m*
seashell-shaped niche	Muschelnische *f*
seat	Platz *m*, Sitz *m*
seated colossus	Sitzkoloss *m*
seated scribe	Schreiberfigur *f*
seat of the gods	Göttersitz *m*
seats	Gestühl *n*
secco painting	Seccomalerei *f*, Sekkomalerei *f*
secession	Sezession *f*
secondary color	Sekundärfarbe *f*
secondary figure	Nebenfigur *f*, Assistenzfigur *f*
secondary motif	Nebenmotiv *n*
secondary scene	Nebenszene *f*
second casting	Zweitguß *m*
Second Coming, the —	die Wiederkunft Christi
section	Abschnitt *m*, Schnitt *m*, Fach *n*, Partie *f*
cross —	Querschnitt *m*
golden —	goldener Schnitt *m*
longitudinal —	Längsschnitt *m*
sectional drawing	Schnittzeichnung *f*
secular	außerkirchlich, weltlich
secular architecture	Profanbau *m*
sedan chair	Sänfte *f*, Tragsessel *m*
sedilla	Dreisitz *m*, Levitenstuhl *m*
seem	scheinen
segment	Abschnitt *m*, Segment *n*
segmental arch	Flachbogen *m*, Segmentbogen *m*, Stichbogen *m*
segment of a circle	Kreisabschnitt *m*
seicento	Secento *n*, Seicento *n*
self-contained	geschlossen

self-containedness	Geschlossenheit *f*
self portrait	Selbstbildnis *n*, Selbstporträt *n*
Seljuk	seldschukisch
semantics	Semantik *f*
semicircle	Halbkreis *m*
semicircular	halbkreisartig, halbrund
semicircular arch	Rundbogen *m*
semidome	Halbkuppel *f*
semi-opaque color	halbdeckende Farbe *f*
semiotics	Semeiotik *f*, Semiotik *f*
semiprecious stone	Halbedelstein *m*
sense	Sinn *m*
sense of touch	Tastsinn *m*
sensitive	1. sensibel 2. empfindlich
sensitive to light	lichtempfindlich
sensitivity	Empfindsamkeit *f*
sensuous	sinnlich
sepia	Sepia *f*
sepia drawing	Sepiazeichnung *f*
sepulchral vault	Grabgewölbe *n*
sepulchre	Grab *n*, Grabmal *n*, Gruft *f*
Sepulchre, Holy —	das Heilige Grab
sepulchrum	Sepulcrum *n*
seraph	Seraph *m*
series	Folge *f*, Reihe *f*, Serie *f*
series production	Serienfertigung *f*
serif	Serife *f*
serigraph	Serigraphie *f*, Siebdruck *m*
Sermon on the Mount, the —	die Bergpredigt
serpent	Schlange *f*
serpentine	Serpentine *m*
set *v.*	1. abbinden 2. einfassen, fassen
set *n.*	1. Bühnenbild *n* 2. Satz *m*, Garnitur *f*

set designer	Bühnenbildner *m*
set painter	Kulissenmaler *m*
set painting	Kulissenmalerei *f*, Dekorationsmalerei *f*
settee	Kanapee *n*, Lehnbank *f*, kleines Sofa *n*
setting	1. Einfassung *f* 2. Fassung *f* 3. Szene *f*
settlement	Niederlassung *f*, Siedlung *f*
set up	aufstellen
Seven Days of the Creation, the —	die sieben Schöpfungstage
Seven Joys of the Virgin, the —	die Sieben Freuden Mariä
seven liberal arts, the —	die sieben freien Künste
Seven Sorrows of the Virgin, the —	die Sieben Schmerzen Mariä
Seven Wonders of the World	die sieben Weltwunder
severe	streng
Severe Style	strenger Stil *m*
severity	Strenge *f*
severy	Gewölbefach *n*, Kappe *f*, Wange *f*
sew	nähen
sewage system	Kanalisation *f*
sfumato	Sfumato *n*
sgraffito	Sgraffito *n*, Graffito *n*, Kratzputz *m*, Kratzputztechnik *f*
shade *v.*	schattieren
shade *n.*	Schatten *m*, Schattierung *f*, Ton *m*
shading	Schattierung *f*, Tönung *f*
shadow	Schatten *m*
shadowy	schattig
shady	schattig
shaft	Schacht *m*, Schaft *m*
column —	Säulenschaft *m*

shaft and chamber tomb	Schachtkammergrab *n*
shaft grave	Schachtgrab *n*
shaft grave circle	Schachtgräberring *m*
shaft-ring	Schaftring *m*, Wirtel *m*
shallow	flach, flächenhaft, oberflächlich
shape *v.*	bilden, gestalten, modellieren, formen
shape *n.*	Form *f*, Format *n*, Gestalt *f*
history of form and —	Formgeschichte *f*
prototype —	Urform *f*
vocabulary of —	Formensprache *f*
shapeable	verformbar
shapeless	formlos
shapelessness	Formlosigkeit *f*
shard	Scherbe *f*, Vasenfragment *n*
clay —	Tonscherbe *f*
sharp	spitz, scharf
sharp-edged	kantig
sheathe	beschlagen, verkleiden
sheathing	Verkleidung *f*
sheet	Blatt *n*
sheet aluminum	Aluminiumblech *n*
sheet bronze	Bronzeblech *n*
sheet iron	Walzeisen *n*
sheet metal	Blech *n*
shell	1. Schale *f*, Schalung *f* 2. Muschel *f*
shellac	Schellack *m*
shell construction	Schalenkonstruktion *f*
shell gold	Muschelgold *n*
shell marble	Muschelmarmor *m*
shepherd	Hirt *m*, Schäfer *m*
sherd	Scherbe *f*, Vasenfragment *n*
shield	Schild *m*
shine *v.*	scheinen, strahlen, erglänzen, glänzen
shine *n.*	Schein *m*, Glanz *m*

shingle	Schindel *f*
shingle roof	Schindeldach *n*
Shingle Style	Schindelstil *m*
ship	Schiff *n*
ship burial	Bootsgrab *n*, Schiffsbestattung *f*
ship-shaped pulpit	Schiffskanzel *f*
shirt	Hemd *n*
shop-work	Werkstattarbeit *f*
short	1. klein, kurz 2. buttrig
shot color	Schillerfarbe *f*
shoulder	Schulter *f*
shouldered arch	Kragsturzbogen *m*, Schulterbogen *m*
show *v.*	darstellen
show *n.*	Ausstellung *f*, Schau *f*
showpiece	Prunkstück *n*
shrine	Schrein *m*
shrink	schrumpfen, einlaufen
shrinkage crack	Schwundriß *m*, Schwundsprung *m*
shutter	Fensterladen *m*
shuttering	Schalung *f*
shuttle	Weberschiffchen *n*, Schiffchen *n*, Schütze *m*
sibyl	Sibylle *f*
siccative	Sikkativ *n*, Trockenmittel *n*, Trockenstoff *m*
sickle	Sense *f*, Sichel *f*
side	Seite *f*, Wand *f*, Wandung *f*
side aisle	Seitenschiff *n*
side altar	Nebenaltar *m*
side apse	Nebenapsis *f*
sideboard	Kredenz *f*
side chair	Stuhl ohne Armlehnen
side chancel	Nebenchor *m*
side panel	Außenflügel *m*, Flügelbild *n*
side view	Seitenansicht *f*, Profilansicht *f*

side wall	Seitenwand *f*, Wange *f*
Sienese	sienesisch
sigillography	Siegelkunst *f*, Sphragistik *f*
sign *v.*	signieren
sign *n.*	1. Zeichen *n*
	2. Signum *n*
	3. Schild *n*
signature	Signatur *f*, Signierung *f*, Namenszug *m*
signet	Petschaft *n*
significance	Bedeutung *f*
signing	Signierung *f*
sign of the zodiac	Sternbild *n*
sileni	Silene *pl*
Silenus	Silen
silhouette	Schattenbild *n*, Schattenriß *m*, Silhouette *f*
silica	Kieselerde *f*
silica gel	Kieselgel *n*, Silikagel *n*
silk *adj.*	seiden, Seiden-
silk *n.*	Seide *f*
silk cloth	Seidenstoff *m*
silk embroidery	Seidenstickerei *f*
silken	seiden, Seiden-
silk screen	Siebdruck *m*, Serigraphie *f*, Schablonendruck *m*
silk screen printing frame	Siebrahmen *m*
silk weaving	Seidenweberei *f*
silky	seidig, weich, glänzend
sill	Sims *n*, Fensterbrett *n*
silver *adj.*	silbern, Silber-
silver *n.*	Silber *n*
silver gray	silbergrau
silverplate	versilbern
silver plating	Silberplattierung *f*
silver point	Silberstift *m*
silver smalto	Silbersmalte *f*

silversmith	Silberschmied *m*
silversmithing	Silberschmiedekunst *f*
silver stain	Silberlot *n*
silver utensil	Silbergerät *n*
silverware	Silbergerät *n*, Silberbesteck *n*
silvery	silbrig
sima	Sima *f*
Simon's Prophecy	die Prophezeiung Simeons
simple	einfach, schlicht
simple-solution varnish	Harzölfirnis *m*
simplicity	Einfachheit *f*
simultaneity	Simultanität *f*
simultaneous contrast	Simultankontrast *m*, Simultanwirkung *f*, optische Überflutung *f*
simultaneous representation	Simultanität *f*
sinew	Sehne *f*
singerie	Singerie *f*
single	einzeln, Einzel-
Single-Grave culture	Einzelgrabkultur *f*
single-leaf print	Einblattdruck *m*
single-leaf woodcut	Einblattholzschnitt *m*
sinking in	Einschlagen *n*
sinopia	Sinopia *f*, Zinnober *m*
sinopia underdrawing	Sinopia *f*
Siren	Sirene *f*
Sistine Chapel	Sixtinische Kapelle *f*
sit	sitzen
site	Ort *m*, Lage *f*, Stätte *f*, Bauplatz *m*, Aufstellungsort *m*
site conditions	Baugrundverhältnis *n*
site plan	Lageplan *m*
situation	Verhältnis *n*, Situation *f*
situla	Situla *f*
size *v.*	grundieren

size n.	1. Größe f, Ausmaß n, Maß n, Format n
	2. Leim m, Grundierung f
actual —	Originalgröße f
skeleton	1. Skelett n
	2. Rohbau m
skeleton construction	Skelettbau m, Skelettbauweise f
skene	Skene f
sketch v.	skizzieren
sketch n.	Skizze f, Studie f, Riß m, Umrißzeichnung f
sketchbook	Skizzenbuch n
sketching easel	Feldstaffelei f
sketchy	skizzenhaft
skew	schief, schräg
skewback	schräges Widerlager n
skill	Kunst f, Kunstfertigkeit f, Geschicklichkeit f
skilled	geschickt
skillful	kunstvoll
skin	Haut f
skin color	Fleischfarbe f, Fleischton m, Teint m
skirt	Rock m
skull	Schädel m, Totenschädel m
skull cap	Kalotte f, Käppchen n
sky	Himmel m
sky blue	himmelblau
skylight	Dachfenster n
skyphos	Skyphos m
skyscraper	Wolkenkratzer m, Hochhaus n
slab	Platte f
slanted	schräg, schief, quer, abschüssig
slanted roof	Steildach n
slat	Lamelle f, Latte f
slate	Schiefer m
slate roof	Schieferdach n
slate slab	Schieferplatte f

Slaughter of the Innocents	der bethlehemische Kindermord, der Kindermord zu Bethlehem
sleeve	Ärmel *m*
slender	schlank, schmächtig
slide *v.*	gleiten
slide *n.*	Dia *n*, Diapositiv *n*
sliding door	Schiebetür *f*
slight	schmächtig, dünn, klein
slim	schmächtig, schlank
slip	Malschlicker *m*, Schlicker *m*, Tonschlicker *m*, Engobe *f*
slope	Böschung *f*, Schräge *f*, Neigung *f*, Giebelschenkel *m*, Giebelschräge *f*
sloped	geböscht, schräg
small	klein, Klein-
small-figured	kleinfigürig
small scale *adj.*	kleinfigürig
small scale *n.*	Kleinformat *n*
small-scale sculpture	Kleinplastik *f*
smalt	Schmalte *f*, Smalte *f*
smalto	Glasmosaikstein *m*, Glasmalte *f*, Schmalte *f*
smooth *v.*	glätten, planieren
smooth *adj.*	eben, glatt, plan
smoothness	Glätte *f*
smudge	Klecks *m*
snail	Schnecke *f*
snail-shaped	schneckenförmig
snail shell	Schneckengehäuse *n*
snake	Schlange *f*
snake cult	Schlangenkult *m*
snuff box	Schnupftabakdose *f*
soapstone	Speckstein *m*
Socialist Realism	Sozialistischer Realismus *m*
socle	Sockel *m*
socle area	Sockelzone *f*

sofa	Sofa n, Kanapee n
soffit	Unterfläche f
soffitte	Soffitte f
soft	weich, sanft, Weich-
soft ground etching	Weichgrundätzung f, Durchdruckverfahren n
softness	Weiche f, Weichheit f
soft paste	Weichporzellan n
soft paste porcelain	Frittenporzellan n, Weichporzellan n
soft resin	Weichharz n
Soft Style	Weicher Stil m
softwood	Weichholz n, Nadelholz n
solar spectrum	Sonnenspektrum n
solder v.	löten
solder n.	Lot n
solid	massiv, Massiv-
solid wood	Massivholz n
solitaire	Solitär m
Solnhofen stone	Solnhofer Kalkschiefer m, Solnhofer Schiefer m
Solomon's seal	Davidstern m, Davidsstern m
solution	Lösung f
Solutrean	Solutréen n
soot	Ruß m
soot black	Rußschwarz n
sopraporta	Supraporte f, Sopraporte f
soujourn	Aufenthalt m
soul	Seele f
sounding board	Kanzeldach n, Kanzelhaube f, Kanzelhimmel m, Schalldeckel m
source	Quelle f, Quellenwerk n, Vorlage f, Ursprung m
documentary —	Schriftquelle f, Quellenwerk n
source book	Quellenwerk n
sovereign	Fürst m, Herrscher m

space	1. Platz *m*, Raum *m*
	2. Lücke *f*, Zwischenraum *m*, Abstand *m*
arrangement of —	Raumordnung *f*
development of —	Raumentfaltung *f*
illusion of —	Raumillusion *f*
organization of —	Raumgliederung *f*
structure of —	Raumgefüge *n*, Raumstruktur *f*
space-defining	raumbestimmend, raumbildend
spaceless	raumlos
space-limiting	raumgrenzend
space-shaping	raumbildend
spacious	großräumig, weiträumig
spaciousness	Räumlichkeit *f*, Weiträumigkeit *f*
spackle	kitten
span *v.*	überspannen
span *n.*	Spannweite *f*
spandrel	Zwickel *m*, Bogenzwickel *m*, Spandrille *f*
sparkle	glänzen, erglänzen, leuchten
spatial	räumlich, Raum-
spatial depth	Raumtiefe *f*
spatial distortion	Raumverzerrung *f*
spatial dynamics	Raumdynamik *f*
spatial effect	Raumwirkung *f*
spatial harmony	Raumharmonie *f*
spatiality	Räumlichkeit *f*
spatial relationship	Raumbeziehung *f*
spatial statics	Raumstatik *f*
spatter	sprenkeln
spatula	Spachtel *m, f*, Spatel *m*
speaker's stage	Rednertribüne *f*
spear	Lanze *f*, Speer *m*
spear bearer	Speerträger *m*
spearhead	Speerspitze *f*
spear thrower	Speerschleuder *f*
specialist	Kenner *m*, Spezialist *m*

spectral color	Spektralfarbe *f*
spectrum	Spektrum *n*
speculum humanae salvationis	Heilsspiegel *m*
sphere	Kugel *f*
spherical	kugelförmig
spherical building	Kugelbau *m*
sphinx	1. Sphinx *f* 2. Sphinx *m*
sphragistics	Sphragistik *f*, Siegelkunde *f*
spinel	Spinell *m*
spiral *adj.*	schraubenförmig, spiralförmig
spiral *n.*	Spirale *f*
spiral-shaped column	Spiralsäule *f*
spiral-shaped ornament	Spirale *f*
spiral stairs	Spindeltreppe *f*, Wendeltreppe *f*
spire	Turmhelm *m*, Turmspitze *f*
broach —	achtseitiger Helm *m*
spirit	Geist *m*
spirit of turpentine	Terpentingeist *m*
spirit varnish	Alkoholfirnis *m*, Harzölfirnis *m*, Spiritusfirnis *m*
splayed	abgestuft, abgetreppt
splendid	prachtvoll, prächtig, herrlich
split	Riß *m*, Spalte *f*
spot	Fleck *m*, Klecks *m*, Tüpfel *m*
spout	Ausguß *m*, Schnabel *m*, Tülle *f*
spray concrete	Torkret *m*
spray gun	Spritzpistole *f*
spray painting	Spritzmalerei *f*
spring	1. Brunnen *m*, Quelle *f* 2. Feder *f*
springer	Bogenansatz *m*
springing	Kämpferlinie *f*
sprinkle	sprenkeln
sprue	Gußkanal *m*, Gußröhre *f*
spur	Eckblatt *n*, Eckknolle *f*, Ecksporn *m*

spur stone	Prellstein *m*
square *adj.*	quadratisch, Quadrat-
square *n.*	1. Quadrat *n*
	2. Platz *m*
square capitals	capitalis quadrata
squared timber	Eckholz *n*, Kantholz *n*
square meter	Quadratmeter *n*
squaring	Quadrierung *f*
squaring off	Quadrierung *f*
squaring-off grid	Quadratnetz *n*
squeegee	Gummiwalze *f*, Rakel *f*
squinch	Trompe *f*
S-shaped profile	Karnies *n*
St.	hl.
stabile *adj.*	stabil, Stabil-
stabile *n.*	Stabile *n*
stable	stabil, Stabil-
stadium	Stadion *n*
staff	Stab *m*
staffage	Staffage *f*, Beiwerk *n*, Figurenstaffage *f*, Assistenzfigur *f*
staffage animals	Tierstaffage *f*
stage	1. Bühne *f*, Schaubühne *f*
	2. Stadium *n*, Stufe *f*
stage designer	Bühnenbildner *m*
stage of development	Entwicklungsstufe *f*
stage painting	Dekorationsmalerei *f*, Kulissenmalerei *f*
stage set	Bühnenbild *n*, Bühnenhintergrund *m*, Kulisse *f*, Dekor *n*, Theaterdekoration *f*
stain *v.*	beizen
stain *n.*	Beize *f*
stained canvas	gefärbte und grundierte Leinwand *f*
stained glass	Glasmalerei *f*
stained glass artist	Glasmaler *m*

stained glass painting	Glasmalerei *f*, musivische Glasmalerei *f*
stained glass window	Glasgemälde *n*, Buntscheibe *f*, Glasfenster *n*, Bleiglasfenster *n*, Buntglasfenster *n*
stainless steel	rostfreier Stahl *m*
stair	Treppe *f*, Stufe *f*
staircase	Treppenhaus *n*, Stiegenhaus *n*
stair foundation	Stufenunterbau *m*, Krepidoma *n*, Krepis *f*
stair riser	Setzstufe *f*, Steigung *f*
stair string	Wange *f*
stair tower	Treppenturm *m*
stair tread	Auftritt *m*
stairs	Treppe *f*, Treppenhaus *n*
exterior —	Freitreppe *f*
stairway	Treppenhaus *n*, Stiegenhaus *n*, Treppe *f*, Stiege *f*
stake	Pfahl *m*, Pfosten *m*
stalls	Gestühl *n*
stamnos	Stamnos *m*
stamp *v.*	einpunzen, prägen, stanzen, stempeln
stamp *n.*	Punze *f*, Stanze *f*, Stempel *m*, Patrize *f*
stamp carver	Stempelschneider *m*
stamp seal	Petschaft *n*, Stempelsiegel *n*
stance	Haltung *f*, Stellung *f*, Schrittstellung *f*
stanchion	Strebe *f*, Stütze *f*, Stützpfosten *m*
stand *v.*	stehen
stand *n.*	Gestell *n*, Untersatz *m*, Halterung *f*
standard	1. Maßstab *m* 2. Standarte *f*, Fahne *f*
stand oil	Standöl *n*
St. Andrew's cross	Andreaskreuz *n*, Schrägkreuz *n*
St. Ann, Madonna and Christ Child	Anna Selbdritt

stanza	Stanze *f*
star	Stern *m*
starch	Stärke *f*
starch paste	Stärkekleister *m*
star of David	Davidstern *m*, Davidsstern *m*, Judenstern *m*
star-shaped	sternförmig, Stern-
state	1. Staat *m* 2. Zustand *m* 3. Zustandsdruck *m*, Etat *m*
statement	Aussage *f*
state of preservation	Erhaltungszustand *m*
static	statisch
statics	Statik *f*, Raumstatik *f*
Stations of the Cross	die Kreuzwegstationen
statue	Statue *f*, Figur *f*, Standbild *n*
column —	Säulenfigur *f*
statue-like	statuarisch, statuenhaft
statue of Memnon	Memnonskoloss *m*
statuesque	statuarisch, statuenhaft
statuette	Statuette *f*
Staufen art	staufische Kunst *f*
stave	Stab *m*
stave church	Stabkirche *f*, Mastenkirche *f*, Reiswerkkirche *f*
stave construction	Mastenbau *m*
stay	Aufenthalt *m*
St. Bartholomew	der hl. Bartholomäus
St. Catherine's wheel	Katharinenrad *n*
St. Christopher	der hl. Christophorus
steatite	Steatit *m*, Speckstein *m*
steed	Reittier *n*
steel	Stahl *m*
steel blue	stahlblau
steel construction	Stahlbau *m*
steel drawing pen	Stahlfeder *f*
steel engraving	Stahlstich *m*

steel frame building	Stahlskelettbau *m*
steel girder	Stahlträger *m*
steel gray	stahlgrau
steel reinforced concrete	Stahlbeton *m*, Eisenbeton *m*
steel skeleton	Tragstahl-Skelett *n*
steel structural element	Stahlbauelement *n*
steel support	Stahlstütze *f*
steeple	Turm mit Spitze
stele	Stele *f*
stellar vault	Sterngewölbe *n*
stellate	sternförmig, Stern-
stem	Stamm *m*, Stengel *m*, Stiel *m*
stencil	Schablone *f*, Matrize *f*, Patrone *f*
step	Stufe *f*
stepped	stufenförmig, gestuft, Stufen-
stepped gable	Staffelgiebel *m*, Stufengiebel *m*, Treppengiebel *m*
step-pyramid	Stufenpyramide *f*
steps	Treppe *f*, Stufen *pl*
step-shaped	stufenförmig, Stufen-
stereobate	Stereobat *m*
stereochromy	Stereochromie *f*, Mineralmalerei *f*, Silikatmalerei *f*
stereometric	stereometrisch
stereometry	Stereometrie *f*
St. Francis of Assisi	der hl. Franziskus
St. George and the Dragon	der Drachenkampf des hl. Georg
St. Gregory at Mass	Gregorsmesse *f*
stiacciato relief	gequetschtes Relief *n*
stick *v.*	haften, kleben
stick *n.*	Stab *m*, Stock *m*, Stange *f*
sticky	klebrig
stiff	steif, starr, hart
stigma	Stigma *n*, Wundmal *n*
Stigmata, the —	die Wundmale Christi
stigmatization	Stigmatisation *f*
still life	Stilleben *n*

stilted arch	gestelzter Bogen *m*
stimulation	Anregung *f*
stimulus	Anregung *f*, Stimulus *m*, Impuls *m*
stipes	Stipes *m*
stipes grave	Stipesgrab *n*
stipple	punktieren, tüpfeln
stirrup handle krater	Bügelhenkelkrater *m*
stirrup jar	Bügelkanne *f*
St. James the Great	der hl. Jakobus
St. Jerome	der hl. Hieronymus
St. John in the Wilderness	Johannes in der Einsamkeit
St. John Preaching	Johannespredigt *f*
St. John the Baptist	Johannes der Täufer
St. John the Evangelist	Johannes der Evangelist
St. Luke	der hl. Lukas
St. Luke painting the Virgin	Lukasmadonna *f*
St. Mark	der hl. Markus
St. Matthew	der hl. Matthäus
stoa	Stoa *f*
stola	Stola *f*
stomach	Bauch *m*
stomp	Wischer *m*
stone *adj.*	steinern, Stein-
stone *n.*	Stein *m*
imitation —	Gußstein *m*
Stone Age	Steinzeit *f*
stone bead	Steinperle *f*
stone chisel	Steinmeißel *m*
stone coffin	Steinsarg *m*
stone inlay	Inkrustation *f*
stone mason	Steinmetz *m*
stone masonry	Steinmetzkunst *f*
stone mason's mark	Steinmetzzeichen *n*, Meisterzeichen *n*
stone mosaic	Steinmalerei *f*

stone sculptor	Steinbildhauer *m*
stone sculpture	Steinplastik *f*, Steinskulptur *f*
stone slab	Steinplatte *f*
stone tool	Steingerät *n*, Steinwerkzeug *n*
stoneware	Steinzeug *n*
stool	Schemel *m*, Hocker *m*
stop	auskitten, kitten
stop out	abdecken
stopper	Stöpsel *m*
storage jar	Vorratsgefäß *n*
storage vessel	Vorratsgefäß *n*
store room	Magazin *n*, Magazinraum *m*, Vorratsraum *m*
storied urn	Hausurne *f*
story	1. Geschichte *f* 2. Stockwerk *n*, Geschoß *n*, Etage *f*, Flucht *f*
blind —	Triforium *m*
story of Creation	Schöpfungsgeschichte *f*
stoup	Weihwasserbecken *n*, Weihbrunnen *m*, Weihbecken *n*, Aspersorium *n*
St. Peter	der hl. Petrus
St. Peter Sinking	der sinkende Petrus
St. Peter's Cathedral	Petersdom *m*
St. Peter's grave	Petrusgrab *n*
straight	gerade
straightedge	Lineal *n*
straight line	Gerade *f*
strain	spannen
strainer arch	Schwibbogen *m*
strapwork	Beschlagwerk *n*
stratigraphy	Stratigraphie *f*
stratum	Schicht *f*
straw-colored	strohfarben
street	Straße *f*
Street Boy Extracting a Thorn	der Dornauszieher

street scene	Straßenbild *n*, Straßenszene *f*
strength	Stärke *f*, Kraft *f*
stretch	1. dehnen, spannen
	2. aufspannen
stretchable	dehnbar
stretcher	Läufer *m*
canvas —	Keilrahmen *m*
stretching	Streckung *f*
stretching frame	Spannrahmen *m*
stretching pliers	Spannzange *f*
striations	Strichelung *f*
strict	streng
strictness	Strenge *f*
string	1. Schnur *f*, Faden *m*
	2. Treppenwange *f*
string course	Fries *m*, Gesims *n*
strip	Streifen *m*, Band *n*, Rute *f*
stripe	Streifen *m*
striped decoration	Streifenornamentik *f*
stroke	Strich *m*, Duktus *m*
stroke-ornamented ware	Stichbandkeramik *f*
stronghold	Festung *f*, Burg *f*, Kastell *n*
strontium yellow	Strontiumgelb *n*
structural	strukturell, baulich, Bau-
structural element	Strukturelement *n*, Bauglied *n*
structure	Struktur *f*, Gefüge *n*, Gebilde *n*, Bau *m*, Baukörper *m*, Aufbau *m*, Anlage *f*
struggle	Kampf *m*
strut	Strebe *f*, Stützbalken *m*, Verstrebung *f*
stucco	Stuck *m*, Stukkatur *f*, Stukkierung *f*
stucco coating	Stuckschicht *f*
stucco relief	Stuckrelief *n*
stucco work	Stukkatur *f*, Stukkierung *f*
stucco worker	Stukkateur *m*

stud	Pfosten *m*
student	Schüler *m*, Student *m*
studio	Atelier *n*, Künstlerwerkstätte *f*, Studio *n*
studio easel	Werkstattstaffelei *f*
study	Studie *f*
stump	Wischer *m*
stun	verhauen
stupa	Stupa *m*
St. Veronica and Her Veil	Veronikabild *n*
St. Veronica's Veil	Schweißtuch *n*, Veronikatuch *n*, das Schweißtuch der hl. Veronika
style	1. Stil *m*, Manier *f*, Mode *f*, Stilform *f*, Stilrichtung *f*, Richtung *f*, Weise *f* 2. Stift *m*, Stilus *m*
breach in —	Stilbruch *m*
change in —	Stilwandel *m*, Stilwandlung *f*
characteristic of a —	Stilmerkmal *n*
history of —	Stilgeschichte *f*
style analysis	Stilanalyse *f*
stylistic	stilistisch
stylization	Stilisierung *f*
stylobate	Stylobat *m*
stylus	Griffel *m*, Ritzgriffel *m*, Stift *m*, Stilus *m*
styrofoam	Styropor *n*
subject	1. Bildthema *n*, Thema *n*, Bildgegenstand *m*, Inhalt *m*, Sujet *n* 2. Fach *n*
subsidiary chapel	Nebenkapelle *f*
substructure	Substruktion *f*, Unterbau *m*
subtractive mixture	subtraktive Farbmischung *f*
successor	Nachfolger *m*
sudarium	Schweißtuch *n*, Veronikatuch *n*
suggestion	Anzeichen *n*, Spur *f*, Andeutung *f*, Einschlag *m*

sulfur yellow	schwefelgelb
Sumerian art	sumerische Kunst *f*
sumptuous	üppig, prächtig, herrlich
sun	Sonne *f*
sunbeam	Sonnenstrahl *m*
sun blind	Sonnenblende *f*
sun break	Sonnenblende *f*
sun chariot	Sonnenwagen *m*
Sunday painter	Sonntagsmaler *m*
sun disc	Kultscheibe *f*, Sonnenscheibe *f*
sun god	Sonnengott *m*
sunken area	Vertiefung *f*
sunk relief	versenktes Relief *n*
sunlight	Sonnenlicht *n*
ray of —	Sonnenstrahl *m*
sun symbol	Sonnensymbol *n*, Sonnenzeichen *n*
super-abacus	Kämpfer *m*
superstructure	Oberbau *m*, Überbau *m*
suppedaneum	Suppedaneum *n*
Supper, the Last —	das letzte Abendmahl
Supper at Emmaus, the —	Christus in Emmaus, das Emmausmahl
Supper in the House of Levi	das Gastmahl des Levi
Supper in the House of Simon	das Gastmahl bei Simon
support *v.*	halten, stützen, tragen
support *n.*	1. Halterung *f*, Auflage *f*, Stütze *f*, Stollen *m* 2. Malgrund *m*
supporter *heraldry*	Schildhalter *m*
support girder	Stützenträger *m*
supporting beam	Stützbalken *m*, Sprieße *f*, Sprießholz *n*
supporting element	Stützelement *n*
supporting steel construction	Tragstahl-Skelett *n*

supporting surface	Lagerfläche *f*
supporting wall	Stützmauer *f*
Suprematism	Suprematismus *m*
Suprematist	Suprematist *m*
surface	Fläche *f*, Oberfläche *f*
articulation of the —	Flächenaufteilung *f*, Flächengliederung *f*
surface structure	Oberflächenstruktur *f*
surplice	Chorhemd *n*
surreal	surreal
Surrealism	Surrealismus *m*
Surrealist	Surrealist *m*
surrealistic	surreal
suspend	hängen
suspended sculpture	Hängeplastik *f*
suspension bridge	Hängebrücke *f*
suspension construction	Hängekonstruktion *f*
swag	Feston *n*
swastika	Hakenkreuz *n*
swelling	Wulst *m*
sword	Schwert *n*, Klinge *f*
sword grip	Schwertgriff *m*
syllabary	Silbenschrift *f*
symbol	Symbol *n*, Sinnbild *n*, Emblem *n*, Sinnzeichen *n*, Zeichen *n*
symbolic	sinnbildlich, symbolhaft, symbolisch, Symbol-
symbolic value	Symbolwert *m*
Symbolism	Symbolismus *m*
symbolism	Symbolik *f*, Symbolsprache *f*
architectural —	Bausymbolik *f*
Symbolist	Symbolist *m*
symbolization	Versinnbildlichung *f*
symbolize	symbolisieren, versinnbildlichen
Symbolkeramik	Symbolkeramik *f*
symbol of fertility	Fruchtbarkeitssymbol *n*
Symbols of the Passion	Passionswerkzeuge *pl*

symbols of the Virgin	marianische Symbole *pl*
symmetric	symmetrisch
symmetrical	symmetrisch
symmetry	Symmetrie *f*
axis of —	Symmetrieachse *f*
plane of —	Symmetrieebene *f*
synagogue	Synagoge *f*
synchronism	Synchronismus *m*
synthetic *adj.*	synthetisch, Kunst-
synthetic *n.*	Kunststoff *m*
synthetic resin	Kunstharz *n*
system	System *n*, Schema *n*, Anordnung *f*
systematic	systematisch
tabernacle	Tabernakel *m, n*, Sakramenthäuschen *n*
table	Tisch *m*
table easel	Tischstaffelei *f*
table leg	Tischbein *n*
Tables of the Law, the —	die Gesetzestafeln
tablet	Tafel *f*
clay —	Tontafel *f*
tableware	Geschirr *n*, Besteck *n*
tablinum	Tablinum *n*
taboo	Tabu *n*
Tachisme	Tachismus *m*
tack	Zwecke *f*
tacky	klebrig
tactile	haptisch
talent	Begabung *f*, Talent *n*
talented	begabt, geschickt, talentiert, talentvoll
talisman	Talisman *m*
tall	hoch, groß
tallboy	Stollenschrank *m*

Talmud	Talmud *m*
tambour	Tambour *m*, Trommel *f*
tambour area	Tambourzone *f*
Tanagra figurine	Tanagrafigur *f*
tankard	Humpen *m*, Krug *m*
tape, pressure sensitive —	Klebestreifen *m*
taper *v.*	sich verjüngen
taper *n.*	1. Verjüngung *f* 2. Kerze *f*
tapestry	Teppich *m*, Wirkteppich *m*, Tapisserie *f*, Bildteppich *m*, Wandteppich *m*, Gobelin *m*
tapestry loom	Wirkstuhl *m*
tapestry manufactory	Bildwirkerei *f*, Gobelinwerkstätte *f*
tar	Teer *m*
tarpaper	Dachpappe *f*
tassel	Quast *m*, Quaste *f*
taste	Geschmack *m*
tasteful	geschmackvoll
tasteless	geschmacklos
tattoo *v.*	tätowieren, tatauieren
tattoo *n.*	Tätowierung *f*
tau cross	Antoniuskreuz *n*, Taukreuz *n*
Taurus	Stier *m*
teak	Teakholz *n*, Tiekholz *n*
team of horses	Gespann *n*
technique	Technik *f*, Verfahren *n*, Werkverfahren *n*
technology	Technik *f*, Technologie *f*
tectonic	tektonisch
tectonics	Tektonik *f*
telamon	Atlant *m*
tempera	Tempera *f*, Temperafarbe *f*
tempera painting	Temperamalerei *f*
template	Schablone *f*
temple	1. Tempel *m*, Tempelbau *m* 2. Schläfe *f*

bent-axis —	Knickachstempel *m*
dipteral —	Dipteros *m*
hypaethral —	Hypäthraltempel *m*
temple chamber	Tempelkammer *f*
temple construction	Tempelbau *m*
temple of Apollo	Apollontempel *m*
temple ruins	Tempelruine *f*
Temptation, the —	die Versuchung
Ten Commandments	die Zehn Gebote, Dekalog *m*
tendon	Sehne *f*
Tenebrae candelabrum	Teneberleuchter *m*
tenebrism	Tenebrosmalerei *f*
tenebrist painting	Tenebrosmalerei *f*
tenia	Taenia *f*
tension	Spannung *f*
tepidarium	Tepidarium *n*
terrace	Terrasse *f*
terracotta	Terrakotta *f*
terra sigillata	Terra Sigillata *f*
terrazzo	Terrazzo *m*
tessellated floor	Mosaikboden *m*
tessera	Würfel *m*
test sculpture	Probeplastik *f*, Versuchsplastik *f*, Bozzetto *m*
tetrahedron roof	Pyramidendach *n*, Zeltdach *n*
tetramorph	Tetramorph *m*
tetrastyle	viersäulig
textile *adj.*	textil, Stoff-
textile *n.*	Stoff *m*
textile dyeing stencil	Färberschablone *f*
textile printing	Stoffdruck *m*, Zeugdruck *m*
textiles	Textilien *pl*
texture	Gefüge *n*, Textur *f*
thatched roof	Strohdach *n*
thatching	Dachstroh *n*
thaumatology	Thaumatologie *f*
theater	Theater *n*

theater stage	Skene *f*, Bühne *f*
theme	Thema *n*
themes	Themenkreis *m*
theophany	Theophaniebild *n*
theory	Theorie *f*, Lehre *f*
thermae	Thermen *pl*
thermoluminescence	Thermolumineszenz *f*
thermoluminescence dating	TL-Datierung *f*
thick	dick, stark, pastos, Dick-
thick glass	Dickglas *n*
thickness	Stärke *f*
Thief on the Cross, the —	der Schächer am Kreuz
thigh	Schenkel *m*, Oberschenkel *m*
thin *v.*	verdünnen
thin *adj.*	dünn, Dünn-
thinner	Verdünnungsmittel *n*
thin-walled	dünnwändig
thixotrophy	Thixotropie *f*
tholos	Rundtempel *m*, Tholos *m*
tholos tomb	Kuppelgrab *n*
thread	Faden *m*, Garn *n*, Faser *f*
threaded glass	Fadenglas *n*, Filigranglas *n*
threading	Fadenauflage *f*
three-aisled	dreischiffig
three-dimensional	dreidimensional, plastisch, raumplastisch, vollplastisch, vollrund
three-dimensional effect	Raumwirkung *f*
three-dimensionality	Dreidimensionalität *f*
three-dimensional sculpture	Rundplastik *f*
Three Magi, the —	die Drei Weisen aus dem Morgenland
Three Marys at the Tomb, the —	die Drei Marien am Grabe
three-quarter view	Dreiviertelansicht *f*
threshold	Schwelle *f*, Türschwelle *f*

throne	Thron *m*
throne room	Thronsaal *m*
throw *pottery*	formen, drehen
thrust	Schub *m*, Schubkraft *f*
lateral —	Seitenschub *m*
vault —	Gewölbeschub *m*
thuja wood	Thuja *f*
thumb	Daumen *m*
thunderbolt	Blitz *m*, Donnerkeil *m*
thurible	Rauchfaß *n*
thyrsus	Thyrsus *m*, Thyrsusstab *m*
tiara	Tiara *f*
tie-beam	Spannbalken *m*
tied arch	Stabbogen *m*
tierceron	Zwischenrippe *f*
tight	straff, knapp, fest, eng
tightness	Straffheit *f*
tile	Fliese *f*, Kachel *f*
tiled floor	Fliesenboden *m*, Kachelboden *m*
tilted	schräg
timber frame house	Fachwerkhaus *n*, Fachwerkbau *m*
timber framing	Fachwerk *n*
time	Zeit *f*
tin	1. Dose *f* 2. Zinn *n*
tin enamel	Zinnglasur *f*
tint *v.*	schattieren, tönen
tint *n.*	Farbton *m*, Schattierung *f*, Tönung *f*
tinted paper	Tonpapier *n*
tin vessel	Zinngefäß *n*, Blechgefäß *n*
tiny	winzig
titanium white	Titanweiß *n*
Titanomachy	Titanomachie *f*
title page	Titelblatt *n*
titular saint	Titelheilige *m, f*
toe	Zehe *f*

toga	Toga *f*
tomb	Grab *n*, Grabmal *n*, Gruft *f*, Grabkammer *f*
tomb inscription	Epitaph *n*, Epitaphium *n*, Grabinschrift *f*
tomb inventory	Grabinventar *n*
tombstone	Grabmal *n*, Grabstein *m*, Grabplatte *f*
tombstone relief	Grabsteinrelief *n*
tombstone rubbing	Grabplattenabdruck *m*
tondo	Tondo *n*
tone	Farbton *m*, Ton *m*
tone value	Tonwert *m*
tongue and dart	Blattwelle *f*, lesbisches Kymation *n*, Wasserlaub *n*
tool	Gerät *n*, Werkzeug *n*
tooth	Zahn *m*
toothed	zackig
toothed chisel	Gradiereisen *n*
topaz	Topas *m*
top coat	Überstrich *m*
top floor	Dachgeschoß *n*
topic	Thema *n*
topographical landscape	Topographie *f*
topography	Topographie *f*
top story	Dachgeschoß *n*
Torah	Pentateuch *m*
torc	Torques *m*
toreutics	Toreutik *f*
torque	Torques *m*
torso	Torso *m*, Rumpf *m*, Oberkörper *m*
tortillon	Wischer *m*
tortoise shell	Schildpatt *n*, Schildkrötenpanzer *m*
torus	Torus *m*
torus profile	Wulst *m*
total effect	Gesamtwirkung *f*

total height	Gesamthöhe *f*
total impression	Gesamteindruck *m*
totem	Totem *n*
totem pole	Totempfahl *m*
touch *v.*	tasten, berühren
touch *n.*	1. Duktus *m*, Handschrift *f*, Pinselführung *f*, Pinselstrich *m*
	2. Einschlag *m*, Andeutung *f*, Anzeichen *n*, Spur *f*
touched up spot	Retusche *f*
touch up	auffrischen, retuschieren, retouchieren
tourmaline	Turmalin *m*
tournament	Ritterspiel *n*
tower	Turm *m*
tower monstrance	Turmmonstranz *f*
Tower of Babel, the —	der Turmbau zu Babel
tower shape	Turmform *f*
town	Stadt *f*, Ort *m*
town hall	Rathaus *n*
town planning	Stadtplanung *f*, Städtebau *m*
trabeated ceiling	Balkendecke *f*
trabeation	Balkenbauart *f*
trace	pausen
tracery	Maßwerk *n*
bar —	Stabwerk *n*
blind —	Blendmaßwerk *n*
trachyte	Trachyt *m*
tracing	Pause *f*
tracing paper	Pauspapier *n*, Transparentpapier *n*
tracing wheel	Pausrad *n*, Punktierrad *n*
tract	Areal *n*, Gebiet *n*
trade fair	Messe *f*, Ausstellung *f*
trademark	Marke *f*
tradition	Tradition *f*, Sitte *f*, Brauchtum *n*, Überlieferung *f*
traditional	traditionell, herkömmlich

traditional costume	Tracht *f*
tragedy	Tragik *f*
train	schulen
train of cloth	Schleppe *f*, Bahn *f*, Stoffbahn *f*
trait	Merkmal *n*, Zug *m*, Eigenart *f*
transept	Kreuzschiff *n*, Querhaus *n*, Querschiff *n*, Transept *n*
transept apse	Querapsis *f*, Querschiffkonche *f*
transept arm	Kreuzarm *m*, Querhausarm *m*
transept conch	Querschiffkonche *f*
transfer *v.*	umspannen, rentoilieren
transfer *n.*	1. Abziehbild *n* 2. Rentoilieren *n*
transfer lithography	Umdruck *m*
transfer paper	Dekalkierpapier *n*, Abziehpapier *n*, Umdruckpapier *n*
Transfiguration, the —	die Transfiguration, die Verklärung Christi
transition	Übergang *m*
transitional phase	Übergangsphase *f*
transitional style	Übergangsstil *m*
translucent	translucent, transluzid, diaphan, durchscheinend
translucent picture	Diaphanie *f*
transmit	überliefern
transom	Holm *m*, Riegel *m*, Sturz *m*
transparency	Durchsichtigkeit *f*
transparent	durchsichtig, transparent
transparent color	Lasurfarbe *f*
transparent paint	Lasurfarbe *f*
transparent paper	Transparentpapier *n*
transparent picture	Transparentbild *n*
transverse arch	Gewölbebogen *m*, Gurtbogen *m*, Quergurt *m*
lateral —	Schildbogen *m*
transverse line	Quere *f*
transverse rib	Ortrippe *f*

transverse ridge rib	Scheitelrippe *f*
trapezoid	Trapez *n*
trapezoidal capital	Trapezkapitell *n*
travertine	Travertin *m*
TRB culture	Trichterbecherkultur *f*
treadle-operated loom	Trittwebstuhl *m*
treasure	Kleinod *n*, Schatz *m*
treasure chamber	Schatzkammer *f*
treasure house	Schatzhaus *n*
treasury	Schatzhaus *n*, Schatzkammer *f*
treat	behandeln
treatment	Behandlung *f*
trecento	Trecento *n*
Tree of Jesse	Jessebaum *m*, der Stammbaum Christi, die Wurzel Jesse
Tree of Life	Lebensbaum *m*
tree-ring dating	Dendrochronologie *f*
trefled	kleeblattförmig, Kleeblatt-
trefled cross	Kleeblattkreuz *n*
trefoil *adj.*	kleeblattförmig, Kleeblatt-
trefoil *n.*	Dreipaß *m*, Kleeblatt *n*, Trifolium *n*
trefoil arch	Dreipaßbogen *m*, Kleeblattbogen *m*
trend	Strömung *f*
trepanation	Trepanation *f*
trepanning	Trepanation *f*
trephining	Trepanation *f*
trial proof	Zustandsdruck *m*, Probeabzug *m*, Probedruck *m*, Etat *m*, Andruck *m*, Epreuve *f*
triangle	Dreieck *n*
triangular	dreieckig, Dreiecks-
triangular composition	Dreieckskomposition *f*
tribe	Stamm *m*
tribune	Tribüne *f*
Tribute Money, the —	der Zinsgroschen

trichora	Dreiapsidenchor *m*, Dreikonchenanlage *f*, Kleeblattchor *m*
triclinium	Triklinium *n*
trident	Dreizack *m*, Trident *m*
triforium	Triforium *m*, Drillingsfenster *n*
triglyph	Dreikerb *m*, Dreischlitzplatte *f*, Triglyph *m*, Triglyphe *f*
trilobe arch	Dreipaßbogen *m*, Kleeblattbogen *m*
trim	schmücken
Trinity	Trinität *f*
trinket	Berlocke *f*, Schmuck *m*
tripod	Dreifuß *m*
triptych	Dreiflügelbild *n*, Triptychon *n*
trireme	Triere *f*
Triton	Triton *m*
triumphal arch	Triumphbogen *m*
triumphal column	Triumphsäule *f*
triumphal procession	Triumphzug *m*
Trojan	Troer *m*
trompe l'oeil	Trompe l'oeil *m*
trophy	Tropaion *n*, Trophäe *f*
troubador	Minnesänger *m*, Troubadour *m*
trough	Rinne *f*, Traufleiste *f*
trousers	Hose *f*
trowel	Kelle *f*
Troy	Troja, Troia
true to nature	naturgetreu
trumeau	Fensterpfeiler *m*, Türpfeiler *m*, Mittelpfosten *m*, Portalpfeiler *m*, Trumeau *m*
truncated roof	Flachdach *n*
Trundholm sun chariot	Sonnenwagen von Trundholm *m*
trunk	1. Rumpf *m*, Torso *m* 2. Stamm *m*, Baumstamm *m* 3. Truhe *f*, Kiste *f*
truss	Dachstuhl *m*

tub	Bottich *m*
tube	Tube *f*
Tudor arch	Tudorbogen *m*
tudor flower	Tudorblatt *n*
Tudor style	Tudorstil *m*
tufa	Tuffstein *m*
tuff	Tuffstein *m*
tuft	Quast *m*, Quaste *f*
tuft of hair	Haarbüschel *m, n*
tula work	Tula-Arbeit *f*
tulip-shaped pulpit	Tulpenkanzel *f*
tumulus	Tumulusgrab *n*, Grabhügel *m*, Hügelgrab *n*
tung oil	Tungöl *n*, Holzöl *n*
tunic	Tunika *f*
tunnel	Stollen *m*, unterirdischer Gang *m*
tunnel kiln	Tunnelofen *m*
tunnel vault	Tonnengewölbe *n*
tureen	Terrine *f*
Turkey red	Türkischrot *n*
turmeric dyestuff	Gelbwurz *f*, Kurkumagelb *n*
turn	1. drechseln 2. drehen
turn of the century	Jahrhundertwende *f*
turnsole dyestuff	Lackmus *n*
turntable	Modellierbock *m*, Modellierstuhl *m*
turpentine	Terpentin *n*, Terpentinöl *n*
spirit of —	Terpentingeist *m*
turquoise *adj.*	türkisfarben
turquoise *n.*	Türkis *m*
turret	Dachreiter *m*, Dachtürmchen *n*, Türmchen *n*
Tuscan order	toskanische Ordnung *f*
tusche	Lithotusche *f*
tusk	Stoßzahn *m*
tutelary spirit	Genius *m*

twilight	Dämmerlicht *n*
twin	Zwilling *m*
twirled rosette	Wirbelrosette *f*
twist	drehen, krümmen, sich winden
twisted	busig, gebust, gewunden
twisted column	gewundene Säule *f*
two-color print	Zweifarbendruck *m*
two-dimensional	zweidimensional, flächig
two-disc fibula	Plattenfibel *f*
two-headed eagle	Doppeladler *m*
two-storied	zweigeschossig, zweistöckig
tympanum	Giebel *m*, Giebelfeld *n*, Tympanon *n*, Türfeld *n*, Bogenfeld *n*
type	1. Art *f*, Typ *m*, Typus *m*, Gattung *f* 2. Letter *f*, Type *f*, Schrift *f*
typeface	Letterart *f*, Schrifttyp *m*
typography	Typographie *f*
typological Bible illustrations	typologischer Bilderkreis *m*
typology	Typologie *f*
Tyrian purple	Purpur *m*
Uffizi	Uffizien *f*
ugliness	Häßlichkeit *f*
ugly	häßlich
ultramarine blue	Lasurblau *n*, Ultramarin *n*
ultraviolet light	Ultraviolett *n*
umber	Umbra *f*, Umber *m*, Schattenfarbe *f*
umbrella	Schirm *m*
umbrella dome	Schirmgewölbe *n*
unadorned	schlicht, schmucklos
unbaked brick	Luftziegel *m*
unblemished	makellos, fehlerfrei, perfekt
unburnished gilding	Mattvergoldung *f*

uncial	Unziale *f*, Unzialschrift *f*
uncial book hand	Unziale *f*, Unzialschrift *f*
uncial letter	Unzialbuchstabe *m*
unciform	hakenförmig
unclothed	unbekleidet
undamaged	unversehrt
undecorated	schmucklos
undergarment	Untergewand *n*
underglaze painting	Unterglasurmalerei *f*
under life-size	unterlebensgroß
underpainting	Untermalung *f*, Untertuschung *f*
undersurface	Unterlage *f*, Unterseite *f*
undressed	1. unbekleidet 2. unbehauen
Unetice culture	Aunjetizer Kultur *f*
unfinished	roh
unfinished building	Rohbau *m*
unguentarium	Salbgefäß *n*
unhewn	unbehauen
unicorn	Einhorn *n*
unit	Einheit *f*
unit of measure	Maßeinheit *f*
unmounted	ungefaßt
unpainted	unbemalt, ungefaßt
unrealistic	wirklichkeitsfremd, unrealistisch
unset	ungefaßt
unsigned	unsigniert
unworked	unbehauen
unworked marble	Rohmarmor *m*
unworked stone	Bruchstein *m*
upholstery	Polsterung *f*
upper	Ober-
upper arm	Oberarm *m*
upper floor	Obergeschoß *n*
upper Paleolithic	Jungpaläolithikum *n*
upper surface	Oberfläche *f*
upright beam	Ständer *m*

Urfirnis	Urfirnisware *f*
urn	Urne *f*
cinerary —	Leichenbrandurne *f*, Aschenurne *f*
house-shaped —	Hausurne *f*
urnfield	Urnenfeld *n*
urnfield culture	Urnenfeldkultur *f*
use	Anwendung *f*, Verwendung *f*, Gebrauch *m*
utensil	Gebrauchsgegenstand *m*, Gerät *n*, Utensilien *pl*
utility ceramics	Gebrauchskeramik *f*
valuable	wertvoll
value	1. Wert *m* 2. Valeur *f*
color —	Farbwert *m*, Valeur *f*
tone —	Tonwert *m*
vanishing point	Fluchtpunkt *m*
vanitas still life	Vanitasstilleben *n*
varnish *v.*	lackieren
varnish *n.*	Firnis *m*, Lack *m*
final —	Schlußfirnis *m*
intermediate —	Zwischenfirnis *m*
varnish coating	Lacküberzug *m*
varnishing day	Vernissage *f*
vary	variieren
vase	Vase *f*
vase painting	Vasenmalerei *f*, Vasenbild *n*
vat	Bottich *m*
Vatican	Vatikan *m*
vault *v.*	wölben
vault *n.*	Gewölbe *n*, Wölbung *f*
annular barrel —	Ringtonne *f*
barrel —	Tonnengewölbe *n*
domical —	Domikalgewölbe *n*, Klostergewölbe *n*

false —	Überkragungsgewölbe *n*, Überkragungskuppel *f*
fan —	Palmgewölbe *n*, Strahlengewölbe *n*
groin —	Kreuzgewölbe *n*, Kreuzgratgewölbe *n*
net —	Netzgewölbe *n*, Zellengewölbe *n*
reticulated —	Netzgewölbe *n*
rib —	Kreuzrippengewölbe *n*, Rippengewölbe *n*
sail —	Hängekuppel *f*, Kreuzrippengewölbe *n*, Segelgewölbe *n*, Stutzkuppel *f*
stellar —	Sterngewölbe *n*
tunnel —	Tonnengewölbe *n*
type of —	Wölbungsart *f*
wagon —	Tonnengewölbe *n*
vault apex	Scheitelhöhe *f*
vault boss	Schlußstein *m*
vault cell	Gewölbekappe *f*, Wange *f*
vault construction	Gewölbebau *m*, Gewölbekonstruktion *f*
vaulted	gewölbt
vaulted ceiling	Gewölbedecke *f*
vaulted roof	Wölbedach *n*
vault groin	Gewölbegrat *m*
vaulting	Wölbung *f*
vaulting shaft	Dienst *m*
vaulting shafts, clustered —	Dienstbündel *n*
vault rib	Gewölberippe *f*
vault support	Gewölbeträger *m*
vault thrust	Gewölbeschub *m*
veduta	Vedute *f*, Stadtvedute *f*, Stadtansicht *f*, Prospekt *m*
veduta painting	Vedutenmalerei *f*
vegetable dye	Pflanzenfarbstoff *m*
vegetable oil	Pflanzenöl *n*
vehicle	Bindemittel *n*, Farbbindemittel *n*
veil	Schleier *m*, Flor *m*

veil of St. Veronica	das Schweißtuch der hl. Veronika, Veronikatuch *n*
vein	Ader *f*
marble —	Marmorader *f*
vellum	Pergament *n*, Pergamenthandschrift *f*
vellum paper	Pergamentpapier *n*, Velin *n*, Velinpapier *n*
velvet	Samt *m*
veneer *v.*	furnieren
veneer *n.*	Furnier *n*, Furnierholz *n*
veneration of the Virgin	Marienkult *m*
Venetian glass	venezianisches Glas *n*
Venetian red	Venezianischrot *n*
Venice	Venedig
Venice turpentine	Venezianer Terpentin *n*
vent	Eingußkanal *m*, Entlüftungskanal *m*, Luftkanal *m*
Venus de Milo	melische Aphrodite *f*
Venus de'Medici	mediceische Venus *f*
verdigris	Grünspan *m*
verdure	Gartenteppich *m*, Verdüre *f*
verge	Dachüberstand *m*, Überstand *m*
Verism	Verismus *m*
vermeil	Vermeil *n*
vermeil red	vermeil
vermilion	zinnoberrot
vernicle	Schweißtuch *n*, das Schweißtuch der hl. Veronika, Veronikatuch *n*
vernis mou	Vernis mou *n*, Durchdruckverfahren *n*, Weichgrundätzung *f*
vernissage	Vernissage *f*
verre de fougère	Waldglas *n*
version	Fassung *f*, Version *f*
vertical	senkrecht, vertikal
vertical line	Senkrechte *f*, Vertikale *f*
vertical section	Vertikalschnitt *m*

vesica	Mandorla *f*
vesica piscis	Fischblase *f*
Vesperbild	Vesperbild *n*
vessel	Gefäß *n*
vessel wall	Gefäßwandung *f*
vestal virgin	Vestalin *f*
vestibule	Vestibül *n*, Vestibulum *n*, Vorhof *m*
vestment	Ornat *n*
vestry	Sakristei *f*
Via Sacra	Prozessionsstraße *f*
vicinty	Umgebung *f*, Nähe *f*
victor	Sieger *m*
Victoria green	Viktoriagrün *n*
victorious	siegreich
victory	Sieg *m*
goddess of —	Siegesgöttin *f*
victory column	Siegessäule *f*
victory stele	Siegesstele *f*
Vienna	Wien
Vienna Sezession	Sezessionstil *m*
view *v.*	betrachten, anschauen
view *n.*	Blick *m*, Ansicht *f*, Anschauung *f*, Ausblick *m*, Prospekt *m*, Perspektive *f*
aerial —	Vogelperspektive *f*
bird's eye —	Vogelperspektive *f*, Draufsicht *f*
partial —	Teilansicht *f*, Ausschnitt *m*
worm's eye —	Froschperspektive *f*
viewer	Betrachter *m*, Beschauer *m*
view from above	Draufsicht *f*, Daraufsicht *f*
viewing, direction of —	Anschauungsrichtung *f*
viewing path	Blickbahn *f*
viewing side, ideal —	Idealansicht *f*
view of the interior	Innenansicht *f*
viewpoint	Betrachtungspunkt *m*
vignette	Vignette *f*

Viking	Wikinger *m*
villa	Villa *f*
vine	Ranke *f*
vine black	Rebenschwarz *n*
vine foliage	Ranke *f*
vine ornament	Weinranke *f*
vine scroll decoration	Rankenwerk *n*
vine scroll pattern	Blattfries *m*, Laubfries *m*, Rankenfries *m*
violet purple	violett
virgin	Jungfrau *f*
symbols of the —	marianische Symbole *pl*
Virgin and Child, the —	Madonna mit Kind, Maria mit Kind
Virgin in the Rose Bower	Madonna im Rosenhag
Virgin of the Rose-Crown	Rosenkranzbild *n*
Virgin on the Crescent	Maria auf der Mondsichel
Virgo	Jungfrau *f*
Virtues and Vices	Tugenden und Laster
visage	Antlitz *n*, Gesicht *n*
viscosity	Dickflüssigkeit *f*, Zähflüssigkeit *f*
viscous	dickflüssig, zähflüssig
visibility	Sichtbarkeit *f*
visible	sichtbar
Visigoth art	westgotische Kunst *f*
vision	1. Phantasiebild *n*, Erscheinung *f* 2. Sehkraft *f*
cone of —	Sehpyramide *f*
line of —	Sehachse *f*
Visitation, the —	die Heimsuchung Mariä, Visitatio *f*
visor	Helmklappe *f*
vista	1. Durchblick *m*, Blick *m* 2. langer Gang *m*, Korridor *m*
visual	bildlich, visuell
visual arts	bildende Kunst *f*
visual cliché	Bildklischee *n*
visual experience	Seherfahrung *f*

vitreous porcelain	Glasporzellan *n*
vitrification	Sinterung *f*
vitrify	sintern
Vitruvian scroll	laufender Hund *m*, Wellenband *n*
vivid	1. anschaulich 2. lebendig, lebhaft
vividness	1. Anschaulichkeit *f* 2. Lebhaftigkeit *f*
vocabulary of figures	Figurenwelt *f*
vocabulary of gestures	Gebärdensprache *f*
vocabulary of symbols	Symbolsprache *f*
volet	Altarflügel *m*, Flügel *m*
volume	1. Band *m* 2. Volumen *n*
volute	Volute *f*, Schnörkel *m*
volute krater	Volutenkrater *m*
Vorarlberg plan	Vorarlberger Schema *n*
votive art	Votivkunst *f*
votive chapel	Votivkapelle *f*
votive image	Votivbild *n*, Weihenbild *n*, Weihbild *n*, Exvoto *n*
votive tablet	Votivtafel *f*
voussoir	Keilstein *m*
V-shaped gouge	Geißfuß *m*
vyse	Spindeltreppe *f*, Wendeltreppe *f*
wagon vault	Tonnengewölbe *n*
wainscot	Wandtäfelung *f*
waist	Taille *f*
walkway	Laufgang *m*
wall	Mauer *f*, Wand *f*, Wandung *f*
curtain —	nicht tragende (Außen-)Wand *f*
enclosing —	Umfassungsmauer *f*, Einfriedungsmauer *f*, Mauerring *m*
fire —	Brandmauer *f*
inner —	Innenwand *f*

outer —	Außenwand *f*
panel —	nicht tragende (Außen-)Wand *f*
retaining —	Stützmauer *f*, Futtermauer *f*
wall anchor	Maueranker *m*, Wandanker *m*
wall articulation	Wandgliederung *f*
wallboard	Faserplatte *f*
wall clamp	Maueranker *m*, Wandanker *m*
wall mosaic	Wandmosaik *n*
wall niche tomb	Wandnischengrabmal *n*
wall offset	Mauerabsatz *m*
wall painting	Wandbild *n*, Wandgemälde *n*, Wandmalerei *f*
wall paneling	Wandtäfelung *f*, Wandverkleidung *f*, Lambris *m*
wallpaper	Tapete *f*
wall pier	Wandpfeiler *m*
wall plate	Fußpfette *f*
wall register	Wandzone *f*
wall rib	Schildbogen *m*, Schildrippe *f*
wall structure	Wandaufbau *m*, Wandstruktur *f*
walnut	Nußbaum *m*
walnut oil	Nußöl *n*, Walnußkernöl *n*, Walnußöl *n*
walrus tusk	Walroßzahn *m*
ware	Töpferware *f*, Keramik *f*
war chariot	Kampfwagen *m*, Streitwagen *m*
warp *v.*	krümmen
warp *n.*	Kette *f*, Warp *m*, Werft *m*
warp beam	Kettbaum *m*, Walzholz *n*, Zettelbaum *m*
warped	busig, gebust, krumm, verbogen
warp threads	Kettenfäden *pl*, Zettel *m*, Längsfäden *pl*
warp-weighted loom	Gewichtswebstuhl *m*
warrior	Krieger *m*, Kämpfer *m*
wash	1. waschen 2. lavieren

wash drawing	lavierte Federzeichnung *f*
Washing of the Feet, the —	die Fußwaschung
watch tower	Wachtturm *m*, Wartturm *m*, Ausguck *m*
watercolor	Aquarell *n*, Wasserfarbe *f*, Wasserfarbenmalerei *f*
water glass	Wasserglas *n*
watermark	Wasserzeichen *n*
water medium coating	Wasserstrich *m*
water pitcher	Wasserkanne *f*
waterproof	wasserfest
water soluble	wasserlöslich
water supply system	Wasserversorgungsanlage *f*
water table	Mauerabsatz *m*
water-tempera brush line	Wasserstrich *m*
wattle	Geflecht *n*
wattle and daub	Geflecht und Lehm, Flechtwerk *n*
wave	Welle *f*
wave decoration	Wellendekor *m*
wave meander	laufender Hund *m*, Wellenband *n*
waves	Wellen *pl*, Wellendekor *n*
wax	Wachs *n*
wax coating	Wachsüberzug *m*
wax crayon	Wachskreide *f*, Wachsmalstift *m*
wax death mask	Imago *f*
waxed paper	Pergamentpapier *n*
wax figure	Wachsfigur *f*
wax impression	Wachsabdruck *m*
wax mask	Wachsmaske *f*
wax model	Wachsentwurf *m*, Modellmännchen *n*
wax modeller	Wachsbossierer *m*
wax modelling	Wachsbildnerei *f*
wax sculpture	Keroplastik *f*, Zeroplastik *f*, Wachsbild *n*
wax statue	Wachsfigur *f*
wax stencil	Wachsschablone *f*

wax tablet	Wachstafel *f*
waxwork	Wachsbildnerei *f*
weapon	Waffe *f*
wear	tragen
weather effects	Witterungseinfluß *m*
weathering	1. Verwitterung *f* 2. Wasserschlag *m*
weather moulding	Kranzleiste *f*
weave *v.*	1. flechten 2. weben 3. wirken
weave *n.*	Gewebe *n*, Webart *f*
weaver	Weber *m*, Wirker *m*
master —	Webmeister *m*, Wirkmeister *m*
weaving	Weberei *f*, Weben *n*, Wirken *n*
weaving method	Webverfahren *n*
weaving mill	Weberei *f*
weaving process	Webverfahren *n*
weaving reed	Riet *n*, Webeblatt *n*
weaving shuttle	Schiffchen *n*, Schütze *m*, Weberschiffchen *n*
Wedding of Cana, the —	die Hochzeit zu Kanaan
wedge	Keil *m*
wedge-shaped	keilförmig, kuneiform, Keil-
Wedgwood ware	Wedgwoodware *f*
weft	Schuß *m*, Weft *n*
weft thread	Schußfaden *m*
Weighing of the Souls, the —	die Seelenwägung
weight-bearing	tragend, Trag-
weight-bearing capacity	Tragkraft *f*
weight-bearing structure	Tragkonstruktion *f*
weight-bearing wall	Tragwand *f*
weld *v.*	schweißen
weld *n.*	Wau *m*
welding, arc —	Lichtbogenschweißung *f*
well	Brunnen *m*

well-levigated	feingeschlämmt
well-shaped	wohlgestaltet
west Roman	weströmisch
westwork	Westwerk *n*
wet	naß
wet-into-wet	naß in naß
wetting agent	Netzmittel *n*
wheel	Rad *n*
wheel window	Radfenster *n*, Rosenfenster *n*, Katharinenrad *n*
whet	schleifen
whetstone	Schleifstein *m*, Wetzstein *m*
white	weiß, Weiß-
white-ground	Weißgrundmalerei *f*
white-ground painting	Weißgrundmalerei *f*
white lead	Bleiweiß *n*, Kremserweiß *n*
white lead in oil	Bleiweißpaste *f*
white-line woodcut	Weißlinienschnitt *m*, Weißschnitt *m*
whitewash *v.*	weißen
whitewash *n.*	Tünche *f*
whiting	Schlämmkreide *f*
whorl rosette	Wirbelrosette *f*
wicker goods	Flechtware *f*
wickerwork	Geflecht *n*, Flechtwerk *n*
wide	breit, weit, Breit-
width	Weite *f*
wife	Frau *f*, Ehefrau *f*
wig	Perücke *f*
wind-blown acanthus	windbewegter Akanthus *m*
window	Fenster *n*
bay —	Erker *m*, Auslucht *f*
casement —	Flügelfenster *n*
lancet —	Lanzettfenster *n*
leaded glass —	Bleiglasfenster *n*
rose —	Fensterrose *f*, Radfenster *n*, Rosenfenster *n*

stained glass —	Bleiglasfenster *n*, Buntglasfenster *n*, Buntscheibe *f*
wheel —	Radfenster *n*
window grating	Fensterkorb *m*
window ledge	Sohlbank *f*, Fensterbrett *n*
windowless	fensterlos
window lintel	Fenstersturz *m*
window screen	Fensterraster *m*, Gitter *n*
window shape	Fensterform *f*
window sill	Fensterbank *f*, Fensterbrett *n*, Sohlbank *f*
window surface	Fensterfläche *f*
wing	1. Flügel *m* 2. Trakt *m*
wing chair	Ohrensessel *m*
winged	geflügelt, Flügel-
winged altarpiece	Flügelaltar *m*, Flügelretabel *n*, Klappaltar *m*, Schreinaltar *m*
winged horse	Flügelpferd *n*
winged lion	Flügellöwe *m*
wire	Draht *m*
wire-reinforced glass	Drahtglas *n*
wire sculpture	Drahtplastik *f*
Wise and Foolish Virgins, the —	die klugen und törichten Jungfrauen
with the grain	in Faserrichtung
woad dyestuff	Waid *m*
woman	Frau *f*
Woman Taken in Adultery, the —	Christus und die Ehebrecherin
Women at the Tomb, the —	die Frauen am Grabe
wood *adj.*	hölzern, Holz-
wood *n.*	Holz *n*
wood beam	Holzbalken *m*
wood-beamed ceiling	Holzbalkendecke *f*
wood block carver	Formschneider *m*
woodcarver	Holzschnitzer *m*, Schnitzer *m*

woodcarver's bench	Schnitzbank *f*
woodcarving	Schnitzkunst *f*, Holzbildhauerei *f*, Holzbildnerei *f*, Holzschnitzerei *f*
woodcarving chisel	Schnitzeisen *n*
woodcarving knife	Schnitzmesser *n*, Holzmesser *n*, Schneidemesser *n*
wood construction	Holzbau *m*
woodcut	Holzschnitt *m*
color —	Farbholzschnitt *m*
polychrome —	Vielfarbenholzschnitt *m*
woodcutting gouge	Hohleisen *n*
wooden	1. hölzner, Holz- 2. steif
wooden ceiling	Holzdecke *f*
wooden core	Holzkern *m*
wooden floor	Holzboden *m*
wooden frame	Holzrahmen *m*
wood engraving	Holzstich *m*, Tonstich *m*
wood engraving block	Holzstock *m*
wooden peg	Holznagel *m*
wooden sculpture	1. Holzbild *n*, Holzplastik *f*, Holzskulptur *f* 2. Holzbildnerei *f*, Holzbildhauerei *f*
wooden structure	Holzbau *m*
wooden tablet	Holztafel *f*
wood frame construction	Ständerbau *m*
wood grain	Faser *f*, Holzmaserung *f*, Maserung *f*
wood plank floor	Bretterboden *m*
wood-pulp paper	Holzpapier *n*
woof	Schuß *m*, Weft *n*, Durchschuß *m*, Einschlag *m*
wool	Wolle *f*
woolen	wollen, Woll-
work	Werk *n*, Arbeit *f*, Opus *n*, Schaffen *n*

work drawing	Werkzeichnung *f*, Visierung *f*
workmanship	Kunstfertigkeit *f*, Arbeit *f*, Ausführung *f*
work of art	Kunstwerk *n*
work procedure	Werkverfahren *n*
workshop	Werkstatt *f*, Werkstätte *f*, Studio *n*, Atelier *n*
workshop piece	Werkstattarbeit *f*
world	Welt *f*
wordly	weltlich
world's fair	Weltausstellung *f*
worm's-eye view	Froschperspektive *f*
worship	Anbetung *f*, Adoration *f*
Worship of the Golden Calf	die Anbetung des goldenen Kalbes
worth	Wert *m*
worthless	wertlos
worthy subject matter	bildwürdiges Sujet *n*
wrapping	1. Drapierung *f* 2. Empaquetage *f*
wreath	Kranz *m*, Blumenkranz *m*
wrinkle	Falte *f*, Runzel *f*
wrist	Handgelenk *n*
wristguard	Armschutzplatte *f*
write	schreiben
writing	Schrift *f*
writing quill	Schreibfeder *f*
written source	Schriftquelle *f*
wrought iron *adj.*	schmiedeeisern, Schmiedeeisen-
wrought iron *n.*	Schmiedeeisen *n*
xanthorrhea	Akaroidharz *n*
x-ray *v.*	durchleuchten, röntgen
x-ray *n.*	Röntgenaufnahme *f*
x-ray style	Röntgenstil *m*
xylene	Xylol *n*

xylographer	Xylograph *m*, Formschneider *m*, Holzschneider *m*
xylography	Xylographie *f*, Holzschneidekunst *f*
xylol	Xylol *n*
yarn	Garn *n*
yellow *v.*	gilben
yellow *adj.*	gelb
yolk	Dotter *n*
young	jung
young fustic	junges Fustikholz *n*
youth	Jüngling *m*, Knabe *m*
Y-shaped cross	Deichselkreuz *n*, Gabelkreuz *n*, Schächerkreuz *n*
zebra wood	Zebraholz *n*
zebrano	Zebraholz *n*
ziggurat	Zikkurat *f*, Zikkurrat *f*, Stufentempel *m*
zigzag *adj.*	zackig, zickzackförmig
zigzag *n.*	Zackenfries *m*, Sägezahnfries *m*
zigzag band	Sägezahnfries *m*
zigzag ornament	Sägezahnfries *m*, Zackenfries *m*
zigzag pattern	Zickzackband *n*
zikkurrat	Zikkurat *f*, Zikkurrat *f*, Stufentempel *m*
zinc	Zink *m*, *n*
zincography	Zinkdruck *m*, Zinkographie *f*
zinc plate etching	Zinkätzung *f*
zinc white	Zinkweiß *n*
zinc yellow	Zinkgelb *n*
zinken	Zinken *pl*
zodiac	Tierkreis *m*, Zodiakus *m*

sign of the —	Tierkreisbild *n*, Tierkreiszeichen *n*
zone	Zone *f*
zoomorphic ornament	Tierornament *n*, Tierornamentik *f*

Wir empfehlen:

Reading Knowledge in German for Art Historians and Archaeologists
Ein englisch-deutscher Lesekurs für Kunstgeschichte und Archäologie

2., durchgesehene Auflage, 152 Seiten, DIN A 5, kartoniert, DM 29,80

Die Autoren haben aus ihrer großen Erfahrung im Deutschunterricht für Ausländer mit diesem Lehrbuch einen sprachlichen Einführungskurs für englischsprachige Studenten vorgelegt, der das Studium der deutschen Kunstgeschichte und Archäologie ermöglicht. Aber auch für andere geistesgeschichtliche Fächer hat sich dieser Lesekurs bereits bewährt. Die Lesefähigkeit deutscher wissenschaftlicher Texte wird in systematisch aufgebauten Lektionen und Übungen erarbeitet. Der erforderliche Wortschatz wird in gezielter Anordnung vermittelt.

Kleines Deutschlandbuch für Ausländer
Wichtige Sachgebiete und ihr Wortschatz

von Rudolf Meldau

11., überarbeitete Auflage, 93 Seiten, DIN A 5, kartoniert, DM 13,80

Dieses erfolgreiche Informations- und Lehrbuch wurde für die 11. Auflage eingehend nach dem heutigen Entwicklungs- und Sprachstand überarbeitet. Das Buch macht den Ausländer mit den wichtigsten deutschen Lebensformen bekannt und vermittelt ihm den entsprechenden Wortschatz.` Die straffe Gliederung leistet dabei eine entscheidende Hilfe. Der Band dient zugleich als Arbeitsgrundlage für deutsche Sprachkurse.

Deutsche Kultur – Eine Einführung

herausgegeben von Heinz Fischer

2., neubearbeitete und ergänzte Auflage, 261 Seiten, 18 Abbildungen und Karten, DIN A 5, kartoniert, DM 17,80

Der Band gibt einen landes- und kulturkundlichen Überblick über die Bundesrepublik und ihre Nachbarländer in ihrer historischen Entwicklung bis zur Gegenwart. Für die vorliegende 2. Auflage wurde diese Einführung völlig neubearbeitet und um wichtige Kapitel ergänzt. Die Einführung dient der allgemeinen Information sowie vornehmlich als Arbeitsmittel beim Deutschunterricht für Ausländer. Behandelte Themenkreise: Geschichte – Wegweiser durch die Bundesrepublik – DDR – Österreich – Schweiz – Landschaft und Wirtschaft – Sprache – Bildungswege – Musik – Volkslied – Kunst – Literatur – Theater – Film – Fernsehen – Folklore – Trachten – Humor – Chronologie.

ERICH SCHMIDT VERLAG

BASKERVILLE SERIE

Verzamelde Gedichten 1

Ida Gerhardt

Verzamelde Gedichten

I

Athenaeum—Polak & Van Gennep
Amsterdam 1992

Kosmos

Voor Marie van der Zeyde

WANDELING IN VLAANDEREN

Het landschap had ons opgenomen,
de dag heeft helder ons behoord;
de open hemel, 't gras, de bomen,
een levend water—en volkomen
de vreugd van woord en wederwoord.

De peppels langs de smalle dijken
bloeiden, bestoven van het goud,
de lucht scheen eind'loos diep te wijken,
maar aan de voet was ons het prijken
van kleine planten welvertrouwd.

O licht over de voorjaarslanden
waarin de leeuw'rik valt en stijgt,
en water dat de oeverranden
bloeiend weerspiegelt en ons bande
in aandacht die zich overneigt,

hoe zacht neemt gij het hart gevangen
en richt het tot zijn stille zin—
de blik zwerft uit, een stout verlangen
spant reeds zijn kracht en zoekt de lange
horizon af; nieuw werk gaat in.

*En dit was met ons langs de wegen
bij 't rustig, gelijkmatig gaan,
beleden soms en soms verzwegen,
maar van elkander in genegen
aandacht begrepen en verstaan.*

*Zon kleurde de verweerde hoeven,
de leiboom bloeide aan de muur,
de boomgaard prijkte — en het toeven
bij deze pracht bood ons te proeven
de volle gaven van het uur.*

*Het landschap staat in mij geschreven,
gras, water, bloemen, ieder ding, —
ook wij, in aandacht weggegeven,
en over al dit bezig leven
het licht in hoge koepeling.*

Vlaanderen, voorjaar '38

Kosmos

KOSMOS

Het spel van lijn en kleur en van schakering
dat leeft in de natuur, het donker en het licht
—wetten van wisseling en wederkering—,
ik vind het terug in het voltooid gedicht.

De groeiwijs van de plant, het levend zich ontvouwen
van vorm na vorm, weer rustend in de regelmaat
die fijn vertakt door bloem en blad en stengel gaat,
is mij een teken dat het stil, geduldig bouwen

van woord aan woord gehoorzaamt aan eenzelfde streven.

—Wij luist'ren: hoorbaar, op ons ademen bewogen,
stuwende en gestadig is het eigen leven

verborgen arbeidend; totdat het diepst verlangen
tot rust wordt in het woord. Dan ligt voor onze ogen
de vorm, waarin het trillende is ingevangen.

MILIUM EFFUSUM*

Een pluimgras-schaduw, neergeschreven
en wiegende over mijn blad;
op het effen papier het beven
der arepluimen, rijke schat
van fijne zaden, kiemend leven;
boven de puntig uitgedreven
gescherpte blaad'ren ijl geheven.

Beeld van het overvele dat
het trillend vers zoekt na te streven
en in zijn eenheid samenvat:
de ranke bouw, het vrije zweven,
der woorden duizendvoudig leven,—
o zinrijk teken, hier gegeven,
gespiegeld op het wachtend blad.

* *milium effusum*—breed gierstgras.

KINDERSPEL

Hij zat nadenkend bij zijn kleine schat,
een doos met schelpen, en met fronsend turen
de namen prevelend zag hij de uren
terug, waarin hij hen gevonden had.

Dagen van open zon, dagen van regen
en vlagen wind, het breken van de zee,
en alle argeloze vreugden, die ermee
verweven waren; tot naar stiller wegen

zijn aandacht boog: het lijnenspel, de kleuren,
het kleine leven dat dit broze bouwde,
het zeediep met het wonderlijk gebeuren
van plant en dier, zoals hij in vertrouwde

verhalen het herlas... en in dit zoet herkennen
nog dieper dalend, sloot hij glimlachend de ogen;
glijdend langs nerf en karteling bewogen
de vingers in een tasten, een gewennen

aan diepste aandacht—Sober spel, omgeven
van een zó grote stilte, dat ook wij gevangen
toezagen,—dan een flitsend even
elkaar aanzien: wij lazen een gelijk verlangen.

DE AKELEI
Dürer

Toen hij het kleine plantje vond,
boog hij aandachtig naar de grond
en dan, om wortels en om mos
groef hij de fijne aarde los,
voorzichtig—dat zijn hand niets schond.

Behoedzaam rondom aangevat
droeg hij het langs het slingerpad
van bos en akker voor zich uit,
en schoof het thuis in 't licht der ruit
zoals hij het gevonden had.

Dan, fluitende en welgezind
mengde hij zoekend eerst de tint;
diepblauw en zwart ineengevloeid,
met enk'le druppels rood doorgloeid,
dat het tot purper samenbindt.

En uur aan uur trok stil voorbij;
zó diep verzonken werkte hij,
dat het hem soms was of zijn hand
de vezels tastte van de plant—
zo glanzend kwam de omtrek vrij.

Totdat het gaaf te prijken stond:
de wortels scheem'rend afgerond,
het uitgesprongen groene blad
scherp in zijn karteling gevat
tegen de lichte achtergrond;

de bloemkroon purper violet,
de hokjes om het hart gebed
en boven de geknikte steel
de honingsporen, het juweel
vijfvlakkig: kantig neergezet.

In 't vallend donker toefde hij
nog dralend bij zijn akelei;
dan, in het laatste licht van 't raam
schreef hij de letters van zijn naam
en 't jaartal glimlachend erbij.

Aanhef

AANHEF

Van heuvel tot heuvel gaat een schalmeien—
een heldere inzet, een dagbegin;
van heuvel tot heuvel gaat een schalmeien,
bergen en hemel sluiten het in.

Zwelt er een tegenroep in de valleien?
Donkerte huist in het dal daar beneden;
schaduwen—tussen de wanden der bomen
ritselt het water, een prevelend stromen;
vochtiger klank in het dal daar beneden.

IJl is de morgen en fonk'lend de landen;
schuivende bundels van licht, dat gaat breken
trekken voorbij, tot hun vluchtende randen
glijdend in 't nevelig dal zijn ontweken.

Zwerft daar een weerglans in donkerder streken?

Wereld, gevat in dit zuivere dagen,
wisselspel over de glooiende landen,
lokt gij de sluim'rende fluit in mijn handen?
Wat wordt mij nader en nader gedragen?

Zal ik het vinden, dit prille beginnen,
stijgende inzet, waarbinnen zich even
in een bewegend schakeren, een zweven,
lichtend verraadt, wat ik spelend zal winnen?

Los uit de donkere oorsprong, geheven,
vormt zich de toon—in een tint'ling, een beven
slaat het tot melodie, wordt het tot leven,—
vrij naar het licht van de heldere morgen.

Stralende aanhef, wat houdt ge geborgen?

SCHERZO

Zachte argeloze vreugd
die ons éénmaal werd beschoren,
toen wij in de dans verloren
deelden in het spel der jeugd.

In de lichte snelle rei
werden wij ook meegenomen,
in de dans voert de volkomen
zorgeloosheid heerschappij.

Helder klonk de korte slag
van de handeklap: de paren
neigden spelend tot elkaar en
weken weer met schaterlach.

In dit dansen werd een licht,
tintelend geluk geboren;
zingt het nu nog, onverloren,
zingt het nog in mijn gedicht?

Een herinneren, een glans
in mijn sober werk gebleven,
soms een glinstering, en èven
de figuren van de dans.

DE FLUIT

Voor Titia Langeveld

Ik ken op aarde geen geluid
zo zuiverend als van de fluit,
een open landschap brengt het mij
jong in de tinten groen nabij,
—schaduw en licht gaan in en uit.

Is het de oorsprong van het hout
dat in zich nog besloten houdt
de boom, gevormd in ring na ring,
het lover in zijn fluistering,
het ruisen dat zich wijd ontvouwt?

Hoor, in de ebben schacht verdoken,
dit stromen, donker en gebroken,
een oerklank stamelend bevrijd,
een zingen in aanvankelijkheid
en dolen, prevelend gesproken.

Een adem schiep de eerste mens
en nu bezielt hij naar zijn wens
dit hout—met rijzen en met dalen
formeert het tastend ademhalen
de tonen. Langs hun zuiv're grens

de reeksen, ijl omhoog getogen
en als in strak azuur ontvlogen
zo licht en bovenaards ontstegen,—
dan dalend in een speels bewegen
tot milder wending omgebogen.

Een heuvelland komt in het licht,
fijn bloeiend gras, trillend gezwicht,
een oeverbocht, het zilver stromen
van een rivier, gehuifde bomen;
rondóm het strenge vergezicht

der naaldhoutbossen. Wat bewoog
er onder de satijnen boog
der treurwilgtakken? Aangelopen,
teer en verwonderd in het open
riviergras dit figuurtje, hoog

sloeg er een vogel, parelend klaar,
er viel een vak van zon — en paar
na paar, een losse rand
kwam te bewegen in het land;
dansende, dwalend door elkaar,

met in ontglippen en ontmoeten
een prille drift, een huiverzoete
ontvoering. Uit het verre lover
waait een versluierd roepen over,
een lachen vlucht op lichte voeten,

een rank, een speelse fantasie.
D'aanvankelijke melodie
wordt strak, in effen trant hernomen
en trekt voorbij: een naderkomen
van 't afscheid dat ik wenken zie.

Een nauw gewaagde klank—nog even
huivert een ademtocht van leven
langs de versmalde parelrij
der gaten, maakt zich stijgend vrij;—
dan dooft omfloerst het lichte zweven.

Als ging het leven zelve uit
zo is het ons nu dit geluid
verstierf—wij zien elkander aan,
nog toevende.

Quo carmine demum

TUIN VAN EPICURUS

Wij kozen soberheid tot bondgenoot.
De geest beheerst als willig instrument
het lichaam, tot die fiere dienst gewend;
gevoed met zuiver water, zuiver brood.

Wij kozen soberheid tot bondgenoot.
Besloten schikt zich in der uren kring
naar strikte trant tot rust en ordening
wat ons het denken, vrijuit zwervend bood.

Wij kozen soberheid tot bondgenoot.
Wij arbeiden in zwijgen en geduld;
de dag is als een honingkorf gevuld
en vriendschap is in onze tuin genood.

Wij kozen soberheid tot bondgenoot,—
en uur na uur draagt ons zijn gave aan,
wij rijpen als de vruchten, als het graan
in 't goede leven tot de goede dood.

LUCRETIUS
...noctes vigilare serenas,
quaerentem dictis quibus et quo carmine demum...

Zonlicht en wolken en de roekeloze pracht
der aarde, uitgebroken, naar het licht
zich tillende en bevend toegericht,—
bloeiende leeft het vóór mij in de stille nacht.

Helderder nog en klaarder, met in het verschijnen
iets bovenaards, een glanzen als het eerste dagen
van wat geschapen is en in een dwingend vragen
mij toegewend.—O, eenmaal argeloos te zijn en

niets dan deel te wezen van dit bloeiend leven,—
zoals het dier, het kind, uiteindelijk ontheven
van wat ik zelf mij koos: dit zwoegen, deze pijnen.

Zal ooit het woord ik zó formeren dat gedreven,
gevormd tot eigen staat, een wereld in het schijnen
van jong ontsprongen licht mijn handen komt ontzweven?

NA DE DAG

Nog bergt de grond gegiste zon
warm onder 't harsig naaldtapijt,—
een dierenspoor heeft naar de bron
en deze stilte mij geleid.
Het spat wat fijne zilverigheid.

De dag was ongemeten wijd,
ik ben doorgloeid van wat ik won,—
vandaag was het of nieuw begon
de aarde in oorspronkelijkheid.

En óók het vers, waarop ik zon,
hoe werd het zó van zelf bevrijd:
elk woord of het niet anders kon
volstrekt in zijn aanwezigheid.

Het ligt zo glanzend uitgespreid
in 't effen rijm, dat het omspon
en gaaf in zijn beslotenheid;
de hartslag van een verre bron
rimpelt het even en verglijdt.

Is dichten slechts aandachtigheid?

MOMENT

De kleine hof ligt in het middaglicht,
de bijen zwermen om de bloesembomen;
een arbeiden in de natuur, in mijn gedicht—
dan zie ik langs het dalend pad haar komen

in zon—en als een vlam doorlicht het ogenblik
mij hel. Dit licht, haar nadering, het stuwend lenteleven,
bloei en bevruchting,—en daarmee verweven
ons beider eenheid en het scheppend ik.

En eens, in stiller dagen van het jaar,
vervulling van dit uur, voldragen leven:
beladen takken en van mij en haar
het overvele in mijn werk geschreven.

MINIATURIST

O zachte glans, getemperd stralen
der uren op het werk gericht,—
de dag met rijzen en met dalen
zegent mij met zijn wiss'lend licht,

dat kleurt het nederig gerei,
het tafelvlak, de effen wanden,
glijdend het perkament voorbij
en 't ingehouden werk der handen.

Achter het raam de fonkeling
van hoven, bos en ploegland buiten;
de horizon in zuiv're ring
getrokken komt mijn rijk omsluiten.

FAUN

Hij staat geleund tegen de stam
en keurt de saamgevoegde fluit,
besprongen door de rosse vlam
van het gewaaierd varenkruid.

Hij toeft, maar ademt elk gerucht,
de geur van lover dat vergaat,
het vallen van een rijpe vrucht
die in de weke aarde slaat.

Het lichaam, in zijn korte rust,
is wreed en teder tegelijk;
de ogen waken, fel van lust,
over het ondoordringbaar rijk.

HERINNERING

Voor mijn Vader

De geur van kruizemunt waait over,—
ik zie mijn vroege kindertijd,
de wei, het slootje en zijn tover
van koelte en doorzichtigheid.

Water en de geheimenissen
die voor het turen opengaan,
scholen van kleine, snelle vissen
in vlucht en onbeweeg'lijk staan.

En planten, fijn vertakt en zwevend,
in heldere rechtstandigheid
beneden in de diepte levend
of op het water uitgespreid.

Spelen, maar met een eerste ontwaren
van d'onvervreemdbaar eigen aard—
O spiegeling—na zóveel jaren,
heb ik het alles gaaf bewaard?

THUISKOMST

Dit is mijn droom—het kleine huis aan de rivier;
het rusteloze scheren van de zwaluw gaat er
langs dak en raam; de roodborst nestelt bij de vlier.
Een schip zeilt traag voorbij; de bel luidt over 't water.

En als ik nader waar de dijk zich buigt door 't land,
richt kort zich op die in de lage tuin gebogen
over de spade staat,—en met de vrije hand
weert zij het helle licht beschuttend van de ogen.

Hoe ken ik dit gebaar, hoe is het mij vertrouwd,
dit sterke opzien van wie daag'lijks naar de lucht en
het wiss'lend, open water turend, rustig oud
werd in dit dijkland en zijn ruime wolkenvluchten.

Er is een scherp herkennen van elkaar en
dan komt zij langs het smalle klinkerpad gelopen,—
maar keert nog terug en stoot de stroeve huisdeur open.
Dit ogenblik—wat tellen zóveel bitt're jaren?

IN MEMORIAM

Met duizend fijne zaden
ving het te sneeuwen aan,
de ongerepte paden
ben ik alleen gegaan.

Roerloos ligt het volkomen
herschapen land om mij,—
die mij werd weggenomen
nu is hij zó nabij,

als nadert een ontmoeten
in deze sneeuwen laan,—
ik zie het spoor der voeten
waar wij tezamen gaan.

Kerstnacht

KERSTNACHT

I

Kerstnacht—het woord is als een lafenis,
een koele sneeuw, glanzend onder het zachte
stralen der sterren—op de landen is
het weerloos stil, een ongerept verwachten.

Kerstnacht—het eenzaam zwerven der gedachten
rondom het oud verhaal, het nimmer uit te spreken
verlangen naar het helder zingen in de nacht en
het opgaan van de ster, een lichtend teken.

Kerstnacht—het sneeuwt op uw geschonden aarde,
dun en verstuivend dekt een huivering
van ijle val, een lichte zuivering
het vragen, dat wij ongestild bewaarden.

KERSTNACHT

II

Kerstnacht, de kentering van 't jaar—
het huis besluit zijn vreugde-en-leed,
en 't schuwe denken aan elkaar,
nu elk de ander wakend weet.

Een vragen, zoekend in de nacht
doolt langs de kamers, gaat en keert—
hebben wij niet elkander zacht
en onverbiddelijk geweerd?

De sterren schuiven langs het raam,
buiten slaat traag het late uur;
een zelfde huis houdt ons tezaam.
Hoe kostbaar lijkt, hoe broos van duur

dit ene soms: bijeen te zijn,—
draagt ieder dan van dag tot dag
dit óók—dit heimwee en de pijn
om de gebroken vleugelslag?

Wij staren zwijgend in de nacht,
in deernis om elkaars gemis,
het hart dat hunkerend verwacht
wat zózeer onbereikbaar is.

Het Veerhuis

Het water

I

Voor mijn Vader

SPREUK BIJ HET WERK

Als ik nu in dit land
maar wat alléén mag blijven,
dan zal de waterkant
het boek wel voor mij schrijven.

Dit is wat ik behoef
en hiertoe moest ik komen,
het simpele vertoef
bij dit gestadig stromen.

Het water gaat voorbij,
wiss'lend gelijk gebleven,—
het heeft stilaan in mij
een nieuw begin geschreven.

Ik weet met zekerheid,
hier vind ik vroeg of later
het woord dat mij bevrijdt
en levend is als water.

EEN LIEDJE VAN HET WATER

Ik lag de lieve lange dag
tussen het bloeiend fluitekruid;
er zweefde een liedje voor mij uit,
nu hoort naar wat ik zingen mag:

Wie nooit de lieve lange dag
bij 't spiegelklare water lag,
zijn uur is kort, zijn vreugd heeft uit,—
want nimmer zag hij wat ik zag
tussen het bloeiend fluitekruid.

Wie naar het klare water gaat
hem zullen de ogen opengaan,
want zeker zal hij hier verstaan,
geknield tussen wat groeit en leeft,
hoe God het schoonste zingen geeft
bij water, bloeiend kruid en riet
om niet!

DE RIT

De hooggewielde wagen
gaat door het spattend grint;
ik voel de korte vlagen
van ruimte, zon en wind

bij 't dravelingse rijden
over de zware dijk;
de stroom is mij bezijden,
de polder ligt te kijk.

De spiegels van mijn ogen
staan open op het licht;
een jong en waaks vermogen
is in mij opgericht.

En bij dit straffe draven,
der hoeven held're slag
ontspringen duizend gaven
den fonkelenden dag.

Feest is er in dit rijden
en lichte zegepraal,—
zó wint mijn drift het wijde
en zó wil ik mijn taal.

SCHEPEN

Florens velis (Lucretius)

Schepen als zeilende bloemen
over de zilv'ren rivier,—
mag ik gezegend mij noemen,
't rijkste ontwaarde ik hier.

Statig hun langzaam verschijnen,
donker van zeil en van boeg;
in de besluiting der lijnen
trots en zich zelve genoeg.

Zeilen als zwellende blaad'ren
aan een ontplooiende kroon;
schaduwen dragend bij 't naad'ren,
donker, verrukkelijk schoon.

Zalig en overgegeven
volg ik hun komen en gaan,—
tot in het hart van het leven
raakt mij hun nadering aan.

HET ANDERE LAND

Zacht is de waterkant
zacht is de groene weide;
maar zachter kleurt het land
ginds aan de overzijde.

Het riet, de oeverrand
fluist'ren te allen tijde
beloften in het land
ginds aan de overzijde.

En staande hand in hand
wij zwijgend turen beiden
naar 't licht bewaasde land
ginds aan de overzijde.

Zo na ons hart verwant
zo ver van ons gescheiden;
het onbereikbaar land
ginds aan de overzijde.

NAAR DE WINTER

De waterkant wordt ruig verweerd,
het rietland goud en roest van dracht;
vandaag heb ik mijn boot gemeerd
bij 't huis dat naar de winter wacht.

Van zwerfse tochten teruggekeerd
draag ik in mij nog al de pracht
der dagen, die thans ongedeerd
over de drempel wordt gebracht.

Laat hier de winter en zijn macht
mij vinden, op het werk gekeerd,
in stilte, overrijk bevracht,—
het nutteloze afgeweerd.

Het water
II

HET VEERHUIS

Als langs de duisterende waterbaan
de veerboot aan de meerpaal is gebracht,
begint het rijkste wat ik ken: te nacht
hoor ik het water aan de schoeiing slaan.

Diep ingenesteld in het donker huis
lig ik te luist'ren naar die trage klop;
en een verbeiden richt zich langzaam op,
speurend—het hart wordt in de stilte thuis.

En wéér hervindt het, door de stroom bespeeld,
zijn ondoorgrondelijk en diep bezit,—
van hemel en rivierland rijst het beeld;
de dag is heerlijk, heerlijker is dit

verholene, wat de daggezichten bindt:
één blinde kern, die schoksgewijs ontstaat,—
en het vertragen dan tot diep beraad
als woord na woord te fluisteren begint.

Daarbuiten leeft de stroom, waarover wijd
der sterrenbeelden pracht is opgegaan;
door 't venster waait een reuk van water aan,—
ik weet geen naam voor dèze zaligheid.

HET ZOLDERVENSTER

Wij stonden voor het zoldervenster saam,—
daarbuiten heersten zon en wind en regen
in vlagen blinkende elkander tegen;
de spitse droppels sloegen aan het raam.

En toen—voorbij de hemel op ons aan
kwam recht een vlucht van wilde ganzen streven—
het licht lag telkens op hun vleugels even
om dan in donkerte weer om te slaan.

Het schreeuwen was vlakbij—het klein vertrek
scheen plots'ling door het voorjaar ingenomen,
zo onverwacht en stormende gekomen
en groeiende in het woordeloos gesprek

dat aanving: alles wat zich nieuw bezint
na donk're maanden—afweer en verlangen
dooreengemengeld; wereld ingevangen
door 't raam, de wanden en het dakgebint.

IN HET SCHIP

Te liggen met gesloten ogen
in 't donkere ruim dat ons omvat
—een wieg van binten, toegebogen—
de goede stroom om 's harten schat.

Eentonig trilt een sidderend schuren
de ketting langs, het krakend hout
slaapt niet—o water, deze ure
wees met het schip en ons vertrouwd,

dat wij tezamen ons bezinnen
hoezeer gij van ons beiden zijt;
want tussen wat wij zó beminnen
en ons is geen gescheidenheid.

Tòt wij ons aan de droom vertrouwen
die diep in ons geborgen is:
't zeil dat omhoog gaat aan de touwen,
als het weer licht en morgen is.

DE WEL

Wij zwommen samen door de kalme stroom
en schoven door een spiegeling van wolken;
toen trok een tinteling van koeler kolken
scherp door de luwe kreken bij de zoom.

Het lokte ons om door die huivering,
die zuil van wellend water heen te schieten;
met lichte schrik, met schaterend genieten
bespeeld door koudes frisse zuivering.

Wij vluchtten wel, als ons tè vast omsloot
om pols en voet de greep van koele ringen,
maar keerden schalks, tot zij ons weer omvingen
en gaven tartend ons de wiss'ling bloot.

Verrukkelijke wijsheid van het spel,
hoezeer zijt gij ons beiden bijgebleven:
het water klaar, de lieve lust te leven
en 't argeloos lachen om die kleine wel.

TROOST DER RIVIER

In droefenis een zuiv're toeverlaat,
o zilveren rivier, waart gij het meest, —
gij zijt de wel van helderheid geweest,
die spiegeldiep, mijn vragen heeft verzaad.

Want wie u trouw blijft, weet hoezeer geneest
het peinzen, dat bij u te rade gaat, —
en zoekt en buigt zich over, tot hij leest
de zin, die in uw stroom geschreven staat.

Wat bleef van opstand aan uw oeverbocht?
wat kleine tranen om een klein verdriet,
verwaaid. — Het land rust mild en wijd.

Dan heeft de oogopslag zijn rijk gezocht, —
en 't eindeloos blinken van uw stroomgebied
omvat hij in een klare zekerheid.

Melodieën

PASTORALE

Over het water,
            over de wei,
die mij de liefste zijt
            wees mij nabij.

Ruisen van water,
            bloeiend het land,
parelende klaarte
            die het omspant.

Daarin een vragen
            zwervende uit,
jubelend klagen
            ontspringt aan de fluit.

Over het water,
            over de wei
speelt het u nader,
            nader bij mij.

Weif'lend in schromen
            tilt zich de voet,
aarzelend komen
            met al vermoed

  weelde der uren
     veilig verwacht,—
diep is hun duren,
    dieper de nacht.

  Over het water,
    over de wei,
die mij de liefste zijt
    wéés mij nabij—

DANS

Wat zingt het popelend refrein?
Kom mede in de snelle rei;
wij dansen op de klaverwei,
met lichte voet, op lichte maat,
totdat de rei verstrengeld staat:
guirlande.

Wat zingt het popelend refrein?
Kom mede in het heerlijk spel;
het uur is kort, de dag is snel,
wij grijpen wat zo rap ontwijkt
als vleugend licht dat overstrijkt
de landen.

Wat zingt het popelend refrein?
Kom mede in de dansfiguur;
wees éne vonk in 't kruisend vuur
van ogenlachen naar elkaar,
tot lief bij liefste, paar na paar,
belanden.

OGENTROOST EN EREPRIJS

Ogentroost en ereprijs
—need'rig bloeisel—zijn in mei
open op de grote wei,
wie bij hen één dag wil toeven
zal geen rijkdom meer behoeven;
als de leeuwerik wordt hij vrij,
als de blik van kind'ren wijs—
ogentroost en ereprijs.

Ogentroost en ereprijs—
glàns en zoete artsenij
zijn hun namen allebei;
wie met hen alléén wil wezen,
méér zal hij dan honing lezen;
zoèk hen in het vroeg getij,
vind verwond'rings paradijs—
ogentroost en ereprijs.

TOT DE SLAAP

Zo kom tot rust. Vertrouw u aan de nacht,
te slapen gaat nu alles op de aarde—
en geef verloren wat uw hart bezwaarde,
langs verre stromen wordt het thuis gebracht.

Zo kom tot rust—en hoor naar het gestadig
ruisen des levens. Al wat is geschapen
doorwoont het, aan zijn hartslag moogt gij slapen:
ook in u zelve arbeidt het genadig.

Zo kom tot rust—en vind de diepe dalen
van slaap. De sterren gaan, de waat'ren stromen;
zo word dan op hun maten meegenomen
gerust.—Nòg wacht de nacht: ùw ademhalen.

KINDERLIEDJE

'k Moest dwalen, 'k moest dwalen
langs bergen en langs dalen;
zo zong het in mijn kindertijd,
nòg wordt het hart mij weerloos wijd
bij 't simpele herhalen,
'k moest dwalen.—

Een vragen, een vragen
werd dwingend meegedragen
als 't zingen door de ronde ging;
een eind'loze verwondering
kwam stilaan in mij dalen,
'k moest dwalen.—

Ontwaren, ontwaren
van verten die er waren,
van heuvels waar de voeten gaan,—
maar eenzaamheid kwam bonzend slaan
in 't hart bij het herhalen,
'k moest dwalen.—

Na jaren, na jaren
hoe bitter werd te ervaren
levens verlangen, levens pijn
gevangen in dit klein refrein,—
geluk nooit te behalen,
'k moest dwalen.—

Herkenningen

GEBOORTE

Wanneer een vers is afgemaakt
en tot zijn eigen vorm gekomen,
dan wordt het èven aangeraakt
en gaat het leven er in stromen.

De kleuren gloeien langzaam aan,
dan komt het aderwerk verschijnen;
de bloedklop doet zijn stuwing gaan
door nerven en vertakte lijnen.

Eén is er, die dit wonder ziet
nog van het eerste waas beslagen:
de maker zelf, die om het lied
zijn pijn en moeite heeft gedragen.

En diep verwonderd, oog in oog
met dit voltooid, bewegend leven,
dankt hij wie hem tot arbeid boog
en zó zijn zegen heeft gegeven.

DE VOGEL

Kwam een vogel gevlogen
in de pracht van zijn vlucht,—
waar zijn wieken bewogen
lag er kleur in de lucht.

Kwam een vogel gevlogen
en mijn hart boog zich neer:
—wat mij zó heeft bewogen,
laat het stem krijgen, Heer.

Kwam een vogel gevlogen
over water en wei;
in het licht van mijn ogen
streek hij neder bij mij.

DE VLINDER

De vlinder kwam van perk tot perk gevlogen,
tot rustend hij de wieken opensloeg,
daar lag op 't blauw, in schemerende bogen,
de sterrenhemel, die hij pralend droeg.

Op gronden van azuur stond uitgeschreven
der sterren stand in fijne stippeling,—
en rond die diepten was een zoom gedreven
van zwart, waarin de blik besterven ging.

Ik sprak, over dit hemelveld gebogen:
'doet gij mij zó de diepste zin verstaan?'
Een stem: 'verstond gij reeds uw eigen ogen
waarin dit alles mag gespiegeld staan?'

DE FAZANT

Waar onverwacht het pad zich buigt
stond op een klein vak open land
tussen de bossen en het ruigt
in 't klare herfstlicht de fazant.

Geruisloos knielde ik op de grond,
mijn hand zocht waar de kijker hing, —
en nader schoof de held're ring
tot scherp het beeld getekend stond.

Goudbruin, waarlangs inademing
verdoffe' en gloeien rusteloos vloog, —
de staart die vleugen purper ving,
de kop met het juwelenoog.

En toen ik fel en feller zocht,
wist ik dat in dit klein stuk glas
de afgebeden lusthof was,
die voortaan ik betreden mocht.

DE HAZELAAR
Voor A. Erichsen

Onverwacht mij tegen
in 't nog winters jaar
op de sprong der wegen
bloeit de hazelaar.

Tegen 't licht gehangen
slingertjes van goud;
aarzelend, bevangen
raak ik aan het hout.

Trillend dwaalt van boven
't fijne wolken los;
en met bloei bestoven
in het naakte bos

blijf ik in een beven
teruggehouden staan,
en ik raak nog even
't donker stamhout aan.

ONHEIL

De wilde roos heeft kort gebloeid dit jaar
langs 't huis waarin wij waren met elkaar.

Niet vol in de aar als anders stond het graan
op 't veld waardoor wij samen zijn gegaan.

De vrucht verschrompelt aan de tak dit keer,—
wellicht zien wij elkander nimmer weer.

ONTWAKEN

In de héle vroege dag
ving de merel aan te zingen,
met een vlijmend-zoet doordringen
van wat diep verborgen lag.

Ving de merel aan te zingen,—
en ik wist: wij waren beiden
in ons samenzijn gescheiden,
toen ik roerloos luisterend lag.

In de héle vroege dag
zong de merel van ons beiden,—
àlles wat ik had verzwegen;
zong hij mij het afscheid tegen
van wie argeloos naast mij lag.

HET VIOLENPERK
Voor Titia en Martien

Het ronde perk met donkere violen,
gevat in groen van zomergeurend gras,—
verzonken wereld waar ik kind in was,
in een verwonderd spelen weggescholen.

Het ronde perk met donkere violen,
purper, onpeilbaar zwart en smeulend bruin—
hier was het hart der paden in de tuin,
het middelpunt van droom en heerlijk dolen.

Het ronde perk met donkere violen,—
hoe boog ik dieper op hun zware gloed
naar het geheim, dat schemerend vermoed,
in hun fluwelen staren bleef verholen.

Het ronde perk met donkere violen,—
daar, turend in een ernstig bloemenhart,
wist ik voor 't eerst, in helle schrik verward,
de gave, slapende in mij verscholen.

WADDENEILAND

Wat ik gezien heb op die éne dag
aan kleurend water en vervloeiend zand,
aan plante' en schelpen, liggend op de hand,
is méér dan nòg mijn hart bevatten mag.

De eigen voetstap trad een ketting af
tussen de vogelprenten op het strand
de duizenden, het was de verste rand
van mensenleven waar ik mij begaf

—tot in de stilte, vloeiend als een ring—

Water en lucht en tijdeloze tijd,
ik dronk het diep—tot aan die pareling
van klaarte openbarend ieder ding:
sterk straalt het in zijn kleur, zijn eigenheid.

En dit aanschouwen wordt zo hemelwijd:
dan meet wie éne schelp te rapen ging
en wegzinkt in die tint, die tekening,
het veld der velen dat hij overschrijdt.

Ars poëtica
Voor M.

TUIN VAN EPICURUS
Voor de vrienden

Gij die in eenvoud wilt tezamenhoren,
de tiende jaarkring sloot om onze dis,—
waar vriendschap open als het zonlicht is
werd ons een ongepeild geluk beschoren.

In arbeid werd der uren goud ontgonnen;
de volle rijkdom van het eigen ik
vindt ieder terug, gespiegeld in de blik
van wie aan hèm zijn klaarte heeft gewonnen.

Zie naar het licht—hoe kleurt het mild en stil
ons samenzijn. Wat grenzen zijn gesteld
aan wie het nodige slechts nemen wil?

Nog ongeweten wegen zult gij gaan.
Vriendschap—gij hebt haar reinigend geweld
alreeds beseft. Zo weet: zij ving pas aan.

STEM VAN EPICURUS

Nu komt de nacht over de diepe tuin
en zijn geheimen, die wij daags betraden,—
reeds rijst de maan voorbij de cederkruin,
wit valt het licht op perk en slingerpaden.

De vrienden rusten—ik wil deze nacht
alleen zijn met de strenge sterrenbeelden,
mij zelve peilend—wat ik heb gebracht
aan wie met mij de volle jaren deelden.

Zij kwamen, blinden in hun vurig streven—
maar wie mijn gaarde en mijn wet verkoos
heb ik der wijsheid held're spreuk gegeven:
voor al uw pijlen zij geluk de roos.

Ik zag hun zin in manlijkheid zich richten;
zij wonnen bij het rijpen van de tijd
die blik, gewet aan vrijheids vergezichten,
waaraan ik klaar de mijnen onderscheid.

Gedachten vonden ongeweten banen
—hoe vlàmden zij bij 't kruisen van elkaar!—
van woord en weerwoord ruisen deze lanen
en van vervuldheid is de nacht er zwaar.

Beladen tuin, die draagt het zoet verzamen
der vrienden, in uw stilte is het goed
het kostbaar snoer te tellen van hun namen,
nu nadert wat hun liefde niet vermoedt.

LUCRETIUS-VERTALING

Een suizelen van regen aan de ruit
en binnen niets dan dit: te zijn gebogen
over de tekst, die voor de vraag der ogen,
de onafgewenden, langzaam zich ontsluit.

En dan de zware stuwing—een bewogen
dwingende arbeid; tot het denken stuit
en luistert: helder hoorbaar het geluid
der eigen stem—het edelste vermogen.

DE BIJEN
Purpureosque metunt flores et flumina libant. (Vergilius)

De donk're bijen brommen om de korven
waar bij de schuur de oude linde staat,—
ik denk aan de arbeid in de korf geborgen,
het langzaam groeien van de honingraat.

En wéér op deze plek—als zóveel dagen—
bestormt mij plotseling een overvloed
van beelden, zó in lichtglans toegedragen,
dat overstelpt ik de ogen sluiten moet.

Uren—terwijl de zoekende gedachten
zich allengs tot verbinding schikken gaan,—
de dag verstrijkt, het zwermen der bevrachte
gonzende dieren houdt gestadig aan.

Tot de avond invalt en ik neergebogen
mij dankend op de rijke dag bezin;
doordringend komt een zoemen langs gevlogen,
een late bij keert nog ter korve in.

VAGANTES

De verre verte blauwt. — Wij trekken door de dalen
en zien der heuv'len oogsten in het heerlijk licht—
broeders in éne spreuk, die zingend wij herhalen:
'der aarde schoonste spiegel is het gaaf gedicht.'

Ons is de goede zon, het ruisen van de regen,
de zoete lindengeur bij 't vallen van de nacht;
bij elke tweesprong waait een nieuwe droom ons tegen
en de gedachte kust het voorhoofd onverwacht.

Zo hebben wij berooid de overvloed gevonden
en 't hechtste dak dat voor de sterv'ling is gebouwd:
bij wind en weer in elk getij te zijn verbonden
met Hem, die zich in 't land en in ons hart ontvouwt.

TOLSTOI PLOEGENDE

Een ongemeten land—in zwoegen gaan de paarden,
de ploeglijn kleurt de grond met donker stremmend schrift;
laag hangt het wolkendek over de vale aarde.
Tolstoi, het ploeghout klemmend. Wat geladen drift
en zwijgenswil aan krachten overzwaar vergaarden
temt hij. De voren worden recht en scherp gegrift.

Als ver het land gekeerd ligt, wordt hem weids hergeven
de rust, zo diep verzadigd als de aarde geurt.
En waar aan 't akkereind hij fronsend stilstaat, even,

eer voor het laatst den grond het grijpend ijzer scheurt,
voelt hij hoe losgewoeld, in siddering van leven,
de werking van het scheppen nieuw in hem gebeurt.

SAPPHO

Nòg staat haar voetstap in het gouden zand
en in de purp'ren branding wordt gesproken
met hàre stem—hel, in de val gebroken—
de donk're omslag ruisend langs het strand.

Zij ging de zware gang: van het praegnant
begin, de vlam van drift ontstoken,
tot strenge en kuise arbeid en beloken
beluist'ren van een goddelijk verband.

Dit maakt ons ademloos bij haar geluid
wanneer het stijgt, of donker zingt en klaagt;
het leven zelve beeft in deze toon.

Zoals de zee, die om dit eiland sluit,
verlangens oerzang naar de kusten draagt.—
Er is geen scheiding in hun beider schoon.

VREUGDE IN HOLLAND

Vreugd is het in de grote wei te staan,
—water en bloei en lucht zo ver men ziet—
het oog speurt hoe de vogels over gaan
en wet zijn scherpte aan een vrij gebied.

Vreugd is het, om waar levend water vliet
te zwemmen, wijd de armen uit te slaan:
dan tint'len de gedachten—men geniet
hun sterke stroom zo vrij te voelen gaan.

En vreugd is in de liefde, gaaf en frank,
voor wie het hart zich koos tot zijn gezel,
de bloei der verten in elkanders ogen—

Maar schoonste vreugd, als dàn des harten dank
zó diep is, dat het op de zuiv're wel
der eigen taal vanzelve wordt gebogen.

Het carillon

HET CARILLON

Ik zag de mensen in de straten,
hun armoe en hun grauw gezicht,—
toen streek er over de gelaten
een luisteren, een vleug van licht.

Want boven in de klokketoren
na 't donker-bronzen urenslaan
ving, over heel de stad te horen,
de beiaardier te spelen aan.

Valerius:—een statig zingen
waarin de zware klok bewoog,
doorstrooid van lichter sprankelingen,
'Wij slaan het oog tot U omhoog.'

En één tussen de naamloos velen,
gedrongen aan de huizenkant
stond ik te luist'ren naar dit spelen
dat zong van mijn geschonden land.

Dit sprakeloze samenkomen
en Hollands licht over de stad—
Nooit heb ik wat ons werd ontnomen
zo bitter, bitter liefgehad.

Oorlogsjaar 1941

Buiten schot

BITTERHEID

De tuinman met zijn kapmes kwam
en snoeide van de appelstam
de uitgesprongen wilde loot,
die zijdelings naar de ruimte schoot.

Dan snoert hij boombast om de wond;
de naakte tak ligt op de grond:
ik wéét, nu zet het gave fruit
zich breder aan de twijgen uit.

Hoe is toch in het vroege jaar
soms alles zo beklemmend zwaar?
Ik wou dat God mij, als die tak,
maar uit hun drukke leven brak.

Buiten schot

BRIEF

Ik hield het huis getrouw in stand.
De hof zult gij nog rijker vinden.
Sterk werd om 't erf de meidoornrand,
—wat stroever snoeit de groene linde.

De welput bleef onaangerand

zo helder, als die morgen puur
dat wij ons op zijn spiegel bogen
en 't water, klaar omhoog getogen,
ten dronk was in het afscheidsuur.

Als zonlicht fonkelt het gerei.

Ik wacht het keren van het tij;
als huis en hof en hemel blinken
op 't schoonste zijt ge hier.
                    Dan drinken
—laat dièp de kruik in 't spiegelen zinken!
wij, lief, de dronk van u en mij.

SPRINGBRON

'Wat van de springbron fris
en rond bedroppeld is
—de kroon, het kartelblad
zijn kamertjes van nat—
o schoonste schoon der hoven!'

'Maar fris van liefdes wel
bedauwd en parelhel
—de ogen, 't zacht gezicht
zijn kamertjes van licht—
o schoon, al schoon te boven!'

WINTERS RONDEEL

Gegroet gij frisse tintelkou
en winterland voor heldere ogen;
de ekster, op het erf gevlogen,
roept: 'wáár dat páár?' in 't vorstig blauw.

Een strakke lucht, het rijpte nauw;
wij gaan als kinderen opgetogen
met stampen in de tintelkou,
—het winterland voor heldere ogen.

Gegroet, gij ijl vertakte bouw
van peppels langs de dijk gebogen,
en verten fijn van rook bevlogen—
Wie die vandaag niet kijken zou?
Gegroet, gij frisse tintelkou!

VAART

Het water kruivend om de boeg
en in het hart de vlam—
dàt is het schoonste wat ik ken,
dàt is het beste wat ik ben,
zó is het dat ik woon en wen
met wie mij nam!

GELUK

Als een rozeruiker zoet
is het zacht ontloken turen,
schat van de ademloze ure
dat het hart zijn liefde ontmoet.

Als een rozeruiker zoet
is het ingetogen zwijgen,
sprakeloos tot elkander neigen
als het hart de liefste ontmoet.

Als een rozeruiker zoet
is het eindeloos mild genezen,
't zalige geborgen wezen
als het hart, vervuld, ontmoet
Liefde en Liefdes overvloed.

NAAR U

Dit is de eerste schuchtere groei,
een zich ontplooien naar het licht.
Eéns is van liefde en geduld
de tijd vervuld,—
dan staat mijn stille tuin in bloei.
En elk aandachtig bloemgezicht
is toegericht
naar u.

VERWACHTING

Weet gij het ook de ganse nacht?
De vogels komen. Aan een geuren
—van wind, van water?—valt te speuren
hoe 't lage land een komst verwacht.

Mórgen het teken aan de lucht
—een frons, een lijn, een krimpend wolken—
en dan, bui van geluid, een vlucht
die dalen gaat: de vogelvolken.

En wéér staan in verwondering
wij tussen dit gevleugeld sneeuwen;
morgen—dan zijn wij, lieveling,
het eerste paar van duizend eeuwen.

VEILIG

Gij ziet mij soms zo donker aan;
dan kán mijn vlucht niet opwaarts gaan.

Zo zwaar slaat vaak te nacht uw hart—
dan dool ik, aan zijn stroom verward.

Maar God weet, dat aan déze vrees
tot sterker vreugd ik steeds genees.

Want immer vindt het eigenst ik
in dezer diepten donkere blik,

aan dezes harten donkere slag
de ingang tot nog schoner dag.

O angsten en geborgenheid—
Wie zijt gij, die mij zó geleidt?

ANGST

Het was een zwaluw, aan het venster doodgevlogen;
ik heb hem in de ronde lampkring neergevlijd,
de wieken nauwlijks van de opvlucht teruggebogen,
de kleuren nog bewaasd van nacht en vochtigheid.

Wat onrust houdt de late uren mij bewogen,
die niet bedaren wil, zelfs nu gij bij mij zijt?—
Ik zie het kleine dier, de streep der toeë ogen,
en in het hart slaat hamerend mij de eenzaamheid.

AAN DE STROOM

De gang der statige rivier
die door de groene landen gaat,
de gang der statige dagen hier
in 't huis dat aan het water staat,
van arbeid, van gestadigheid
en liefdes begenadigdheid
zo overzwaar—
en hoorbaar, dóór der wateren maat,
te nacht het levend hart—God, laat
ons bij elkaar!

SLAPENDE

Schoon sterk gelaat, mij diep vertrouwd,
naar denkens verten uitgebouwd,
gekorven met de stroeve lijn
van wie verborgen zwoegend zijn,—
geev' God dat geen onedel schrift
ik in uw zuivere velden grift.
Waar in der ogen diepe nis
de vlam van ons geheimenis
stil achter donker fronsen brandt,
o, worde 't licht nooit aangerand
door mij—

Slaap goed, ik zie u niet meer aan—
uw droom moet naar zijn diepten gaan,
zijn verten,—vrij.

AANSCHOUWING

Elkander aanzien, tot het eigen beeld
te schijnen staat in levendheldere ogen,
een gouden zelf, aan aarde en tijd onttogen,
van wellend licht fijn fonkelend doorspeeld,—
o zichtbaarheid van liefdes alvermogen!
—Klein brandpunt binnen iris' kleurenbogen,
wat wereld is ons in u toebedeeld?

INZET

De vroege dag is zonder breuk of smet.
Gij hebt uw beitel en burijn gewet,

maar toeft ter werkbank, bij de noorderruit:
het lage land strekt zich zo eindeloos uit.

Levend van vlam, met sterke wrongen kleur,
het nieuw stuk hout, nog bitterwild van geur—

Een flits. Was dit een vogel langs het raam?
Uw oog licht op,—gij vat de arbeid aan.

HET VOGELHEEM

Gij werkt,—op het gelaat de fijne drift gespannen,
de sterke donkere hand bestuurt de tekenstift;
de ring van onze rust heeft uur en tijd gebannen
—niets dan het blanke blad, het bloesemende schrift.

Water dat leeft en glanst. Een plant met sterke nerven
weerspiegelt zich; jong kruid staat prijkend opgericht;
dáár, in de diepe bocht waar licht en schaduw zwerven,
is, wildernis van pracht, der vogelen heem gesticht.

Daar ligt hun wereld, trots en in zichzelf besloten,
in waters helderheid een kern die kleurt en straalt,
—onder de hemelkom van tijdeloos licht doorvloten
als op de vroegste dag,—naar Scheppers wet bepaald.

Vogels.—Ik zie de scherpe tekening der veren:
leigrijze tinten; bruin als ribbelig oeverzand,
zilver en weifelend blauw; het regenboogschakeren
van splinterend licht; een rood dat in de ogen brandt.

Gij werkt.—Hebben wij méér dan deze rust van node?
Hier mogen met ons diepst bezit wij samen zijn;
tot stilte en arbeid onvoorwaardelijk ontboden
en onaantastbaar binnen liefdes hecht domein.

MIDZOMERWENDE

Speel, kleine daemon met verschoten haar
die op je scheerlingfluitje zit te knerpen;
midzomerdag—de hoge, schelle, zerpe—
de zeis door 't gras, de kentering van 't jaar.

Hooioogst! en wij in 't veld, een tartend paar:
't lot gùnde ons om dubbel zes te werpen—
Tot in het hart gaat mij het trillend snerpen;
o kind, hoe speelt ge ons zo van elkaar!

Speel, kleine daemon met verschoten haar!
Gaat dan—zó vroeg—ook onze zomer neigen?
Speel, laat ons schuilgaan in elkanders zwijgen.
't Gras is gemaaid. Het graan rijpt in de aar.

DANKZEGGING

Ik houd het linnen blank. Maar als ik in de laden
de geurige stapels strakker in hun vouwen schik,
treedt Gij soms achter mij. De glans van Uw genade
glijdt over werk en hand, en zoekt het wachtend ik.

Een reuk van eeuwigheid is vleugend om die uren,
dat werkeloos geleund tegen de donkere kast,
gereinigd door de rust van dit verzonken turen,
ik tot de stilte ontwaak en naar Uw gaven tast.

Het valt mij soms zo zwaar, 't werk in zijn stugge ronden.
Maar het voldragen vers zegt voor die strengheid dank,
zo vaak Uw trouw mijn huis, mijn arbeid heeft gevonden.
Gij weet mij bij mijn werk: ik houd het linnen blank.

SAPPHISCH

Vergeef mij dat de schoonste nachten
niet immer van ons beiden zijn:
mijn vriend, het zijn zo grote machten,
waardoor wij sòms gescheiden zijn.

Wanneer ik in de hof mag dwalen
waar 's hemels roos mij opengaat,
dan ducht ik zelfs ùw ademhalen,
uw hart dat in den donker slaat.

Láát mij—in eenzaamheid—de uren,
dat ik mijn diepste wet aanvaard.
Hun pracht, die onverwelkt zal duren,
zij wordt alleen voor u vergaard.

TWEESPRAAK

ENO
Waar waart gij in uw droom?
UNA
Op de asphodelenweide
waar wij de vroege lentedagen zijn gegaan.
Waar waart gíj in uw droom?
ENO
Tussen het gouden graan.
De maaiers stonden recht; het was het oogstgetijde.

Waart gij bij wáter ook?
UNA
Er was een heldere beek,
de spiegel trilde als de zwaluw overscheerde.

ENO
Er flitsten zilveren vissen in de diepe kreek,
zwaar woog het net mij toen ik langs de rietzoom keerde.

UNA
Waar waart gij bij het kraaien van de vroege haan?
ENO
Voor het ravijn, waarover smal de houtbrug leidde.
UNA
Ik zou over 't ravijn een smalle houtbrug gaan.
Tweemaal kraaide de haan, toen ik...
BEIDEN
...uw komst verbeidde.

BUITEN SCHOT

Godlof,—de rietwouw heeft zijn vleugelen uitgeslagen
en staat weer sterk en statig boven de rivier.
Ik vreesde nacht en dag het aangeslopen jagen;
zij zwierven om ons erf,—nòg staat hun voetstap hier.

Hij koos zich óns domein,—heemvogel van ons beiden!
Wij sloegen in verbond zijn vorstlijk zwenken ga.
Van duizend vogels blinkt de lucht en zingt de weide,
—géén was ons hart als deze stoute stijger na.

Ontzweefd. Ik moet mij voor mijn hete tranen schamen;
zie mij niet aan,—dit schot ging rakelings ons voorbij.
Hoe hèbben zij gejaagd op 't schoonste van ons samen—

'en niets ons aangedaan. Ook onze vlucht is vrij'.

Glans en weerglans

SPEL VAN TWEE

Gij hebt mijn blad beschreven, Heer,
met wolken, water, wind en licht,
der aarde bloei, der vogelen heir,—
de afglans van Uw aangezicht.

En ik—in schuw ontzag—wat kan
mijn dank dan U ten dienste zijn?
Maar soms, als ik op 't strafst mij span,
hoe doèt die brandende aandacht pijn.

Tot—weer!—Uw zachte hand mij stuit—
en zalig volg ik uur na uur
het buitelen van een fris geluid,
de passen van een dansfiguur.

CONTRAPUNT

Het tokkelt op de donkere grond—
Neem uw schalmei, verscholen herder,
en vorm, met toegeronde mond,
het regendroppelen spelend verder.

Het tokkelt op de donkere grond—
Hoort gij de tonen van de regen?
Blaas nu de volle stem ertegen;
God luistert naar uw schoon verbond.

DE GRASSEN

Als ik nog ouder ben, en helderder mijn ogen
door zachte tranen en zacht geluk gewassen zijn,
dan valt veel arbeid stil—dàn zal ik toeven mogen
waar op de zomerwei de hoge grassen zijn.

Veel schoons heb ik aanschouwd, veel zware vreugd gedragen,
en wél was elk seizoen tot aan de rand gevuld;
maar dit vraagt klare rust, de vree van late dagen,
de stilte en de wijsheid van een rijp geduld.

Daar ligt de weide, trillend, schemerend van schrifturen
waarin door de eeuwen eend're wetten staan verteld;
ik zie hen tegen 't blauw in ongebroken uren,
getakte tekenen op een azuren veld.

Oneindig is de rijkdom der verscheidenheden
van haakjes, tittels, lijntjes in het strakke schrift,
soms zwevend overdonsd—bij het naar buiten treden
der bloeisels, grijs op grijs—met stippelende stift.

En ik zal, als een kind, dit langzaam leren lezen,
tot vast in mij geprent de ranke aren staan;
en in het donk're huis zal 's avonds òm mij wezen
de wiegeling der grassen vóór het slapen gaan.

DE VLINDERS

Wanneer de lentevelden welken
en zomers hoven opengaan,
vangt over kronen en honingkelken
het hoogtij van de vlinders aan.

In ondoorgrondelijk donker groeide
wat thans met licht en hemel speelt—
de kleuren, aan de zon ontgloeide,
de tekening, scheppings evenbeeld.

Twee kleine vleugelen, opgeslagen
of zwichtend, trillende in het licht,
aanziet hoe zij de weerglans dragen
der werken in Zijn hof verricht:

de zon, de maan, de hemelbanen
waar 't sterrestof zijn strepen slaat,
het purperblauw der oceanen,
de tinten van de dageraad;

het spel van duizend elementen
geaderd in verstrengeling,
van der seizoenen gang de prenten,
strak, of in teed're mengeling.

Der lente parelmoeren luchten
zag ik, de brand van zomerdag,
een herfst met vegen vogelvluchten,
en — schoonste schoon — een oogopslag.

Vlinders, hoe heb in gouden uren
ik uw kortstondige pracht gezocht. —
Maar of beturende uw figuren
ik vele raadselen peilen mocht,

en Atalanta's cijferen lezen
en schouwen in het oog der pauw, —
liefst is mij 't kleine wiekewezen
van niets dan Gods oneindig blauw.

ONTMOETING

        SAPPHO
Zijt gij gegaan de hoven der gedachte?
Nog hangt hun morgenlijke geur u aan.

        THALES
Zijt gij de hoven van de droom gegaan,
dat nacht en rozen u de wrong bevrachtten?

        BEIDEN
    O koninklijk bestaan!

        SAPPHO
De paden traadt gij door geen voet begaan;
ben ooit uw oogst te schatten ik bij machte?

        THALES
't Geheimenis waar vorsende ik naar trachtte
onthult gij in een donker oogopslaan.

        BEIDEN
    O zon der nachten!

        SAPPHO
Wentelt mijn wereld in een heller baan?

        THALES
Is dít de dageraad, de lang verwachte?

BLINDE GROENLING

Gij kleine groenling ingekooid,
gehangen aan de kalken wand,
van ruimte en ogenlicht berooid,
gij zijt nog enkel stem
voor Hem.
Maar zongt gij ooit,
banling aan blinde muur,
als in dit uur?
Gij valt Hem aanstonds in de hand
voltooid—

Sonnetten van een leraar

Aan de nagedachtenis van mijn collega
J. P. F. Nelck

*Ergo si quis exstiterit, qui sese laesum clamabit,
is aut conscientiam prodet suam aut certe metum.*

Erasmus, *Laus Stultitiae*

ZUEIGNUNG

Dag Pegasus!—Wat doe jìj hier in het gebouw?
Ik ben met zaterdagse thema's nagebleven.
Kijk niet: mijn kleren zijn vol krijt, mijn ogen grauw;
en rode inkt blijft altijd aan m'n vingers kleven.

Ja, dit is zogezegd de school.—Wat wil je nou?
Ik heb mezelf al zoveel maanden afgeschreven...
Of dacht je dat we—God, wat is het buiten blauw!—
door de kapotte tuimelramen konden zweven?

Jij hoort daarbuiten, Pegasus, en hier hoor ik.
O, doe dàt niet, kniel niet op deze planken vloer
vol stof—en dat voor mìj, mijn trots, mijn prachtig dier.

Pegasus—laat mij, dat ik in je manen snik.
Wist jìj dan hoeveel malen ik mijzelf ontvoer,
nochtans, om deze kind'ren?—Dráág mij: ik ben hier.

WOESTIJN

Geen enkel raam dat werkt. De tocht der buitendeur
tot in de laatste hoek der schilferige gangen.
En zwijg van de wc's.—Een nameloze geur
blijft veertig weken aan de klamme muren hangen.

Lokalen, vaalgeworden platen: vochtvlek, scheur.
Flarden gordijnen schuiven langs verroeste stangen.
Orpheus—met inktmop-ogen—slaakt zijn laatste zangen.
De Gratiën, kromgetrokken, oefenen horreur.

Zet u niet op die stoel: ge valt, als Eli, dood;
tussen de zitting en de leuning geen synthese—
Steun op de tafel niet: hij heeft een manke poot.

Wat op de banken staat, moet ge vooral niet lezen.
—Trek recht uw rug en arbeid voor uw dagelijks brood.
Gij kunt, aan dèze tucht, tot eerlijkheid genezen.

DEPARTEMENT

Vergeet uw kaartje niet. Houd het vàst in uw hand.
Dat is voor Charon: hij geleidt u naar de doden.
Geen mens komt zonder kaartje naar de overkant.
Vrees Charon niet. Spreek hem gewoon maar aan met 'bode'.

Ontschoei uw handen, wanneer gij zijt aangeland
in 't fluisterhuis, waar—in het zwart—stoeten genoden
u vóór zijn. Uren kucht de hangklok aan de wand
eer er weer één tot Hades' kameren wordt ontboden.

Het is uw beurt. Gà maar: het is al lang beslecht.
Stel u vooral niets voor van weegschaal of gevecht.
Vergeet vooral de zaak, waar gij uw hart aan gaf.

Dan komt ge wel weer buiten in de zon terecht.
En, maal nooìt over 't opschrift op dit stenen graf:
'Wat heden stond in bloei viel gisteren reeds af.'

1933-1939
1943-1947

BIECHT

Ruzies met mijn collega's hebben niets om 't lijf.
Ik mag hen graag; vooral de krommen en de scheven.
—ik sta ook trouwens zelf van de gebreken stijf—
Alleen, die éne Streber kan ik niet vergeven.

Mijn rector gunt me veel; en zèlfs wel dat ik 'schrijf'.
De school gaf ik de beste jaren van mijn leven.
Sòms zeg ik dat ik ga, toch weet ik dat ik blijf.
Alleen, die éne Streber kan ik niet vergeven.

Hij is correct; hij heeft mìj waarlijk niets misdreven.
Maar gruwelijk strooit distels tussen 't kiemend zaad
hij, die maar één beginsel heeft: zijn eigen voordeel.

't Is om dit minne onkruid, dat ik hem zo haat.
Ik werd de laatste tijd toch zachter in mijn oordeel...
Vergeef het mij, ik kan... ik kàn hem niet vergeven!

BIJ EEN EINDEXAMENFOTO

Een Streber, jongens, strebt omdat hij streben moet.
Want dat is zijn natuur: zo moet een bunzing stinken.
Bijbels: hij heeft zijn ziel verkocht voor werelds goed.
Klassiek: hij zal zijn eigen vleugelpaard verminken.

Een Streber, jongens, strebt omdat hij streben moet.
Mocht één van jullie ooit tot dàt bestaan verzinken
—mijn klas, die ik met Plato's Phaedros heb gevoed—
dan zie ik liever, dat hij eerlijk zal verdrinken.

Ik heb dat alles wèl nooit op het bord gezet.
Ik heb het je, uit schuwheid, nooit zozeer verteld.
De ethica bleef steeds zwijgend verondersteld.

Nu word ik achteraf door dit verzuim gekweld.
Mijn knappe klas—ik zie met zorg naar je portret.
Laat het niet nodig zijn.—Vergeef mij dit sonnet.

PORTRET

Een stoere Urkerknul, vaak met negotie
—schol, bot of poon—met vader aan de dijk.
Zijn ouders zijn een zon op de promotie:
met karpoetsmuts en vlammend jak te prijk.

Zijn beurt baart altijd enige emotie.
Want, naast een stukkezak van beddetijk,
voert hij een ruig schrift, waar—zwàrt van devotie—
wendingen in staan, die ìk nooit bereik.

Soms kan hij Plato als een lier vertalen,
om dan—dat blijft in toga zo!—kalm-an
zijn neus met ratelslagen op te halen.

Ik las de Phaedros: het gevleugeld span.
Stil wees hij bij. Zéér groot, zéér recht. Een man
die verten ziet: idee en idealen.

DAEMONEN

Kindlief, nu wil ik àlles voor je doen;
maar doe het mìj dan—alsjeblieft—niet aan,
dat ik je als een ancilla—goor met groen
gevlekt—naar dat examen op zie gaan.

Om zo'n examen-daemon te verslaan,
is kwestie van een diep intern fatsoen.
Jouw angst is tegenpool van eigenwaan.
Schud niet je hoofd: mijzelf paste jouw schoen.

Ik was een angsthaas van de ergste soort.
Bevend vloog ik door de tentamens voort,
tot, om een ander, ik mijzelf vergat:

Op mijn promotie, in een volle zaal.
Toen tàrtte ik de toga's, allemaal,
omdat daarginds mijn grijze vader zat.

PSYCHE

Ik las de Phaedo met mijn vijfde klas;
en in de tekst kwam het woord ψυχή voor:
ik legde, aan 't nog kinderlijk gehoor,
uit waarom ψυχή 'ziel' èn 'vlinder' was.

Terwijl ik nòg eens de passage las
was er ineens een ritseling, en een spoor
van glanzen kwam, van 't raam, de ruimte door.
Er zat een grote vlinder voor het glas.

Het was een dagpauwoog. En ieder zag
de purperen gloed, die op zijn vleugels lag;
de ogen, waar het aetherblauw in brandt.

Ten laatste—hij zat rustig op de hand—
bracht hem een jongen weg. Onaangerand,
zei hij, was hij ontweken naar het blauw.

A EN Ω

Lucas II : *49*

Het mooiste werk: Grieks in het eerste jaar.
Het Griekse alphabet staat op het bord.
'Kijk, kinderen, Ψ: dat is een kandelaar.
Maak dat de Omega gaaf getrokken wordt.'

Behoed dit eerst beginnen voor gevaar;
dat niet het werk, nauwelijks ontkiemd, verdort.
—Zie, als het buiten vroege lente wordt,
liggen de kleine Griekse bijbels klaar.

Pasen: een jongen leest met heldere stem
van Jezus, twaalf jaar, in Jeruzalem;
en hoe hij voor de schriftgeleerden las.

En elk kind in de luisterende klas
begrijpt het vragend: 'Wist gij niet?' van Hem,
die in de dingen van zijn Vader was.

WERKLOOSHEID

Drie jaar nu al. Ik kom nog in 't gesticht.
Kon ik ze thuis ontslaan van mijn bestaan!
Mijn kleine zusje ziet me nauwelijks aan.
't Is of de meid het woord niet tot mij richt.

Ieder leeft op, als ik mijn hielen licht.
Het beste kon ik bij Van Nelle gaan.
Alleen: dan is het met m'n vàk gedaan.
Voor leraar krijg ik een te oud gezicht.

Vanmorgen ben ik naar de kerk geweest.
'God zal u, als op adelaarsvleugelen, dragen.'
Maar ík heb zitten zweten als een beest.

Want steeds zag ik, toen de gemeente zong,
die werkeloze, die het raam uitsprong
en, van vier hoog, te pletter is geslagen.

Rotterdam: 1933, 1934, 1935

EINDVERGADERING

Terrarium. Verwaarloosd en geronnen
een gruwzaam leven in de dorre spleten;
het kruipen van de tijd geeft niets gewonnen
voor wie van moeheid niet te sterven weten.

De groene wanden zijn met slijm besponnen.
Er is geen water. Geen weet hoe zij heten.
Vertraagd zit een zijn eigen poot te vreten.
Twee zijn voorzichtig aan elkaar begonnen.

Genade, God,—o, laat mij toch ontwaken!
Verschrikkelijk is het rond dit groene laken.
'Wij gaan thans over tot de derde klas.'

Sigaren staan in scharen en in kaken.
Aanzie toch, wat wij van elkander maken!
Suf hokt de ziel in een verdord karkas.

CODE D'HONNEUR

Bezie de kinderen niet te klein:
Zij moeten veel verdragen—
eenzaamheid, angsten, groeiens pijn
en, onverhoeds, de slagen.

Bezie de kinderen niet te klein:
Hun eerlijkheid blíjft vragen,
of gij niet haast uzelf durft zijn.
Dàn kunt ge 't met hen wagen.

Laat uw comedie op de gang
—zij weten 't immers tòch al lang!—
Ken in uzelf het kwade.

Heb eerbied voor wat leeft en groeit,
zorg dat ge het niet smet of knoeit.—
Dan schenk' u God genade.

TUSSENUUR

Midwinterdag.—De geur van oude jassen,
de gang met kalken licht om in te dwalen;
een schateren—grindstorting—uit een klasse;
en dan hoort men de school weer ademhalen.

Dit is mijn land. Ik zal niet meer verkassen:
Dr I. G. M. Gerhardt, oude talen.
Vergeef mij, God, mijn duizendvoudig falen.
Ik kon dit nimmer in mijn schema passen.

En rebelleerde.—Maar ik ben gezwicht:
Te sterk zag mij mijn werk in het gezicht.
Het is mijn prachtige, mijn hondse baan.

Waar staat van 'wandelen voor Uw aangezicht'?
Een tussenuur. In deze geur, dit licht.
Het is mijn arbeid, en Gij ziet mij aan.

KARAKTER

Wanneer ik eenmaal mijn pensioen zal halen
en 't stadje làten, waar ik leraar was,
dan zal, als ze mijn gage uitbetalen,
mijn hart zijn overstempeld als een pas.

Het kleinste kind zette er initialen,
zijn onuitwisbaar merk iedere klas;
soms tekens, die geen sterveling zal vertalen.
'Χαρακτήρ', kinderen, betekent: 'kras'.

Het zij zo—Maar ik raak in alle staten,
als paedagogen zo hartroerend praten
van wat één leraar aan de kinderen geeft.

Zo God het wil, zet hij in alle klassen
zijn stempel—mooi of lelijk—in de passen:
maar het is hij, die duizend stempels heeft.

De Argelozen

*Tussen de rozeslingers en het groen
danste een rei van kinderen in 't plantsoen.
Zij zongen: 'Herder, laat je schaapjes gaan!'
Wat zult gíj, land, tegen de wolven doen?*

CHARIS

In de slaap geschreven
wordt het schoonst gedicht,
tussen dood en leven;
stil bij U verricht
wordt het ons gegeven
met het licht.

EERSTE VERJAARDAG
Geert Bomhoff, 10 augustus 1947

Eén jaar de aarde om de zon
sinds dit klein licht zijn loop begon,
dat, nu vandaag zijn eerste ronde
zich sloot, tezamen heeft gebonden
een toegenegen rei, gericht
naar dit klein stralend aangezicht.
——Een kring voltooid, een herbegin
zet lachend bij de koren in.
Dat ik dit argeloos feest wou meten
aan 't spel van zonnen en planeten
vergeef mij.——'k Zag zijn kleine baan
vannacht tussen de sterren staan.

DE GROENE LAAN
voor Rie Bomhoff-van Rhijn

Zwarte zwanen, witte zwanen,
rozerank van kind aan kind—
Argeloos schrijft het spel zijn ronde,
tot de strofe is gewonden
en het referein begint
als een wimpel, als een lint.
Zwarte zwanen, witte zwanen—
Dansen door de groene lanen.
Argeloos uit kindermonden
woorden, die geen wijsheid vindt,
tot een rondedans gebonden:
en het spelen herbegint
als een wimpel, als een lint.
Dansen door de groene lanen—
Zwarte zwanen, witte zwanen.

HET KIND

Het orgel uit de Warmoesstraat,
met rinkelbom en belletrom
en Kerstliederen op de plaat
die van de koperen rol komt glijden,
kon door de sneeuw niet verder rijden.
Kinderen dromden er rondom.
De orgelman greep om het even
het wiel: 'De witte vlokken zweven'...
het stokte in de vierde maat.
Plotseling schreide zó verlaten
het kleinste kind in sneeuw en kou,
dat ik het thuisbracht door de straten.
——Maar toen ik daarna, in de stage
stuifjacht, de hoek was omgeslagen,
lag blank de sneeuw en onbegaan:
Ik zag alleen zíjn sporen staan.

VAN EEN KIND

Argeloos voor de zicht:
ogentroost, mèt het graan
weggemaaid, maar, vederlicht
opgeraapt—Hiervandaan
ginds naar de weide gegaan.
Ogentroost, om te staan
schoon van kroon, in het licht.

MICHIEL MATTHAEUS
sept. 1938-dec. 1944

Nu slaapt hij in zó liefelijke staat,
dat geen meer ziet, hoezeer hij werd geschonden,
het deerlijke in linnen weggewonden;
de wimpers liggen op het zacht gelaat.
Hij was, zei men, verminkt.—Maar nimmer vonden
wij schoner schoon dan in zijn ernstig oog,
en in zijn handje, dat zich nog bewoog
naar ons, toen wij hem niet meer helpen konden.

OVER DE WEIDE

Zèker zal hij er zijn,
die wij op aarde beschreiden,
komende over de weide,
lachend en zonder pijn.
Kniediep in bloemen, klein,
komende over de weide,
lopende tussen ons beiden.—
En in zijn wijze geleide
zullen wíj kinderen zijn.

Komende over de weide,
zèker zal hij er zijn.

KELTISCH GRAFSCHRIFT

Die voor zichzelf niets vroeg,
wier liefde bij mij was,
rust in het hoge gras.
Ik gaf haar pijn genoeg.
Wier liefde bij mij was,
die ik van huis verjoeg,
zij, die mijn kinderen droeg,
rust in het hoge gras.

BRIEF AAN DE GROOTOUDERS
(Keltisch)

Het kind, waarom wij vurig vroegen,
had éne dag zijn aardse staat.
Het sneeuwde al, toen wij het droegen
waar nu het kruis gekorven staat.
Ik heb de akkers mogen ploegen.
De aarde draagt het winterzaad.

VERJAARDAG
Betty Boeke - 28 april 1954

Tussen april en mei
staat in het licht en het groen,
tussen der kinderen rei,
tussen der kinderen festoen,
schuchter dragende zeventig jaar,
schuchter dragend het zilveren haar,
zij, om wier liefde de ronde
deze dag wordt gewonden;
die het geheim heeft gevonden:
'Wordt als de kinderen, gij...'
Tussen april en mei.

ZONDAGMORGEN

De zon begint met muntjes licht
te spelen op het beddelaken;
de dag is argeloos van gezicht
en stemmen in het huis ontwaken.
De aanslag van een zachte lach,
en van een kind het pril geschater
op de ondertoon van plonzend water:
Zij heft het naar de nieuwe dag.

WEERZIEN OP ZOLDER

Wel te rusten, Vader Beer!
Het kind is hier vandaan.
Van al zijn spelen
en al zijn strelen
is haast je haar vergaan,
je lijf kaal tot de naden.
Het gaat op donkere paden
die jij en ik niet weten
—om wat er met zijn liefde is gedaan.
Met ogen die niet meer bestaan,
Beer, zie mij niet zo aan.

HET EGELTJE

De egel komt in 't eendere schemeruur
schuifelen langs de plavuizen van de schuur.

De ademsporen van zijn spitse snuit
gaan op de kille stenen aan en uit

omtrent de stille mens, die met geduld
zijn schuwheid went en de aarden schotel vult

en wacht, totdat een kleine ruige hand
zich tastend vastgrijpt aan de schotelrand.

Dan drinkt het dier. Even, als in verstaan,
zien twee bevredigden elkander aan.

SPIEGELING

Spieg'lend in omgekeerde stand
beweegt de groene varenplant
binnen het rimpelende licht,
en tussen dit vertakte wuiven
gaan kleine visjes—schitterschicht—
door kamertjes van schaduwig huiven.
Zie! zij gaan open, zij gaan dicht.

DE OUDE DICHTER

Niets vraag ik, dan dat gij mij
in uw zorgeloze spelen,
in uw jubelen laat delen:
ga mij niet uit schroom voorbij.

Geef mij niets: gij kúnt niets geven
dan het lachen, dan het leven,
dan het dansen van uw rei.

Naar mijn arbeid wilt niet vragen.
Zie, hoe van de bloemenwei
gaaf het blad ligt opgeslagen:
dans de regelen voor mij.

WATERMOLEN

Toevend op de groene treden
—waterkoelte, waterraderen;
diep geluk dat wordt beleden
bij het onbenoembaar naderen
van het groenbemoste rad...
groene koelte, groene raderen—
Waterval—wat schemerschat
houdt ge in uw geheim bevat!

AFSCHEID

Goudstof van vlinderwieken,
welhaast is het vergaan;
der vogelen zoet muzieken,
welhaast is het gedaan.
En in de vruchten slaapt het zaad.
Toon mij nog ééns uw schoon gelaat,
éér straks in 't graan de maaiers staan,
éér 's nachts de vogels over gaan,
—o zomer, éér gij gaat.

Kwatrijnen in opdracht

In opdracht

Van scheppens pijn de onverhoedse stoot;
liefde en haat, tot op de wortels bloot.—
Hoe hèbt gij, God, mij met dit volk verbonden,
dat gij mij tot zó bitter werk ontboodt.

I

I

's Nachts wakker in het uitgestorven huis
hoorde ik het bezig water van de sluis.
Toen riep men mij met name—twee, drie maal.
Een slaan van luiken en een groot geruis.

11

Zoek in mijn verzen heulsap noch venijn.
Het zijn de scheuten van een felle pijn;
de doodsangst om mijn land, mijn volk, mijn taal,
wringt in het onverbiddelijk kwatrijn.

III

Het late jaar, de eendere waterwegen,
het stampend licht in vlagen mist en regen.
Een aanklacht roept de brulboei van het rak.—
De nood van Holland zelf heeft stem gekregen.

IV

Stroomop, stroomaf der schepen donkere boeg;
door de bevrijde aarde snijdt de ploeg.
Arbeid en brood. En toch dit smartelijk derven.—
O staf, die water uit de rotsen sloeg!

V

Rivier en sterren in een heldere droom:
waar de Moerdijk zich spant over de stroom
stond Marsman, en zijn norse kijken mat
het land van oeverzoom tot oeverzoom.

VI

Nòg murmelen de schelpen: Gorters Mei.
Zijn naam ruist op de brandingskam voorbij.
De landwind antwoordt niet.—Een voze reuk
waait van de troosteloze duinenrij.

VII

Het schoon van Holland: welhaast doodgesnoeid;
de vogel zwijgt, de rank is uitgebloeid.
Een harde zon schijnt op de koolaspaden,
waarlangs gekneusde dovenetel groeit.

VIII

De minnaar van de blauwe ereprijs,
de grijze Thijsse, hebt gij naar 's lands wijs
—hoe argeloos stond hij bij uw zwarte hulde—
met eer gekroond, verwoest zijn paradijs.

IX

Op Groenoord werd, bij nacht en najaarsvlagen,
tweemaal de klopper op de deur geslagen.
Ontken het niet: het is Verster geweest,
die van de schuldigen rekenschap kwam vragen.

X

Bij iedere nieuwe schending van uw grond
sluipt als een gif de wanhoop in mij rond.
Haat, drift: ik kan mijn arbeid vàn mij spuwen.
De taal wordt mij tot alsem in de mond.

XI

Ten laatste heeft de stad haar schrikbewind
op mij gelegd, en afgesneden vind
ik iedere uitweg. Dagelijks loop ik blinder
het raadsel van haar stratenlabyrinth.

XII

Mijn vesting neemt ge niet: het blauw bazalt,
de kribben, waar het water rijst en valt,
waar — sterk als ik — doornrank en bitterzoet
hun wortels wringen tussen kier en spalt.

XIII

Soms waait er over mijn gekorven land
nog rinse geur van riet en voorjaarsplant,
en vogelen, aan de oude plek getrouw,
dalen in zwermen op rivier en strand.

II

XIV

Hier, telkenmale als ik het zeil omhaal,
hoor ik, aanvlagende over de Waal,
Van Schendels stem.—Herberg mij, elementen!
Hier leef ik vrij: dit water, deze taal.

XV

Klaroenstem in der steden nameloos grauw,
profetisch, Nijhoff, uw 'voor Dag en Dauw'.
Nòg wordt in de woestijn die stem vernomen
van statige vreugde en van fors berouw.

XVI

Gezegend wie, als hij de taal aanslaat,
zijn hart voelt hameren en in vrezen staat.
—Eén witte toon uit de volstrekte stilte,
één witte vogel die het rif verlaat.

XVII

De adelaar die zijn snavel heeft gewet
aan het bazalt—zijn nest blijft onverlet.
Zo wees bedacht op het u toevertrouwde
en hard uw kracht: geen rover nadert het.

XVIII

De erfenis der meesters slecht beheerd,
het ambacht van de kunstenaar verleerd,
het hoog geheim verraden in de herberg:—
De vlam gedoofd, de kracht der jeugd verteerd.

XIX

Reeds voelt de veile schare uw onvermogen:
kringende gieren, pikkend naar uw ogen.
Genadeloos is, voor wie zijn kunst verried,
het grauw, dat hij met aas heeft groot getogen.

XX

Ik zag de kunstenaars in zwarte stoeten
elkander in het stadion ontmoeten.
De auto's stonden op de asfaltweg.
—Een lachen vluchtte heen op zilv'ren voeten.

XXI

De slanke marter, in de boom gevlogen,
de tanden bloot, het moordlicht in de ogen,—
hoe heeft hij mij, in uw vereend bedrijf
bijna gekooid, met schaamrood overtogen!

XXII

Wie zelf de wijde wateren is gewend
laat zwijgend de ander in zijn element.
Men groet elkaar met de ogen. In de Lekbocht
heb ik als kind een visotter gekend.

XXIII

Heel Rotterdam, zijn huizen en zijn kaden,
bestond voor mij bij Leopolds genade.
Ik zag—een kind—hem in de avondstad
als Cheops door de sterrentuinen waden.

XXIV

De uitgebrande stad blijft hem herhalen.
Ik zag zijn voetstap om de puinen dwalen;
om de doorschoten toren waait zijn stem—
De driftige stroom schrijft zijn initialen.

XXV

Weer zijn vannacht de doden omgegaan.
Aangeklaagd, tot het kraaien van de haan,
hebben er stemmen.——Bij het grauwe dagen
zag ik de schuimstreep op de waterbaan.

XXVI

Vernuftige pijlers, ontrouw en verraad
dragen de brug. Gij die behaaglijk gaat
op haar plankier, buig nimmer naar het water:
gij mocht de spiegeling zien van uw gelaat!

XXVII

Gestreden heb ik levenslang met U.
Ik vind geen andere vrede dan bij U.
Hitte des daags, weder zijt gij geweken.
Oase van de avond, thans bij U.

III

XXVIII

Verkaveld werd, mijn lief, de laatste hof.
Het blinken van de wateren zelfs werd dof.
Mij blijft de toevlucht van uw levende ogen
voor hun alarmen en hun waaiend stof.

XXIX

De welput, en de lege emmer daalt;
het water, schommelend omhooggehaald,
een lichtend vlak tussen de donk're wanden...
Zalig wie de gelijkenis vertaalt!

XXX

Aan de andere kant hoor ik u al arbeiden
en mìjn houweelslag zal straks ù bevrijden.
O donkere watergang van Siloah,
hoe smalle wand houdt nog ons hart gescheiden.

XXXI

Toen kwam het kind mij stamelend verhalen:
'ik zag vannacht de wilde zwanen dalen'.
En fluisterend ik: 'vóór de ochtend nog zag ik
de leeuwerik voedsel voor zijn broedsel halen.'

XXXII

Bij 't strenge fonkelen van de winternacht
werd mij een toefje liederen toegebracht.
Bij 't nachtegalenlied uit de jasmijnen
heb ik het bitter doodslot overdacht.

XXXIII

Wanneer de zwaluw aan de balken bouwt,
de ooievaar zijn breedste vlucht ontvouwt,
de koekoek in de wilgen niet kan zwijgen...
Kùs het geluk, dat u is toevertrouwd!

XXXIV

De eerste dag dat men de zeisen haart,
het grote ruisen door de halmen vaart.—
Wat roept de koekoek, kort en dof geworden?
Rijk was de lente—en wat hebt gij vergaard?

XXXV

Een hoge kreet trekt scherp zijn zilvervoor.—
Dan gaat de vogel in de nacht teloor.
Ik ben ontwaakt. Gij hebt mij opgeroepen.
En ademloos volg ik uw lichtend spoor.

XXXVI

Verlaat uw velden, broeders! Snèl en snèl!
Een ranke zuil, een zilverhelle wel
aanzie!—staat levend in het dode water,
omhooggetogen—eindelijk—door mijn spel!

XXXVII

Waar zich de tweesprong van de stroom ontvouwt,
het huis: op storm en wassend tij gebouwd.
Geen wereld zal ons hier, mijn lief, vervreemden
van de opdracht, onvoorwaardelijk toevertrouwd.

XXXVIII

Terwijl een golf tot aan de muren sloeg,
een bruisend licht ons naar de ramen joeg,
zeilde de trotse schoener langs,—en jubelend
stond Samothrace's Nike op de boeg.

XXXIX

Bazuinen stoten in de ochtendlucht.
Wat wedervaart ons? Deze zwanenvlucht,
die hoos van glans en donker bij hun dalen...
Stuivende wateren ruisen van gerucht.

XL

Van Zuiderkruis naar Poolster, Grote Beer,
schuift in de ijle nacht der vogelen heir
zijn baan van leven onder langs de sterren.
Straks dalen zij als meteoorstof neer.

XLI

Soms, als ik tot mijn diepste diepte keer,
hergeeft gij mij het Holland van weleer.
Kuis gaan de kleuren open, en door tranen
zie ik het in de klaarte van Vermeer.

XLII

Uw doortocht door dit volk brengt geen in kaart.
Niets dan de tekenen dat gij mèt ons waart:
over het werk der edelsten uw naglans,
de bliksemflitsen van uw nedervaart.

XLIII

Voorwaardelijke troost, Godlof, ontkomen,
door het verrafeld landschap opgenomen,
hoorde ik een ruisen, dóór mijn opstand heen:
de harpslag van de eeuwenoude stromen.

XLIV

Geklommen op de donkere torentrans
zag ik mijn land in bovenaardse glans.
De zee in reven fonkelde om de kust.
De stromen togen met het licht ten dans.

XLV

Gij die in eigenwaan bijkomstig acht
des dichters werk, gìj zijt de dode vracht
aan boord vanouds. Die kent sextant noch dieplood.
Terwijl gìj slaapt loopt hìj de hondewacht.

XLVI

Een urn, een grafsteen—mìj zegt het niet veel.
Gij doet maar. Een herinnering is mìjn deel:
een oud Iers kerkhof—wilde bijen bouwden
hun honingraten in een bekkeneel.

XLVII

Door storm ontworpen, in der wateren tucht,
eeuwen beschreven door der wolken vlucht,
Gij trots domein der levende rivieren, —
bid om de geest, die u opnieuw bevrucht!

Het levend Monogram

Voor Marie van der Zeyde

Deel 1
In Memoriam Matris

AAN ALLEN

Ik heb dit donkere boek geschreven,
want God heeft het mij opgelegd.
Geen uur ben ik alleen gebleven
dat het mij nièt werd aangezegd.
Ik—vriend van stilte, dier en plant,
schreef naar zijn wil, met grijze haren,
de gruwelen van mijn kinderjaren

op deze doortocht naar zijn land.

I DE GESTORVENE

Hier rust, met stof gevuld de mond,
zij, die mij heeft gedragen;
zij, die mij naar het leven stond
in al mijn levens dagen.

En nu haar lichaam moet vergaan,
nu is zij in mij opgestaan.

—Ik kan haar niet verslaan.—

II TEGENSTEM

Gij zijt uit haar: aanzie de steen:
de nàmen zelfs hebt gij gemeen.
Aanvaard uw deel.—Ik zie u aan.
Tot zij in vree zal slapen gaan.
Tot gij in vrede hier zult staan.

KINDERHERINNERING

Vóór wij vertrokken naar de zwarte brandersstad,
ging gij nog eenmaal met mij naar de uiterwaarden.
Er was een wollig schaap, dat witte lammeren had;
een veulentje stond bij de grote blonde paarden.

Opeens voelde ik, dat gij mij naar het water trok.
Gij zijt gekeerd, omdat ik wild en angstig schreide.
Wit liep gij op de dijk; ik hangend aan uw rok.
Moeder en kind: vijanden en bondgenoten beide.

HET GEBED
de grootouders

Drie maal per dag, naar vaste wetten,
nemen zij de eigen plaatsen in,
en gaan zich rond de tafel zetten;
van haat eendrachtig: het gezin.

De vader heeft het mes geslepen,
de kinderen wachten, wit en stil.
De moeder houdt haar bord omgrepen
alsof zij het vergruizelen wil.

Een grauw: dan vouwen zij de handen,
de disgenoten in het huis:
van tafelrand tot tafelranden
geschikt tot een onzichtbaar kruis.

KAPITALE BOERENPLAATS

Wie geld bewaart is wélbewaard:
Tweehonderd jaren onbezwaard.

Een achterdochtig onverstaan
wrokt in de sombere olmenlaan.

Van trage haat en lust bevracht
het geile water in de gracht.

Den vreemdeling behoede God—
De heemhond vliegt hem naar de strot.

KLEIN GRAFMOMUMENT

Dolle kervel, bitterzoet,
oevergroei van Hollands Lethe—
hier heeft eens het kind gezeten,
vechtend om de laatste moed.

Dolle kervel, bitterzoet,
—vijftig jaren bloeien uw planten—
't waarde radeloos langs de kanten,
kervel om de klompenvoet.

Dolle kervel, bitterzoet:
tien geslachten zullen weten
hoe een kind, klein maar verbeten,
zich de dood at in het bloed.

TRISTIS IMAGO

Wat staat gij naast mijn bed, Moeder van gene zijde?
Wat doet gij in mijn kamer in de zwarte nacht?
Kan mijn bestaan zich nooit van uw bestaan bevrijden,
dat gij mijn slaap nog met uw heimelijkheid bevracht?

Wat praat gij tegen mij, Moeder van gene zijde?
Ik wìl niet wakker worden, als gij naast mij staat.
Het hart zal mij stukhameren, als ik moet lijden
het schrikkelijk verwijt op uw geblust gelaat.

DE AFGRONDEN

Kerstmis en Oudejaar,
de afgrond, het gevaar.
Met touwen aan elkaar.
Verboden dood te vallen
alléén: want elk trekt allen.
Messcherp de rand, waarop wij staan.
—God, zie ons aan.—

DE RATTEN

's Nachts hoorden wij in 't holle huis
de ratten rennen langs de binten.
Zij scheurden spaanders van de plinten;
in kasten viel de kalk tot gruis.

De Rotte gistte van bederf.—
Uw fierheid heeft geen kamp gegeven:
ge hebt het vaal gespuis verdreven,
nòg: de boerin op eigen erf.

Maar later, 's nachts in het gewelf
der kelders hoorden wij u vloeken;
uw bezem bonkte—in lege hoeken:
De ratten zaten in uzelf.

DE MANTEL

Met uw zwarte mantel aan
door de witte sneeuw gegaan:
aan het einde van de laan
ligt het wit gesticht.

Met uw zwarte mantel aan
door de witte gang gegaan
in het naakte licht.

Met uw zwarte mantel aan
hebt gij aan de wand gestaan,
door uw kinderen gericht,
die gij baarde
naakt in 't licht.

Toen uw mantel werd ontdaan
zijn wij heengegaan.

VERGEEFS VERZET

Gij ging in bittere opstand heen.
—De vlinders spelen om uw steen.

Versteend uw afgewend gelaat.
—Zie, hoe de treurroos opengaat.

De dag, de nacht zaagt ge niet aan.
—Uw graf beschijnen zon en maan.

SONNET VOOR MIJN MOEDER

Gij hebt, Moeder, dit leven zwaar gedragen.
Gelijk ik het zwaar draag. Wij zijn verwant.
Wij horen in dit stormbevochten land
van kavels, tussen dijk en stroom geslagen.

Ik heb uw gang: die driftige en toch trage
voetstap, die onverzettelijke trant.
Uw harde hand herken ik in mijn hand,
onwrikbaar om de schrijfstift heengeslagen.

Machtig zijn wij, in liefde en in haat.
Gij hebt u dóódgehaat, hatend het meest
uzelve, om de liefde die gij schond.

Ik ben genezen van het bitter kwaad.
En eer in stugheid, wie gij zijt geweest:
van mijn talent de donkere moedergrond.

DE AANSTOOT

Hamer, kleine bonte specht;
stoot uw snavel op de stammen.
In dit bos van molm en zwammen
klinkt uw hard geluid oprecht.

Hamer in het gistend woud—
In mijn hart en in mijn oren
dringt uw tikken en uw boren.
Hamer op het harde hout.

Hamer, kleine bonte specht;
straks—zij zullen God wel danken!—
timmert men voor mij zes planken.
Dan is alle twist beslecht.

SAMENZWERING

Het water praatte deze nacht
om huis.
      Rondom de vlonder
was babbelen en lachen zacht,
—een donk're spot daaronder.

Het water praatte deze nacht
om huis.
      Tot aan de muren
was het—o bitt're overmacht—
een lispelen en schuren.

Het water praatte deze nacht—
Nu ga ik als een blinde
door 't huis, dat op het dagwerk wacht.

Ik kan mijn vree niet vinden.

Deel II
Daemonen

Over zwarte karresporen,
over greppels, over voren,
zweeft het witgepluisde zaad
van de nooit gerooide doren;
zweeft, gevleugeld, al mijn haat.
Eér het kiemt tussen het koren,
God, verlos mij van het kwaad!

HUISELIJK LEVEN

Ik bracht mijn kind een buks mee naar huis;
hij schouderde hem en schoot
eer ik het kon verhinderen
de zeven poppekinderen
van het poppenhuis
morsdood.

Schiettent op de Boul'Miche
en verbaasde kinderogen
van borden, ogen gelogen.
—Wie woont er in dat huis?—
Ah, je m'en fiche!
Zeven borden aan gruis.

WEERZIEN OP ZOLDER

Welterusten, Vader Beer!
Het kind is hier vandaan.
Van al zijn spelen
en al zijn strelen
is haast je haar vergaan,
je lijf kaal tot de naden.
Het gaat op donkere paden
die jij en ik niet weten
—om wat er met zijn liefde is gedaan.
Met ogen die niet meer bestaan,
Beer, zie mij niet zo aan.

HET BORD

Ingekooid—op een tronk verdord,
de slagpen hoekig opgestoken,
snavel en oog in rouw verdoken,
de doffe vederen saamgeschort
de adelaar, in zijn vlucht gebroken
en in het slagnet neergestort.
Wandelaars lezen op een bord:
'Bergarend, vlucht 2.80 M.'
De kinderen naderen eendrachtig
wanneer er aas geworpen wordt.

MARCHE FUNÈBRE

Fanfarecorps in de avondstraten
bij walmend fakkellicht—
De liefde heb ik lang verlaten.
God, houd met mij gericht.
De tuba schalt, de trommels slaan.
Ik heb geen huis om in te gaan.

Licht over levende gelaten,—
Er is geen mens, waar ik van hou.
Tegen de muur in de avondstraten.
God, ziè mij met mijn zwart berouw,

met mijn gekeerde doodsflambouw.

GRIJZE ZEE

De zee trekt langzaam dicht
in regen en in mist.
Mijn hart trekt langzaam dicht
in grijze mist en regen.
Er zijn tot u geen wegen,
tot u.

RADIOBERICHT

Te Grave beneden de sluis
voorbij de zware deuren
mag mij het water sleuren
en kantelen met geruis.
—Grave beneden de sluis.

'Wij geven de waterstand.'

O God, hoe kon het gebeuren—
gesloten het venster, de deuren,
gebannen uit liefde en huis.
—Grave beneden de sluis.

'Wij geven de waterstand.'

Grave, dat is groen land
en water, dat draagt mij thuis.

'Grave beneden de sluis.'
Grave, beneden de sluis.

DE GEDULDIGEN

De groene snoek, gevangen
na wild en sterk verzet
en dan, naar visserswet,
tegen de wilg geslagen
die hem de kop verplet—
het beeld vervolgt mij dagen.

Mijn lèvende verlangen:
houd gij het van hun trage
aassnoeren, God, gered!

ZONSONDERGANG

De vogelen heb ik zien komen
voorbij het zonneoog.
Ik heb hen neder zien stromen:
de ganse aarde bewoog
van vleugelen wit en zwart,
van kreten wild en verward.
Tot de zon was ondergegaan.
Toen heb ik hen óp zien staan.
Duizenden vleugelen, geslagen,
waren als één vogel,—gedragen,
zwart, langs nachts baan.

NASCHRIFT

Deze winter is Eén
met mij overgebleven
in het verlaten gebied.
Anderen hardden mij niet:
het ging op dood of op leven.
Weet dat dit boek is geschreven
onder zijn 'ja' en zijn 'neen'.

Deel III
Hoefprent van Pegasus

SCHRIFTUUR

Schriftuur moet bloeien als een plant,
de regelen als ranken gaan,
de strofen winden tot hun rand
en inperking. Uw hoog vermaan
verlicht mij dat niets kan bestaan
wat het oorspronkelijk verband
verbrak.—Ontsprongen aan mijn hand
vangt thans het eigenlijk schrijven aan.

MANTIEK

Blijf, vogelen, uw vluchten schrijven
boven ons tijdeloos verblijven.

Uw maningen gestaag herhalen,
die wij vertalen telkenmale.

Wij hebben aarde en tijd verlaten—
wilt naderen tot de zilveren platen,

dat taal en teken ons omstromen.
Wij wachten naar uw naderkomen.

ZUM TODE

Soms laat gij mij een eb en vloed alleen.
Uren vergaan met schrijven in het zand.
Zo weer ik mij, krijsvogels om mij heen,
vergankelijk, uitgestoten aan de rand
der aarde.——Water komt en gaat, het strand
ligt nat en gladgewist gelijk voorheen.

TUSSENSPEL

Soms zijt ge omgeven door de kleinste dieren,
vogeltjes trippen om uw flank hun spoor;
er speelt een hazenpaar, en bij uw oor
blijft eindeloos de leeuwerik tierelieren.

De bijen komen u met goud versieren;
buitelend breekt de kleur van vlinders door,
die in een wolk van stuifmeel bruiloft vieren.
Dit is uw spel. Ik kom er niet in voor.

O lieflijkheid—Muziek, muziek, muziek,
dit spelen om uw hoofd en witte wiek,
dat gij gedoogt, een berg begroeid met bloemen,

genadig toevend in dit zachte zoemen
en kwetteren—Kan zó de tijd bestaan?
Verwijl nog; laat uw vleugelen niet opengaan.

SLAPENDE
Voor Peter Gumbert

Zwijg, aarde, rond het grote witte paard
waar hij zijn plek tot rusten heeft verkoren—
Gij dalen, houdt zijn naglans welbewaard
en bergen, geeft zijn lichtspoor niet verloren.
Hij is geweldig over u gegaan.
Nu zijn de sterrevleugelen toegedaan.
Stil, Nacht—en wil dit zachte staan
niet storen.

DE PAARDEN

Daags drinken bij het wed
de grote aardse paarden.
Hoefprenten staan op de aarde,
het gras is zilt geplet.

Te nacht, als sterren en maan
in zachte diepten spiegelen,
beweegt het wak een wiegelen:
twee vleugelen ruisen aan.

Het water ligt vervaard,
als witte manen zinken:
rimpelend om het drinken
van een geweldig Paard.

Later draagt het, weer blak,
de adem in nevelvegen
van 't Paard dat, reeds ontstegen,
dronk uit een sterrenwak.

ΠΟΙΗΣΙΣ

De strofen komen toegevlogen
gelijk de vogelen overgaan.
Soms tot figuren streng getogen,
soms vegen grijs op grijs vergaan.
Mij geldt hun rakelingse baan.
Ik ben niets dan één groot vermogen.
Ik ben alleen en roep hen aan.

THRACISCH I

Ginder het wrak, bij de stranding
diep in de zandplaat gewoeld;
hier, met de kantelende branding
is het boegbeeld aangespoeld.

Een gekromd zeepaard, verbonden
met vier snaren: de Lier;
en de naam—Grieks ongeschonden—
'Orpheus', in slingers van wier.

Te avond heb ik het hergeven
aan het scherp trekkende tij.
Toen het uit zicht was gedreven,
ruisten de liederen in mij.

THRACISCH II

De aanhef van de ebben fluit:
en zie! de trotse golveranden
kantelen, brekend op de stranden,
alreeds de machtige maatgang uít.

Het lied, dat jubelend moduleert:
Aanzie! de witte vogelen komen
en schrijven over het kruivend stromen
de frasen, die de fluit schakeert.

ORPHISCH

Als Orpheus voor de dieren speelt,
de aardgeboren volken,
verschijnt hun levend evenbeeld:
in 't kruiven van de wolken
stuwt leeuw en lam en adelaar aan.
En dèze en gindse karavaan
glanst in de stroom, die stil bleef staan
tot spiegelen en vertolken.

HET MOTIEF

Het is een zwaluwnest,
leemhut boven de beken;
één kan het brood er breken
en slapen, op z'n best.

Wie heeft, in eenzaam uur,
hier dit motief geschreven:
'Lièf, leven van mijn leven',
rank op de witte muur?

's Ochtends, langs dauwig spoor,
moest ik de wand afdalen;
in eindeloos herhalen
—de val en de vocalen—
ging het mij jubelend voor.

DE WELLEN

In diepten, sluierfijn
rechtstandige tuil der wellen,
asparagus van snelle
lichtranken in groene schijn.
Het kiezel, kristallijn
betrest met waterbellen,
is wiegelend, waar de helle
oorsprongen zijn.

HERFST

Grootmachtige vlagen,
grootmachtig licht,
najaar, wij dragen
u, ongezwicht.
Buien achterhalen
ons tot het hart;
ploegakkers stralen,
zilver en zwart.
Verweer, herfstdagen,
ons aangezicht.—
Grootmachtige vlagen,
grootmachtig licht:
zo wij versagen,
houd kort gericht.

ZELFPORTRET

De wouw, die hier zijn standplaats heeft,
heeft zijn beschermer overleefd,
die neergeslagen is bij het maaien
en aan wiens brauw het zweet nog beeft.
Zijn vleugelen blinken lichterlaaie
terwijl hij om de dode zweeft.

EROOS

Aan de steenwand grauw
wij, verslagenen in staren.
Dáár, ontzaglijk te ontwaren,
macht viervleugelig opgevaren,
parende de adelaren
vóór het blauw.

ANIKATE MAXAN

Schud de vleugelen, dat hun zwart
't zwartste van de nachten tart.
Zwart met blauwige weerschijnen.
Schud de vleugelen, dat het hart
haast begeeft. Adelaarspracht.
Span de krachten, vier de bogen,
laat hen opengaan, getogen
—macht schaduwend tegen macht—
naar de nacht.

AFSCHEID

Bittere brandingsslagen
tuimelen aan op de kust.
Duininwaarts vindt het klagen
van de stormvlagen geen rust.
Herfst en het kenteren der dagen.
Eenzaamheid, bitter belagen.

Moge mijn hart niet versagen
dat Gij tot deze stage
opgang zo groots hebt ontrust.

Deel IV
Het levend Monogram
ΙΧΘΥΣ

ΙΧΘΥΣ

De vis, getrokken door mijn hand
en èven vrij nog van de golven,
zal straks gewist zijn van het strand
en door de grote vloed bedolven.
Maar in het water, dat hem nam
zwemt levende het Monogram.
Geheime trek van tij en maan:
Hij zal op alle kusten staan.

AD TE CLAMAVI

De adelaar is neergeschoten.
Hij daalde cirkelend: heel het dal
zag met ontzetting naar zijn val.
Een land door bergen ingesloten.
Mijn ziel door bergen ingekraagd.
Vleugelen had ik uitgeslagen—
God, wil mij op uw adem dragen;
aanzie mij, God, ik ben belaagd.

ΨΥΧΗ

Eén vleugel nog in de cocon
en één, gekreukeld, die gaat gloeien.
Ik wist niet dat het zó begon,
zó deerlijk—
        God, laat niet verschroeien
mij schaamte voor uw aangezicht,
dat ik mijn blik, tóch, heb gericht
toen hij vrij wilde en niet kon...

Het was een schepsel in uw licht.

PREEK OP TERSCHELLING
'Want zij waren vissers.' Matth. 4 : 18

Raak mij niet tot in het hart
met uw starend vragen;
mij, in kleren zwaar en zwart
aan de wand geslagen,

vissers, met uw stroef gebed
en uw simpele wetten;
als bij 't meer Genésareth
komend van de netten.

Die het woord 'Komt achter mij'
eenmaal hoorden spreken,
vissers waren zij, als gij.
En de Vis is teken.

Vis en Visser ken ik niet,
die voor u moet bidden.
Die mijn zwarte armoe ziet,
Hij zij in uw midden.

STAKING

De ploeg van het ontginningsland
heeft wéér de spade neergesmeten
en zit tussen de vale keten
zwijgend het trage brood te eten.
Smakeloos zout vreet aan het strand.
Eén slaapt al. Op de zondagskrant
die om de hompen heeft gezeten
staat bij de tekst: 'Geef gìj hun te eten'
gigantisch breed zijn voet geplant.

UITTOCHT UIT RUSLAND
Aan de Mennonieten uit Rusland

Onder der wolken gang
de exodus der schamelen,
die bij het vlek verzamelen.
Een wekroep, een gezang

slaat op. De trage maat
vaart in de zware voeten,
tot, door de laatste stoeten
het machtig Paaslied gaat.

De kinderen aan de hand.—
Onder de gang der wolken:
een strééprje onder de volken,
die talrijk zijn als zand.

UITTOCHT

Toen Pharao het volk verbood te gaan,
deelde een staf de wateren, en de stroom
hield in. Droogvoets bereikten zij de zoom,
het oeverriet der Schelfzee.—Zó ving aan
de uittocht.
          Telken nanacht in de droom
zie ik de wateren omgebogen staan.
Wij wandelen verwonderd, hand in hand.
En hoog boven de strook waarlangs wij gaan,
hoog boven waterwand en waterwand
een strook van ruisen en een reppend slaan
van vogelwieken. Trekvogels, hun baan
recht boven ons, naar het beloofde land.

GREEN PASTURES

Wij die wandelden in het licht
van het zacht getijde,
het verwonderd aangezicht
naar de pracht der weiden,
elkaar leidend bij de hand
door het lieflijk groene land—
niet zal Hij ons scheiden.

Wie heeft onze gang geleid
langs de koele stromen,
ons in liefde en licht geweid
aan de groene zomen,
ons van tranen en angst bevrijd?
Wat met schromen werd verbeid
is met schroom gekomen.

In de zomen van het licht
gaan wij aardse beiden;
komend voor zijn aangezicht
aan het eind der tijden
zien wij eindelijk, ongedeeld,
wat geen aardse wei verbeeldt:
Glans in glans, door glans omspeeld
op de groene weiden.

BRIEF UIT DE GEMEENTE

Als in de kring het lamplicht wordt ontstoken,
het witte tafellaken is gespreid
en de gebeden worden uitgesproken,
weten wij dat ge in ons midden zijt.
Altijd wordt, ook voor u, het brood gebroken.
Wij werken voort als gij. Hij kent de tijd.

APOCALYPS
1 *Cor.* 13 : 12

Ik zat in de wachtkamer van de trein
op dit veilig terrein God te ontkomen.
Toen zag ik, dat de zaal vol goud ging stromen
en engelengelijk werden in die schijn

de wachtenden.—Die met het fretgezicht,
het kind dat met zijn limonade knoeide
en al de elkaar aanstarende vermoeiden
toefden als zaligen in een baan van licht.

'Verzet de wissel, wachter baanvak zeven;
laat men zich aanstonds naar 't perron begeven':
uit de oude vouw rijst elk in 't grauwe licht.

Het laatst zag ik de wandspiegel beslaan.
Eénmaal, van aangezicht tot aangezicht...
als ik versta, gelijk ik bèn verstaan.

WIJNSTOK

Zonder mij kunt gij niets doen. Joh. 15 : 5

Het was de hovenier,
die in het vroege licht
de ranken heeft gericht,
diep in elkaar verward,
vervreemdend van het hart,
de wortelstok.

Geen zag wat zich voltrok
in het zeer vroege licht.
Hij raakte hen slechts aan:
zij zijn vaneengegaan,
ontbonden
ontwonden.

Het was de hovenier.
Verwonderd, in vroeg licht,
gescheiden ongescheiden
de door zijn hand geleide
hartranken.
          —Aan ons beiden
hebt gij het, God, verricht.

DE DISGENOTEN

Het simpele gerei,
het brood, dat is gesneden,
de stilte, de gebeden—
Want de avond is nabij.

Uit tranen en uit pijn
dit samenzijn verkregen:
bij sober brood de zegen
twee in ùw naam te zijn.

Waar aan de witte dis
uw teken wordt beleden
verschijnt Gij—: 'u zij vrede'.
gij Brood—gij Wijn—gij Vis.

HET ROZEBLAD

Het blad, gedwarreld op uw graf,
—gij gaaft het één, gij gaaft het al—
ligt als een bloeddrop bij uw naam;
rozeblad in vertraagde val,
rozeblad op de witte steen.
Gij gaaft het al, gij gaaft het één.
Ik ben tot liefde niet bekwaam.
Mijn bladeren vallen nimmer af.

STEM VAN DE DICHTER

'Wat ik mijn lief heb misdreven
heeft zij vergeven
zeven maal zeventig maal.
Toen ik in vrees en beven,
God, uw balans zag zweven,
lei zij haar hart in mijn schaal.'

BEGRAFENIS M. NIJHOFF

Gedenk nu de aarde opengaat
het kind, dat leefde in zijn gelaat
en dat de lei heeft volgeschreven.
God alleen wist dat het nadien
de grote nieuwe brug wou zien.
De engelen gaven vrijgeleide.

Hij is reeds aan de overzijde.

IN MEMORIAM PATRIS

Waar is mijn Vader? Is hij in het licht?
Hij lag verheerlijkt, toen hij was gestorven.
Ziët hij, van aangezicht tot aangezicht?
Zijn aardse liefde was op haar gericht,
die nooit op aarde vrede heeft verworven.
Is hem, ginds, het volmaakte aangericht?

VALLEI VAN DE DOOD

In de droom de zachte vallei
des doods aanschouwd;
beloken de bloemenwei,
het gras bedauwd.
Zéér morgenlijk, zilverfris.
Hoè tijdelijk dit respijt!
Vallei—en te worden verbeid
als wit het haar—zilver—is.

FINIS

Wat ziet gij, liefste, mij aan?
Nòg kan ik donker vervaren
om het kwaad der donkere jaren
dat, donker, ik u heb gedaan.
Wat ziet gij, liefste, mij aan?
Geen sterveling weet wat zij waren
dan gij, die dit donkere, zware
door liefde te niet hebt gedaan.

De Hovenier

Aan de nagedachtenis van mijn zuster Truus

MET VOLSTREKTE EER

Er kwamen paarden in de witte sneeuw
te Wassenaar voorbij het dorpskerkhof
de dag dat daar mijn zuster was begraven.
——Zij kende slechts één liefde: de volstrekte.——
En komende ter hoogte waar het was,
ving één paard aan te knikken met het hoofd,
beamende hetgeen zij heeft gedaan.
En al de anderen in de witte sneeuw
inhoudend waar de smalle vore was,
zij trantelden en neigden, en bewezen
de laatste eer.

Het kengetal

HET KENGETAL

Ontzettend is het uit de verre verte
met vingers, die het schrijven aan de muur
de ander op te roepen door de wand,
de opgeschrikte.—Als zijn adem komt,
staat radeloze liefde naast de daad.
Dan vangt het wederzijdse roepen aan:
flarden uiteengerukt door een ontijdelijk
bruisen of een woelen zonder naam.
Plotseling schuift een zwarte stilte dicht.—
En aan dit eindelijke doodsravijn
aanhoor: het dolen van het eigen hart
dat ruisend stuwt en stuwt de éne naam.
Geen antwoord.
Catherine waart om Wuthering Heights.
Saul, bevend, wacht te Endor Samuel.

SAPPHO

Schoon gelaat, van droppels nog overfonkeld,
trotse tranen om het volmaakt geboren
strofisch lied dat, jong aan het licht gesprongen,
opent de ogen.

Dit uw dracht van brandingomvlaagde dagen,
nachten dat gij slapeloos weer der sterren
straling zag vergaan, als het klare maanlicht
àlschijnend opkomt.

Wie kan leed u doen?—Aan de strofen ontstijgen
zeedoorwaaide geuren van thijm en bijen,
ook het openkomen der grote rozen
nimmer genaderd.

LEOPOLD

Adelaar was hij tot de laatste strofe,
toppen òverzwevende waar geen sterveling
ooit genaakt, of naar de verlaten horstplaats
statig weer dalend.

Onverschrokken kantelend langs ravijnen,
vochtomvlaagd door daverend levend water,
schrijvende zijn vederenschaduw daar waar
eeuwige sneeuw ligt.

God zij lof om dit nimmer aangerande
trots vermogen, dat zóveel barre winters
heeft getart en de sterke vleugels wette:
Trots ongebroken.

THASOS

Een eiland als een ezelsruggegraat.
De geiten rukken aan het wrede gras,
de zee komt sissend langs de spitse kust.
Mij is het goed, het meest bij noordenwind.
Op deze stenen wordt de voet gehard,
hier, hoog tegen de rotsen, wet zijn kracht
op ruimte en licht, ontstegen aan het nest,
roofvogeljong, het scherp gevlerkte vers.

SAPPHISCH

Gekanteld aan de appelaar
bij treden door geen voet genaakt
amphore, waaruit water vliet
dat wellend niet ten einde raakt:
der goden dodengave aan haar,
de steeds ontstegene in het lied,
de donkere appel aan de tak,
die geen hand uit het lover brak.

HET DAGWERK

Ik loop in de Maeander van het dagwerk,
het heilig en verschrikkelijk motief,
met vastgesloten mond houd ik mij vaardig
voor deze eindeloze tranteldans
van gaan en keren, schouderwenden, haaks
staan op de lijn die tot een hoek verspringt
—de windingen keren in zichzelve weer—
Maeander van het dagwerk dat mij heeft
genomen; voetenstrak en feilloos loop
het heilig en verschrikkelijk motief
bij ieder einde ik de Maeander in.

DE OUDERDOM
Eert uw vader en uw moeder

Dit is hun tijdeloos seizoen.
Het vroege blad verdorde,
het dorre is jong geworden.
Uw hand stelle geen orde.

De tekenen verhelen
het raadsel van hun doen,
nog met geen zwaard te delen.

Slechts waagt, om méé te spelen,
uw kind zich uit het groen.

...gelijk een kind, spelende op het strand,
dat alles maken kan: een vogelbeest,
een vis, een mens, een huis en een barkas.
God geeft het hem in zilte lijnen aan
wanneer de vloed terugloopt op het zand.
Het kind stort zich met hartstocht op zijn schop
of tekent met de vingers vin en veer.
's Avonds staat het te kijken hoe het tij
weer opzet en zijn maaksels vóór en na
doet slinken en met ruisen overspoelt.
'Geprezen!' Morgen komt er wéér een dag.
Dan komt het terug, het schopgeschouderd kind.
Het weet: de Geest blaast tòch waarheen hij wil.

KRINGLOOP

Lichtfonkelend in de archipel
het schelpeneiland, waar geen voet
het vastgevoegde strand betreedt.
De kleuren spelen met het licht.

De golven kantelen om en om
de welving en de karteling,
totdat bij ribbelige eb
zich hecht de horen en de harp.

Maar later, als de maan opgaat,
worden zij zwevend opgelicht
in randen kantelende naar
de lichtdoorglansde archipel.

PARNASSUS

Dit:
aan de sneeuwgrens staan.
Wind en licht
raken aan.
Bladen en stift
zijn al ontgleden,
in paden beneden
staat het gegrift.

CLARA HASKIL
Mozart Pianoconcert in A-dur

Gebracht langs donkervlietende
rivieren, langs ravijnen
van brokkelig gesteente
naar de eindelijke weiden van de rust.
De beek spreekt in zichzelve, gentianen
dragen de droppels op het ernstig blauw,
varens zijn nog gefronst.
En steeds het prevelen, prevelen van water.
—Zijt gij daar, die op aarde naast mij was?
O liefste, liefste, hoe aanzie ik thans
uw eigen staat, en weet ik wie ik zelve
mag zijn.—Herken het tekenschrift
der vlinders en der purperen honingmerken:
strofen op aarde onontraadselbaar.
Dit is het, wat wij nimmer uit te spreken
vermochten, wat thans op de lippen ligt
van zelve.
Hoor, het water vraagt
dat wij nog zwijgen, want de wind heft aan,
vlagen van snaren, ruisend, en daarachter
een donker stromen, waar de oorsprong
verholen is.

HET VERRAAD

Van het verraad onpeilbaar ogenblik.—
De vogel van het hart kwam toegevlogen
waar takken zich over het water bogen:
de argeloze worgt de hennepstrik.

DE LICHTBAK

De bijt is in het ijs geslagen,
de lamp blijft branden bij het wak.
Een knaap heeft de lantaarn gedragen.
Straks komen naar het rimpelend vak
de stille vissen, lichtomspeeld,
die men met haken op zal halen.
Verraad, o gruwelijk evenbeeld,
gelijkenis, nauwelijks te vertalen.—
Het komt, gelokt uit bodemlagen,
het starende en stom verlangen.

Tot hen, die met de lichtbak vangen.

FORLORN

Ik kan niet vinden waar gij zijt.
Langs uw gelaat gaat noodweer aan;
de bittere branding zie ik slaan,
met zilt dat in de ogen bijt.
Ik kan niet vinden waar gij zijt,
noch waar ik zelf ben in mijn pijn.
O onmacht van dit samenzijn,
verholen riffen, blind ravijn
en dieplood van het zelfverwijt—
Ik kan niet vinden waar gij zijt.

NADERING

Aan de andere kant hoor ik u al arbeiden
en mijn houweelslag zal straks ù bevrijden.
O donkere watergang van Siloah,
hoe smalle wand houdt nog ons hart gescheiden.

DE VERSTOTENE
(Keltisch)

Het dorp begint mij te vermijden
en mompelt sinds zij mij verliet.
De kinderen wijken schuw terzijde,
de hond gromt sinds zij mij verliet.
De dominee komt de Heer belijden,
als hij mijn land verwaarloosd ziet.
Wat raken mij de jaargetijden?
't Is winter sinds zij mij verliet.

ALLEEN
(Keltisch)

De tafel en het bed zeggen: alleen.
De donkere kleren aan de muur: alleen.
Om huis en stallen sluipt het woord—een moordenaar
die men het mes hoort wetten op de steen.

DERTIG EEUWEN
Voor mijn leerlingen

Toen Patroklos gelegd was op de baar,
werd hij door alle jongens uitgedragen.
Ik zag hen kinderlijk de dode schragen,
een haag van jonge eiken naast elkaar.

Maarts voorjaar joeg de wolken langs het goud.
Er donderde een phalanx straaljagers over,
toen op de brandstapel omfloerst met lover
zij hem legden en de vlam sloeg in het hout.

Myriaden jaren op de palm der hand.—
Ik dorst niet opzien naar wie was ter zijde,
lieflijk en stil, Briseïs aller tijden,
toen hij verbrand werd in dit lage land.

PHOENIX

Voor Maurits van Boetzelaer

Tienduizend maal heb ik het myrrhe-ei
in kringvluchten gedragen over Arabië,
tot ik het hief zo moeiteloos als mijn eigen
gevederte.—Toen kwam ik waar hij lag,
mijn dode vader, streng tesaamgevouwen;
de ogen in de sombere verenkrans
gesloten tot een streep, geklemd de snavel,
de klauwen hiëratisch teruggebogen
in afweer voor het hart.—De strakke dode
gebed op ademloze steen.
Ik nam hem op, zwevende met hem over
de invalspoorten van het hooggebergte,
het rotsplateau waartoe geen voet genaakt,
de zandwoestijnen en, van groen omstrookt,
de grote stroom, de Nijl.—Onafgebroken
richtend mijn vlucht naar Heliopolis
daalde ik neer en gaf hem aan de god
die zon en zenging is; hij, vuur en vlam.
Ontstijgende heb ik niet omgezien:
Eindelijk waar hij hoort te zijn.—Hij is
mijn Vader en ik ben zijn zoon.

RONDEEL
VOOR HENRIËTTE ROLAND HOLST
Zalig die hongeren en dorsten naar de gerechtigheid;
want zij zullen verzadigd worden. Matth. 5 : 6

De helft was haar niet aangezegd
—eenzaam te leven en te sterven—
die opgesleten tot de nerven
door vreemde handen is afgelegd.

Na het verloren aards gevecht.
Want macht gaat uit om macht te werven.
De helft was haar niet aangezegd:
eenzaam te leven en te sterven.

Godlof, aan de aardse staat onthecht
die tijd noch wereld kan onterven.
Zij zal gerechtigheid niet derven
ginder in glans haar weggelegd:

De helft is haar niet aangezegd.

RONDEEL VOOR LEOPOLD

Offert Asklepius een haan;
want hij is tot de dood genezen,
die door zijn volk is uitgewezen
en ongeweten heengegaan.

Wat komt gij samen òm hem staan?
Het woord is bitter: onvolprezen.
Offert Asklepius een haan,
want hij is tot de dood genezen.

Geen die het laken terug zal slaan
nu hij niet meer te wéér kan wezen.
Geen stilte is zo stil als deze.—
Hij kwam aan de overzijde aan.

Offert Asklepius een haan.

DE DRIE PHARAOHS

Toen was er, midden in het stadsgewoel,
een man en op de hand droeg hij
een valk.
En mensen dromden rond dien Pharaoh,
die met een ketting om de voet
in onbewegelijke trots het eigen lot
bestaarde. Hij was als bazalt.
O, gelijk deze zag ik in zijn stad
kort voor zijn dood, een vastgeketend vorst,
de mensen overstarend op een plein,
die Cheops schiep, den dichter Leopold.

HET ONWEER

Verscholen in de holle wilgenstam
zie ik de bliksem zigzaggen in de rivier.
De donder schudt het land.
Ik ben doorweekt tot op de huid
en mateloos gelukkig—tot de kern
des harten.
Uit de vochte stomp
met lichtend mos komt geur van kistenhout.
En plotseling zie ik mijzelf gestrekt:
de vinger draagt de ring nog, al het andere
siddert tot helle as.
—En schreeuwende ontstijgt
het adelaarsjong.

Schlüszli

In memoriam Cor Sassen

*Haar vriendschap zonder aandrang of verraad
naderden mens en dier in vrije staat.
Haar hart was als haar kamer: waar de vogel,
de schuwe, in en uit het venster gaat.*

SCHLÜSZLI

Het dorp ligt wit
—wàt een sneeuw!—
Ik klim naar boven met twee
verse broden onder mijn arm.
Ze luiden, het is
acht uur.
Het begint weer, witte
vlokken en witte
woorden, het daalt zó maar.
O zie, het is wóórd geworden!—
op mijn donkere mouw
het kristal.

LENTE

Voorzichtig beginnen te spelen
binnen een groenende koelte,
de bloemen met name te groeten
en van het hart te ontsluiten
aarzelende kamers.
Het brood met elkander te delen,
de koele beekval te voelen.
En in de avond te wachten
de bevende witte vlinders:
de kamperfoelie gaat open.

VERJAARSWENSEN

Bronwater, uit de hand
gedronken, licht en schaduw,
en al de hoge grassen
gepluimd, nog groen.
En dat de vrienden komen
met enkel de geschenken
van hun verrukkelijk lachen;
met 's avonds van hun zwijgen
de dauw.

ZOMERAVOND

Langzaam over het land
in de avond de trompet
van de andere boerderij.
Het praten op de bank
sterft uit, de witte roos
laat stille bladeren vallen.
Het kind, te bed gebracht,
slaapt niet, achter het hart
der luiken luistert het.

WINTER

De sterren wintertintelen
en de maan
doorschijnt de melkwegnacht.
Het kraakt van sneeuw op de aarde
waar ik ga,
een nieteling, een adem wit,
een ademdamp van liefde en poëzie.

EB

Grauwgrijze schapenkudden trekken
de wadden langs.—Een hekatombe
van koeien staat half in het water.
De damp slaat van de wieren af.
Verder landinwaarts naderen grazend,
staartzwaaiende de grote paarden,
zó langzaam dat volmaakt archaïsch
dit trage kleien onland wordt.

THUISKOMST IN HOLLAND

De groene oevers nog van de ochtend overtogen
de geur van wind en water weer onder bereik.
De machtige stroom, de spanning van de stalen bogen
nadert: de vroege trein rijdt over de Moerdijk.

De naam

DE NAAM

Een kind dat niet òplet
en met afwezige ogen,
van de anderen afgebogen,
initialen zet.

Het zelf—ontwaard met schrik
en trots—geeft eindeloos seinen,
meldende zijn verschijnen
in code: dit ben ik.

Wolken gaan langs het raam.
Het klein gezicht trekt saam.—
Van de overzijde het sein:
'Ik heb u bij de naam
geroepen. Gij zijt Mijn.'

DE SCHRIJVER

Men zette op de boerderij
in de opkamer het bed voor mij.

En daar ik vreemd ben aan hun taal
brengt men mij zwijgende het maal.

Ik ben alleen: een eenzaamheid
die tot in huid en haren bijt.

Het licht verschuift aan het beschot.
Ik worstel zwijgende met God.

GRÜSZ GOTT
Ik wandelde en sprak met de Heer.

Wij wandelen naast elkaar,
de Vader en het kind
dat het nog niet begrijpt.
Het waagde nauw de vraag.

Nog met de ochtenddauw
zijn wij op pad gegaan:
Hij nam mij bij de hand.

De bloemen groeten Hem
—Yes Lord—de schuchtere beek
houdt haast zijn kabbelen in.
De bergen worden licht.

Wij wandelen naast elkaar,
de Vader en het kind.
Ik zie Hem niet, maar Hij
is mij zó dicht nabij
als geen op aarde ooit was.

LES PIEDS-BOTS

Komende met de graanschop langs de schuren om,
de horrelvoet met zijn gebarentaal.
Hem is de tong sinds zijn geboorte stom.
Hij wijst mij, dat er een zwaar onweer komt
en ik beduid dat ik hem heb verstaan.
Ik, die hinkend in heel dit leven faal
en spreek, vanaf de moederschoot verstomd.

STEEN-INSCRIPTIE

Dit is de stoet der Joden, saamgesnoerd met touwen,
de blote zolen op het rotsplateau geplant;
de mannen stom gefnuikt, de lastbeladen vrouwen
met kinderen geklemd aan de gebonden hand.

De daad van Pharaoh in het graniet geschreven;
trotse hiëroglyphen melden stam en tal.
Ik zie een grauw perron, de Joden saamgedreven,
de rijen ogen links, naar Pharaoh beval.

De steenhouwer zou één fout met de dood bekopen:
er mag geen naam ontbreken in de slaventrein.
Opdat zìj zouden gaan, schroefde ik de schrijfstift open,
de letters zettend die nooit uit te wissen zijn.

Ariër-verklaring 1941

DE ERFVIJAND

Hij stapt eenzelvig op de werf
en kerft met hees gekras mijn naam;
hij tikt vermanend aan het raam:
dan zijn er mensen op het erf.
De zwarte kraai, die Gerhardt heet,
die wreed men beide vlerken sneed,
die diep mij in de vinger beet
toen ik zijn kooi los deed.

DE AARDE

Moeilijk is het achter de ploeg te gaan,
altijd te denken aan de arbeid en het zaad,
de handen stroef te klemmen om de ploegstaart.

Moeilijk is het: de kluiten kantelen,
na iedere vore komt een nieuwe vore.
De paarden geven hitte af en zweet.

Moeilijk is het: te merken dat men zelf
werd tot een ploeg, met pinnen vastgezet;
het kromgebogen ploeghout van het lijf,
de scherpgesleten ploegschaar van de geest.

DE REINIGING

De uitgeholde stam met varens overgroeid
waardoor het water gaat dat op de bergen smelt,
weerspiegelend gans het dal, de lente nauw ontbloeid,
en met de groene geur, die regenval voorspelt.

Het water spelend met het onvergankelijk licht,
de stille stamelvraag, stromende door een boom,—
Tot, wie hier naderde en òverboog met schroom
de handen durft te dompelen en het aangezicht.

FACULTAS MEDICA

Hij die het mes en het lancet hanteert
kan onverschrokken zijn wanneer hij vreest
met heilige vrees. Het edelste, de geest,
wordt in dit uur beveiligd of gedeerd.

Zie het gelaat van wie zich niet verweert,
een open boek. Wie, zelfverblind, niet leest
richt diep het letsel aan dat niet geneest.
Hij heeft de adel van het ambt onteerd.

Gezegend die het weten van zijn grens
belijdt: zijn hand vertoont die vaste trek,
zijn ziel de schroom die adeldom verraadt.

Met instrumenten werkend aan een mens
opent hij nog de sluitklink van het hek
waardoor de ander naar de vrijheid gaat.

ZONDAGMORGEN

Het licht begint te wandelen door het huis
en raakt de dingen aan. Wij eten
ons vroege brood gedoopt in zon.
Je hebt het witte kleed gespreid
en grassen in een glas gezet.
Dit is de dag waarop de arbeid rust.
De handpalm is geopend naar het licht.

HET ONTSPRINGENDE
Voor M.

Die
in huis
het brood snijdt
en het linnen laat blinken,
laat tegelijkertijd
alle zware en lichte
klokken los.
Duiven vliegen in en uit,
het trappenhuis wordt flamboyant en
ik zit onder springende
luchtbogen mee te zingen
   —dat kan zij
dat kan zij—
crypten onder de voeten
en een dakruiter
   —Lobet den Herrn—
in het blauw.

AANVANG
8 Febr. 1959

Die het kindje het aanzijn geeft
geeft het aanzijn aan alles
nooit door woorden noembaar,
dat slaapt onder schedeldons
als een perzik.
Vlinders slapen er, bloemen
met tippen toegevouwen,
bladerenfronsels, een handje
openend.
Tuiltjes van water slapen.
En ook de verten slapen,
verten met donkerblauwe
rivieren, met grote bomen,
even bewegend, daarachter
stil in het aanvangslicht
slapen de hemelweiden.

WIEG

Geur van honing
en jonge melk,
van een nestdiertje
dat slaapt.
Een ademhalen van dons.
En speurbaar
aan de neusvleugels
de geur van wat gebeurd is:
geboorte,
geheim.

TERUGKOMST UIT HET ZIEKENHUIS

Het onverbiddelijke is
in huis.
Het schudt de kussens op
en trekt de lakens recht.
Linnen is uitgelegd.
Hartbrekend komt
bloemengeur langs
de trappen.—Boven
wordt gesloten
haar deur.
Alles is nu gereed:
de zieke wordt
straks thuis verwacht.

VÓÓR ONS
Henk † 1956

Slaap, jongensspeelgoed, boek en bal.
Slaap, grote mensen—'t Is nog nacht.
Een kind is zonder tijd of tal:
hij heeft ons uur niet afgewacht.

—Nòg brak de dageraad niet aan.—

Vóór ons.—Hij wilde niemand storen,
al hoorden wij de deur wel gaan,
toen hij, heel stil, is opgestaan
om de eerste vogels, ginds, te horen.

GROSZSTADT

Vliegtuigen trekken in de nacht hun spoor.
Ik luister: ik ben van Uw hart vervreemd.
De treinen gaan onder mijn voeten door.
Ik luister: ik ben van Uw hart vervreemd.
Vèr van mij, die ik naast mij ademen hoor.
Ik luister: ik ben van Uw hart vervreemd.

DE VERLATENE

Vroeg valt de avond in het dal. Vannacht
is onverwacht de eerste sneeuw gevallen.
Nu komt de winter en de stilte,—
de tijd dat ik in huis het brood zal bakken
en in de diepe sneeuw het pad zal graven
tot aan de deur. Hij zal niet keren.
Hij zal met mij het brood niet breken.

GEBOORTE

Gods liefde op aarde neergedaald
ligt in een stal op stro te slapen.
De stille herders van de schapen
zij hebben het alom verhaald.

De ster staat boven Bethlehem.
De Koningen uit het Oosten vonden
een kind in windselen gewonden
en os en ezel zien naar hem.

Hier slaapt, der wereld toevertrouwd,
die was vóór de aanvang van de tijden,
het kind waarom Maria schreide,
waarover elk de handen vouwt.

LICHT UIT LICHT

De liefde bidt voor wie
niet weten wat zij doen;
gekruisigd blijft zij stil
voor wie de hamer heft.

En na de sabbath keert
zij tot de treurenden,
verrezen uit het graf
wandelt zij in de hof.

Onherkend zit zij aan,
met hen, met u, met mij
te Emmaüs, tot het brood
door Hem gebroken wordt.

KOMEND VOORJAAR
Truus † 13 Februari 1960

Gebroken licht, en wolken drijvende aan de lucht,
de levende rivier, bevlaagd van wisselend weer
en, reppende in een wig, een wildeganzen-vlucht.
Lente in dit lage land. Gij ziet het nimmermeer.

Hier, aan het water, durf ik denken aan uw dood.
Ik kon niet om u schreien: onze liefde is stom
wanneer wij zijn geboren uit één moederschoot.
Gìj zoudt begrijpen wat mijn hete tranen ontsloot:
de boerse groet, u zózeer lief: 'de wind is om'.

Moerdijk, Maart 1960

DE VEERPONT

Hier bij de vlonder en de overhaal
het stommelen van de pont op het plankier
denk ik aan hem, die met mij de rivier

zo vaak hier zocht.—Hoe zwijgend hij genoot
bij 't gaan en keren van de kettingboot
en soms iets zeide in zijn simpele taal:

over het licht, de wolken en de wind.

Hij was mijn Vader en ik ben zijn kind.
O God, hoe heb ik hem tekort gedaan,
die met het grote veer is meegegaan.

HET VERLOREN KIND

Onder de sneeuwwitte bloemen
slaapt tussen wuivend gras,
nimmer met name te noemen
die mij de speelgenoot was.

Die uit de schoot is geboren
waaruit ik zelf ben ontstaan;
toen, bij de tweesprong, verloren.
Vragende zag het mij aan.

Onder de sneeuwwitte bloemen
slaapt, nog één heuvel voorbij,
die mij met name zal noemen
als ik mij naast hem vlij.

BUXTEHUDE

Nu zwijgt zijn serafijnse spelen.
Hij wekte elk instrument met name
tot mensen en engelen tesamen
rondom het kleine orgel kwamen.

Slaapt, klarinetten, fluiten, veêlen
in 't hout: herrijzend, òm hem, alle
dien dag dat zich de hemelen delen,
als buiten de bazuinen schallen.

VROEG FRESCO
und hat ein Blümlein bracht

De wortel Isaï.
Tegen de witte muur
de kleur van bloemen in
een oude kruidentuin.
Den slapende ontspringt
geworteld in het hart
stil der gezichten rank,
verbleekt tot zinnia's
violen uitgewist
verplozen distelen.
Bovenaan wiegt het kind
zijn anjerhoofdje en heft
een vinger naar het licht.

CHRISTUS ALS HOVENIER
Zij dacht dat het de hovenier was. Joh. 20 : 15

Eén Rembrandt kende als kind ik goed:
de Christus met de grote hoed
wandelend in de ochtendstond.
En, naar erbij geschreven stond:
Hij was een hovenier.

En nòg laat ik mijn tranen gaan
als in de gaarde ik Hem zie staan,
en—wat terzijde—in stille schrik
die éne, zij die dacht als ik:
Het was de hovenier.

O kinderdroom van groen en goud—
géén die ontnam wat ik behoud.
De laatste hoven naderen schier
en ijler wordt de ochtend hier.

Hij is de hovenier.

De Slechtvalk

Aan de nagedachtenis van Theodora van Buuren
9 januari 1906-19 januari 1962

*Het sneeuwt, en in dit witte zweven
dat naar de aarde dralend gaat,
een schemeren is er, een gelaat
naar 't schijnsel van mijn raam geheven;
eindelijk de laatste eer te geven
vraagt het in zijn ontslapen staat.*

De Slechtvalk

PORTRET THEODORA VAN B.

De vrouw, die ordent in het ochtendlicht
bloemen, instrumentarium en boek,
tipt nog een droppel met de witte doek
en stelt de stoel, die stijgt zonder gewicht.

De morgenruiker houdt nog knoppen dicht.
De kamer wacht, gereed, het vroeg bezoek.
Het nadert, kaatseballend, om de hoek:
het kind komt binnen met een fris gezicht.

Er is bedrijvigheid. Het vult het glas
en zet zich ernstig in de goede stand.
Het wacht de handelingen die het kent.

Tussen zacht babbelen tikt het instrument.
Zij wonen samen in dit veilig land.
Het blonde kind. De vrouw in witte jas.

FACULTAS MEDICA

Hij die het mes en het lancet hanteert
kan onverschrokken zijn wanneer hij vreest
met heilige vrees. Het edelste, de geest,
wordt in dit uur beveiligd of gedeerd.

Zie het gelaat van wie zich niet verweert,
een open boek. Wie, zelfverblind, niet leest
richt diep het letsel aan dat niet geneest.
Hij heeft de adel van het ambt onteerd.

Gezegend die het weten van zijn grens
belijdt: zijn hand vertoont die vaste trek,
zijn ziel de schroom die adeldom verraadt.

Met instrumenten werkend aan een mens
opent hij nog de sluitklink van het hek
waardoor de ander naar de vrijheid gaat.

NACHTWAKE

Doof, hoop, uw fakkel uit.
Hoe eindeloze uren
moet zij de pijn verduren
die stil de ogen sluit.

In huis is geen geluid.

Even of er iets was,
een ritseling langs de ruiten:
een vlinder wil naar buiten.
Hij fladdert aan het glas.

DE SNEEUWHAAS

Zij schoten op de witte haas.
Ik vond hem met gezonken oren
bloedend tussen het groene koren,
de ogen in het licht verbaasd.

Toen klaagde hij met een kinderstem
en stierf. Tussen het groene koren
doofde het laatste licht aan hem.
Het glanzen dat hier niet mocht horen.

Wier zuivere staat men moest verstoren
hoe, in den dood, geleekt gij hem.

DE DONKEREN

Treedt, donkere mensen, zacht
die haar hebt omgebracht
en bergt uw donker wapen.
Zij ligt zo stil te slapen,
ontkomen aan uw macht.

Niet rake uw donker kwaad
die boven aarde staat,
de laatste stille dagen
eer zij wordt uitgedragen.
En zwijgt wanneer zij gaat.

Als is verbrand tot as
die onaantastbaar was,
keert, op uw donkere sporen.
Zij wil u niet verstoren
die uw gedachten las.

SCHRIFTUUR

Al maanden staat het huis verlaten,
haastig onttakeld en verdaan.
De ijsbloemen staan op het raam.
In scherpgenerfde varenbladen
schittert, onuitgewist, uw naam.

DE TERUGGEWEZEN GAVE

't Was winter en al schemerig in de stad.
Ik wilde het Janskerkhof over gaan,
eigenlijk om bij Anne Frank te leggen
een bosje bloemen dat ik bij mij had.
Ik had ze al van het papier ontdaan,
maar week terug. Het beeldje op het plein
in deze schemering leefde en zag mij aan
en stille lippen wilden mij iets zeggen,
terwijl ik onbewegelijk bleef staan.
Niets stoorde dit ontijdelijk samenzijn.
Tot hoorbaar werd haar woordenloos vermaan,
zij, een Joods kind dat weet van eeuwen heeft:
'Gij waart daarbij. Ook nu zij niet meer leeft.'

HET ONHERROEPELIJKE

Gij slechtvalk met het onyx oog,
gehouwen uit korrelig porfier,
weer keerde ik waar gij zijt. Gedoog
mijn nadering, zwijgend koningsdier.
Eeuwigheid, overstaar mij hier
die nauwelijks te ademen waag,
die in het hart mijn dode draag
in de gesloten sarkophaag.

Keltisch

THE DIVINER

*Ik ben die de gevorkte tak,
die in mijn hand begint te beven,
voel kantelen waar de wel van leven
zich doortocht door de steenwand brak.
Het siddert in mijn vingertoppen
wat nadert in verholen staat;
tot in mijn hartekameren gaat
de donkere toon, het manend kloppen:
het water houdt met mij beraad.*

DE OPGEROEPENEN

Eindelijk laat mij alleen,
schuifelend om huis als het duistert,
komend om samen te scholen—
Langer hard ik dit niet.

Vreemdeling, in ons gebied
hebt ge met waren en dolen
onraad gemaakt, ons verstoord.
Noem ons, en dàn gaan wij heen.

Rusteloos zijn wij tot gij hoort.

KELTISCH GRAFSCHRIFT

Die voor zichzelf niets vroeg,
wier liefde bij mij was,
rust in het hoge gras.
Ik gaf haar pijn genoeg.
Wier liefde bij mij was,
die ik van huis verjoeg,
zij die mijn kinderen droeg,
rust in het hoge gras.

BRIEF AAN DE GROOTOUDERS

Het kind waarom wij vurig vroegen,
had éne dag zijn aardse staat.
Het sneeuwde al, toen wij het droegen
waar nu het kruis gekorven staat.
Ik heb de akkers mogen ploegen.
De aarde draagt het winterzaad.

TILL DEATH US DO PART

Zolang gij er zijt,
het brood voor mij snijdt,
de legerstee spreidt,
mag God het mij geven,
het lichaam, het leven.
Hier ben ik. Altijd.

AND AFTER

Gegroet van gene zijde
mijn eigen lieveling,
gegroet van gene zijde
die lang al van mij ging.
O wil mij nog verbeiden
gij reeds aan gene zijde,
zwevende, zwevende met uw voet.
Mij die mijn ketenen slepen moet.

DE VERSTOTENE

Het dorp begint mij te vermijden
en mompelt sinds zij mij verliet.
De kinderen wijken schuw terzijde,
de hond gromt sinds zij mij verliet.
De dominee komt de Heer belijden,
als hij mijn land verwaarloosd ziet.
Wat raken mij de jaargetijden?
't Is winter sinds zij mij verliet.

ALLEEN

De tafel en het bed zeggen: alleen.
De donkere kleren aan de muur: alleen.
Om huis en stallen sluipt het woord—een moordenaar
die men het mes hoort wetten op de steen.

HET VUUR
de doodgraver spreekt

De kleine Matthew Jones, dàt was er een:
de dominee stond verslagen van zijn vragen.
En rood haar dat hij had! Zó rood, daar kon
hij wel de brand mee in de hoeve steken.
Dit is zijn steen. Dat wordt alweer vijf jaar.
Wie het gedaan heeft is nooit uitgekomen.
Zijn vader noemde hem 'mijn zwavelstok',
zijn moeder zei altijd: 'mijn vurige jongen.'

OUDEJAARSAVONDPREEK

Het kerkpad over zerken.
De koster trekt het touw.
De kerkbanken op zerken.
O angst, o bittere kou;
kervend tot het gebeente
de zang van de gemeente.

De preek. Het schuifelen, zuchten,
het kraken van gewrichten,
het haperen van mijzelf.
Schaduw van vale vlerken:
gebarend boven zerken
roep ik in het gewelf.

DE PREDIKANT

De uil is mijn kameraad
op deze stille hoeve,
waar mijn herstel zijn stroeve
en trage maten slaat.

De vrouw die 's avonds komt
zegt, naar haar landsaard sprekend,
'het vuur is ingerekend,'
waarbij mijn hart verstomt.

Onder het dakgebint
stel ik 's nachts eindeloos orde
op wat as is geworden
en nimmer wederkeert.

HET BROOD

De dominee wist van niets.
Hij las altijd in boeken.
En ik wist ook van niets.
Ik was toen zestien jaar:
Ik bracht het brood.

Het kind is dood.

Wie oordeelt het gezin
ginds ver de heuvelen in?
Ik breng het brood.

DE DAGLOONSTER

Tussen de voegen woekert gras.
Ik had het gisteren weggewied.
Het scherpste mes verdelgt het niet:
tussen de voegen woekert gras.
Zij woekert voort die derde was
in iedere voeg sinds ze ons verliet.
Ik wees haar uit. Ondelgbaar schiet
ze achter mij op: een kort, wreed gras.

DE DAGLOONSTER (II)

Wat deed ze op de boerderij?
Met pest en plaag zijn wij bezocht,
uit iedere muur slaat klam het vocht,
geen ziekte ging het vee voorbij.
Wat deed ze op de boerderij?
Het noodweer heeft de oogst geveld,
ons kind werd tegen de eg gekneld
en is verminkt. O duivelsbruid
die mij bezat met haar en huid,
laat af, laat af! God, wijs haar uit!

FEEST VAN DE KINDEREN

Ringelreie rozenkrans
danst onze rei de dodendans.
Wij kwamen feestelijk uitgetreden,
het paard, verblind van zonneglans,
heeft ons in het ravijn gereden.
Dwaallichtjes in het dal beneden
leiden wij 's nachts elkaar ten dans.

FAIR CERIDWEN

Die mij ontwijkt
is die ik graag win;
die voor mij prijkt
is die ik niet min.
Die mij ten dans vraagt
wil ik niet tot man.
O, dat zijn kans waagt
hij die het niet kan!

WIEGELIEDJE

Ademend, ademend,
't hoofdje op de hand,
in het omwademend
tijdeloos land.
Ademend, ademend,
vademen diep
waren de wateren
waarin het sliep;
die weer omsluiten
den slapensgenoot.
Ademend, ademend,
stil in de schoot.

HET ARMHUISKIND

Ik was het kind dat ieder schuwde,
dat met twee gekken slapen moest
die het niet wekte met zijn hoest,
dat bloedig op de vloeren spuwde.

En in de kerk wees men mij aan.

Aanzie mijn vrouw, mijn huis, mijn graan,
de kinderen uit mij ontstaan:
God liet zijn onkruid niet vergaan.

De Japanse visser

*Het kind dat streng mijn gave heeft versmaad
en mij het schaamrood joeg naar het gelaat,
wist wie gij waart. Onder de grote doden
zijt gij geteld, die aanzien zocht noch staat.*

DE JAPANSE VISSER

Over de smalle brug
als nog de sterren staan
ga ik bij u vandaan,
de netten op de rug.

Mijn manden dragende aan
de bamboe keer ik terug,
als er al sterren staan.
Om weer tot u te gaan
over de smalle brug.

HET FREGATSCHIP

Wij naderden de naakte witte klip,
maar aan de steenwand sloeg een gloed ons tegen:
een wolk van bloemen, wilde rode regen,
omgaf met geuren allen in het schip.
O bittere tranen om wat werd onthecht,
om wat, tot aan de laatste dag ontzegd,
achter de wal der tanden wordt verzwegen,
en wilde geur om lippen en om haar.
Hoe voeren wij, afgewend van elkaar,
als schreienden voorbij de bloesemregen.

DE GESTORVENE

Zeven maal om de aarde te gaan,
als het zou moeten op handen en voeten;
zeven maal, om die éne te groeten
die daar lachend te wachten zou staan.
Zeven maal om de aarde te gaan.

Zeven maal over de zeeën te gaan,
schraal in de kleren, wat zou het mij deren,
kon uit de dood ik die éne doen keren.
Zeven maal over de zeeën te gaan—
zeven maal, om met zijn tweeën te staan.

VOOR M.

In diepten van mijzelf waar aan
anderen lang ik ben ontwend,
hoor ik de zware branding gaan,
het onvervreemdbaar element
waaraan ik leef en leven moet.

En zijn triomf is onbetwist.

O gij, die gelijk geen mij kent,
ik weet dat gij die stem vermoedt,
dit donkere kantelen en slaan.
Gij, enige die mijn hart behoedt,
enige die weet af te staan.

EEN LIED VAN ALKMAN
in poëtas non poëtas

Zwaluw, doorklief de lucht!
Nù is de grote trek.
Vergeet het late broed,
dat met gesperde bek
in 't nest verhongeren moet.
Een eeuwenoud gericht
verwierp het voor de vlucht.

Wiekslag, doorklief de lucht!
Wat zwak is kan
het niet bestaan.
Phalanx, sluit aan!

ACHILLES MET XANTHOS

Gereinigd door de zee
geroskamd door de wind
het sterk Thessalisch kind
de hengst. Die op de stee
bij herfst de merries dekt
en edel ras verwekt.

En stappend naast het paard
in ongenaakbaarheid
de trotse jonge zoon
der hofstee, die de kroon
der stallen onvervaard
vast aan de halster leidt.

ROCK

Hij wordt de vogel Rock gelijk
mijn vader, grauw en uitgeloogd,
die krassend mij te zeggen poogt
de waarheid waarvoor eens ik wijk.
Mijn naam heeft zijn geslacht verhoogd.
Maar ergens is dat laatste rijk:
een bergland dat geen vrouw gedoogt.

ULTIMA THULE

Schapen en wolkendrachten
vachten in elkander verwist,
blaten en dalende mist.
Regengeladen de nachten,
nevelige dageraad.
De nog met water bevrachte
aardeschijf. Aanvangsstaat.

ANAMNESIS

Teruggekomen eer hij werd verwacht,
over de bergen, uit het zuiderland
van akkerstroken en rimpelende Nijl:
de vogel met de rode poten, tureluur.
Ginds heeft, wanneer het oeverriet ontsteeg
het wielend roepen, in zijn ronde boot
van wilgenribben en huid de Nijlvisser
het kenterend getij gespeurd en weet gehad
en niet gehad, van kleuren van een land
dat hij nooit zag: een groene uiterwaard,
de planten op een blauw bazalten krib,
de regenwolken waar het licht door breekt.

DE APOCALYPTISCHE EZEL
quidquid latet apparebit

Midden in een landschap zonder eind,
aan een verrafeld touw gelijnd
balkt hij. Het was mij nooit verteld
dat dit bestond in zijn geweld.
De klank verscheurt mij hart en oren.
O God, het is een alpenhoren,
't paard Honger uit de Openbaring,
de diepe oerkreet van de paring.
Dan — tanden bloot — een tubastoot:
een schetteren, mirum spargens sonum,
dat heel de hemel ervan splijt,
het 'per sepulcra regionum'
dat mij tot in het merg doorsnijdt.
Dat bokken van de schapen scheidt.

DENKEND AAN ISRAËL

Een stem is opgegaan in de Jordaan.
Het draagt van de omwolkte Hermonwand
tot waar de vaderen over zijn gegaan,
achter de ark naar het beloofde land.

Bergbeken breken naar het keteldal.
Toornig stort het in donkere gronden neer,
en komt dan donderend van de overwal:
'Hoor, Israël, hoor. Ik ben een Enig Heer.'

KRATER VAN KYRTOS

Weg van de klippen westwaarts vaart
—het snelle schip gaat voor de wind—
de listige met de spitse baard,
Odysseus.—Op het eiland waart
dien hij het oog heeft uitgeblind,
stokstrompelend; de reus verdwaasd
van pijn en blatend als een kind.
De schapen wijken uit, verbaasd,
als hij hun vachten tracht te strelen.
Waar zee en eiland zich verdelen
staat zij, Athene, en heft de hand.
Wat dreef u, bultenaar, te penselen
dit raadsel op de kraterwand?

VOGELVRIJ

Kinderen van een prachtig ras
—ik kwam hun noordelijk dorp voorbij—
scholden en achtervolgden mij
en één smeet raak met een pol gras.

En toen ik hen ontkomen was
zat ik tussen een wilgenrij,
een oude vrouw in de maand mei
en sloeg de kluiten van mijn jas.

Kinderen zijn oprecht en wreed:
zij zagen mij de dichter aan
en deden frank, wat meer discreet
de wereld dagelijks heeft gedaan.

DE WEERLOZEN

Zij zijn nooit weg, zij zien mij dagelijks aan:
de eekhoorn in de stalen klem gekneld,
het krimpend hert waarbij de jagers staan,
't kind dat zijn radeloos heimwee niet vertelt.
Dat wat zo argeloos was en werd gekweld
en vroeg met de ogen om nog te ontgaan.

Eer het toesloeg. Eer het werd aangedaan.

STEM VAN DE HERFSTREGEN

    Wees niet bevreesd wanneer de vlagen gaan
        rondom uw huis—het is uw aards verblijf.
    Wees niet bevreesd als ziekte u komt slaan—
        uw lichaam was altijd een aards verblijf.
    Zonder bekommernis laat u ontgaan
        roem, eer en staat; zij zijn een aards bedrijf.
    Maar wees bevreesd wanneer de tranen gaan,
        de bevende, om wat is aangedaan
            door u.
    De liefde is uw eeuwige verblijf.

CHINESE TEKENING

Dicht bij de waterzoom
onder een wilgeboom
twee vrienden witgebaard,
en op hun knieën staat
een schaakbord, zwart en wit.
De een verzet het paard,
de ander, tijdeloos, zit
te glimlachen. Hij denkt.
Verder de stroom af zwenkt
een net dat overgaat.

AAN HET WATER

Liefelijk waart gij in het wilgendal:
uw spreken donker en de zilveren val
van lachen als wij aan het water kwamen.
Hoe kort, hoe kort. O, noem het niet met name—
en de echo telkens van de overwal.

DE TWEE ZUSTERS

Geworpen op de laatste klip
de onontwijkbaar witte wand,
hoor 's nachts ik uit het andere land
de bel van een gezonken schip,—
het dingdong donker voortgeplant.

O, die reeds zonk naar donker zand
en die mij uit uw diepten groet,
haast doven ook mijn vuren uit.
Ik weet—wij beiden van één bloed—
dat gij voor mij het dingdong luidt.

DE AANZEGGING

Wees niet bevreesd wanneer de knokkel op
de deur, de kort herhaalde klop
van wie tot wachten nimmer was gezind,
er is. Schuif weg de grendelbout
en zorg dat gij uw gast rechtop begroet
en, als hij zegt wat hij u zeggen moet,
dat gij hem niet één woord ten kwade houdt.
Hij kwam dat gij u voorbereiden zoudt.

VERANTWOORDING. ZES KWATRIJNEN

Een hoge kreet trekt scherp zijn zilvervoor.
Dan gaat de vogel in de nacht teloor.
Ik ben ontwaakt. Gij hebt mij opgeroepen.
En ademloos volg ik uw lichtend spoor.

Gestreden heb ik levenslang met U.
Ik vind geen andere vrede dan bij U.
Hitte des daags, weder zijt gij geweken.
Oase van de avond, thans bij U.

Waar vindt de hoge vreugde onderkomen,
de smart wanneer het schoonste is ontnomen?
O gij, die jong tot zelftucht Ik verkoos:
binnen de strofe en haar trotse zomen.

Vernuftige pijlers ontrouw en verraad
dragen de brug. Gij die behaaglijk gaat
op haar plankier, buig nimmer naar het water:
gij mocht de spiegeling zien van uw gelaat.

Toen kwam het kind mij stamelend verhalen:
'ik zag vannacht de wilde zwanen dalen.'
En fluisterend ik: 'Vóór de ochtend nog zag ik
de leeuwerik voedsel voor zijn broedsel halen.'

Gij vader van het vers, wees onvervaard.
Bedil het niet. Laat het naar eigen aard
zich grillig als een hagewinde slingeren,
of feilloos sluitend zijn: gezwaluwstaart.

IN DEN BEGINNE

Ik zet mijn verzen als een schelpdier aan
in diepten waar geen sterveling mij kent,
ik adem in en uit, en zij ontstaan
uit stille kernen, in het element
dat was van den beginne. Altijd blijft
het grote stromen in mij overgaan.
Ik ben alleen. Een maatgang schrijft en schrijft:
ademende zet ik de mantelen aan.

AFVAART

The love I lived, the dream I knew (Yeats)

Vaarwel die aan de einder wijkt,
ik mag uw pracht in mij bewaren,
groen eiland dat een harp gelijkt,—
geen rooft u aan mijn laatste jaren:
welving die edel zich versmalt,
waar rijst het tij, het tij vervalt,
waaierend gras en zwart bazalt.

'wijl God niet eeuwig met zijn maaksel twist'

RIETVELD †

Toen zonk het potlood, schetsende op schaal.
Een siddering vaart door het skelet van staal
en het betonblok. Rondom rouwt de Domstad
om wie ontviel, de maker integraal.

BEGRAFENIS VAN GERRIT ACHTERBERG
Voor C. Achterberg-van Baak

Te armoedig nog om bij elkaar te horen
en in onszelf en in elkaar verward,
waren wij daar, een hand litteratoren.
Toen de familie in het kerkezwart
en met een boerse waardigheid verscheen,
werd onze vaalheid nog meer openbaar.

De bloemen overdekten kist en baar.
Daar was hij die ons niet meer nodig had.
Ik zag terzijde van het middenpad
zijn vader, ouder dan Methusalem,
zijn schouders haast gekromd tot aan zijn kruis.
O, toen hij opzag, hoe geleek hij hem
die schreef: 'daar woonden wij met man en muis.'
Hij hield de handen om zijn doornen stok.
Maar toen de stoet opstommelde en vertrok,
bleef hij alleen. De doornstok in zijn hand
begon te schrijven op het blauw plavuis.
God sta ons bij.—'En Jezus schreef in het zand.'

VOOR DAG EN DAUW
In memoriam M. Nijhoff

Wel elke ochtend ligt de dauw
over uw verzen, als dien dag
dat morgenlijk uw hand hen schiep.
De donkere wereld merkt het nauw,
maar wie niet tot de morgen sliep
leest tussen maan en dageraad
de bladzij die hij éénmaal zag
en sedert leest met de ogen dicht.

'Er staat geschreven wat er staat.'

En wat uw taal heeft aangeraakt,
thans is het aan uzelf verricht:
de dag, die uit de nacht ontwaakt,
de dauw, het ongerepte licht.

DE GESTORVENE

Gij zijt gelijk een korrel in de grond
en bezig om in oogsten op te staan.
De stille tekenen zijn mij niet ontgaan.

Niets is onmogelijk. Harsverzegeld stond
in Chefrens pyramide een kruik met graan,
en een die na millennia het vond

zaaide ervan. 't Werd avond, het werd dag
over de Nijlstrook.—Tot hij de ochtend zag
dat zich de kiemplant uit de korrel wond.

De Ravenveer

TERUGKEER

Machtig baken, lichtende in de nachten,
wenk het schip, dat veilig de kust bereike
die de vaart, de eenzame, haast volbracht heeft,
lang in den vreemde.

Zwerveling aan kusten bevolkt met vogels,
zelve zij geschapen met zware wiekslag.
Die, beschroomd als zij, ik vermag te geven
niets dan dit éne:

Ingehuld te staan op de donkere aarde,
liefdeblind, en zwijgend het schip verbeiden,
ademloos welhaast als het langzaam nadert
onder de sterren.

Verzen van Holland

HET ERFGOED

Vooroudertrots: goed ingeklonken land.
Ik heb een aard die ingeklonken is
en uitverweerd. Waarin gezonken is
tot zware grond een laag van tegenstand.

MOERDIJK

Aalscholvers braken door de wolken heen.
En vliegend vormden zij een sterrenbeeld.
Cassiopeia. Het bleef onverdeeld
tesamen, tot het boven Dordt verdween.

IN MEMORIAM PATRIS

Mijn vader heeft de waterlaarzen aan.
Wij samen zijn de Lekdijk afgekomen.
Ik ben voor mijn verjaardag meegenomen:
hij moest vandaag bij het gemaal langs gaan.

Gemaal: dat is je vader horen noemen
die vreemde woorden van een andere taal
als hij de waterstand leest van de schaal;
te ademen in het onbenoembaar zoemen
dat gonzend omgaande aanwezig is.
Èn, niets te zeggen als hij bezig is:

'Dàt is een man, daar kun je staat op maken.'
Als op de zaken orde is gesteld
doen wij op huis aan. Een lucht van geweld:
Gorcum ligt al door wolken overkraagd.
Geen noodweer en geen wereld kan mij raken
als hij, het laatste stuk, mij op de schouder draagt.

DE ERFGENAMEN

De vleugels wijd, het hoofd hoog opgestoten,
immer trotserend wat te naderen waagt,
een wilde zwaan, in zijn domein belaagd:
het boegbeeld. Licht en donker overvloten
kroont hij het schip, dat immer uitgedaagd
door verten achter verten, schuimomvlaagd
zijn weg ploegt.—Dat de in zichzelf besloten
werende naam 'De drie gezusters' draagt.

DE ZWARE LAST

Er zijn soms maanden dat ik nooit alleen
mag zijn en ik verdraag het zonder klagen:
gehangen om mijn hals een molensteen.
Zo zag ik eens een hond een baksteen dragen
die om zijn nek hing aan een knellend touw;
hij wilde telkens zwerven, zei de vrouw,
daartegen hielpen etensbak noch slagen.
En schuw zocht hij mijn hulp, slepend zijn steen.

Mijn broeder hond, het mag niet dat gij zwerft,
of sterft diep in het stille bos alleen.
Uw broeder mens als hij ten leste sterft,
hij draagt als gij zijn steen, vel over been:
de zware mensen, legerend om hem heen.

ONDER DE BRANDARIS

Dit is het huis genaamd de duizend vrezen.
Hij die er slapen wil hij zal er waken.
Een oppermachtig licht slaat er zijn kruisen.
Met interval van donkere seconden
waarin de branding zwaarder schijnt te ruisen
verschijnt een mene tekel op het laken:
en wat geweest is, het wordt zwart bevonden.
Ik was hier 's nachts, ik was in duizend vrezen,
vrezen des doods, waarvan ik niet kan spreken,
in een gericht van licht alleen gelaten.
En aan de dageraadsrand alleen gebleven,
met licht getekend en genoemd met name,
van onuitwisbaar licht het zegel dragend.
Wat ik geschreven heb heb ik geschreven.
Hij doopt met licht. Ik waag het hem te vrezen.

CONSTELLATIE

Een woord van Achterberg: het sterrengrint.
Geen sterveling dan hij zou het bedenken
en een melkweg in drie syllaben schenken;
hoe meer je kijkt, hoe meer je er in vindt.
Was het kiezelpad rondom zijn huis
dat werd tot sterrenstelsel onverwacht?
Of heeft hij buiten in de heldere nacht
—edelman, bedelman, wichelaar, kind—
gedacht aan figuraties van wit grint?

HET VERS VAN GORTER

Het vers van Gorter heeft de geur van graan
dat bloeit en stuift: die reuk van hemels zoet
met erdoorheen het aardse evengoed;
dat zegt de tarwe en het brood al aan.

En koren geurt weer uit het brood vandaan.
Hij schreef vanuit die kringloop overvloed
 — het waait ons uit de woorden tegemoet—
het vers dat in het zonlicht kan bestaan,

de volle dag trotseert. Het voedt als brood
en bloeit als koren, stuifmeelovertrild.
Het vers van Gorter: franke gulheid noodt

dat wie hier nadert toch de honger stilt
die hij verborg of nimmer uit kon spreken.
Brood met de geur van graan. Gij moogt het breken.

SEGHERS

Septemberlicht door de wolken,
diafaan, tot stralen gebroken,
of zalig worden gesproken
dit laagland en wie het bevolken.
Licht waarvan geen vreemde kan weten,
het verzadigde, waterbevrachte.
Die Hercules was geheten,
hij was het te etsen bij machte.

AFSCHEID VAN HOLLAND

Twintig jaar vrijheid, twintig jaar verraad
aan het edelste. Ik hard u, Holland, niet
met dìt gelaat, waarop geschreven staat:
ziehier die zich voor geld aan ieder biedt.

Het valt mij zwaar dat ik mijn land verlaat.
't Ware tè zwaar als ik het nìet verliet:
gelijk een mens die van een mens weg gaat,
niet hardend dat hij hem ontluisterd ziet.

Ik had u lief en leerde u verachten,
Holland. Ik groeide op onder uw stem:
het water dat als kind mij wakker riep

wanneer het stormde onder Woudrichem.
Nòg gaan de wolken over het Hollands Diep.
Gij zijt mijn land, gij blijft in mijn gedachten.

DE DAGERAAD
and death shall be no more

Zwanen, steekt de trompet:
heft schallend het Halleel aan;
gij zijt de vogelaar ontgaan.
Zijn netten had hij gezet.

Hij heeft u geen veder geroofd:
op de grens van de nacht en de dag
vliegt gij, met bruisende slag,
met al morgenrood om het hoofd.

Ik ben op de aarde maar klein;
ik kan naar u opzien alleen,
die trekt, recht over mij heen,
naar de meren om vrij te zijn.

aan de nagedachtenis van twee joodse vrienden,
gevallen in het verzet, 1942

DE TEMPELROOF

Ik zou wel aan de klaagmuur staan
om u, mijn land, als er een was:
maar ik, ik weet niet waar.
Ik weet alleen:
waar goud en brons het licht kon zijn,
liggen de vreemden in het gras
en drinken uit ùw schaal de wijn,
heffen ùw kandelaar.

EEN HOLLANDS ONWEER

Ik sta te schuilen onder het wagenkot;
het rommelt nog, maar is haast afgebuid.

De boer verschijnt, kijkt of het al wat wordt
en zet de emmers voor het melken uit.

'Volk op het erf, ik hèb het er niet op'
lees ik uit het verzetten van zijn pet.

Roepend alvast 'we hebben het gehad'
rep ik mij langs de plassen van het erf

en wring mij zijdelings door het knarsend hek
dat ik, gelijk geschreven staat, goed sluit.

Ik zie dit sedert welhaast dagelijks terug:
ik zou nog iedere grashalm kunnen tekenen.

Er is iets anders wat ik niet bevat.
Terwijl het was, wist ik met zekerheid:

'Ik ken het al. Eigenlijk was het eerder.'

DODENHERDENKING

De namen der gevallenen
die wij zo snel vergaten
worden soms nog gezongen
bij monde van de stormwind.

Dan: luister aan de palen.

Ik hoorde het eens vervaarlijk
onder Zalk en Veecaten —
te zwaar haast voor de masten
en de metalen draden.

Verzen van overzee

ULTIMA THULE

Daar waar de zware nevels hingen
waarden zij om als nevelingen,
de trage schapen, met geblaat
klagende om de dageraad.
En nevens ieder was het lam.
Alleen de eenzame bleef stom,
de heerser, voerende zijn staat,
de zwaargevachte machtige ram.
Homerisch is dit land. Er gaat
van het toevallige niets om.

DE ZALMEN

Zij zijn gegaan. Na middernacht.
Stroomop, in voortstuwende stoeten—
stroomopwaarts: op de gronden aan.
Waar het bereid getij verwacht
die krachtens ingeschapen moeten
elf stroomversnellingen bestaan,
de waterval met staarten slaan;
die tartende de zwaartekracht
tegen de katarakt opgaan.

DE AFWIJZING

Ik schrijf u met de ravenveer,
Mijnheer.
Mijn eer uw eer
uw hart mijn hart
heeft nìets gemeen.
Ik schrijf u met de ravenveer.
Ik schrijf u met het ravenzwart
het teken: neen.

WAYSIDE INN

Een man die op een narwal lijkt
en somber naar mij koeterwaalt,
staande niet van mijn tafel wijkt
terwijl mijn kaak het voedsel maalt.
Vast gaat het over vis en vangen.
Hoe gaarne zag ik hem gehangen
die heel mijn heimwee hier vertaalt.

EILEEN

Het is een feeks, een helleveeg,
zij haalt mijn erf van bloemen leeg,
steekt snel haar tong uit voor het raam,
leest een boeket van woorden saam
als distels, om mij toe te gooien.
Komt later aan de keuken schooien,
een klein geraamte van vier jaar.
En als de sneden zijn verslonden,
geeft zij één tel haar ogenpaar
vrij.——Ergens in die groene gronden
lijkt zij op mij, lijk ik op haar.

DE DAGERAAD

Ik zag een kalfje bij de moeder drinken,
een stille handeling die hier nog mag.
Zij stonden in de aanbrekende dag
half slapend in dit drinken te verzinken,
wazig in nevelen, nog haast verborgen.
Over het witte gras heen kwam de morgen.
Bevreesd waadde ik weg van wat ik zag.

JULINACHT

De dag was nog bevracht
met geuren. Onverwacht
de omslag van het weer.
Jaarkentering en keer.
Orion dooft zijn pracht.
Langzaam valt in de nacht
de statige regen neer.

FRAGMENT

Als grote rozen voor een donkerend raam
de strofen, met het weggeborgen hart
van purper, haast versomberend tot zwart.
Als grote rozen voor een donkerend raam.
Sappho, de ondoorgrondelijke naam.

ZOMERNACHT

Onder de Archipel der sterren
lig ik op de allene heuvel,
lig ik bij de allene woning.
Ik woon alleen, ver van de mensen.
Waar denk ik aan? Dat ik moet sterven,
want alle schepselen moeten sterven.
En dat die éne ik zó liefheb
dat deze liefde niet zal sterven,
maar wordt gesteld onder de sterren.

BRIEVEN DER VRIENDEN

Achter een woord verscholen
leeft het geheime leven.
Gij moet u daar niet begeven.

Ge zoudt er kunnen verdwalen
in grote verlatenheden,
of gentianen vertreden.
Of er was misschien een moeras.

Ik heb mij daar ééns gewaagd.
Altijd is mij bijgebleven
het hert dat ik op had gejaagd.

HET DOODSBERICHT

Langzaam zie ik hen gaan
die ik nog bij mij had,
de bocht om van het pad.
Wat gouddoorschenen stof,
dan wordt het in de hof
nog stiller dan voorheen.
De liefsten.—Eén voor één.

ROUWTIJD
blow, blow, thou winter wind

Blaas, blaas, oostenwind,
onbarmhartig door ons heen:
beter met de storm alleen
dan dat doodsgeur blijft omwaren
onze huid en onze haren.
Beter koud in merg en been.

Blaas, blaas, oostenwind.
Mocht die vlijmend wij ontberen
ongezien hier wederkeren,
dat zij het huis gezuiverd vindt
—onveranderlijk het hare—
kuis en helder, wit van wind.

TWEESPRAAK

De vogel eenzaam op het dak
spreekt tot de wind om het huis:
'Daarbinnen leeft een
die is alleen,
en toch hoorde ik dat zij sprak.'

En dan spreekt de wind om het huis
tot de vogel eenzaam op het dak:
'Daarginder leeft een
die liet haar alleen.
Zij zegt het woord dat hij brak.'

DE HERSCHEPPING

Als Orpheus bij de lier zong gingen stenen
bewegen, takken van machtige eiken
wilden met handen naar elkander reiken,
de wilde dieren van het bos verschenen,
die luisterend zich bij hem nedervlijden
en bomen kwamen nader op de tenen.
Een witte wolk is daar zómaar gedaald.
Dit had mijn ouder zusje mij verhaald;
zij zei: 'Hij zingt het, maar het heeft géén woorden.'
En die nacht droomde ik van een groot geruis,
en dat, terwijl ik Orpheus spelen hoorde,
mijn ouders wandelden door het trappenhuis.

HET VERLATEN HUIS

Steeds rond het uur van middernacht,
gelijk de schim van Hamlets vader
verschijnt hij en komt slepend nader,
stokoud, afzichtelijk van verval,
een ezel met verflarde vacht
en al ontblote tandenwal.
En heffend het skeletgelaat
hijgt hij met hese en doffe zuchten
de aanklacht van wie is gesmaad
en doet mij wraak en onheil duchten,
het aan mijn muren schurend dier.
O Hamlets vader, o King Lear,
vertwijfeld mij uw aanklacht maakt
om wat ik schrikkelijk heb verzaakt.
Mijn vader, mijn vader die ik verliet,
wiens ouderdom ik verstiet!

HET ROTSEILAND

De kust komt onder zware luchten,
Atlantisch, en bij vallend tij
scharen zich sombere vogelvluchten
tot de afreis. Straks vertrekken zij.

Het nadert dat ook ik moet keren
van deze golfbesprongen grond.
Als het wintert zullen zij mij weren
van haard en broodkorf: vreemde hond.

AVONDHEMEL

Daar, aan het westelijk zwerk,
in wolken, onverwacht,
Hendrickje Stoffels, thàns geschapen werk
van Rembrandt, dat mij door zijn macht
ontzet. Zìj is het, geen dan zij,
lieflijk en groots. In wolken onverwacht.
Ik heb geschreid om Holland deze nacht.
Waarom van overzee verschijnt gij mij?

HET VERS

Langs de nachthemel komen
de zomen van de morgen.
Het slaapt nog, bij mij geborgen;
het slaapt nog—ongenomen.

DE SCHRIJVER

Geduldig is het papier:
met tekenen wordt het beschreven,
met leven en dood overweven;
het papyrusblad van de Rivier.

Dragend, het geduldig papier,
de syllaben binnen zijn rand;
en tot de rol wordt het gewonden,
met het zegel tot stomheid gebonden.
Straks rust het onder het zand.

Draag gij, geduldig papier,
de woorden door mij geschreven,
de enige mij gebleven
sedert zìj van mij ging:
'slaap vredig, mijn lieveling.'

Het Weerzien

INCANTATIE

Ik draai gestadig de getallen.
Steden en straten zijn vervallen

opdat de éne mag verschijnen
die in het kruispunt is der lijnen.

Ik draai gestadig de getallen

en er verduisteren blokken huizen,
dat, waar de laatste lijnen kruisen,

moge verschijnen huis en naam.
Daar, achter het verlichte raam,

is, in het hart van de getallen,
de stem—de enige van allen.

HET BONDGENOOTSCHAP

Wie zelf de wijde wateren is gewend
laat zwijgend de ander in zijn element.
Men groet elkaar met de ogen. In de Lekbocht
heb ik als kind een visotter gekend.

HET WEERZIEN

Immer vervaarlijk blijft het schilderij.
Rivierlandschap van Salomon Ruysdael.
Rivierlandschap met veer en overhaal.
De zomer is voorbij. Octoberlicht.
Statig vaart onder wolken, tegen tij,
het grootzeil op, ik denk komend van Dordt,
een machtige tjalk. Licht wordt er uitgestort
in gouden banen, maar de atmosfeer
draagt al verandering. Er komt onweer.
Van overzee, in tweespalt levenslang,
aanzie ik Holland, in dit groots gericht
van licht en donker.—Vóór zijn nedergang.

STUDENTENKAMER

Daar, in de Donkere Gaard,
waar mijn eerste kamer ik had,
diep in de binnenstad,
zat ik te werken: ik las
over het woord quintessens.

En in die donkere Gaard
strekte ik mijn hand uit; ik at
van de boom van goed en van kwaad:
en het vers werd mij geopenbaard.
Ik zag het neerslaan, ontstaan.

Een vreemdeling ben ik op aarde.
Dit is in haar donkere gaarde
waarvoor ik sedert besta:
het vers—een kristal, een heelal:
quinta essentia.

DE DADER

Zwarte regelen op het wit papier.
En niets anders had ik ooit te geven.
Wilt gij laken wat er staat geschreven,
sla het blad slechts op: en het is hier.
Zwarte regelen op het wit papier.
Jong een dwaas en oud een dwaas gebleven.
Wilt gij oordelen over mijn leven,
sla het blad slechts op: en ik ben hier.

VERWACHTING

Smeltwater uit de bergen, raak mij aan:
de sterren kenteren en de nieuwe maan
voorzegt de lente. Winterlang verstoken
van u, smeltwater aan de sneeuw ontloken,
wacht ik u, om in bloemen op te staan.

Twee uur: de klokken antwoordden elkaar

Wanneer gij zegt: 'geen waarheid, maar een droom', dan antwoord ik: 'een waarzeggende droom'.

TWEE UUR: DE KLOKKEN ANTWOORDDEN ELKAAR

    Ik zag bij toeval, als er toeval is,
een happening aan het meer van Neuchâtel.
Gymnasiasten zochten daar na twaalf
verpozing in hun vaste areaal:
er was, zei men mij later, niets beraamd.
Doch plotseling sloeg het uur een bladzij om.
    Een donkere jongen hield zijn schreden in,
bezon zich kort en legde op de plek
waar vier arduinen palissaden staan
een stijf omsnoerde stapel schriften neer.
'Het is hoog tijd!'—waarop een kameraad,
zijn schriften grissend uit zijn legertas,
—een derde reikte hem een hennepriem—
bewees dat hij het ogenblik verstond:
dit alles ging reeds rond per ijlbericht.
    En géén bleef achter bij dit driemanschap:
want allen stormden tassenzwaaiend aan,
schreeuwend als meeuwen en ontdeden zich
gezwind van wat op slag had afgedaan.
Na een bewogen krijgsraad sloot het plan.
Er werd een vierkant basement gelegd,
de grondslag voor een hoekige kolom
uit stapels saamgevoegd, met een techniek
die aan hun intellect geen twijfel liet:
schaakbordsgewijs versprongen in elk blok
naar vast systeem massief en luchtkanaal.
    De opwinding, intussen, buide af,
maar de aanpak hièld het koppig nu-of-nooit
dat door obstakels slechts wordt uitgedaagd

en schijnbaar spelend het probleem oplost.
Aan bouwmateriaal was geen gebrek:
het werk rees veelbelovend uit de grond;
doch de verankering moest sluitend zijn,
het blok—zag elk—moest deugdelijk omsnoerd.
Zo werden das en fietsriem omgeschoold
tot klampen in een kruiselings verband.

Er kwam, frank stappend, een jong meisje aan,
zo lieflijk als de bloemen die zij droeg.
En zij, snel radend, zonder aarzeling,
trad toe en stond haar Schotse haarlint af.
Een hel metalen jubel steeg omhoog,—
o Hellas, o epheben, gij zijt hier:
een nieuw geboren vrijheid werd gevierd
in die triomfkreet, die zijn tijding zond
tot aan de andere oever van het meer.

Het werk vroeg met dit al een strak beleid;
want middelerwijl was de kolom manshoog.
Twee jongens, sterk als stammen, stonden pal
terwijl een derde op hun schouders klom
en, aangevuurd door menig hartig woord,
de afsluiting met een zwaai een feit deed zijn.
Het was, wees mijn horloge, kwart voor één:
men scheen naar iets of iemand uit te zien,
eerst korzelig, dan met stampend ongeduld.
Een knetterende verwensing brandde los.
Doch daar kwam dravende, met wapperend haar,
de schuldige jonge Hermes aangesneld
en hief omhoog wat hij veroverd had.
Behoedzaam nu, gij die de kan hanteert:

dat ieder blok gelijkelijk wordt doordrenkt;
en gij, die daar gereed staat met uw twijg,
dóóp hem, opdat hij lichterlaaie brandt.
   Thans, allen in den ronde, achteruit!
De vuurvlam spoot als een fontein omhoog.
Schouder aan schouder hadden zij hun stand,
verbonden jonge strijders wier besluit
de ruggespraak veracht had.—Zie, zij stond
bereid, feestelijk haast, tussen hen in,
het jonge meisje, opziend wimperlicht.
   Wat mij verscheen bij deze helle brand
—vlagen herinnering, vlagen vergezicht,
vol raadselen en tekenen dooreen—
joeg door zijn macht mij vreugde aan en vrees.
En zij? Verstonden zij dit ogenblik
slechts als bezegeling van een verbond,
slechts als triomf, uiteindelijk gevierd?
Hoe het ook zij: niets wat de ring verbrak,
noch trad er onrust op toen onverwacht
de vlam neersloeg en zwarte rook ontsteeg
aan wat het wrekend vuur hier overliet:
een stapel naamloos zwartgeschroeid papier.
Het smeulde nog: symbool van een régime
dat door zijn eigen inteelt werd verstikt,
gericht door een verbeten jong geslacht
dat sterk is, en berooid tot op het bot.
   Er luidde, ergens ver, een harde bel,
gebiedender bij iedere klepelslag.
En zonder haast ontbond de cirkel zich
en zonder haast bedekte men de plek
waar immer nog een vale walm opging,
met kiezel van de oever weggehaald.

De donkere jongen wenkte—ieder zocht
uit de ordeloze stapels de eigen tas,
en groepsgewijs begaf men zich op weg:
volgens eenparig woordeloos besluit
nièt naar het grijsgepleisterde gebouw
waar stellig een verbolgen rector stond,
die alreeds bij verstek was afgeschud,
maar noordwaarts, waar de wind der vrijheid woei.

En ik bleef achter. Laak mijn tranen niet:
wie oud geworden is in dèze eeuw
draagt in zijn denken vele eeuwen mee.
Gelaagd is hij, gelijk een bergwand is,
en heeft, eenzaam, van die gelaagdheid weet.
Ik dacht aan de verrukkingen van mijn jeugd,
aan dichters die mij brood en beker zijn:
zanger der zangers die Homerus heet,
en zij, als sterren aan het firmament,
Sappho, Alcaeus, Alcman, Pindarus,
wier strofen zelve sterrestelsels zijn,
stralend in hun gestrenge samenhang;
werelden wederrechtelijk ontzegd
aan hen wie dagelijks geboden was
een bladzij op te slaan waarvan de zin
door wiè gebood verduisterd was voorgoed.

En aan mijn land dacht ik—aan zijn bewind,
dat lafweg zijn verwoestingen voltrok,
decenniën reeds bevreesd ten dode toe
voor wat waarachtig is en uit de geest.
Een grondeloos heimwee greep mij naar het hart:
vervreemd is alles en de wereld dor.

Jeugd, afgesneden van de wortelstok,
twist met de ouderen, reeds moegetergd:
een hees geredekavel.—Eenzaam staat
wie nog bevroedt waaròm gestreden wordt
in blinde onmacht: eerbied voor elkaar,
dit simpelste, nog altijd onbereikt.
Nog onbereikt, en wenkende nochtans:
voor dèze inzet streed ik levenslang.
Maar nooit was mij de twijfel zo nabij
als in dit vreemde uur, op vreemde grond.
Toen zag mij Plato's Theaetetus aan:
sober en statig van belettering
de Griekse tekst binnen de strakke rand.
Een groene twijg, een lauwer ongerept
lag overlangs het blad—kronend de plaats
waar zij, een machtig denker en een knaap,
tesamen peilen wat mathesis is,
en waar hun beider adel het bestaat
elkaar tot hulp te zijn, zodat niet faalt
de opdracht steeds gesteld: de dialoog.

Een lichte wind stak op vanuit het meer;
de plek waar ik nog altijd zat werd kil.
Ik zocht wat ik had meegevoerd bijeen
en sloeg de damweg in die stadwaarts leidt.
Twee uur: de klokken antwoordden elkaar.

Die uw verkorenen hebt aangeraakt,
hun voorhoofd hebt getekend met uw licht,
gìj weet wat mìj te weten is ontzegd:
of wat ontsprong aan hun verwondering
en stralend de millennia doorscheen,

naamloos zal onder gaan in roet en as,
of morgenlijk, als gij de hand opheft,
vervaarlijk zal herrijzen naar het licht.

Zwitserland, Mei 1971

BASKERVILLE SERIE

Verzamelde Gedichten II

Ida Gerhardt

Verzamelde Gedichten

II

Athenaeum—Polak & Van Gennep
Amsterdam 1992

Vijf Vuurstenen

Voor Marie van der Zeyde

Autochthoon

VERNOMEN TIJDENS EEN ONWEER

Vijf vuurstenen gaf ik u in de hand:
een harde jeugd, die ziel en ribben treft,
een sterk talent, in eenzaamheid beseft:
aanstoot blijft het voor vrienden en verwant.
Het ongeëerd zijn in uw eigen land.
Dat zich de minste boven u verheft.

Vijf oerstenen: vijf kansen die ik gaf.
Mijn wet is: kwarts op kwarts en hard op hard.
Vuur schuilt in stenen, van de schepping af.
Het slaapt totdat het wakker wordt getart.

BIOGRAFISCH I

De taal slaapt in een syllabe
en zoekt moedergrond om te aarden.

Vijf jaren is oud genoeg.
Toen mijn vader, die ik het vroeg,

mij zeide: 'dat is een grondel',
—en ik zàg hem, zwart in de sloot—

legde hij het woord in mij te vondeling,
open en bloot.

Waarvoor ik moest zorgen,
met mijn leven moest borgen:

totaan mijn dood.

BIOGRAFISCH II

In de donkere romp, in de molen,
—en van angst leek mijn bloed te bevriezen—
dáár heb ik als kind mij verscholen,
toen het winnen was of verliezen.
Toen het winnen was of verliezen.

Die daarboven ik òm hoorde gaan,
zij stortten, stortten het graan;
gemalen, gemalen werd het,
tussen stenen te pletter geplet:
dat er brood, dat er brood zou ontstaan.

En ik stond daar, ik zag wat ik zag:
—en zij stortten, stortten het graan—
het vergrauwde licht van de dag,
de balk met stof en spinrag;
en overdwars lag het touw.

Een kind is een muis in het nauw
als de machtigen samenspannen,
als de machtigen samenspannen,
als zij wachten: met ogen en handen.
Ik stond daar: ik zag wat ik zag.

En zij maalden, maalden het graan,
tussen stenen te pletter geplet.
Moed komt uit een afgrond vandaan.
Toen ik ging, met mijn kraag opgezet,
wìst ik: ik zal ze verslaan.

DE VOOROUDERS

Ik kan niet van hen spreken,
stel hen niet in gebreke;
ik werd achter mijn tanden stom.
Hun liefde en hun veten
gaan niet meer in mij om.
Er bleef alleen het teken:
brandmerk en adeldom.
Als een fossiel in zwarte lei.
Zij slapen. Eeuwen diep in mij.

AUTOGRAM

Handtekening,
ik zet u neer:
weerhaak en kerf,
penkras en nerf.
Code van eer.

In tegenweer
—zwaard tegen zwaard,
aard tegen aard—
werd gij gewet.
Doorgrond mij, Heer,
als ik signeer.

Ik heb gezet.

WINTERNACHT (BIOGRAFISCH III)

Oudjaar en nieuwe maan,
kou die ik nauwelijks hard:
de strenge vorst houdt aan.

Boötes, fonkelend, tart
mijn onmacht met zijn macht,
zijn ploegend ossenpaar.

O bitterkoude nacht,
gij kromt mij in elkaar.
O vore, diep en zwart:

de ploegschaar van een jaar
door lichaam heen en hart.

HET VERLAAT (BIOGRAFISCH IV)

Onder de groene bomen
daar ademt het verlaat,
het tijdeloze stromen
dat in zichzelve praat.

Onder de groene bomen—
o, vèr van mensen vandaan;
het water heeft woning genomen,
het ruist er, de sluisdeur staat aan.

Met tranen ben ik gekomen,
ik ben met tranen gegaan:
onder de groene bomen
ten tweede male ontstaan.

HET AARDS GELUK

Het toegangspad, tussen de meidoornhagen.
Een kwikstaart komt naar onze namen vragen.

De diepe tuin, vol groen geheimenis,
waar in het hart een rozendoolhof is.

Het vriendenhuis, benedendijks gebed.
Men speelt er zondagsavonds strijkkwartet.

Zaltbommel 1972

MELANCHOLIA

Gaan vissen tussen Rossum en Hurwenen,
achter een krib, alleen met zijn verlangen.
Goed aas aanslaan, gezind om niets te vangen.

Aken zien naderen en hun naam ontcijferen,
die éne lezen en het weer betwijfelen.
Neen, niet.—Het meegebrachte brood gaan eten,

zichzelve uit een fles de koffie schenken.
Wegstaren en de Waterman gedenken.
Staan vissen tussen Rossum en Hurwenen.

Weet hebben wáár precies hij is verdronken
van wie er staat—hij die daar is gezonken—
dat hem het water goed zat aan de benen.

STANDBEELD

Daar staat zij, ongebroken en paraat,
de landsmoeder die zij ons altijd was;
krijgshaftig in haar vormeloze jas:
'Wij Wilhelmina', zéér tegen de draad.
Waag u, binnen haar krachtveld, op het gras:
gij zult een souvereine wil ontmoeten
die u gedoogt en tegelijk weerstaat.
Zij slaat u met een zwaarte in de voeten
alsof ge tegen rijzend tij ingaat.

beeldhouwer: Mari Andriessen
plaats: Wilhelminapark, Utrecht

ANNO DOMINI 1972

Er is te Heiligerlee een klok gegoten
en het was in de inzet van zijn stem:
of aarde en hemel samen vrede sloten;
hij zong—de wil des makers wekte hem.
En met de macht van zijn metalen mond
riep hij mij aan met name waar ik stond.
En stemmeloos heb ik het uitgestoten:
'Géén, Holland, heeft als gìj mijn hart doorwond.'

AUTOCHTHOON

Ik draag een haat vol liefde voor mijn land,
waarin ik onverzettelijk sta geplant:
door hellegronden boort de boom zijn wortels.
En heft zijn kroon tot licht en wolkenrand.

DIJKWACHT 1973

Wie huis en herberg had
aan de oude aartsrivier
bij krib en uiterwaard,
en nergens anders aardt;
en haat met bittere haat
het minne schrikbewind
der lafheid dat welhaast
zijn land bracht tot den val:
hij neemt elk teken waar.
Het trekt hem naar de Lek.

Zoals een schipper wijst:
'het weerlicht al. Het zit
daarginds bij Loevesteyn',
zo sta ik en ik speur.
De peppelrijen langs
vaart fluisterend beraad;
de stroom, verdonkerend, heeft
reeds van het noodweer weet,
het naderend ontzet.
De wolken kruien. Er
komt werking in het zwerk.

AANZEGGING

Er nadert schaarste van graan.
Tè lang is de gave getart.

De dag zegt het aan de nacht:
'er zit al zwart in de halm.'

De zon zegt het aan de maan:
'het ìs al in het gewas.'

De aar verteert in de schacht,
de tarwe is ziek in het hart.

En de wind zegt het in zichzelf:
'het sterft op plekken al af.'

Een vreemd overspelig gras
legt op de akkers beslag.

Graaft met nàgels waar het eens was,
waar de aarde wit was van graan:

als er àl te veel is begaan
zal de dag zwart zijn als de nacht.

Dan slaat het zaad niet meer aan.

LOF VAN HET ONKRUID

Godlof dat onkruid niet vergaat.
Het nestelt zich in spleet en steen,
breekt door beton en asfalt heen,
bevolkt de voegen van de straat.

Achter de stoomwals valt weer zaad:
de bereklauw grijpt om zich heen.
En waar een bom zijn trechter slaat
is straks de distel algemeen.

Als hebzucht alles heeft geslecht
straalt het klein hoefblad op de vaalt
en wordt door brandnetels vertaald:

'gij die millioenen hebt ontrecht:
zij kòmen—uw berekening faalt.'
Het onkruid wint het laatst gevecht.

ZIEKENBEZOEK

Wanneer een mens, door pijn getatoueerd,
afwerensmoe zich op de zijde keert,
het zweet nog tracht te wissen met het laken:
wellicht, wellicht—dat ge eíndelijk zwijgen leert.

TESTAMENTAIR

Ver van de plek die ik niet ken,
waar ik, zegt men, woonachtig ben,
vreemdeling, bijwoner, renegaat—
ver van de zelfverzekerden
is onderdak en toeverlaat;
een diepte tussen dal en wand:
berekuil, niemandsland.

Gij die mij duldt in dit gebied,
met vuur getekend door uw hand,
die nooit mij stamelaar verstiet—
Geef, als de dood mij overmant,
dat ik hièr val. Dat men mij vindt
op steen gebed, de ogen blind.

VOLTOOIING

Diep in de kern van het vers,
daar waar de strengen ontstaan,
hoort het al niet meer aan mij,
breken de krachten zich baan;
steigeren, vinden bestand.
Machtig in rijmen en rand,
hoor! stem en branding gaan aan:
werking van trek en van tij.
Diep in de kern van het vers
scheurt het zich naakt van mij vrij.

DE NAZATEN

Soms, nachten lang, zijn er signalen:
een raadselig zoeken en ontwijken;
ik kan de zin niet achterhalen,
kan geen verbinding meer bereiken.

Vervreemd ben ik van hen, verlaten,
de verzen die mij zijn geboren:
kinderen die niets laten horen,
met wie men in de droom blijft praten.

Maar als ik, wereld, lig verslagen
dan zullen zìj er zijn, mijn zonen,
om als een wacht, die stille dagen,
rond mij onder mijn dak te wonen.

MAART

Vanwaar ik stond zag ik twee vissen gaan,
de snelle stroom met wendingen trotseren
en bij een woud van waterplanten keren,
met waaierende vinnen waakzaam stáán.
Toen raakten ze elkander èven aan:
een lichte schok. Naderen en afweren.
Het rommelde. Met zwarte regensperen,
met steigerend licht brak zich het voorjaar baan.

LIEFDESVERKLARING

O land dat eindeloos in uw opdracht faalt,
ik blijf het kind dat blind in u geloofde:
om licht waarbij geen licht ter wereld haalt,
de geur van water om uw havenhoofden,
een aalscholver die op een ducdalf daalt.

Voorjaar

ZES DAGBOEKBLADEN

DANK AAN EEN EZEL

Gij met uw zachtzinnige oren
en uw geduldig gezicht:
ik ben u zeer verplicht.

Dat gij het hebt aan willen horen
hoe toenmaals het is geschied;
en hoe mij de ander verried.

En dat ge zelfs niet hebt bewogen,
mij slechts hebt getroost met uw ogen.
Dat kunnen de mènsen niet.

PASEN

Een diep verdriet dat ons is aangedaan
kan soms, na bittere tranen, onverwacht
gelenigd zijn. Ik kwam langs Zalk gegaan,
op Paasmorgen, zéér vroeg nog op den dag.
Waar onderdijks een stukje moestuin lag
met boerse rijtjes primula verfraaid,
zag ik, zondags getooid, een kindje staan.
Het wees en wees en keek mij stralend aan.
De maartse regen had het 's nachts gedaan:
daar stond zijn doopnaam, in sterkers gezaaid.

RONDEEL

Leigrijs kan de lente zijn,
winterdag als appels blozen,
herfsttij jong als witte rozen,
zomer donker fronsend zijn.

Mei, de bruid, in kristallijn,
heeft een krans van rijp verkozen;
leigrijs kan de lente zijn,
winterdag als appels blozen.

Komt en zorgt erbij te zijn!
Als 't getij eens wil verpozen,
gùnt uw ogen het festijn.
Spelbrekers zijn uit den boze:
Leigrijs mag de lente zijn.

FUGATISCH

Onderlangs en bovenover
gaat het water en zijn tover
vast gelijnd in klim en val
rond langs de terrassenwal;
bloemen, fonkelend overtogen,
kijken op met grote ogen.

Tussen kruidige duizendschonen
waarin ronde droppels wonen,
langs het fronsen der violen,
toegewend en wegverscholen,
gaan wij het gewonden pad,
zelf in schromen ingevat.

Stil van jaren, wit van haren
herbeleef uw wedervaren,
al wat kwam en al wat was—
water gaat langs het terras.
Schrei niet om wat is ontvallen;
water gaat langs groene wallen.

DE HUISGODIN

For old Tom and Margy

Onder een loverhut,
gebouwd tegen de gloed
des middags, ligt beschut,
beslaande gans haar huis,
herkauwend en voldaan
de koe, de overvloed.

Tweemaal per etmaal is
er snel en spits geruis
van melken. Het bestaan
is zij. En zij is goed.
Zij ìs er: zo gewis
als sterren, zon en maan.

VROEG OP WEG

Goede morgen, winterkoning:
'k Ziè u, kleintje in de heg!
'k Ziè u, reiziger op weg!

Telt gij ze wel, winterkoning,
het stel jongen in het nest?
Negen in het nest is best!

Staartje als een boterspaantje!
Waaikuif als een legervaantje!

Had ik het niet mogen vragen?
Had ik u niet mogen plagen?

Negen jongen, negen honger.
Zonder kinderen honderd hinderen.

Au, uw spreuk is bar en boos...
Win een roos!

Koninkje, gìj hebt gewonnen!
Zo gewonnen zo geronnen:
negen—zeven voor de kat.

Trànen—als 'k ze had gehad.

God zij mèt u, weggeling!
God zij mèt u, heggeling!

Ballingschap tot het vers

BUITENGAATS

Dit is het schip de Vis,
een ribbekast van staal,
een kop van staal, een staart.
De waterbaan ligt vrij,
de loods is al van boord.
Het vaart recht voor de wind.

En ik sta op het dek.
Ik ben weer in de vaart.
De sibbe is van boord;
ik adem en ik leef.
Dit is het schip de Vis;
ik vaar: ik heb mijn zin.

EERSTE AVOND OP NORTHROCK

Ik die hier eindelijk te schrijven zit
—'t was vijf uur varens van de overkant—
ben weer gewend. Want nauwelijks geland
liep ik vijf mijlen voor een lampepit.
Niets raakt ooit, sinds St Patrick, uit zijn stand
in dit gehucht waarvoor ik dagelijks bid.
Thans is het avond. En de lamp: hij brandt.
Komt, zuster stilte, zuster eenzaamheid,
gij enigen die mij vertrouwelijk zijt:
behoedt mij. Hoedt de lampkring en mijn hand.

BRIEFKAART AAN M.

Een zilte westenwind.
Veel mist: een zilte mist.
De schelpenbank bij eb
geeft nevels af van zilt.

Géén mensen.—Als je zwemt
wèl herfstig. Danig fris.
Het werk komt vrij: een vis
in zijn zilt element.

WEERBERICHT UIT NORTHROCK

Hang uw scheepsroer aan de schouw,
stort het zaaizaad in de mand;
't wordt met varen niet te klaren,
lang al wacht het naakte land:
zaaiweer is het, zilvergrauw.
Zaaiweer, als er buien drijven,
najaarsbuien, waterzware,
die straks hemd en huid niet sparen.
Gà, en leer het aan den lijve:
natte kluiten, groene aren.

ATLANTISCH

Over kanteltrappen van steen
is het pad naar de klip te begaan.
Nog een uur—en ik zal er staan:
met de zee en de meeuwen alleen.

Zal er staan, als ik het behaal,
en, windomwaaid op de rots
weer proeven met bittere trots
de smaak van zilt en metaal.

DE AFGEZANT

Een vis met incarnaten voorhoofdsband,
met aan de vinnen incarnaat een teken,
zwom tot de donkere meerpaal waar ik stond,
sprong naar mij op en was in zwart ontweken.
Aan u dacht ik; aan wat is omgebracht.

Nòg strijdt ge in uw sterreloze nacht
stom om uzelve, om verloren pracht,
om al wat, stralende, had kunnen zijn.
Aan u denk ik, ik denk aan u altijd
en wis het zilt dat in de ogen bijt.

IN NEVELEN

Mijn pen, te lang terzij gelegd,
terzij, gelijk ik zelf wou zijn,
had taal en teken mij ontzegd
en gaf, vol stolselen, geen begin.
Ik doopte hem in water in.
En in de schaal met water zonk
de droppel, het ultramarijn,
en heeft zich zwevende verdeeld.

En uit het nevelend blauw ontstond
een langzaam losgewonden beeld,
de eindelijke, de moeder mijn,
lieflijk van ogen en van mond.
Hoe zacht en ernstig zag mij aan
wier kind, wier blijdschap ik mocht zijn,
nieuw en van donkerte ontdaan.
—En wenkte nog en was vergaan.

DE EENZAME

Ik volg de sterrebanen,
de omdoling der planeten,
tel turende hun manen:
ik kan u niet vergeten.

Mijzelf heb ik versleten
naar melkwegstelselen starend;
ik cijfer in lichtjaren:
ik kan u niet vergeten.

Ik nader ongeweten
en laatste samenhangen.
De nacht is vol verlangen:
ik kan u niet vergeten.

IN TEKENEN

Met het gespleten riet,
met de gepunte veer,
met stift of wiggespijker
zet hij zijn noden neer,
de mens, de povere schrijver.
Eenzaam is alle schrift.

Het blijft hiëroglief,
bereikt de ander niet
die, in zichzelf gekeerd,
weghurkt of zich verweert.
Het heeft in tekenen lief.
Eenzaam is alle schrift.

Zie de aderen van de steen,
de nerven van het blad,
het sterrenfirmament:
Eén schrijft bij nacht en dag.
Zie op de kust bij eb
zijn hand, zijn palimpsest.
Eenzaam is alle schrift.

TRIOMF

Staal brult als het de smeltoven ingaat.
Het vers staat steil van angsten éér de staat,
de ingeschapene, zal zegevieren:
éér het, voltooid, de maker zèlf verslaat.

IN ROOD EN ZWART
J. H. Leopold ter ere

Twaalf mannen zag ik dansen
—het was bij vlagend najaar—
hun zwaard- en Morrisdansen.
Van overzee gekomen
de vreemdgetaalde schare.
Zij dansten: strakke passen
en gekanteelde standen,
met raadselig eerbetonen
van zwaarddiagonalen.
Gold het een vorst, een zanger?

O grootste onzer zonen—
Had rechtens in dit laagland,
zijn stamland, hij ontvangen
de lauwertak, de zware,
waren genood de twaalven
hem koninklijk te dansen:
hoe hàd hij het genoten
met manlijk trotse tranen.
—Dàn was de smart, de zwarte,
hem van het hart genomen.

JONGENSVRIENDSCHAP

Zien wat niemand ooit aanschouwde,
gaan waar niemand is gegaan;
ver van òns. Op kusten aan
waar geen zeil zich nog vertrouwde.

Wat de zeewind meldt verstaan.

IJlend, ijlend naast elkaar,
klaar de stormen te verduren:
een helogig vogelpaar
koersend op de Dioscuren.

THRACISCHE JONGENSDANS

Die bars de schildpadlier bespant,
het Thracisch lied weet aan te slaan,
hij, Chiron, danig grijs gebaard,
gebiedt de dansers in de baan.
Steigerend komt hun branding aan,
verdeelt zich in vervoerde vaart,
wisselt de standen naar de trant,
laat cirkels om elkander gaan.
Met handgeklap, met voetgestamp,
met kreten vogelhoog ontsneld
en door de bergwand teruggemeld.
Rond hem die, danig grijs gebaard,
de dans regeert met oog en hand
en hoefslagdavering van geweld,
die onbarmhartig oordeel velt.
Die bars de schildpadlier bespant.

MORGENSCHEMERING

Met vragende vocalen,
met stamelende syllaben,
ontwaken in de nanacht.
Een samenhang ontraadselen
met donker stokkend pogen.
De dageraad zien naderen.
Hóóg, hóóg boven vermogen
eenzaam het vers behalen.

ZELFPORTRET

Oud ben ik en verweerd.
Ik tel mijn jaren niet.

Zij zijn over mijn hoofd
als vlagen wind vergaan.

De taal der mensen werd
mij waaiend stof en as.

Ik tel mijn moeiten niet.
Arktisch welhaast de tucht

waarvan geen wereld weet:
ballingschap tot het vers.

BIJ HET RAVIJN

Gij die de naam draagt
waarvan de toonval
donker bezwerend
mij tot een troost is
bij het onpeilbaar
raadsel des doods:
ik ken uw maning.

Ver in de bergen
hebt ge uw standplaats
waar ge u handhaaft
zonder verbastering.
Donker van adel.
Akelei purper,
akelei zwart.
Atropurpurea.

ALCYONISCH

Veerman, mag ik overvaren?
Als ge het veergeld in mijn hand geeft.
Veergeld heb ik niet te geven:
die ik aanhing nam mij alles.

Zing mij dan het lied, vrouw Naamloos,
van de ijsvogel bij de tweestroom,
van zijn nest, het onontdekte—
gij, die hem vermocht te naderen.

Ik, die hèm vermocht te naderen,
die de koningstooi mag dragen,
het kobalten vederenkleed,
Veerman Dood, ik ben gereed:
wat gij hebt gewaagd te vragen
zingt u die vrouw Naamloos heet.

Een herfstavond

In memoriam Brendan Joyce 1903-1972
a faithful shepherd

HET BERICHT

De dag van het schapenscheren
—lees ik in nauw te ontcijferen
en telkens stokkend handschrift—
die dag van zware hitte
werd hem een dag des onheils.

Na vijven viel er onweer:
en hij, doorweekt en zwetend,
de stroeve schaar hanterend,
was plotseling neergeslagen.
Hij stierf diezelfde avond.

Mij is daar in de verte
een bondgenoot ontvallen
met wie ik telken jare
bij brood en beker zwijgend
de gastvriendschap vernieuwd heb.

Hij schonk mij zonder woorden
wat gij mij, grauwe wereld,
nimmer vermocht te geven,
wat gij, zo gij de macht had,
mij schamper zoudt ontnemen.

EEN HERFSTAVOND

Stamvader van de kudde,
in eenzaamheid gehulde,
ik hoor hier van het vastland
somtijds de sombere noodhoorn
van uw geronnen roepen,
als ander weer op til is
of regen zich laat wachten,
en weet u aan de rotswand
wegstarende landinwaarts,
balling op het schiereiland.
En twijfel overvalt mij
of ik u waarlijk vrijkocht.

Heer Ram, ik waag het zelden
uw areaal te naderen
waar gij, hooghartig stappend,
met voetgestamp gebiedend,
aanvangt mij terug te drijven,
vellend de veelgekromde,
de raadselige horens.
Oud en verweerd geworden,
steengrauw allengs van mantel,
maar steeds als vorst herkenbaar
wenst gij alleen te blijven
in uw domein: wreed gras,
bazalt en wirwarstruiken.

Ongunstig leek uw teken
dien grauwe maartse morgen.

Op het veld, nog wit van nachtvorst,
wierp de ooi onder de sleedoorn
een lam, bevend van naaktheid
en kou, erbarmelijk blatend.
En blindelings in zijn jammer
zocht het de moederwarmte;
doch het werd teruggestoten,
verhief zijn aanklacht, vragend,
tot de ooi, wrokkig genaderd,
het eindelijk bij zich duldde.
Hard ras handhaaft zich koppig:
een kleine ram, manhaftig,
hoog op de sterke hoefjes,
wist op het schrale onland
gras en kruipwilg te vinden,
leerde in geselregen
en barre wind of somber
mokkende onweersdagen
verduren en verweren.
Seizoen versloeg seizoen
en de omloop der getijden
zag hoe een eenling, afweegs,
van de anderen verbannen,
zijn paden wond, zijn doling,
onder de gang der wolken
tot volle wasdom groeide.
Tot in de derde jaarkring
herders een steendam slechtten,
de sterke thans verschenen
van zijn domein bezit nam.
    Trantelend in sneeuwen mantel
een jonge vorst verkoren,

een danser vóór de ooien;
voortrekker en beschermer,
waakzaam van oog, gebleken
standvastig in de stormloop;
met doffe horenstoten
nors de rivaal rammeiend
die bij de omgrenzing dóórbrak.
Een minnaar straks, een heerser.

En in de opgaande jaren
van steeds wassende sterkte
een stamvader geworden;
bij elk verschenen voorjaar
omringd door lentelammeren,
witte—als meidoornbloesem,
gevlekte—als kiezelstenen.
 Dan maanden zich afzonderend,
geen nadering gedogend,
traag grazende, of roerloos
aan een bemoste steenrand
wegstarende, weerspiegelend
de ommegang der uren,
de zware wolkenstoeten,
de nachtelijke gesternten;
nochtans, naar mij verhaald werd,
bij naderend noodweer nimmer
de angstigen verzakend,
doch een die machtig opdaagt,
die wijkplaats wijst en wering,
met zware roep vermanend.

Hoè kort, hoè kort het hoogtij!
Want na de trotse jaren
waarin onaangevochten
het vast bewind gevoerd werd;
na een volzware herfstmaand,
seizoen van oppermachtig
heer zijn en onderwerper,
onmerkbaar ingetreden
een kentering, een verebben.
En bij de uittocht westwaarts,
de trek totaan het rietgras,
een gaan met trager schreden,
een vaker rust gedogen
en, onverhoeds, de omfloersing
diep in de roep, verradend
genadeloos.—November
zag afweegs een verstoteling,
een doler dien het messcherp
gekerfd had met de oorkeep,
het teken van verwerping
en dood.
   Ik ben een vreemde
in deze warse streken,
somtijds geduld en somtijds
argwanend waargenomen;
een die, geweerd, zijn heil weet
in zwijgen, aldus mijdend
elk woord te zijnen laste.
Maar dìt geding kon kort zijn:
wie, slechts de koopsom vragend,
loven en bieden afwijst
houdt de eer aan zich.—En nochtans:

geld neergeteld in norsheid
en weggeveegd in norsheid
is kwaad van klank. Het zij zo.
Ik handelde althans niet
in voze onoprechtheid,
in onverstand dat weigert
het tègen af te wegen:
de strijd, het eenzaam einde.
Mij dreef dit éne: eerbied.
En heilzaam was te weten
dat wat de macht der mensen
berekenend beraamd had
gedelgd was; dat de onttroonde,
de banneling met de ogen
van gouddoorschenen barnsteen,
met waardigheid zou dragen
herfsttij en barre winter,
zijn weg zou gaan ten einde,
voltooiend onaantastbaar
de ingeschapen kringloop.

Geladen is deze avond
waarin het telkens weerlicht,
van vreemde voorgevoelens,
van rekenschap en afscheid:
mij wacht een andere opdracht.

Vaarwel, Heer Ram, niet ken ik
de tijd u toegemeten;
ginder, waar thans de nacht valt,
zult ge, als uw kracht gaat stremmen,
aan mensenmacht onttrokken

uw eigen einde vinden:
wellicht doordat ge insneeuwt,
of stortte van een steenwand,
of zómaar ingeslapen.
   Hoe brandend kan een wens zijn
die stom wordt omgedragen.—
God, die mij kent, bescherm mij:
laat het mij niet ontzegd zijn
om, als het komt, gevrijwaard
voor overmacht van mensen
en het oneerbaar uitstel
mijn eigen dood te sterven.

Het Sterreschip

Voor Johan Polak
donum natalicium

BIJ EEN DONUM NATALICIUM

*Ik heb een dag door Amsterdam gewandeld
als was ik naar Jeruzalem getogen,
en heb Polak mijn manuscript gebracht.*

*Hij was sinds kort weer op het werk gebogen,
een man die lichaamspijn al niet meer acht.
Hij was veranderd en ook niet veranderd.*

*En binnenskamers, bij de boekenwanden
der uitgaven, een ingekeerde pracht,
trok stil mijn ergste ongewendheid over.*

*Zo las ik dan wat ik had uitgekozen
en gaf hem toen ik ging mijn werk in handen.
——En daarna, wandelend langs de Keizersgracht,*

*een vreemdeling naar Jeruzalem getogen,
heb ik iets bij mijzelve overwogen.
'Ik denk dat ik het doe' heb ik gedacht.*

DE PROFUNDIS

Hadden wij nimmer nog zwanen gezien,
zòuden wij hen op het water ontwaren,
o, wij zouden van vreugde vervaren—
lachen en schreien misschien.

Hadden wij nimmer nog zwanen gezien,
vlogen zij òver met ruisende slagen,
o, wij zouden dit duister verjagen—
eindelijk bevrijd zijn misschien.

ONDER GORCUM

Torenhaan, haan van gehamerd metaal,
boven de stad van de Maas en de Waal,
over wie wéér het gerucht is gegaan
'hij trekt de stormen en onweren aan',

haan van de stad die mij wenkt en mij weert,
gìj zijt het die op uw spits mij tempteert,
zwaaiend en draaiend, vervaarlijke haan,
wijzende mij dat de wind om zal gaan.

Weet gij van mij wat geen sterveling weet,
tergt ge mij om wat het leven mij deed?
òf maakt het u zo vervaarlijk vervaard
dat ik het baarlijke woord heb ontwaard

en dat mij sedert de taal heeft gefaald?
Werd gij niet zèlf daar omhoog achterhaald,
sidderende van de staart tot de kam
toen er een hoos de rivier over kwam?

Haan, die een nimmer verwrikbare wet
heeft tussen aarde en sterren gezet,
vogelvrij zijt ge voor nood en geweld.
Het zijn de sterken die bloot zijn gesteld,

die buiten staat zijn de Geest te weerstaan,
godlof verslagen, en niet te verslaan.

Stormen en onweren trekken wij aan.

OVER DE EERBIED I

Gij moet het eenzaam laten
het zaad dat ligt te slapen
en dat al kiem gaat maken.

Dit eerstelingsbewegen
van leven binnen leven
vermijd het te genaken.

Laat het stil in zijn waarde,
zaad in de donkere aarde;
zaad in de donkere aarde.

En het zal groen ontwaken.

OVER DE EERBIED II

Ik heb mijn eigen ouders heen zien gaan,
heb anderen de laatste dienst gedaan.
Maar vraag mij niet hoe het is toegegaan:
sterven is iets waarover men niet spreekt.

Al weet ik dat ik stilaan raak onthecht,
dat zich de schaduw om mijn liefste legt
en ons nog korte tijd is toegezegd:
sterven is iets waarover men niet spreekt.

God, die mij langs ravijnen hebt geleid,
ik draag, nu mij de aardse staat ontglijdt,
een eerst vermoeden van uw majesteit.
Sterven is iets waarover men niet spreekt.

ONVOORWAARDELIJK

Als ge oud en schamel zijt,
het tergend lot u slaat,
als ieder u verlaat
en gij uw pijn verbijt;
en van uw eenzaamheid
laat nacht en dag niet af
de wind, die wreed en straf
recht op de ramen staat,
Waak! het is wakenstijd.
Waak en besta de strijd:
de machtige wanner scheidt
de korrel van het kaf.

GEORGICA
Labor improbus

Ik ben een tuinman, niets dan dat,
met aarde en met mest bespat;
ik buig mij neer, ik richt mij op,
ik klem de schoffel en de schop.

Ik wied, ik volg mijn diepste wet
als ik de naakte zaailing zet;
ik richt mij op, ik buig mij neer.
Een tuinman ben ik en niets meer.

Ga ik met donker stram naar huis,
de pijn spaart schouderblad noch kruis.
Ik waak nog als ik rusten mag.
Mijn land, mijn land: het is kort dag.

Delft straks uw spa voor mij de wig,
vergeet waar ik geborgen lig.
Voorbij mijn moeite, nood en pijn
moet er een tuin van sterren zijn.

DE GROTE STILTE
Doodzwijgen, door een hamerslag vernield.
(Ballade van de gasfitter)

Het uur dat Achterberg is heengegaan
en zijn gereedschapstas moest laten staan,

is binnen in de taal iets los geschokt.
Hoor met uw oor: de doorverbinding stokt.

Alles had stem en ging over en weer.
Het is veranderd in de atmosfeer.

Geen woord bleef waar hij bezig was ontheemd.
Er is geen sterveling die het overneemt.

VOOR M. VASALIS

Soms lijken uw verzen uit oerleem,
een aarde zwaar van gehalte,
nog vochtig van wegtrekkend water.
Het leem van de eerste mens Adam.

Soms naderen zij mij als nevelen,
damp van de waterwoestijnen
des aanvangs. Het raam van mijn kamer
wordt wit; er is mist aan mijn haren.

En soms zijn zij adem en windvlaag.

Maar mijn tranen zijn om die enkele
die ontstijgen alreeds bij de aanhef.
De ontzegden: óók aan uzelve.
Zij vinden hun weg naar de sterren.

DICHTERSPREUKEN I

Mijn zoon, zo ge dichter wilt worden,
gewen uw pen om te delgen.

Hebt ge zeven woorden geschreven,
gij zult er zes met de ban slaan.

En zo zich het zevende handhaaft,
het is van godswege een leenwoord.

Gewen uw pen om te delgen,
mijn zoon, wees tègen uzelve:

Dat wat een vers tot een vers maakt
is niet van sterfelijke oorsprong.

Wie dichter is zorgt dat hij staan laat,
mijn zoon, wat nièt van zijn hand is.

DICHTERSPREUKEN II

Mijn zoon, zo ge dichter moogt worden,
bedenk: er is een ontzegging,

er bestaat een onthechting des harten
die het adelsmerk van het vers is.

Hafiz, de grootvorst der dichters,
hij vond, mijn zoon, op een morgen

onherkenbaar de roos die zijn trots was:
met het scherp van de stam afgeslagen.

En hij zweeg. Hij heeft het verbeten.
Strenger pracht nog gewerd zijn vers sedert.

Ik bid u, mijn zoon, niet te vrezen.
Hij geeft de geest niet met mate.

HET SCHIP

Er kwam een schip gevaren;
het kwam van Lobith terug,
met grint en rivierzand geladen.
Het richtte zijn boeg naar de brug.

De scheepsbel was helder te horen,
de brugwachter kwam al in zicht;
een halfuurslag viel van de toren.
Het schip voer door schaduw en licht.

Met boegbeeld en naam kwam het nader,
de ophaalbrug ging omhoog;
een deining liep door het water
dat tegen de schoeiing bewoog.

Er stond een kind op de kade
—ik was het, ik was nog klein—
het had niets meer nodig op aarde
om volkomen gelukkig te zijn.

DE AFDALING

Op de Elisabeth van Maasbracht
heb ik gevaren, drie nachten drie dagen;
trappen van water daalden wij af.
Veertig meter gaat het omlaag
vanaf Maastricht tot Grave.

Met de Elisabeth van Maasbracht.
Sterk is het ancestrale, het water:
trappen van water dalen er af
tot in de dood en zijn krochten omlaag,
's nachts, als de dromen ontwaken.

Op de Elisabeth van Maasbracht—
schaduwen, raadselen, wolkengevaarten;
trappen van raadselen daalde ik af:
zeventig jaren ben ik gesmaad
door wie één naam met mij dragen.

Met de Elisabeth van Maasbracht
rijzend en dalend nog laat in de sluizen
—trappen van water daalde zij af—
meerden wij. Het was stil op de kade,
wit was om de lantarens de mist.

'Als alle tranen zijn afgewist'
staat er in de Openbaring.

DE EENLING

Dwalend over het barre rotsenzadel
stootte ik op een onverwacht gewas.
En ik zag dat het een akanthus was.
Zijn eigenmachtige eeuwenoude adel
had zich tot in de nerf gehandhaafd. Een
die stug de ingeschapen wet voltrok:
te breken naar het licht dwars door de steen.
Acht schachten stoelden op zijn wortelstok.
Een warse plant, met zon en maan alleen.

AETATE SUA LXX

Iets wat ik had willen zeggen,
wat, al toen ik kind was, telkens
aarzelend trachtte stem te vinden,
heeft in mij zijn plek verlaten.
Sarren doet het hart verstenen.

Of het ergens in de bergen
staat in zwart bazalt gebeiteld,
vreemd verweerd en onontcijferd;
aan de rotswand stom geworden.
Sarren doet het hart verstenen.

Zeventig, zo staat geschreven,
is de leeftijd van de sterken.
God weet dat hun sarren nochtans
wèl zijn eer aan mij behaald heeft.
Sarren doet het hart verstenen.

DAGERAAD

Verrader is het woord in onze taal.
Verraden heb ik zelf. Het was drie maal.

En drie jaar was het dat ik het niet wist.
Drie jaar heb ik geleefd als in een mist.

Tot het die nanacht in de slaap gebeurde.
De hanen kraaiden en de nevel scheurde.

HOOGGEBERGTE

Stijgende tegen de wand
tarten het doodsgevaar,
grijpen met haak en met hand.
Richel bereiken en rand.
Tweezaam, de voeten geplant,
uitzien, geschraagd aan elkaar:
adem en ogenpaar.

KINDERPORTRET

Het kind verloren en beschreid
verstilde in mij. Als een camee;
profiel dat lieflijk is van snee,
overwaasd van een tederheid
die èven naar bedroefdheid zweemt.

En vragen legt er zich omheen.

Beeltenis met de zachte boog
der slapen en het ernstig oog
dat weet al heeft van het verraad,
ik eer uw ongerepte staat.

Ik draag u bij mij, onvervreemd.

IN MEMORIAM

Door de stroming wordt een wieg gesneden
midden in het water en zijn banen,
dat het kindje slapen mag; zijn tranen
zijn gestild, zijn angsten zijn geleden.

Lichtend in de donkere onderstromen
van het water komt een wieg gevloten,
door verbaasde vissen aangestoten;
en het kindje glimlacht in zijn dromen.

In het water wordt een wieg gesneden.
Varend tussen wieren en guirlanden
slaap gerust, mijn lieveling, slaap in vrede,
eindelijk bevrijd uit mensenhanden.

IN VLAANDEREN

Dovenetel, honingdrager
bloem der bermen, korf van gulheid,
acht mijl door de polderlanden
liep ik, en gij waart weerszijden.

Waart weerszijden, en bij wolken
overzwermden u de bijen,
bloem der bermen, korf van gulheid,
dovenetel honingdrager.

Hoe zij tastten langs uw bloeikrans—
en ik mèt hen, ik beken het,
zocht uw nectar zèlf bijtijden.
Hoogtij viert ge als het Mei is,
honingdrager dovenetel!

HET HEMELS WELKOM

Met stralend weer gegaan,
met regen thuis gekomen,
om straks met zware zomen
nat op de mat te staan.

Met hoofdschuddend vermaan
wordt men nog aangenomen.
Zo stralend uitgegaan,
zo druipnat thuis gekomen.

Nu 't welhaast is gedaan
heb ik zo schone dromen:
Ik klop: ik hoor met schromen
het zware slot omgaan.
'Met stralend weer gekomen!'

NACHTLIEDJE

Er leeft een boom onder water,
een boom van wieling en stroming,
lichtgroen, in de diepte der zeeën;
hij rijst omhoog als het tij komt,
en is er niet meer als het eb is.
Ik heb hem zien prijken bijtijden
bij Silf, als het heldere maan was.

Er leeft een boom onder water,
ik ken hem, hij is vol geheimen;
hij vouwt zich open in tuilen,
in loverstromen van bladeren.
Ik zìng niet voor groten der aarde,
ik zing voor simpelen en dwazen,
en voor kinderen als zij gaan slapen.

JUNINACHT
tekst voor een ballet

Vreemd aan de ander in war doorelkander
danst om de rozen die raadselen zijn.
Wars is de wijn op de bodem der kelken,
groene festoenen zij moeten verwelken:
danst door de doolhof van lachen en pijn.

Naderen, kruiselings wisselen, keren;
tegen verlangen kan géén zich verweren:
vraagt het de rozen die raadselen zijn.

Dansen is dolen, is derven en zwerven,
aarzelend verkiezen en rakelings verliezen,
handen in handen staan bij het refrein;
zingen en springen, de tranen verdringen:
danst om de rozen die raadselen zijn.

ZWALUWENLIEDJE

Vaarwel, vaarwel o zwaluw,
rep u naar warmer landen;
de zomer is vervlogen,
de grote reis begonnen,
en pijlsnel gaat het Nijlwaarts.
Vaarwel, vaarwel o zwaluw,
wìj hier kunnen niet weten
of gij ginds in Egypte
door ibis en flamingo
soms scheef wordt aangekeken
—bijwoners, vreemdelingen—
òf welkom wordt geheten.

Hòe de ontvangst mag wezen,
de Nijl zij u goedgunstig
met dikke groene muggen.
Maar als het zuidenwind wordt,
kom terug, kom terug o zwaluw,
keer weder uit den vreemde;
maak dat wij u weer dapper
zien scheren langs het water,
zien metselen aan de dakrand
het nestje voor het legsel;
en horen hoe gij kwetterend
de grote zomer aanzegt.

NIKÈ

Kraanvogels met machtige slag,
kraanvogels in vliegende vlucht
boven Hellas, hoog aan de lucht,
de snavels in falanx gericht;
drie wiggen in splinterend licht,
met het scherp door de zeewind gewet.

En zij hebben triomf getrompet
waar in fonkeling Sounion lag,
waar ik stond en hen hoorde, hen zag
en hun paean vervaard heb vertaald:
op de donkere nacht heeft de dag
de gevederde zege behaald.

DE BULTENAAR

Ik ben van de moederschoot af
tot een kruipend wezen verminkt:
met voeten waarop ik niet ga
en een rug die mijn schaduw is.

Maar ik ken de hitte des daags
en het slapeloos uur van de nacht
waarin de beslissing valt.
En de zorg om het dagelijks brood.

En de éne—die niet naar mij ziet;
die ik nooit naar mijn eigen gebied,
naar mijn steilten ontvoeren zal.
Met mijn bergtouw, met mijn houweel.

ONVERVREEMDBAAR

Dit wordt ons niet ontnomen: lezen,
en ademloos het blad omslaan,
ver van de dagelijksheid vandaan.
Die lezen mogen eenzaam wezen.

Zij waren het van kind af aan.

Hen wenkt een wereld waar de groten,
de tijdelozen, voortbestaan.
Tot wie wij kleinen mogen gaan;
de enigen die ons nooit verstoten.

HET VLIEGEND HERT
Fragment

Heeft hij bij mij asyl gezocht, de vreemdeling,
voor het vervloekte spuitgif? Vlak voordat ik
de ramen sluiten wilde schoot iets gonzend
mijn kamer binnen, stiet tegen mijn voorhoofd
en viel dan loodrecht neer. Een grote kever,
vervaarlijk prachtig, in kuras gepantserd,
lag op mijn schrijfpapier, trachtte te vliegen,
wond zich, vergiftigd, krimpend om zichzelve,
kroop zigzag langs het witte blad, verstrakte
en trok de poten wigsgewijze samen.
Des doods—ik kon mijn oog niet vàn hem wenden.
En met zijn harnas, en zijn werend masker
geleek hij mij een opgebaarde koning
uit een vervlogen rijk.—Zijn adelswapen
beslaat het schild. Hij is aan gene zijde.
Doch ook een hert geleek hij; ook een aardgeest
met vreemd gekromd gewei, een fabelwezen
voortijdelijk, een drager van geheimen.

Werd daar een zeis gehaard in verre verten?
Of gold het mìj, dit ijl metalen seinen,
dit gescandeerd 'waar zijt gij?', afgebroken
en weer herhaald?—Zie, wat verschoof er
aan de balans? Wie had het oervermogen
zich te verschansen in de tegenkrachten
gewekt? De voelsprieten bewogen.

O God, hoe vaak heb ik mijn wacht verslapen.
Mìj ging dit aan. Mìj, thans en bovenmate.
En hem aanrakend bracht ik blindelings over,
met tranen haast, wat kern is van mijzelve;
wat met mijn hartslag mij is ingeboren:
aanslagen te weerstaan, verraad te laten
voor wat het is, en het geheim te hoeden.

Wat mij gebleven is. Niet méér, niet minder.

De schaduwen trokken af, het pantser glansde.
En aan het raam begon de wind te waaien.

Toen rechtte zich de uit de dood gewekte,
een elf, een Erlkönig in staal gestoken,
en hief het hoofd, het raadselig gekroonde,
en vouwde de metalen vleugels open.
En hij ontweek naar andere gewesten.

DE TIJDING

Naderend in de vroegte van de dag
het berggehucht boven het Arvendal
zag ik dat het als uitgestorven lag;
een stilte hing om huis en schuur en stal.

Een stokoud man wees dalwaarts op mijn vraag:
een dode werd het bergpad af gebracht.
Met vier droeg men de zware baar omlaag.
Mannen en vrouwen volgden, streng in dracht.

Ik zag dat in de stoet een kind mee liep,
en dat het bloemen plukte onder het gaan.
De laatste daling wachtte, steil en diep.
Beneden ving een klok te luiden aan.

De dragers rustten. Op dat ogenblik
ging er onzichtbaar iets aan mij voorbij;
luisterend met al mijn zinnen hoorde ik
mijn vader fluisteren: 'het is goed met mij.'

ARCHAÏSCHE GRAFSTEEN

In het verscholen thijmdal,
domein der honingbijen,
de dodensteen, de stèlè.
'Mētoon wijdt deze grafsteen
aan zijn verkoren Aktè,
de moeder zijner zonen,
die stierf, oud twintig jaren.
Zij heeft het brood gebakken,
zij heeft de wol gesponnen,
het huis in stand gehouden.'
De wind beweegt, de bijen
zoemen de stilte stiller;
zij arbeiden, zij fluisteren:
'het huis in stand gehouden,
het huis in stand gehouden.'

HET NOODWEER

Als zij de blauwzwarte rijksdaalders liet zien
'van de watersnood, van de watersnood'
die zij mee had gemaakt in dat rampjaar,

dan vlogen trots en angsten mij aan,
om de watersnood, om de watersnood;
om het licht dat verschoot in haar ogen.

Trots en angst, en daar ònder verholen verzet.
Bij de watersnood, bij de watersnood
in de zwarte nacht luidt de stormklok.

De springvloed sloeg haar en sloeg mij in dat jaar
van de watersnood, van de watersnood;
dat jaar dat zij mij heeft gedragen.

TEKST OP EEN RIVIERBAKEN

God weet: ik heb mijn verzen uitgestort
voor wie ik nimmer zag noch ooit zal zien.
Opdracht vol raadselen. Het uur is kort.

Misschien is het een erfgenaam: nadien,
wanneer ik zelf tot stof zal zijn verdord.
Een kind dat in dit land geboren wordt.

ONDER VREEMDEN

Het speelt het liefste ver weg op het strand,
het kind dat nooit zijn eigen vader ziet,
die overzee is in dat andere land.

Het woont bij vreemden en het went er niet.
Zij fluisteren erover met elkaar.
Heimwee huist in zijn kleren en zijn haar.

En altijd denkt het dat hij komen zal:
vandaag niet meer; maar morgen, onverwacht—
en droomt van hem en roept hem in de nacht.

Ik wacht u, Vader van de overwal.

GENESIS

Oud worden is het eindelijk vermogen
ver af te zijn van plannen en getallen;
een eindelijke verheldering van ogen
voordat het donker van de nacht gaat vallen.

Het is een opengaan van vergezichten,
een bijna van gehavendheid genezen;
een aan de rand der tijdeloosheid wezen.
Of in de avond gij de zee ziet lichten.

Het is, allengs, een onomstotelijk weten
dat gij vernieuwd zult wezen en herschapen
wanneer men van u schrijven zal: 'ontslapen'.
Wanneer uw naam op aarde is vergeten.

Het Sterreschip

HET STERRESCHIP

Aan de watergang geboren,
aan de grote stroom getogen,
met verholen het vermogen
om zijn tijdingen te horen,
om de maningen van zijn gronden
na te stamelen bij monde,

blijf ik het verbond bewaren.
Bij de wereld in gebreke
blijf ik naar het water aarden;
mag ik met het water spreken,
ademen zijn ademhalen,
zijn voorzeggingen vertalen.

Een die ancestraal het water
als de aartsbelager haatte
hield mij in haar schoot besloten,
heeft wat mij was ingeschapen
in het donker omgedragen;
kon mij, uit haar schoot gestoten,

slechts vervolgen ongenadig.
Maar genadig is het water,
troost is het en openbaring;
en een kind hervindt zijn dromen
als er werelden van wolken
met hun wonderen overvaren:

adelaren, karavanen;
door de buien heen verschenen
torensteden, lichtomvloten.
En wanneer de zwaargeladen
aken statig stroomaf kwamen
kon geen overmacht mij roven

het onstilbare verlangen
—vrees en zaligheid tesamen—
naar die éne, steeds verwachte,
zelden op de Waal te ontwaren,
dragende de naam der namen
ondoorgrondelijk, Aldebaran.

Aldebaran, om met vragen
aan uw raadselnaam te raken,
of van u gewag te maken
heb ik steeds als kind vermeden.
Bij uw nadering, Aldebaran,
werd het heden vreemd, ontledigd,

hield een kentering oppermachtig
intocht binnen mijn gedachten
en doorvoer mij een vermoeden
—opgestoten uit de gronden
van het weten ongeweten—
van verborgen samenhangen;

van dat Ene dat moest wezen
in de stuwing van de stromen,
in het trekken van de vogels;
in het in zichzelf gekeerde
oud geheimenis der woorden.
En, verscholen, in mijzelve.

Want de vlagen van het water,
donker door u opgeworpen,
spraken, ruisend langs de rietkraag,
Aldebaran, van de machten
die verwierpen en verkozen,
mij bezwerende bij name.

Hoor! het was voor nu en later:
op genade of ongenade.
—En dàn, na die korte spanne
tijds van uw verbeid verschijnen,
was over het krimpend water
reeds de eenzaamheid gekomen,

had zich ook in mìj voltrokken
de vervreemding—en op eenmaal
bleven, grondeloos verlaten,
trots en dwarse wanhoop over,
plotseling in bittere tranen,
bittere wanhoop omgeslagen.

* * *

Om een laatste antwoord is het,
dat ik, oud en grijs geworden,
door mijn naasten haast verslagen,
ééns nog intrek heb genomen
in de stad van mijn geboorte.

In een herberg onherbergzaam,

waar zodra er afgeruimd is
het door anderen stuurs verwachte,
het onwennige gewende
dóór mij áán mij wordt voltrokken:
eenzaam de balans opmaken,
zwijgend het gelag betalen,

mompelend goeden avond zeggen,
stommelen naar een zolderkamer
waar geen hond of kat zou aarden;
waar verlatenheid als buiten
één voor één de lichten aangaan
's avonds in het hart komt huizen.

Maar er laat zich door het venster
een riviergezicht ontwaren
nauw voor ogen te geloven.
Uit een ondoorgrondelijk voormaals
als het donkert roept de roerdomp,
en er trekken wulpen over

bij het dageraads ontwaken.
—Uit het water werd geschapen
toen de Geest daarover zweefde,
staat geschreven, al wat leefde;
nog in nevelen verborgen.
Het werd avond. Het werd morgen.

Die mij vormde in het verborgen,
die mijn lot gebood en opdracht,
wees mijn eenzaamheid indachtig.
'Toen ge nog een kind was wist ge,
met het water stil te rade,
wat dit is: In den beginne.

Blijf, om wie Ik ben, verwerpen,
wijs het af om Mijnentwille
het bedachte eigenmachtig.
Wind en watergang weerleggen
wat gij zèlf had willen zeggen;
wat geoordeeld is tevoren.

Luister slechts—en uit de verte,
ginder waar het tij gaat rijzen,
komt het baarlijk woord ter ore:
aan geen wereld onderhorig,
door geen mensenmacht te temmen.
Aan zijn afkomst te herkennen.'

* * *

God, mijn God, ik kan u enkel
danken met mijn blinde tranen,
nauw beseffend dat het wáár is.
Langs de donkere overzijde
kwam hij als een ster gevaren,
mij herkenbaar aan het toplicht;

zoon des vaders, Aldebaran,
die, als Aldebaran toenmaals,
voert, zijn haven raadselig latend,
slechts een naam en ster als boegbeeld;
die—o droom die ik gedroomd heb
in mijn bittere kinderjaren—

aan het venster mij vermoedend
mij gegroet heeft uit de verte:
driemaal zwenkend de lantaren,
stotende drie horenstoten.
Die ik hier, bevrijd uiteindelijk,
al het andere ontkomen,

heb zien heengaan in de avond,
bij het baken afgebogen.

Dolen en Dromen

Voor mijn vrienden

Misschien is het een erfgenaam: nadien...

Ik ben zómaar met groot verlof geweest,
anderhalf etmaal op een paar uur na;
en tevens werd mij onverwacht verleend
een helderheid van horen en van zien
waaraan ook het geringste niet ontging,
al was het maar een varentje in de voeg
van een vervallen muur.——En tegelijk
was ik volkomen uit de tijd getild:
gisteren, morgen of vandaag——och kom!
Anderhalf etmaal ben ik omgegaan
——mijzelf ontkomen, eindelijk mijzelf——
dolend en dromend in een kleine stad,
waar àlles stem kreeg, àlles open ging.
Steeds wetend: zó kan het maar éénmaal zijn.

Ik kom hem telkenmaal in Zutphen tegen,
een kind dat stil zijn weg gaat door de stad,
nadenkelijk van voorhoofd en van ogen.
Ik schat hem tien of elf en denk bijtijden
dat het er veel van weg heeft dat hij spijbelt,
doch leg dit in mijzelf het zwijgen op.

Hoe vaak heb ik als kind de school vergeten
voor Rotterdam? Volleerd allengs in zwerven,
vertrouwd geraakt met binnenstad en havens
en nochtans immer op ontdekking uit.
Daarom: proficiat, kleine reiziger,
wiens naam ik zelfs niet weet. Tot wederziens.

Het herfstseizoen zet in. Er zal vanavond
—hoezeer heeft deze kleine stad allure—
kamermuziek zijn in de Refterzaal.
Elk zoekt, er zijn ook kinderen, zich een plaats,
luisterensgraag. Men raadpleegt zijn programma
of partituur. Het is op slag van achten.

De voorzitter, gebarend, wenkt. Een jongen
—ik heb hem dadelijk herkend—voltrekt
de feestelijke aanvangsceremonie
en steekt de kaarsen naast het podium aan.
Er wordt geklapt: het blaaskwintet komt binnen.
Verwachting spreidt zijn vleugelen over ons.

Wat brengt gij, jonge spelers, met uw fluiten,
uw trotse pentagram, in mij teweeg?
Hier is dan uur noch tijd. Hier is alleen,
of het een bergtocht gold, het hartsverlangen
om stijgend langs uw steilten mee te gaan
en uw vermetel spoor niet te verliezen.

de tijden kunnen gerust terug
hun uren gaan en zon en maan
hun banen terug door dag en nacht

En nù—de nacht lang heeft dat vragend thema,
echo tot echo, mij geen slaap gelaten—
waarom alweer verdeeld? Waarom mijzelf
weer wijsgemaakt dat ik de stad in moest?
In deze tweestrijd kies ik, op het kruispunt
bij de Overwelving, voor de Kloostertuin.

Er is geen mens. Een lichte najaarsnevel
geeft aan de atmosfeer die tijdeloosheid
die er in een besloten hof kan zijn.
Een heimwee—heet het wellicht Sisley?—legt
zijn hand op mij, maar laat weer van mij af.
Even soulaas. Het hoeft niet lang te zijn.

Het is zeer kort: het vrij kwartier barst los.
Vlak langs mij stormt een horde van scholieren
de Turfstraat in. Vluchtend voor hun tumult
bereik ik zigzag binnendoor de Zaadmarkt,
waar het museum met een nieuw affiche
mij wenkt.—Staat het mij welbeschouwd niet vrij?

En reeds ben ik, verwachtingsvol, op doortocht
en groet de geefster in het voorportaal.
—In deze witte ruimte woont het licht
en raakt de dingen aan: hun staat verschijnt;
zó vindt wie schromend binnentreedt een welkom
waaraan hij zich bevrijd gewonnen geeft.

Als immer ga ik, ter initiatie,
rechts van de trap de kleine zijzaal in.
Hier ìs het, onveranderd. Ameland
van Dora Esser. Frank en ongetemd
verwijst het windomwaaid naar open zee—
en laat, als steeds, het antwoord aan mij over.

Ben ik hier boven eigenlijk alleen?
Nog in gedachten loop ik regelrecht
naar de achterzaal. Ik schrik: ìs hij het nu,
of droom ik het zomaar? Hij is het wèl;
hij staat, beschroomd en ernstig, bij een wand
met aquarellen van de Walburgskerk.

Laat ik niet in de weg zijn. Het besef,
praegnant, van er-te-zijn kan in een kind
in gronden leven die geen dieplood haalt.
Maar hij bemerkt mij, en hij fronst en aarzelt.
Ik zie het: hij bedoelt mij, hoe dan ook,
iets van zichzelf te zeggen. Als een teken

dat hij mij wel herkent van dat concert.
'Mijn vader', zegt hij, 'is een architect.'
'Dat dacht ik wel', zeg ik. Na dit gesprek
keren wij, met genegenheid, en steeds
er op bedacht elkander niet te storen,
terug naar wat er is tentoongesteld.

God zij met hem.—Ik heb mij niet vergist.
Hoe argeloos voert dit kind een opdracht met zich
die nog verzegeld is; die hij eerst later
met mannelijke ernst ontcijferen zal.
En dan herinnert hij, tezelfdertijd,
zich woord voor woord wat hier vandaag gezegd werd.

Er ziet in deze zaal een achtervenster
zijdelings op de Walburgstoren uit.
Ìk houd mij bij de etsen. Hij gaat telkens,
altijd vermijdend mij het zicht te nemen,
van de aquarellen naar het raam en terug.
Hij vergelijkt.—Ik ga nog vóór hem weg.

de tijden kunnen gerust terug
hun uren gaan en zon en maan
hun banen terug door dag en nacht

Er is buiten een losse bui gevallen.
Verrukkelijk fris. Ik heb naar huis gebeld
dat ik vooreerst niet kom.—Het ruikt naar floxen,
een honinggeur. Onder het poortje door
betreed ik, een verbolgen hommel volgend,
het Bornhof, waar twee metselaars bezig zijn.

Dáár staan de triomfante onderhuurders
van restauratiepanden: nachtschade,
springbalsemien, manshoog en vol met luis,
zevenblad enzovoort. Onkruid vergaat niet.
En bij die muur daarginds een ware Dürer
van weegbree, paardebloem en wilde grassen.

Ik kom graag in het Bornhof. Maar dat opschrift
boven de poort—'t mag dan historisch zijn—
is mij te klam: de hardsteen zweet ervan.
'Hier vloeit een springbron van *gerechtigheid*':
misschien staat dàt nog eens, als eerbaar inschrift,
midden in Zutphen op een gevelsteen.

―――――

'Die mortel', zegt de metselaar, 'is een pest.'
'Man, zwijg ervan. Ik werk óók voor de kost.'
'Dàt kunnen ze in Zutphen', zegt hij: 'werken.'
—Het weer heeft zich bedacht. Het is haast zomers
in de octoberzon. Bij een kop koffie
zit ik wat in de tuin van 's Gravenhof:

een mens alleen heeft er de Walburgstoren
toch als gespreksgenoot.—Ten laatste meld ik
dat ik moet gaan. Thuis ligt veel werk en vast
veel post. Misschien is er die brief wel bij
waarop wij wachten, jaar en dag. Dan vloeit
een springbron van gerechtigheid. Wie weet.

Zeer vroeg naar bed gegaan beland ik aanstonds
van moeheid in een soort van schemertoestand:
ik kan niet slapen en niet wakker worden,
steeds dromend en weer wetend dàt ik droom.
Eerst weer die angstdroom dat ik nog altijd
mijn doctoraal moet doen. Het buitenbusje
bevat een ambtelijk ultimatum dat
met grimmigheid naar bijlagen verwijst.
Dan word ik plotseling naar de IJsselkade
verplaatst waar, tegenstrooms, een zeilschip nadert
met op de steven twee gekruiste fluiten.
—Daar is, luister! dat hemels thema weer.—

Traag of ik waad, steeds achter kabels hakend,
streef ik, het water langs, in duizend vrezen,
om bij het schip niet achter te geraken.
Dan merk ik dat er naar mij wordt gewenkt.
Een auto stopt: of ik soms mee wil rijden?
De slag van het portier maakt mij klaar wakker.

Het is half vier. Ik sta wat voor het raam:
een lichte maan, een heldere lucht vol sterren,
en vrijwel windstil,—ik zet de balkondeur
wijd op de haak; de koelte komt naar binnen.
Mijn moeheid wijkt. O, nù te mogen slapen...
En ik slaap in, en in de slaap gewordt mij

een morgendroom. Zo een die vóór het dag wordt
de zwoeger mens eens langs het voorhoofd strijkt.
Ik droom ik sta in Zutphen voor het raadhuis.
Een aantal burgers—ik zie veel notabelen—
heeft zich daar in de vroegte opgesteld.
Mijn beste vrienden zijn op het appèl.

Men kijkt reeds op horloges. Er verschijnt
uit het stadhuis iemand van kennelijk aanzien;
hij treedt ons groetend tegemoet en spreekt:
'Welkom, aanwezigen. Wij maken heden
een morgenwandeling langs enkele gevels,
van het raadhuis uit, alwaar een tekenaar

vandaag verjaart. Hijzelve wenst zich niet
genoemd te zien. Wie zich geroepen voelt
sluite zich aan; een jonge stadgenoot
opent de stoet.' 'Die jongen', zegt iemand,
'ken ik. Hij speelt heel aardig klarinet.'
Op 't zelfde ogenblik komt er beweging

in iedereen. Wij horen een fanfare
die er mag zijn. De speler gaat voorop.
Neen, het ìs Hameln niet, maar veeleer Zutphen.
'O', bid ik in de slaap gelijk een kind,
'o, laat mij, laat mij nù niet wakker worden;
laat mij die ommegang maken: mèt mijn vrienden;

ik houd zoveel van hen; ik heb vrijwel
nooit tijd voor hen; en zij, wat weten zij
nu godsterwereld van een dichterschap?'
Door de Proostdijsteeg, waar is stilgestaan
ter ere van pand één, zwenkt onze optocht
af naar 't Bolwerck en Ruiter Kortegaerd.

De arts twee rijen vóór mij wijst naar boven.
'Zonder De Jonge', zegt hij, 'lag het zaakje
allang tegen de wereld.' En waarachtig,
dat zul je altijd zien, daar komt hij aan.
Mr de Jonge zelf; hij wil alreeds
hoffelijk zijn hoed afnemen, maar hij heeft

net geen hoed op. Men ziet hem aan hoezeer
hij dit impasse in stilte savoureert.
Dan glimlacht hij. Precies zo keek hij toèn
—die mengeling van blijdschap en distantie
waarmee hij op die foto staat, u weet wel—
toen hem de zilveren anjer werd gereikt.

de tijden kunnen gerust terug
hun uren gaan en zon en maan
hun banen terug door dag en nacht

En dan, ineens, begint het beeld te beven;
alles verwaast—de droom vervluchtigt snel.
't Kind met de klarinet, dat is het laatste
wat nog te ontwaren is. De hanen kraaien.
Dàg dappere Steeds-op-weg! Misschien zie ik
je niet meer terug.—Ik ben al duizend jaren.

De Zomen van het Licht

Opgedragen aan Gerard en Hermien Brantas

GRENSGEBIED I

Nog nevelig in de tuin. 't Is net half zes.
Ik hoor de melkboer, bezig bij het hek,
de flessen wisselen in het flessenrek.
'Morgen, Mevrouw', zegt hij: "t is anders fris.'
Dan denkt hij na, en bij een zaklantaarn
telt hij de posten op; het saldo klopt.
Alvorens hij weer wegrijdt merkt hij op
dat er alweer een r. is in de maand.
   Ik neem het rek en berg het wisselgeld;
't is altijd goed, ik ga het maar niet na.
Toch onbegrijpelijk dat ik nog besta:
ik word straks zesenzeventig, welgeteld.

1980

Eroos ter ere

Die weigert wat gij dag aan dag verwacht,
waarom ge in uw kussen schreit bij nacht,
die u met het verlàngen heeft bedacht,—
hij peilt hen die hij zijner waardig acht.
Eroos, die de veroveraar onttroont
en de verslagene met de lauwer kroont.

DE OPROEP
Groningen, 11 november 1938

Sint Maarten.—Het lichtende lint
van de kinderoptocht, de rij
die zijn liedje zingt, huis aan huis,
bij de ommegang met lampions.
  Geposteerd op de welvende brug
van de gracht waar zij gaan om de bocht,
zie ik halverwege de stoet
hem naderen met dansende gang,
de havenjongen, het kind
dat hier soms, als er feest is, verschijnt
en mij door zijn schoonheid vervaart.
Ik volg hoe hij voetelings komt,
en hìj kijkt omhoog naar de plek
waar ik sta.—Het heeft zo moeten zijn:
en hij roept, als een vogel, triomf.

En ik kàntel het van mij af,
het onzalig voordien; en ik weet,
als wie dakloos is na een brand,
dat ik niets meer èn alles bezit.
  Hij ìs het: ik heb hem herkend,
herkend aan de tweelingster
van zijn ogen, en aan de kroon
van het stralende, waaiende haar.
En met lachende jongenstrots
heft hij omhoog als een toorts
zijn lampion aan de stok,
en draagt hem zingend ten toon.
Eroos Anikètos, de zoon
van Penia en Poros.

EROOS TER ERE

Te werken aan het vers
dat in de steigers staat:
dàt is waarvoor ik dien,
al was het dag en nacht.
Ik leef pas als het mij,
krachtens de Eroos van
het onvoltooide, weet
te zetten naar zìjn hand.

O, de Domtoren als
hij in de steigers stond,
en schemerde er doorheen.
Diep in gedachten liet
hij toe dat hij rondom
met werkvolk was bezet
tot op de transen: mìts
aan hèm bleef het gezag.

MUSISCH I

Wie heeft de tekenen gemerkt,
alvast de nacht voor dag verklaard?
de zwarte merel op zijn tak.
Bij late maan ving hij al aan
met zijn praeludiën, dauwbewaasd,

eert thans de dageraad met een reeks
van fuga's, viert met een motief
de eerste tinten van het licht,
herhaalt het jubelend, aarzelt, vindt
een variant en herbegint,

met wervend lentelijk geluid.
O zanger die de ban verbrak,
er staan nog sterren, maar gij zingt:
gij zingt mijn hart zijn kerker uit.
Het kentert, het is westenwind.

MUSISCH II

Daar waar het stenen trapje is,
brokkelig, en nog géén voet breed,
huist in een schemerige spleet
muziekverliefd de hagedis,
die komt als ik een wijsje fluit

en zit gespitst op het geluid:
reptiel dat, roerloos, hevig leeft.
In prachtbrokaat, smaragd met goud,
fonkelend jong en eeuwen oud;
of Orpheus hem betoverd heeft.

Wiens kloppend keeltje bijna faalt,
wiens kleine hart het nauwelijks haalt
als het wijsje komt, en rijst en daalt,
dat hij voor altijd uitverkoos.
Hoor! 'daar was laatst een meisje loos.'

BIJ PLATO'S PHAEDRUS

Crux in de tekst.—Ik faalde als tolk.
Een zoon van Schoklands poldervolk,
die steevast, uren voor òns uur,
bij dauw zijn vaders koeien molk,
vond een brillante conjectuur:
de strakke woorden schoten vuur.
Het opgetogen koor ving aan
een roffel op de bank te slaan.

En het wàs of wij daarginds hem zagen,
bij de Ilissus in het gras;
die Eroos in het hart bleef dragen,
die wist wat een efebe was,
en nooit één veder zou ontwijden
van wie de vleugels tracht te spreiden.
Die zelf onaangerand ontkwam
toen hij de bittere scheerling nam.

HET SYMPOSION

Ik was zeer laat. En ik ben altìjd vervaard
als de draaideur gaat draaien om zijn as.
Helaas.—Mijn vaste plaats was al bezet.
Een imponerend iemand, zwaargebaard.
Een vreemdeling? Wàt een Silenuskop!
Hij nam mij, niet onhoffelijk, even op.
De ober kwam met borden en servet.
Ik keek steeds aan zijn table à deux voorbij,
maar merkte desondanks met schrik dat hij
alleen zat of hij met z'n tweeën was.

Opeens schoof hij het nagerecht kort weg
en hief—de wijn ving nog wat late zon—
tot zijn gespreksgenoot het fonkelend glas.
Hier was geen twijfel mogelijk: hij begon
thans met de ander het symposion.
Ik had nog niets besteld: ik kòn nog gaan.
Reeds ving, diep in mijn hart, dat branden aan
dat ik zo vrees, en dat maar niet geneest.
Eergisteren.—Wie kan het zijn geweest
die, toen hij zo herkennend naar mij keek,
op Socrates en op Verlaine leek?

HET LIED VAN TEREUS

Steeds schroom ik om die strofen op te slaan,
het hooglied door een sterveling bestaan.
De maan verbleekt, de dag begint te komen,—
de koningsvogel roept de liefste aan.

GRIEKSE DAGERAAD

Uw goddelijk geduld en ongeduld
dat, wáár ik ga, zijn werk aan mij verricht,
heeft in de droom mijn hartewens vervuld:
in Hellas was ik, waar ik nimmer was.
Het Parthenon, in morgenmist gehuld,
zag ik verschijnen in het rijzend licht.
En vluchten vogels zag ik over gaan
tussen de nevelen, in de nieuwe dag;
zich reppende met roep en vleugelslag
naar waar, in cirkeling, het theater lag
van Dionysus. Duidelijk dáárvandaan
woei vlagend op de wind een juichen aan.

Dan meldde een helle oproep het begin;
en volk na volk zetten de zangers in.
Honderden.—In het vroege ochtenduur
opgaande in de tekst en partituur
van Aristophanes' *Vogels*; ongestoord
en vurig.—Hoe zij zòngen, grieks getaald!
zó zuiver Attisch werd wel nooit gehoord.
—En steeds nog staat in mij die jubel op
die aan de sterveling Eroos openbaart:
wanneer de fluit de steile hemelvaart
waagt,—als de solo inzet en de hop
zijn liefde aan de nachtegaal verklaart.

CYCLADENVAART

'Zeilende schepen zijn de wagens van de zee.'
'Gehuifde wagens zijn de schepen van de wegen.'
Hel zongen het de jongens, windomwaaide twee;
het heerlijk keervers ging het heerlijk keervers tegen.
En ik, met schuim bespat, ik zong het met hen mee:
'zeilende schepen zijn de wagens van de zee.'
Ik povere, ik heb een hoog geschenk verkregen.

VERGETELHEID

Zo mij werd toegestaan een wens te wagen:
mochten de snoeren in mijn late dagen
mij vallen in het land der Lotophagen.
Alles vergeet die van de lotos eet:
zijn herkomst zelfs en hoe de liefste heet.

Voorgoed te toeven bij de Lotophagen,
zalig en van mijzelve zonder weet,
—alles vergeet die van de lotos eet—
om lachende mijn lasten af te staan.
Ik liep langs zee en zag de wolken gaan.

TWEESPRAAK

Ik ken u—en ik ken u niet,
die mij inleidt in uw gebied;
die als een vader met mij praat
en straks argwanend naar mij ziet.

Ik kende u—en ik kende u niet
—een kind nog in mijn prille staat—
gij die mij onverhoeds verried.

Ik ken u—en ik ken u niet,
die mij toont hoe een vers ontstaat,
en lacht als het aan stukken slaat.
Die Leopold zijt.—En ook niet.

ANONIEM

Een vers dat met 'schoon lieveke' begon,
een kind dat het die wintermiddag las,
en dat zijn ogen niet geloven kon.
Er onder stond een donkere naam: ANON.

Het wachtte zich te vragen wie dat was.
—En zwijgzaam blijf ik in mijn ouderdom;
ik vond een kleinood, een onpeilbaar woord:
ADESPOTON. Dat wat aan niemand hoort.

Een vers: geen sterveling weet van wie het is.

Geen macht die er de hand op legt.—Het heeft
datgene wat alleen beloken leeft:
de adel van het aartsgeheimenis
alles te schenken en niets prijs te geven.

En wat ervan gezegd wordt of geschreven
schendt met zijn gissingen de eenzaamheid
van de verborgene, wiens identiteit
de eeuwen door onkenbaar is gebleven.

ULTIMA THULE

Dit is hun eiland. Zij zijn autochthoon;
in zwarte lompen en met zwarte voeten.
Ik denk, mijns ondanks, wèl bij het ontmoeten
aan wat zich op hen vestigde metterwoon.

Hun kinderen zijn traag van taal en spel,
en lijken halfweg in de grond gezonken;
een soort kobolden, laag van kruis en schonken.
Hun taak is water halen uit de wel,

een mijl van het schamele gehucht vandaan.
Het meeste grijpen mij de ouderen aan:
met okeren gelaat en okeren handen;
door jicht gebroken tot de vreemdste standen,

een Zadkine als zij trachten op te staan.

BRIEF VAN OVERZEE

Nu alles tègen is geweest,
en ge moest vechten als een beest:
kom hier—want hier huist geen verraad.
En eet, en zet u bij de haard,
opdat ge straks weer Shakespeare leest.

Gìj zijt, als weinigen, het waard:
dat steile steigeren van de taal,
dat als het steigeren van een paard
bijtijden door de verzen vaart.
Een middel dat spartaans geneest.

HERKENNING

't Wordt voorjaar langs de IJssel bij Veecaten.
Wolken en licht, in wisselende staten,
scheppen een Voerman: een opalen zwerk
dat hemels is en Hollands bovenmate.

VOORJAARSMORGEN

Voorjaar, ten langen leste onverslagen,
hoe heerlijk is uw intocht, nu de zon
na gramme kou en maartse hagelvlagen
het triomfantelijk van de nachtvorst won.

Het dak ontwaakt, de muren krijgen oren,
de windvaan weet de tekenen te verstaan.
De liefste zag de liefste lang niet aan:
nu hebben beiden hun gelijk verloren

en strakjes zal het op een lachen gaan.
Schud, hoeve, àf uw laatste sneeuwen last;
de grendels weg: er is een hoge gast

dien hier een ongezeglijk tweetal vast
wel met een blozend welkom mag bekoren.
Voor wie een kransje aan de deurpost past.

Tien ontmoetingen

Zóveel tart het begrijpen: de mens bovenal tart ieder begrip.
Sophocles, *Antigone* vs. 332

HIER IN MIJN KAMER
In memoriam Jacob van Looy

Het is een kind. Het tekent alles wat er is:
een man, een vrouw, een huis, een holenbeer; een vis,
een brede bladerenboom, die uit één lijn ontschiet.
Het kind gaat stil zijn weg. Het komt, en stoort mij niet.

Ik kijk vervaard naar wat het kleurkrijt doet ontstaan:
een rode vos komt uit zijn vossehol vandaan;
de hoefsmid grijpt de hoef: hij moet het paard beslaan.
Het kind gaat stil weer weg. Het ziet mij nimmer aan.

Wat zoekt gij mij, klein weeskind met uw vuurrood haar?
Gij waart vóór mij: een aera scheidt ons van elkaar.
Nochtans, geen dag word ik uw nadering nìet gewaar.
Van éne ster zijn wij, ver achter uur en jaar.

BIJ EEN FAMILIEPORTRET

Mijn vaders pleegouders. Een waardig paar:
een stille man, een ingetogen vrouw;
om een jonge verwante in de rouw:
mijn vaders moeder. Zij stierf in Tarnau.

Van dèze twee stamt wat ik weet van haar.

Wie gaf zó antwoord als een kind iets vroeg?—
eerbiedig, bijna schromend haaromtrent
die zelve heen moest gaan, maar haar talent
op het behouden zoontje overdroeg.

'Het komt van háár. Hij heeft haar nooit gekend',
zegt bij 't verschemerende raam een stem.
En dan: 'en bij u drieën weer van hem.'

ONVERBROKEN

Geen die daarginds uw graf nog vindt;
er rest van u portret noch brief.
Maar ik die kind ben van uw kind
ik heb u uit de verte lief.
En gij mìj, onbetwijfelbaar.

Er is een weten van elkaar
dat tijd en afstand overwint.

Soms grijpt ge even in; ik merk
het aan een stremming in het werk,
een wenk: ik leg de schrijfstift neer;
die lichte wijziging komt van u.
Het vers handhaaft zich continu.

Er is bericht, over en weer.

IN MEMORIAM
HANS BRÜGGEN, BENEDICTIJN

Ik droomde dat de vijand binnentrok.
Hij kwam langs de Sint Adelbert-Abdij
in Egmond. En hij vorderde de klok.
'Ik geef de monniken vijf uur', zei hij.

Wèg was hij en liet ieder waar hij stond.
Toen gromde het: 'die protser! Kinderspel!
Mannen, het dondert niet. Ik zìng het wel.'
En òf hij zong; zong als een klokkemond.

In heel de omtrek ging de mare rond:
"'t Is hèm, Hans Brüggen: hoor toch wat een stem!'
—En ik werd wakker en ik merkte dat

ik in de slaap alles verwisseld had.
Een droom: wat maakt dan exegese uit?
Ginds zingt hij die wij hebben uitgeluid.

PORTRET VAN CORNELIA DE VOGEL
aetate sua LXXV

Nooit uitgedacht.—Of in die grote kop
een bijenvolk zijn intrek heeft genomen.
't Gonst dag en nacht; de arbeid kan niet op.
Het wemelt er van driftig gaan en komen.

En een steeds omgaand denken vergewist
zich of geen post voortijdig is verlaten.
Hier wordt geen nectar achteloos verkwist,
noch was verspild bij het metselen van de raten.

Gij slaat het blad om.—Door de jaren heen
zijt ge gebleven die ge altijd was;
de tekst beturend door het brilleglas,

of plotseling er van opziend, in gedachten:
met door die scherp geslepen lenzen heen
de straling van uw opstandingsverwachten.

ANNO 1982 I

Zij zaten, twee mannen, twee vrouwen,
in wisseling van partner bedreven,
in het bosrestaurant voor élite
hun jonge haasjes te eten,
die, zó uit het nest, hen voldeden.
De gérant stond glimlachend ter zijde
en vroeg of het was naar genoegen.
'Heeft u wellicht', vroeg de minnaar,
'na deze vier gangen nog andere
culinaire specialiteiten?'

ANNO 1982 II

Gij die met gemaskerd gelaat
het kind uit het moederlijf sneed
—het heeft nog èven geleefd—
en het, toen de daad was gedaan,
naar de afvalemmer verwees,

ik heb u gezien: pal daarna;
in uw pak met visgraatmotief,
gebieder van de kliniek,
dalend van het bordes
als waart ge God zelf.

Ik ken hen van de reliëfs,
de Assyriër en de Hethiet:
ùw expressie—het zij u gezegd,
clean shaven barbaar—
bezaten zij niet.

VADER EN ZOON
Dedicated to Sean O'Mally, nine years old.
With highest esteem.

Die ik negen jaren gekend heb,
die ik nooit dan verworpen gekend heb,
graatmager van haat en van hunkering—
hij staat ìn mij geprent, onuitwisbaar:
het kind met de roofvogel-ogen.

In de hoefsmederij van zijn vader,
waar een vosruin moest worden beslagen,
hurkte hij bezijden de blaasbalg
en zag mìj—ik stond in de poortgang—
metéén, met de blik van een sperwer.
Waarom bleef ik waar ik niet hoorde,
nog verhaastend wat zich heeft voltrokken;
wat mij najaagt tot in mijn dromen?
 Van zijn aambeeld vandaan kwam de hoefsmid
met gezag naar het paard aan de muurring,
en hij sprak met zijn basstem ertegen
overredend of het een mens was;
en het hinnikte, het hief gewillig
de hoef voor het inslaan der nagels.
Doch toen miste de man bij zijn arbeid
—en ik merkte het, ik werd angstig—
een vijl, en hij riep er de knecht om.
Maar het kind, opgesprongen, was eerder:
het griste uit de werkbak een vijl weg,

en schoof die, in vrees en verwarring,
langs de grond met de voet naar zijn vader.
 En het was of een hoos, of een noodweer
door de smidse voer, of het weerlicht
insloeg en de grondslagen schokte.
En de hoefsmid, asgrauw van woede,
verwenste met daverend vloeken
zijn zoon, die zich dìt had vermeten
en hij trapte hem tegen de schenen.
En het kind, blind van pijn en vernedering,
stiet een schreeuw uit, spoog naar zijn vader,
schoot weg naar een hoek van de smidse
en sloeg brullende tegen het estrik.
In de as lag het, in het veegsel,
in de schroeilucht van hoorn dat verzengd is,
en het kromde zich of het een beest was.
O God—en ik kon hem niet helpen.

HET VERSTOORDE WERELDBEELD

Hoe kàn dat: dagpauwogen in de hof
van Breeklenkamp naast ons?—Niet te geloven.
Hun wiekenpracht gaat het verstand te boven:
vier zonnen op een veld van sterrestof.

Hij had dit jaar brandnetels in het gras,
de oude boer, wat achterop met werk,
daar er een erfenis met ruzie was:
pauwogen fladderen van perk tot perk.

Hij cijfert achter de gordijnen uren
terwijl ze nectar uit zijn tuintje puren.
Zondags zit hij—zijn zaak is vóór geweest—

stil op de bank voor huis, verkalkt en blauw;
dan zitten er pauwogen op zijn mouw,
wier tekenen hij bevreemd en bevend leest.

TOEN HOLLAND ANTWOORD GAF

Dat mij dit nog gewerd:
 van mijn werk de late erkenning,
dreef in verbijstering mij
 tot een tocht door dit ingedijkt laagland;
wit van mist als het was
 en door twisten en zorgen geteisterd.
Ik liep en liep: tot ik kwam
 waar de grote, de grijze rivier stroomt.

1979

Bij dag en nacht

Nalatenschap

Dappere morgenhaan,
gij bode van het licht,
haan van een Hollands erf:
zeg mij het dagwerk aan.
En ben ik heengegaan,
meld dan, hoog opgericht,
met roep en vleugelslaan
aangaande mijn versterf:
dat het is opgestaan.

BIJ DAG EN NACHT

Hoe had ik ooit dit leven overleefd
wanneer de droom mij niet geschonken was?
de vreemdeling, die met de toverkap,
die omgaat in de mens bij dag en nacht;
de kenner van zijn hartsgeheimenis.
Ik droom, vergrijsd, zovéél; ik weet somtijds
niet meer of wakend ik of slapend ben.

Ten tijde dat ik de *Georgica*
vertaalde, werkend aan het Bijenboek,
en overal leek mij geur van thijm te zijn,
—want ik zat met de tekst kort bij een plek
waar een iemker zijn rieten korven had—
droomde ik soms dat ik Vergilius zag,
het pad afkomend: een schroomvallig man,
wat boers en tevens zeer voornaam: geheel
de dichter van dat ingehouden vers:
'*rijk in mijn werk, in stilte teruggetrokken.*'
Hij ging voorbij, hij zag niet op of om;
tòch dacht ik dat hij van mijn arbeid wist,
en dat ik hem niet vreemd was.—En reeds toen
heeft het *Ultima Thule* in één vers
van hèm, Vergilius, in mij gewekt
een raadselig heimwee naar die grijze kust,
dat nevelige eiland over zee
dat Eyre heet;—en waar ik heb gewoond,
waar ik mij met mijn opdracht bergen mocht.

—Toen mij, veel jaren later, overmacht
daar stee en erf ontnomen had voorgoed
en ziekte zich diep in mij had verschanst,
droomde ik des nachts, vechtend voor mijn behoud,
eindeloos van het Huis: dat Ierse huis
ons onvergetelijk.—Zo bouwvallig als
een huis maar zijn kan; èn zo prachtig dat
ik vaak dacht: 'Shakespeare's *Cymbeline* speelt hier.'
Zeer eenzaam lag het, naar het meer gekeerd:
de deur een zwaarbeslagen poort, de muur
van grof behouwen steen; het dak een ark
voor al wat rent op poten, kruipt of vliegt.
Naar dìt huis kroop in nood—de wezel was
hem aan de hals geweest—het haasje, dat
steeds piepend, en steeds trachtend om mij iets
te zeggen, in mijn handen stierf.

Van de gruwzame dromen spreek ik niet;
noch van die trap waarvan men plotseling
dreigt af te storten—want er is een tree
van weggehaald—noch ook van dat perron
waarlangs men radeloos met een koffer holt.
De klok verspringt: de Express vertrekt. Straks staat
de liefste mens daarginds en wacht vergeefs.

—Een godsgeschenk: de aloude dromen die
behoren bij het kenterend jaargetij;
vaak dromen van bevrijding, als de mens
door anderen gekooid of door zichzelf,
verlangt naar storm, en in de blinde nacht
hoopt op de troost van regen aan het raam.

En als het kòmt, dat ritselende schrift,
vindt hij zijn rust—en weet het in de slaap
dat het ook waaien gaat: hoor, het wordt herfst!
En in zijn dromen wordt hem aangezegd
dat het begonnen is: de vogeltrek,
de exodus der volken aan het zwerk,
hoog boven deze aarde.—Zie, dit zijn
de weken naar de najaarsevening toe.

Zelden droom ik van wie zijn heengegaan
—o vráág het niet, zelfs van mijn vader niet—
maar die mij hier op aarde lief zijn, zie
ik telkens in de droom. En het is alsof
de lasten van hen afgenomen zijn.
Zij lachen, en zij wandelen in licht,
licht dat hen tussen lover door omspeelt:
het heeft iets van een ingetogen feest.

Soms is de droom ook heelmeester, en dan
grootmoedig als Asklepius.—Het was
in dat fatale jaar dat slag op slag
ons trof, dat het niet om te harden was;
dat ons bij dag de strijd om het bestaan,
bij nacht de zorg, die rover van de slaap,
vervreemdden van onszelf en van elkaar.—
Wat heeft mij toen gewenkt, wat nam mij mee
de bergen in, waar ik hervonden heb
de hoogdag der hoogdagen van voordien?:
nieuw, ongerept, en transcendent bijna,
die sneeuwen tocht over de Alpenpas.
Twee mensen, langzaam stijgend, enkel met

een bergstok, zwijgend op elkaar bedacht
bij het wisselen van vóór- of achter gaan,
of bij het zigzagpad, waar men haast niet
naar de ander waagt te zien.—En stap voor stap
wint men het vergezicht, waarnaar het hart
de donkere winter lang is uitgegaan.
    O wie heeft daar geen weet van: het moment
dat bij een splitsing de één zich heeft vergist
en plotseling met bonzend hart bemerkt
dat hij de tochtgenoot is kwijtgeraakt,
en roept: 'bèn je daar nog?' En dan, gekaatst
van wand naar wand, de tegenroep: 'ik kòm!'

—Vlak voor de invasie, toen het op het scherp
stond van een mes, zag ik 's nachts in de droom
de slag bij Salamis, naar Aeschylus'
beschrijving in *De Perzen*. Tegelijk
hoorde aldoor, bij vlagen, ik muziek;
fragmenten: uit het strenggetoomde koor
dìe statige passages die welhaast
alleen bestaan uit namen, adelszwaar;
meldend de afkomst en het weids gezag
van Xerxes' admiraals, krachtens het lot
voorbestemd op de rotsen te vergaan.
    Eens, ons een inzicht openend terloops,
zei Leopold: 'de namen-symphonie.'
    Met bijna zwijgen heeft hij mij destijds
na afloop van de les, toen ik iets vroeg,
tot het besef gebracht van het geheim
der woorden. Zonder aarzeling. Zeggend nog
terzijde, bij het afgaan van de trap:

'toen waren vers, muziek, en dans nog één;
begrìjpt zij wel?' En wendde zich.

Thans komen zìj, bij nanacht wel het meest,
van raadselen zwaar, èn vol betekenis:
de dromen van de hoge ouderdom.
Koppig van aard en straf, als oude wijn
die, lang gekelderd in zijn aarden kruik,
het niet verdraagt te worden aangelengd,
en zijn uniciteit bewaart.——Slechts Eén,
hij die de sterren in hun banen leidt
en het verborgen hartsverlangen peilt,——
hìj kent de door géén mens geweten plek
die ik, als zich de overgang voltrekt
van droom naar dood, nog éénmaal hoop te zien;
waar ik gestaan heb, waar de adelaar
nog huist en zich op vleugelen verheft:
bij Olbia aan de Borysthenes.

HET PLOEGSCHRIFT

Boustrophèdon is het schrift;
ossekerelingsgewijze
in de zwarte steen gegrift,
als de voren van een span
ploegende ossen, die een man
maant met donkere roep te maken
de ommezwaai, als zij geraken
zwoegende aan de akkerrand:
oerschrift, eeuwen eender ploegschrift.
Boustrophèdon, welke hand
heeft de tekenen ingedreven,
donker opgaand, stremmend even
en verlangzaamd aan de rand?

HOLLAND

Ik werk graag op een klein bestek;
gewoon een weiland: zo'n perceel
begrensd door sloten en een hek.
Dichter, vraag voor uzelf niet veel,
maar vecht voor uw gerechte deel:
houd u de wereld van de nek.

Ik stèl wel graag een vaste grens:
het Hollands polderland gewend
zit ik—ik kèn dat drassig gras—
content te werken op mijn jas,
en kom op gang. Ik hèb mijn wens:
hoe kleiner veld hoe scherper lens.

SIGNALEN

Schippersinstinct, oeroud, voor wind en weer;
dichtersinstinct, oeroud, voor taal en teken,
springlevend, en bij 's werelds beter weten
tartend op slag en dwars tegen de keer;

zin voor het woord en zin voor atmosfeer,
mij even eigen als mijn huid en haren:
maakt gìj mij bij het klimmen van de jaren
tot een eenzelvig zwerver, meer en meer?

Zo een die bij het òpspringen van een vis
of het plotseling zwenken van een vogelvlucht
denkt: 'en tòch zit er onweer in de lucht',
of: 'met dat vers van gisteren is iets mis.'

Vrienden zijn somtijds om zijn lot beducht
daar hij wat zonderling aan het worden is.
Láát mij—ik wàndel niet in duisternis.
Ik kom alleen steeds zintuigen te kort,

daar mij bij voortduring bericht gewordt.

Οὐτιδανὸς Οὖτις

Ik lees veel sprookjes, zonder hoop
—het hèlpt niet, Andersen of Grimm—
en wen niet aan de voze troost
'je kunt het werkelijk niet zien.'
Een onontkoombaar woord: Cycloop.

Voor een jong en gespitst gehoor
vertaalde Leopold het voor:
boek ix van de Odyssee—
'die mij het oog heeft uitgeblind.'
Ik was nog onbeproefd, een kind,

maar het ging mij door alles heen.
Het heelt niet.—En geen arts geneest
het wèten wie het is geweest
die mij dit vlijmend leed aandeed:
een die, ongrijpbaar, Οὖτις heet.

KWADE DAGEN

Ga niet naar anderen als dàt leed u slaat
dat de mens kromt, of als een wig hem splijt;
ga niet naar anderen: raak uw kracht niet kwijt,
die harde kern waarmee ge het bestaat.
En houd uw huis in stand, gelijk altijd.

Ga niet naar anderen: hun blik verraadt
weigering te beseffen wat er is.
Straks woelt hùn onrust om in uw gemis.
Mijd hun bedisselen, hun ergernis
dat ge u blijkbaar nièt gezeggen laat.

Zoek het bij een goed vriend, u toegewijd,—
een die u niets verwijt, niets vraagt, niets raadt,
maar u verdraagt met uw beschreid gelaat.
Die, zèlf zwijgzaam, u kent voor wie gij zijt,
en merkt dat het, nog bevend, berg-op gaat.

HET DISTELZAAD

Ik hoorde een vrouw; zij zeide tot haar kind,
zómaar op straat: "'t Was heel wat beter als
jij nooit geboren was.' Het zei niets terug,
het was nog klein, maar het begon ineens
sleepvoetig traag te lopen; als een die
in ballingschap een juk met manden torst
en radeloos merkt dat zij zwanger is.
In Babylon misschien of Nineveh.

Ja, het wàs zwanger, zwanger van dat woord.
Dat was, in duisternis ontkiemd, op weg:
tot in het derde en vierde nageslacht.

EEN LOFLIED MIDDEN OP STRAAT
van de voorzanger

Rabbi Jehuda, hij práát!
hij práát, de zoon van mijn zoon:
één jaar oud, en hij roept mijn naam,
die dageraadsvogel; soms praat
hij als tokkelsnaren, en soms
is het, wat zèg ik, een fluit.

En opmèrkzaam! hij hoort elk geluid:
hij lacht als een specht als mijn zoon
uit de kan de wijnkruik bijschenkt.
 Ach, was het niet Ráb Uzziēl,
die zei dat een schuldeloos kind
alle talen der wereld omvat?

Rabbi, ù is muzikaal:
u moest eens zien hoe dat kind
stil ligt te luisteren wanneer
zijn moeder—geprezen zij zij!—
te zingen loopt door het huis,
of zijn vader het Hallēl aanheft.

HET WINTERONWEER

Uit zichzelf in de avond stalwaarts keerden de koeien,
bergaf onder de val van de gestadige sneeuw.
Ach! Therimachus slaapt naast de eik zijn
ononderbroken slaap.—Ter ruste gelegd heeft hem
het vuur van omhoog.

uit het Grieks vertaald

WINTER ONDER SCHELLINGWOUDE

Immer in dit drassig laagland
handhaaft zich het spitse rietgras;

's zomers wuivend met zijn pluimen
wordt het met de herfst eenkennig.

Rietgras om zich te verschansen;
om de medeminnaar listig

in een hinderlaag te lokken:
ergens waar de bodem wegzinkt.

Rietgras, werend als het wintert;
als men eenzaam, zich vemannend,

op de scherpgeslepen ijzers
rijdt, gekromd, tegen de wind in.

Ontoegankelijk het rietland,
ontoegankelijk de sterveling:

menigmaal heb ik hier Breero
rakelings voorbij zien schaatsen,

grauw, verbeten.—Door die éne
ongenaakbaar afgewezen.

SPOEDOPNAME

Leg het nu hier maar neer:
horloge, sleutelbos,
het mes met stalen veer,
de vulpen en het geld.
Alles wat niet meer telt;

leg het hier zo maar los.
Of neen, berg het maar op,
maak avond en ga heen.
—Zó is het goed. Alleen
met ring en harteklop.

DE PROFUNDIS

De mens die waar zijn dode slaapt
de anderen zachtzinnig weert,
opdat de liefste niets geschiedt;
en zwijgt, en binnengaat wanneer
waar het met bloemen is verfraaid
de schroeven worden aangedraaid,—
om hèm heb ik mij afgevraagd
zo làng ik leef, en altijd weer,
mij afgevraagd waarom gij niet
—wachter, wat is er van de nacht?—
komt en uw engelen ontbiedt.

HET VOLMAAKTE

Ik gaf mijn kind een zilveren bal.
Het werd zijn één, het werd zijn al;
en hij die steeds met ieder deelt,
hij schreit als iemand er mee speelt.

Ik sprak tot hem met zacht vermaan;
hij zag mij lang verwonderd aan
en liet toen stil zijn tranen gaan.

Ik gaf mijn kind een zilveren bal:
bracht ik zijn onschuld nu ten val?
Of ben ik blind?—Het goddelijk kind
hield in zijn handjes het heelal.

ONTKOMEN

Diep in de stilte binnengedaald—
zoals een vis
zoals een vis
binnen het water ademhaalt,
water dat adem en aanvang is.

Diep in de stilte—en vrij geraakt,
zoals een vis
zoals een vis
zwaarteloos vaart met vinnen en staart,
voelend wat water en koelte is.

Diep in de stilte eenkennig gewend
—zoals de vis
zoals de vis
enkel kent zijn element—
kennend de Ene die was en is.

POËTA LAUREATUS I

Het wijkt als het mijn nadering vermoedt;
het is mij vóór, ik ben het achterna,
het vers dat als ik er het oog op sla
alreeds aan glans zal hebben ingeboet.
Eenhoorn, die zich aan mìj niet toevertrouwt.

Mijn hart trekt samen als de ander rouwt.
En ik werf om wat zó steil weerstreeft—altijd,

het vers dat hem van droefenis had bevrijd
en, mocht het zìjn, vernieuwd van hoofd tot voet.
Waarom ik heb gebeden en geschreid.
O raadselachtig woord: 'ik taal ernaar'—
o nietig leven dat ten einde spoedt!

POËTA LAUREATUS II

De verzen die een glanzen dragen
en waarin keuren zijn geslagen,
waaraan mijn vorst zijn hart verpandt,—
van ù ontvingen zij gestalte
die toetst het goud op zijn gehalte:
Gìj weet: zij zijn nìet van mijn hand.

Een naam in schelpen

NA DE VLOED

Vroeg banjeren langs het strand. Terugtrekkend tij.
Nog geen vijf uur. Zie, zie! schreeuwen de meeuwen.
O God, dit kan niet waar zijn.—Afgezet
op het ebstrand, immens, een alphabet.
Hebreeuwse quadraturen, uitgedreven
in ribbelige ruggen natte klei,
zich rijend in reliëf: het Bᵉrešit bārā.
Zoutfonkelend, oeroud.—Met vleugelslaan
ontstijgt, de golfkam langs, een zwerm van sternen
en stòrt zich in het licht.—Ik laat
voet voor voet af van wat geschreven staat.

Παρὰ θῖνα θαλάσσης

Drie woorden slechts van Homerus,—
    o hóór het kantelen en ruisen
dat er in schuilt;—als een kind
    dat gelovig de schelp aan het oor legt.
Hoorde ge eigenlijk nooit
    dat komen en gaan, gaan en komen:
hoorde ge eigenlijk nooit
    de zee in het vers van Homerus?

VAN DE BRUG AF GEZIEN
voor Rembert

Wij lijken, ouder wordend, op elkaar,
gij stille man daarginds met uw sextant
—een zeeman die liefst op de sterren vaart
en het schip had willen noemen *in Gods hand*—
en ik: enkeling die op verzen vaar.

'Een werkelijk vers is eigenlijk een ster',
denk ik altijd: 'merk hoe het licht uitstraalt.'
En hoger inzicht heb ik nooit behaald:
wat gééft het of een mens daarvoor betaalt?
Genoeg: ook daarin staan we elkaar niet ver.

Gij die het houdt op 's hemels sterrekaart,
ik die in kenteringen van het jaar
als staat te vrezen dat het lot toeslaat,
op zolder mij op Shakespeare's Songs verlaat,
of op twee regels van Vasalis vaar.

TWEE MANNEN

Op dat ongenadig onland
—vlijmscherp, manshoog is het rietgras—
bij de Hont of Westerschelde,
meldde de metalen lichtmast
telkens fluitend: er is storing.

Vlak langs waar ik lag te lezen
kwamen over de bazaltdijk,
ieder met een tas, twee mannen.
Naderden de lichtmast, hielden
kort beraad en klommen aanstonds

feilloos, spijl voor spijl, het staal in.
Wandelende langs de spanten,
werkend met engelse sleutels,
zaten zij ten laatste weerzijds
schrijlings op twee leidingdraden.

De een: 'dáár! radicaal versleten:
àlles slijt.'—'O ja?' de ander.
En zijn maat: 'man, zul je dáár nou
eeuwig over blijven malen?'
'Mooi gezegd!—ik hàd haar jawoord.'

'Koekoek, koekoek' riep de koekoek
spottend uit het elzenbosje;
'bakboord' klonk het van de sluizen.
En zij werkten, balancerend,
voort aan de hoogspanningsdraden,
bij de Hont of Westerschelde.

HERFST AAN DE SCHELDE
voor mijn zuster Mia

Hier meren schepen uit vier hemelstreken.
De kade is een Babel aller talen.
Nog in de late nacht komt van de sluizen
met een metalen stentorstem de maning
tot wie de haven naderen bij het baken.

Hier, in het huis *de Scheepslantaarn* geheten
slaap ik de oerslaap van mijn kinderjaren
droomloos en diep, opnieuw.—Om nochtans aanstonds
—de slaap heeft, als het water, vele lagen—
te ontwaken door een schok van verre herkomst

wanneer de schepen met de schepen spreken,
of bij slecht zicht elkaar, voor anker liggend,
schor op de misthoorn om compassie vragen.
Maar niemand rekent hier de nacht naar uren,
of tèlt het uit de slaap te zijn gestoten.

Want hòe ook weer en wind: vroeg in de vroegte,
nog vóór de meeuw zijn visvangst is begonnen,
heeft reeds het waaks instinct de wacht betrokken
en waarschuwt, als het raderwerk der sluizen
is aangeslagen, om het uur der uren,

de nieuwe dageraad voor wie gaan en komen,
niet blind en doof lichtvaardig te verzuimen.
Reeds gaan de ochtendnevelen zich verdelen;
ik sla de ramen naar de kade open,
—o geur van hennep, plaatijzer en teer—
de hemel in het oosten wordt ontsloten.
Aan het havenhoofd beginnen de bevelen.
Hóór! Eén voor één de vreemdgetaalde namen,
aanroep en antwoord gaan over en weer:
'Sally, Namur, Osaka, Raamsdonkveer!'

En gescandeerd: 'Osaka, wij herhalen!'
Apocalyptisch haast, van andere orde.
Zo mij geen dageraad meer zou geworden
dan deze, na de nacht der najaarsevening,
ik was bereid—ik had geen wensen meer.

EEN NAAM IN SCHELPEN

Mijn diepste eerbied geldt een kind
dat onaanrandbaar naar de zee
verlangt, en het niet merken laat
aan anderen.—Dat de werking weet
van vloed en eb, en het gedrag
kent van de vogels langs de kust.

In welk millennium, dat telt
niet, en al evenmin of het
op Chios of op Tessel is.
Het loopt de vloedlijn langs; het zoekt
schelpen van dat verzonken blauw:
het prachtigst als zij zilt nog zijn;

of speelt het eeuwenoude spel
van zich te meten met de zee.
Het bouwt een bolwerk, bakent met
de schop de omtrek af, en stòrt
zich op het graven van de gracht;
en werpt een wal op, om verwoed

die met de spa gelijk te slaan.
 Zó verstrijkt uur na uur, totdat
de vesting is voltooid.—Het zet
zich neer en dènkt: hoe alles ìs
en later zijn zal—en dan waait
de wind dat weg: het hoèft nog niet.

Mijn diepste eerbied geldt dit kind.

En het wordt avond—het bemerkt
dat ginds het wentelende licht
is aangegaan en maant en maant:
het kent het ouderlijk gebod.
De zon is weg; de dag is om.

En het vermant zich, en verlaat

zijn burcht aan zee, het bastion
waarop zijn naam in schelpen staat,
en dat—hij weet het—nog vannacht
als het tij opzet wordt geslecht.

Het neemt zijn schop op en het gaat
op stroeve voeten havenwaarts.

IN NEVELEN

Heimwee dat overwonnen moet.
Waartegen ik vertwijfeld vecht.
Vergeefs.—Ik beef van hoofd tot voet
als iemand het woord Ierland zegt.

HET AFSCHEID

Nu zwaarder wordt der jaren last
verschijnt mij vaak een droomgezicht:

een haven waar een schoener ligt,
en ik: ik ben een varensgast.

En hoor: zij zìngen al aan boord,
en taal wordt mij hun vreemde taal.

'Vaarwel, mijn liefste en mijn land;
ik ben het beste in het want.

Vaarwel, houd mij geen ontrouw na;
ik ben het beste in de ra.

Vrienden, vaarwel! Ik ben het best
daarboven in het kraaienest.'

Ik heb geen wensen meer: ik ben
een varensgast, en één van hen.

De horen meldt met grote stem
de afvaart en het nieuw begin.
De bootsman haalt de loopplank in.

GRENSGEBIED II

Ik kan hem soms wanneer ik wakker lig
als was het door een verrekijker zien:
de vuurtoren hier mijlen ver vandaan,
die van het zeedorp waar mijn wijkplaats is;

waar thans zijn wenteling de kust bestrijkt
met wiggen duisternis, met wiggen licht;
naar de seconden van het interval
met even en oneven om en om.

En volgend deze ronde in de nacht,
de cirkeling der wiggen om hun as,
nog tellende mijns ondanks èn alreeds
ervarende dat er geen tijd bestáát,

besef ik bij dit wijlen aan de grens
het raadsel van de hoge ouderdom:
het prijsgegeven zijn en alreeds vrij.
Het raken aan de zomen van het licht.

1982

De Adelaarsvarens

Negen verzen van zonsopgang

Aan mijn vrienden
11 mei 1985

ER STOND BIJ: VERTAALD UIT HET FRANS

Ik las het eindeloos als kind:
er was een man en hij had
levenslang. Onschuldig. Hij zat
gevangen: hij had geen verhaal.
Maar hij had een lepel van tin.

Hij vijlde ermee in de nacht;
hij kraste krassen, hij nam
een jaar voor één staaf van het raam.
Totdat de kracht hem begaf.
Al had hij een lepel van tin.

Maar toen kreeg hij hulp: van een rat,
een zwarte rat uit de gracht,
die voor hem vrat aan de kalk,
aan de lijst van het tralieraam.
En hij nam weer zijn lepel van tin.

Toen brak, op een nacht, er iets af;
en het wàs er; het was er, het gat.
En hij stond geschramd op de kant
van de gracht, de gevangene. Hij heeft
nog gezien dat de dageraad kwam.

WINTERMORGEN IN IERLAND

Het wintert. Witberijpt komt thuis
die dapper de fourage torst
—en immer sterrestelsels morst
van melkstippels op het plavuis—
en meldt bedaard zes graden vorst.

Nadien daagt uit het nergens op
de bedelaar die om koffie klopt
en binnenscharrelend blaast en stampt,
ontdooit, en keurt wat geurt en dampt,
met tintelvingers om de kop.

De roodborst in zijn kleine taal
roept aan het raam om zìjn onthaal,
en door een muurspleet van het huis
verschijnt de bruine hazelmuis
en neemt een nootje van de schaal.

Hoedt nu het vuur, en hoedt elkaar
dat ge in de kentering van het jaar,
als straalt Arkturus aan de lucht,
de gouden uren niet ontvlucht.
Kom, winter, met uw kou, uw tucht.

DE ZWARTE KAT

Hij voert onmerkbaar het gezag,
de kat: om hem wentelt de dag;
het werk wordt op het erf hervat
als híj komt uit het keldergat

die, wéér op veldtocht in de nacht,
zijn rattental heeft omgebracht,
vervolger van het vaal gespuis
van hooizolder tot onderhuis.

Nog woedt het in hem na: hij kromt
de sterke zwarte rug en gromt;
wie zag toen heel de hoeve sliep
de kwade kansen die hij liep?

De zon komt op: zijn feilloos oog
ontwaart de stijging van haar boog;
het starend zwart, nu klimt het licht,
versmalt van cirkel tot ellips.

Treed terug voor zijn geheimenis,
dat gij met uw verstand niet vat.
Of hij van voor de tijden is:
van mensen wars—Ramses de kat.

WINTERWENDE

Een zonsopgang als een archaïsch schild,
met wakken goud en koperrood en zwart;
barbaars en prachtig.—En diagonaal
steeds vluchten wilde ganzen, wigsgewijs.
Ik heb het goud der Thraciërs gezien,
verbijsterd omgaand langs die weidse pracht,
welhaast in tranen om de lovertak,
de lauwerkroon van bladgoud die er lag.
Doch aards was het nochtans. Maar dit wat ik
u te vertellen tracht,—het was een wenk
van gene zijde reeds.—Mijn liefste, niet meer lang.

BRUILOFTSSPEL
Allegro ma non troppo

Ik zag in alle vroegte op een holle weg
in het zilvergrijze zand een choreografie.

Twee duiven hadden hier, en niemand die het wist,
met trippelende pas een minnedans gedanst,

in een zeer hoofse trant: een préambule wellicht;
het snoer der voetjes was te volgen op het pad.

Hier speelden zij hun spel, de doffer en de duif;
de doffer die zijn duifje buigend noodt ten dans,

het duifje dat coquet haar kuisheid spreidt ten toon,
het hoofdje schuin, de voetjes spits als tot verweer.

En midden in het snoer, tussen twee berken in,
was er een plek van enkel cirkels om elkaar.

Van alles wat hier bij zonsopgang was geschied,
heb ik dan mogen zien, eer het werd weggewist,

de choreografie: als een Japanse prent;
het hiërogram der werving, in het zand geëtst.

BERGWERELD

Hoor! de herder blaast zijn horen;
uit de witte nevelen heffen
zich met traag geblaat de schapen;
aan de hemel in het westen
gaat de maansikkel verbleken.

Lente-evening in de bergen,
wending na een nacht vol sterren.

Hoor! de herder blaast zijn horen;
voor de schapen gaat de hamel.

In het klimmend daglicht opent
zich het uitzicht op de dalen,
de maeander van het water.

HET SCHIP DE NOORD
In honorem J.H. Leopold

Een jongen, haast nog kind, heeft het gegeven,
als eergeschenk: het varen 's morgens vroeg;
de wind die in de ochtend gaat herleven,
het breken van het water op de boeg;

de zon die op de schemering gaat winnen,
en—of er iets van vroeger werd geheeld—
de vreugde om de dag die mag beginnen,
het licht dat met het vlietend water speelt.

De zaligheid van staande op de steven,
te ontwaren in dat rimpelende schrift
het vers, aan moeite en pijn en tijd ontheven,
dat werd geschreven met de zilverstift.

GEDICHT GEVONDEN IN EEN LADE

Zevenster van zeven regels,
door een kinderhand geschreven.
Zonder naam en zonder jaartal.
Zeven: en juist in het midden
komt die argeloze wending;
een enjambement dat spelend
mij ontwapent—dat ik reken,
vechtend met mijn dwaze tranen,
tot die morgenlijke wonderen
die de nieuwe dag voorafgaan,

die het grote kwaad ontkrachten.

HET DOCHTERTJE VAN JAÏRUS

Zij zagen haar verwonderd aan,
het meisje dat was opgestaan.

Alsof zij slechts geslapen had.
Hij hield haar bij de hand gevat.

Het rouwmisbaar, het klaaggeluid,
de stoornis is het huis al uit.

Stil nu: hij stelt als simpele wet
dat haar wat brood wordt voorgezet.

—Dat wat een wonder is van taal
ik las als kind het honderdmaal

en wist: 'en 's avonds was er feest,
er zijn vriendinnetjes geweest.'

Daar waar de dood zich had verschanst
werd bij de zilveren fluit gedanst.

De Adelaarsvarens

Voor Marie van der Zeyde

Een kind slaapt naast zijn schelp, nog ongeschonden,
de winnaar naast de lauwer hem gewonden;
ik lig nog wakker: stil beschijnt de lamp
het blad—uw brief van overzee gezonden.

Steeds weer Uw opdracht. Wat weet ìk
omtrent de tijd mij nog vergund?
Gij alleen kent mijn hete schrik
en het ondeelbaar ogenblik
dat ik opnieuw de stilus punt.

Langzaam opent zich het inzicht
dat een werkelijk vers iets levends
is, van stonden aan een wonder.

Langzaam opent zich het inzicht
dat het licht van binnenin is
wat die wisseling geeft van tinten.

Langzaam opent zich het inzicht
dat geen mensenkind kan weten
waar de herkomst van het vers ligt.

TOT SAPPHO

Kostbaar is mij alles van u;
ik nader het niet dan met schroom.
Maar ik buig onvoorwaardelijk het hoofd
voor wat eigenlijk niet is voltooid;
alsof het nog woont in de droom,
alsof het nog is in het vlies.
—Het onvoldragene dat leeft
in de schoot van de moeder; het heeft
bewogen, het kondigt zich aan.

Voor de balletmeester

Alles is pas aangevangen.
Ongemeten zijn de kansen:
Orpheus liet de stenen dansen.

APOLLINISCH

Sneller dan de mensen zijn de herten,
sneller dan de herten is de zwaluw;
sneller dan de zwaluw mijn gedachten,
die naar verre verten, ijlings, ijlings
uitgaan, liefste, om u te bereiken.

Die een godheid in zijn vlucht bijtijden
kruist, en zwenkende herschept tot verzen
die, mij nieteling ontvliedend, derwaarts
ingaan in de reidans, in de cirkeling.
Die ik zelf nog zag, met hete tranen.

De grote zomer heeft zijn tijd gehad,
de herfst begint, het vallen van het blad.
Het is voor het eerst, als het begint te dagen,
dat het palet des hemels zwart bevat.

IN DROEFENIS

Geen die het mensenhart begrijpt.
De mei was in de bloesembomen
toen mij de liefste werd ontnomen.
Geen die het mensenhart begrijpt:
de tranen wilden mij niet komen.

Geen die het mensenhart begrijpt:
het weer had 's nachts zijn keer genomen,
ik zag de wereld wit berijpt.
En ik liet vrij mijn tranen stromen.
Geen die het mensenhart begrijpt.

AEQUINOCTIUM

Die kortste dag, die langste nacht,
zij doen voor mij, een stokoud mens,
in feite niet veel meer ter zake.
Ik heb nochtans een hartewens:
dat haast onmerkbaar rijzen en dalen,
die lichte schommeling der schalen,
voorjaars- en najaarsevening,
nog éénmaal mee te mogen maken.

HET ZEEPAARDJE

Raadsel der raadselen achter glas,
zeepaard dat staande rijst en daalt
en in het water ademhaalt;
een Parthenon-paard van Phidias,
maar dan oneindig fijn verkleind
en door de oceaan gelijnd.

Raadsel der raadselen; wie van ons,
wezens van ander element,
sprakeloos voor dit paard van brons
dat ogen heeft van amethyst,
staat níet aan de aanvang en erkent
dat hij nog nooit iets zeker wist?

ΔΟΣ ΜΟΙ ΠΟΥ ΣΤΩ

Hoe moeten wij onszelf verstaan,
een wars en Prometheïsch ras,
vervreemd en uit uw hand vandaan?
De ode die van Sappho was
lichtte geen aarde uit haar as.
Geen Hooglied wijzigde haar baan.
En eenzaam is zijn weg gegaan
die Cheops schiep.—Hij riep u aan;
hij zocht het punt waar hij kon staan.

VOORTEKENEN
Rotterdam 1939

Van Koblenz af was er steeds mist geweest.
De Baseler nachttrein meldde zich vertraagd
in Rotterdam. Onder de stalen kap
riep de portieren langs een spoorwegman:
'Niet uitstappen! Het laatste stuk moet nog
over de wissel heen.' De trein stond stil.
En ik zag bij de klok van het perron
mijn vader staan. Hij zag mij pas toen ik
vlak bij was. Kou kwam van zijn winterjas.
'Dag vader! Heeft u al die tijd gewacht?'
'Dat viel best mee. Geef mij die tas maar vast.
Zeg kind, wat ben ik blij dat je er bent.'
Wij liepen het perron af. 'Vader, was
mijn kaart uit Basel er?' 'Dat medaillon
van Holbein van Erasmus? Nu en of!
Geef mij een arm. Ze breken in zijn stad
het asfalt alvast op. Het zint mij niet:
de tijd is ongewis.' Een rode zon
verscheen in vlammen aan de oosterkim,
een lichtelaaie zwartgerande brand.
Een aanzegging boven de havenstad.

Ierse nacht

De sterrennacht gaat haast het oog te boven.
De lichten op de verre hoeve doven.
Tussen de brem vervolgt de vos zijn tocht
om, nu de herder slaapt, een lam te roven.

DE SLACHTLAMMEREN

De hondsdagen met rosse hitte,
van onweer drachtig, en geladen
met onbestemde haat en angsten,
voorzeggen dat het onderweg is.
—En in de nacht tevoren is er
dat vragend blaten van de lammeren
en het schorre antwoord van de ooien:
een voorgevoel van naderend onheil.
En, steeds weer overrompelend, is het
er 's morgens: het vervaarlijk schreeuwen,
het driftig klappen van de hekken;
het nors cordon dat stokkenzwaaiend
de lammeren opeist, de onnozelen.
—En onder duizendvoudig blaten
van de beangste moederschapen
en het hinniken van schichtige paarden
wordt gemelijk het bevel voltrokken;
tot aan de ontdekte allerlaatste,
de kleine smekende verstekeling,
gehaast in het wagenkrat geworpen.

En zij zijn weg gelijk zij kwamen,
de mannen met de dorenstokken.

Om huis en stallen hangt beklemmend
een stank van zweet en mest en modder;
wij mijden zwijgend, als bij afspraak,
het drassig land vol wagensporen.

Volgen, als steeds, de twee etmalen
des aanklagens: het koor der ooien.
Om hen die niet meer zijn schreit Rachel.
En op de derde morgen, steevast,
of er geen kindermoord geschied was,
is heel de kudde aan het grazen.
   Doch als wij trachten door de modder
ons stap voor stap een weg te banen,
is bij het hek de wacht betrokken.
Twee machtige rammen. Vast voornemens
hun horens door ons heen te stoten.

A FAIRY TALE

Op de witte steen gezeten
midden in het groene veld,
doet kabouter Aulos weten
nu hij honderd jaren telt,
dat hij deze dag der dagen
zijn muziek wil overdragen.

En de wind verspreidt de mare:
vrolijk op dit minnelijk teken
komen uit vier hemelstreken
jong en oud, een bonte schare,
en verwerft zich deze ure
een bouquet van partituren.

Kleine kinderen, hen verblijden
liedjes van vier jaargetijden,
statige cantoren talen
naar motet en madrigalen;
schuchtere jonge liefdesparen
vragen iets voor fluit en snaren.

Tot het donkert.——Leeggegeven
als een zonnebloem van zaden,
wetend zich in Gods genade,
legt na honderd jaren leven
hij zich op het mos te slapen.
Wie die hem straks op zal rapen?

Als een veertje is zijn gewicht.
Elfen, komt: uw last is licht.

DE REISKAMERAAD

Op een onaards uur vertrokken,
wars van alles, zonder reisplan,
elke overlegging mijdend
en mij weidend in mijn vrijheid
bij het dansen van de draden,
weet ik feestelijk in mijn jaszak
het kompas, dat onder Arkel
ik als kind eens op een morgen
heb gevonden in de wegberm.

Dat mijn trots was, dat het nog is,
dat ik Boreas gedoopt heb.
Waaraan nooit iets gemankeerd heeft.
Of ik zuidwaarts ga of zigzag,
onomkoopbaar, onverbiddelijk
richt zich de magneetnaald noordwaarts.
Eindelijk reizen wij weer samen,
twee die bij elkander horen,
twee die aan elkaar gewaagd zijn.

1980

BRIEFKAART AAN M.

Bericht van hier: de rogge heeft gestoven.
Weer onverwacht, weer elk begrip te boven.
Een wolk van stuifmeel en van zonnegloed;
een geur van brood, warm uit de bakkersoven.

In nevelen

Opgedragen aan Ben Hosman

RONDEEL
Voor mannenstem

Ik heb mij in mijn liefste vergist;
ik ga mijn wegen in nevel en mist.
Zij was in mijn dromen bij dag en bij nacht,
zij is niet gekomen, ik had haar verwacht.

Zij heeft mij gesmaad om mijn povere staat.
Ik werk, ik vind mijn brood niet op straat.
Ik heb mij in mijn liefste vergist;
ik ga mijn wegen in nevel en mist.

Ik heb eens gevonden in weer en in wind
een schelp ongeschonden, ik was nog een kind.
Ik had hem verkoren, zijn glans ging verloren;
ik weet voor mijn leven iets wat ik niet wist.
Ik heb mij in mijn liefste vergist.

Vredesoptocht (Amsterdam, 21 november 1981)

De dag van het verzet is aangebroken:
de voeten gaan, de toortsen zijn ontstoken.
In kinderharten is, half dromend nog,
de trots van mee te mogen gaan ontloken.

Utrecht, Janskerkhof

November. Allerzielen. Lichte maan.
De binnenstad verstilt, de kerk gaat aan.
Een klok begint te luiden. Allerwegen
ziet men gebogenen met bloemen gaan.

HET BELOOFDE LAND

Een koopman met een tros ballonnen
riep op de Dam: 'wie maakt me los?'
Een man werd door zijn roep gewonnen
en kwam en kocht de hele tros.

En mensen, elk met zijn gedachten,
zonder te weten wat hen trok,
vormden een kring rondom en wachtten
of de tros los kwam van de stok.

En die hem kocht en vrij mocht geven
trad zwijgend midden in de kring.
Het werd zeer stil. Hij wachtte even
en trok de koorden van de ring.

En dansend was hij al ontstegen,
die van ons ieder medenam
wensen een leven lang verzwegen,
en zweefde boven Amsterdam.

Hoog, hoog boven de Westertoren
zagen wij hem in de avond gaan;
tot wij hem uit het oog verloren,
de druiventros van Kanaän.

DE ZESTIGSTE VIERING

Te middernacht daalt stap voor stap
de prior van de keldertrap,
en kiest waar de gewelven zijn
een fles belegen rode wijn.

Het klooster slaapt, de poort is dicht;
de lange gang is zonder licht.
Hij vindt de refter op de tast
en neemt twee glazen uit de kast.

En schikt waar het kapittel is
de kelken in een vensternis.
In het ondeelbare moment
wordt er een bladzij omgewend.

En hij en de afwezige ander
beleven het weer met elkander:
het uur der vriendschap, het verbond
dat zelfs de bittere dood niet schond.

Bijeen: in ernst en argeloosheid,
er wordt gelachen en geschreid;
dan, na het lang verbeid begin,
zet de muziek der stilte in.

Een verre haan betrekt de wacht
en meldt de kentering van de nacht
alom. Het komend ogenblik
ontrooft het gij, ontrooft het ik.

De maan verbleekt, de dag breekt aan.
Voorbij,—de ander is gegaan.
Gegaan. Hij is een jaar reeds ver,
verdwenen met de morgenster.

Neen, niet de ouders die ons vroeg verloren;
zelfs niet de liefste die ons heeft verkoren.
De vriendschap is het die de vrijheid wekt
waartoe wij uit het donker zijn geboren.

JONGENSVRIENDSCHAP

Zien wat niemand ooit aanschouwde,
gaan waar niemand is gegaan;
ver van òns. Op kusten aan
waar geen zeil zich nog vertrouwde.

Wat de zeewind meldt verstaan.

IJlend, ijlend naast elkaar,
klaar de stormen te verduren:
een helogig vogelpaar
koersend op de Dioscuren.

Van de meester-beeldhouwer

Kies wat uw beitel nìet bevalt:
het bar graniet, het zwart bazalt.

PELGRIMSTOCHT

Hervonden na tien jaren tijds
de plek waar geen sterveling komt.
Waar het stil is als in een crypt.
Waar zij zijn, in blauw-zwarte lei.
Twee adelaarsvarens, manshoog,
vereeuwigd fossiel in de steen.
Ik adem, ik heb het bereikt.

Er komt mistige kou van de wand
waar hun werend domein is, waar zij
ongenaakbaar, met zwijgend gezag,
mij doen weten dat ik nìets weet.

Het wandtapijt dat heel de zaal beslaat
is door de mot geschonden, draad na draad;
de jonge vorst, door zorgen aangevreten,
verliest zijn glans, zijn koninklijke staat.

DE WIJNKRUIK SPREEKT

Wat zal u straks ontzegelen, edele wijn,
een bruiloftsmaaltijd of een oogstfestijn?
Wordt gij geplengd voor een beweende dode,
geheven bij een vriendensamenzijn?

Bewaard voor vorsten en hun disgenoten
zal ik worden vermorst, zinloos vergoten,
waar, bij een hooggelopen woordentwist,
een vriend het lemmet door zijn vriend zal stoten.

HET SIGNAAL

Het onweer heeft mij haast ontzind.
Het sloeg, een hoeve verder, in.
Nu, bij het aarzelend dagbegin,
rammeit er een op luik en blind
en wijt mij dat hij mij niet vindt,
en gaat met hagelstenen aan.

En maant en maant mij, te verstaan:
'doe open! het wordt zuidenwind.'

DE MAALTIJD
17 december 1987

Bewaard de gave tafelronde
der vrienden, die elkaar hervonden.
Een samenzijn als in de tuin
van Epicurus. Ongeschonden.

De toverwoorden

Opgedragen aan Ad ten Bosch

HET HUIS 'DE DRIE ABEELEN'

Nog als voorheen. Een ongeschonden droom.
De witte hoeve aan de waterzoom.
Nog als voorheen, vertakt boven de voordeur,
sterk en voornaam gesmeed de levensboom.

DE TOVERWOORDEN
Het huis De drie Abeelen, 1912

Een sprookjesboek dat open lag,
een kind dat heel die zomerdag
verdoken in het rietgras lag.
En nu ligt het, te bed gebracht,
niet talend nog naar slaap of nacht,
klaar wakker: om alleen te wezen
met wat daarginds het heeft gelezen.
Hoe het begon en verder ging;
en toeft in de herinnering.
Hoe was het toch, dat wat zij las,
dat einde dat zo prachtig was?
Vlakbij is het, en ook ver af.

Het laatste zonlicht is vergaan,
het donkert aan het zolderraam.
En in de schemering hervindt
zij als vanzelf wat zij zag staan.
Het ritselt in het dakgebint:
'Dat is de wind, het hemelse kind.'

Herfsttij. Het groen der bladeren is vergaan;
de uittocht van de zwaluwen vangt aan.
De trotse zwaan ziet de opvlucht van zijn jongen,
om dan hen aan de ruimte af te staan.

CONFRONTATIE
Rijksmuseum Amsterdam

De Zwaan van Asselijn die levensgroot
het hele doek diagonaal beslaat
en uitwijst met gezag, de vleugels wijd,
die waagt te naderen tot zijn areaal.

Een aartszwaan, strijdbaar op het nest bedacht,
waar driftig wat nog amper is beveerd
het daglicht zoekt en tikt tegen de schaal.
En straks zich onvervaard te water waagt.

En wie hier achteloos denkt voorbij te gaan
of omkeert op zijn schreden en blijft staan,
hij wordt gedagvaard tot een kort geding.
Het eindeloos verdaagd verhoor vangt aan:
'Wat hebt gìj met uw kinderen gedaan?'

OMZIEN IN DEERNIS

Zij die geboden en verboden
liggen onder de groene zoden.

En gij, aan wie het is geschied,
hun kind—laat hen niet zo alleen,
wanneer ge op de grijze steen
hun jaartallen en namen ziet.

BEKENTENIS

Ik kan langs vlakke velden gaan,
ik kan op hoge bergen staan,—
ik kan geen ogenblik vergeten
wat kinderen is aangedaan.

HET MEISJE MET DE ZWAVELSTOKKEN
(Andersen)

Zij was van kind af mij nabij,
het meisje met de zwavelstokken;
en nu sinds kort zij blijkt vertrokken
is het wat vreemd en leeg in mij.

Misschien word ik te oud. Misschien
—het gaat mij beter dan tevoren—
heb ik haar uit het oog verloren.
Ik weet: ik zal haar niet meer zien.

IN MEMORIAM

Van zijn boek opziend vroeg het kind:
'Wat is dat toch, een labyrinth?'
Mijn kleine prins, gij rozendoolhof,
geen mens die meer uw paden vindt.

DE BESCHERMER

Hij heeft het weer geklaard. Zijn vlieger staat:
een adelaar boven de waddenplaat.
Tot hem zendt dit vereenzaamd kind zijn vragen:
briefje na briefje, opwaarts langs de draad.

THE CHILD IS FATHER OF THE MAN

Kent gij het spel der lente wel?
dat neigen van een bloemenveld
waarover licht en schaduw snelt;
de kleurenwisseling van de wei
gevat binnen de heuvelrij.

En er komt een voorbij, een kind,
en ziet het meegaan met de wind
en blijft verbaasd, grootogig staan.
Het zucht, het kan de pracht niet aan,
en is gelukkig en alleen.

Dan maant een klokslag en hij gaat.
Het dooft, het lichtend klein gelaat.
—Gedenk de jongen met zijn tas,
het schoolkind dat een kroonprins was,
als gij uw Shakespeare openslaat.

INTOCHT

Kampen, april 1946

Zij komen uit de verte aan,
gereed er zich weer door te slaan,
de werkers van het eerste uur,
die steeds met vieren naast elkaar
en pal gebogen op het stuur,
uit Genemuiden en Zwartsluis
windomwaaid en met wapperend haar
het laatste schoolkwartaal ingaan.
Vooraan bereiden hun de baan,
de bijnaam dragend van 'het gruis',
die straks hun eerste Grieks verslaan.
Ik krijg hen in dit vroege licht,
hier waar ik op de kade sta,
steeds duidelijker in het zicht.
Daar komen er waarachtig twee
—zij doen de anderen uitgeleide—
die, teugels losjes om de pols,
een ongezadeld paard berijden.
Boers en klassiek, niet te geloven.

Toen was het, waar ik stond alleen,
dat mij het Parthenon-fries verscheen:
te paard te voet de ephebenstoet,
opgaand, Athene tegemoet;
vereeuwigd in de marmersteen.
Het was er even en verdween.

En weer gewend naar wie daar kwamen
—en ik zag hen door tranen heen—
wist ik dat ook dit Hellas was.
De tijden waren niet gescheiden.
Heeft één van hen dit ook geweten?
En nader kwamen zij en nader.

Ik ben, ook zelf een poldermens,
het tot op heden niet vergeten,
wat ik te zeggen nauw vermag:
die winderige lentedag
dat ik het fries van Phidias,
dat ik The Elgin Marbles zag.

RUYSDAEL

Terwijl de meid de was spoelt bij de vlonder,
ziet het kind, meegelopen, hoe er onder
het water ook weer witte wolken zijn.
En knotwilgen: het hollandse godswonder.

IN HET VOORBIJGAAN

Gisteren heb ik zomaar een naam gespeld,
een Rijnaak onder Ochten langsgevaren.
In één moment kon ik het woord ontwaren:
Argo, helwit op een azuren veld.

Toch nog?—Mijzelf in blindlezen bekwamen?
De halve nacht spelde ik arkennamen.

EEN GRAFSCHRIFT

Geloof van mij, gij die mijn naam hier leest,
ik heb de dood van kind af nooit gevreesd.
Hij was vertrouwd.—Het ondoorgrondelijk leven
is mij de donkere despoot geweest.

DE SIDDERAAL

En toen het Paasvacantie was,
ontwaarde ik op een maartse dag
ergens in zo'n versmald kanaal
—men zegt hier ook wel trek of tocht—
een middelgrote sidderaal.
De sloot was schoon, de lucht zo klaar
dat hij in het water werd weerkaatst.
En in dat omgekeerd gewelf
stond, of het in een spiegel was,
dit schepsel van de vijfde dag.

Steeds strevende omhoog beseft
het, kronkelend van staart tot kop,
dat het niet uit zichzelf kan treden;
alleen, bevreesd, een raadselbeest.
En wie het aanraakt krijgt een schok.
En als het zich in kronkels wringt,
schrijft het mij: 'is het leven dan
een levenslang van angst en pijn?'
Wie ik dan niet of wel mag zijn,
bescherm mij, God, tegen mijzelf.

RIVIERBAKEN
Gorcum, 22 april 1988

Daar waar het water was,
daar waar het, later, wás
wat ik als kind al wist.

Daar waar het water is,
daar waar het baken is
waarin het is gegrift.

CAFÉ HET PUTTERTJE

Het is een klein en landelijk café,
dat door een stokoud echtpaar wordt beheerd.
Het is er 's avonds stil. Men praat er niet.
Tenzij er iets opmerkelijks geschiedt:
een schaker die te laat zijn dame ziet
schaak staan. Een plotseling collé.

Men ziet welwillend op bij mijn entree;
ik groet, ik houd mij strikt aan mijn gebied.
Er is een tafeltje gereserveerd.
Eindelijk. Einde van de Odyssee.
Koffie. Denken en werken, ongedeerd.

Het Boerenbedrijf

Een vertaling van Vergilius' *Georgica*

Aan de nagedachtenis van
dr. Johanna Goekoop de Jongh († 25 november 1946)
—*haar laatste arbeid was de revisie van dit manuscript*—
en aan
dr. Marie H. van der Zeyde
—*haar dankt deze vertaling ontstaan en voltooiing.*—

Andes, bij Mantua, waar het landgoed van den ouden Maro bloeit. *De schuren staan er tot berstens toe gevuld met de veldvrucht, krachtige slaven verrichten den arbeid, het blanke vee gedijt op de vochtige weiden, de ranken van de wijndruif slingeren zich door de olmkroon, en Ceres zegent den akker. Toch is er een zorg, die den meester de wenkbrauw doet fronsen. 'Vergilius' roept hij luid door het woonhuis, 'de bijen gaan zwermen, kom, leid ze naar een rustplaats met den bekkenslag.' Doch een antwoord wordt er niet vernomen. Een andermaal draagt hij een knecht op, zijn jongen voor het brandmerken der bokjes te halen, maar er wordt vergeefs gezocht op het erf en in de bijgebouwen. De seizoenen rijen zich als tot een schoonen dans aan elkander; de dag komt, dat men de geiten en schapen naar het woud en naar het grasland moet drijven, de teenen honingkorven uit moet rooken, en ze voor de kracht van den zongloed met frisch loof moet bedekken; de tijd breekt aan, dat de maaiers naakt naar het veld gaan, en de sikkels door de halmen doen zingen, dan volgt de maand, dat de Falernische druif wordt gesneden; echter onder de herders en oogsters vindt men Vergilius niet.*

Intusschen schuilt hij, wiens naam vragend genoemd wordt, achter den koestal bij den hagedoorn, en niemand merkt daar de kleine en magere gedaante in den grauwen hemdrok op. Vanuit de plek, waar hij zich verborgen houdt, overziet hij de vlakte; maar het is niet om naar het grazige landschap en het opflikkeren van den door de zon beschenen stroom te kijken, dat hij hier neerduikt. Hij wacht op een heuglijker wonder, en het verlangen er naar doet hem huiveren. Dagelijks wordt het langs het weipad aan de haag voorbijgeleid. Een baardeloos man met de statuur van een godheid voert het voor aan den breidel. Hij is jeugdig en krachtig en breed in de schouders; o, maar het paard zelf, Vergilius heft er aanbiddend de handen voor op. Het praalt in de kleur van de sneeuw op een bergtop, en als het de heg is genaderd, spert het de neusgaten open; lillend schuim bespat de flanken, en steigerend rijst het als een zeegolf voor de blauwte van de strakke zomerlucht.

Vaak doet de jonge Maro navraag bij de slaven, maar geen die van den hengst of zijn bezitter te berichten weet. Zoo gaat de tijd voort, en draagt den innigen geur van een onbevredigd begeeren. Tot, op een avond, nadat moeder voor het laatst haar schietspoel door de schering heeft geworpen, en vader de schuren heeft gegrendeld, en voor de knechten versch stroo om de haardplaat heeft gespreid, Vergilius zacht uit het huis sluipt. De maan is opgestegen en beschijnt de geweldige hoefprenten, die op de klei staan ingeplant. Dit spoor wordt gevolgd, terwijl het hart den knaap in den boezem zoo wild is als een vogel, die de vlerken tegen de spijlen van zijn kevie slaat. Plotseling weergalmt een luid schallend brieschen, en een toornig stampen werpt den omgewoelden bodem op. Maar als het witte paard, dat een blauwen glans krijgt in het licht van den avond, den knaap herkend heeft, die hem achter de stallen bij de meiheg heeft bespied, nadert het langzaam, legt den kop op Vergilius' schouder, buigt dan de knieën en zoodra hij den last op den rug voelt, spreidt hij twee purperen vleugelen open, doet de donkere aarde onder een slag van de hoeven verzinken, en draagt zijn berijder omhoog naar de sterren.

Aart van der Leeuw

Georgica

De akkers

Wat rijkdom geeft van graan, bij welke ster de akker,
Maecenas, moet gekeerd en om de olm de wijnrank
geleid, wat zorg het vee vereist en 't schapenhouden
en hoe gekend wil zijn het spaarzaam volk der bijen,—
dit wil ik zingen.—Gij, stralende wereldlichten,
die langs het firmament 't verschuivend jaar wilt leiden;
Liber en milde Ceres, als op aarde uw gave
Chaonië's eikel voor de gulle aar verruild heeft
en de Acheloüs-drank mengt met de ontdekte druiven;
ook gij, wier macht en hulp de boer gewaar wordt, Faunen
—danst aan tezamen, Faunen en Dryadenmeisjes—:
ik zing uw gaven. Help ook gij, die in de aanvang
het briesend paard de grond uitsloeg met zware drietand,
Neptunus; woudbewoner dan, voor wie op Ceos
sneeuwblank driehonderd stieren 't sappig blad afgrazen;
Pan zelf, laat uw vertrouwde bos op de Lycaeus,
schapenbeschermer: als de Maenala uw zorg heeft,
verschijn en help, Tegeër; en gij, die de olijf schiep,
Minerva; knaap die de gebogen ploeg ons aanbracht;
Silvanus, een ontworteld jong cypresje dragend:
goden en godinnen alle, die beschermt genegen
het veld, die nieuwe planten ongezaaid laat groeien
en 's hemels regenruisen op het zaad doet dalen.
Dàn gij—in welke godenraad gij eens zult tronen
is ondoorgrond nog, Caesar; voert uw tocht door steden,
wilt gij de landen hoeden en mag de grote aarde

[27-57]

als gever van de wasdom, heer van weer en winden
u groeten, als Venus' zoon met myrte u bekransend?
Of komt ge als god der wijde wateren, eert de zeeman
uw macht alleen en buigt voor u het verre Thule,
en brengt u Tethys' dochter 't zeeënrijk als bruidsschat?
Of voegt ge als nieuw gesternte u bij de trage maanden,
waar 't sterrenbeeld der Maagd en Scorpio daarnevens
plaats biedt,—reeds trekt tesaam de Schorpioen, hoe fel ook,
zijn scharen en laat uw teken overmaat van ruimte.
Wat god gij wordt (u vraagt geen Tartarus tot koning,
zomin gij zulk onzalig heersen zoudt begeren
—al wordt Elysium door Griekenland verheerlijkt
en keert Proserpina niet weer op moeders vragen—):
geef mij een goede tocht en steun mijn stout beginnen
en wees—in deernis voor de landman en zijn dwalen—
mijn gids, nu reeds vertrouwd met der geloften aanroep.

Vroeg in het voorjaar, als de sneeuw op 't grijs gebergte
smelt en bij westenwind de grond weer gaat ontdooien,
moet de os al door de zware bodem trekken, zwoegend,
de ploeg, 't gesleten ijzer blinken in de vore.
En hoe inhalig ook, de boer houdt niets te wensen
bij 't land dat tweemaal zon en tweemaal kou gevoeld heeft;
zijn oogst is meer dan rijk en doet de schuren kraken.
Maar eer ons kouter grond, nog onbekend, gaat scheuren,
moet wèl van wind en weer de wisseling geleerd en
van grondgesteldheid en bewerking de traditie:
wat een speciale streek graag heeft en wat er nièt gaat.
Hier is het goed voor graan, daar doet de druif het prachtig,
elders wordt fruit geteeld en groent vanzelf het grasland.
Gij ziet, de Tmolus schenkt ons reukwerk van saffranen,
Indië ivoor, zijn wierook het verfijnde Scheba;

[58-89]

naakt delft Chalybië ijzer, bevergeil narcotisch
heeft Pontus; paarden—Elis' prijswinnaars—Epirus.
Zo heeft aanstonds haar eeuwige wet en vaste grenzen
natuur gesteld aan elk gebied, sinds dat Deucalion
over de ontvolkte aarde slingerde zijn stenen,
waaruit de mens ontstond, een hard geslacht. Welaan dan:
een vette grond moet dadelijk, in de vroegste maanden,
gekeerd door sterke ossen; en de open kluiten
kan in de zomer dan de volle zon verpulveren.
Maar is de bodem schraal, dan kan—vlak voor Arcturus'
opgang—volstaan er los de ploeg doorheen te halen:
zo krijgt op zware grond het graan geen last van onkruid,
en uit het schrale zand haalt ge niet alle vocht weg.
Ge kunt het stoppelland ook om 't jaar laten liggen,
dat de vermoeide grond op krachten komt als braakland;
òf—als het jaar gaat kenteren—gouden tarwe zaaien
waar ge eerst de dikke, rammelende bonenpeulen
plukte of wik met platte vruchtjes en de bittere
lupine—brosse stelen en ritselende zaden.—
Schraal immers maakt het vlas de grond en schraal de haver;
schraal de papaver, zwaar van slaap en doods vergeten.
Toch, wisselbouw is makkelijk: wees niet te kieskeurig
alleen om dorre grond flink te bemesten of over
't van dracht vermoeide land het asvat om te keren.
Ook zo krijgt de akker rust, door wisseling van producten,
en 't land, schoon onbeploegd, is toch niet zonder luister.
Vaak helpt men uitgeputte grond ook door te branden
en 't knettervuurtje door het stoppelstro te jagen:
't kan dat daaruit de grond verborgen voedingssappen
en krachten haalt, òf dat het vuur wat niet deugt grondig
uitbrandt en 't overtollig water kan verdampen.
Of wel, die hitte maakt meer poriën en luchtkanalen

vrij ondergronds, waardoor 't gewas nieuw sap kan trekken;
tenzij dit juist de open aderen strakker afsnoert:
geen motregen, geen stekend felle zonneblakering,
geen scherpe noorderkou vreet dan zich in de bodem.
—Om natte zomers bidt en heldere winters, boeren:
een poederdroge winter geeft de beste tarwe.—
Vooral wie met zijn hark de taaie kluiten fijnstoot,
of wilgenhorden erlangs trekt, hèlpt zijn grond: niet ziet hem
om nièt de blonde Ceres van Olympus' hoogten;
zo óók wie de aarderuggen, die het kouter opwierp,
nòg eens doorsnijdt, zijn ploeg in schuine richting kerend,
gestaag de grond bewerkt en hem zijn wil doet voelen;
dàn wordt het goed.—
         Slechts Mysië roemt zonder ontginning
zich rijk; Gargara zelf kan nauw zijn oogst geloven.—
Merk wie, als 't graan gestrooid is, aanpakt en—geen stukje
gronds overslaand—de pulverig droge bergjes platharkt;
dàn over 't veld de beek leidt, vlug vertakt in stroompjes,
en, als 't geblakerd land zijn planten slap laat hangen,
zie!—van een heuvelfrons een pad van afwaarts water
te voorschijn lokt!—Het valt, het ruist met schuren over
de gladde steen—een parelen koelt de dorre velden.
Ik prijs wie—dat de halm, te zwaar van aar, niet doorknikt—
van tè vroeg graan de jonge scheuten af laat grazen,
als 't juist boven de voor uitkomt,—ook wie bij drasland
door zuigend zand 't in plassen staande water afvoert;
vooral in kenteringsmaanden, als tot overstroming
het water wast en diep in 't land een slijklaag afzet,—
er blijven poelen staan, die klamme damp uitwasemen.

Maar toch, al hebben mens en dier met zwoegen de akker
gekeerd—de kwade gans, kraanvogels van de Strymon

[120-151]

en cichorei met bittere vezels zijn niet minder
een schade, of zonloos weer. De Vader zelf—hij wilde
moeizaam ontginnings gang; hij liet het eerst met kunde
het land bewerken, 's mensen geest door zorgen scherpend:
het slaperig bot versuffen duldt hij in zijn rijk niet.
Vóór Juppiter was er geen boer, die de akker ploegde;
afbakenen zelfs van land of met een wal verkavelen
werd niet geduld: gemeenschap kreeg de oogst en de aarde
droeg ongevraagd vanzelve alles des te guller.
Hij gaf de zwarte slang zijn dodend gif, hìj stuurde
de wolf op roof, hìj bracht de branding in de zeeën;
de honing schudde hij het blad af, sloot het vuur weg
en heeft gestuit de wijn, die overal vloot bij beken,
dat nood zich—zinnende—zou smeden tal van kunsten
allengs: de korenhalm zou speuren in de vore
en slaan uit vuursteenaderen de verborgen vonken.
Toèn voelde 't water de eerste bootjes, holle elzen,
toen vond de zeeman groepen en namen voor de sterren:
—Pleiaden, Hyaden en Lycaons heldere Arctos.—
Toen ging men 't wild met strikken, met de lijmstok vogels
verschalken, 't diepe bos omsingelen met de meute;
reeds gooit de visserman plat op de stroom zijn werpnet
breeduit,—een ander trekt het vochtig sleepnet zee door.
Toen kwam het harde ijzer, 't gieren van het zaagblad
—tevoren kloofde men het splijtbaar hout met wiggen—,
toen vaardigheden velerlei. Sterker dan alles
was koppig werk en nood, nijpend in harde tijden.
Ceres was 't, die de mens met ijzer leerde keren
de grond, toen 't heilig bos al haagappels en eikels
te weinig bood en hem Dodona niet meer voedde.
Nu kreeg het koren ook zijn plagen: aan de halmen
vrat kwade brand, en op het land stond stug en stekelig

de distel. Weg is de oogst, het ruigt schiet op bij plekken
—klis en driedistel—, midden in het gouden graanland
gaan hard raaigras en schrale wilde haver tieren.
Als gij niet met uw schoffel achter 't onkruid aanzit,
de vogels opschrikt met lawaai, een schaduwzware
boomgroep wat uitsnoeit en met bidden roept om regen,—
ach!—dan helpt straks geen kijken naar een anders voorraad:
't wordt in de bossen eikels schudden voor de honger.

Ook het gereedschap van de werkse boer vraagt aandacht;
want zonder dat zaait men geen graan en ziet geen wasdom:
de ploegschaar eerst, de ploeg, gebogen, van zwaar eiken,
traag dokkerende karren—Moeder Ceres heilig—,
dorswagen en dorsslee, de machtig zware eggen;
dan Celeos' nederig gerei uit wilgetwijgen,
horden van takken en de mystieke wan van Iacchus,—
vergeet niet alles lang te voren klaar te hebben,
wilt van 't gezegend land gij niet de glorie derven.
Al vroeg wordt in het bos met macht en kracht gebogen
een olm tot ploegboom, naar de kromme vorm zich voegend;
een dissel daaraan vast, acht voet vanaf de wortel,
twee oren en een ploeghout met een dubbele welving.
Men kapt nog eerst voor juk een lichte linde,—een beukschacht
voor handvat, dat 't beloop der voor van achteren regelt;
hang 't hout boven de haard: het vuur beproeft zijn weerstand.

Veel ouderwetse raad zou ik nog voor u hebben,
als gij uit ongeduld bij 't kleine werk niet wegloopt.
Zo dient de dorsvloer met de zware wals geëffend,
dan handgekeerd en met potaarde taai gebonden:
daar komt geen onkruid door, dat trekt geen scheuren uit droogte
en—kwaad gespuis heeft dan geen kans: een heel klein muisje
heeft dikwijls ondergronds èn huis en voorraadschuren;

[183-213]

hun gangen graven daar de mollen, dood van ogen,
of men vindt in zijn hol de pad—zoveel raar ontuig
komt uit de grond—; door hooggetaste tarwe werkt zich
de korenworm, de mier, benauwd voor late armoe.
En zie, als zich de amandel in het bos met weelde
van bloesems tooit en buigt de geur-beladen takken:
bij overdaad van bloei prijkt straks het graan gelijkelijk,
een volle zomer komt en vol valt er te dorsen.
Maar is de boom te dicht van blad, te zwaar van schaduw,
om niet komt—dik van kaf—het graan straks op de dorsvloer.
Vaak zag ik boeren zaad behandelen vóór het zaaien,
—er gaat een scheut natron of oliedroesem over—
om in de loze peul een dikker boon te krijgen,
die, ook boven een matig vuurtje, gauwer gaar komt.
Zaaigoed, zorgzaam gekeurd en eerste soort, ik zag het
tòch achteruitgaan, wanneer mensenhand niet jaarlijks
ijverig de grootste zaden uitlas. Hoe toch alles
onder een noodlot slechter wordt en machteloos afglijdt!
Het is of iemand moeizaam stroomopwaarts een schuitje
werkt met zijn riemen; èven laat hij de armen zakken—
mèt raakt hij in de zuiging en wordt meegetrokken.

Voorts gaat de sterrenstand—Arcturus, of de dagen
der Bokjes en de helle Draak—òns aan, zo goed als
de zeeman op zijn thuisvaart, die bij storm de Pontus
durft tarten en de straat van 't oesterrijk Abydus.
Zodra de Weegschaal effent dag- en slapensuren,
en deelt de wereld half in licht en half in schaduw,
uw ossen, boer, aan 't werk—uw gerst gezaaid op de akker,
vóór de eerste regens, inzet van de norse winter.
't Is zaaitijd ook voor vlas en voor papavers—Ceres
gewijd—, en tijd om voort zich op de ploeg te buigen;

[214-245]

nu kan het nog: de grond is droog, de wolken hangen.
't Voorjaar begint met bonen; in de rulle grond gaat
ook gij, luzerne, en dàn komt het seizoen voor gierst aan,
als weer de witte Stier met gulden horens opent
het jaar en dalend wijkt de Hondsster voor zijn naderen.
Maar als voor tarweoogst of forse spelt gij de akker
bereidt—wilt ge bepaald een veld van enkel aren—,
wacht dàn tot de Pleiaden ondergaan bij morgen
en terugtrekt Cnossos' stralend sterrenbeeld Corona,
eer ge 't benodigd zaad bergt in de voor,—vertrouw niet
onwillige aarde vóór de tijd de hoop des jaars toe.
Velen begonnen éér Maia onderging: bedrogen
heeft hen het lang verwacht gewas met loze aren.
Zo ge echter wik wilt zaaien of gewoon maar peulen
en teelt van linzen uit Pelusium niet te min vindt,
dan geeft Boötes dalend u zijn helder teken:
van dan af kunt ge zaaien en doorgaan tot het wintert.
Zo heerst in het heelal, verdeeld in vaste zônen,
de gouden zon, en trekt zijn baan door twaalf tekens.
Het hemelruim beslaan vijf velden: één ligt immer
ros in het zonneflitsen, door het vuur geblakerd;
rondom, ten versten rand, zijn links en rechts getrokken
de somber blauwe, star van ijs en zwart van regen.
Twee, tussen rand en midden, dankt het zwoegend mensdom
der goden gunst; hiertussen is de baan gesneden,
waarlangs in schuine stand de dierenriem kan wentelen.
De hemelkoepel, steil naar Scythië en 't Riphaeisch
gebergte rijzend, welft, en daalt naar 't Libysch zuiden.
Eén pool is steeds hoog boven ons, éen—onder onze
voeten—zien donkere Styx en diepe schimmenwereld.
Ter noordpool glijdt de lange Draak met kronkelbochten
als een rivier rondom en tussen beide Beren,

de Beren, schuw te duiken in Oceanus' wateren.
Ter zuidpool heerst, zo wordt gezegd, òf diep en zwijgend
eeuwige nacht—een wand van ondoordringbaar duister—
òf met de dag die ons verlaat rijst ginds de morgen,
en als ons vroeg het briesend zonnespan beademt,
ontsteekt dáár, roodgetint, Vesper de late lichten.
Zo kunnen wij het goed seizoen te voren weten
ook bij onzekere lucht: de zaaitijd en de maaitijd;
wanneer de riemslag door 't verraderlijke water
mag gaan, wanneer de vloot, getuigd, weer uit mag lopen,
of in het bos de pijnboom—goed op tijd—gekapt kan.
Niet vruchteloos volgt het oog de omloop der gesternten
in de evenmaat des jaars,—vier wisselende seizoenen.

Wanneer kil regenweer de boer een keer in huis houdt,
dan kan er veel, wat later bij goed weer gehaast moet,
alvast mooi vroeg gedaan: hij klopt de harde ploegschaar
die stomp werd bij; hij holt een boomstam uit tot troggen,
of geeft zijn schapen een merk, zijn korenhopen een nummer.
Anderen punten palen en gaffels, of verwerken
rijs uit Ameria tot bindteen voor de wijnrank.
Ook kunt ge vast uit twijgen lichte korfjes vlechten,
vast koren roosteren, vast het malen tussen stenen.
Zelfs op gewijde dagen is bepaald soort arbeid
geen zonde of overtreding: schoonmaken van greppels
hoeft u niet te bezwaren, een heg zetten om bouwland
màg—net als vogels strikken, dorenstruiken afbranden
of 't blatend schapenvolk in heilzaam water baden.
Op 't stapvoets ezeltje laadt vaak de drijver vrachten
olie of goedkoop fruit, en brengt een grof gebikte
molensteen of een klomp zwart pek terug uit stad mee.
De maan geeft ook een bonte rij van dagen, gunstig

voor arbeid. Schuw de vijfde: Eumeniden en vale
Orcus zijn toen verwekt; toen baarde Terra—gruwzaam—
Coeüs, Japetus, de vreselijke Typhoëus
en de tot 's hemels afbraak saamgezworen broeders.
Driemalen trachtten ze—stout stuk—op Pelion Ossa
te wentelen, en op Ossa 't woudgebergte Olympus,
driemalen spleet des Vaders bliksemschicht de stapeling.
De zeventiende dag kunt ge goed wingerd planten,
het jongvee vangen en temmen, en een nieuwe schering
opzetten. Negen is mooi voor drossers, kwaad voor dieven.
Veel werk ook laat zich beter in de koele nacht doen,
of als de zon opgaat en ochtenddauw op 't land ligt:
bij nacht wordt stoppelstro, bij nacht een droog stuk weiland
het best gemaaid; de nachtdauw maakt de halmen willig.
Soms blijft er een lang op, als 's winters laat de lamp brandt
en zit met een scherp mes fakkels uit hout te kerven.
Zijn huisvrouw in die tijd, haar lange taak met zingen
kortend, haalt door 't getouw de kam—een hoge trilling—
of laat boven het vuur de zoete most inkoken
en schuimt met blaadjes 't borrelend wijnsap in de pan af.
—Maar in midzomer wordt gemaaid het rosse koren,
in midzomer gedorst de zongerijpte garven.
Ploeg naakt, zaai naakt: de boer z'n luie tijd is 's winters.—
Als 't koud is mag de landman graag zich wat te goed doen,
of geeft om beurt de buurtschap welgezind een feestje.
Het winters gul onthaal doet alle zorg vergeten;
—zó komt een rijk bevrachte vloot wel thuisgevaren
en hangt het scheepsvolk blij de kransen om de stevens.
Toch—het is pluktijd nu voor eikels, laurierbessen,
olijven en bloedrode myrt; 't seizoen om strikken
te zetten voor kraanvogels, netten voor de herten,
te jagen op haas langoor en—met suizend touw van

[309-339]

de Baleaarse slinger—'t damhert neer te vellen,
als hoog het sneeuwdek ligt, als de rivieren kruien.

Herfsttij,—moet van zijn stormen en sterren ik verhalen,—
hoe, als de dagen korten en de zomer terugloopt,
de werker waaks moet zijn?—waaks ook als lente aanstormt
met regens, als reeds stug de aren op het veld staan,
en in de groene halmen zwelt de melken korrel?
Vaak heb ik, als de boer in 't gouden graan de maaiers
losliet en door de brosse gersthalm al de zicht ging,
de volle kracht der winden op elkaar zien stoten;
de zware aar met losgetrokken wortels sloegen
ze ver de lucht door,—dan nam in een donkere zuiging
de storm het mee: licht kaf en dwarrelende strootjes.
Vaak nadert aan de lucht een zware sleep van water;
tot boos noodweer, tot zwarte slagregens verdichten
de buien zich uit zee. Het uitspansel—aan flarden—
spoelt in een wolkbreuk de oogsten en het werk der ossen
weg. Greppels lopen vol, diepe rivieren wassen
hoorbaar,—het bruist in zee van wielingen en kolken.
En midden in die nacht van wolken voert de Vader
het schelle weerlicht,—slagen, waar de ganse aarde
bij siddert; dieren kruipen in hun holen, doodsangst
doorvaart de volken en trekt de mens het hart tesamen.
Zijn vlammenschicht treft Athos, Rhodope, het steile
Ceraunia; wilder wordt de storm, de regen dichter.
Bossen en stranden kreunen onder de zware vlagen.
Bescherm u dus: bereken sterren en seizoenen;
waar zich—in verre kou—de ster Saturnus terugtrekt,
hoe aan de lucht Mercurius zwerft in vuren banen.
Bovenal: eer uw goden; vier het jaarlijks feest van
de grote Ceres, offerend in het groene weiland,

[340-370]

kort na des winters uittocht, bij al helder voorjaar.
Dan zijn de lammeren vet, de wijn fluwelig zacht, dan
slaapt men zoet—diep is de schaduw in de bergen.
Laat heel het jonge landvolk rond u Ceres vieren,
smelt raathoning voor haar in melk en zachte wijn en
driemaal ga 't offerdier—tot zegen—rond het nieuwe
gewas. De ganse rei van juichende gezellen
volge, met het refrein 'Ceres, betreed dit huis' en
niemand sla de sikkel in het rijpe koren
vóór hij, het hoofd omkranst met eikeblaren, Ceres
eerde met boerse dans en met de aloude wijzen.

En, opdat wij het weten kunnen aan vaste tekens
als regen komt of hitte of gure wind, bepaalde
de Vader zelf wat uit de maanstand valt te lezen,
wat wijst op kalmer weer, bij welk verschijnsel—vaak al
gezien—de boer zijn vee dicht bij de stal moet houden.
De zee begint al dadelijk, als er storm op til is,
deinende op te lopen,—in de bergen schuurt het
en kraakt; of op de kusten hoort men ver de branding
daveren,—in de bossen wordt het ruisen sterker.
Dan vooral beukt de branding de gebogen boten,
wanneer uit zee de duikers driftig op gaan vliegen—
men hoort hun schreeuwen op 't strand—de meeuwen op het droge
scharrelen en de reiger, zijn moerasgebieden
verlatend, trots van vlucht boven een hoge wolk stijgt.
Vaak ook, als er bar weer op komst is, ziet gij sterren
flitsend verschieten in de lucht en in het nachtelijk
donker een lange streep van witte vlammen trekken;
soms stuift het ook fijn kaf; het vallend blad blijft dwarrelen,
of losjes op het water spelen lichte pluisjes.
Maar als het weerlicht aan de kant van 't grimmig noorden,

als donderen de zuid-westrevieren, komt het hele
land blank van wassend water, en op zee bergt iedere
schipper het kletsnat zeil. Te overvallen hoeft ons
de regen nooit: kraanvogels vluchten voor de bui uit
de diepe dalen in; de vaars—de kop ten hemel
getild—staat met gesperde neus de lucht te snuiven;
ijl roepend scheert de zwaluw 't waterbekken over,
en uit de modder kwaakt 't naargeestig koor der kikkers.
Vaak ook haalt diep uit 't mierennest de mier zijn eitjes
—z'n paadje vlijtig heen en weer—, er staat een grote
regenboog en de raven gaan bij hele troepen
krassend hun aasveld uit met korte vleugelslagen.
Zeevogels, bont gekleurd, en wat op wei en drasland
van Azië's Cayster in zoet water voer zoekt,
ze schudden druk een bui van druppels langs de veren:
't is kopje onder gaan, inrennen op de golflijn,—
het eindeloos herhaalde spelletje van baden.
Dan roept de sombere kraai met hard geluid om regen,
of stapt eenzelvig op het drooggewaaide strand om.
En zij, de meisjes die bij nacht haar taak afspinnen,
merken de storm wel—als de olie in de tuitlamp
knetterspat en de pit gaat kromtrekken en roeten.
Maar evengoed kunt gij bij regen blauwe hemel
en zon voorspellen—let slechts op de vaste tekenen:
de tinteling der sterren straalt dan ongesluierd,
de maan die opkomt leent van broeders licht geen schijnsel
en aan de lucht geen tere schapewolkjes drijven;
noch drogen op het strand ijsvogels—Thetis' vreugde—
hun vleugels in de luwe zon; de vuile varkens
vergeten met hun snoet in 't losse stro te woelen.
De nevels zakken laag, de damp staat op de velden;
en, wachtend dat de zon wegzinkt, zit op de daknok

in de avondval de nachtuil eindeloos te roepen.
Hoog in de klare lucht verschijnt de sperwer, Nisus,
en Scylla die moet boeten voor de purpren haarlok,
en wáár haar snelle wiekslag deelt de lichte aether,
zie—suizend nadert door het luchtruim, wrekend, grimmig
haar achtervolger Nisus; en waar Nisus rondkringt,
deelt vluchtend zij met wiekslag snel de lichte aether.
Dan roepen uit gesmoorde keel de raven driemaal
en viermaal scherp en hel,—vaak op hun hoge horsten
rumoeren ze in de takken met elkaar, in zoete
en onbegrepen drift,—blij, nu de regen afdrijft,
weer bij de jongen op 't vertrouwde nest te wezen.
Ik dacht niet dat zo'n dier begaafd is van Godswege,
of van nature dieper voelen kan wat nadert;
maar wanneer wind en weer en wisselende neerslag
gekenterd zijn, en Juppiter in storm en regen
verdicht de ijle sfeer, verijlt de dichte luchten;—
dan slaat de stemming om: het hart voelt zich bewogen
zo ànders nu, dan toen de wind de wolken voortjoeg;
daarom dat koor van vogels buiten, deze blijdschap
in 't weiland en die triomfante roep der raven.

Maar let ge op de felle zon en hoe de manen
elkaar opvolgen, dan verrast u nooit het weer van
morgen; een heldere nacht wordt u niet tot een valstrik.
De nieuwe maan vergaart de teruggekomen vuren:
omvat zij nu een zwart stuk lucht met flauwe sikkel,
dan hebben land en zee een zware bui te wachten;
maar als op haar gelaat een maagdelijke blos komt,
dan wordt het wind: wind kleurt altijd het gouden maanlicht.
Zo ze echter op de vierde avond—dat mist nimmer—
puur is en langs de hemel gaat met scherpe punten,

[434-464]

dan krijgt de dag van morgen en die zich daaraan rijen
totdat de maand afloopt, geheel geen wind of regen;
straks wijden zeelui op het veilig strand hun gave
aan Glaucus, Panopea en Ino's Melicertes.
Maar ook de zon—bij opgang èn als hij in zee zinkt—
voorspelt: met hem gepaard gaan onmiskenbare tekens,
waarneembaar 's morgens vroeg en als de sterren rijzen.
Wanneer zijn jonge licht met vlekken is getekend,
en hij, in nevel schuil, verwist zijn schijf in 't midden,
reken op regen: want van zee komt onweerhoudbaar
dan zuiderstorm,—een ramp voor vee, gewas en bomen.
Maar als, tegen het dagen, tussen dichte nevels
straalbreking zich vertoont, of van Tithonus' leger,
het crocus-gouden, bleek Aurora oprijst,—ach dan
zal 't wingerdloof maar slecht de tere tros beschermen,
zó vinnig tikt en springt de hagel op de daken.
En dit, als na zijn hemeltocht de zon gaat dalen,
is meer nog aandacht waard: wij zien zo dikwijls over
het zongelaat in weifeling allerlei soort kleuren:
somberblauw wijst op regen, vurig ros op stormweer;
maar gaan over die rosse gloed nog vlekken lopen,
dan barst straks alles tegelijk in storm en regen
los,—die nacht krijgt geen sterveling mij op zee, ik laat mij
door niets bewegen dàn de kabels los te gooien.
Maar is de zonschijf puur—of hij de dag nu brengt of
onttrekt—, ducht van bewolking dan geen kwaad; straks ziet ge
bij noordenwind en heldere lucht de bossen wuiven.
Eindelijk: wat brengt de late avond, welke wind komt
met witte wolken, wat beraamt de vochte Auster?—
De zon voorspelt het u. Wie durft de zon te zeggen:
'Gij liegt'?—
          Zij waarschuwt vaak voor ondergrondse woeling;

dat dreigt verraad of oorlog, gistend in 't verborgen.
Zij rouwde ook om Rome na de moord op Caesar,
toen ze haar stralend hoofd met valig zwart omfloerste
en dit ontaard geslacht voor eeuwige nacht gevreesd heeft.
Toen trouwens gaven aarde en oceaan hun tekenen—
huilende honden, sombere vogelvluchten spelden
onheil. Hoe dikwijls barstte de Etna uit,—wij zagen
over 't Cyclopenland kokende lava schuiven;
hoog sloegen stukken vuur op en gesmolten stenen.
Zo ver Germania reikt, liep langs de lucht geluid van
wapenen—door de Alpen voeren vreemde schokken;
ook in de stille bossen werd vernomen telkens
een grote stem. In het voornachtelijk uur verschenen
onwezenlijke spookgestalten; dieren spraken
—gruwzaam!—het levend water stokt, de grond splijt open;
der tempelbeelden brons is klam,—'t ivoor schreit tranen.
In dolle kolken draait de bossen van hun wortels
Eridanus, der stromen koning; heel de streek door
spoelt hij èn vee èn stallen weg. Werden in die dagen
offers geslacht,—steeds spelde onheil 't angstaanjagend
geweide. Bloed bleef wellen uit de putten; steden
in 't bergland hoorden 's nachts het huilen van de wolven.
Nooit had men vaker bij een heldere hemel inslaand
weerlicht of felle schrik door vlammende kometen.
Zo zag Philippi dan ten tweeden male elkander
Romeinse legers tarten met gelijke wapenen.
De goden was 't geen aanstoot, dat ons bloed tweemalen
Emathia drenkte en de wijde Haemus-vlakte.
En stellig komt eenmaal de tijd, dat in die streken
de boer, met de gebogen ploeg zijn akker kerend,
werpspiesen vindt door schilferige roest vervreten,

[496-514]

stuit met zijn zware eg op lege helmen, en beenderen
ontwaart, gigantisch groot, uit blootgekomen graven.

Goden van dit ons land, Romulus, Moeder Vesta,
—behoedend Rome's Palatijn, Etrurië's Tiber—
gun ons althans, dat deze held de ontwrichte tijden
zij tot een stut. Genoeg hebben wij lang reeds bloedig
geboet de meineed van 't Laomedontisch Troje.
't Hemels paleis misgunt u ons te lang al, Caesar,
en klaagt dat gij triomfen zoekt bij mensen;—daar toch
verkeerden goed en kwaad. De aarde in oorlog—misdaad
grijnst overal ons aan! De ploeg geraakte in oneer,
verlaten ligt het land, de boer is in den vreemde;
tot vlijmend zwaard wordt omgesmeed de kromme sikkel.
Hier dreigt Germanië, ginds de Euphraat met een aanval;
steden, vlak bij elkaar, breken de band en grijpen
de wapenen: door de wereld raast de wrede oorlog.—
Zo kiest het vierspan, als de stallen openzwaaien,
de ruimte en neemt de menner mee, die radeloos rukt aan
het toom. De wagen luistert niet meer naar de teugels.

De bomen

Dit van de akkerbouw en van de stand der sterren.—
Een nieuw lied voor u, Bacchus, voor het wild geboomte
en voor de jonge olijf, die langzaam komt tot wasdom.
Verschijn, Vader Lenaeus, hier—waar alles prijkt met
uw gaven; in het najaar, rijkbetrost, is fonkelend
dit land van u: de wijnoogst schuimt de kuipen over.
Verschijn, Vader Lenaeus; dans met ons blootsvoets en
met jonge most bespat,—ontbind uw kostbaar schoeisel.

Eerstens verschilt voor iedere boom de eigen groeiwijs.
Er zijn er die vanzelf, terwijl de mens niet ingrijpt,
opschieten—in 't open veld, of met de oeverbochten
meegaand: de kruipwilg en de bremtak, taai en buigzaam,
peppels en wilgenschot, het blad matgroen en zilver.
Sommige kiemen uit gevallen zaad: de hoge
kastanje en wintereik—een koning in het loofbos
van Juppiter—en de eik, orakelboom der Grieken.
Bij andere maakt de wortel tal van jonge loten:
bij wilde kers en olm, en ook Parnassus' lauwer
is eerst een tengere spruit in moeders zware schaduw.
Zo liet natuur vooreerst het groeien: al het kleinhout,
de stammen en van 't heilig woud de zware reuzen.
Maar de ervaring vond geleidelijk nòg meer wegen.
Soms breekt men van de gave moederboom de stekken
en plant ze in greppels uit; soms steekt men diep in de aarde
stevige takken, scherp gepunt of met vier kepen.

[26-56]

Sommige bomen vragen om de loot te buigen,
die wortelt áán de stam en in de eigen aarde.
Andere doen het zonder wortels en de snoeier
steekt onvervaard de toploot in de grond. 't Gebeurt zelfs,
als blokken zijn gezaagd, dat zo'n stuk droog olijfhout
—een wonder noem ik het—een uitloper gaat maken.
Het hout van de ene boomsoort kan door enting rustig
in d'andere overgaan; de perestam draagt appels,
de pruimen purperen aan de stenige kornoelje.
Aan 't werk dus, kwekers—leert voor iedere soort de eigen
teeltwijs; veredelt door cultuur de wilde vruchten.
Laat grond nooit ongebruikt: de Ismara één wijngaard,
heel de Taburnus één olijvenkleed—hoe prachtig!
Gìj naast mij: laat ons saam voltooien 't werk dat aanving,
mijn sieraad, die met recht mijn naam de schoonste kroon zijt,
Maecenas—thans met volle zeilen zee gekozen.
Ik mag niet hopen alles in mijn lied te omvatten,
al had ik honderd tongen, honderd monden, een ijzeren
geluid.—Help mij en schere ons schip dicht langs de kusten,
—het land onder bereik; ik zal niet voor verdichtsels,
uitweidingen of breed begin uw aandacht vragen.

Wat zich vanzelve tilt te voorschijn naar de zomen
des lichts, zet wel geen vrucht, maar tiert gezond en welig.
Dat doet de groeikracht in de grond. Nochtans, bij enting
of bij verplanting in goed omgespitte kuilen
verdwijnt de wilde aard; bij doorgezette teelt voegt
zo'n boom geredelijk zich tot alle variëteiten.
Zelfs de onvruchtbare sprant, die onder bij de wortel
ontspringt, dòet het—mits uitgeplant op open akker;
nu maakt de moederboom, van tak en lover donker,
vrucht zetten onmogelijk of verstikt het eerst beginsel.

[57-87]

Ten leste: een boom die uit gevallen zaad gekiemd is,
heeft weinig schot; zijn schaduw is pas voor uw kleinzoon.
De vrucht, verbasterend, kent het sap niet meer van vroeger;
wat schriele trosjes draagt de druif—goed voor de vogels.
Iedere boom vraagt feitelijk zorg: gij moet ze alle
uitplanten en geen moeite sparen voor veredeling.
Dit slaat het beste aan: een stuk hout bij olijven,
bij druiven een rank, een sterke tak bij Paphos' myrte.
Uit stekken kweekt men harde hazelaars, stoere essen,
en—kroon van Hercules—de schaduwzware abelen;
zo groeit de eik van Dodona's god, de slanke palmboom,
de den, die straks de zee ziet en haar avonturen.

Nu wat men ent: amandel op de wilde arbutus;
de onvruchtbare plataan prijkt met gezonde appels;
kastanjes draagt de beuk, de es is van perebloesem
sneeuwwit; de varkens kraken eikels onder de olmen.
Voorts ent en oculeert men op meer dan één wijze.
Want waar de knoppen zich dwars door de schors heen werken
—het tere weefsel scheurend—maakt men juist in 't vruchtoog
een holletje en duwt daar 't vruchtoog van een andere
boom in: dat moet dan met de vochte bast vergroeien.
Of men maakt juist op gladde stam een snee en drijft diep
tot in het harde hout met wiggen een spleet; daarin wordt
de vruchtbare ent geklemd. En 't duurt niet lang of prachtig
verheft zich naar het blauw een boom met rijke takken,
verbaasd om zijn veranderd blad en vreemde vruchten.
Dan zijn er ondersoorten: bij de forse olmen,
bij wilg, bij lotosboom, bij de cypres van de Ida;
en ook de vette olijf vertoont meer dan één type:
Ovalen, Staafjes en de Pausia, wrang van vruchten.
Veel soorten heeft Alcinoüs' hof,—niet van één stam zijn

[88-118]

peren uit Crustumium, Syrië, de zware pondspeer;
aan ónze wijnstok hangen andere druivetrossen
dan van Methymna's ranken Lesbos' plukkers oogsten.
Uit Thasos zijn er druiven, witte uit Marea,
—de één geschikt voor zware grond, voor lichte de ander—
Psithia, fijn voor sec; Lageos, klein van druiven,
—daar komt een voet die struikelt van, een tong die stamelt!—;
de Purpertros, de Praecia en—hoe prijst mijn lied u,
Rhaetiër? Toch—Phalernermost wint u de krans af.
Wijn van Aminnea is er ook—en zeer belegen!—
waarvoor de Tmoliër nijgt en zelfs de kroon van Phanae;
de kleine Argitis—als die druif is er geen tweede:
zó vol van sap, zó jaren duurzaam. U, de goden
bij 't nagerecht gevallig, sla ik ook niet over,
Rhodiër, en Bumastos met uw volle trossen.
Doch alle soorten die bestaan en alle namen
zijn ongeteld: waartoe hun aantal ook te ramen?
Wie hiernaar vraagt kan óók aan 't Libysch strand gaan zoeken
hoeveel zandkorrels daar bij westenwind verstuiven,
of, als de oosterstorm de vloot beloopt, staan kijken
hoevele brekers naar de kust van Ionië rollen.

Niet iedere grond kan echter iedere boomsoort hebben:
de wilg staat aan het water, elzen in slijk en poelen,
op steengrond in de bergen de onvruchtbare essen;
myrte groeit prachtig op het strand, en Bacchus eindelijk
kiest open heuvels; taxis 't noorden en de koude.
Zie aardes grenzen door de mens beheerst—in 't oosten
Arabië's tenten, ginds Geloni, bontbeschilderd:
iedere boom hoort in zijn land: alleen in Indië
zwart ebbehout, alleen in Scheba wierookstokjes.
Kent gij het geurig harshout van de balsembomen,

van de mimosa, altijd groen, de ronde vruchten,
het Aethiopisch woud, wit van de donzen wolvrucht?
De Seres kammen van boombladeren zijvlokken;
vlak langs de Oceanus heeft Indië zijn bossen,
een verre baai der wereld,—weet ge dat geen boogschot
daar hoger dan de bomen vrije lucht kan halen?
en toch—dit volk grijpt wakker naar de pijlenkoker.
Medië heeft het zure sap, de stroeve wrangheid
van de citroen; er is geen sneller werkend middel
als kwade stiefmoeders een drank vergiftigd hebben
met kruidenmengsel en met boze toverspreuken;
probaat drijft het de donkere giffen uit het lichaam.
Een zware boom is het, die sterk op een laurier lijkt;
als hij geen andere geur—doordringend scherp—verspreidde,
wàs 't een laurier. Het blad waait nimmer af, de bloem houdt
zich zeer lang goed; de Mediërs nemen tegen slechte adem
citroen en het helpt oude mensen bij benauwdheid.

Nochtans, het land der Meden, zwaar begroeid met wouden,
de trotse Ganges en de Hermus, gouddoorwemeld,
raakt aan Italië's pracht niet; Bactrië noch Indië,
noch gans Panchaia's zanden, kostelijk van wierook.
Dit land is niet door stieren—vurige adem blazend—
geploegd; van draketanden droeg het nimmer zaaisel;
hier stond geen stugge oogst van krijgshelmetten en speren.
Maar prachtig prijkt het graan, de Massicus draagt druiven
zó rijk—en overal zijn olijven en bonte kudden.
Hier draaft het oorlogsros met trotse nek het veld in;
hier trad het sneeuwblank vee—de stier als statigst offer—
zo vaak, besprenkeld met uw zuiverend nat, Clitumnus,
de triomfale stoeten vóór naar Rome's tempels.
Hier is het lente altijd; de zomer gaat zijn maanden

[150-180]

te boven—tweemaal draagt het schaap, tweemaal de vruchtboom.
Vreemd zijn dit land de wrede rovers leeuw en tijger,
de monnikskap, zijn plukker jammerlijk verradend,
de slangen, langs de grond hun zware kronkels trekkend,
of schubbig saamgerold tot machtige spiralen.
Dan zoveel steden overschoon en grootse werken,
zovele sterkten op de steile rots gestapeld,
en onder de oude muren glijdend de rivieren.
De hoge zee noem ik op onze kust, de lage;
de grote meren: u, heerlijk meer Larius, u ook,
Benacus, hoog van golven, bruisend als de branding.
Kent gij de havens en de dam van de Lucrinus?—
zwaar gaat het verontwaardigd water aan, waar brekend
de zee met daveren terugstroomt uit het Julisch water
en het Tyrrheense tij zich stort in de Avernus.
Dan zijn in dit ons land ontsloten zilverbeken
en kopererts en goud in overrijke aderen.
Een wakker vechtersras—Marsi, jonge Sabelli,
Liguriërs, fel gehard, de piekeniers der Volsci
droeg het: een Decius, Marius, der Camilli adel,
Scipiones—stugge strijders—en u, Caesar, grootste,
die nu reeds, triumfant in 't verre land van Azië,
de Indiër, weerloos, keert van de Romeinse burchten.
Heil, grote Moeder van het graan, land van Saturnus,
aan helden groot—'k betreed om u dit veld van oude
vermaarde kunst en durf de heilige bronnen ontsluiten:
het lied van Ascra zing ik in Romeinse steden.

En thans over de soorten grond: de kracht van ieder,
zijn kleur en welk product er aanslaat van nature.
Een stugge grond vooreerst en schrale heuvels—dun is
de kleilaag daar; 't is steentjes en wirwar van struiken—

[181-212]

heeft graag een groep van Pallas' krachtige olijven.
De dichte groei van wilde olijven op zo'n bodem
bewijst het; heel de grond ligt vol met wilde vruchten.
Maar vette grond, van zoete vochtigheid verzadigd,
een vlakte met dicht gras en overvloedig vruchtbaar
(zoals wij in een bergvallei soms in de diepte
zien—hierheen stroomt het water boven van de rotsen
met vruchtbaar slib), en land, dat toegekeerd naar 't zuiden
veel varens heeft—voor de gekromde ploeg een hinder—
dat zal u straks een kerngezonde wingerd geven,
met volle trossen; dat is goede grond voor druiven,
voor wijn, gelijk wij die uit gouden schalen plengen,
als bij 't altaar de zware Etruriër het ivoor blaast,
't geweide, opgedragen, rookt in wichtige schotels.
Maar als ge liever koeien en kalveren wilt houden,
of lammeren, of—dat geeft dorre velden—geitjes,
zoek dan de verre bergwei van het rijk Tarente;
of laagland zoals 't arme Mantua moest derven;
de stroom, met groene oevers, draagt de sneeuwen zwanen,
de kudden vinden welig gras en zuivere wellen
en wat de beesten afgrazen in de lange dagen,
hergeeft het koele dauwen in de korte nachten.
Een zwarte grond, waar zwaar de druk van 't kouter door komt
en rul van boven (zoals ook de ploeg het rul maakt)
is opperbest voor koren; uit geen landschap ziet ge
méér zware ossenkarren traagzaam huiswaarts keren;
zo óók grond, waar de boer verwoed het bos gerooid heeft:
het hout heeft hij gekapt, dat jaren lang niets opbracht
en de oude vogelhuizinge tot de naakte wortels
gesloopt. Zij kringen in de lucht, van 't nest verdreven,—
maar in de barre grond flitst de ingedreven ploegschaar.
Maar hellingen met kale kiezels geven nauwelijks

[213-243]

de bijen rosmarijn en wat lavendelstruikjes.
Van ruwe tuf en kalksteen,—van reptielen donker
vervreten—mag gezegd, dat geen grondsoort zo kostelijk
slangen aan voedsel helpt en diepe kronkelgangen.
Een land dat dunne mist uitdampt en ijle nevels,
vochtigheid indrinkt en—wanneer het wil—weer afscheidt,
zich dekt van zelve met een altijd groene grasmat,
en 't ijzer niet met scherpe roest of schilfering aantast,
dat zal een rijke wingerd om de olmen winden;
't is beste olijvengrond; gij vindt het bij ontginning
voor kleinvee goed en voor de kromme ploegschaar willig.
Zulk bouwland heeft rijk Capua, 't Vesuvius-landschap,
de Clanius, bedreigend het ontvolkt Acerrae.

Nu hoe ge iedere grondsoort kunt leren onderscheiden.
Vraagt gij u af of grond los of bijzonder vast is
(daar 't een voor koren goed is en voor wijnbouw 't ander
—voor Ceres vastere, zeer losse voor Lyaeus—)
kijk het terrein goed aan en laat in de effen bodem
daar diep een kuil uitsteken; daar gooit ge alle aarde
weer in en stampt het met de voeten aan van boven.
Komt er te kort, dan is het losse grond—juist heerlijk
voor kleinvee en voor volle wijn; maar wil de aarde
er niet meer in, teveel voor de gedichte kuil, dan
is 't vast; reken op taaie kluiten, forse ruggen
bij 't ploegen en scheur zo'n bodem met een sterk span ossen.
Echter een zilte grond, of—als de term luidt—bitter,
voor koren ongeschikt (de ploeg maakt hem niet handzaam,
hij laat geen wijn zijn adel, geen vrucht zijn vermaardheid)
verraadt zich zó: haal stijf gevlochten wilgenmanden
of wijnpers-zeven van de rokerige zoldering;
druk daar die slechte grond, vermengd met zoet bronwater,

[244-275]

in tot de rand; dan werkt natuurlijk al het vocht zich
naar buiten—dikke droppels dringen door het vlechtwerk.
Dan zegt de smaak genoeg—bitterheid onversneden
zal, als ge ervan proeft, u wrang de mond vertrekken.
Evenzo zien we als volgt direct wat vette grond is:
die laat zich nooit, hoe hard men knijpt en kneedt, verpulveren,
maar blijft als pek bij 't pakken aan de vingers hangen.
Op natte grond groeit alles hoog, ja overdadig.
Heus, laat het land voor mij niet al te vruchtbaar wezen,
niet zijn teveel aan kracht tonen in 't jonge koren.
Het stom gewicht alleen al zegt wat zware grond is,
wat lichte. Met één blik herkent ge zwarte aarde
en iedere aparte kleur.—Dat grond niet deugt en zuur is
blijkt niet direct. Soms ziet gij 't slechts aan de begroeiing:
pijnbomen, giftige taxis en de donkere klimop.
Vergeet—na deze inspectie—niet de grond eerst danig
te luchten en langs de helling geulen uit te steken;
stel de gekeerde kluiten aan de noordenwind bloot,
alvorens ge er zo'n vruchtbare wijngaard zet. Het beste is
rul bouwland: daarvoor zorgen wind en rijp en vrieskou
en die op de akker wrikt en trekt, de sterke spitter.
Maar als ge werkers hebt, die waaks zijn tot in 't kleinste,
dan zoeken ze eerst ééhnzelfde grondsoort voor het aanslaan
en voor de plek waar straks de aanplanting te staan komt,
dat niet 't gewas, ineens verzet, zijn moedergrond mist.
Nog sterker: de oriëntatie geeft men op de bast aan,
dat iedere plant zijn stand—hoe hij de zuiderwarmte
opving, hoe hij de rug toekeerde naar het noorden—
hervindt: zó weegt gewoonte bij het jonge wezen.
Kijk eerst of ge uw wijngaard 't beste in de vlakte
of op de heuvels zet. Bakent ge een zwaar stuk grond af,
plant dicht opeen: dichte aanplant maakt de druif niet schraler.

[276-306]

Maar kiest ge glooiend wijnland op een heuvelhelling,
gun dan de rijen ruimte en feilloos blijv' de plaatsing,
waarbij diagonaal de rijen op het pad staan.
Zó, bij 't geweld des krijgs, ontplooit wel zijn cohorten
het trekkend legioen na 't halt in de open vlakte;
de rijen zijn gericht, de aarde één brede golving
van spiegelend brons—nòg ving het gruwzame gevecht niet
aan, maar weifelend waart Mars tussen beide legers.
Steeds zij tussen de rijen evenredige afstand:
niet slechts opdat het ongebonden denken rust vindt
in 't perspectief, maar anders geeft de grond niet allen
eendere kracht en wint de rank geen vrije ruimte.
En nu vraagt ge allicht hoe diep de kuil moet wezen:
een wijnstok durf ik nog wel in een smalle greppel
te zetten, maar een boom moet stevig diep de grond in.
De wintereik vooral—zo hoog als hij zijn kruin heft
in 't blauw, zo diep reiken in de Tartarus zijn wortels.
Zo kan geen winter hem, geen stormstoot en geen wolkbreuk
ontwortelen: onwrikbaar, kinderen en kindskinderen
verslaande, staat hij, pal bij 't wentelen der geslachten.
Zó, allerzijds zijn kroon en sterke takken strekkend,
—zelf machtig middelpunt—draagt hij zijn zware schaduw.

Echter, uw wijnberg moet niet op het westen liggen;
zet ook tussen de wijn geen hazelaar; kies geen ranken
van boven, breek niet boven uit de top uw stekken—
(de wijn hoort bij de grond!)—beschadig nimmer loten
met een bot mes en ent geen tamme olijf op wilde.
Een herder, achteloos, laat wellicht een vonkje vallen,
dat ongemerkt tussen de vette schors blijft smeulen;
het hout vat vlam; het vuur slaat in de hoogste takken
en loeit tegen de lucht; dan grijpt het om zich heen en

viert in de volle kroon door alle takken hoogtij.
De brand grijpt stam na stam en drijft een dikke rookzuil
de hemel toe, die roeterig zwart op alles neerslaat,
het meest wanneer de wind met vlagen op het bos valt
en de opgestoken storm het kolkend vuur aanwakkert.
Na zo'n brand is het vruchthout weg; zelfs omgekapt kan
de olijf zich niet herstellen en loopt niet bij de grond uit;
de onvruchtbare houdt het veld, wrangbladige oleaster.
Laat geen autoriteit, hoe knap ook, u belezen
de harde grond bij scherpe noordenwind te spitten:
dan trekt de vorst de aarde dicht en krijgt het stekje
geen kans om aan te slaan met zijn verkrompen wortel.
Het best plant men de wijn, als in de purperen lente
de witte ooievaar verschijnt, de slangenjager;
of tegen de eerste herfstkou, als de zonnewagen
nog niet de winter heeft bereikt, zomer al heenging.
Lente is de tijd van 't groenend bos, de bloei der hoven,
bij lente werkt de grond en vraagt kiemkrachtig zaaisel.
Dan daalt met vruchtbare regens alvermogend Aether,
de Vader, in de schoot der zalige Aarde en alles
wat groeit ontvangt het leven uit die machtige paring;
dan zingt het onbetreden bos van luide vogels;
dan weet ook 't vee zijn tijd en zoekt het Venus weder.
Het milde land wil dragen en bij de zoele zephyr
ontsluit zich 't veld; in alles gist het jonge groeisap
en in de nieuwe zon durft zich de kiemplant veilig
te wagen, en de wingerd vreest geen zuiderstormen
of regen, langs de lucht gejaagd uit 't machtig noorden:
zijn knoppen breken uit, hij vouwt elk blaadje open.
Niet anders scheen het licht over de jonge wereld
op de eerste dag, en zó was het seizoen bestendig,
droom ik mij—; het was lente,—lente vierde al het

[339-369]

geschapene, de oostenwind hield in zijn vorstige adem,—
toen de eerste dieren 't licht indronken, en de mensen,
der aarde kroost, opkwamen uit de stugge bodem,
het bos vol dieren stormde, 't hemelruim vol sterren.
Nooit had dit pril geheel de groeipijn kunnen dragen,
als tussen warmte en kou niet zulk een rust kwam heersen,
niet 's hemels mildheid veilig de aarde hield omvangen.

Voor 't overige, wat ge ook voor boompjes in de grond zet,
geef ze flink mest, dek ze vooral met goed wat aarde,
doe in de kuil poreuze steen of ruwe schelpen:
die immers laten 't water door, dan kan van onderen
de lucht er bij en zal uw boom het doen. Men vindt er
die stenen bovenop of goed wat zware scherven
stapelen; dat dekt af tegen de hevige regens
en barre hitte als 't land, geblakerd, scheurt van droogte.
Na 't planten heeft men telkens de aarde op te harken
tot aan de vork; blijf ook de harde hak hanteren
of drijf het kouter in de grond,—laat gaan en keren
uw ossen, het weerstrevend span, tot in de wijngaard.
Geef wijn de gladde rietstok, dan 't gestripte rijshout,
de essehouten staak, de gaffel om te stutten,—
geleidelijk werkt hij zich omhoog en vreest geen schade
van wind; tot in de olmtop reiken zijn terrassen.
Zolang de eerste groei nog in zijn jonge blad komt,
voorzichtig, het is teer!—Zelfs als de rank zich welig
de lucht inwindt, in 't blauw teugelloos uitgeschoten,
sla dan nòg nergens 't snoeimes aan, maar pluk voorzichtig
wat weg met duim en vinger om het blad te dunnen.
Maar maakt hij eenmaal, sterk van stam de olm omslingerend,
nieuw lot, zet dan de schaar er in, knot dàn zijn armen
(daarvóór is 't mes te bar!), voer dan gerust een krachtig

regiem, en ongenadig kort zijn kronkeltakken.
Zet ook een takkenheg en houd de beesten buiten,
vooral zolang het tere loof nog niets kan hebben.
Behalve zonnebrand en nachtvorst is de moedwil
van buffels en brutale geiten een bezoeking,
de schapen vreten 't loof, en 't jongvee, nooit verzadigd.
De kou, al heeft het stevig ruiggevroren, hitte
die op de dorre hoogten neerslaat, is zo erg niet
als dit gedierte en zijn venijnige harde tanden
—scherp staat in d'aangeknaagde stam het merk getekend—.
't Is daarom dat men Bacchus brengt op alle altaren
een bokkenoffer—'t spel verschijnt op het proscaenium
als eertijds; Theseus' zonen gaan langs dorp en kruisweg,
talent ontvangt zijn prijs, en lustig bij de beker
wordt in de malse wei glibberend zak-gesprongen.
Ook 't volk van Troje uitgegaan, Italië's boeren,
viert in 't rustieke vers zich uit met daverend lachen,
't grijnzend mombakkes voor, in boomschors uitgesneden;
u, Bacchus, roept hun lied uitbundig, u ter ere
hangen in de pijnboomtop de kleine wassen maskers.
Nu komt de rijpenstijd, de prachtig volle trossen;
wijn overgroeit het dal, de diepte der valleien,—
wijn, wáár de god zijn heerlijk hoofd heeft omgedragen.
Dies zullen, naar de wijs, wij 't aloud loflied zingen
Bacchus ten prijs; de schaal met offerkoeken beuren;
gegrepen bij de horens staat de bok voor 't altaar,—
aan 't hazelhouten spit roostert het vet geweide.

Er is bij wijnbouw nog een andere vaste arbeid
die vraagt en vragen blijft: 't losmaken van de bodem,
drie- viermaal in het jaar;—de kluiten moeten eindeloos
met de omgekeerde hak verpulverd—, èn het dunnen

op de aanplant. Voor de landman trekt het werk zijn ronde,
't jaar schrijft zijn eendere kring, en wentelt naar zijn oorsprong.
Eindelijk heeft de wijn zijn laatste blad verloren,
de tooi der bossen valt, de wind komt uit het noorden.
Nu is de boer paraat: over het komend jaar gaat
zijn denken—met het krom Saturnus-kapmes houdt hij
de naakte wingerd kort; zo snoeit hij er model in.
Spit vroeg uw grond, steek vroeg de brand in 't takkenafval;
wees er vroeg bij uw staken in de schuur te bergen.
Oogst laat,—de wijn wordt tweemaal door zijn loof verduisterd,
tweemaal verdwijnt de bodem onder 't ruige onkruid;
dus dubbel werk, en zwaar:—geef statige domeinen
uw lof, hoùd klein bedrijf.—Dan moet ge aan het snijden:
't riet van de waterkant, de muisdoorn uit de bossen;
wèrk is er, waar de wilg in 't wild is opgeschoten.
Nu is de druif geleid, nu mag het snoeimes rusten,
nu staat de gaardenier aan 't eind der zuivere rijen
en zingt.—Maar 't harken blijft: dan komt het stof naar boven;
en is de druif straks rijp, veel kans dat het stortregent.

Heel anders de olijf: die eist geen kweek, die vraagt niet
om 't kromme mes, noch om de hark met taaie tanden,
zodra hij wortel heeft en tegen weer en wind kan.
De grond geeft, enkel met de hak gebroken, 't plantje
al vocht genoeg,—geploegd, levert hij volle vruchten.
—Kweek dus de vette olijf, zij is ook Pax gevallen.—
De vruchtboom ook, als hij zich eenmaal sterk van stam voelt
en zelf zijn weerstand heeft, schiet naar de sterren driftig
omhoog uit eigen kracht en vraagt geen hulp van mensen.
Zo is het ook in 't wild; zwaar hangt de tak van vruchten,
de vogelwildernis kleurt bloedrood van de bessen;
de dieren vinden er pijlbrem, 't hoog geboomt geeft harshout,

[432-462]

—dat voedt de lampen in de nacht, hun ronde lichtkring.—
En aarzelt dan de mens te zaaien en te zorgen?—
Maar waartoe 't grote juist? De wilg, de lage bremstruik,
zij geven toch de geiten voer, de herders schaduw,
een haag om de aanplant heen, en honing voor de bijen.
—Een vreugd: Cytorus' golvend buxusbos te aanschouwen,
Narycia's pijnboomwoud—heerlijkheid van een landschap
nog door geen werktuig, door geen mensenhand geschonden!
Kaukasus' kammen zelfs en maagdelijke wouden,
waar blazende oosterstorm rusteloos breekt en brijzelt,
't draagt zijn verscheidenheid: draagt timmerhout—voor scheepsbouw
de spar, voor huizen ceder en cypres. Uit hout schaaft
de boer het spakenrad, uit hout het zware karwiel;
uit hout ook wordt gebouwd de scheepsromp en zijn welving.
De wilgen geven rijs, de olm zijn lovertakken,
de myrte sterke schachten—ook kornoelje is prachtig
voor speerhout. De Ituraeër kromt een boog uit taxis.
Linde en palmhout, zacht en glad onder de beitel,
ook zij krijgen model, als 't scherp metaal hen uitholt.
Hoe drijft de elzen boot licht op de stroomversnelling
de Padus af; hoe bouwt het bijenvolk zijn raten
in schorsholten of diep in een vermolmde steeneik.
Wat gave bracht ons Bacchus, zózeer waard te loven?
Bacchus dreef ook tot schuld; de woedende Centauren
sloeg hij ten dode, Rhoetus, Pholus en Hylaeus,
die met het zware mengvat de Lapithen dreigde.

Zózeer gelukkig, als ge uw eigen rijkdom kende,
volk van het land! Vanzelve, ver van 't schendig woelen,
doet gul de goede aarde voedsel voor u groeien.
Hier stuwt geen statig huis in 't morgenuur bezoekers
bij golven door de trotse deur uit volle zalen;

geen aangegaapte pracht,—schildpad van deurpanelen,
het kostbare, Ephyra's brons, en stoffen, gouddoorspeelde.
De witte wol wordt niet door 't rode Syrisch kleurgif,
de zuivere olijvensmaak door kruiden niet bedorven.
Hier onbezorgde vrede, een argeloos open leven
vol bonte vreugden, en de rust van 't wijde buiten,
zijn grotten, zuivere meren en zijn koele dalen.
Een koe die loeit... Hoe zoet is 't onder 't schaduwlover
te mogen slapen.—Land van bossen, waar het wild huist,
van jong volk, sober opgegroeid, dat weet van werken,
hoe eert ge uw goden, eert ge uw vaderen.—Ontwijkend
liet hièr gerechtigheid op aard' haar laatste voetspoor.

En ik—één wens: dat, hoogste heerlijkheid, de Muzen
mij, die haar schatten draag, doorwond van groot verlangen,
aanvaarden, wijzend mij der sterren hemelbanen;
hoe zich de zonneschijf verduistert, taant het maanlicht;
door welke kracht de aarde beeft, de zee in vloedgolf
de dam vernielt en dan weer in zichzelve terugzinkt;
waarom in d'Oceaan de winterzon zo haastig
wegduikt en wat de nachten talmend in doet vallen.
Doch mag ik dit gebied der schepping niet betreden,
doordat te koud het bloed om 't hart mij stroomt, zo laat mij
mijn vreugd in 't land, het sprankelend water der valleien,
voor stroom en bos mijn liefde—in nederigheid:—O laagland,
Spercheüs en, van Sparta's dochteren doordanste,
Taÿgetus!—O, wie in Haemus' koele bergdal
mij brengt; in stilte en schaduw van zijn zware bomen!
Gelukkig wie der dingen oorzaak mocht doorgronden,
die alle angsten en het onverbiddelijk noodlot
dwong aan zijn voeten en Acherons roofgierig ruisen.
Gelukkig ook wie kent de landelijke goden:

[494-525]

Pan zelf, de oude Silvanus en de zusters nymfen.
Geen bijlenbundels van het volk, geen koningspurper
raakt hem; geen tweedracht, broeders tot verraad ontrustend,
geen Daciër en zijn horden, dalend van de Donau;
niet Rome's macht, noch tronen, wankelend. Hem kwelt niet
de haat tegen wie heeft, de deernis met de arme.
De vruchten van de tak, de oogst die de goede aarde
gul geeft van zelve, plukt hij,—vreemd blijft hem het ijzeren
recht, het bezeten forum en de staatsgebouwen.
Rusteloos roeien anderen op blinde zeeën, tarten
het zwaard of dringen door tot 's vorsten hof en drempelen.
Men ondergraaft de stad, de hulpeloze haardstee
voor een juweelbokaal, een Tyrisch purperen rustbed;
de vrek begraaft zijn schat om op zijn goud te slapen.
De gapers staan de rostra rond; 't applaus, verdubbeld,
dat door de rijen vaart van senatoren en volk doet
het velen aan. Men roemt, bevlekt met bloed van broeders,
om—balling dan—van huis en eigen haard verstoten,
ginds onder vreemde zon een vaderland te zoeken.
De boer, hij scheurt met zijn gekromde ploeg de aarde.
Zo groeit het werk des jaars, dat erf en jong gezin draagt;
zo groeit zijn veebeslag, gedijt zijn trouwe ploegspan.
En onuitputtelijk schenkt het jaar zijn rijkdom: vruchten,
de lammetjes, de geitjes, volle korenschoven;
de dichte oogst der voren kan de schuur niet bergen.
't Wintert—de olijf van Sicyon wordt geperst, de varkens
komen van eikels dik naar huis; haagappels hangen
in 't bos,—nu gaan de bonte najaarsvruchten vallen.
Hoog op de bergen rijpen in volle zon de druiven.
Een lief stel kinderen hangt hem aan, hij kust ze alle
en 't huis bewaart zijn kuisheid rein.—De koeien dragen
de zware volle uier en waar 't gras al hoog staat

[526-541]

stoeien de stevige bokjes, speels, met stootse horens.
Zijn feesten viert de boer. Behaaglijk in het grasland
    —het altaar rookt, zijn makkers winden om 't mengvat kransen—
plengt hij en roept u aan, Lenaeus.—Voor zijn herders
is er een wedstrijd: spieswerpen—een olm is doelwit.
Zó leefden eens in oude tijden de Sabijnen,
zó Remus en zijn broer; zó groeide Etrurië stellig
tot macht en zó werd Rome, schoonste stad ter wereld,
dat ene ringmuur trok rondom zijn zeven heuvelen.
Lang voor het rijk van Dicte's vorst, lang voor de mensen,
ontaard, hun runderen slachtten om het vlees te eten,
leefde in de gouden eeuw Saturnus zó op aarde.
Nog nimmer was gehoord de krijgstrompet, nog nimmer
't geklink van zwaarden—hameren op het harde aambeeld.
    —Maar achter ons strekt reeds de baan zich ongemeten:
't is tijd het schuimend span de halster af te nemen.

Het vee

U, Pales oud-eerwaard, en u, Admetus' herder
der sage, een zang, u, bos en beken van Arcadië.
Een ander lied, dat wis toegankelijke oren boeide,
het werd reeds elks bezit. Weet één niet van Eurystheus
de kwelgeest, van Busiris en zijn schandelijk altaar?
Wie zong de tedere Hylas niet, Latona op Delos,
Hippodamia en Pelops, glanzend de elpen schouder,
een menner scherp... Ik waag de kamp, dat ook mijn vlucht gaat
omhoog, en glorierijk mijn naam van mond tot mond vliegt.
In 't eigen land mag ik, zo mij de jaren resten,
de Muzen binnenvoeren van Aonië's toppen—
mag ik, mijn Mantua, de palm der palmen u reiken.
Daar rijst dan in het groene land de marmeren tempel
bij 't water, waar de Mincius, breed, met trage bochten,
zich slingert tussen 't ranke riet der oeverzomen.
En in het hart des heiligdoms zal Caesar tronen.
Ik houd voor hem in 't feestgewaad met purperen randen
een ren langs de rivier met honderd vierspanwagens.
Heel Hellas komt naar hier—verlaten wordt Olympia,
Molorchus' woud—ten wagenren, ten stuggen vuistkamp.
En zelf, bekranst met een gesnoeide olijftak, breng ik
mijn gaven. Nu reeds ziet mijn droom de plechtige stoeten
door mij geleid ten heiligdom, de offerstieren;
hoe de toneelwand wijkt door draaiende décors en
Brittanni op 't gordijn de purperen voorhang heffen.
In goud en zwaar ivoor prijkt op de tempeldeuren

de Ganges, waar Quirinus' wapenen triomferen,
de Nijl, die golft van oorlog in zijn machtig stroombed—
men ziet de statige zuilen uit het brons der snebben.
Dan Azië's steden onder 't juk, Armenië machteloos,
in listige ren de Parth, die ruggelings zijn pijl schiet;
triomf tweevoudig: hier, en ver aan vreemde stranden.
Binnen staan beelden, ademend, van Parisch marmer:
heroën van een gens bij Juppiter begonnen,
Assaracus, stamvader Troos, en Cynthius, bouwer
van Troje. Onzalige Nijd, van vrees verkrompen, ziet bij
de Hellestroom de Furiën, Ixions schrik'lijk
beslangde rad, de steen die Sisyphus geen rust laat.
Maar zoeken wij vooreerst de onbetreden boswei,
der nymfen paden,—uw wens, Maecenas, die mijn wet is.
Geen opvlucht zonder u; o breek dit werkeloos wachten;
het roept met duizend stemmen u en mij: Cithaeron,
Laconië's jachtstoet, Epidaurus, dat zijn paarden
africht; weerkaatsend schalt de echo uit de bossen.
Maar ééns wijd ik aan Caesars fel bevochten zege
een lied, en maak zijn naam vermaard door zóveel eeuwen
als Caesars aera van Tithonus' oorsprong afligt.

Wie paarden fokt en zich Olympia's palm als prijs droomt,
wie runderen fokken wil, sterk om de ploeg te trekken,—
zijn eerste zorg zij een goed moederdier. Het beste is
stug soort: zo'n beest is lomp van kop, van nek gedrongen,
met kwabben aan de hals die tot zijn poten hangen.
De romp is van formaat enorm, 't is alles machtig,
van hoef tot kruin; 't ruige oor zit onder kromme horens.
Het mag wat mij betreft best een witbonte wezen,
een die het juk niet wil en soms gemeen kan stoten,
en haast iets van een stier heeft; een die hoog van schoften

[59-90]

bij 't gaan zijn staartkwast zwiepend over 't eigen spoor slaat.
De goede tijd voor dekking, en voor 't kalven loopt tot
het tiende jaar, begint na 't vierde; eerder
of later deugt een koe niet voor de dracht, zomin als
voor veldwerk. Is nu 't vee jong, weelderig en springgraag,
dan prompt de stieren in de wei, de drift der dieren
gevierd; zo krijgt men jaar op jaar de nieuwe kalveren.
—De beste tijd is voor wat leeft en lijdt op aarde
zo ras voorbij; er komen ziekte, vale grijsheid
en pijn; tot straks de dood zonder genade toeslaat.—
Wel zijn er altijd bij, waaraan ge iets vindt mankeren;
blijf daarom schiften en kies, dat gij niet straks onthand zit,
intijds fokdieren voor uw kudde uit het jongvee.
Niet minder is 't bij paarden zaak te selecteren.
Vooreerst moet gij de dieren, die gij wilt bestemmen
tot fokpaard, van jongsaf bijzondere aandacht geven.
Een veulentje van ras heeft dadelijk in de weide
een hoger gang en zet zijn pootjes eleganter.
Direct durft hij de weg op, in het boze water;
een vreemde brug stapt hij in goed vertrouwen over
en wordt niet schichtig van lawaai.—De hals is rijzig
en sierlijk 't hoofd, de rug gevuld en kort de buiklijn.
De spieren spelen op de trotse borst. Het hoogst geldt
een vos, een appelschimmel; niet gewild zijn wit en
vuilgeel. Een raspaard kan bij krijgsrumoer, hoe ver ook,
niet stilstaan, spitst zijn oren, rillingen gaan over
zijn lijf,—hij briest, een zuil van vurige adem blazend.
De manen, dicht en kruivend, vallen rechts, de wervels
trekken een dubbele lijn de lende langs; hij krabt in
de grond, dan valt de zware hoef neer dat het davert.
Zó 't paard van Amyclae, door Pollux straf geteugeld,
Cyllarus of, bezongen in het Griekse epos,

[91-121]

Mars' tweespan en de rossen van de fiere Achilles.
Langs zulk een hals liet eens—een sterke hengst—Saturnus
zijn manen stromen en vluchtende bij Rhea's nadering
liet hij van scherp gehinnik Pelions hoogten schallen.

Verliest uw paard zijn vuur, komt de ouderdom met kwalen,
houd hem bij huis; 't aftandse beest moet uitgebannen.
De vlam is uitgedoofd en Venus' dienst verricht hij
moeizaam en zonder vrucht,—en waagt hij ooit een aanval,
het wordt, zoals de lichte brand vliegt door de stoppels,
een loos strovuur. Dus let op temperament en leeftijd
vóór alles, daarna ook op eigen aard en stamboom,
of 't paard bij nederlaag gekrenkt zich toont, bij zege
gestreeld. Dat ziet men als in wilde ren de wagens
het veld instuiven, zwaaiende uit de open stallen,
de menners scherp staan op de eindtriomf, de spanning
nijpt in het bonzend hart. Het zweepkoord giert, zij jagen
met losse toom, voorover,—de as loopt warm in 't wervelen.
Nu eens schijnen zij laag en dan weer hoog, een zweven
van de aarde los door 't luchtruim, steigeren naar de hemel.
Eén jagen is 't, één ijlen; een wolk van gouden stofzand
gaat op, met vlokken schuim bespat hen de achtervolger;
dat doet de roem, dat doet het hunkeren naar de zege.
Het eerst dorst Erichthonius met de vier te rijden,
hij, recht en triomfant boven 't geflits der spaken.
Maar Pelions Lapithen legden 't bit aan, reden
als ruiter volte en leerden om in volle rusting
te galopperen en hoog in trotse draf te vallen.
't Vraagt allebei dressuur. Voor allebei behoeven
de temmers een jong beest—vurig, een scherpe draver—
jòng,—spijts een ander, die triumfen vierde op 't slagveld,
als vaderland Epirus melden mag of 't grootse

[122-152]

Mycene en zijn stamboom tot Neptunus terugvoert.

Zo geeft men acht op alles: nadert nu de bronsttijd,
dan dient er waakse zorg besteed, en stevig krachtvoer
aan het toekomstig fokdier, leider van de kudde.
Men snijdt hem welig gras, men put hem levend water,
voert tarwe bij, dat hem zijn zoete taak niet zwaar valt
en niet een krachteloos kroost van vaders honger 't merk draagt.
De merries evenwel houdt men met opzet mager.
En als de paringsdrift voor 't eerst zich in hun onrust
verraadt, is 't voorschrift: géén groen blad en weg van 't water.
Zelfs afgereden worden ze en geplaagd met hitte,
wanneer de dorsvloer dreunt bij 't kloppen op de schoven,
als op een westerbriesje 't lichte kaf gaat stuiven.
Dit doen ze dat van overgrote weelde de akker
niet voor het zaad zich sluit en lui de voren dichttrekt,
maar 't neemt met gretigheid en veilig houdt geborgen.
Maar nu is 't rijk der vaders uit, de tijd der moeders
breekt aan. Zij lopen in de wei de volle maanden
der dracht. Geen mens zal dan het dier voor zware karren
aanspannen; 't mag niet springen dwars over een weg heen,
op hol slaan in het land of zwemmen in trekkend water.
Zij grazen in de vree der dalen, langs de volle
rivieren. Daar is mos en heerlijk groenende oevers,
grotten om te schuilen, koelte slaat er van de rotswand.
Daar waar de Silarus stroomt door 't woud en op de Alburnus
de steeneik groeit, vliegt een insect bij zwermen, dat asilus
te onzent heet (de Grieken noemen 't anders: oistros),—
kwaadaardig beest, schril gonzend, waarvoor hele kudden
het bos uitvluchten; dol wordt van het stotend loeien
èn lucht èn bos, en de opgedroogde stroom Tanager.
Met deze plaag heeft Juno, schrikkelijk in haar woede,

de vaars Io—wier ondergang zij zocht—, geteisterd.
Bescherm—immers zij steken 't felst bij middaghitte—
ook hiervoor 't drachtig vee en weid uw kudde kort na
zonsopgang, of als 't met de eerste sterren nacht wordt.

Maar zijn de kalveren er, dan gaat alle aandacht over
op hen: men brandmerkt ze direct, één merk voor de afkomst
en één al naar men ze tot fokdier op wil kweken,
ze heilig houden voor 't altaar of laten scheuren
de grond, en 't ruggenveld tot losse kluiten keren.
't Gewone vee mag grazen in het groene weiland;
maar die ge africhten wilt voor de praktijk van 't veldwerk,
wen die al jong aan tucht (dè weg dat gij ze goed krijgt)
als de aard nog soepel is, het jonge beest nog handzaam.
Begin met ze om de hals een lichte ring van rijshout
losjes te leggen; later, als hun vrije nekken
't juk zijn gewend, vorm dan—door 't koppelen van die halsters—
een span, en dwing uw ossen samen stap te houden.
Laat ze óók vast, voor en na, een lege wagen trekken
langs het terrein (het spoor staat los in 't stof getekend),
en later, zwichtend onder 't zwaar gewicht en krakend,
de beuken kar, tweewielig, met beslagen dissel.
Geef onderwijl uw halfwas rund'ren niet uitsluitend
gras, wilgenloof (een schrale kost is dat), moerasgras,
maar trek een handvol nog groen gras uit; laat de kalfkoe
niet, naar de oude trant, de emmers sneeuwblank vullen,
maar al haar goede melk aan 't kalfje mogen geven.

Droomt ge veeleer van krijg, van trotse ruiterscharen,
wilt ge—in 't licht gerij Alpheüs' zomen scherend—
bij 't woud van Juppiter uw vliegend span besturen,
dan moet uw paard eerst wennen: aan het woelend slagveld,

[183-213]

't geschal van de trompet, het knarsen van het wiel dat
hij trekt en—in de stal—aan 't rinkelen van het hoofdstel;
al meer en meer is hij gestreeld bij 'n prijzend woordje
en blij wanneer de baas hem stevig op de nek klopt.
Zó moet het veulen, als 't eenmaal van moeder af is,
gewend; dan—nieuwe plicht—steekt hij in een zacht halster
zijn kop,—nog weerloos, sidderend, nog beduusd van jonkheid.
Zijn er drie zomers om en is de vierde in aantocht,
dan moet hij voltes maken en met heldere hoefslag
straf draven—of beurt om beurt de poten sierlijk buigen;
men ziet, hij zwoegt er op.—Dàn mag de wind hij tarten,
dàn stuiven over 't open veld, als kent hij teugel
noch toom,—in 't losse zand staat nauw het spoor getekend.
—Zó komt hoog uit het noorden een bolle wind geblazen,
het boze weer uit Scythië en de droge wolken
verwaaien; 't hoge graan—een wiegelende vlakte—
ritselt op 't zwellend ademen; in de bossen ruisen
de toppen—lange golven stuwen naar de kusten.
Vóórt vliegt de wind—hij strookt het land, hij strookt het water.—
Nu komt hij uit, het paard, langs Elis' wijde grasbaan;
hij rent—bezweet, de bek beschuimd met bloedige vlokken—
of draaft met soepele nek voor lichte Belgen-sulkies.
Pas dàn, na de dressuur, mogen ze stevig krachtvoer;
dat zet goed aan. Sterk voeren vóór 't dresseren maakt hen
geweldig koppig, en rebels—als men ze aanpakt—
tegen de zweep die striemt, de punten van het wolfsbit.

Maar niets bewaart de krachten beter dan zorgvuldig
Venus te weren en wat de blinde driften prikkelt;
hetzij men runderen houden wil of liever paarden.
De stieren worden dus naar afgelegen weiden
verbannen—een berg voorbij of achter brede stromen,

òf wel ze staan op stal, aan goed gevulde ruiven.
Het zien van 't wijfje toch verteert stilaan hun krachten
als vuur—om háár wordt loof en groenend kruid vergeten
voor zoeter lokking, en de trotse minnaars dwingt zij
herhaaldelijk het op de horens uit te vechten.
In 't grote woud van Sila weidt een prachtig koebeest:
zij vechten—stoot om stoot—in dolle drift, de stieren;
vaak is het raak—het zwarte bloed loopt langs de lijven;
't wordt kop aan kop een duwen met de horens—loeien,
gerekt, galmt na in 't bos en langs Olympus' ketens.
Het vechterspaar blijft nimmer in één stal: de éne,
die het verloor, gaat weg—in vreemde streek een balling—
diep kreunend om de smaad, de afstraffing door de trotse
die won en 't wijfje dat hij, machteloos, verspeeld heeft;
omkijkend naar de stal verlaat hij 't oude erfland.
Nù heeft hij maar één wil: zijn krachten oefenen—koppig
ligt hij tussen de rotsen op de naakte bodem,
verkiest geen voer dan stekelig blad en scherpe biezen
en traint zich àl zijn drift te richten naar de horens.
Hij viert zich bonkende op een boomstam uit,—met stoten
tart hij de lucht, zand stuift—zó krijgt de strijd zijn voorspel.
Dan, als zijn sterkte is saamgebald, hersteld zijn krachten,
voorwaarts!—in dolle ren op de argeloze vijand.
Zó, midden in zee, begint een brandingskam te schuimen
verweg; de golf loopt op, kromt zich—en omgeslagen
dondert hij op de kust de stenen langs, een kanteling
steil als de rotswand zelf;—maar diep in 't water kookt het
en kolkt,—hoog wordt het donkere grondzand opgeworpen.

Ja, al wat leeft op aarde: mensen, wilde dieren,
wat zee bevolkt en weiden, en vogels bont van veren,
zij tuimelen blind in 't vuur: 't is de éne drift bij allen.

[245-275]

Venus' seizoen—nooit feller zwerft door de woestijnen
los van haar welpen de leeuwin, moorden zó zinloos
de lompe beren; overal ligt vol dode beesten
het bos; dan is de ever wild en vals de tijger;
onzalig dan wie trekt door de eenzame Sahara.
De paarden—zie, hun hele lijf langs gaan de rillingen
wanneer slechts een bekende geur komt overwaaien;
dan houdt geen mens met toom, met straffe zweep hen tegen;
geen rotsen of ravijn, zij stáán niet voor de slagboom
der bruisende rivier, die losse blokken kantelt.
Zelfs het Sabellisch zwijn breekt los; hij wet de houwers,
krabbelt in de aarde en schuurt zijn bast tegen een boomstam;
zó hardt hij, links en rechts, zijn schoeren voor de stoten.
En dan de màn, die brandende diep-in voelt woelen
de stugge drift?—'t Is vliegend weer, hol staat de branding;
maar hij zwemt over, laat, in blinde nacht. En boven
dondert het aan de zware hemelpoort, het water
brult, brekende op de rots.—Niets houdt hem terug, zijn ouders
niet in hun smart, zijn lief niet, die om hèm zal sterven
een wrede dood.—
         Zie Bacchus' bontgevlekte lynxen,
het wolvenpak, de honden, 't schuwe hert—toch strijdbaar;
maar weet: het allerscherpst merkt men de bronst bij merries.
't Was Venus zelf, die deze driften schiep: te Potniae
toen Glaucus werd verscheurd door 't eigen bijtend vierspan.
Bronst jaagt hen over bergen en bruisende rivieren,
—zij klauteren op de kam, zij zwemmen 't stroombed over.—
Nauw slaat de vonk in 't gretig lichaam aan—bij voorjaar
vooral (bij voorjaar keert de warmte in 't bloed),—of allen
staan met de koppen westwaarts op de rotsige steilte
en snuiven de ijle lucht. Menigmaal zonder énige
paring drachtig—door de wind bevrucht, o wonder!—

slaan zij in draf: het puntig rotsgebergte over
of door 't geplooide dal,—niet oostelijk, naar zonsopgang
maar noordelijk en noord-west, of zuidelijk waar de stormwind
zwart losbarst en de lucht met kou en vocht versombert.
In die tijd wordt hippomanes (de rake term van
de herders), giftig slijm, door 't lichaam afgescheiden;
hippomanes—hoe vaak verzameld door een boze
stiefmoeder en gemengd met kruiden en toverspreuken!
—Voorbij vliegt middelerwijl de tijd, voorbij ongrijpbaar,
wijl onze ronde toeft, geboeid, bij al 't bijzondere.

Dit van het grootvee—de andere helft van 't werk blijft over:
behandeling van 't gewolde schaap, de ruige geiten.
Hier wacht een taak: hier, wakkere boer, valt naam te maken.
Wel ben ik mij bewust hoe zwaar 't is dit in woorden
te vangen en een klein bedrijf zijn glans te geven;
maar toch—Parnassus' strenge steilten over draagt mij
verlangen zoet. O weelde een bergland te betreden,
waar géén tevoren 't glooiend spoor vond naar Castalia!
Thans, Pales oudeerwaard, met volle toon gezongen.

Mijn eerste voorschrift is het schaap met hooi te voeren
in een beschutte stal, tot weer het zomers loof groent,
en op de kille vloer dik stro en bossen varens
te leggen, dat zo'n beest—'t is teer—niet heeft te lijden
van vorst—want dat geeft schurft en kwade pootgezwellen.
Dan nog een verdere raad: geef geiten overvloedig
haagappelloof, en om te drinken levend water.
De stal—rug naar de wind—moet zó staan dat hij 's winters
de zon vangt, pal op 't zuiden; want straks komt de kou, als
de Waterman gaat dalen, 't late jaar doordrenkend.
De geit vraagt, net zo goed als 't schaap, om zorg en aandacht

en brengt niet minder in—ofschoon, wol van Milete,
gekleurd met Tyrisch purper, is prijzige marktwaar;
een geit wèrpt meer, een schaap is kostelijk als melkgeefster:
hoemeer de emmer schùimt wanneer er wordt gemolken,
te rijker zal de melkstroom uit de uiers vloeien.
De bokken—hùn scheert men ook graag de grijze kinnebaard;
zo aan de Cinyps, waar het stugge haar verwerkt wordt
voor de kazerne of 't schamel zeevolk aan een cape helpt.
Een geit vindt best zijn voer in 't bos en op de bergtop
—de stekelrank der braam, de struiken van de steilte—,
en keert vanzelf op tijd ter kooi; 't jong volgt de moeder,
die nauw de zware uier tilt over de drempel.
Bescherm ze dus met zorg voor vrieskou en voor stuifsneeuw
—juist omdat zij van mensen niet zovéél verlangen—,
voer bij met ruime hand, met esse- of wilgelover
en houd de schaapskooi, heel de donkere winter, open.

Maar lokt de westenwind, en noodt de goede zomer
èn geiten èn schapen naar de weide op de bergen,
dan, met de morgenster, geplukt de friste buiten;
nòg is de ochtend jong, het grasland wit van nevelen,
de dauw op 't fijne kruid een weelde voor de dieren.
Als 't vierde hemeluur dan schrompelende dorst brengt,
en 't schel cicaden-sjirpen scheurend uit het hout breekt,
ga bij een put of diepe poel uw beesten drenken,
waar 't vlugge water langs een eiken goot geleid wordt.
Zoek een vallei met schaduw in de middaghitte,
zo een, waar stoer van stam een machtige oude eik staat
die breed zijn takken spreidt, of waar een donkere bosrand
—steeneiken dicht gegroept—in schaduw ligt en stilte.
Voer naar de waterlopen wéér uw kudde en weid ze
tot aan zonsondergang; de avond valt en mild wordt

[337-367]

de lucht,—in manedauw gaat de natuur verademen,
—ijsvogelroep aan 't strand, een vinkenslag in 't hakhout.—

Zal ik van Libye's herders zingen, van hun steppen
en hoe zij huizen, eenzaam, in verstrooide hutten?
Vaak dag en nacht, gerijd tot maanden, trekken kudden
grazende door die grote verlatenheid en vinden
geen onderdak—het land is eindeloos. De herder
in Africa neemt alles mee op trek: hut, huisraad,
zijn wakkere hond, zijn koker bovenstbeste pijlen,—
zoals, sinds eeuwen her, ook Rome's strijders trekken,
marcherend overzwaar bepakt; de vijand ziet hen
opeens vóór zich—dan stáát het kamp al—in formatie.
Anders waar 't Scythenvolk woont rond het meer Maeotis,
en kolkende de Donau 't blonde zand doet wielen,
de Rhodope—die pal naar 't noorden toe ligt—ombuigt;
dáár blijft het vee op stal, daar groeit geen sprietje gras op
de vlakte en nergens is een loofboom. Troosteloos eender
met bergen opgewaaide sneeuw en hard bevroren
strekt zich het land—tot zeven ellen rijst het sneeuwdek;
't wintert altijd en altijd snerpt de koude vrieswind.—
En nooit doorbreekt de zon de bleke nevelen, niet als
hij met zijn span de hemelsteilte oprijdt, niet als
zijn wagen dalende in 't rosse spiegelen wegzinkt.
Opeens zet in de levende rivier een ijskorst
zich af, en 't water draagt meteen de ijzeren wielband
—ééns was het schip daar thuis en nu de lompe karren—;
't brons springt zomaar kapot en áán het lijf bevriezen
de kleren, met een bijl moet men de wijnen hakken;
het binnenmeer bevriest massief tot op de bodem
en in de ruige baarden glinsteren ijskristallen.
En altijd eender blijft het uit de hemel sneeuwen;

er sterven schapen; logge runderen, ruw berijpt, staan
bewegingloos—een koppel herten, saamgedrongen,
kleumt onder 't vreemde dek, 't gewei juist even zichtbaar.
Die jaagt men niet met net en losgelaten honden,
of—'t maakt hen wild van angst—het koord met purperen veren,
neen, waar zij worstelen om de sneeuwhoop weg te werken
treft hen van vlakbij 't mes, en onder deerlijk gillen
afgemaakt, worden ze in triomf naar huis gedragen.
De mensen graven zich in holen in, diep onder
de grond en leven er zorgeloos en lui,—een stapel
houtblokken vlamt, hele olmen rollen in de vuurhaard;
hier slijten zij de nacht bij 't spel en lustig gaat er
hun wijn rond: gerstebier met zure lijsterbessen.
—Zó leeft een volk onder de noordersterrenhemel,
verwilderd, door de barre winterstorm gegeseld,
om 't lijf de ruige gele vachten van zijn schapen.

Houdt ge het schaap voor wol, pas op voor ruwe planten,
klis en driedistel—, mijd terrein met ruige grassen
en selecteer direct: wit soort met zachte vachten.
En als de ram—zijn wol mag van het puurste wit zijn—
ook maar een zwarte tong heeft onder 't vocht verhemelt,
dan moet hij weg; zo'n beest bezorgt de nieuwe lammeren
vlekken op de vacht: zoek uit de grote kudde een ander.
Een sneeuwen vacht—als waar 't verhaal is—overmocht u,
Diana, en door Arcadië's Pan liet gij u vangen
—een roepen diep in 't bos, roep sterker dan uw hoogmoed.—
Voor melkvee moet ge volop citysus en klaver
aandragen en wat zout door 't groenvoer in de ruif doen;
dat geeft een groter dorst—dùs meer gespannen uiers,
en in de melk is even nog de zoutsmaak merkbaar.
Niet zelden gaat direct het jong weg van de moeder

en krijgt een muilkorf met hard ijzer voor zijn snoetje.
Melk, bij het rijzend licht des daags gemolken, stremt men
bij nacht; maar die van avondval en eerste schemer
brengt vóór het daagt de herder weg in houten vaten
naar stad: of, ìets gezouten, wordt het kaas voor 's winters.

Zorg, en niet in de laatste plaats, goed voor uw honden,
snelle Spartaanse brakken, bassende Molossiërs:
wei is best voer. Met zulke wachters zijt ge veilig
voor dieven in de stal bij nacht, voor wolven buiten,
voor de aanval—in de rug—van 't roofvolk uit de bergen.
En dan is er de drijfjacht;—als de onager wegstuift,
de meute zal de haas, de meute 't damhert jagen;
de ever uit zijn wildernis en wentelpoelen
wordt opgeschrikt met blaffen, en langs hoge bergen
hitst gij 't geweldig hert met schreeuwen in de netten.
Nu nog een raad: brand in uw stallen geurige ceder
en rook met galbanum de schadelijke reptielen uit;
vaak zit—raak haar niet aan!—onder de zware kribben
een adder weggekropen, dodelijk schuw voor 't daglicht.
Dan zoekt de ringslang graag een donker hoekje—dàt is
zo'n pest voor 't vee!—met gif besmet hij, aangeschuifeld,
de beesten. Pak een steen of pak een knuppel, herder:
als hij, boos sissend, met gezwollen hals zich opheft,
sla raak.—
      In doodsangst duikt de kop weg in het donker;
de windingen van zijn lijf, de ringen van zijn staartpunt
zijn lam, een laatste kronkel trekt zijn trage bochten.
Gevaarlijk evenzeer de bos-slang uit Calabrië,
die uit zijn opgerolde schubbenlijf een voorstuk
opsteekt, gemerkt met grote vlekken langs de buiklijn.
Zolang nog uit de bronnen water welt en nat is

de grond bij vochtig voorjaar, zuidenwind en regen,
huist hij in poelen aan de kant, waar hij vraatzuchtig
vis en kwakende kikkers in zijn zwarte keel propt.
Maar het moeras wordt droog, de dorre grond gaat scheuren:
dan schiet hij op het droge—vuur doet de ogen flikkeren—
en doet zijn kwaad dáár; wild van dorst, getergd van hitte.
Bekruip' mij dan geen lust om buiten zacht te slapen,
behaaglijk, op de boskam, mij in 't gras te strekken,
als hij, nieuw uit zijn huid gekropen, jong en glanzend
spiraalt, of—buiten 't hol met eieren of jongen
steil in de zon—zijn tong, driemaal gevorkt, laat trillen.

En nu de ziekten: 'k leer u oorzaak en symptomen.
Een schaap loopt schurft op—een kwaad ding—wanneer hij nat is
en koud tot op het bot, of door en door bevroren
en ruig van vorst; ook als men hem na 't scheren vuil laat
en hij dan 't zweterig lijf aan scherpe stekels ophaalt.
Met water uit de beek wassen daarom de herders
hun kudde en kopje-onder gaat de ram de kolk in,
kletsnat—dan, losgelaten, drijft hij met de stroom mee.
't Geschoren schaap wordt óók wel ingesmeerd; een mengsel
van bitter olieschuim, zilverglid, zuivere zwavel
roert men door zalf van zachte was en pek; en daardoor
gaat zeeajuin, scherp nieskruid en donker bitumen.
Toch is tegen de kwaal geen middel zó doeltreffend
als dat het mes ingrijpt en blootlegt waar het zeer zit;
het kwaad leeft dóór en woekert in 't verborgen verder
zolang de herder schuwt behandeling toe te passen,
iedere verbetering lijdelijk van de goden vragend.
Jà, nog iets: als de pijn, diep in het dier genesteld,
te keer gaat en de hoge koorts het doet vermageren,
is 't goed, als men de koortsgloed zakken laat door tussen

de hoef, daar waar de ader klopt, een snee te geven;
zo doen het de Bisalten en strijdbare Geloni,
—horden over de Rhodope, door Getië's steppen—
volk waar gestremde melk met paardenbloed de drank is.

Een schaap, dat ge van verre àl te vaak de schaduw
ziet zoeken, dat met lange tanden van het gras vreet
en achteraan komt, of midden in 't land, bij 't grazen
gaat liggen, dat alléén, diep in de avond, afzwerft—
zo'n kwade plek moet dadelijk uitgesneden, vóórdat
besmetting moordend sluipt in de argeloze kudde.
Veelvuldiger dan vlagen op zee bij naderend stormweer
valt ziekte op het vee. En de besmetting teistert
niet beest voor beest, maar grijpt de hele zomerweide
inééns—het lam, het schaap, heel 't volk tot aan de wortel.
Dat weet wie de Alpensteilten kent, Noricums dorpjes
in 't hoogland, de Timavus, stroom van Istrië's vlakte:
nù nog, na zóveel tijd, ziet hij hoe 't rijk der herders
vereenzaamd is, de bergwei overal verlaten.
Hier heerste eenmaal ziekte in de lucht—afschuwelijk
werd de atmosfeer, heel 't warme najaar bleef het gisten;
elk dier moest sterven—op de weide, in de bossen;
het water werd besmet, aan 't grasland vrat de schimmel.
Geen rechte wegen koos de dood; had koortsgloed, jagend
door de aderen, het arme lijf verdord van droogte,
dan stróómde weer het etterig vocht, dat al de organen
stuk voor stuk aantastte en geleidelijk ondermijnde.
Vaak, ìn de plechtige dienst, is 't offerdier voor 't altaar
—juist strikte men met sneeuwen lint zijn wolband—tussen
der dienaars traag gebaren stervend neergeslagen.
En àls de priester nog tevoren een dier geslacht had,
dan wilde het geweide op 't altaar niet branden

en kon de ziener, hoè men vroeg, geen uitspraak geven;
't aangelegd offermes wordt nauw door bloed gekleurd en
er spatten in 't losse zand donker wat droppels etter.
Nu moeten in 't welig gras de kalfjes overal sterven
of 't zoete leven laten voor de volle kribbe;
de aanhalige huishond, hij wordt dol—van blaffend hoesten
schokken de varkens, ziek, de zere keel gezwollen.
Strompelend, verraden in zijn vreugden, taalt het prijsros
niet naar het gras of 't frisse water meer; zijn hoef bonkt
onrustig neer, de oren liggen plat; bezweet rilt
het lijf—kil als de doodsstrijd komen gaat en dor is
de huid, die bij 't aanraken hard voelt en weerspannig.
Dit zijn, vóór 't sterven, de symptomen in de eerste dagen;
maar als in zijn proces de ziekte gaat verergeren,
dan schitteren de ogen; de adem—diep gehaald uit
de borst—is soms beklemd van zuchten, zware snikken
spannen het onderlijf en uit de neus spuit donker
het bloed; de tong zit rasperig voor het dichte keelgat.
Wel bracht een middel—door een trechter wijn ingieten—
soms baat; het gold in stervensnood als enige uitkomst;
maar achteraf bleek 't juist funest: want, bijgekomen,
in hete razernij bij 't naderen van de doodsstrijd
—spaar dìt de vrome, goden, sla die waan uw haters!—
scheurden zij 't eigen lijf met blote tanden aan stukken.

Zie, voor de stugge ploeg gaat dampende de trekstier—
neer slaat hij, braakt een golf van schuimig bloed—en geeft dan
zijn laatste zucht. De ploeger spant, terneergeslagen,
de trekos uit, die treurt om zijn gestorven makker
en midden in de voor laat hij de ploegschaar steken.
Niets lokt het beest, de koelte niet der diepe bossen,
het zachte gras, het stroompje, schietend langs de rotsen,

dat zuiverder dan zilver 't laagland zoekt; de flanken
zijn ingezonken, de ogen staren dof, omfloerst met
stompzinnigheid, de nek zakt zwaar omlaag naar de aarde.
Wat baat hun nu hun vlijt, hun trouwe dienst bij 't ploegen
van taaie grond? En dan doet zich een beest geen schade
met Bacchus' gaven of met overdaad van schotels;
zij voeden zich met loof en 't simpel gras der weiden,
hun dronk is water uit de klare bron, de driftige
gang der rivier,—geen zorg breekt hun gezonde slaap af.
Een boze tijd.—Er was, verhaalt men, in die streken
geen koe voor Juno's dienst meer; 'n ongelijk paar buffels
trok voor de kar de gaven naar de statige tempels.
Zo breekt de hak moeizaam de grond; de blote nagels
krabben de kuilen voor het zaad; langs 't bergpad kraken
de karren—mannen trekken, straf de nek gespannen.
De wolf zoekt niet met list de schaapskooi in te sluipen,
noch waart hij bij de kudden om des nachts—tè fel is
de greep der ziekte; schichtige herten, schuwe gemzen
tussen de honden komen ze om de huizen zwerven.
En later, al wat zwemt, het volk der oceanen—
als stukken wrakhout spoelt de branding bij de vloedlijn
hen aan—de robben wijken uit naar de rivieren.
Nu sterft, vergeefs gekropen in zijn kronkelgangen,
de adder, en de slang—verstard, met stijve schubben.
Zelfs voor de vogels is de lucht onrein, zij tuimelen in
hun vlucht en laten hoog onder een wolk het leven.
Verandering van wei geeft ook niet meer, en hééft men
een middel, 't werkt verkeerd—de meesters staan verslagen:
Chiron zelfs de Centaur, Melampus zelfs de ziener.
Verschrikkelijk rijst in 't licht, Doods donkerte onttogen,
Tisiphone, vaalbleek, die vóór zich ziekte en angsten
uitjaagt en dagelijks hoger 't wrede hoofd gaat dragen.

[554-566]

Blaten en stotend loeien komt van de rivieren,
de oevers—nu verdord—de zachtgelijnde heuvelen.
Straks slaat het kùdden tegelijk: tot in de stallen
liggen, afschuwelijk gistend, rottende cadavers,
tot—wijzer—men ze in kuilen bergt en dekt met aarde.
Immers onbruikbaar was het leer; het vlees kon niemand
met water zuiveren of boven 't vuur bereiden;
zelfs niet geschoren kon, door ziekte en vuil vervreten,
de vacht; het weefsel, nauwelijks aangeraakt, verpulvert.
Wie tòch de ongeluksvacht wou dragen—hij bekocht het
met jeukende uitslag: 't lijf ging stinken van een kleverig
zweet en kort daarna—snel ingetreden einde—
vervrat het folterend vuur het aangetaste lichaam.

De bijen

Over de honing, gave van des hemels dauwen,
een nieuw lied.—Schenk, Maecenas, ook dit werk uw aandacht.
Hier ligt te kijk een kleine wereld en haar wonderen:
aanvoerders onversaagd, een ganse staat,—zijn volken,
zijn levenswijze, driften en strijd wil ik ontvouwen.
Klein is het arbeidsveld, niet klein zijn roem, als gunstig
de goden willen zijn, Apollo hoort mijn vragen.
Begin met voor de bijenstand een plek te zoeken
buiten de wind (beladen komen zij waar wind staat
de korf niet in) en waar geen schaap, geen bokje stoeiend
trapt op de bloemen, of een koe die loopt te grazen
de dauw afschudt en poten op het jonge gras zet.
Geen schubbig hagedisje, scherp getekend, hoort bij
de voorraadplaats; geen vogels ook, de bijenwolf of
de zwaluw, 't keeltje bloedbevlekt door Procne's wandaad,
—want dat zijn grote rovers, die liefst ook het bijtje
snappen in hun vlucht: goed voer voor hun vraatzuchtig broedsel.
Een klare bron, een meertje in zijn groene mosrand,
dàt graag,—een smalle, vlugge beek door 't gras, en schaduw
van palm of zware oleaster bij de vliegplank.
Als dan de zwerm, voor 't eerst, de nieuwe koning volgend,
zijn lente houdt en 't jongvolk, uit de raat gelaten,
speelt, roept dichtbij weldadige koelte van het water,
en 't gastvrij bladerdak geeft onderweg een rustpunt.
Leg midden in 't water, of het stromend is of stilstaand,
wat wilgen overdwars en een paar grote stenen,

[27-58]

dan kunnen ze in de zon hun vleugels zitten drogen
op al die bruggetjes, wanneer soms bij het rusten
een windvlaag hen natspatte of in de beek deed tuimelen.
Ook bloeie er groen vijfvingerkruid en thijm, sterk-reukig
daar in de buurt, voorts aromatisch bonentoekruid
volop en, van de springbron fris, een plek viooltjes.
De woning zelf, hetzij gevoegd uit repen boomschors,
hetzij een korf, die ge uit buigzaam rijshout saamvlecht,
moet nauw van ingang zijn; want honing stremt bij vrieskou,
terwijl ze omgekeerd bij hitte smelt en uitloopt.
Twee even kwade dingen voor de bijen; 't is niet
om nìet dat ze in hun huis de fijnste spleetjes ijverig
met was bestrijken, en met maagdenwas uit bloemen
de naden dichten,—kleefstof tot dit doel vergaard en
bewaard—taaier dan mare en pek van Phrygië's Ida.
Ze graven zelfs wel—als het waar is—holen en wonen
behagelijk daar ondergronds; men vindt ze in gaten
binnen in 't puimsteen of in een vermolmde boomtronk.
Maar zorg ook zelf goed: geef hun luchtig huis een laagje
van aangestreken klei; gooi wat los groen er over;
staat bij de korven taxis, kap ze; en rooster nimmer
daar kreeften rood. Mijd plaatsen, waar een diep moeras is,
een mestvaalt stinkt, of waar de rotswand bij het kloppen
weergalmt, en als gij roept de echo kaatsend terugspringt.
Thans dit: zodra de gouden zon de winter terugdrijft
onder de aarde, en met zomers licht de hemel
ontsluit, begint hun trek: de bossen door, de bergwei,
purend de purpren bloemen af, de waterspiegel
licht rakend.—Dan vervoert een onverklaarde drift hen
tot zorg voor korf en broed; de nieuwe raten bouwen
zij kunstig, stijf gevuld met kleverige honing.
Nadien, ontwaart ge een zwerm, de korf nu uitgevlogen,

[59-90]

voorbij het zomers blauw hoog aan de hemel drijvend
—zwart wolkje, dat verbaasd ge op de wind ziet meegaan—
let op: vast zoeken zij zoet water en beschutting
van lover. Strooi dan daar welriekend kruid naar voorschrift:
citroenkruid fijngewreven en wasbloem, simpel groeisel.
Nu rinkel met metaal, ga rond met Cybele's cymbels:
vanzelf vallen ze bij die kruidenplek, vanzelf ook
hervinden ze hun trant en kruipen in de cellen.
Maar zwermen ze uit ten oorlog—dikwijls toch komt tweedracht
tussen twee koningen, met hevige beroering—
dan kunt ge dit metéén voorvoelen: aan de stemming
bij 't volk, hun popelende strijdlust,—de achterblijvers
roept dreigend schril gezoem met koperen signaalklank;
er gaat geluid als korte stoten op klaroenen.
Zij troepen wemelend samen, trillend met de vleugels,
hun wapens wettend met de snuit, hun pootjes poetsend.
Vlak voor de koningscel, rondom de koning warrelt
de dichte zwerm, met luid gegons de vijand tartend.
Dan, als het voorjaar helder wordt, de hemelen open,
rukken zij uit;—'t gevecht begint: hoog in het luchtruim
zoemt het—de strijd verdicht zich tot een warrelend kluwen.
Zij tuimelen sneuvelend: hagel valt niet dichter, nimmer
regent de steeneik, fors geschud, zó'n bui van eikels.
De koningen, kern der rijen, kenbaar aan hun vleugels,
voelen een grote moed in 't kleine lichaam werken;
zij weten van geen wijken, zó lang tot verpletterend
de overwinnaar één partij doet zwenken en vluchten.
Die opgewondenheid en dit verbitterd vechten—
gooi slechts een handvol stof, en het is stil gevallen.
Hebt gij de aanvoerders beide zó het halt geboden,
dan moet de onooglijkste, dat hij geen parasiet wordt,
geofferd: koning zij aan 't ruime hof de schoonste.

[91-122]

De één is fonkelend van fijne gouden schubjes
—een stralend rosgoud pantser—maar de ander, borstelig
en traag, moet smadelijk zijn zware lichaam slepen.
Dus koningen tweeërlei en tweeërlei soort volken:
het een vuil-ruig en lelijk, of door 't stof der wegen
een reiziger kwam getogen en wat drabbig speeksel
uitspuwt verdorst—; het ander licht, met vlugge vonken,
met vlekjes vurig goud symmetrisch overstippeld.
Dat is het beste broed, zó wint ge als 't seizoen komt
een zoete honingsoort; niet zoet alleen,—wat meer is:
ook zuiver, die de smaak van straffe wijn kan temperen.
Maar wordt het doelloos vliegen en spelen langs de hemel,
versmaadt de zwerm de raat en staat de korf vereenzaamd,
verbreek dit zinloos spel van ongedurigheden.
't Is licht verbroken: trek de koningen hun vleugels
uit; kunnen zij niet weg, dan durft geen bij zich wagen
aan steiler vlucht, of de uittocht uit het kamp beginnen.
Nu moet een tuin, waar crocus bloeit en geurt, hen trekken,
waar—dieven en vogels werend—met zijn wilgen snoeimes
hun schutspatroon staat, Hellespontus' god Priapus.
Een ijverig ymker haalt zijn thijm, zijn sparren zelve
hoog van de berg, om ze overal rond de stand te planten;
zelf pakt hij stevig aan en eigenhandig zet hij
de vruchtbare stekken, die hij sproeit met weldoend water.

En ik—zo 'k niet, bijna aan 't einde van mijn arbeid,
de zeilen reefde en reeds de steven landwaarts wendde,—
ik zong misschien van rijke tuinen, welverzorgd van
sierplant, de dubb'le bloei van Paestums rozenhoven,
ook van de andijviestruiken, fris gedrenkt aan 't water,
van oevers, groen van eppe en hoe, door 't gras gekronkeld,
komkommers buikig groeien. 'k Zweeg niet van de narcis

[123-153]

—laat met zijn tooi—of van de krullige acanthus,
de lichte klimop en—struik van het strand—de myrte.
Want in de stad Tarente, aan de voet van 't bolwerk,
waar stroomt door 't blonde land de donkere Galaesus,
kende ik een oude man uit Corycus, die 'n stukje
overgeschoten land had: voor de ploeg onwillig,
geen beste grond voor vee en niet geschikt voor wijnbouw.
En toch—zijn rijtjes groente tussen 't hout verzorgend,
zijn randje witte lelies, ijzerhard, papaver,
was hij rijk als een koning, en laat in de avond
weer thuis, had hij voor niet een rijk beladen tafel.
De eerste voorjaarsroos had hij, de eerste vruchten
in 't najaar en ten tijde als nog de barre winter
de stenen stukvroor en het levend water stremde,
stond hij zijn kleine irisjes al uit te plukken,
mopperend: 'het blijft maar guur, de wind zit in het noorden.'
Hij had ook 't eerste bijenbroed, de eerste zwermen
bij wolken en vroege honing, schuimend uit de raten
geperst; zijn linde en sneeuwbal bloeiden overdadig;
en wat zijn boomgaard vroeg in lentetooi beloofde,
vervulde hij bij najaar in de rijpe vruchten.
Olmen, al uitgegroeid—hij plantte ze op rijen,
peren, stevig van stam, de sleedoorn met zijn pruimen
en de plataan, prieel reeds waar de beker rondgaat.
Maar ingesloten binnen strikte grenzen mag ik
niet toeven hier,—dit worde een lied voor anderen na mij.

Thans verder: 'k wil ontvouwen de aard der bijen, gave
van Vader Juppiter, omdat zij—aangetrokken
door een muziek van brons, 't gekletter der Cureten—
in Dicte's grot de hemelkoning voedsel brachten.
De bijen alleen bezitten samen kroost en samen

de bijenstad; zij leven onder strenge wetten
en weten van een eigen heem, een vaste haardstee;
op winters komst bedacht werken zij 's zomers vlijtig
en wat zij garen gaat bij de gemene voorraad.
Eén groep gaat over 't voedsel, volgens vaste regeling
bij 't veldwerk bezig,—anderen, binnenin de korven,
bouwen uit Narcistranen en kleverige boomhars
't raatfundament, waaraan—van boven naar beneden—
zij hecht de cellen metselen. Eén groep kweekt het broed op
—de hoop des volks—en brengt het groot; weer anderen persen
de zuivere honing, pure nectar, in de cellen.
Ook zijn er door het lot poortwachters aangewezen;
zij letten—om de beurt—op neerslag en bewolking,
ontlasten wie beladen aankomt, òf—in phalanx—
weren zij 't luie tuig, de darren, van de korven.
Het werk krioelt, het geurt naar thijm en honingreuken.
Zó hameren de Cyclopen uit massa's smeltmetalen
het weerlicht. Bij de leren blaasbalg staan er, pompend
de luchtstroom in en uit; en bij de koelbak, 't sissend
brons dompelend. Hamers slaan op 't aambeeld, de Etna davert.
Zij heffen op de maat in wisselslag de armen
met forse zwaai en kantelen 't ijzer met de grijptang.
Niet anders—als men klein met groot mag vergelijken—
doen Cecrops' bijen in hun aangeboren drift tot
bezit. Elk heeft zijn werk: de oudsten dragen zorg voor
de stad—de bouw der raat met kunstig fijne cellen.
De jongeren komen moe des avonds laat op huis aan,
de pootjes vol met thijm; afpurend her en der nog
haagappel, wilgenkatjes, crocus-goud, lavendel,
de gulle linde, de ijzerblauwe hyacinthen.
Voor allen geldt één tijd van werk, één tijd van rusten.
Vroeg zwermen ze uit, bedrijvig staag, tot hen de avond

terugroept—dralend afscheid van de bloemenweide;
dan keren zij ter korf, dan komen ze aan zichzelf toe.
Het zoemt en gonst en bromt rondom de plank en 't vlieggat.
Dan, als elk in zijn cel gekropen is, valt nachtelijk
de stilte en dekt de goede slaap het moede lichaam.
Nooit echter gaan zij ver van huis als er een bui hangt;
dreigt oostenwind, dan wil de hemel hun niet aanstaan:
zij halen water dicht onder de veilige stadsmuur,
wagen slechts korte vluchten en nemen dikwijls steentjes
—zoals een wankel bootje op de golfslag ballast—
aan boord, voor 't evenwicht in de ijle wolkenvelden.
Dan nòg iets heel merkwaardigs in het bijenleven:
zij zoeken niet de paring, die de krachten ontzenuwt
in Venus' dienst, noch baren zij in pijn hun jongen.
Die plukken ze gewoon van geurig kruid en bladeren
—zó simpel komt een koning met zijn jonge burgers,
waarvoor een nieuw paleis en rijk in was gebouwd wordt.
Soms, op hun tochten, schuren ze aan harde stenen
de vleugels stuk,—soms zelfs bezwijken ze aan hun lasten,
zó trekt de bloem hen en de trots op 't honing winnen.
Daarom, al is hun zelf een korte spanne levens
gemeten—immers 't reikt niet meer dan zeven jaren—
de soort sterft nimmer uit; de staat van 't huis duurt reeksen
van jaren en men telt voorouders van voorouders.
Hun koning wordt vereerd, meer dan vorsten in Egypte,
Lydië, of 't Parthenrijk bij Medië's Hydaspes.
Randt niets de koning aan—heel 't volk heeft één gezindheid;
sterft hij, dan breekt de band: erger, zij slaan aan 't plunderen
der honingcellen en slopen 't metselwerk der raten.
Hij houdt toezicht op 't werk; hij is hun held en allen
omzwermen hem,—een dichte wolk van donker gonzen.
Vaak gaat hij op de schouders en zij dekken op 't slagveld

hem met het lijf, om schoon te sterven aan hun wonden.
Men zegt wel, afgaand op die tekenende gedragslijn,
dat bijen iets hebben van goddelijke geest en aethers
fluïdum; want de godheid woont in alles: de aarde,
de banen van de zee, de diepten van de hemel.
Hieruit ontvangen dieren in wei en bos èn mensen
bij de geboorte elk de ijle levensadem;
hierheen keert alles, als het is ontbonden, zeker
terug; er ìs geen dood,—alleen levend ontstijgen
naar 't sterrenheir, een naderen tot de hoogste sferen.
Gaat ge de heilige korf, de schat der honingkameren
ontsluiten,—put eerst water, dat ge uzelf besprenkelt,
reinig uw mond en zwaai de vlugge rook der fakkel.
Tweemaal is vol de oogst, twee malen gaart men honing:
ééns als Taÿgete de aarde haar schoon gelaat toont
en achteloos met de voet zich aan d'Oceanus afstoot,
en ééns als zij, het waterteken van de Vissen
ontwijkend, flauwer wordt en daalt in zee bij winter.
Zijn bijen boos, dan is het èrg: hun plagers steken
zij giftig en de angel blijft verborgen zitten
diep in het vlees,—hun zelve kost de steek het leven.
Ducht gij een strenge winter, kan het niet veel lijden,
wekt hun onrust en hun geplunderd huis uw medelij,
met thijm roken en de lege stukken raat wegsnijden
moet wel: misschien zit ergens, vretend van de honing,
'n sterhagedis, een nest lichtschuwe pissebedden,
of wel een luie dar, die teert op and'rer voorraad.
Soms sluipt een horzel in (die vecht op sterker wapen)
of vieze kakkerlakken,—soms weeft voor de ingang
een spin, Minerva's vijandin, haar ijle webben.
Hoe meer ze zijn geplunderd, des te toegewijder
werkt heel 't getroffen volk aan het herstel der schade,

[250-280]

de gaten dichten, 't mozaïek der raten leggen
uit maagdenwas. Maar zijn de bijen—even kwetsbaar
in hun bestaan als wij—door ziekte mat, niet tierig,
metéén kunt gij het zien aan stellige symptomen.
Daad'lijk hebben de zieken een andere kleur: zien mager
en zonder glans; de doden worden uitgedragen
buiten de korf, en de anderen volgen in de rouwstoet.
Zij hangen—pootjes in elkaar gehaakt—voor de ingang,
of wel zij sluiten 't huis en blijven samen binnen,
van honger lusteloos en van trage kou verkrompen.
Dan hoort men ze: een somber en eentonig gonzen;
zo suist het, als er sterke wind staat, in de bossen,
zo ruist de zee, wanneer een brandingskam terug stroomt
en snort het felle vuur binnen de ovenwanden.
Is 't zó, dan raad ik geurig moederhars te branden,
door rietjes honing in de korf te druppelen. 't Montert
de zieken op en lokt ze naar de wei van vroeger.
Goed werkt een vleugje geur er door van fijngestampte
galappels en dor rozeblad, moststroop op vlammend
vuur ingekookt, of psithiawijn van trosrozijnen,
sterk duizendguldenkruid en thijm van de Hymettus.
Dan groeit er in de wei een bloem, die bij de boeren
amellus heet. De plant is makkelijk te herkennen:
uit éne pol schiet op een dikke bos van stelen.
't Bloemhart is goud, de dichte stralenkrans van blaadjes
rondom zweemt naar het donker purper van violen.
Vaak, in festoenen, siert hij voor de goden 't altaar;
de smaak proeft wrang,—de herders plukken hem op weigrond
in 't dal en langs de Mella met zijn slingerbochten.
Neem hier de wortels van, kook ze in een geurig wijntje
en richt bij de ingang hun een rijkelijke dis aan.

Maar zit men plotseling zonder bijenbroed, niet wetend
hoe de oorsprong van een nieuwe stam verwekt moet worden,
ontvouwen wil ik dan de wondere ontdekking
des meesters uit Arcadië: als een vaars geslacht is,
ziet telkens uit het rottend bloed men bijen komen.
Ziehier 't verhaal gevolgd tot aan zijn vroegste oorsprong:
Waar in Egypte het gezegende Canopus,
stad van de Nijl die spiegelend de velden blank zet,
vaart rond zijn akkerland in bonte, smalle bootjes;
waar de nabijheid drukt van 't pijlenschietend oosten,
waar met zijn donker slib de Nijl het land doet groenen
en stroomt en splitsend zich vertakt in zeven monden,
stuwend zijn wateren heel van bij de ebben Zwarten,
zoekt gans het land vertrouwend baat bij die methode.
Men kiest een kleine ruimte—voor dit doel opzettelijk
beperkt—met laaggezolderd pannendak en tussen
vier enge wanden; dan in iedere wand een raampje
met schuin invallend licht,—naar de vier hemelstreken.
Een kalf, waarvan de horens zich al om gaan buigen,
tweejarig, neemt men nu, en stopt, hoe 't beest ook worstelt,
zijn neusgaten en bek stijf dicht; 't wordt doodgeslagen—
de huid blijft gaaf en 't murwgebeukte vlees gaat rotten.
Zo blijft het liggen in dat schuurtje, onder 't lichaam
wat afgebroken takken, verse thijm, lavendel.
Dit als de westenwind voor 't eerst het water rimpelt,
vóórdat het weiland gloeit van jonge kleuren, voordat
de zwaluw 't nestje bouwt, al kwetterend, aan de balken.
Geleidelijk ontbindt het lijf, de lauwe vochten
gaan gisten en er verschijnen zonderlinge diertjes:
eerst zonder poten nog, al spoedig vleugelsnorrend;
één klomp,—dan maakt zich de één na de ander vrij de lucht in,
tot ze—als een zomerwolk uitregent in een stortbui—

[313-342]

losbarsten, of als pijlen van de pees gesprongen
wanneer de Parthen flitsend 't eerste salvo geven.
Wat godheid, Muze, smeedde ons deze edele kennis?
Waar nam der mensen wondere ervaring aanvang?

De herder Aristaeus, Tempe's dal ontvloden,
waar, naar de sage luidt, hem al zijn bijen stierven
door ziekte en honger—aan Peneüs' bronhoofd stond hij
en klaagde bitter, en zijn woord klonk tot zijn moeder:
'Cyrene, moeder mijn, die woont diep in de bronwel,
waarom ben ik—van edele godenstam geboren,
(gij zegt toch: Thymbra's heer, Apollo, is mijn vader)
zó door het lot belaagd op aarde—uw zoon? Waar bleef uw
liefde voor mij? Wat gaaft ge me uitzicht op de hemel?
Zie, zelfs de simpele eer van dit mijn leven als sterveling,
met waakse zorg voor vrucht en vee in eindeloos pogen
verworven, moet ik missen—en gij zijt mijn moeder!
Ontwortel nu maar zelf,—waarom ook niet?—mijn boomgaard,
steek wreed mijn stallen aan, verniel de oogst te velde;
de brand in 't koren, hak met harde bijl de wingerd
kapot, als gij u zózeer stoot aan mijn vermaardheid!'

Zijn moeder in haar kameren diep, onder het stroombed,
ving het geluid.—Rondom haar zat een ring van nymfen
te spinnen: kostbare wol, van zeegroen diep verzadigd;
Phyllodoce en Drymo, Xantho en Ligea,
—tegen het blank der halzen golft en glanst het hoofdhaar—
Cydippe en de blonde Lycorias—de ene kind nog,
met de eerste ervaring van Lucina's pijn de andere;
Clio en Beroë, Oceaniden beide,
met goud gegord en bonte vachten omgeslagen;
Opis en Deiopeia, Ephyre en—eindelijk

liet zij haar pijlen rust—de snelle Arethusa.
Eén, Clymene, vertelde: van Vulcanus' hulpeloos
jaloers verdriet, Mars' listen en zijn steelse vreugden;
tellend, van Chaos af, der goden minnarijen
bij reeksen. Zij, geboeid, spinnen de zachte woldraad
àf van het rokken, tot—weer!—Aristaeus' weeklacht
zijn moeders oor treft. Allen, in haar doorzichtige zetels,
zijn stil. Maar Arethusa, vóór de andere zusters,
ziet uit en beurt het blonde hoofd boven het water
en turende: 'Met reden ontstelde u deze smartkreet,
zuster Cyrene. Hij, uw lieveling Aristaeus,
staat daar verslagen bij vader Peneüs' bronhoofd
en schreiende beticht hij ù van harteloosheid.'
En Aristaeus' moeder, in een helle ontsteltenis:
'Breng hier hem, hier naar ons. Hìj mag der goden drempel
betreden.' Op haar wenk gaan wijd de diepe wateren
uiteen en vormen een geëffend pad. De golven
staan, omgekruld, aan beide kanten als een bergwand;
hij daalt de diepten in en komt tot onder 't stroombed.
Nu ziet hij haar paleis en vochtige revieren,
meren besloten in grotten en murmelende bossen;
verbaasd, bij 't schrijden, om de zware gang der wateren,
als aller stromen loop onder de grote aarde
hij merkt, in richting afgesplitst: Phasis en Lycus,
het bronhoofd waar de diepe Enipeus breekt te voorschijn,
de wel van vader Tiber en de Anio-beken,
Hypanis, kiezel-schurend, Mysië's Caïcus
en—met zijn stierenhoofd en 't paar der gulden horens—
Eridanus, rivier die langs der landen weelde
mondt in de purperen zee als driftigste der stromen.
Hij treedt in de gewelfde druipsteengrot; Cyrene
haar zoon aanhorend, weet: onnodig deze tranen.

[375-405]

Nu reiken, naar de wijs, de zusters helder water
en glad geschoren doeken voor het handen wassen;
andere beladen rijk de dis en dragen telkens
de bekers op: 't altaar geurt van Panchaia's wierook.
Zijn moeder: 'Vul met Bacchus' druifnat de bokalen,
Oceanus geplengd.' Zij zelf bidt, tot Oceanus,
vader van al wat is en tot de zusters nymfen,
honderd in 't woud en honderd in de stromen wonend.
Driemalen sprenkelt zij op 't brandend haardvuur nectar
en driemaal slaat, hoog tegen het verwulft, de weerschijn.
Bemoedigd, op dit teken, vangt zij haar verhaal aan:

'Bij Carpathos leeft, in Neptunus' rijk, een ziener,
Proteus, zeekleurig, wijde wateren rijdt hij over;
zijn wagen trekt een span, half vis half tweepootpaarden.
Hij zoekt nu juist Emathia's havens en zijn stamland
Pallene op. Verering vindt hij bij de nymfen,
bij Nereus zelf, oeroud.—Want, ziener, weet hij alles:
wat is, wat is geweest, wat in de toekomst nadert;
dit door Neptunus' gunst: diens vissenvolken talloos
en plompe robben hoedt hij in de waterbanen.
Hem vangen moet gij, zoon, en binden—dat hij blootlegt
de wortel van het kwaad en uitkomst geeft ten beste.
Zijn raad geeft hij u nimmer zonder dwang; verbidden
laat hij zich niet: aanpakken hard, en stevig snoeren
zijn boeien: hierop strandt zijn loze list ten laatste.
'k Zal zelf u, als de zon ontsteekt de middaghitte,
de planten dorsten en de schapen schaduw zoeken,
zijn schuilplaats wijzen, waar hij oud, vermoeid van 't water,
zich terugtrekt: in zijn slaap kunt gij hem licht verrassen.
Maar hebt ge hem gegrepen en geboeid—dàn werkt hij
zich listig los, een tovenaar met dierenmaskers.

[406-435]

Ineens wordt hij een borstelig zwijn, een boze tijger,
een draak gepantserd of een leeuw met rosse manen;
óók, met de felle knettering van vuur, ontsnapt hij
de touwen of loopt weg als water uit uw handen.
Maar in hoemeer gedaanten bont hij zich verandert,
te straffer snoer, mijn zoon, hem in de sterke touwen;
totdat hij, omgetoverd, weer de Proteus is die
ge zaagt, toen hij de ogen look in eerste sluimer.'

Zij sprak, een reine geur van ambrozijn verspreidend,
die wademde om het lichaam van haar zoon. Een vleugen
van zoetheid woei van zijner haren pracht; een sterkte
voer lenig in zijn lijf.
     Er is een grot, geweldig,
uitgehold in de bergwand, waar de zeewind injaagt
het zware water, dat in losse golven terugrolt;
van ouds een veilige ree voor 't schip door storm belopen.
Daar houdt zich Proteus schuil achter een machtige steendam.
En hier wordt Aristaeus door de nymf, van 't licht af,
verstopt; zij zelve treedt iets terug, gehuld in nevelen.
De Hondsster, blakerend het dorstig Indië, brandde aan
de hemel fel; de zonschijf had zijn baan ten halve
beschreven,—dor was 't gras, de stromen in hun bedding
dampten, met droge monding, lauw tot op de slijklaag,
toen uit de zee Proteus de grot, naar zijn gewoonte,
opzocht en om hem heen het volk der wijde wateren;
het schudt zich af en spat een bui van zoute droppels;
de robben strekken zich, verspreid, op 't strand te slapen.
Hij zelf—als in de bergen bij zijn hut een herder,
als 's avonds stalwaarts keren van de wei de kalfjes,
de lammeren, blatend, terging voor de wolf,—zo zet hij
zich op een rots in 't midden en telt hun aantal over.

[436-466]

En Aristaeus, nu de kans zich biedt, laat nauwelijks
de grijsaard tijd het matte lichaam neer te leggen;
toè schiet hij met een schreeuw en boeit hem, achterover,
metéén. Maar Proteus weert zich, met zijn oude loosheid;
hij transformeert zich in de wonderlijkste dingen:
een vuur, een vreselijk beest, de golven van het water.
Maar als geen listigheid een uitweg opent, zwicht hij,
wordt weer zichzelf en spreekt met mensenstem uiteindelijk:
'Wie is het die u, jongeling overkoen, gelastte
te naderen mijn verblijf? Wat zoekt ge hier?' Hij antwoordt:
'Dat weet gij, Proteus, zelf. Want ù kan niets misleiden,
zo doe het ook niet ons. Op raad der goden kom ik
u voor mijn stervend werk om een orakel vragen.'

Hij sprak. De ziener eindelijk, met geweld zich dwingend,
—groen vuur schiet uit zijn vlammende ogen—knarsetandend,
opent de mond en doet orakelend zijn uitspraak:
'Wel is het van een god, dat u de wraakzucht teistert;
gij boet een zware fout. Orpheus, rampzalig—schuldeloos
nochtans—met deze straf blijft hij, zo 't lot niet ingrijpt,
u slaan, diep wrokkend om de vrouw hem afgenomen,
Eurydice. In vlucht voor ù, rap langs het water,
zag zij niet voor haar voet—een kind in doods nabijheid—
de grote slang, in 't hoge oevergras verscholen.
En de Dryaden, rei van speelgenoten, riepen
over de bergen, vèr; de hoge toppen schreiden
—Pangaea, Rhodope—, het vechtersland van Rhesus,
de Donausteppen en zij, Athene's Orythuia.
Zelf zocht hij met zijn lier te sussen 't ziek verlangen,
zingend, o liefste, op 't verlaten strand eenzelvig
van u bij 't rijzend licht, van u als de avond daalde.
Zelfs door de Hellekrochten, Hades' diepe poorten,

geschreden door het woud, spokig van donk're nevelen,
trad hij voor 't schimmenrijk, de koning der verschrikking,
de harten voor het menselijk smeken zonder deernis.
Zie, door zijn lied geroerd, ontzweefden donkers diepten
de schimmen ijl, van licht verstoken schijngestalten,
— zo komen in een boom honderden vogels schuilen
voor de avondval of voor een onweer uit de bergen—:
moeders en vaders, fiere helden, afgestorven
van dit bestaan; kinderen, meisjes vóór haar bruidstijd;
zonen, tot as verbrand voor de ogen van hun ouders.
Rondom hen, slijkig zwart met haveloze biezen,
ligt de Cocytus, sombere poel van stilstaand water,
en negen malen strikt de Styx hen in zijn kronkels.
Hij zingt: de hoven van de dood, de Orcus zelve,
de Erinyen—blauwig kronkelen door het haar de slangen—
zijn ademloos; het blaffen smoort in Cerberus' kelen,
Ixions wentelrad blijft, nu de wind zwijgt, stilstaan.
Reeds keerde Orpheus terug, aan elk gevaar ontkomen,
terwijl de weergegevene naar het licht geleid werd,
Eurydice, nà hem, Proserpina gehoorzaam.
Toen plotseling overmocht hem weerloos het verlangen
—hoezeer vergefelijk, als de Hel vergeving kende—
staan bleef hij en zag om, reeds op de grens van 't daglicht,
naar haar, Eurydice, roekeloos—ach!—bezweken.
Te niet zijn tocht, geschonden van de wrede heerser
't verdrag: drie donderslagen klonken uit de Avernus.
En zij: "hoe kondt ge mij verderven en u zelve,
Orpheus, zozeer verblind! Genadeloos roept opnieuw mij
het noodlot terug, het donker dekt mijn brekende ogen;
een laatst vaarwel—de grote nacht heeft mij gegrepen,
'k strek machteloos naar u, niet meer van u, mijn handen."
Zij sprak—en uit zijn ogen, zoals rook vernevelt,

[499-528]

dun in de lucht ontweek zij. Tastend in het ijle,
nog zóveel woorden op de lippen, ontwaarde Orpheus
Eurydice niet meer—en Orcus' veerman laat hem
ten tweeden male niet over het scheidend water.
Wat kon hij? Waar vindt woon die tweemaal dierf het liefste?
Verbad zijn stem de dood, zijn tranen deze machten?
Zij, in doods kilte, voer reeds in de boot van Charon.
En hij—gaat het verhaal—heeft zeven volle maanden,
waar steil de rotswand rijst, bij de verlaten Strymon
geschreid en in de koele grot zich uitgezongen;
de tijgers strekten zich, de eiken kwamen tot hem.
Zo klaagt de nachtegaal, in schaduw van een peppel,
om zijn verloren jongen, die een boer, hardvochtig,
loerend heeft uitgehaald—kaal uit het nest; de vogel
snikt heel de nacht—droef, op zijn tak, begint hij telkens
de melodie en vult ver de omtrek met zijn klachten.
Geen vrouw, geen liefde wist zijn hart te winnen—eenzaam,
de ijsvlakten van het noorden over, Tanaïs' sneeuwveld,
en de altijd ruig berijpte barre steppen zwierf hij
en treurde om zijn verlies—Eurydice en Hades'
geschonden gave—trouw die de Bacchanten krenkte.
Bij Bacchus' riten, in nachtelijke orgie, is Orpheus
verscheurd; zijn lichaam lag verstrooid over de velden.
En nòg, toen van de marmeren hals het hoofd gescheiden
mee met de Hebrus dreef en wentelde in zijn wieling,
bleef toch "Eurydice" de stem, het stervend spreken
"arme Eurydice" het wijkend leven roepen,—
"Eurydice" weerkaatsten langs de stroom de oevers.'
Proteus' verhaal: dan dook hij met een sprong de zee in
en maakte, waar hij sprong, een kolk van kruivend water.

Cyrene echter bleef en sprak, zijn vrees begrijpend:
'Mijn zoon, uw hart mag vrij zijn rouw en zorg vergeten;
hier wortelt al het kwaad: hierom sloegen de nymfen,
met wie zij diep in 't bos ten reidans ging, met ziekte
uw bijenvolk. Breng gij in nederigheid uw gaven,
vraag om vergeving, smeek der dalen zachte zusters
eerbiedig: dan verstilt haar toorn, zijn ze u genadig.
Maar hoè gij hen verbidt, wil voegzaam eerst ik melden:
Zo kies vier prachtige stieren, statig van gestalte,
—zij grazen bij uw kudde op Lycaeus' bergwei—
en—nimmer heeft het juk hen aangeraakt—vier koeien.
Richt vier altaren op, waar 't heiligdom der nymfen
verrijst en offer 't bloed van de geslachte dieren,
maar laat hen zèlf in 't bos onder de bladeren liggen.
Later, wanneer het daglicht rijst ten negenden male,
breng Orpheus' schim uw gave—de vergetenszware
papaver—slacht een donker schaap, hervind de bosplek;
Eurydice, verzoend, wijdt ge een kalfje als offer.'
Aanstonds vervult hij ijverig zijn moeders opdracht:
ten tempel opgegaan bouwt hij 't altaar naar voorschrift
en leidt vier prachtige stieren, statig van gestalte,
daarheen en—nimmer raakte 't juk hen aan—vier koeien.
En later, als de dag verrijst ten negenden male,
keert hij—na 't Orpheus-offer—weder naar de bosplek.
En daar—een wonder, onverwacht en ongelofelijk,
vertoont zich; 't rottend vlees der koeielijven wemelt
van bijen, bruisende uit de doorboorde flanken.
Het groeit tot grote wolken, die dan in een boomtop
neerslaan; er hangt een tros, waarvan de boomtak doorbuigt.

Dit was mijn zang: de akkerbouw, de zorg voor 't vee en
de bomen, terwijl Caesar, machtig, bij de Euphraat

met oorlog flitst en triomfant de willige volken
richt naar zijn wet, zijn baan aanstuurt op de Olympus.
En ik, Vergilius, was toen een kind van 't heerlijk
Napels, rijk in mijn werk, in stilte teruggetrokken;
ik, die mijn herdersverzen speelde en, frank van jonkheid,
Tityrus, zong van u in brede beukenschaduw.

Aantekeningen

BUITEN SCHOT

104 De naam Una is ontleend aan een der 'Tales' van Edgar Allan Poe. Eno en Una zijn *de* man en *de* vrouw, evenzeer verwant als verschillend. Het vers speelt zich af op de grens van droom en waken, maar op een meer verborgen wijze ook aan de grens van het aardse leven: het zijn de heengeganen, die bij de Grieken over de asphodelenweide wandelen; welke bloem men zich daarbij in feite moet denken, is onbekend.

105 *Rietwouw*: een locale benaming van de bruine kiekendief.

112 Sappho, de dichteres, en Thales, de geniale denker, hebben elkaar stellig niet gekend, al waren zij ongeveer tijdgenoten. Elk van hen 'ontmoet' echter in de ander een benadering van de werkelijkheid, die de eigene aanvult en zelfs te boven lijkt te gaan; een ontmoeting die wordt beleefd met bewondering en met diepe vreugde.

SONNETTEN VAN EEN LERAAR

117 *Pegasus*: het gevleugelde paard der poëzie.

118 *Orpheus*: zanger, wiens lied en spelen op de lier zelfs stenen ontroerde.

Gratiën: de drie Gratiën symboliseren de bevalligheid.

119 *Charon*: veerman in de onderwereld, die de doden overzet.

121 *Vleugelpaard, Phaedros*: In Plato's dialoog *Phaedros* wordt de ziel vergeleken met een wagenmenner, die een span gevleugelde paarden bestuurt.

123 *Ancilla*: slavin, dienstbode.

124 *Phaedo*: een dialoog van Plato over de onsterfelijkheid van de ziel (psyche).

125 A en Ω: eerste en laatste letter van het Griekse alfabet. Men zie hierbij Openbaring 22:13. Ψ: uit te spreken: psi.

130 *Χαρακτήρ*: (Charaktèr): kras, stempel, karakter.

DE ARGELOZEN

De verzen *Keltisch Grafschrift* en *Brief aan de grootouders* zijn later opgenomen in de cyclus 'Keltisch' in de bundel *De Slechtvalk*. Het vers *Weerzien op zolder* is later opgenomen in de bundel *Het levend Monogram*.

KWATRIJNEN IN OPDRACHT

De *Kwatrijnen in opdracht* werden geschreven in het tweede en derde jaar na de bevrijding. De neiging 'alles waarin een klein land groot kan zijn' te sacrifiëren was reeds toen zichtbaar. Besef van de—nu een kwart eeuw lang—aangerichte schade wordt de laatste jaren wakker en mobiliseert de besten van ons volk.

164 Aan Jacob Thijsse werd in 1922—hij was toen 57 jaar oud—door de universiteit van Amsterdam het doctoraat honoris causa in de biologie verleend.

165 De schilder Floris Verster zag in 1926 zijn huis en tuin Groenoord, waar hij sinds 1892 werkte, door de gemeente Leiden gevorderd: voor een doel dat nooit verwezenlijkt is. Kort voor de onteigening overleed Verster. Men vond hem in de tuin van Groenoord.

172 M. Nijhoff, Sonetten 'voor Dag en Dauw'. Zie Verzameld Werk, deel I, p. 439.

130 In de dagen van de profeet Jesaja werd, dwars door het rotsmassief, een tunnel gegraven om het water van de bron Gihon naar Jeruzalem te leiden. Een inscriptie op de tunnelwand, in 1880 ontdekt, vertelt hoe twee arbeiders aan weerszijden eindelijk elkaars houwelen hoorden.

HET LEVEND MONOGRAM

217 *Tristis imago*: de sombere schim.

236 *Pegasus*: het gevleugelde paard, dat de dichter draagt.

243 Ποίησις: schepping.

252 'Ανίκατε μάχαν: deze woorden zijn ontleend aan een koor uit Sophocles' *Antigone* en betekenen '(Eroos) onoverwinnelijke in de strijd'.

254 *Het levend Monogram:* het teken der vroegste Christenen was een vis. De letters van het Griekse woord Ichthys (vis) zijn de beginletters van de vijf Griekse woorden, waarvan de vertaling luidt: 'Jezus Christus, Zoon Gods, Heiland'.

ΙΧΘΥΣ: het Christus-symbool: de Vis.

256 *Ad Te clamavi:* tot U blijf ik roepen (aanhef van Psalm 140).

257 Het Griekse woord ψυχή betekent 'ziel' en 'vlinder'.

264 De tekst uit 1. Cor. 13:12 luidt: 'Want nu zien wij nog door een spiegel, in raadselen,—doch straks van aangezicht tot aangezicht.'

DE HOVENIER

279 *Saul... Samuel:* Zie 1 Samuel 28.

280 Dit vers heeft, evenals het volgende, de Sapphische strofevorm. De Griekse dichteres Sappho leefde ± 600 v. Chr.

282 'als een ezelsruggegraat': woorden ontleend aan de Griekse dichter Archilochus.

283 *amphore:* kruik.

293 *Watergang van Siloah:* In de dagen van de profeet Jesaja werd, dwars door het rotsmassief, een tunnel gegraven om het water van de bron Gihon naar Jerusalem te leiden. De tunnel is ruim 500 m lang. Een inscriptie op de tunnelwand, in 1880 ontdekt, vertelt hoe twee arbeiders aan weerszijden eindelijk elkaars houwelen hoorden.

296 *Patroklos:* Griekse held, vriend van Achilles, gesneuveld voor Troje.

Briseïs: geliefde slavin van Achilles.

297 *Phoenix:* Het verhaal bij de Griekse schrijver Herodotus luidt: Hij (de vogel Phoenix) komt uit Arabië en brengt zijn vader, in myrrhe gewikkeld, naar de tempel van Helios, terwijl hij hem overbrengt op de volgende wijze. Hij maakt een ei van myrrhe, zo groot als hij maar dragen kan en beproeft dan het te dragen. Wanneer hij zich geoefend heeft, dan holt hij het ei uit en legt zijn vader erin.

299 De Grieken offerden bij genezing de god Asklepius vaak een haan. De laatste woorden van Sokrates—de door zijn volk veroordeelde—zijn: 'Krito, wij zijn Asklepius nog een haan schuldig'.

305 *Schlüszli:* 'sleuteltje', (fictief) Zwitsers dorp.

310 *hekatombe:* kudde. Homerisch woord.

321 *Facultas:* de grondbetekenis van het woord facultas is 'mogelijkheid' (positief en negatief). Zo betekent 'medische faculteit' hier: *waartoe de arts in staat is* (positief en negatief).

336 *De wortel Isaï:* de stamboom van Christus, beginnend bij Isaï, de vader van David. De even naïeve als indrukwekkende uitbeelding is: uit het hart van Isaï, die ligt te slapen, ontspringt een rank, die de gezichten der stamvaders draagt.

337 *Christus als hovenier:* Op dit schilderij van Rembrandt ziet men de opgestane Christus, wandelend op Paasmorgen in de hof van Jozef van Arimathea. Hij draagt een grote tuinmanshoed van stro. Terzijde Maria Magdalena, die 'dacht dat het de hovenier was' (Joh. 20:15).

DE SLECHTVALK

350 *Slechtvalk:* Egyptisch, oude Rijk.

352 *Keltisch:* deze verzen zijn geïnspireerd door een oud kerkhof met Keltische grafkruisen. Wales, ± 1800.

353 *Diviner:* wichelroedeloper. Tevens van de dichter gezegd.

357 *Till death us do part:* uit het huwelijksformulier.

368 *Ceridwen:* meisjesnaam uit Wales.

379 *Alkman:* dichter uit het oude Sparta. Het onderhavige vers is geen vertaling en gaat niet op enige klassieke tekst terug, maar het is geschreven in de geest van Alkmans reidansen.

380 *Xanthos:* het paard van de Homerische held Achilles, hier nog een jongen op de vaderlijke hoeve.

382 *Ultima Thule:* eiland aan de uiterste rand van de wereld (Vergilius).

383 *Anamnesis:* een kennis die op voor-persoonlijke herinnering teruggaat.

384 *De apocalyptische ezel:* de Latijnse citaten zijn uit het Dies irae, onderdeel van de Requiem-mis.

386 *Kyrtos:* de gebochelde. De naam is, evenals de voorstelling op de krater (= mengvat), fictief.

399 'Wijl God niet eeuwig met zijn maaksel twist': laatste regel van Achtderbergs gedicht 'Begrafenis' (*Maatstaf* 1e jaargang 1953).

TWEE UUR: DE KLOKKEN ANTWOORDDEN ELKAAR

Dit gedicht is bedoeld als declamatorium; ik stel mij voor dat de gedeclameerde tekst tegelijkertijd door dans, spel of eventueel projectie kan worden zichtbaar gemaakt. De tekst bedoelt niet—ik zeg dit om misverstand te voorkomen—een pleidooi te zijn voor de klassieke opleiding. Evenmin—ook dit om misverstand te voorkomen—betuigt de tekst adhaesie aan het z.g.n. 'rode boekje': dat treurig specimen van slimme en platte consumenten-mentaliteit.

VIJF VUURSTENEN

472 *grondel:* zoetwatervisje. Zwemt en 'staat' graag dicht bij de bodem.

476 *Boötes:* 'de ossendrijver', het sterrenbeeld Arcturus.

477 *verlaat:* schutsluis.

479 Zie Arthur van Schendel: *de Waterman.*

'dat hem het water goed zat aan de benen': vgl.het einde van hoofdstuk IV (evenzo voor de namen Rossum en Hurwenen) en van hoofdstuk XV.

'daar is gezonken': nl. bij Sleeuwijk onder Gorcum.

481 *Heiligerlee:* vele, waaronder vermaarde, klokken zijn gegoten in de klokkengieterij te Heiligerlee (Gron.).

491 *ducdalf:* aaneengeklonken paalwerk om schepen aan vast te leggen; favoriete plek om te rusten voor meeuwen en aalscholvers.

496 *fugatisch:* in fugavorm.

498 *weggeling:* letterlijke vertaling (gemunt door Leopold) van het Griekse woord ὁδίτης = die langs de weg gaat.

509 *palimpsest:* handschrift waarin de oorspronkelijke schriftuur is uitgewist om plaats te maken voor ander schriftuur.

511 *zwaard- en Morrisdansen:* beide volksdansen van Engelse bodem, waarbij in laatstgenoemde het gevaarlijke zwaard was vervangen door een stok.

512 *Dioscuren:* de tweelingbroeders Castor en Pollux, zonen van Zeus, beschermers der zeelieden, die zich naar hun dubbelster richtten.

513 *Chiron:* de centaur (paard-mens) Chiron was de vereerde en geduchte leermeester van jonge Homerische helden, met name van Achilles.

schildpadlier: het dekschild van de schildpad, met snaren bespannen, is de oudste vorm van de Griekse lier.

515 *Arktisch:* van de Poolstreek.

516 *Atropurpurea:* zwartpurperen.

517 *Alcyonisch:* van de ijsvogel, de vogel met kobaltblauwe veren.

HET STERRESCHIP

532 *De profundis:* 'Uit afgronden (roep ik u, Heer).' Aanhef van psalm 130.

533 *stad die mij wenkt en mij weert:* mijn geboortestad Gorcum.

537 *Labor improbus:* koppig werk. Vgl. *Vergilius' Georgica (Het Boerenbedrijf)* I 146.

541 *Hafiz:* Perzische dichter (± 1325-1390).

549 *In memoriam:* Gaarne zou ik de lezer willen behoeden voor de misvatting dat in dit vers het water het verraderlijke element is, waarin een kind is omgekomen. Veeleer zijn het 'de wateren der rust', die het kind ('eindelijk bevrijd uit mensenhanden') dragen. Dit vers en het voorafgaande *Kinderportret* horen bijeen.

552 *Silf:* gefingeerde naam.

554 *Zwaluwenliedje:* het rhythme is geïnspireerd door dat van een anoniem Grieks zwaluwenliedje, behorende tot de zgn. Anacreontea (± 100 n. Chr.).

555 *Nikè:* de gevleugelde godin der overwinning (Grieks).

Sounion: kaap op de zuidpunt van Attica.

paean: overwinningshymne.

561 Archaïsche grafsteen: Het grafschrift is, afgezien van de reminiscens aan het antieke *domum servavit lanam fecit,* fictief.

568 *Aldebaran:* ster van de eerste grootte in het sterrebeeld Taurus.

Ten aanzien van de gehele bundel: Het menen te weten (subs. het menen te moeten weten) 'which is which' e.d. kan ik de lezer niet genoeg ontraden. Met een dergelijke instelling verspert men zich, van het begin af, de toegang tot het vers.

DOLEN EN DROMEN

Het gedicht 'Dolen en Dromen' omvat, in zijn aaneenschakeling, op een paar uur na anderhalf etmaal: vanaf het avondconcert 'op slag van achten' tot het ontwaken op de overvolgende morgen, als de hanen kraaien.
De tegenstem, die enkele malen hoorbaar wordt, is de stem van de dichter Achterberg. De cursief gedrukte verzen na strofe V, VII en XXXI zijn van hem. (Zie Gerrit Achterberg, *Verzamelde Gedichten,* Querido, Amsterdam, pag. 63.)

'Dolen en Dromen' is geen hommage aan Zutphen, ondanks mijn gehechtheid aan deze stad; en evenmin een hommage aan een harer burgers. Zelfs de identiteit van 'het kind met de klarinet' blijft onkenbaar.—Het gedicht gaat over een wijze van ervaren die de mens soms—bij hoge uitzondering—ten deel mag vallen: het bekende en vertrouwde opent zich voor hem. Het onthult zijn wonderen en verborgen samenhangen en geeft nochtans zijn laatste geheimenis niet prijs.

Het motto vóór in de bundel is ontleend aan het vers *Tekst op een rivierbaken* in 'Het Sterreschip'.

580 r. 8 *pentagram:* Het getal vijf kreeg voor mij door de opstelling der jonge spelers, en meer nog door hun spel, een bijna magische betekenis.

581 r. 4 *Sisley:* de schilder Alfred Sisley, behorend tot de kring der Franse Impressionisten.

581 r. 11 *het museum:* bedoeld is het Museum Henriëtte Polak.

581 r. 14 *de geefster:* Wie het museum binnenkomt wordt onmiddellijk geconfronteerd met een portret in brons van de schenkster.

582 r. 8 *het besef, praegnant, van er-te-zijn:* Het nog slapende bewustzijn-van-zichzelf kan door een betekenisvolle ervaring bij een kind plotseling ontwaken.

582 r. 14 *'Mijn vader', zegt hij, 'is een architect.':* Dat deze regel de sleutel is tot het hele gedicht heb ik zelf pas ontdekt toen het was voltooid.

584 r. 1 en 2 *dat opschrift boven de poort:* Het opschrift (anno 1723) boven de poort van het Bornhof luidt:
HIER VLOEIT EEN SPRING BORN VAN NOOTWENDIGH ONDERHOUT
VOOR OUDE BURGERS, 'T ZIJN DAN MANNEN OFTE VROUWEN;
DES HEREN BORREN HOF IN ZUTPHENS STADT GEBOUT
KAN DIE VERVALLEN ZIJN MILTDADIG ONDERHOUWEN.

De bewoners van het oude Borrenhof, dat thans in restauratie is, en bestemd is om een aantal wooneenheden te bevatten, zijn sinds 1962 gehuisvest in het nieuw gebouwde bejaardenhuis 'Het Bornhof'.

587 r.6, *'t Bolwerck en Ruiter Kortegaerd:* Het Bolwerck (1549), gebouwd in de overgangstijd naar de Renaissance, en het pand Ruiter Kortegaerd (1639) daarnaast, zijn beide door het Wijnhuisfonds prachtig gerestaureerd. 'Kortegaerd' is een verbastering van Corps de garde.

587 r.8 *De Jonge:* Mr. M. de Jonge, een immer onvermoeid vechter voor het behoud van Zutphens stadsschoon. Op 28 juni 1978 werd hem door de Regent van het Prins Bernhard-fonds de Zilveren Anjer uitgereikt.

587 r.17 *die foto:* De foto i.c. staat in het jaarverslag 1978 (zie pag. 3) van het Wijnhuisfonds te Zutphen.

DE ZOMEN VAN HET LICHT

Ter oriëntatie

Ik heb, vanaf mijn laatste gymnasium-jaren, altijd een voorkeur gehad voor de dialogen van Plato, en in het bijzonder voor het *Symposion*.

Op de avond van 11 november 1938 (een datum die men op blz. 596 van deze bundel vindt) ontwaakte ik, door een schijnbaar toeval, plotseling tot het inzicht dat de rede van Socrates in Plato's *Symposion* een onontkoombare opdracht voor mij inhield. Ik zou afstand moeten doen—op dìt moment en voorgoed—van de min of meer uitgestippelde en beveiligde toekomst die ik mij, na vele jaren van bijna smadelijke armoede, niet zonder verlichting had voorgesteld. Veeleer zou het de poëzie zijn die mij, hoè ik dan ook in mijn onderhoud zou moeten voorzien, voortaan gebiedend de wet zou stellen. De zo geheten 'persoonlijke verlangens' waren hiermee nietig verklaard.

Het mag de lezers van het vers 'De oproep' mogelijk ongeloofwaardig voorkomen dat het toevallig passeren van een kind in een juist langskomende St. Maartens-optocht ('de havenjongen, het kind/dat hier soms, als er feest is, verschijnt') de oorzaak zou zijn van deze revelatie,—wat geschied is blijft daarom niet minder waar.

Deze uitheemse passant (ik schatte hem op ongeveer veertien jaar), een jongen van uitzonderlijke schoonheid, was buiten twijfel een Griek. Een efebe,[1] zoals deze soms wel op antieke Griekse vazen worden afgebeeld; een enkele maal met het bijschrift Eroos.[2]

Tevens was hij, hoe jong ook, geheel de Eroos zoals hij in het *Symposion* getekend wordt: 'arm, schraal, schamel gekleed...levend in gebrek'; en tegelijk bijna koninklijk imponerend: 'dapper en energiek..., een die alles wil begrijpen...',[3] Eroos, de zoon van twee ouders, zo wordt ons verteld, die elkaars tegengestelden zijn: van Penia, de berooidheid, de armoede; en van Poros, de rijkdom, de overvloed.

Ik zou wel willen dat ieder die Nederlands kent, en helder en zuiver denken niet is ontwend, het zichzelf niet ontzegde die enkele bladzijden te lezen die men kan vinden in *Poëtica* van de dichter Bloem. Zij dragen de titel 'Het Verlangen'[4] en zijn in hun doorleefdheid en voornaamheid onovertroffen. En mocht hij, denk ik dan, het zichzelf daarnà niet ontzeggen de Eroos-rede van Socrates in het *Symposion* te lezen; zo mogelijk in het oorspronkelijk Grieks, en anders in een vertaling.

Beide stukken getuigen, op authentieke en onaantastbare wijze, van het eeuwigheidsverlangen dat in de mens is gelegd, de goddelijke onvervuldheid (het woord is van Bloem) die hem vermag uit te heffen boven het toevallige, en boven de slagen van het lot.

Socrates geeft in zijn rede deze goddelijke onvervuldheid de naam Eroos en, op indrukwekkende wijze, ook de gestalte van de mythische Eroos.—Er staat van Socrates, die een voor ons nauwelijks voorstelbare denkarbeid heeft ver-

1 *efebe*: zie de aantekeningen bij 'Bij Plato's Phaedrus' (pag. 600).
2 *Eroos*: de zoetelijke voorstelling van Eroos als een aanvallige putto, uitgerust met een miniatuur-boog en dienovereenkomstige pijlenkoker, is van later tijd.
3 Ik citeer hier de vertaling van Gerard Koolschijn, Amsterdam 1980, die het *Symposion* op zeer originele en meeslepende wijze heeft weergegeven. De vertaler houde mij ten goede dat ik de vertaling van Poros door 'Succes' zeer betreur, mede omdat de hele passage daardoor zinloos wordt. Ook de woorden 'drank en seks' (pag. 15) geven een vertaling die niets met het origineel van doen heeft en bovendien in dèze vorm ten aanzien van het werk van Aristophanes ook nog een notoire onwaarheid bevat.
4 J.C. Bloem, 'Het Verlangen' in *Poëtica*, Amsterdam 1969.

richt en voor talloos velen, vooral jongeren, nieuwe verten heeft geopend, in het *Symposion*[1] een aangrijpende uitspraak over zichzelf. Aangrijpend omdat er in die enkele woorden waarmee hij zichzelf tekent—ὃς οὐδέν φημι ἄλλο ἐπίστασθαι ἢ τὰ ἐρωτικά ('ik die graag wil verklaren dat ik/enkel versta wat van Eroos is')— zóveel ligt vervat.

Een grote bescheidenheid en tevens het besef een geroepene te zijn; een zachtzinnige en tegelijk ongenadige ironie tegenover wie zichzelf 'algemeen ontwikkeld' achten; èn een lichte, doch tegelijk niets verhelende, zelfspot. Maar het is toch het meest een welhaast onbereikbare eenzaamheid die ons in dit getuigenis treft. Bovenal het onopvallende οὐδέν ἄλλο ἢ ('enkel', 'alleen maar'): zó simpel en praegnant uitgesproken dat men het hoofd buigen moet.

Dit was het dan, alleen maar dìt, waarvan hij—naar zijn eigen getuigenis— wèrkelijk zeker was, waarvan hij *weet had*, naar de diepste betekenis van dat woord. Eroos, het onstilbaar verlangen, dat hem steeds weer tot zijn werk opriep—zoals het ook de kunstenaar rust noch duur laat—en dat hem tenslotte op een doodvonnis is komen te staan.

Altijd opnieuw is het mij, in de jaren dat ik docent was, opgevallen met welk een feilloze intuïtie jonge mensen, soms bijna nog kinderen, het gehalte van een passage als de boven geciteerde weten te schatten. Het was een zestienjarige die mij indertijd ten aanzien van dit οὐδέν ἄλλο ἢ de weg wees.

En ik dacht er wederom aan hoe gaarne Socrates met jongeren sprak, hoe vaak zij hem inspireerden, gelijk hij hèn inspireerde. Naïef waren deze jonge gesprekspartners allerminst, maar zij waren onbedorven. En: zij wisten wat schroom is. Αἰδώς, die kostbare eigenschap (door Socrates en eveneens door Plato zo hoog geschat) die een voornaam en sterk karakter kenmerkt.

Wie nu mogelijk 'Het Verlangen' van Bloem en Socrates' Eroos-rede in het *Symposion* niet ongelezen hebben gelaten—tot hen richt ik mij nog een keer. Ik zou hun de bladzijde willen wijzen waar het te vinden is: Aristophanes' 'Lied van Tereus', dat ik een hooglied heb genoemd.[2] Een hooglied, een Eroos-lied—het

[1] Zie Plato's *Symposion* 177d (ed. Burnet vol. II).
[2] Aristophanes, *De Vogels* vs. 209 e.v.

is maar kort, het omvat maar veertien regels—zó volmaakt dat ik, altijd weer, nauwelijks kan geloven dat het zómaar op het blad staat.

Het lied van Tereus, eenmaal een Thracisch koning, doch door de goden in een hop veranderd, voor zijn uitverkorene, de nachtegaal—zij die eens een Atheense koningsdochter was. En, als het ware op de achtergrond, wordt een ander motief hoorbaar: de dodenklacht om het tragisch omgekomen kind, om het jonge prinsje Itys.

Ik moet, helaas, dit lied niet of nauwelijks vertaalbaar achten, in welke taal dan ook. Bovenal omdat dan ook de *taalmuziek* van het Griekse origineel, die uniek is, moet worden prijsgegeven.

Ik heb dan het hoge voorrecht gehad het Tereus-lied, voorafgegaan door een veelstemmig vogelkoor, in de droom te mogen horen: in het Grieks, en door de dubbelfluit begeleid.[1] Of zo'n droom in feite maar enkele minuten duurt of heel veel langer—dat zal wel niemand weten. Mijzelf leek de 'generale repetitie' van de jubelende vogels (die 'vroeger' niet alleen zongen, maar ook konden spreken, zo leert ons de dichter) overheerlijk lang te duren. En het Tereus-lied?— hier was geen uur of tijd meer in het geding—alleen een tijdeloze en bovenaardse volkomenheid.

Aantekeningen

600 De dialoog *Phaedrus* is genoemd naar de hoofdpersoon Phaedrus, een jonge aanzienlijke Athener.

crux: moeilijkheid in de tekst die de geleerden niet kunnen oplossen.

conjectuur: gissing > voorstel dat, zonder veel ingrijpen, tot een betere lezing leidt.

hem: Socrates.

Ilissus: riviertje ten zuiden van Athene.

efebe: een jongen in de jaren tussen kind en man, in wie de belofte en de glans der jeugd nog ongeschonden zijn.

scheerling: in 399 v.Chr. werd Socrates veroordeeld tot de dood door de scheerlingbeker (scheerling = dolle kervel).

[1] Zie het vers 'Griekse dageraad' op pag. 603 van deze bundel.

601 Het woord symposion betekent 'het tesamen drinken', de voortzetting van een gemeenschappelijke maaltijd bij een glas wijn. Soms was er muziek; maar in intellectuele kringen gaf het symposion vaak gelegenheid tot discussies over filosofische of literaire onderwerpen.

Silenus: metgezel en opvoeder van Dionysus,de god van de wijn. Silenus ziet er uit als een oude, kaalhoofdige en gebaarde Satyr.

of hij met z'n tweeën was: de onzichtbare tweede is Eroos.

602 *het hooglied door een sterveling bestaan:* het lied van de hop voor zijn uitverkorene, de nachtegaal (zie Aristophanes, *De Vogels*, vs. 209 e.v.).

603 *het theater van Dionysus:* te Athene, aan de voet van de Acropolis. Aanvankelijk waren het toneel en de tribunes voor de toeschouwers nog van hout. In 330 v.Chr. werd het stenen Dionysus-theater gebouwd.

Aristophanes' Vogels: De komedie *De Vogels* van Aristophanes ($\pm$ 445-388 v.Chr.) werd in 414 v.Chr. te Athene opgevoerd. Het woord komedie moet men niet verstaan in zijn tegenwoordige betekenis. Daarvoor zijn met name de koren en de bovenvermelde solo te indrukwekkend, en de (maar al te gegronde) kritiek van de dichter op de politiek van Athene in de laatste decenniën te ernstig.

604 *gehuifde wagens:* Vgl. Homerus, *Odyssee* VI 70, waar een huifkar wordt beschreven.

een hoog geschenk: de vaart van het schip zelf èn het élan van de beide keerverzen zijn tesamen voor de genodigde een geschenk dat in het Grieks γέρας, d.i. een eergeschenk, zou heten.

605 *Lotophagen:* 'Lotus-eters' die zich voeden met een plant (vrucht?) die degene die ervan proeft alles doet vergeten 'wat achter hem ligt' en hem vervult met het verlangen voor altijd bij de Lotophagen te blijven.

607 *Een vers dat met 'schoon lieveke' begon:* verwijst naar een oud Nederlands 'Meilied', dat aldus begint:

Schoon lieveke, waar waardegij
den eersten meienacht
dat gij mij genen mei en bracht?

Anon: afkorting voor anoniem. Ik zag als kind in dit Anon een geheimzinnige eigennaam.

Adespoton: letterlijk: iets zonder heer (eigenaar), dit met de dubbele betekenis

'van een onbekende auteur' en 'waar niemand de hand op kan leggen'.
608 *Ultima Thule:* eiland (of eilandengroep) in het uiterste noorden van Europa > afgelegen en eenzaam eiland.
610 *een Voerman:* Jan Voerman (1857-1944), Nederlands schilder, vooral van riviergezichten. Nog altijd kan men ter hoogte van Zalk en Veecaten, bij de bocht van de IJssel, 'een Voerman' zien ontstaan, vooral bij wisselende bewolking.
613 *een holenbeer:* zie Van Looy, *Jaapje* (het hoofdstuk 'De Beer').

een rode vos: de kleine roodharige Van Looy werd in het Haarlemse weeshuis door de andere kinderen vaak voor 'rooie vos' gescholden. Hierdoor èn door het bijbelvers 'de vossen hebben holen'... (Matth. 8:20) dat hij uit het hoofd kent, is het kind steeds door 'de rode vos' gepreoccupeerd. (Zie *Jaapje*, het hoofdstuk 'De Brief'.)

614 *Mijn vaders pleegouders:* Mijn vader, wiens moeder kort na zijn geboorte (Tarnau, 24 december 1871) stierf, was tot zijn twaalfde jaar te Schiedam in huis bij een broer van zijn vader en diens vrouw. Beiden hebben hun taak als pleegouders voortreffelijk vervuld.

Het komt van háár: het opmerkelijk zuiver taalgevoel dat mijn vader bezat, stamt zeer waarschijnlijk van zijn moeder.

u drieën: bedoeld zijn: mijn beide zusters en ik.

616 Johannes (Hans) Brüggen (1920-1980) werd in 1947 tot priester gewijd. Hij behoorde tot de monnikengemeenschap van de Sint Adelbert-Abdij te Egmond, waar hij cantor en organist was. De toonzetting van de, door Marie van der Zeyde en mij vertaalde, Hebreeuwse psalmen is grotendeels zijn werk.

617 Prof. Dr. C.J. de Vogel (geb. 1905); in 1947 benoemd tot hoogleraar in de wijsbegeerte van de klassieke oudheid en de Middeleeuwen aan de Rijksuniversiteit te Utrecht, waar zij later ook de oud-christelijke wijsbegeerte doceerde. Door haar talrijke publicaties op theologisch en filosofisch gebied en haar vele gastcolleges ook buiten Europa (o.a. in de Verenigde Staten en in Japan) een geleerde van internationale betekenis.

622 *brandnetels in het gras:* de dagpauwoog legt zijn eieren graag op brandnetelbladeren, waar men dan later de rupsen van deze vlinder vinden kan.

627 De Latijnse dichter Vergilius (70-19 v.Chr.) verbleef zeer gaarne op de boerderij van zijn vader bij Mantua. Toen deze boerderij in het jaar 41 van

staatswege onteigend dreigde te worden, vond hij een beschermer in Maecenas, die bevriend was met de jonge Octavianus (de latere keizer Augustus), aan wie Vergilius werd voorgesteld. Het contact met Maecenas deed bij Vergilius de wens ontstaan een leerdicht te schrijven over de landbouw, of eigenlijk over het gehele boerenbedrijf. Dit boek, waarvan het laatste gedeelte over de bijenteelt handelt, kreeg de Griekse naam *Georgica*.
Ultima Thule: Zie aantekening bij pag. 608.

629 *Asklepius:* de god der geneeskunde.

630 *Salamis, Aeschylus, De Perzen:* In 480 v.Chr. werd de geweldige vloot waarmee de Perzische koning Xerxes Griekenland dacht te onderwerpen, door de— zoveel kleinere—Griekse vloot bij het eiland Salamis vernietigend verslagen. De Griekse tragediedichter Aeschylus (± 525-456 v.Chr.) wijdde aan deze indrukwekkende gebeurtenis zijn tragedie *De Perzen*, in 472 v. Chr. te Athene opgevoerd.

631 *Olbia aan de Borysthenes:* plaats aan de noordkust van de Zwarte Zee, bij de samenvloeiing van de rivieren Hypanis en Borysthenes. Toen ik, als jeugdig gymnasiast, in mijn *Atlas antiquus* het gebied van de Zwarte Zee zag, werd ik onmiddellijk gefascineerd door de kustvorming bij Olbia. Bij een zwerftocht langs de Ierse meren ontdekte ik een plek waar de eigenaardige kustvorming nauwkeurig gelijk was (zij het op kleinere schaal) aan die bij Olbia.

633 *Boustrophèdon* ('als de ploegossen kerend') is de naam van een zeer vroeg Grieks schrift. De regels gaan heen en weer—zoals de ploeger met zijn span—van links naar rechts, en daarna van rechts naar links.

636 De cycloop (rondoog, eenoog) Polyphemus wordt, terwijl hij ligt te slapen, door Odysseus en diens gezellen blind gemaakt. Zij boren hem een scherpgepunte gloeiende paal in het oog. Vóór hij deze daad beging, heeft Odysseus zich, met listige opzet, aan de cycloop voorgesteld als Οὖτις(Niemand). Een 'nietige niemand' (Οὐτιδανός Οὖτις) zegt de blinde reus verbitterd. (Homerus, *Odyssee* IX 460.)

640 Naar een Grieks origineel (*Anthologia Palatina* VII 173) in de oorspronkelijke versmaat, en met toevoeging van een titel, vertaald.

641 *Breero:* De dichter Gerbrant Adriaensz. Brederode (1585-1618) is in de winter van 1617-1618 op een tocht van Amsterdam naar Haarlem—mogelijk op de schaats, mogelijk per slede—door het ijs gezakt. Het kwam hem op een

longziekte te staan. Drie maanden later stierf hij.

643 *De profundis:* 'Uit afgronden (roep ik u, Heer)'—aanhef van psalm 130.

644 *een zilveren bal:* In de twintiger jaren werden er op straat soms luchtballonnen verkocht die verzilverd waren, glanzend als een spiegel. Zij waren veel groter dan de gewone 'luchtballonnetjes', niet met gas maar met lucht gevuld, en zeer resistent.

hield in zijn handjes het heelal: Het goddelijk kind wordt in de Nederlandse en Vlaamse primitieve schilderkunst wel afgebeeld met de wereldbol in de handen. In die wereldbol spiegelt zich dan weer de kamer, of het landschap, waarin het kind zich met zijn moeder bevindt.

646 *Eenhoorn:* de eenhoorn is een fabelwezen (vgl. de vogel Phoenix), een zeldzaam en prachtig wonderdier. Het gelukt de mens niet de eenhoorn te vangen. Als dit wonderwezen zich ooit gewonnen zal geven, dan zal het zijn aan een vrouw met een *volmaakt* zuivere intentie (la Dame à la Licorne). Zie ook A. Roland Holst, *Verzameld Werk.* Poëzie I, Amsterdam 1981, pag. 465, eerste strofe.

649 *quadraturen:* letters in kwadraatvorm.

B^{E}REŠIT BĀRĀ: 'In den beginne schiep', de aanvangswoorden van het Boek Genesis.

650 *Παρὰ θῖνα θαλάσσης:* letterlijk vertaald: 'langs het zand (de zandkust) van de zee'. De val van de Griekse hexameter, dat machtige zeerythme, kan in het Nederlandse vers niet dan zeer onvolkomen worden weergegeven.

653 '*koekoek*' en '*bakboord*': beide woorden, luide uitgeroepen, suggereren een nederlaag: het laatste woord mede door de associatie 'bakzeil halen'; de koekoeksroep omdat de koekoek vanouds voor spotziek, wispelturig en ontrouw heeft gegolden (vgl. ook het Engelse *cuckold* en het Franse *cocu* = een bedrogen echtgenoot). De twee mannen, de een gekarakteriseerd door zijn nuchtere constatering 'àlles slijt', de ander door zijn woedende repliek 'O ja?', zijn elkaars 'maats' èn elkaars antipoden.

DE ADELAARSVARENS

664 *Negen verzen van zonsopgang:* werd in mei 1985 met de hand gezet en gedrukt door de Regulierenpers te Amsterdam in een oplage van zeventig exemplaren.

plaren. Hiervan volgde een fotografische herdruk in een oplage van vierhonderdvijftig exemplaren, uitgegeven door uitgeverij Hosman & Ten Bosch, Amsterdam/Zutphen.

685 *Het Zeepaardje:* Parthenon-paard van Phidias. Onder leiding van Phidias zijn de sculpturen van het Parthenon—in het bijzonder van het fries, dat ook jonge ruiters op prachtige paarden te zien geeft— tot stand gekomen.

686 ΔΟΣ ΜΟΙ ΠΟΥ ΣΤΩ: Geef mij het punt waar ik kan staan (en ik licht de aarde uit haar as). Woorden vaak toegeschreven aan Archimedes.

690 *De Slachtlammeren:* Om hen die niet meer zijn, schreit Rachel. Het Hebreeuwse woord rachel betekent schaap (ooi). Bij de profeet Jeremia verschijnt de stammoeder Rachel als de moeder die schreit om haar verloren kinderen. Bij het verhaal van de Bethlehemse kindermoord (Matth. 2:18) wordt hiernaar verwezen.

699 *Het beloofde Land:* het land dat door Jahwe aan het Joodse volk was toegezegd. Wanneer zij het dicht zijn genaderd, brengen twee uitgezonden verspieders uit het land Kanaän, ten teken hoe vruchtbaar het beloofde land is, een grote druiventros mee, die zij samen aan een stok over de schouders dragen.

De avondroep van de straatkoopman 'wie maakt me los' betekent: wie koopt mij het restant van mijn koopwaar af, zodat ik—eindelijk—naar huis kan gaan. Het motief van het losmaken, bevrijden, de vrijheid geven, speelt voortdurend door het vers heen.

700 *De zestigste viering:* Twee monniken van hetzelfde klooster hebben ieder jaar de dag gevierd waarop hun vriendschap tijdens het noviciaat tot stand kwam. Nu een van hen is gestorven, wordt deze viering als vanzelf in niets geschonden.

703 *Jongensvriendschap:* Dit vers is overgenomen uit de bundel *Vijf Vuurstenen*.

De Dioscuren: In de klassieke mythologie twee zonen van Zeus, Castor en Pollux, tweelingbroers. Na hun dood als dubbelster aan de hemel geplaatst, helpen zij de zeelieden hun koers te bepalen.

707 *De Wijnkruik spreekt:* De twee kwatrijnen van dit vers bevatten een reminiscens aan de geschiedenis van Alexander de Grote, die aan het eind van zijn leven en zijn veroveringstochten zijn omgeving steeds meer ging wantrouwen en tenslotte zijn vriend Kleitos in een vlaag van woede en dronkenschap doodde.

709 *De maaltijd:* De wijsgeer Epicurus (341-270 v.Chr.) trok door zijn leer en zijn innemende persoonlijkheid vele leerlingen tot zich. Allengs vormde zich om hem heen een kring van ook onderling trouwe vrienden. Van 306 tot aan zijn dood was hij burger van Athene, maar zijn lievelingsplek was de 'tuin', waar hij met zijn volgelingen samenkwam; en waar men ook gaarne samen de maaltijd gebruikte.

715 *Confrontatie:* Jan Asselijn (1610-1652). Allegorische voorstelling van een vervaarlijke zwaan, wiens nest door mensen wordt bedreigd.

718 *Het meisje met de zwavelstokken:* sprookje van Andersen. Het kleine meisje dat op Kerstavond aan de voorbijgangers haar lucifers tracht te verkopen — maar niemand die ze koopt —, wordt door de kou bevangen en sterft op het bordes van een rijk huis, waar binnen de kerstboom brandt.

721 *The child is father of the Man:* regel uit het gedicht 'My heart leaps up' van William Wordsworth. Met 'the child' is hier het kind Shakespeare bedoeld. Vergelijk ook het 'verborgen zelfportret' in *As you like it*, 2e bedrijf, 7e toneel: 'with his satchel, and shining morning face.'

722 *Intocht:* In het begin van de vorige eeuw, tijdens de Napoleontische oorlogen, verwierf zich Lord Elgin, destijds Engels ambassadeur aan het Turkse hof, een aanzienlijk aantal beeldhouwwerken van het Parthenon (vergelijk de aantekening bij pag. 685), die na allerlei avonturen tenslotte eigendom zijn geworden van het Brits Museum. Zij zijn bekend gebleven onder de naam The Elgin Marbles.

725 *In het voorbijgaan:* Sinds 1983 is mijn gezichtsvermogen zodanig achteruit gegaan, dat er van lezen geen sprake meer is. Hierop heeft het vers 'In het voorbijgaan' betrekking.

728 *Het Rivierbaken:* Op 22 april 1988 is mij door mijn geboortestad Gorcum een rivierbaken aangeboden, waarop het vers 'Tekst op een Rivierbaken' (uit de bundel Het Sterreschip) in steen gebeiteld staat.

VERGILIUS/HET BOERENBEDRIJF

Publius Vergilius Maro (70-19 v. Chr.) werd te Andes, niet ver van Mantua, geboren uit welgestelde boerenouders. De begaafde jongen mocht studeren: hij ging school te Cremona en Milaan en voltooide zijn opleiding te Rome, waar de colleges in de rhetorica hem maar matig trokken; veeleer ging zijn liefde naar de wijsbegeerte uit. In zijn studententijd maakte Vergilius zich vele, vooral litteraire, vrienden.

Afgestudeerd bleef hij een tijd lang op de boerderij van zijn vader, tot in 41 een moeilijk jaar voor het gezin aanbrak. Na jaren van burgeroorlogen, tijdelijk beëindigd in 42, moesten vele gedemobiliseerde soldaten erf en land hebben; er werd op grote schaal onteigend en ook Vergilius' boerderij kwam op de lijst. Bij zijn vroegere leermeester, de Epicurist Siro, vond hij tijdelijk onderdak. Enkele jaren na deze gebeurtenissen publiceerde Vergilius zijn eerste bundel: *Bucolica* (Herderszangen) getiteld. Dit gave, ofschoon nog zeer jonge werk, verzen geschreven in de trant van de Griek Theocritus, maakte hem meteen beroemd.

Middelerwijl was de jonge dichter door vrienden voorgesteld aan Maecenas, de voorname beschermer van zo menig kunstenaar. Maecenas, de vriend en litteraire raadsman van Caesars erfgenaam Octavianus—die over enkele jaren keizer Augustus zal zijn—bracht ook het contact tussen Octavianus en Vergilius tot stand. En uit een gesprek tussen Maecenas en de dichter rijpte in Vergilius het plan een uitvoerig leerdicht te schrijven over de landbouw, of liever: over het ganse boerenbedrijf, welks herleving Italië zozeer van node had. Dit onderwerp was én Vergilius, met zijn jeugdherinneringen en zijn liefde voor het Italische landschap, én Octavianus, die Romes beste tradities ook in deze zin wilde voortzetten, uit het hart gegrepen; voor het talent van Vergilius was het als geschapen.

Na jaren van intensieve arbeid kon Vergilius—soms wisselde Maecenas hem bij de lectuur af—het werk aan Octavianus, die hij reeds zozeer had leren vereren, voordragen. Dit was in het jaar 29. *Georgica* heette, met een Griekse naam, het boek dat de samenkomst der drie vrienden heeft gewijd.

Verklaring van eigennamen

De akkers
5 *Stralende wereldlichten:* Zon en Maan.
7 *Liber:* of Bacchus, god van de wijn.
Ceres: godin van het graan.

8 *Chaonië:* het gebied van de eikenbossen van Dodona, in Noord-Griekenland.
9 *Acheloüs:* grootste rivier van Griekenland. 'Acheloüs-drank' betekent dus: rivierwater.
10 *Faunen:* Faunus was een mythisch koning van het Italische landschap Latium. Na zijn dood werd hij vereerd als god van veld en bos, beschermer der kudden. Hij wordt ook wel met de Griekse Pan (zie bij vers 16) vereenzelvigd. Zijn zonen zijn de Faunen, evenals de Griekse Satyrs voorgesteld met horens, staart en bokspoten.
11 *Dryaden:* boomnymfen.
14 *Neptunus:* god van de zee. Hij schiep door een slag met zijn drietand het paard.
Woudbewoner: Aristaeus, zoon van Apollo en de nymf Cyrene, beschermer van landbouw, veeteelt en bijenteelt. Gaarne toeft hij op Ceos, een der Cycladen.
16 *Pan:* herdersgod, vooral in het Griekse landschap Arcadië vereerd. Pan wordt voorgesteld met horens, staart en bokspoten. De Lycaeus en de Maenala (vers 17) zijn bergen in Arcadië.
18 *Tegeër:* Arcadiër. Tegea is een stad in Arcadië.
19 *Knaap die de gebogen ploeg ons aanbracht:* Triptolemus, een koningszoon uit Eleusis, in het Griekse landschap Attica, werd door Ceres in het gebruik van de ploeg onderricht.
20 *Silvanus:* bos- en veldgod. Silvanus doodde per ongeluk zijn vriend Cyparissus, die in een cypres werd veranderd.
25 *Caesar:* Octavianus, de latere keizer Augustus. Het geslacht der Julii, waartoe hij behoorde, heette rechtstreeks van Venus af te stammen. Aan Venus, godin van schoonheid en liefde, is de myrte gewijd.
30 *Thule:* eiland in het uiterste noorden.
31 *Tethys:* gemalin van Oceanus, de wereldzee.
33 *Maagd en Scorpio:* tekens van de Dierenriem.
36 *Tartarus:* onderwereld, hel.
38 *Elysium:* verblijfplaats der gelukzaligen in het dodenrijk.
39 *Proserpina:* dochter van Ceres, werd door Pluto, god der onderwereld, geschaakt. Ceres zocht overal haar dochter, die nadien, als Pluto's gemalin, zes maanden van het jaar beneden de aarde vertoeft. Gedurende zes maan-

den, lente en zomer, keert Proserpina op de aarde terug en bloeit de natuur.

56 *Tmolus:* berg in Lydië, landschap in Klein-Azië.
57 *Scheba:* streek in Arabia Felix.
58 *Chalybië:* streek ten zuiden van de Zwarte Zee of Pontus.
59 *Elis:* landschap in Zuid-Griekenland, met de stad Olympia, waar de Olympische spelen werden gehouden.
Epirus: landschap in Noord-Griekenland.
61 *Deucalion:* werd bij de zondvloed met zijn vrouw Pyrrha gespaard. Op goddelijk bevel, aan beiden gegeven ('werpt het gebeente uwer Moeder achter u') slingerden zij stenen achter zich, waaruit nieuwe mensen ontstonden.
67 *Arcturus:* ster van de eerste grootte in het sterrenbeeld Boötes. Gaat in september op.
98 *Olympus:* berg in Noord-Griekenland, verblijf der goden.
102 *Mysië:* landstreek in Klein-Azië, beroemd om zijn vruchtbaarheid.
103 *Gargara:* top van de berg Ida in Mysië.
119 *Strymon:* rivier in Thracië, landschap ten noordoosten van Griekenland.
138 *Pleiaden:* Zevengesternte.
Hyaden: Regengesternte: zeven sterren in de kop van de Stier. Opgang en ondergang, in lente en herfst, vielen in de regentijd.
Lycaons heldere Arctos: Callisto, dochter van Lycaon, koning van Arcadië, werd door Juppiters gemalin Juno uit jaloezie in een berin veranderd, maar door Juppiter als het sterrenbeeld Arctos, de Grote en de Kleine Beer, aan de hemel geplaatst.
149 *Dodona:* zie aantekening bij vers 8.
163 *Moeder Ceres:* aan Ceres zijn de landbouwwerktuigen a.h.w. gewijd.
165 *Celeos:* vader van Triptolemus (zie vers 19).
166 *Iacchus:* naam van Bacchus in de Eleusinische mysteriën, de plechtigheden waarbij het sterven en herleven der natuur symbolisch werd voorgesteld. De in de mysteriën ingewijden hoopten de onsterfelijkheid deelachtig te worden. De wan is een zuiveringssymbool.
205 *Bokjes:* twee sterren in de Voerman.
Draak: tussen Grote Beer en Kleine Beer.

207 *Abydus:* stad aan de Hellespont (Dardanellen).
208 *Weegschaal:* teken van de Dierenriem. De zon komt 23 september in dit teken.
217 *Stier:* teken van de Dierenriem. De zon komt 22 april in dit teken.
218 *Hondsster:* Sirius, die na eind april niet meer zichtbaar is.
222 *Cnossos' sterrenbeeld Corona:* Toen Bacchus de Cretensische koningsdochter Ariadne tot zijn bruid maakte, bood Vulcanus, smid en edelsmid der goden, een gouden kroon aan. Deze werd door Bacchus als sterrenbeeld aan de hemel geplaatst. Corona gaat in het begin van de winter onder.
Cnossos: stad op Creta, residentie van Ariadnes vader Minos.
225 *Maia:* een der Pleiaden.
228 *Pelusium:* stad aan de Nijlmond. Linzen werden in Egypte veel verbouwd.
229 *Boötes:* sterrenbeeld dicht bij de Grote Beer.
240 *Scythië:* land ten noorden van de Zwarte Zee, tussen Ister (Donau) en Tanaïs (Don).
't *Riphaeisch* noorden, het uiterste noorden van Scythië.
243 *Styx:* rivier der onderwereld.
251 *Vesper:* de avondster.
265 *Ameria:* stad in het Italische landschap Umbrië.
277 *Eumeniden:* wraakgodinnen uit de onderwereld, die de misdadiger vervolgen.
278 *Orcus:* of Pluto, god van de onderwereld.
Terra: de Aarde, gehuwd met Uranus, de hemel.
279-283 *Coeüs, Japetus, enz.:* Coeüs en Japetus zijn zonen van de Hemel en de Aarde. *Typhoëus* of *Typhon* is een vuurspuwend monster, door Juppiter met de bliksem getroffen en onder de Etna bedolven. De 'saamgezworen broeders' zijn de *Giganten,* geweldige reuzen, die een strijd begonnen tegen de goden van de Olympus. Zij stapelden in die strijd hele bergen, zoals de Pelion en de Ossa in Noord-Griekenland, op elkaar.
309 *Baleaarse:* de slingeraars van de Balearen waren beroemd.
332 *Athos:* berg op de landtong Chalcidice, Macedonische kust.
Rhodope: bergketen in Thracië (zie bij vers 119).
333 *Ceraunia:* of Acroceraunia, berg aan de noordwestkust van Griekenland.
336 *Saturnus:* was, volgens de ouden, van de planeten het verst van de zon verwijderd.

337 *Mercurius:* planeet met de kortste omlooptijd.
339 *Het feest van Ceres:* de Ambarvalia, gevierd in mei, waarbij men het offerdier rond de velden leidt en zegen vraagt op het gewas.
384 *Cayster:* rivier in Klein-Azië, niet ver van Ephesus uitmondend; vele vogels leven in zijn moerasgebied.
398 *Thetis:* een zeegodin, dochter van *Nereus*.
404 *Nisus:* koning van Megara, die door koning Minos van Creta (zie bij vers 222) in de vesting Nisaea belegerd werd. Zijn dochter *Scylla* werd op Minos verliefd en beroofde haar vader van de purperen haarlok, waarvan zijn leven afhing. Nisus stierf en de stad viel. Nisus werd door de goden in een sperwer veranderd, Scylla in een hop. Nog steeds ziet men de vader de dochter vervolgen.
437 *Glaucus, Panopea, Melicertes:* Glaucus en Melicertes, zoon van *Ino*, waren stervelingen, die in zeegoden werden veranderd. Panopea is een der Nereïden, of dochters van Nereus.
438 *De zon:* de vertaling behoudt hier het mannelijk geslacht van het Latijnse woord sol: zon en zonnegod.
446 *Tithonus:* de sterfelijke gemaal van Aurora, godin van de dageraad.
462 *Auster:* de zuidenwind.
472 *'t Cyclopenland:* het gebied van de Etna. De Cyclopen, eenogige reuzen, helpen Vulcanus, de smid der goden, bij zijn werk.
482 *Eridanus:* de Po.
489 *Philippi:* stad in Thracië. In 42 voor Chr. versloegen Octavianus en Antonius daar Caesars moordenaars. In 48 had Caesar bij Pharsalus, in Thessalië, zijn tegenstander Pompeius verslagen. Beide plaatsen liggen in de toenmalige provincie Macedonië. Twee malen zag dus Macedonië, dit is bedoeld met Philippi, Romeinse legers tegenover elkander staan.
492 *Emathia:* landschap in Macedonië.
Haemus: berg in Noord-Thracië.
498 *Romulus:* de legendarische stichter van Rome.
Vesta: godin van de huiselijke haard, maar ook van het haardvuur van de ganse staat, dat in haar tempel steeds brandend werd gehouden.
499 *Palatijn:* een der zeven heuvelen van Rome, waar het oudste Rome lag en waar later keizer Augustus zijn paleis had.

Etrurië: landschap in Italië, waardoor de bovenloop van de Tiber stroomt.
500 Deze held: Octavianus.
502 't Laomedontisch Troje: Laomedon, koning van Troje, bedroog de goden Neptunus en Apollo, die de muren van zijn stad bouwden, en onthield hun de beloofde beloning. De Romeinen, als afstammelingen der Trojanen, moeten voor Laomedons schuld boeten.
503 Caesar: Octavianus.
509 Germanië en Euphraat: symbolisch voor westen en oosten.

De bomen

4 Lenaeus: Bacchus.
16 Orakelboom: in het ruisen van Dodona's eikenbossen hoorde men orakeltaal.
18 Parnassus: berg bij Delphi in Thessalië, verblijfplaats van Apollo en de negen Muzen.
37 Ismara: berg in Thracië.
38 Taburnus: berg in het Italische landschap Samnium.
64 Paphos: de myrte was gewijd aan Venus, die te Paphos, een stad op het Griekse eiland Cyprus, bijzonder werd vereerd.
66 Kroon van Hercules: met abelelover omkranste zich Hercules, toen hij de helhond Cerberus uit de onderwereld had gehaald.
67 Dodona's god: Juppiter, orakelgod van Dodona's eikenwoud.
86 Pausia: een olijf, waarvan de even wrange smaak door kenners werd gewaardeerd.
87 Alcinoüs: bij Homerus (Odyssea VII 112 e.v.) wordt de prachtige boomgaard van Alcinoüs, de koning der Phaeaken, beschreven.
88 Crustumium: plaats in het Italische landschap Latium.
90 Methymna: plaats op het Griekse eiland Lesbos.
91 Thasos: Grieks eiland, tegenover Thracië.
  Marea: stad in het westen van de Nijldelta.
93 Psithia: een wijnstok, waarbij men de wijn uit de gedroogde druiven perst.
  Lageos: eigenlijk 'Hazewijn', naar de kleur der druiven.
95 Praecia: wordt evenzo geperst als de Psithia.
96 Rhaetiër: wijn uit de omstreken van Verona.
  Phalernermost: het Phalernische land, beroemd om zijn wijn, ligt in het Italische landschap Campanië.

97 *Aminnea:* wijnstok, die uit Griekenland in Italië werd geïmporteerd.
98 *Tmoliër:* van de berg Tmolus (zie bij 'De akkers', vers 240).
 Phanae: voorgebergte van het Griekse eiland Chios.
99 *Argitis:* misschien een wijnstok met witte druiven.
102 *Rhodiër:* van het Griekse eiland Rhodos.
 Bumastos: een wijnstok met bijzonder volle trossen.
115 *Geloni:* volk in Scythië, dat zich tatoeëerde.
120 *Aethiopië:* land ten zuiden van Egypte.
121 *Seres:* Oostaziatisch volk, zijdebewerkers.
134 *Mediërs:* volk in Azië, ten zuiden van de Kaspische Zee.
137 *Hermus:* rivier in Klein-Azië, die goudstof meevoert.
138 *Bactrië:* oostelijke provincie van het Perzische rijk.
139 *Panchaia:* fabeleiland ten oosten van Arabië, hier: Arabië.
143 *Massicus:* berg in Campanië.
147 *Clitumnus:* kristalheldere zijrivier van de Tiber.
159 *Larius:* Como-meer.
160 *Benacus:* Garda-meer.
161 *Lacus Lucrinus:* meer aan de kust van Campanië, door een dam van de zee gescheiden.
163/4 *Het Julisch water:* verbindt twee Campaanse meren: de Lacus Lucrinus en de Lacus Avernus.
167 *Marsi:* volksstam in Latium.
 Sabelli: oud-Italisch volk, in de buurt van de Latijnen.
168 *Liguriërs:* volksstam bij het tegenwoordige Genua.
 Volsci: volksstam in Latium.
169 *Decius, Marius, Camilli:* Publius Decius Mus, C. Marius en M. Furius Camillus, beroemde veldheersnamen uit Romes strijd om Italië.
170 *Scipiones:* de familie der Scipionen onderscheidde zich in de oorlogen tussen Rome en Carthago (3e en 2e eeuw v. Chr.).
172 *De Indiër:* in 31 voor Chr. ging Octavianus naar het oosten tot de Euphraat.
173 *Saturnus:* oud-Italische god van de landbouw, later vereenzelvigd met Kronos, de vader van Juppiter. Toen Saturnus een tijd lang op aarde toefde, heerste er vrede en overvloed.
176 *Ascra:* Hesiodus van Ascra ($\pm$ 700 v. Chr.) schreef in het Grieks een leerdicht over de landbouw.

181 *Pallas*: de wijnstok is geschonken door en ook gewijd aan de maagdelijke godin Pallas Athene (Minerva).
193 *Etruriër*: fluitspelers uit Etrurië begeleidden vaak de gewijde ceremoniën.
198 *Mantua*: over de grondonteigening bij Mantua zie blz. 830.
225 *Clanius*: rivier in Campanië, die door een overstroming de stad Acerrae ontvolkte.
229 *Lyaeus*: Bacchus. Hier: de wijnstok.
325 *Aether*: het ijlste gedeelte van de atmosfeer, hier vereenzelvigd met Uranus, de hemel.
380/4 *Bacchus*: na de wijnoogst werd in Attica feest gevierd. Processies trekken 'langs dorp en kruisweg'; er zijn pantomimes en improvisaties, terwijl het plezier ten top stijgt bij het zakspringen: op één been dansend moet men zich in evenwicht houden op een volle, geoliede zak. Uit deze feesten zijn de Griekse tragedie en komedie voortgekomen. Het *proscaenium* betekent letterlijk vóór-toneel, hier: toneel. Met *Theseus' zonen* zijn de Atheners bedoeld. Theseus was een Atheens koning.
406 *Saturnus-kapmes*: zo geheten naar de god Saturnus (vergelijk bij vers 173).
425 *Pax*: de godin des vredes, die een olijftak draagt.
437 *Cytorus*: berg in Klein-Azië, rijk aan buxusbomen.
438 *Narycia*: of Locri, een stad in het pijnboomrijke Italische landschap Bruttium.
448 *Ituraeër*: Ituraea ligt in het noordoosten van Palestina.
452 *De Padus*: de Po.
455/7 *Centauren*: de Centauren, half mens half paard, raakten—bij een bruiloft— slaags met de Lapithen, een volk in Thessalië.
464 *Ephyra*: oude naam voor de Griekse stad Corinthe.
465 *Syrisch kleurgif*: Phoenicische purperverf.
487 *Spercheüs*: rivier in Thessalië.
488 *Taÿgetus*: bergketen in het Griekse landschap Laconica, waarin de stad Sparta ligt.
497 *Daciër*: de Daciërs, tussen Donau en Zwarte Zee, bedreigden het Romeinse gebied steeds met een invasie.
506 *Tyrisch*: van Tyrus, stad in Phoenicië.
508 *Rostra*: spreekgestoelte op het Forum.

519 *Sicyon:* stad dicht bij Corinthe.
532 *Remus en zijn broer:* de tweelingbroeders Romulus en Remus, stichters van Rome.
535 *Dicte's vorst:* Juppiter, die als kind in een grot van de berg Dicte op Creta voor zijn vader verborgen werd gehouden.

Het vee

1 *Pales:* beschermgodin van herders en kudden.
  Admetus' herder: Apollo diende Admetus, koning van Thessalië, negen jaar als herder.
4 *Eurystheus:* koning van de Griekse stad Mycene, die de held Hercules twaalf, bijkans onuitvoerbare, opdrachten gaf. Hercules moest Eurystheus dienen als boete voor een verkeerde daad.
5 *Busiris:* koning van Egypte, die vreemdelingen die in zijn land kwamen, placht te offeren. Hercules doodde hem.
6 *Hylas:* lieveling van Hercules, door bronnymfen geroofd.
  Latona op Delos: Latona bracht Apollo en Artemis ter wereld op het eiland Delos. Zeus was hun vader.
7 *Hippodamia en Pelops:* Oenomaus, koning van het Griekse landschap Elis, beloofde zijn dochter Hippodamia als vrouw aan diegene die hem in de wagenren overwon. Pelops, een zoon van koning Tantalus van Phrygië (in Klein-Azië), won de wedstrijd door list. Deze Pelops had een ivoren schouder. Tantalus had hem namelijk gedood en de goden als maaltijd voorgezet om hun alwetendheid te beproeven. Demeter, treurend om Proserpina, at iets van Pelops' schouder. Door de goden in het leven teruggeroepen, kreeg Pelops een ivoren schouder.
11 *Aonië:* het landschap Boeotië in Midden-Griekenland, Hesiodus' geboorteland. In Boeotië ligt de berg Helicon, verblijfplaats der Muzen.
14 *Mincius:* rivier die langs Mantua stroomt.
20 *Molorchus' woud:* woud bij de stad Nemea in Zuid-Griekenland, waar Hercules de Nemeïsche leeuw versloeg. De herder Molorchus gaf Hercules daar gastvrijheid.
  Bij Nemea werden de Nemeïsche spelen gehouden.
25 *Brittanni:* bij het toneel werd het doek niet neergelaten, maar, van de grond

af, opgetrokken. Brittanniërs, op het doek geschilderd of geborduurd, symboliseren wellicht de gehoopte onderwerping van Brittannië aan Rome.

27 *Quirinus:* Romulus, waarmee hier Octavianus wordt bedoeld.

28/29 *De Nijl:* toespeling op Octavianus' overwinning op Antonius en Cleopatra, koningin van Egypte, in 31 v. Chr. Uit het brons der vijandelijke schepen, (een 'sneb' wordt gevormd door drie balken met zware metalen kop, om het vijandelijk schip lek te stoten) liet Octavianus zuilen maken.

30/31 *Azië, Armenië, de Parth:* symbolisering van de gehoopte definitieve onderwerping van het oosten. De Parthen, ten zuidoosten van de Kaspische Zee, waren oorspronkelijk nomaden. Zij waren voortreffelijke ruiters en boogschutters. Schijnbaar vluchtend keerden zij zich op hun paarden om en troffen zó de achtervolger.

36 *Assaracus...Troos:* stamvaders der Trojanen, dus ook, naar de legende, van de Romeinen.

Cynthius: Apollo, geboren bij de berg Cynthus op het Griekse eiland Delos, bouwer van Trojes muren.

37 *Onzalige Nijd:* een allegorie: de burgeroorlogen, symbolisch voorgesteld door de vrouwenfiguur van de Nijd, zijn ten einde. De Nijd is verbannen naar de Tartarus, waar misdadigers als Ixion, gebonden aan een rad, of Sisyphus, die eindeloos een steen tegen een rots moet opwentelen, verblijven.

43 *Cithaeron:* bergketen in Midden-Griekenland.

44 *Laconië:* landschap in Zuid-Griekenland.

Epidaurus: stad in het Zuidgriekse landschap Argolis.

48 *Tithonus:* gemaal van Aurora, broer van koning Priamus van Troje. Hij had het eeuwige leven, doch niet de eeuwige jeugd.

89/90 *'t Paard van Amyclae:* Amyclae is een stad in Laconica. Hier bracht Leda de Dioscuren, Zeus' zonen, Castor en Pollux ter wereld. Beiden waren vermaard als paardentemmers. Cyllarus is een van hun paarden.

Ook de jonge Griekse held Achilles bezat een prachtig, zelfs onsterfelijk, span paarden.

92/4 *Saturnus:* veranderde zichzelf in een hengst, om zijn avontuur met de Oceanide Philyra te verbergen en zó zijn gemalin Rhea te bedriegen.

97 *Venus' dienst:* de bevruchting.
113 *Erichthonius:* koning Erechtheus van Attica.
146 *Silarus:* rivier in Midden-Italië, tussen de landschappen Apulië en Campanië.
Alburnus: berg in Apulië.
148 *Oistros:* horzel.
151 *Tanager:* zijriviertje van de Silarus.
153 *Io:* dochter van Inachus, de koning van het Griekse landschap Argos. Juppiter, die haar begeerde, veranderde haar in een koe om haar zo aan de vervolging van Hera te onttrekken. Toen kwelde Hera Io met een kwaadaardige horzel.
180 *Alpheüs:* rivier die langs Olympia stroomt.
219 *Sila:* bosrijk gebergte in Zuid-Italië.
258 vv *de man, die:* bedoeld is Leander, die iedere nacht over de Hellespont zwom, om Hero, zijn geliefde, te ontmoeten. Hero, priesteres van Aphrodite te Sestos, ontstak elke avond licht op de toren. In een stormnacht woei het licht uit; Leander verdronk en Hero stortte zich in zee.
264 *Bacchus...lynxen:* Bacchus' wagen werd door lynxen getrokken.
267/8 *Potniae...Glaucus:* Glaucus, koning van de Griekse stad Potniae, minachtte de macht van Venus. Venus maakte toen de paarden van Glaucus zó wild, dat zij hem verscheurden.
291 *Parnassus:* berg der Muzen bij de Griekse stad Delphi.
293 *Castalia:* bron op de Parnassus.
304 *Waterman:* teken van de Dierenriem.
306 *Milete:* stad aan de Kleinaziatische westkust.
312 *Cinyps:* rivier op de noordkust van Africa.
349 *Het meer Maeotis:* de zee van Azov.
392 *Diana:* of Artemis, godin der jacht.
409 *Onager:* wilde ezel.
451 *Bitumen:* aardpek.
461 *Bisalten...Geloni:* de Bisalten zijn een Thracische, de Geloni een Scythische stam.
462 *Getië:* gebied in Thracië.
474 *Noricum:* gebied tussen Donau en Alpen.

475 *Timavus:* riviertje bij Triëst.
550 *Chiron:* een Centaur, uitmuntend door wijsheid en rechtschapenheid. Vele jonge helden, ook Achilles, werden door hem opgevoed.
552 *Tisiphone:* een der Eumeniden (verg. 'De akkers', vers 277).

De bijen

15 *Procne:* gemalin van koning Tereus. Zij doodde uit wraak, omdat Tereus haar zuster Philomela had onteerd, haar eigen zoontje Itys. Tereus vervolgde haar; Procne werd veranderd in een zwaluw, Tereus in een hop, Philomela in een nachtegaal. Nòg heeft de zwaluw een rode vlek op het keeltje.
41 *Phrygië's Ida:* het Ida-gebergte, bij de stad Troje in Klein-Azië.
64 *Cybele:* de Magna Mater, de grote Moeder van alle leven in de natuur. De priesters van Cybele slaan met cymbalen.
111 *Priapus:* de god Priapus, van de Hellespont gekomen, beschermt de tuinen. Zijn attribuut is een snoeimes met wilgehouten greep.
119 *Paestum:* stad in Zuid-Italië; beroemde rozenkwekerijen.
127 *Corycus:* stad in Klein-Azië, bekend om haar tuinbouw.
151 *Cureten:* Cretensische goden, wier wapendans het schreien overstemde van de kleine hemelgod Zeus (Juppiter), die in de Dicte-grot op Creta voor zijn vader Kronos (Saturnus) verborgen werd gehouden. De bijen brachten het kind honing, de geit Amalthea bracht hem melk. Deze Cureten zijn later met de priesters van Cybele (vgl. vers 64) geïdentificeerd.
160 *Narcistranen:* een kleverige vloeistof uit de bloem.
177 *Cecrops:* eerste koning van Attica. Cecrops' bijen dus: Attica's bijen. De honing van de met tijm begroeide berg Hymettus in Attica was beroemd.
211 *Hydaspes:* rivier in Medië.
232 *Taÿgete:* een der Pleiaden.
234 *De Vissen:* teken van de Dierenriem.
247 *Minerva's vijandin:* Arachne durfde Minerva tot een wedstrijd in het weven uitdagen. Tot straf werd zij in een spin veranderd.
278 *Mella:* zijrivier van de Po.
284 *Des meesters uit Arcadië:* Aristaeus, wiens geschiedenis thans volgt.
287 *Canopus:* stad aan de Nijlmond.

317 *Tempe:* vruchtbaar dal in Thessalië.
319 *Peneüs:* rivier in Thessalië.
321 *Cyrene:* nymf, dochter van Peneüs. Zij is moeder van Aristaeus, Apollo's zoon.
323 *Thymbra:* stad niet ver van Troje, met een tempel van Apollo.
339 *Lucina:* godin die de barende vrouwen bijstaat.
340 *Oceaniden:* dochters van Oceanus.
343 *Arethusa:* nymf van de bron Arethusa bij Syracuse op Sicilië.
344/5 *Vulcanus' verdriet:* Vulcanus' vrouw, Venus, bedroog hem met de oorlogsgod Mars.
346 *Chaos:* de vormeloze stof, waaruit de wereld werd geschapen.
366 *Phasis en Lycus:* rivieren bij de Zwarte Zee.
367 *Enipeus:* rivier in Thessalië.
369 *Hypanis:* rivier in Sarmatië, thans de Bug.
Caïcus: rivier in Mysië, landschap in Klein-Azië.
386 *Carpathos:* eiland tussen Creta en Rhodos.
389 *Emathia:* oude naam voor Macedonië.
390 *Pallene:* schiereiland van Macedonië.
414 *Ambrozijn:* de spijs der goden, een overheerlijke, geurige materie.
453 *Orpheus:* Thracische zanger, wiens lied en spelen op de lier zelfs stenen ontroerden.
461 *Pangaea, Rhodope:* gebergten, resp. in Macedonië en Thracië.
Rhesus: krijgshaftig Thracisch koning.
462 *Orythuia:* Atheense koningsdochter, door Boreas (de noordenwind) geschaakt.
478 *Cocytus:* rivier der onderwereld.
486 *Proserpina:* verg. 'De akkers', vers 39.
501 *Orcus' veerman:* Charon, die de doden overzet.
507 *Strymon:* rivier in Thracië.
516 *Tanaïs:* rivier in Scythië (Don).
519 *Bacchanten:* vrouwen die, in extatische opwinding, de god Bacchus volgen.
523 *Hebrus:* rivier in Thracië.
565 *Tityrus:* naam van een herder uit Vergilius' eerste Herderszang. De Herderszangen beginnen met een vers dat bijna gelijkluidend is aan dit laatste vers van de *Georgica*.

Waar de uitgang-*en* met de daaropvolgende lettergreep versmelt (bv. 'De akkers', vers 35, 76 enz.) zijn de verbindingsboogjes om typografische redenen uitgevallen.

Het proza van Aart van der Leeuw is uit *Vluchtige Begroetingen*. (Nijgh en Van Ditmar, Rotterdam 1940).

Inhoud

KOSMOS (1940)

Wandeling in Vlaanderen 6

Kosmos
Kosmos 9
Milium effusum 10
Kinderspel 11
De akelei 12

Aanhef
Aanhef 15
Scherzo 17
De fluit 18

Quo carmine demum

Tuin van Epicurus 23
Lucretius 24
Na de dag 25
Moment 26
Miniaturist 27
Faun 28
Herinnering 29
Thuiskomst 30
In memoriam 31

Kerstnacht
Kerstnacht I 33
Kerstnacht II 34

HET VEERHUIS (1945)

Het water I
Spreuk bij het water 39
Een liedje van het water 40
De rit 41
Schepen 42
Het andere land 43
Naar de winter 44

Het water II
Het veerhuis 47
Het zoldervenster 48
In het schip 49
De wel 50
Troost der rivier 51

Melodieën
Pastorale 53
Dans 55
Ogentroost en ereprijs 56
Tot de slaap 57
Kinderliedje 58

Herkenningen
Geboorte 61
De vogel 62
De vlinder 63
De fazant 64
De hazelaar 65
Onheil 66
Ontwaken 67

Het violenperk 68
Waddeneiland 69

Ars poëtica
Tuin van Epicurus 71
Stem van Epicurus 72
Lucretius-vertaling 74
De bijen 75
Vagantes 76
Tolstoi ploegende 77
Sappho 78
Vreugde in Holland 79

Het carillon
Het carillon 81

BUITEN SCHOT (1947)

Bitterheid 85

Buiten schot
Brief 87
Springbron 88
Winters rondeel 89
Vaart 90
Geluk 91
Naar u 92
Verwachting 93
Veilig 94
Angst 95
Aan de stroom 96
Slapende 97
Aanschouwing 98

Inzet 99
Het vogelheem 100
Midzomerwende 101
Dankzegging 102
Sapphisch 103
Tweespraak 104
Buiten schot 105

Glans en weerglans
Spel van twee 107
Contrapunt 108
De grassen 109
De vlinders 110
Ontmoeting 112
Blinde groenling 113

SONNETTEN VAN EEN LERAAR (1951)

Zueignung 117
Woestijn 118
Departement 119
Biecht 120
Bij een eindexamenfoto 121
Portret 122
Daemonen 123

Psyche 124
A en Ω 125
Werkloosheid 126
Eindvergadering 127
Code d'honneur 128
Tussenuur 129
Karakter 130

DE ARGELOZEN (1956)

Tussen de rozeslingers... 134
Charis 135
Eerste verjaardag 136
De groene laan 137
Het kind 138
Van een kind 139
Michiel Matthaeus 140
Over de weide 141
Keltisch grafschrift 142

Brief aan de grootouders 143
Verjaardag 144
Zondagmorgen 145
Weerzien op zolder 146
Het egeltje 147
Spiegeling 148
De oude dichter 149
Watermolen 150
Afscheid 151

KWATRIJNEN IN OPDRACHT (1948)

In opdracht 155

I
I 's Nachts wakker... 157
II Zoek in mijn verzen... 158
III Het late jaar,... 159
IV Stroomop, stroomaf... 160
V Rivier en sterren... 161

VI Nòg murmelen... 162
VII Het schoon van Holland:... 163
VIII De minnaar... 164
IX Op Groenoord... 165
X Bij iedere nieuwe schending... 166
XI Ten laatste... 167
XII Mìjn vesting... 168
XIII Soms waait... 169

II

XIV Hier, telkenmale... 171
XV Klaroenstem... 172
XVI Gezegend wie,... 173
XVII De adelaar... 174
XVIII De erfenis... 175
XIX Reeds voelt... 176
XX Ik zag de kunstenaars... 177
XXI De slanke marter,... 178
XXII Wie zelf... 179
XXIII Heel Rotterdam,... 180
XXIV De uitgebrande stad... 181
XXV Weer zijn vannacht... 182
XXVI Vernuftige pijlers,... 183
XXVII Gestreden heb ik... 184

III

XXVIII Verkaveld werd,... 187
XXIX De welput,... 188

XXX Aan de andere kant... 189
XXXI Toen kwam het kind... 190
XXXII Bij 't strenge fonkelen... 191
XXXIII Wanneer de zwaluw... 192
XXXIV De eerste dag... 193
XXXV Een hoge kreet... 194
XXXVI Verlaat uw velden,... 195
XXXVII Waar zich de tweesprong... 196
XXXVIII Terwijl een golf... 197
XXXIX Bazuinen stoten... 198
XL Van Zuiderkruis... 199
XLI Soms, als ik... 200
XLII Uw doortocht... 201
XLIII Voorwaardelijke troost,... 202
XLIV Geklommen op... 203
XLV Gij die in eigenwaan... 204
XLVI Een urn,... 205
XLVII Door storm ontworpen,... 206

HET LEVEND MONOGRAM (1955)

Deel I *In Memoriam Matris*
Aan allen 211
I De gestorvene 212
II Tegenstem 212
Kinderherinnering 213
Het gebed 214
Kapitale boerenplaats 215
Klein grafmomument 216
Tristis imago 217
De afgronden 218
De ratten 219

De mantel 220
Vergeefs verzet 221
Sonnet voor mijn moeder 222
De aanstoot 223
Samenzwering 224

Deel II *Daemonen*
Over zwarte... 226
Huiselijk leven 227
Weerzien op zolder 228
Het bord 229

Marche funèbre 230
Grijze zee 231
Radiobericht 232
De geduldigen 233
Zonsondergang 234
Naschrift 235

Deel III *Hoefprent van Pegasus*
Schriftuur 237
Mantiek 238
Zum Tode 239
Tussenspel 240
Slapende 241
De paarden 242
Ποίησις 243
Thracisch I 244
Thracisch II 245
Orphisch 246
Het motief 247
De wellen 248
Herfst 249
Zelfportret 250

Eroos 251
'Ανίκατε μάχαν 252
Afscheid 253
Deel IV *Het levend Monogram*
ΙΧΘΥΣ 255
Ad Te clamavi 256
Ψυχή 257
Preek op Terschelling 258
Staking 259
Uittocht uit Rusland 260
Uittocht 261
Green pastures 262
Brief uit de gemeente 263
Apocalyps 264
Wijnstok 265
De disgenoten 266
Het rozeblad 267
Stem van de dichter 268
Begrafenis M. Nijhoff 269
In memoriam patris 270
Vallei van de dood 271
Finis 272

DE HOVENIER (1961)

Met volstrekte eer 277

Het kengetal
Het kengetal 279
Sappho 280
Leopold 281
Thasos 282
Sapphisch 283

Het dagwerk 284
De ouderdom 285
Achterberg 286
Kringloop 287
Parnassus 288
Clara Haskil 289
Het verraad 290
De lichtbak 291

Forlorn 292
Nadering 293
De verstotene 294
Alleen 295
Dertig eeuwen 296
Phoenix 297
Rondeel voor Henriëtte Roland
  Holst 298
Rondeel voor Leopold 299
De drie pharaohs 300
Het onweer 301

Schlüszli
Haar vriendschap... 304
Schlüszli 305
Lente 306
Verjaarswensen 307
Zomeravond 308
Winter 309
Eb 310
Thuiskomst in Holland 311

De naam
De naam 313

De schrijver 314
Grüsz Gott 315
Les pieds-bots 316
Steen-inscriptie 317
De erfvijand 318
De aarde 319
De reiniging 320
Facultas medica 321
Zondagmorgen 322
Het ontspringende 323
Aanvang 324
Wieg 325
Terugkomst uit het ziekenhuis 326
Vóór ons 327
Groszstadt 328
De verlatene 329
Geboorte 330
Licht uit licht 331
Komend voorjaar 332
De veerpont 333
Het verloren kind 334
Buxtehude 335
Vroeg fresco 336
Christus als Hovenier 337

DE SLECHTVALK (1966)

Het sneeuwt,... 341

De Slechtvalk
Portret van Theodora van B. 343
Facultas Medica 344
Nachtwake 345

De sneeuwhaas 346
De donkeren 347
Schriftuur 348
De teruggewezen gave 349
Het onherroepelijke 350

Keltisch
The diviner 353
De opgeroepenen 354
Keltisch grafschrift 355
Brief aan de grootouders 356
Till death us do part 357
And after 358
De verstotene 359
Alleen 360
Het vuur 361
Oudejaarsavondpreek 362
De predikant 363
Het brood 364
De dagloonster 365
De dagloonster (II) 366
Feest van de kinderen 367
Fair Ceridwen 368
Wiegeliedje 369
Het armhuiskind 370

De Japanse visser
Het kind... 373
De Japanse visser 375
Het fregatschip 376

De gestorvene 377
Voor M. 378
Een lied van Alkman 379
Achilles met Xanthos 380
Rock 381
Ultima Thule 382
Anamnesis 383
De apocalyptische ezel 384
Denkend aan Israël 385
Krater van Kyrtos 386
Vogelvrij 387
De weerlozen 388
Stem van de herfstregen 389
Chinese tekening 390
Aan het water 391
De twee zusters 392
De aanzegging 393
Verantwoording (zes kwatrijnen) 394
In den beginne 396
Afvaart 397
Rietveld † 400
Begrafenis van Gerrit Achterberg 401
Voor dag en dauw 402
De gestorvene 403

DE RAVENVEER (1970)

Terugkeer 407

Verzen van Holland
Het erfgoed 409
Moerdijk 410
In Memoriam Patris 411

De erfgenamen 412
De zware last 413
Onder de Brandaris 414
Constellatie 415
Het vers van Gorter 416
Seghers 417

Afscheid van Holland 418
De dageraad 419
De tempelroof 420
Een Hollands onweer 421
Dodenherdenking 422

Verzen van overzee
Ultima Thule 425
De zalmen 426
De afwijzing 427
Wayside inn 428
Eileen 429
De dageraad 430
Julinacht 431
Fragment 432
Zomernacht 433
Brieven der vrienden 434

Het doodsbericht 435
Rouwtijd 436
Tweespraak 437
De herschepping 438
Het verlaten huis 439
Het rotseiland 440
Avondhemel 441
Het vers 442
De schrijver 443

Het Weerzien
Incantatie 445
Het bondgenootschap 446
Het weerzien 447
Studentenkamer 448
De dader 449
Verwachting 450

TWEE UUR: DE KLOKKEN ANTWOORDDEN ELKAAR (1971)

Twee uur: de klokken antwoordden
elkaar 457

VIJF VUURSTENEN (1974)

Autochthoon
Vernomen tijdens een onweer 471
Biografisch I 472
Biografisch II 473
De voorouders 474
Autogram 475
Winternacht (Biografisch III) 476

Het verlaat (Biografisch IV) 477
Het aards geluk 478
Melancholia 479
Standbeeld 480
Anno Domini 1972 481
Autochthoon 482
Dijkwacht 1973 483

Aanzegging 484
Lof van het onkruid 485
Ziekenbezoek 486
Testamentair 487
Voltooiing 488
De nazaten 489
Maart 490
Liefdesverklaring 491

Voorjaar
Dank aan een ezel 493
Pasen 494
Rondeel 495
Fugatisch 496
De huisgodin 497
Vroeg op weg 498

Ballingschap tot het vers
Buitengaats 501
Eerste avond op Northrock 502

Briefkaart aan M. 503
Weerbericht uit Northrock 504
Atlantisch 505
De afgezant 506
In nevelen 507
De eenzame 508
In tekenen 509
Triomf 510
In rood en zwart 511
Jongensvriendschap 512
Thracische jongensdans 513
Morgenschemering 514
Zelfportret 515
Bij het ravijn 516
Alcyonisch 517

Een herfstavond
Het bericht 520
Een herfstavond 521

HET STERRESCHIP (1979)

Bij een donum natalicium 531
De profundis 532
Onder Gorcum 533
Over de eerbied I 534
Over de eerbied II 535
Onvoorwaardelijk 536
Georgica 537
De grote stilte 538
Voor M. Vasalis 539
Dichterspreuken I 540

Dichterspreuken II 541
Het schip 542
De afdaling 543
De eenling 544
Aetate sua LXX 545
Dageraad 546
Hooggebergte 547
Kinderportret 548
In memoriam 549
In Vlaanderen 550

Het hemels welkom 551
Nachtliedje 552
Juninacht 553
Zwaluwenliedje 554
Nikè 555
De bultenaar 556
Onvervreemdbaar 557
Het vliegend hert 558
De tijding 560

Archaïsche grafsteen 561
Het noodweer 562
Tekst op een rivierbaken 563
Onder vreemden 564
Genesis 565

Het Sterreschip
Het Sterreschip 567

DOLEN EN DROMEN (1980)

Ik ben zómaar... 578

Ik kom hem telkenmaal... 579

DE ZOMEN VAN HET LICHT (1983)

Grensgebied I 593

Eroos ter ere
Die weigert... 595
De oproep 596
Eroos ter ere 597
Musisch I 598
Musisch II 599
Bij Plato's Phaedrus 600
Het Symposion 601
Het lied van Tereus 602
Griekse dageraad 603
Cycladenvaart 604
Vergetelheid 605
Tweespraak 606
Anoniem 607

Ultima Thule 608
Brief van overzee 609
Herkenning 610
Voorjaarsmorgen 611

Tien ontmoetingen
Hier in mijn kamer 613
Bij een familieportret 614
Onverbroken 615
In memoriam Hans Brüggen,
Benedictijn 616
Portret van Cornelia de Vogel 617
Anno 1982 I 618
Anno 1982 II 619
Vader en zoon 620
Het verstoorde wereldbeeld 622

Toen Holland antwoord gaf 623

Bij dag en nacht
Nalatenschap 625
Bij dag en nacht 627
Het ploegschrift 633
Holland 634
Signalen 635
Οὐτιδανὸς Οὖτις 636
Kwade dagen 637
Het distelzaad 638
Een loflied midden op straat 639
Het winteronweer 640
Winter onder Schellingwoude 641
Spoedopname 642
De profundis 643

Het volmaakte 644
Ontkomen 645
Poëta laureatus I 646
Poëta laureatus II 647

Een naam in schelpen
Na de vloed 649
Παρὰ θῖνα θαλάσσης 650
Van de brug af gezien 651
Twee mannen 652
Herfst aan de Schelde 654
Een naam in schelpen 656
In nevelen 658
Het afscheid 659
Grensgebied II 660

DE ADELAARSVARENS (1988)

Negen verzen van zonsopgang
Er stond bij: vertaald uit het Frans 665
Wintermorgen in Ierland 666
De zwarte kat 667
Winterwende 668
Bruiloftsspel 669
Bergwereld 670
Het Schip De Noord 671
Gedicht gevonden in een lade 672
Het dochtertje van Jaïrus 673

De adelaarsvarens
Een kind slaapt... 675

Steeds weer... 677
Langzaam opent zich... 678
Tot Sappho 679
Voor de balletmeester 680
Apollinisch 681
De grote zomer... 682
In droefenis 683
Aequinoctium 684
Het zeepaardje 685
Δός μοι ποῦ στῶ 686
Voortekenen 687
Ierse nacht 689
De slachtlammeren 690
A fairy tale 692

De reiskameraad 694
Briefkaart aan M. 695

In nevelen
Rondeel 697
Vredesoptocht (Amsterdam, 21 november 1981) 698
Utrecht, Janskerkhof 698
Het beloofde land 699
De zestigste viering 700
Neen, niet de ouders... 702
Jongensvriendschap 703
Van de meester-beeldhouwer 704
Pelgrimstocht 705
Het wandtapijt... 706
De wijnkruik spreekt 707
Het signaal 708
De maaltijd 709

De toverwoorden
Het huis de 'De Drie Abeelen' 712
De toverwoorden 713
Herfsttij. Het groen... 714
Confrontatie 715
Omzien in deernis 716
Bekentenis 717
Het meisje met de zwavelstokken 718
In memoriam 719
De beschermer 720
The child is the father of the man 721
Intocht 722
Ruysdael 724
In het voorbijgaan 725
Een grafschrift 726
De sidderaal 727
Rivierbaken 728
Café het Puttertje 729

Vergilius HET BOERENBEDRIJF (1949)

De akkers 737
De bomen 755

Het vee 773
De bijen 793

AANTEKENINGEN 813
REGISTER 857
BIBLIOGRAFISCHE AANTEKENING 889

Register

A en Ω 125
'Ανίκατε μάχαν 252
Δός μοι πού στώ 686
ΙΧΘΥΣ 255
Ούτιδανός Ούτις 636
Παρά θίνα θαλάσσης 650
Ποίησις 243
Ψυχή 257
A en Ω 125
A fairy tale 692
Aalscholvers braken door de wolken heen. 410
Aan allen 211
Aan de andere kant hoor ik u al arbeiden 189, 293
Aan de steenwand grauw 251
Aan de stroom 96
Aan de watergang geboren, 567
Aan het water 391
Aanhef 15
Aanschouwing 98
Aanvang 324
Aanzegging 484
Achilles met Xanthos 380
Achter een woord verscholen 434
Achterberg 286
Ad Te clamavi 256
Adelaar was hij tot de laatste strofe, 281
Ademend, ademend, 369

Aequinoctium 684
Aetate sua LXX 545
Afscheid 151
Afscheid 253
Afscheid van Holland 418
Afvaart 397
Al maanden staat het huis verlaten, 348
Alcyonisch 517
Alleen 295
Alleen 360
Alles is pas aangevangen. 680
Als een rozeruiker zoet 91
Als ge oud en schamel zijt, 536
Als grote rozen voor een donkerend raam 432
Als ik nog ouder ben, en helderder mijn ogen 109
Als ik nu in dit land 39
Als in de kring het lamplicht wordt ontstoken, 263
Als langs de duisterende waterbaan 47
Als Orpheus bij de lier zong gingen stenen 438
Als Orpheus voor de dieren speelt, 246
Als zij de blauwzwarte rijksdaalders liet zien 562
Anamnesis 383
And after 358
Angst 95
Ανίκατε μάχαν 252
Anno Domini 1972 481
Anno 1982 I 618
Anno 1982 II 619
Anoniem 607
Apocalyps 264
Apollinisch 681
Archaïsche grafsteen 561
Argeloos voor de zicht: 139
Atlantisch 505

Autochthoon 482
Autogram 475
Avondhemel 441
Bazuinen stoten in de ochtendlucht. 198
Begrafenis M. Nijhoff 269
Begrafenis van Gerrit Achterberg 401
Bekentenis 717
Bergwereld 670
Bericht van hier: de rogge heeft gestoven. 695
Bewaard de gave tafelronde 709
Bezie de kinderen niet te klein: 128
Biecht 120
Bij dag en nacht 627
Bij een donum natalicium 531
Bij een eindexamenfoto 121
Bij een familieportret 614
Bij het ravijn 516
Bij iedere nieuwe schending van uw grond 166
Bij Plato's Phaedrus 600
Bij 't strenge fonkelen van de winternacht 191
Biografisch I 472
Biografisch II 473
Bittere brandingsslagen 253
Bitterheid 85
Blaas, blaas, oostenwind, 436
Blijf, vogelen, uw vluchten schrijven 238
Blinde groenling 113
Boustrophèdon is het schrift; 633
Brief 87
Brief aan de grootouders 143
Brief aan de grootouders 356
Brief uit de gemeente 263
Brief van overzee 609
Briefkaart aan M. 503

Briefkaart aan M. 695
Brieven der vrienden 434
Bronwater, uit de hand 307
Bruiloftsspel 669
Buiten schot 105
Buitengaats 501
Buxtehude 335
Café het Puttertje 729
Charis 135
Chinese tekening 390
Christus als Hovenier 337
Clara Haskil 289
Code d'honneur 128
Confrontatie 715
Constellatie 415
Contrapunt 108
Crux in de tekst.—Ik faalde als tolk. 600
Cycladenvaart 604
Daags drinken bij het wed 242
Daar, aan het westelijk zwerk, 441
Daar, in de Donkere Gaard, 448
Daar staat zij, ongebroken en paraat, 480
Daar waar de zware nevels hingen 425
Daar waar het stenen trapje is, 599
Daar waar het water was, 728
Daemonen 123
Dag Pegasus!—Wat doe jij hier in het gebouw? 117
Dageraad 546
Dank aan een ezel 493
Dankzegging 102
Dans 55
Dappere morgenhaan, 625
Dat mij dit nog gewerd: 623
De aanhef van de ebben fluit: 245

De aanstoot 223
De aanzegging 393
De aarde 319
De adelaar die zijn snavel heeft gewet 174
De adelaar is neergeschoten. 256
De afdaling 543
De afgezant 506
De afgronden 218
De afwijzing 427
De akelei 12
De akkers 737
De apocalyptische ezel 384
De beschermer 720
De bijen 75
De bijen 793
De bijt is in het ijs geslagen, 291
De bomen 755
De bultenaar 556
De dader 449
De dag van het schapenscheren 520
De dag van het verzet is aangebroken: 698
De dag was nog bevracht 431
De dageraad 419
De dageraad 430
De dagloonster 365
De dagloonster (II) 366
De disgenoten 266
De dominee wist van niets. 364
De donkeren 347
De donk're bijen brommen om de korven 75
De drie pharaohs 300
De eenling 544
De eenzame 508
De eerste dag dat men de zeisen haart, 193

De egel komt in 't eendere schemeruur 147
De erfenis der meesters slecht beheerd, 175
De erfgenamen 412
De erfvijand 318
De fazant 64
De fluit 18
De gang der statige rivier 96
De geduldigen 233
1 De gestorvene 212
De gestorvene 377
De gestorvene 403
De geur van kruizemunt waait over,— 29
De grassen 109
De groene laan 137
De groene oevers nog van de ochtend overtogen 312
De groene snoek, gevangen 233
De grote stilte 538
De grote zomer heeft zijn tijd gehad 682
De hazelaar 65
De helft was haar niet aangezegd 298
De herschepping 438
De hondsdagen met rosse hitte, 690
De hooggewielde wagen 41
De huisgodin 497
De Japanse visser 375
De kleine hof ligt in het middaglicht, 26
De kleine Matthew Jones, dàt was er een: 361
De kust komt onder zware luchten, 440
De lichtbak 291
De liefde bidt voor wie 331
De maaltijd 709
De mantel 220
De mens die waar zijn dode slaapt 643
De minnaar van de blauwe ereprijs, 164

De naam 313
De namen der gevallenen 422
De nazaten 489
De opgeroepenen 354
De oproep 596
De oude dichter 149
De ouderdom 285
De paarden 242
De ploeg van het ontginningsland 259
De predikant 363
De profundis 532
De profundis 643
De ratten 219
De reiniging 320
De reiskameraad 694
De rit 41
De schrijver 314
De schrijver 443
De sidderaal 727
De slachtlammeren 690
De slanke marter, in de boom gevlogen, 178
De sneeuwhaas 346
De sterren wintertintelen 309
De sterrennacht gaat haast het oog te boven. 689
De strofen komen toegevlogen 243
De taal slaapt in een syllabe 472
De tafel en het bed zeggen: alleen. 295, 360
De tempelroof 420
De teruggewezen gave 349
De tijding 560
De toverwoorden 713
De tuinman met zijn kapmes kwam 85
De twee zusters 392
De uil is mijn kameraad 363

De uitgebrande stad blijft hem herhalen. 181
De uitgeholde stam met varens overgroeid 320
De veerpont 333
De verlatene 329
De verre verte blauwt.—Wij trekken door de dalen 76
De verstotene 294
De verstotene 359
De verzen die een glanzen dragen 647
De vis, getrokken door mijn hand 255
De vleugels wijd, het hoofd hoog opgestoten, 412
De vlinder kwam van perk tot perk gevlogen, 63
De vlinder 63
De vlinders 110
De vogel eenzaam op het dak 437
De vogel 62
De vogelen heb ik zien komen 234
De voorouders 474
De vroege dag is zonder breuk of smet. 99
De vrouw, die ordent in het ochtendlicht 343
De waterkant wordt ruig verweerd, 44
De weerlozen 388
De wel 50
De wellen 248
De welput, en de lege emmer daalt; 188
De wijnkruik spreekt 707
De wilde roos heeft kort gebloeid dit jaar 66
De wortel Isaï. 336
De wouw, die hier zijn standplaats heeft, 250
De zalmen 426
De zee trekt langzaam dicht 231
De zestigste viering 700
De zon begint met muntjes licht 145
De Zwaan van Asselijn die levensgroot 715
De zware last 413

De zwarte kat   667
Denkend aan Israël   385
Departement   119
Dertig eeuwen   296
Deze winter is Eén   235
Dicht bij de waterzoom   390
Dichterspreuken I   540
Dichterspreuken II   541
Die   323
Die bars de schildpadlier bespant,   513
Die het kindje het aanzijn geeft   324
Die ik negen jaren gekend heb,   620
Die mij ontwijkt   368
Die voor zichzelf niets vroeg,   142, 355
Die weigert wat gij dag aan dag verwacht,   595
Diep in de kern van het vers,   488
Diep in de stilte binnengedaald—   645
Dijkwacht 1973   483
Dit: 288
Dit is de eerste schuchtere groei,   92
Dit is de stoet der Joden, saamgesnoerd met touwen,   317
Dit is het huis genaamd de duizend vrezen.   414
Dit is het schip de Vis,   501
Dit is hun eiland. Zij zijn autochtoon;   608
Dit is hun tijdeloos seizoen.   285
Dit is mijn droom—het kleine huis aan de rivier;   30
Dit van de akkerbouw en van de stand der sterren.—   755
Dit wordt ons niet ontnomen: lezen,   557
Dodenherdenking   422
Dolle kervel, bitterzoet,   216
Doof, hoop, uw fakkel uit.   345
Door de stroming wordt een wieg gesneden   549
Door storm ontworpen, in der wateren tucht,   206
Δός μοι ποῦ στῶ   686

Dovenetel, honingdrager 550
Drie jaar nu al. Ik kom nog in 't gesticht. 126
Drie maal per dag, naar vaste wetten, 214
Drie woorden slechts van Homerus,— 650
Dwalend over het barre rotsenzadel 544
Eb 310
Een diep verdriet dat ons is aangedaan 494
Een eiland als een ezelsruggegraat. 282
Een grafschrift 726
Een herfstavond 521
Een hoge kreet trekt scherp zijn zilvervoor.— 194
Een hoge kreet trekt scherp zijn zilvervoor. 394
Een Hollands onweer 421
Eén jaar de aarde om de zon 136
Een jongen, haast nog een kind, heeft het gegeven, 671
Een kind dat niet òplet 313
Een kind slaapt naast zijn schelp, nog ongeschonden 675
Een koopman met een tros ballonnen 699
Een lied van Alkman 379
Een liedje van het water 40
Een loflied midden op straat 639
Een man die op een narwal lijkt 428
Een naam in schelpen 656
Een ongemeten land—in zwoegen gaan de paarden, 77
Een pluimgras-schaduw, neergeschreven 10
Eén Rembrandt kende als kind ik goed: 337
Een sprookjesboek dat open lag, 713
Een stem is opgegaan in de Jordaan. 385
Een stoere Urkerknul, vaak met negotie 122
Een Streber, jongens, strebt omdat hij streben moet. 121
Een suizelen van regen aan de ruit 74
Een urn, een grafsteen—mij zegt het niet veel. 205
Een vers dat met 'schoon lieveke' begon, 607
Een vis met incarnaten voorhoofdsband, 506

Eén vleugel nog in de cocon 257
Een woord van Achterberg: het sterrengrint. 415
Een zilte westenwind. 503
Een zonsopgang als een archaïsch schild 668
Eerste avond op Northrock 502
Eerste verjaardag 136
Eileen 429
Eindelijk laat mij alleen, 354
Eindvergadering 127
Elkander aanzien, tot het eigen beeld 98
En toen het Paasvacantie was, 727
Er is te Heiligerlee een klok gegoten 481
Er kwam een schip gevaren; 542
Er kwamen paarden in de witte sneeuw 277
Er leeft een boom onder water, 552
Er nadert schaarste van graan. 484
Er stond bij: vertaald uit het Frans 665
Er zijn soms maanden dat ik nooit alleen 413
Eroos 251
Eroos ter ere 597
Facultas Medica 321
Facultas Medica 344
Fair Ceridwen 368
Fanfarecorps in de avondstraten 230
Faun 28
Feest van de kinderen 367
Finis 272
Forlorn 292
Fragment 432
Fugatisch 496
Ga niet naar anderen als dàt leed u slaat 637
Gaan vissen tussen Rossum en Hurwenen, 479
Geboorte 61
Geboorte 330

Gebracht langs donkervlietende 289
Gebroken licht, en wolken drijvende aan de lucht, 332
Gedenk nu de aarde opengaat 269
Gedicht gevonden in een lade 672
Geduldig is het papier: 443
Geen die daarginds uw graf nog vindt; 615
Geen die het mensenhart begrijpt 683
Geen enkel raam dat werkt. De tocht der buitendeur 118
Gegroet gij frisse tintelkou 89
Gegroet van gene zijde 358
Gekanteld aan de appelaar 283
Geklommen op de donkere torentrans 203
...gelijk een kind, spelende op het strand, 286
Geloof van mij, gij die mijn naam hier leest, 726
Geluk 91
Genesis 565
Georgica 537
Gereinigd door de zee 380
Gestreden heb ik levenslang met U. 184, 394
Geur van honing 325
Geworpen op de laatste klip 392
Gezegend wie, als hij de taal aanslaat, 173
Gij die de naam draagt 516
Gij die in eenvoud wilt tezamenhoren, 71
Gij die in eigenwaan bijkomstig acht 204
Gij die met gemaskerd gelaat 619
Gij ging in bittere opstand heen. 221
Gij hebt mijn blad beschreven, Heer, 107
Gij hebt, Moeder, dit leven zwaar gedragen. 222
Gij kleine groenling ingekooid, 113
Gij met uw zachtzinnige oren 493
Gij moet het eenzaam laten 534
Gij slechtvalk met het onyx oog, 350
Gij vader van het vers, wees onvervaard. 395

Gij werkt,—op het gelaat de fijne drift gespannen, 100
Gij ziet mij soms zo donker aan; 94
Gij zijt gelijk een korrel in de grond 403
Gij zijt uit haar: aanzie de steen: 212
Ginder het wrak, bij de stranding 244
Gisteren heb ik zomaar een naam gespeld, 725
God weet: ik heb mijn verzen uitgestort 563
Godlof dat onkruid niet vergaat. 485
Godlof,—de rietwouw heeft zijn vleugelen uitgeslagen 105
Gods liefde op aarde neergedaald 330
Goede morgen, winterkoning: 498
Goudstof van vlinderwieken, 151
Grauwgrijze schapenkudden trekken 310
Green pastures 262
Grensgebied I 593
Grensgebied II 660
Griekse dageraad 603
Grijze zee 231
Grootmachtige vlagen, 249
Groszstadt 328
Grüsz Gott 315
Haar vriendschap zonder aandrang of verraad 304
Hadden wij nimmer nog zwanen gezien, 532
Hamer, kleine bonte specht; 223
Handtekening, 475
Hang uw scheepsroer aan de schouw, 504
Heeft hij bij mij asyl gezocht, de vreemdeling, 558
Heel Rotterdam, zijn huizen en zijn kaden, 180
Heimwee dat overwonnen moet. 658
Herfst 249
Herfst aan de Schelde 654
Herfsttij. Het groen der bladeren is vergaan; 714
Herinnering 29
Herkenning 610

Hervonden na tien jaren tijds   705
Het aards geluk   478
Het afscheid   659
Het andere land   43
Het armhuiskind   370
Het beloofde land   699
Het bericht   520
Het blad, gedwarreld op uw graf,   267
Het bondgenootschap   446
Het bord   229
Het brood   364
Het dagwerk   284
Het distelzaad   638
Het dochtertje van Jaïrus   673
Het doodsbericht   435
Het dorp begint mij te vermijden   294, 359
Het dorp ligt wit   305
Het egeltje   147
Het erfgoed   409
Het fregatschip   376
Het gebed   214
Het hemels welkom   551
Het huis de 'De Drie Abeelen'   712
Het is een feeks, een helleveeg,   429
Het is een kind. Het tekent alles wat er is: 613
Het is een klein en landelijk café,   729
Het is een zwaluwnest,   247
Het kengetal   279
Het kerkpad over zerken.   362
Het kind   138
Het kind dat streng mijn gave heeft versmaad   373
Het kind verloren en beschreid   548
Het kind, waarom wij vurig vroegen,   143
Het kind waarom wij vurig vroegen,   356

Het landschap had ons opgenomen, 6
Het late jaar, de eendere waterwegen, 159
Het licht begint te wandelen door het huis 322
Het lied van Tereus 602
Het meisje met de zwavelstokken 718
Het mooiste werk: Grieks in het eerste jaar. 125
Het motief 247
Het noodweer 562
Het onherroepelijke 350
Het ontspringende 323
Het onverbiddelijke is 326
Het onweer 301
Het onweer heeft mij haast ontzind. 708
Het orgel uit de Warmoesstraat, 138
Het ploegschrift 633
Het ronde perk met donkere violen, 68
Het rotseiland 440
Het rozeblad 267
Het schip 542
Het Schip De Noord 671
Het schoon van Holland: welhaast doodgesnoeid; 163
Het signaal 708
Het simpele gerei, 266
Het sneeuwt, en in dit witte zweven 341
Het speelt het liefste ver weg op het strand, 564
Het spel van lijn en kleur en van schakering 9
Het Sterreschip 567
Het Symposion 601
Het toegangspad, tussen de meidoornhagen. 478
Het tokkelt op de donkere grond— 108
Het uur dat Achterberg is heengegaan 538
Het vee 773
Het veerhuis 47
Het verlaat (Biografisch IV) 477

Het verlaten huis   439
Het verloren kind   334
Het verraad   290
Het vers   442
Het vers van Gorter   416
Het vers van Gorter heeft de geur van graan   416
Het verstoorde wereldbeeld   622
Het violenperk   68
Het vliegend hert   558
Het vogelheem   100
Het volmaakte   644
Het vuur   361
Het wandtapijt dat heel de zaal beslaat   706
Het was de hovenier,   265
Het was een zwaluw, aan het venster doodgevlogen;   95
Het water kruivend om de boeg   90
Het water praatte deze nacht   224
Het weerzien   447
Het wijkt als het mijn nadering vermoedt;   646
Het winteronweer   640
Het wintert. Witberijpt komt thuis   666
Het zeepaardje   685
Het zoldervenster   48
Hier bij de vlonder en de overhaal   333
Hier in mijn kamer   613
Hier meren schepen uit vier hemelstreken.   654
Hier rust, met stof gevuld de mond,   212
Hier, telkenmale als ik het zeil omhaal,   171
Hij die het mes en het lancet hanteert   321, 344
Hij heeft het weer geklaard. Zijn vlieger staat: 720
Hij staat geleund tegen de stam   28
Hij stapt eenzelvig op de werf   318
Hij voert onmerkbaar het gezag,   667
Hij wordt de vogel Rock gelijk   381

Hij zat nadenkend bij zijn kleine schat, 11
Hoe had ik ooit dit leven overleefd 627
Hoe kàn dat: dagpauwogen in de hof 622
Hoe moeten wij onszelf verstaan, 686
Holland 634
Hooggebergte 547
Hoor! de herder blaast zijn horen; 670
Huiselijk leven 227
ΙΧΘΥΣ 255
Ierse nacht 689
Iets wat ik had willen zeggen, 545
Ik ben die de gevorkte tak, 353
Ik ben een tuinman, niets dan dat, 537
Ik ben van de moederschoot af 556
Ik ben zómaar met groot verlof geweest, 578
Ik bracht mijn kind een buks mee naar huis; 227
Ik die hier eindelijk te schrijven zit 502
Ik draag een haat vol liefde voor mijn land, 482
Ik draai gestadig de getallen. 445
Ik droomde dat de vijand binnentrok. 616
Ik gaf mijn kind een zilveren bal. 644
Ik heb dit donkere boek geschreven, 211
Ik heb een dag door Amsterdam gewandeld 531
Ik heb mij in mijn liefste vergist; 697
Ik heb mijn eigen ouders heen zien gaan, 535
Ik hield het huis getrouw in stand. 87
Ik hoorde een vrouw; zij zeide tot haar kind, 638
Ik houd het linnen blank. Maar als ik in de laden 102
Ik kan hem soms wanneer ik wakker lig 660
Ik kan langs vlakke velden gaan, 717
Ik kan niet van hen spreken, 474
Ik kan niet vinden waar gij zijt. 292
Ik ken op aarde geen geluid 18
Ik ken u—en ik ken u niet, 606

Ik kom hem telkenmaal in Zutphen tegen, 579
Ik lag de lieve lange dag 40
Ik las de Phaedo met mijn vijfde klas; 124
Ik las het eindeloos als kind: 665
Ik lees veel sprookjes, zonder hoop 636
Ik loop in de Maeander van het dagwerk, 284
Ik schrijf u met de ravenveer, 427
Ik sta te schuilen onder het wagenkot; 421
Ik volg de sterrebanen, 508
Ik was het kind dat ieder schuwde, 370
Ik was zeer laat. En ik ben altijd vervaard 601
Ik werk graag op een klein bestek; 634
Ik zag bij toeval, als er toeval is, 457
Ik zag de kunstenaars in zwarte stoeten 177
Ik zag de mensen in de straten, 81
Ik zag een kalfje bij de moeder drinken, 430
Ik zag in alle vroegte op een holle weg 669
Ik zat in de wachtkamer van de trein 264
Ik zet mijn verzen als een schelpdier aan 396
Ik zou wel aan de klaagmuur staan 420
Immer in dit drassig laagland 641
Immer vervaarlijk blijft het schilderij. 447
In de donkere romp, in de molen, 473
In de droom de zachte vallei 271
In de héle vroege dag 67
In de slaap geschreven 135
In den beginne 396
In diepten, sluierfijn 248
In diepten van mijzelf waar aan 378
In droefenis 683
In droefenis een zuiv're toeverlaat, 51
In het schip 49
In het verscholen thijmdal, 561
In het voorbijgaan 725

In memoriam 31
In memoriam 549
In memoriam 719
In memoriam Hans Brüggen, Benedictijn 616
In Memoriam Patris 270
In Memoriam Patris 411
In nevelen 507
In nevelen 658
In opdracht 155
In rood en zwart 511
In tekenen 509
In Vlaanderen 550
Incantatie 445
Ingekooid—op een tronk verdord, 229
Intocht 722
Inzet 99
Jongensvriendschap 512, 703
Julinacht 431
Juninacht 553
'k Moest dwalen, 'k moest dwalen 58
Kapitale boerenplaats 215
Karakter 130
Keltisch grafschrift 142, 355
Kent gij het spel der lente wel? 721
Kerstmis en Oudejaar, 218
Kerstnacht, de kentering van 't jaar— 34
Kerstnacht I 33
Kerstnacht II 34
Kerstnacht—het woord is als een lafenis, 33
Kies wat uw beitel niet bevalt: 704
Kinderen van een prachtig ras 387
Kinderherinnering 213
Kinderliedje 58
Kinderportret 548

Kinderspel 11
Kindlief, nu wil ik àlles voor je doen; 123
Klaroenstem in der steden nameloos grauw, 172
Klein grafmomument 216
Komend voorjaar 332
Komende met de graanschop langs de schuren om, 316
Kosmos 9
Kostbaar is mij alles van u; 679
Kraanvogels met machtige slag, 555
Krater van Kyrtos 386
Kringloop 287
Kwade dagen 637
Kwam een vogel gevlogen 62
Langs de nachthemel komen 442
Langzaam opent zich het inzicht 678
Langzaam over het land 308
Langzaam zie ik hen gaan 435
Leg het nu hier maar neer: 642
Leigrijs kan de lente zijn, 495
Lente 306
Leopold 281
Les pieds-bots 316
Licht uit licht 331
Lichtfonkelend in de archipel 287
Liefdesverklaring 491
Liefelijk waart gij in het wilgendal: 391
Lof van het onkruid 485
Lucretius 24
Lucretius-vertaling 74
Maart 490
Machtig baken, lichtende in de nachten, 407
Mantiek 238
Marche funèbre 230
Melancholia 479

Men zette op de boerderij 314
Met duizend fijne zaden 31
Met het gespleten riet, 509
Met stralend weer gegaan, 551
Met uw zwarte mantel aan 220
Met volstrekte eer 277
Met vragende vocalen, 514
Michiel Matthaeus 140
Midden in een landschap zonder eind, 384
Midwinterdag.—De geur van oude jassen, 129
Midzomerwende 101
Mijn diepste eerbied geldt een kind 656
Mijn pen, te lang terzij gelegd, 507
Mijn vader heeft de waterlaarzen aan. 411
Mijn vaders pleegouders. Een waardig paar: 614
Mijn vesting neemt ge niet: het blauw bazalt, 168
Mijn zoon, zo ge dichter moogt worden, 541
Mijn zoon, zo ge dichter wilt worden, 540
Milium effusum 10
Miniaturist 27
Moeilijk is het achter de ploeg te gaan, 319
Moerdijk 410
Moment 26
Morgenschemering 514
Musisch I 598
Musisch II 599
Na de dag 25
Na de vloed 649
Naar de winter 44
Naar u 92
Nachtliedje 552
's Nachts hoorden wij in 't holle huis 219
's Nachts wakker in het uitgestorven huis 157
Nachtwake 345

Naderend in de vroegte van de dag 560
Nadering 293
Nalatenschap 625
Naschrift 235
Neen, niet de ouders die ons vroeg verloren; 702
Niets vraag ik, dan dat gij mij 149
Nikè 555
Nog als voorheen. Een ongeschonden droom. 712
Nog bergt de grond gegiste zon 25
Nòg murmelen de schelpen: Gorters Mei. 162
Nog nevelig in de tuin. 't Is net half zes. 593
Nòg staat haar voetstap in het gouden zand 78
Nooit uitgedacht.—Of in die grote kop 617
November. Allerzielen. Lichte maan. 698
Nu alles tègen is geweest, 609
Nu komt de nacht over de diepe tuin 72
Nu slaapt hij in zó liefelijke staat, 140
Nu zwaarder wordt der jaren last 659
Nu zwijgt zijn serafijnse spelen. 335
O land dat eindeloos in uw opdracht faalt, 491
O zachte glans, getemperd stralen 27
Offert Asklepius een haan; 299
Ogentroost en ereprijs 56
Ogentroost en ereprijs 56
Omzien in deernis 716
Onder de Archipel der sterren 433
Onder de Brandaris 414
Onder de groene bomen 477
Onder de sneeuwwitte bloemen 334
Onder der wolken gang 260
Onder een loverhut, 497
Onder Gorcum 533
Onder vreemden 564
Onderlangs en bovenover 496

Onheil 66
Ontkomen 645
Ontmoeting 112
Ontwaken 67
Ontzettend is het uit de verre verte 279
Onverbroken 615
Onvervreemdbaar 557
Onverwacht mij tegen 65
Onvoorwaardelijk 536
Op dat ongenadig onland 652
Op de Elisabeth van Maasbracht 543
Op de witte steen gezeten 692
Op een onaards uur vertrokken, 694
Op Groenoord werd, bij nacht en najaarsvlagen, 165
Orphisch 246
Oud ben ik en verweerd. 515
Oud worden is het eindelijk vermogen 565
Oudejaarsavondpreek 362
Oudjaar en nieuwe maan, 476
Οὐτιδανὸς Οὖτις 636
Over de eerbied I 534
Over de eerbied II 535
Over de honing, gave van des hemels dauwen, 793
Over de smalle brug 375
Over de weide 141
Over het water, 53
Over kanteltrappen van steen 505
Over zwarte karresporen, 226
Παρὰ θῖνα θαλάσσης 650
Parnassus 288
Pasen 494
Pastorale 53
Pelgrimstocht 705
Phoenix 297

Poëta laureatus I 646
Poëta laureatus II 647
Ποίησις 243
Portret 122
Portret van Cornelia de Vogel 617
Portret van Theodora van B. 343
Preek op Terschelling 258
Psyche 124
Ψυχή 257
Raadsel der raadselen achter glas, 685
Raak mij niet tot in het hart 258
Rabbi Jehuda, hij prάάt! 639
Radiobericht 232
Reeds voelt de veile schare uw onvermogen: 176
Rietveld † 400
Ringelreie rozenkrans 367
Rivier en sterren in een heldere droom: 161
Rivierbaken 728
Rock 381
Rondeel 495
Rondeel 697
Rondeel voor Henriëtte Roland Holst 298
Rondeel voor Leopold 299
Rouwtijd 436
Ruysdael 724
Ruzies met mijn collega's hebben niets om 't lijf. 120
Samenzwering 224
Sapphisch 103
Sapphisch 283
Sappho 78
Sappho 280
Schapen en wolkendrachten 382
Schepen 42
Schepen als zeilende bloemen 42

Scherzo   17
Schippersinstinct, oeroud, voor wind en weer;   635
Schlüszli   305
Schoon gelaat, van droppels nog overfonkeld,   280
Schoon sterk gelaat, mij diep vertrouwd,   97
Schriftuur   237
Schriftuur   348
Schriftuur moet bloeien als een plant,   237
Schud de vleugelen, dat hun zwart   252
Seghers   417
Septemberlicht door de wolken,   417
Signalen   635
Sint Maarten.—Het lichtende lint   596
Slaap, jongensspeelgoed, boek en bal.   327
Slapende   97
Slapende   241
Smeltwater uit de bergen, raak mij aan: 450
Sneller dan de mensen zijn de herten,   681
Soms, als ik tot mijn diepste diepte keer,   200
Soms laat gij mij een eb en vloed alleen.   239
Soms lijken uw verzen uit oerleem,   539
Soms, nachten lang, zijn er signalen: 489
Soms waait er over mijn gekorven land   169
Soms zijt ge omgeven door de kleinste dieren,   240
Sonnet voor mijn moeder   222
Speel, kleine daemon met verschoten haar   101
Spel van twee   107
Spiegeling   148
Spieg'lend in omgekeerde stand   148
Spoedopname   642
Spreuk bij het water   39
Springbron   88
Staal brult als het de smeltoven ingaat.   510
Staking   259

Stamvader van de kudde, 521
Standbeeld 480
Steeds rond het uur van middernacht, 439
Steeds schroom ik om die strofen op te slaan, 602
Steeds weer Uw opdracht. Wat weet ik 677
Steen-inscriptie 317
Stem van de dichter 268
Stem van de herfstregen 389
Stem van Epicurus 72
Stijgende tegen de wand 547
Stroomop, stroomaf der schepen donkere boeg; 160
Studentenkamer 448
Te armoedig nog om bij elkaar te horen 401
Te Grave beneden de sluis 232
Te liggen met gesloten ogen 49
Te middernacht daalt stap voor stap 700
Te werken aan het vers 597
11 Tegenstem 212
Tekst op een rivierbaken 563
Ten laatste heeft de stad haar schrikbewind 167
Terrarium. Verwaarloosd en geronnen 127
Teruggekomen eer hij werd verwacht, 383
Terugkomst uit het ziekenhuis 326
Terwijl de meid de was spoelt bij de vlonder, 724
Terwijl een golf tot aan de muren sloeg, 197
Testamentair 487
Thasos 282
The child is the father of the man 721
The diviner 353
Thracisch 1 244
Thracisch 11 245
Thracische jongensdans 513
Thuiskomst 30
Thuiskomst in Holland 311

Tienduizend maal heb ik het myrrhe-ei 297
Till death us do part 357
Toen hij het kleine plantje vond, 12
Toen Holland antwoord gaf 623
Toen kwam het kind mij stamelend verhalen: 190, 395
Toen Patroklos gelegd was op de baar, 296
Toen Pharao het volk verbood te gaan, 261
Toen was er, midden in het stadsgewoel, 300
Toen zonk het potlood, schetsende op schaal. 400
Toevend op de groene treden 150
Tolstoi ploegende 77
Torenhaan, haan van gehamerd metaal, 533
Tot de slaap 57
Tot Sappho 679
Treedt, donkere mensen, zacht 347
Triomf 510
Tristis imago 217
Troost der rivier 51
Tuin van Epicurus 23
Tuin van Epicurus 71
Tussen april en mei 144
Tussen de rozeslingers en het groen 134
Tussen de voegen woekert gras. 365
Tussenspel 240
Tussenuur 129
Twaalf mannen zag ik dansen 511
Twee mannen 652
Twee uur: de klokken antwoordden elkaar 457
Tweespraak 104
Tweespraak 437
Tweespraak 606
Twintig jaar vrijheid, twintig jaar verraad 418
U, Pales oud-eerwaard, en u, Admetus' herder 773
Uit zichzelf in de avond stalwaarts keerden de koeien, 640

Uittocht 261
Uittocht uit Rusland 260
Ultima Thule 382
Ultima Thule 425
Ultima Thule 608
Utrecht, Janskerkhof 698
Uw doortocht door dit volk brengt geen in kaart. 201
Uw goddelijk geduld en ongeduld 603
Vaart 90
Vaarwel die aan de einder wijkt, 397
Vaarwel, vaarwel o zwaluw, 554
Vader en zoon 620
Vagantes 76
Vallei van de dood 271
Van de brug af gezien 651
Van de meester-beeldhouwer 704
Van een kind 139
Van het verraad onpeilbaar ogenblik.— 290
Van heuvel tot heuvel gaat een schalmeien— 15
Van Koblenz af was er steeds mist geweest. 687
Van scheppens pijn de onverhoedse stoot; 155
Van zijn boek opziend vroeg het kind: 719
Van Zuiderkruis naar Poolster, Grote Beer, 199
Vanwaar ik stond zag ik twee vissen gaan, 490
Veerman, mag ik overvaren? 517
Veilig 94
Ver van de plek die ik niet ken, 487
Verantwoording (zes kwatrijnen) 394
Vergeef mij dat de schoonste nachten 103
Vergeefs verzet 221
Vergeet uw kaartje niet. Houd het vàst in uw hand. 119
Vergetelheid 605
Verjaardag 144
Verjaarswensen 307

Verkaveld werd, mijn lief, de laatste hof. 187
Verlaat uw velden, broeders! Snèl en snèl! 195
Vernomen tijdens een onweer 471
Vernuftige pijlers, ontrouw en verraad, 183
Vernuftige pijlers ontrouw en verraad 395
Verrader is het woord in onze taal. 546
Verscholen in de holle wilgenstam 301
Verwachting 93
Verwachting 450
Vijf vuurstenen gaf ik u in de hand: 471
Vliegtuigen trekken in de nacht hun spoor. 328
Vogelvrij 387
Voltooiing 488
Voor dag en dauw 402
Voor de balletmeester 680
Voor M. 378
Voor M. Vasalis 539
Vóór ons 327
Vóór wij vertrokken naar de zwarte branderssstad, 213
Voorjaar, ten langen leste onverslagen, 611
Voorjaarsmorgen 611
Vooroudertrots: goed ingeklonken land. 409
Voortekenen 687
Voorwaardelijke troost, Godlof, ontkomen, 202
Voorzichtig beginnen te spelen 306
Vredesoptocht (Amsterdam, 21 november 1981) 698
Vreemd aan de ander in war doorelkander 553
Vreugd is het in de grote wei te staan, 79
Vreugde in Holland 79
Vroeg banjeren langst het strand. Terugtrekkend tij. 649
Vroeg fresco 336
Vroeg op weg 498
Vroeg valt de avond in het dal. Vannacht 329
Waar is mijn Vader? Is hij in het licht? 270

Waar onverwacht het pad zich buigt 64
Waar vindt de hoge vreugde onderkomen, 394
Waar waart gij in uw droom? 104
Waar zich de tweesprong van de stroom ontvouwt, 196
Waddeneiland 69
Wandeling in Vlaanderen 6
Wanneer de lentevelden welken 110
Wanneer de zwaluw aan de balken bouwt, 192
Wanneer een mens, door pijn getatoueerd, 486
Wanneer een vers is afgemaakt 61
Wanneer ik eenmaal mijn pensioen zal halen 130
't Was winter en al schemerig in de stad. 349
Wat deed ze op de boerderij? 366
Wat ik gezien heb op die éne dag 69
'Wat ik mijn lief heb misdreven 268
Wat rijkdom geeft van graan, bij welke ster de akker, 737
Wat staat gij naast mijn bed, Moeder van gene zijde? 217
'Wat van de springbron fris 88
Wat zal u straks ontzegelen, edele wijn, 707
Wat ziet gij, liefste, mij aan? 272
Wat zingt het popelend refrein? 55
Watermolen 150
Wayside inn 428
Weer zijn vannacht de doden omgegaan. 182
Weerbericht uit Northrock 504
Weerzien op zolder 146
Weerzien op zolder 228
Wees niet bevreesd wanneer de knokkel op 393
Wees niet bevreesd wanneer de vlagen gaan 389
Weet gij het ook de ganse nacht? 93
Weg van de klippen westwaarts vaart 386
Wel elke ochtend ligt de dauw 402
Wel te rusten, Vader Beer! 146
Welterusten, Vader Beer! 228

Werkloosheid   126
Wie geld bewaart is wélbewaard: 215
Wie heeft de tekenen gemerkt,   598
Wie huis en herberg had   483
Wie zelf de wijde wateren is gewend   179, 446
Wieg   325
Wiegeliedje   369
Wij die wandelden in het licht   262
Wij kozen soberheid tot bondgenoot.   23
Wij lijken, ouder wordend, op elkaar,   651
Wij naderden de naakte witte klip,   376
Wij stonden voor het zoldervenster saam,—   48
Wij wandelen naast elkaar,   315
Wij zwommen samen door de kalme stroom   50
Wijnstok   265
Winter   309
Winter onder Schellingwoude   641
Wintermorgen in Ierland   666
Winternacht (Biografisch III)   476
Winters rondeel   89
Winterwende   668
Woestijn   118
't Wordt voorjaar langs de IJssel bij Veecaten.   610
Zacht is de waterkant   43
Zachte argeloze vreugd   17
'Zeilende schepen zijn de wagens van de zee.'   604
Zelfportret   250
Zelfportret   515
Zèker zal hij er zijn,   141
Zeven maal om de aarde te gaan,   377
Zevenster van zeven regels,   672
Ziekenbezoek   486
Zien wat niemand ooit aanschouwde,   512, 703
Zij die geboden en verboden   716

Zij komen uit de verte aan, 722
Zij schoten op de witte haas. 346
Zij was van kind af mij nabij, 718
Zij zagen haar verwonderd aan, 673
Zij zaten, twee mannen, twee vrouwen, 618
Zij zijn gegaan. Na middernacht. 426
Zij zijn nooit weg, zij zien mij dagelijks aan: 388
Zijt gij gegaan de hoven der gedachte? 112
Zo kom tot rust. Vertrouw u aan de nacht, 57
Zo mij werd toegestaan een wens te wagen: 605
Zoek in mijn verzen heulsap noch venijn. 158
Zolang gij er zijt, 357
Zomeravond 308
Zomernacht 433
Zondagmorgen 145
Zondagmorgen 322
Zonlicht en wolken en de roekeloze pracht 24
Zonsondergang 234
Zueignung 117
Zum Tode 239
Zwaluw, doorklief de lucht! 379
Zwaluwenliedje 554
Zwanen, steekt de trompet: 419
Zwarte regelen op het wit papier. 449
Zwarte zwanen, witte zwanen, 137
Zwijg, aarde, rond het grote witte paard 241

Bibliografische aantekening

De eerste druk van de *Verzamelde Gedichten* van Ida Gerhardt uit 1980 verscheen ter gelegenheid van de haar toegekende P.C.Hooftprijs. Deze uitgave bevatte alle tot dan gepubliceerde verzenbundels, het tijdgedicht *Twee uur: de klokken antwoordden elkaar*, het gedicht *Dolen en Dromen* (een co-produktie met A.P.ten Bosch, uitgever te Zutphen) en de Vergiliusvertaling *Het Boerenbedrijf*. Het in 1978 verschenen *Vroege Verzen*, waarmee de verzamelbundel opent, is op zichzelf een keuze uit het jeugdwerk.

In 1985 verscheen een herdruk, onder toevoeging van de bundel *De Zomen van het Licht* uit 1983. De editie 1985^2 werd in 1988 vrijwel ongewijzigd herdrukt. De vierde druk uit 1989 is, behoudens enkele correcties, een integrale herdruk van de editie 1988^3.

Deze editie, waarin tevens de in 1988 verschenen bundel *De Adelaarsvarens* is opgenomen, werd van nieuw zetsel vervaardigd. De tekst volgt, behoudens enkele nieuwe correcties, de laatste door de dichteres zelf gecorrigeerde drukken van de afzonderlijke bundels. De bundels *Kosmos, Het Veerhuis, Buiten Schot, Sonnetten van een leraar* en *De Argelozen* uit *Vroege Verzen* zijn hier als afzonderlijke werken beschouwd; de verzameltitel *Vroege Verzen* kwam daarmee te vervallen. De dichtbundels zijn chronologisch opgenomen, met dien verstande dat de genoemde titels uit *Vroege Verzen* achter elkaar zijn geplaatst en de vertaling *Het Boerenbedrijf* buiten de volgorde van het oorspronkelijk werk is gehouden. Verder werden de dichtbundels typografisch met elkaar in overeenstemming gebracht en zijn de aantekeningen bij de diverse bundels alle achterin het tweede deel geplaatst.

Deze vijfde druk werd op aanwijzing van Jacques Janssen door Drukkerij Nauta te Zutphen gezet en op getint offsetpapier gedrukt, en gebonden door Boekbinderij De Ruiter. 125 exemplaren zijn gedrukt op Simili Japon en door de auteur gesigneerd.

Athenaeum—Polak & Van Gennep is een imprint van Em. Querido's Uitgeverij B.V., Amsterdam.

Copyright © *1980, 1985, 1988, 1989, 1992 by Ida Gerhardt.* Niets uit deze uitgave mag worden verveelvoudigd en/of openbaar gemaakt, door middel van druk, fotocopie, microfilm of op welke andere wijze ook, zonder voorafgaande schriftelijke toestemming van Em. Querido's Uitgeverij B.V., Singel 262, 1016 AC Amsterdam. *No part of this book may be reproduced in any form, by print, photoprint, microfilm or any other means, without written permission from Em. Querido's Uitgeverij* B.V., *Singel 262, 1016* AC Amsterdam.

ISBN 90 253 5030 5 / CIP / NUGI 310